Annotated Models

A Brief Walkthrough of *Contemporary Business Communication* Second Edition, by Scot Ober

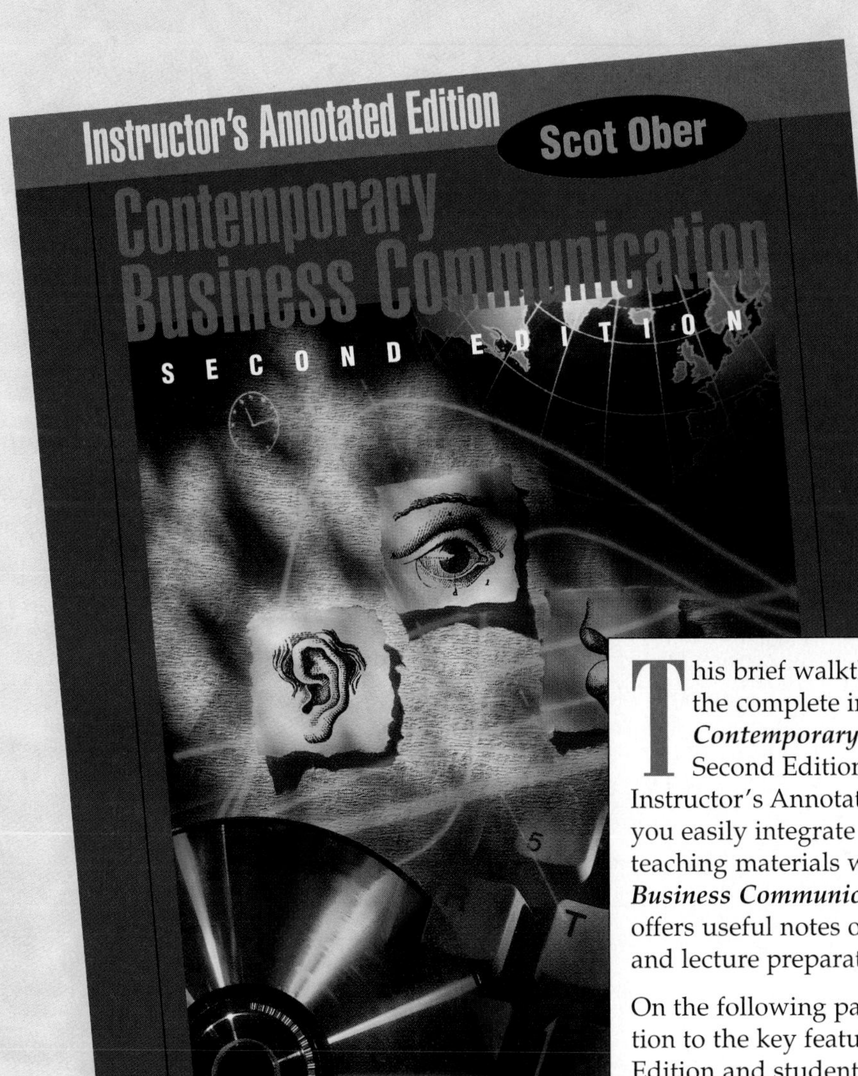

This brief walkthrough will introduce you to the complete instructional package for ***Contemporary Business Communication,*** Second Edition. The package includes this Instructor's Annotated Edition, designed to help you easily integrate into your course the wealth of teaching materials which accompany ***Contemporary Business Communication,*** Second Edition. It also offers useful notes on the text material for course and lecture preparation.

On the following pages, you will find an introduction to the key features of the Instructor's Annotated Edition and student text, as well as a description of the support items available with the text for both you and your students.

Each element in this instructional package was developed to help you create a successful course by helping students gain the effective communication skills they need to succeed in their careers.

An approach to teaching research and extensive

Scot Ober recognizes that, to communicate successfully in the workplace, students must not only develop basic writing skills and master the various forms of business communication, but also develop the ability to analyze the specific needs of a business situation and compose an appropriate communication. As a result, **Contemporary Business Communication,** Second Edition, helps you prepare students for the real world challenges of communicating in business.

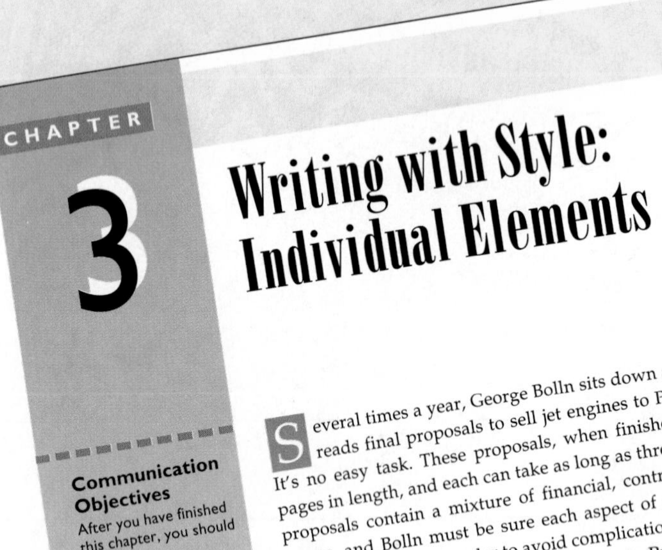

CHAPTER

3

Writing with Style: Individual Elements

Communication Objectives

After you have finished this chapter, you should be able to

1. Write clearly.
2. Prefer short, simple words.
3. Write with vigor.
4. Write concisely.
5. Prefer positive language.
6. Use a variety of sentence types.
7. Use active and passive voice appropriately.
8. Keep paragraphs unified and coherent.
9. Control paragraph length.

Several times a year, George Bolln sits down at his desk and carefully reads final proposals to sell jet engines to Pacific Rim governments. It's no easy task. These proposals, when finished, are often *hundreds* of pages in length, and each can take as long as three months to prepare. The proposals contain a mixture of financial, contractual, and technical language, and Bolln must be sure each aspect of a proposal is examined in painstaking detail in order to avoid complications down the road.

Bolln is manager of Advanced Military Programs for Massachusetts-based General Electric Aircraft Engines—Lynn. He is one of thousands of U.S. executives who are, with increasing frequency, doing business with Korea, Taiwan, Japan, the Philippines, and the People's Republic of China. For G.E. Aircraft Engines, the Pacific Rim business is worth quite a bit; the Korea fighter program is worth $500 million in initial sales alone.

The rules for doing business in the Pacific Rim vary with each country, but there is one constant. The reports must be written in such a way that those who speak English as a second language will not have problems understanding them.

"We obviously avoid using language that's known to only a select group of people in the United States," said Bolln, specifically referring to acronyms that are casually used throughout the military supply business. Bolln must also make sure the language is kept simple, that "flowery" descriptions are simplified. When Bolln spots something in a report, presentation, or proposal that has the slightest chance of being misunderstood, he makes sure the sentence is rewritten.

56

informed by current classroom experience

MEMO TO: Business Communication Colleagues
FROM: Scot Ober
DATE: September 1994
SUBJECT: A Delicate Balance

Over the course of my twenty years of teaching business communication to thousands of students, I have used almost a dozen different textbooks. While each book had its strengths, I never found a text that achieved the delicate balance I was looking for: a text that was informed by theory, yet was clear and accessible for students; one that provided the solid, practical guidance that students need to develop business communication skills, without becoming rigidly prescriptive; and one that would help students analyze context and propose creative solutions to realistic communication challenges while reinforcing basic writing skills.

What I have tried to write is a text that achieves that balance: one that is grounded in the theory and research from the academic disciplines of business communication, organizational behavior, human psychology, composition, and rhetoric; one that teaches students that effective communication is more than the mere absence of grammatical error; and one that recognizes that while the basic principles of business communication are not carved in granite, neither are they written in sand.

As you take this brief walkthrough of *Contemporary Business Communication*, Second Edition, I think you will agree that the text will provide your students with the human, technical, and conceptual skills they will need to communicate effectively in the complex and ever-changing contemporary business environment.

College of Business • Ball State University • Muncie, IN 47306-0335 • Phone: 317-285-5227

A truly integrated instructional outstanding support for classroom

New! Instructor's Annotated Edition helps you see *at a glance* the supporting materials available for your use in the classroom.

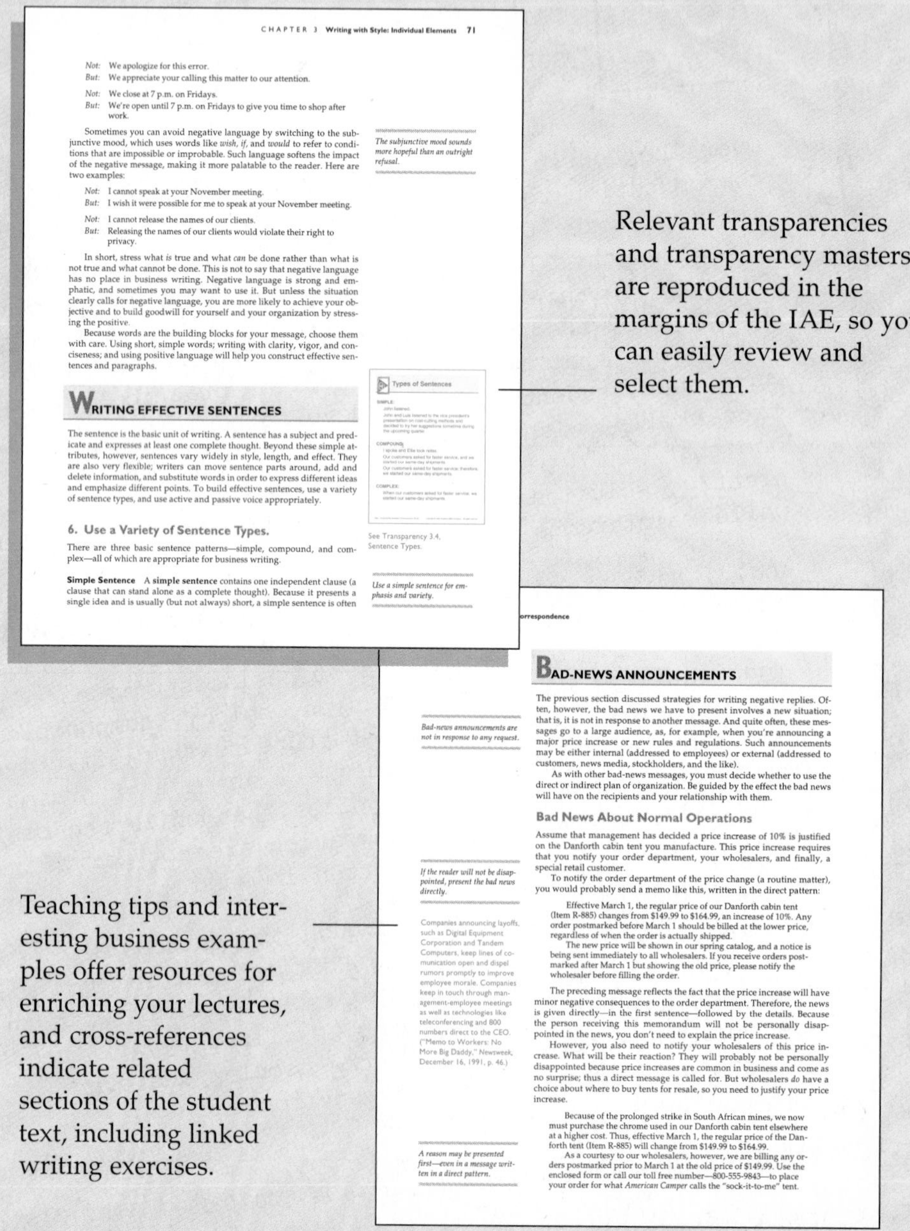

Not: We apologize for this error.
But: We appreciate your calling this matter to our attention.

Not: We close at 7 p.m. on Fridays.
But: We're open until 7 p.m. on Fridays to give you time to shop after work.

Sometimes you can avoid negative language by switching to the subjunctive mood, which uses words like *wish, if,* and *would* to refer to conditions that are impossible or improbable. Such language softens the impact of the negative message, making it more palatable to the reader. Here are two examples:

The subjunctive mood sounds more hopeful than an outright refusal.

Not: I cannot speak at your November meeting.
But: I wish it were possible for me to speak at your November meeting.

Not: I cannot release the names of our clients.
But: Releasing the names of our clients would violate their right to privacy.

In short, stress what *is* true and what *can* be done rather than what is not true and what cannot be done. This is not to say that negative language has no place in business writing. Negative language is strong and emphatic, and sometimes you may want to use it. But unless the situation clearly calls for negative language, you are more likely to achieve your objective and to build goodwill for yourself and your organization by stressing the positive.

Because words are the building blocks for your message, choose them with care. Using short, simple words; writing with clarity, vigor, and conciseness; and using positive language will help you construct effective sentences and paragraphs.

See Transparency 3.4, Sentence Types.

WRITING EFFECTIVE SENTENCES

The sentence is the basic unit of writing. A sentence has a subject and predicate and expresses at least one complete thought. Beyond these simple attributes, however, sentences vary widely in style, length, and effect. They are also very flexible; writers can move sentence parts around, add and delete information, and substitute words in order to express different ideas and emphasize different points. To build effective sentences, use a variety of sentence types, and use active and passive voice appropriately.

6. Use a Variety of Sentence Types.

There are three basic sentence patterns—simple, compound, and complex—all of which are appropriate for business writing.

Use a simple sentence for emphasis and variety.

Simple Sentence A **simple sentence** contains one independent clause (a clause that can stand alone as a complete thought). Because it presents a single idea and is usually (but not always) short, a simple sentence is often

BAD-NEWS ANNOUNCEMENTS

Bad-news announcements are not in response to any request.

The previous section discussed strategies for writing negative replies. Often, however, the bad news we have to present involves a new situation; that is, it is not in response to another message. And quite often, these messages go to a large audience, as, for example, when you're announcing a major price increase or new rules and regulations. Such announcements may be either internal (addressed to employees) or external (addressed to customers, news media, stockholders, and the like).

As with other bad-news messages, you must decide whether to use the direct or indirect plan of organization. Be guided by the effect the bad news will have on the recipients and your relationship with them.

Bad News About Normal Operations

Assume that management has decided a price increase of 10% is justified on the Danforth cabin tent you manufacture. This price increase requires that you notify your order department, your wholesalers, and finally, a special retail customer.

If the reader will not be disappointed, present the bad news directly.

To notify the order department of the price change (a routine matter), you would probably send a memo like this, written in the direct pattern:

> Effective March 1, the regular price of our Danforth cabin tent (Item R-885) changes from $149.99 to $164.99, an increase of 10%. Any order postmarked before March 1 should be billed at the lower price, regardless of when the order is actually shipped.
>
> The new price will be shown in our spring catalog, and a notice is being sent immediately to all wholesalers. If you receive orders postmarked after March 1 but showing the old price, please notify the wholesaler before filling the order.

Companies announcing layoffs, such as Digital Equipment Corporation and Tandem Computers, keep lines of comunication open and dispel rumors promptly to improve employee morale. Companies keep in touch through management-employee meetings as well as technologies like teleconferencing and 800 numbers direct to the CEO. ("Memo to Workers: No More Big Daddy," *Newsweek*, December 16, 1991, p. 46.)

The preceding message reflects the fact that the price increase will have minor negative consequences to the order department. Therefore, the news is given directly—in the first sentence—followed by the details. Because the person receiving this memorandum will not be personally disappointed in the news, you don't need to explain the price increase.

However, you also need to notify your wholesalers of this price increase. What will be their reaction? They will probably not be personally disappointed because price increases are common in business and come as no surprise; thus a direct message is called for. But wholesalers *do* have a choice about where to buy tents for resale, so you need to justify your price increase.

A reason may be presented first—even in a message written in a direct pattern.

> Because of the prolonged strike in South African mines, we now must purchase the chrome used in our Danforth cabin tent elsewhere at a higher cost. Thus, effective March 1, the regular price of the Danforth tent (Item R-885) will change from $149.99 to $164.99.
>
> As a courtesy to our wholesalers, however, we are billing any orders postmarked prior to March 1 at the old price of $149.99. Use the enclosed form or call our toll free number—800-555-9843—to place your order for what *American Camper* calls the "sock-it-to-me" tent.

Relevant transparencies and transparency masters are reproduced in the margins of the IAE, so you can easily review and select them.

Teaching tips and interesting business examples offer resources for enriching your lectures, and cross-references indicate related sections of the student text, including linked writing exercises.

package offers
success

Instructor's Resource Manual with Transparency Masters provides additional teaching materials, including chapter overviews, lecture and discussion notes, suggested answers to and/or teaching tips for *all* review and discussion questions, writing exercises and case problems, additional *Microwriting* exercises with formatted solutions, answer key to grammar and mechanics exercises, **New!** Fully formatted solutions to *all* letter-writing assignments, **New!** Sample long report and memo report, and **New!** over 50 transparency masters provide solutions to selected in-text exercises.

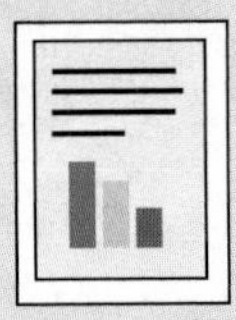

100 Acetate Transparencies include summaries of key concepts, good/bad paired examples, text figures, and supplementary information.

Test Bank and ***Computerized Test Bank*** (IBM and Macintosh) contain approximately 1,200 test items including multiple-choice, short-answer, true-false, revision, and writing items.

Video Case Studies reinforce business communication concepts and introduce students to the changing communication environment at companies such as Lotus, Chiat/Day, and Chemical Bank. For each video, discussion questions and suggested writing assignments are provided.

A systematic approach helps competence as communicators

Real world situations . . .

- ***Microwriting*** is Scot Ober's unique method for helping students learn how to analyze a business communication problem, by modeling, step-by-step, the problem-solving process, and then presenting an appropriate "solution," whether it be a memo, letter, report, or oral presentation. A Microwriting activity appears in every chapter from 5 through 17, and is reinforced by an unsolved Microwriting problem in the chapter exercises.

- ***Chapter-opening vignettes*** introduce students to business professionals who describe their own communication challenges and strategies.

- ***Spotlights on Technology, Law and Ethics,*** and ***Across Cultures*** provide integrated, up-to-date coverage of important issues in the rapidly changing environment of business communication.

- ***Urban Systems Continuing Case Problems*** introduce students to the communication challenges faced by the staff of Urban Systems, a small start-up company whose product is Ultra Light, a flexible, paper-thin light source. Each case is followed by Critical Thinking questions and Writing Assignments. As students solve these problems in context, they face communication problems similar to those they will ultimately face on the job.

A Simple Memo

MICROWRITING

PROBLEM

Today is December 3, 19—, and you are Alice R. Stengren, president of the Entrepreneurial Association of Reed Northern College. *EARN* is the newest of the six student organizations in the school of business and has 38 members. It was formed two years ago when the department of management instituted a major in entrepreneurship. The purposes of EARN are (1) to provide opportunities for members to learn more about entrepreneurship, primarily through monthly meetings that feature guest speakers; (2) to provide social interactions for future entrepreneurs; and (3) to promote entrepreneurship as a major or minor course of study at the college.

To further the third purpose, the association recently voted to institute a $1,000 EARN scholarship. The scholarship will be awarded on the basis of merit to a junior or senior business student majoring in entrepreneurship at Reed Northern. Funds for the scholarship will be raised by selling coffee and doughnuts each day from 7:30 to 10:30 a.m. in the main lobby of the school of business building. Write a memo to Dean Richard Wilhite, asking permission to start this fund-raising project in January.

PROCESS

1. What is the purpose of your memo?

   Convince the dean to let EARN sell coffee and doughnuts in the main lobby from 7:30 to 10:30 a.m. daily, beginning in January.

2. Describe your primary audience.

   Dean Richard Wilhite:
   - Former president of Wilhite Energy Systems (started the company—an entrepreneur himself)
   - 46 years old; has been business dean at RNC for six years (very familiar with the school and college)
   - Nationally known labor expert
   - Holds tenure in the department of management (same department as entrepreneurship major)
   - Has spoken about the need to increase scholarships
   - Devotes a great deal of time to lobbying the legislature and raising funds (recognizes the need for fund-raising)
   - Doesn't know me personally but is familiar with EARN

3. Is there a secondary audience for your memo? If so, describe.

   No secondary audience.

students gain confidence and in the world of business

. . . and solid practical instruction

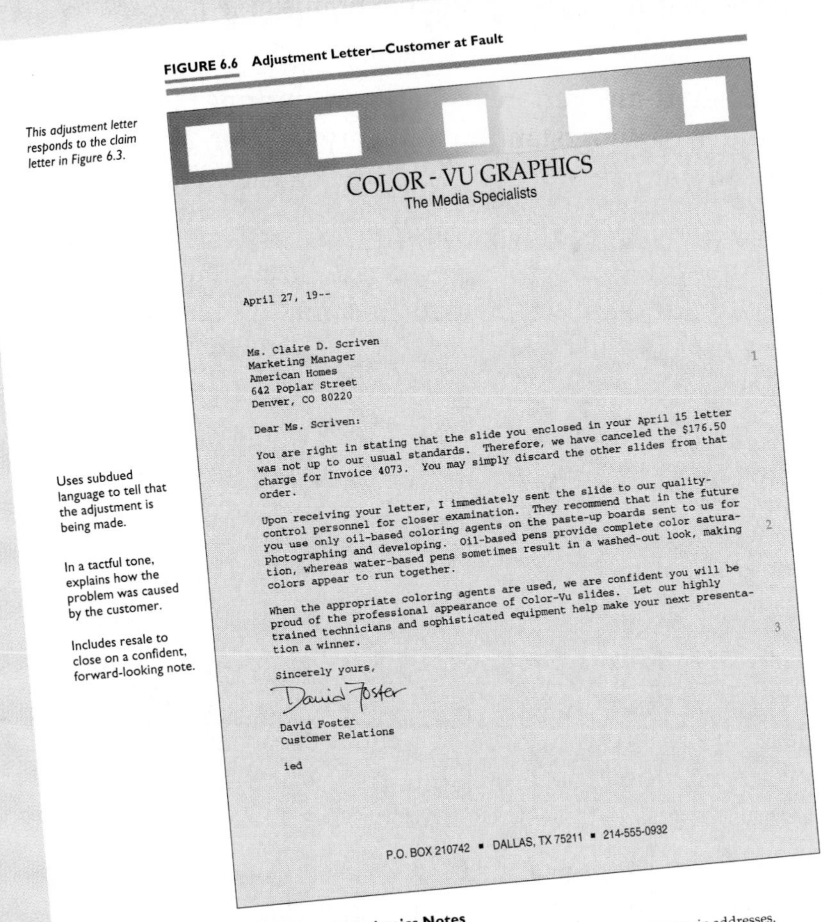

FIGURE 6.6 Adjustment Letter—Customer at Fault

This adjustment letter responds to the claim letter in Figure 6.3.

COLOR - VU GRAPHICS
The Media Specialists

April 27, 19--

Ms. Claire D. Scriven
Marketing Manager
American Homes
642 Poplar Street
Denver, CO 80220 1

Dear Ms. Scriven:

Uses subdued language to tell that the adjustment is being made.

You are right in stating that the slide you enclosed in your April 15 letter was not up to our usual standards. Therefore, we have canceled the $176.50 charge for Invoice 4073. You may simply discard the other slides from that order.

In a tactful tone, explains how the problem was caused by the customer.

Upon receiving your letter, I immediately sent the slide to our quality-control personnel for closer examination. They recommend that in the future you use only oil-based coloring agents on the paste-up boards sent to us for photographing and developing. Oil-based pens provide complete color saturation, whereas water-based pens sometimes result in a washed-out look, making colors appear to run together. 2

Includes resale to close on a confident, forward-looking note.

When the appropriate coloring agents are used, we are confident you will be proud of the professional appearance of Color-Vu slides. Let our highly trained technicians and sophisticated equipment help make your next presentation a winner. 3

Sincerely yours,

David Foster
Customer Relations

ied

P.O. BOX 210742 ▪ DALLAS, TX 75211 ▪ 214-555-0932

Grammar and Mechanics Notes

1 Use the capitalized two-letter Postal Service abbreviation for state names in addresses.
2 *whereas* is one word. 3 *Sincerely yours,*: Capitalize only the first word in a complimentary closing.

162

- ***More than 45 fully-formatted sample documents,*** listed on the endpapers for easy reference, include marginal annotations that discuss how the writer has approached a communication problem, and grammar and mechanics footnotes that provide practical instruction in context.

- ***Easily accessible tabbed reference section*** includes grammar and mechanics review exercises, formatting information for all types of documents, and spelling lists.

- ***A wealth of realistic and engaging exercises*** provide ample practice for developing business communication skills.

- ***Checklists*** feature helpful summaries of key concepts, and are listed on the endpapers for easy reference.

Tools for student success in and beyond the classroom

Study Guide with *The Job Seeker's Handbook*—A Special Value for Students
This specially priced student resource effectively reinforces the learning process and includes a valuable bonus: *The Job Seeker's Handbook.*

- Objective, short-answer, revision, and writing exercises extend students' understanding of every chapter, and additional drills reinforce grammar and mechanics skills.
- *The Job Seeker's Handbook* provides practical career planning guidance through interactive exercises, as well as additional resources for developing effective resumes, cover letters, and interviewing skills.

CBC Grammar Review Software supplements the grammar and mechanics coverage in the text through interactive review exercises.

***American Heritage College Dictionary,* Third Edition, at a special low price.** The new edition of this acclaimed dictionary is an invaluable aid to student writing. It is available for just $9.00 net to the bookstore, when ordered together with *Contemporary Business Communication*, Second Edition, or any Houghton Mifflin College text.

Contemporary Business Communication

SECOND EDITION

Contemporary Business Communication

INSTRUCTOR'S ANNOTATED EDITION

SCOT OBER
Ball State University

HOUGHTON MIFFLIN COMPANY **Boston** **Toronto**
Geneva, Illinois Palo Alto Princeton, New Jersey

Sponsoring Editor: Kristin Watts Peri
Basic Book Manager: Susan Warne
Senior Project Editor: Cathy Labresh Brooks
Senior Production/Design Coordinator: Sarah Ambrose
Manufacturing Coordinator: Marie Barnes
Marketing Manager: Robert Wolcott

Cover design: Linda Manly Wade
Cover image: William Whitehurst, New York City

Library of Congress Catalog Card Number: 94-76539

ISBN: 0-395-70745-5

Instructor's Annotated Edition ISBN: 0-395-70993-8

123456789-DW-98 97 96 95 94

To my five sons, with deep affection—

Jeff

Andy

Ken

Tony

Casey

Brief Contents

Contents

PART II

Developing Your Writing Skills 55

CHAPTER 3 Writing with Style: Individual Elements 56

CHAPTER 4 Writing with Style: Overall Tone 87

CHAPTER 5 The Process of Writing 108

PART III

Basic Correspondence 141

CHAPTER

6 Routine Messages 142

CHAPTER

7 Persuasive Messages 177

CHAPTER

Bad-News Messages 215

CHAPTER

Special Messages 250

PART IV

Report Writing 291

CHAPTER

Planning the Report 292

CHAPTER

13 Writing the Report 401

PART V

Oral Communication 451

CHAPTER

14 Business Presentations 452

CHAPTER

15 Other Types of Nonwritten Communication 494

Preface

Students don't have to be convinced of the need for high-level communication skills. By the time they enter business communication classes, they know enough about business to appreciate the critical role communication plays in the contemporary organization and the role it will play in helping them get a job and be successful on the job. To sustain this inherent interest, students need a textbook that is current, fast paced, and interesting—just like business itself. Thus, the first objective of *Contemporary Business Communication* (*CBC*) is to present comprehensive coverage of real-world concepts in an interesting and lively manner.

At the same time, we know that many students have difficulty recognizing how to shape communications to meet the needs of a business situation. They need to be guided through the process of analyzing the problem and tailoring the message to their purpose. Thus, the second objective of *CBC* is to help students develop the analytical skills they will need on the job.

The response to the first edition of *Contemporary Business Communication* has been gratifying, especially the helpful comments and suggestions received from users around the country. Based on this feedback, changes in the discipline, and changes in the business workplace, this edition of *CBC* has been extensively revised to provide students with the skills they need to communicate effectively in the complex and ever-changing contemporary business environment.

FEATURES NEW TO THIS EDITION

Several features have been added to make this edition of *CBC* more effective for the student and more convenient for the instructor.

Instructor's Annotated Edition

Complementing the "easy-to-learn" approach of the first edition is the "easy-to-teach" approach of the second edition, made possible in large part by the addition of an *Instructor's Annotated Edition.* The IAE provides specific teaching aids right at the point where you need them; for example:

- Miniature copies of the transparencies and transparency masters are shown in the chapter margins of the IAE so that you can see immediately what enrichment materials are available for each section of the text. The 100 color transparencies and the 50 transparency masters included in the *Instructor's Resource Manual* are all new and all contain original material, such as summaries of key concepts, additional bad/good paired examples, and additional model documents.
- Marginal notes refer you to appropriate sections in the teaching support package for suggested solutions to text exercises, additional Microwriting exercises, additional examples, and the like.
- Teaching tips and interesting business examples offer resources to enrich your lectures.

"Say it *directly*"

Today's managers are busy and must make every minute count. They prefer—indeed, many even *demand*—directness in messages from their subordinates. Thus, for the first time, this text teaches a direct organizational plan (major idea first) for *all* messages (including persuasive and bad-news messages) that travel up the organization from subordinate to superior. Messages from superiors to subordinates continue to follow the familiar direct organizational plan for good news and routine messages and indirect plan for persuasive and bad-news messages.

Reference Manual

New to this edition is a 63-page built-in Reference Manual that students will use throughout the course and throughout their professional lives. The Reference Manual contains the following sections:

- Rules, examples, and exercises for correct *grammar, punctuation,* and *number usage;*
- Detailed *formatting standards* for all aspects of correspondence and reports;
- A *spelling list* of the 1,000 most commonly misspelled words in typical business writing;
- Appropriate methods for *documenting sources* (including footnotes, endnotes, and author/year citations) in both APA and MLA styles
- A list of *proofreading symbols* and commonly used grading symbols (including cross-references to related sections in the text).

Streamlined Content

Students learn to communicate by practicing communicating—not just by *reading* about communicating. Thus, the second edition of *CBC* has been streamlined in a number of ways to provide more efficient instruction. Every chapter has been tightened to present the needed information in the most useful format. The report unit has been decreased from five to four chapters by deleting the chapter on specialized reports (proposals, policies, and procedures have been retained and are now covered in Chapter 10). In addition, all formatting instructions for letters, memos, and reports have been moved out of the text chapters and into the new Reference Manual, where they are available for easy reference.

These changes, combined with the smaller, more convenient physical size of the text, will help your students learn in a productive environment.

RETAINED FROM THE PREVIOUS EDITION

In addition to these features new to the second edition, many of the features introduced in the first edition have been expanded to make them even more effective.

Microwriting

Microwriting activities—detailed studies of typical communication tasks—proved to be one of the most popular features of the first edition, and they have been expanded in the present edition. Beginning with the first writing chapter (Chapter 5), each chapter contains a three-part Microwriting activity, which includes the *problem* (a situation that requires a communication task), the *process* (a series of questions with answers that provides step-by-step guidance for accomplishing the communication task), and the *product* (a fully formatted finished document). Microwriting activities require students to focus their efforts on developing a strategy for the message before beginning to compose the message, and they serve as a step-by-step model for composing the end-of-chapter exercises.

The Microwriting activities in each chapter all contain the answers to the process questions. New to each chapter in this edition is an end-of-chapter Microwriting exercise that poses process questions and then requires the student to provide answers, thus more actively engaging the student in the problem-solving process. The *Instructor's Resource Manual* contains additional Microwriting exercises

Spotlight on Contemporary Issues

Chapter 2 of the present edition continues the first edition's introduction of three contemporary issues that are having an impact on business communication: the increasing international and intercultural nature of contemporary business, technology in the workplace, and the growing importance of the legal and ethical dimensions of business.

In addition, throughout the text, boxed features called Spotlights show how these issues affect the specific topic covered in each chapter. These Spotlights (entitled *Spotlight Across Cultures, Spotlight on Technology,* and *Spotlight on Law and Ethics*) have been updated and expanded—from 17 in the first edition to 24 in the present edition.

The Spotlights are specifically designed to reinforce criteria from the American Assembly of Collegiate Schools of Business (AACSB) for teaching the international, technological, and ethical dimensions of business. As a matter of fact, the entire text has been designed to meet AACSB Accreditation Standard C.1.2.c, which now states directly that "the business curriculum should include written and oral communication as an important characteristic" (*Standards for Business and Accounting Accreditation,* American Assembly of Collegiate Schools of Business, St. Louis, MO, 1991).

Urban Systems: An Ongoing Case Study

As in the first edition, every chapter in the present edition ends with a case study involving Urban Systems (US), a small entrepreneurial company whose primary product is Ultra Light, a new paper-thin light source that promises to revolutionize the illumination industry. A company profile (complete with a photograph of each major player) is contained in the Appendix to Chapter 1, and each chapter presents a communication problem faced by one of these managers. As students systematically solve these 17 case studies, they face communication problems similar to those typically found in the workplace.

The continuing nature of the case study provides these positive learning experiences:

- Students are able to use richer contextual clues to solve communication problems than are possible in the shorter end-of-chapter exercises.
- Students become intimately familiar with the managers and the company and must select what is relevant from a mass of data, thereby learning to deal with information overload.
- Because the same situations frequently carry over into subsequent chapters, students must face the consequences of their earlier decisions.
- Many cases require students to solve the same communication problem from two different perspectives.
- The cases provide excellent opportunities for practicing collaborative communication.

New to this edition is the addition of a Critical Thinking section to each case, which requires higher-order reasoning skills to analyze the situation before beginning to communicate.

Continuing Examples and Exercises

Continuing examples are often used throughout the chapter (or even carried forward to the next chapter) in both the text and in the end-of-chapter exercises. For example, in Chapter 6, students first assume the role of buyer and write a claim letter and later assume the role of seller and answer the same claim letter by writing an adjustment letter.

These continuing examples and exercises show that communication problems are not solved in a vacuum. They're more realistic because they give a sense of following a problem through to completion; they're more interesting because they provide a continuing thread to the chapter; and they reinforce the concept of audience analysis because students must first assume the role of sender and later the role of receiver for the same communication task.

Full-Page Annotated Models

Even more full-page models of each major writing task appear in this edition (now more than 60 in all, including 17 models in the Reference Manual). Each model is shown in complete, ready-to-send format so that students become familiar with the appropriate format for each kind of writing assignment. A variety of correct styles are illustrated and annotated, and each model provides step-by-step composing notes in the side margin. Unique to this text are the grammar and mechanics notes in the bottom margin, which call attention to specific illustrations of the grammar and mechanics rules presented in the Reference Manual.

Efficient Organizational Plan

The present edition follows the same logical organizational plan introduced in the previous edition:

- Part I—Communicating in Business (Chapters 1–2) presents basic communication theory in a nontechnical manner and introduces three contemporary issues that affect business communication.
- Part II—Developing Your Writing Skills (Chapters 3–5) introduces and illustrates basic writing principles, with one complete chapter devoted to the writing process.
- Part III—Basic Correspondence (Chapters 6–9) provides instruction and many annotated, fully formatted models of routine, persuasive, bad-news, and special messages. Audience analysis and legal/ethical implications are discussed throughout.
- Part IV—Report Writing (Chapters 10–13) includes separate chapters on data collection and on data analysis. The implications of technology are covered at each stage of the reporting process, including computerized data searches, computerized data analysis, and document design (desktop publishing).
- Part V—Oral Communication (Chapters 14–15) takes students completely through planning and giving a business presentation. Also covered are business meetings (including parliamentary procedure), listening skills, telephone communication (including voice mail), dictation, and business etiquette.
- Part VI—Employment Communication (Chapters 16–17) covers every part of the job-search process, including the legal and ethical dimensions of the job campaign.

Other Student Aids

CBC contains the following additional features to help students master the concepts presented:

- The end-of-chapter exercises have been updated and substantially expanded, with 50% more exercises than in the first edition. They deal with such current real-world problems as environmental concerns, smokers' versus nonsmokers' rights, NAFTA, Carpal Tunnel Syndrome, and AIDS in the workplace.
- Chapter-opening vignettes illustrate the communication tasks of actual managers at real corporations. New to this edition is an end-of-chapter exercise that relates specifically to the corporation introduced in the opening vignette.
- Nineteen checklists provide brief, step-by-step outlines for completing specific types of communication tasks.
- Five self-instructional LABS (Language Arts Basics) in the Reference Manual cover standard English usage in short, easy-to-manage installments. Each LAB presents the most important rules for that topic, plenty of illustrations of each rule, and exercises to test student mastery.
- Each chapter is packed with practical, easy-to-understand illustrations of each concept introduced.
- Marginal notes summarize the important points in the chapter, and a list of key terms at the end of each chapter defines all technical vocabulary introduced in the chapter.
- The revision stage of the writing process receives full attention, beginning with detailed instructions in Chapter 5 and reinforced in the report chapters and in every Microwriting activity.
- A lively and crisp writing style speaks directly to the student.

COMPLETE PACKAGE OF SUPPORT MATERIALS

In addition to the Instructor's Annotated Edition, the teaching and learning package for *Contemporary Business Communication*, Second Edition, includes:

- *Instructor's Resource Manual* with 50 transparency masters
- 100 acetate transparencies
- *Study Guide* with *The Job Seeker's Handbook*
- *Test Bank* with approximately 1,200 questions
- *Computerized Test Bank*
- Video case studies for *Contemporary Business Communication*
- *CBC Grammar Review Software*

Instructor's Resource Manual

The Instructor's Resource Manual presents useful guidelines and additional teaching materials, including chapter overviews, answers to review and discussion questions, suggestions for and sample solutions to chapter exercises, fully formatted solutions to all letter-writing exercises, solutions to Urban Systems cases, sample reports, additional Microwriting samples, and answers to all exercises in the Reference Manual. Over 50 transparency masters include solutions to selected in-text exercises.

Acetate Transparencies

100 acetate transparencies include summaries of key concepts, good/bad paired examples, text figures, and additional model documents.

Study Guide with The Job Seeker's Handbook

This specially priced student resource reinforces the principles of successful business communication, and provides valuable career-planning guidance. To extend students' understanding of every chapter, The *Study Guide* offers objective, short-answer, and revision exercises. Additional drills strengthen grammar, mechanics, and spelling skills. The *Study Guide* contains diverse samples of real-world correspondence.

The Job Seeker's Handbook included in the *Study Guide* provides to-the-point coverage of important job-hunting techniques, useful tips on self-assessment, and a wide variety of practical exercises. It includes special sections on developing a powerful résumé, writing persuasive cover letters, successful interviewing, follow-up tactics, and results-oriented career strategies.

Test Bank

The all-new *Test Bank* contains approximately 1,200 test questions for 17 chapters, including multiple-choice and true/false items, short-answer questions, revision exercises, and writing cases.

Computerized Test Bank

This microcomputer program aids instructors in preparing examinations consisting of any quantity and combination of questions. With the program, the instructor selects questions from the *Test Bank* and produces a test master—and alternate versions, if desired—for easy duplication.

Video Case Studies

Five video case studies reinforce business communication concepts, covering such topics as oral communication, new communication technologies, business writing, and intercultural issues. The case studies introduce students to the changing communication environment at companies such as Au Bon Pain, Ronald McDonald Children's Charities, and Chemical Bank. For each video, discussion questions and suggested writing assignments are provided.

CBC Grammar Review Software

The concise explanations, clear examples, and nearly 300 interactive exercises in this review program supplement the grammar and mechanics coverage in the text. This software is available for IBM and Macintosh computers.

American Heritage Dictionary

The American Heritage Dictionary is an invaluable resource for college and career success. The best-selling third edition is the most complete, up-to-date, and heavily illustrated dictionary available. Instructors may order the hardcover, thumb-indexed *American Heritage College Dictionary,* Third Edition in a shrink-wrapped package with *Contemporary Business Communication.* Also available is a brief hardcover version, *The American Heritage Concise Dictionary,* Third Edition, which also may be shrink-wrapped with *Contemporary Business Communication.*

ACKNOWLEDGEMENTS

During the revision of this text, it has been my great pleasure to work with a dedicated and skillful team of professionals at Houghton Mifflin, and I gratefully salute the editorial, design, production, and marketing staff for the major contributions they made to the success of this text. Although it is always dangerous to name names, I would be remiss if I did not specifically acknowledge with deep gratitude the special assistance of Sue Warne, Cathy Brooks, Kristin Watts Peri, Nandana Sen, and Bob Wolcott. What a genuine pleasure it has been to work with this talented team.

In addition, I wish to thank the following reviewers for their thoughtful contributions:

Carl Bridges, Ohio University
Annette Briscoe, Indiana University Southeast
Mitchel T. Burchfield, Southwest Texas Junior College
Janice Burke, South Suburban College (IL)
Anne H. Colvin, Montgomery Community College (PA)
Doris L. Cost, Metropolitan State College of Denver (CO)
L. Ben Crane, Temple University (PA)
Ava Cross, Ryerson Polytechnic University (Ontario)
Nancy J. Daugherty, Indiana University-Purdue University, Indianapolis
Rosemarie Dittmer, Northeastern University (MA)
Graham N. Drake, State University of New York, Geneseo
Kay Durden, The University of Tennessee at Martin

Phillip A. Holcomb, Angelo State University (TX)
Larry R. Honl, University of Wisconsin, Eau Claire
Alice Kinder, Virginia Polytechnic Institute and State University
Richard N. Kleeberg, Solano Community College (CA)
Lowell Lamberton, Central Oregon Community College
E. Jay Larson, Lewis and Clark State College (ID)
Michael Liberman, East Stroudsburg University (PA)
Marsha C. Markman, California Lutheran University
Diana McKowen, Indiana University, Bloomington
Maureen McLaughlin, Highline Community College (WA)
Wayne Moore, Indiana University of Pennsylvania
Gerald W. Morton, Auburn University at Montgomery (AL)
Rosemary Olds, Des Moines Area Community College (IA)
Karen Sterkel Powell, Colorado State University
Jeanette Ritzenthaler, New Hampshire College
Betty Robbins, University of Oklahoma
Joan C. Roderick, Southwest Texas State University
Sue Seymour, Cameron University (OK)
Sherry Sherrill, Forsyth Technical Community College (NC)
John R. Sinton, Finger Lakes Community College (NY)
Curtis J. Smith, Finger Lakes Community College (NY)
Randall L. Waller, Baylor University (TX)
Maria W. Warren, University of West Florida
Betty Rogers Youngkin, University of Dayton (OH)

PART I

Communicating in Business

CHAPTER 1

Understanding Business Communication

CHAPTER 2

Contemporary Issues in Business Communication

CHAPTER 1

Understanding Business Communication

Communication Objectives

After you have finished this chapter, you should be able to

1. Describe the components of communication.
2. Explain the major types of verbal and nonverbal communication.
3. Explain the directions that make up the formal communication network.
4. Describe the characteristics of the grapevine and provide guidelines for managing it.
5. Identify the major verbal and nonverbal barriers to communication.

To Deedy Taylor, communication means many things. As employee services manager at The Home Depot, Inc., the largest home hardware store chain in the United States, Taylor is responsible for communicating the company's benefit, wellness, and employee assistance programs to more than 25,000 employees in 100 locations. But to Taylor, communication means more than simply sending relevant information from corporate headquarters in Atlanta to retail stores all over the country. To Taylor, communication means motivating people, breaking down boundaries, and directing the flow of information and ideas that encourage people to think in new ways and to act more effectively.

Communication, the way Taylor sees it, is the lifeblood of the modern business. How well a communication system works determines how readily ideas are shared. It's especially important, says Taylor, that employees understand that ideas flow every which way, not just from the top down. "The key to communicating effectively is to not dictate anything. Since we rely on independent outlets, we are not a hierarchy. Our interactions with the operators of the retail outlets are circular—we work with them, they work with us."

Another key to communicating effectively is knowing when to use which medium to get your message across. Taylor uses many media—letters, telephones, face-to-face contact, and video—and she takes great care to choose the medium that is most appropriate to her particular message.

"The way we pass along information is critical to our employee relations," says Taylor. "We use video in conjunction with more informational media to set tones, to deliver feel-good messages that letters don't do as well. But video doesn't tell a whole story; it gives highlights of your message and sends broader messages. For instance, Home Depot uses video to provide employee training seminars on product use and presentation."

In other cases, Taylor says, the appropriate medium is more concrete. To build relationships with company managers, for example, Taylor will write letters, which are more personal and more authoritative. "When we are communicating with managers, we have to excite them," says Taylor. "We want them to go and excite others. This means that we have to ignite the managers' interest with our writing, which is sometimes difficult to do. In the first sentence I tell them what's in it for them. I go on from there to tell them just what the program is that we want them to get behind. The third thing I tell them is that they don't have to do very much at all to make the program a success. Then I tell them how to do it, and give them a contact name if they have any problems or would like any help."

Deedy Taylor
Employee services manager, The Home Depot, Inc., Atlanta, Georgia

A chapter overview appears in the *Instuctor's Resource Manual*, pp. 2–5.

Unfortunately, says Taylor, the most effective form of communication—the face-to-face meeting—is seldom used. "Many business people make the mistake of avoiding human contact," says Taylor. "Too much is done in writing. The telephone is good, but in-person is preferable. Nothing beats face-to-face communication, even today."

However you communicate, says Taylor, the most important thing is to do it constantly, to keep the communication channels open. If a company recognizes the value of communication and keeps channels open, employees will fill those channels with new ideas—meaning new business.

"When you communicate effectively," says Taylor, "it's intoxicating. It's the greatest feeling in the world. When you mess up, it can be disastrous. That's the risk and excitement of communication."

COMMUNICATING IN ORGANIZATIONS

Communication is necessary if an organization is to achieve its goals.

Walk through the halls of a typical modern organization, and what do you see? Managers and other employees reading reports, drafting electronic mail on their computers, attending meetings, conducting interviews, talking on the telephone, conferring with subordinates, holding business lunches, reading mail, dictating correspondence, and making presentations. In short, you see people *communicating*.

An organization is a group of people working together to achieve a common goal, and communication is a vital part of that process. Indeed, communication must have occurred before a common goal could even be established. And a group of people working together must interact; that is, they must communicate their needs, thoughts, plans, expertise, and so on. Communication is the means by which information is shared, activities are coordinated, and decision making is enhanced.

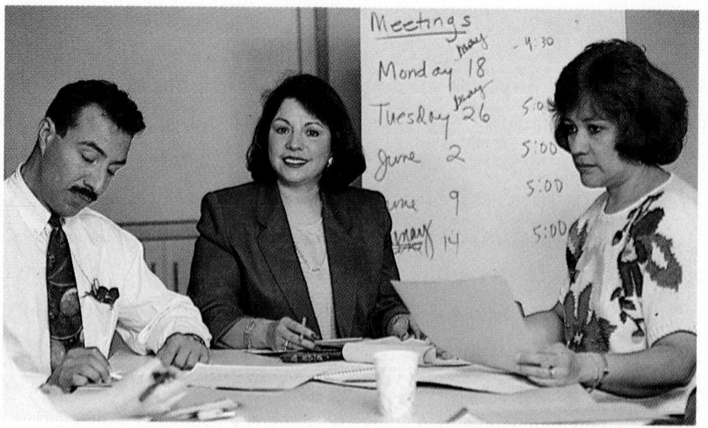

Communication changes as the workforce changes. In response to changing demographics, Ester Fuentes (center) founded an Oregon-based firm specializing in training employees to work in a more diverse workplace.

Understanding how communication works in business and how to communicate competently within an organization will help you participate more effectively in every aspect of business. Consider these recent research findings—all of which come from studies conducted within the past five years:[1]

- A survey of 224 recent business graduates ranked communication as the most important area of knowledge both for securing employment after graduation and for advancement and promotion once on the job.
- A survey of 6,000 people conducted by *Young Executive* magazine found that the most annoying habit of American bosses was poor communication.
- A survey of 200 corporate vice presidents reported they spend the equivalent of nearly three months a year writing letters, memos, and reports.
- A survey of 1,000 white- and blue-collar workers found that the most frequent cause of workplace resentment and misunderstandings is poor communication.
- Eighty percent of the managers at 402 firms surveyed nationwide say most of their employees need to improve their writing skills, up from 65% the previous year. But only 21% of the firms offer training in writing skills.

For more on good communication skills, see the supplemental lecture/discussion notes in the *Instructor's Resource Manual*, beginning on p. 5.

Clearly, good communication skills are crucial to your success in the organization. Competent writing and speaking skills will help you get hired, perform well, and earn promotions. If you decide to go into business for yourself, writing and speaking skills will help you obtain venture capital, promote your product, and manage your employees. These same skills will also help you achieve your personal and social goals.

THE COMPONENTS OF COMMUNICATION

Because communication is such a vital part of the organizational structure, our study of communication begins with an analysis of its components. **Communication** is the process of sending and receiving messages—sometimes through spoken or written words and sometimes through such nonverbal means as facial expressions, gestures, and voice qualities. As illustrated in Figure 1.1, the communication model consists of five components: the stimulus, filter, message, medium, and destination. Ideally, the process ends with feedback to the sender, although feedback is not necessary in order for communication to have taken place.

Communication is the sending and receiving of verbal and nonverbal messages.

To illustrate the model, let us follow the case of Dave Kaplan, a chemical engineer at Industrial Chemical, Inc. (We'll become quite familiar with Dave and his company in the coming chapters.) In 1989, in the process of working on another project, Dave developed Ultra Light, a flat, electroluminescent sheet of material that serves as a light source. Dave could see the enormous business opportunity offered by a paper-thin light fixture such as Ultra Light, which was bendable and could be produced in a variety of shapes and sizes.

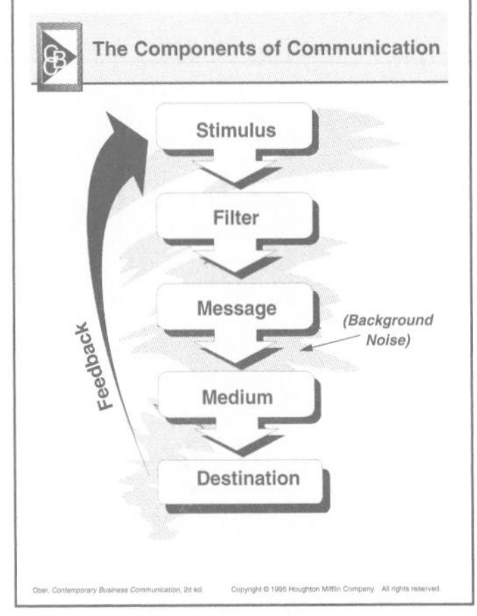

See Transparency 1.1, The Components of Communication.

The market for lighting is vast, and Dave, even though at the time an engineer and not a businessman, felt the sting of inventing a device that had great potential but that belonged to somebody else (Industrial Chemical, Inc.). He was disappointed in IC's eventual decision not to manufacture and market this product. As we learn what happened to Dave Kaplan after IC's decision, we'll examine the components of communication, one at a time.

Incident	*Communication Component*
Dave receives a memorandum from the head of R & D.	Dave receives a *stimulus.*
He interprets the memo to mean that IC has no interest in his invention.	He *filters* the stimulus.
He decides to relay this information to his brother.	He forms a *message.*
He telephones Marc.	He selects a *medium.*
His brother receives the call.	The message reaches its *destination.*
Marc listens and tells Dave his reaction.	Marc provides *feedback.*

FIGURE 1.1 The Components of Communication

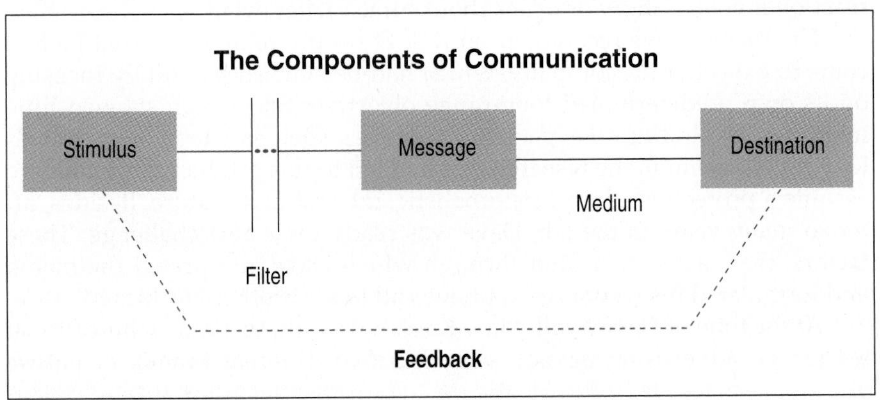

The Stimulus

Step 1: *A stimulus creates a need to communicate.*

In order for communication to take place, there first must be a **stimulus,** an event that creates within an individual the need to communicate. This stimulus can be internal or external. An internal stimulus is simply an idea that forms within your mind. External sources come to you through your sensory organs—your eyes, ears, nose, mouth, and skin. A stimulus for communicating in business might be a memo you just read, a presentation you heard at a staff meeting, a bit of gossip you heard over lunch, your perception that the general manager has been acting preoccupied lately, or even the cold air that is slipping in from a drafty office window.

You respond to the stimulus by formulating a message, either a **verbal** message (written or spoken words), a **nonverbal** message (nonwritten and nonspoken signals) or some combination of the two. For Dave Kaplan, the stimulus for communication was a memorandum he received from the head of the research and development (R & D) department informing him that IC was not interested in developing Ultra Light but would, instead, sell the patent to some company that *was* interested.

The Filter

Step 2: *Our knowledge, experience, and viewpoints act as a filter to help us interpret (decode) the stimulus.*

If everyone had the same perception of events, your job of communicating would be much easier; you could assume that your perception of reality was accurate and that others would understand your motives and intent. Unfortunately, each person has a unique perception of reality, based on his or her individual experiences, culture, emotions at the moment, personality, knowledge, socioeconomic status, and a host of other variables. These variables act as a **filter** in shaping everyone's unique impressions of reality.

Once your brain receives a message, it begins to interpret the stimulus to derive meaning from it so that you will know how to respond or whether any response is even necessary. Stimuli that reinforce existing beliefs are likely to create a more lasting impression and to generate a stronger response than those that call into question your existing beliefs.

Likewise, stimuli are affected by your current emotional or physical frame of reference. An event that might normally cause you to react strongly might not even register if you're suffering from a bad cold or from lack of sleep. Or a remark made innocently might cause a strong negative reaction if you're angry or upset about some earlier event.

The memo Dave received from R & D simply reinforced what he had come to expect at his company, which had become successful by focusing on its own predetermined long-range objectives and which showed little interest in exploiting unexpected discoveries such as Ultra Light. Dave's long involvement in the research that had led to this product caused him to assume a protective, almost paternalistic, interest in its future. Besides, after so many years in the lab, Dave was ready for a new challenge. These factors, then, acted as a filter through which Dave interpreted the memo and formulated his response—a phone call to his brother in Chicago.

At the time of Dave's call, Marc Kaplan was sitting alone in his office at a Chicago advertising agency sampling five different brands of cheese

FIGURE 1.2 An Example of Communication at Work

pizza (see Figure 1.2). As a marketing manager in charge of a new pizza account, he was preoccupied with finding a competitive edge for his client's product, and his perception of Dave's message was filtered by his current situation.

To hear his scientist brother, the MIT graduate who all his life had preferred to pursue solitary scholarly research, suddenly erupting over the phone with the idea of starting a business contradicted Marc's lifelong preconceptions about Dave and acted as a strong filter resisting Dave's urgent message. Furthermore, Marc's emotional and physical frame of reference—hunkered down as he was over several cheese pizzas—did not put him in a receptive mood for a grand scheme that would take tens of thousands of dollars and many years of hard work. But Marc's background—his economic status, his education, and his current job—added another point of view, in this case a highly favorable filter for taking in Dave's message.

If Dave is good enough at communicating his message, he might be able to persuade Marc to join him in buying the Ultra Light patent from IC and starting a business of their own.

The Message

Step 3: *We formulate (encode) a verbal or nonverbal response to the stimulus.*

Dave's message to Marc was, "Let's form our own company." The extent to which any communication effort achieves its desired goal depends very directly on how well you construct the **message** (the information to be communicated). Success at communicating depends not only on the purpose and content of the message but also, just as important, on how skillful you are at communicating, how well you know your **audience** (the person or persons with whom you're communicating), and how much you share in common with your audience.

As a scientist, Dave Kaplan did not have an extensive business vocabulary. Nor did he have much practice at oral business presentations and the careful pacing and selective reinforcement required in such circumstances. In effect, Dave was attempting to make an oral business proposal, unfortunately without much technique or skill.

"You're crazy, Dave. You don't know what you're talking about." This initial response from Marc made it clear to Dave that his message wasn't getting through. But what Dave lacked in skill, he made up for in knowing his audience (his kid brother) backward and forward.

"You're chicken, Marc" had always gotten Marc's attention and interest in the past, and it worked again. Dave kept challenging Marc, something he knew Marc couldn't resist, and kept reminding him of their common ground: all the happy adventures they had shared as kids and adults.

The Medium

Step 4: *We select the form of the message (medium).*

Once the sender has encoded a message, the next step in the process is to transmit that message to the receiver. At this point, the sender must choose the form of message to send, or **medium.** Oral messages might be transmitted through a staff meeting, personal conference, telephone conversation, press conference, voice mail, or even such informal means as the company grapevine. Written messages might be transmitted through a memorandum, report, letter, contract, brochure, bulletin-board notice, electronic mail, company newsletter, press release, or addition to the policies and procedures manual. And nonverbal messages might be transmitted through facial expressions, gestures, or body movement.

Because Dave is in the process of talking with Marc over the phone, his medium is a telephone conversation.

The Destination

Step 5: *The message reaches its destination and, if successful, is perceived accurately by the receiver.*

The message is transmitted and then enters the sensory environment of the receiver, at which point control passes from the sender to the audience. Once the message reaches its destination, there is no guarantee that communication will actually occur. You are constantly bombarded with stimuli and your sensory organs pick up only part of them. Even assuming your receiver *does* admit your message, you have no assurance that it will be interpreted (filtered) as you intended. Your transmitted message becomes the source, or stimulus, for the next communication episode, and the process begins anew.

After Dave's enthusiastic, one-hour phone call, Marc promised to consider the venture seriously. Marc's response provided **feedback** (reaction to a message) to Dave on how accurately his own message had been received. In time, it led to many more versions of the communication process, both written and oral, before the two brothers founded Urban Systems, a small, "start-up" company whose primary product is Ultra Light and which employs 178 people at its corporate headquarters in Ann Arbor, Michigan, and in a completely automated manufacturing plant in Charlotte, North Carolina.

The Dynamic Nature of Communication

From our look at the components of communication and the model presented in Figure 1.1, you might erroneously infer that communication is a linear, static process—flowing in an orderly fashion from one stage to the next—and that you can easily separate the communicators into senders and receivers. That is not the case.

Two or more people often send and receive messages simultaneously. While you are receiving one message, you may at the same time be sending another message. For example, the look on your face as you are receiving a message may be sending a new message to the sender that you either understand, agree with, or are baffled by the message being sent. And the feedback thus given may prompt the sender to modify his or her intended message.

Thus, artificially "freezing" the action in order to examine each step of the communication process separately causes us to lose some of the dynamic richness of that process in terms of both its verbal and nonverbal components.

Urban Systems: A Continuing Case Study

As we join Urban Systems (US) in its second decade, Dave and Marc's company now has annual sales in the $30 million range, with a net profit last year of $1.4 million. It is considered a progressive company by the investment community, with skillful management and healthy earnings potential. The local community considers US to be a good corporate citizen; it is nonpolluting, and its officers are active in community affairs.

You will be seeing more of the Kaplan brothers and Urban Systems in the chapters ahead, as communication within the organization serves as an ongoing case study for each of the major areas of business communication—from this basic model of communication all the way through to the final chapter. You'll have the opportunity to get to know the people in the company and watch from the inside as they handle every type of business communication in concrete terms. Right now, you can learn more of the background of Urban Systems by reading the Chapter 1 Appendix, an overview of the company's history, products, financial data, and its all-too-human personnel.

TYPES OF COMMUNICATION

For more on verbal and non-verbal communication, see Video Case Study 1, Chiat/Day.

We have defined communication as the process of sending and receiving messages. The different types of messages that can be sent and received are shown in Figure 1.3.

Verbal Communication

Verbal messages are composed of words—either written or spoken.

It is the ability to communicate by using words that separates human beings from the rest of the animal kingdom. Our verbal ability also enables us to learn from the past—to benefit from the experience of others.

FIGURE 1.3 Types of Verbal and Nonverbal Communication

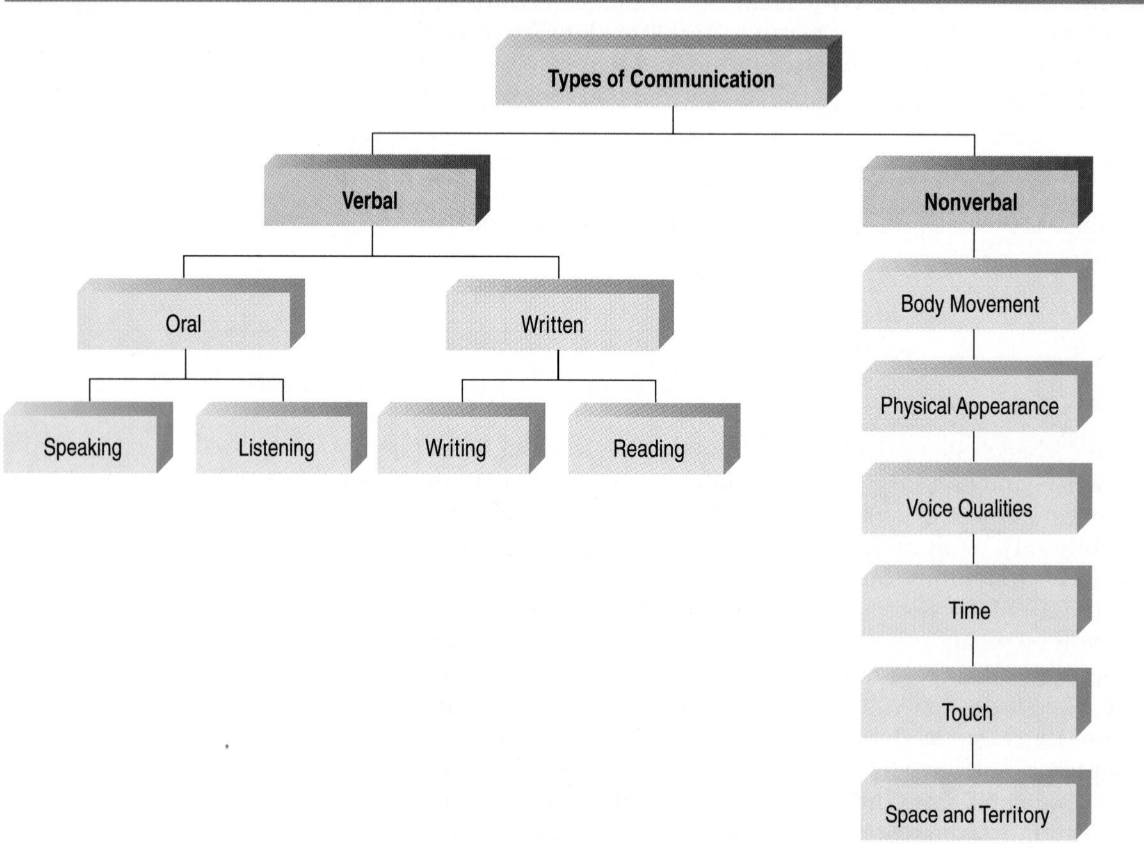

Oral Communication Oral communication is one of the most common functions in business. Consider, for example, how limiting it would be if a manager could not attend meetings, ask questions of colleagues, make presentations, appraise performance, handle customer complaints, or give instructions.

Oral communication is different from written communication in that it allows more ways to get a message across to others. You can clear up any questions immediately; use nonverbal clues; provide additional information; and use pauses, accents, and voice tone to stress certain points.

For oral communication to be effective, a second communication skill—listening—is also required. No matter how well crafted the content and delivery of an oral presentation, it cannot achieve its goal if the intended audience does not have effective listening skills. Some research has found that nearly 60% of all communication problems in business are caused by poor listening.[2]

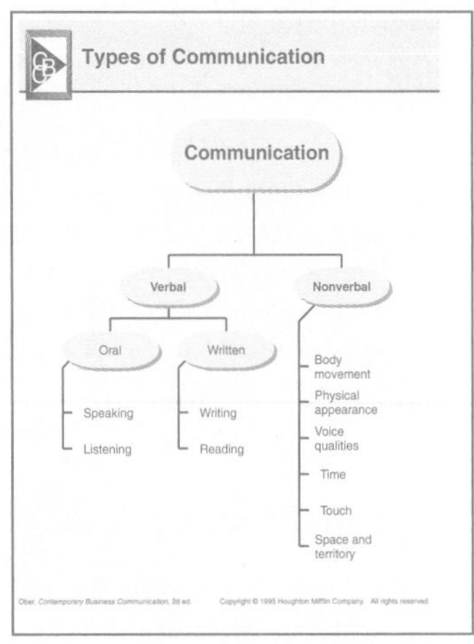

See Transparency 1.2, Types of Communication.

Written Communication Writing is more difficult than speaking because you have to get your message correct the first time; you do not have the advantage of immediate feedback and nonverbal clues such as facial expressions to help you achieve your objective. Examples of typical written communication in industry include the following:

- *Memorandums:* A **memorandum** is a written message sent to someone working in the same organization; it is often sent via computer (electronic mail) in automated offices.
- *Letters:* A **letter** is a written message sent to someone outside the organization; it also can be sent by computer via commercial electronic mail networks, such as MCI or CompuServe.
- *Reports:* A **report** is an orderly and objective presentation of information that assists in decision making and problem solving. Examples of common business reports include policies and procedures, status reports, minutes of meetings, financial reports, personnel evaluations, press releases, and computer printouts.
- *Miscellaneous:* Other examples of written communications include all types of contracts, sales literature, newsletters, and bulletin-board notices.

Writing is crucial to the modern organization because it serves as the major source of documentation. A speech may make a striking impression, but a memorandum leaves a permanent record for others to refer to in the future in case memory fails or a dispute arises.

Most oral communication is temporary; written communication is permanent.

For written messages to achieve their goals, they must be read. The skill of efficient reading is becoming more important in today's technological society. The abundance of widespread computing and word processing capabilities, along with the proliferation of convenient and economical photocopying and faxing, has created *more* paperwork rather than less. Thus, information overload is one of the unfortunate byproducts of our times (see Spotlight on Technology). These and other implications of technology on business communication are discussed in Chapter 2.

SPOTLIGHT ON TECHNOLOGY

Overcoming Information Anxiety

Executives, like nearly everyone else in this information-laden society, are being bombarded by more data than they can absorb. According to Richard Wurman, author of *Information Anxiety*, in order to function in business we are being forced assimilate a body of knowledge that is expanding by the minute.

THE BLACK HOLE

Trying to process all this information can induce "information anxiety"—apprehension about the ever-widening gap between what we understand and what we think we *should* understand. In other words, it is the black hole between data and knowledge. Here are some symptoms of information anxiety as Wurman describes them:

- Nodding your head knowingly when someone mentions a book, artist, or news story that you have actually never heard of.
- Feeling guilty about that ever-higher stack of periodicals waiting to be read.
- Blaming yourself for not being able to follow the instructions for putting a bike together.
- Feeling depressed because you don't know what all the buttons on your VCR do.

Wurman believes that "the System" is at fault—too many people are putting out too much data. For example, about 9,600 periodicals are published in the United States each year. Wurman believes it's a myth that the more choices you have, the more freedom you enjoy. More choices simply produce more anxiety. So as you decrease the number of choices, you decrease the fear of having made the wrong one.

NOBODY KNOWS IT ALL

The first step in overcoming information anxiety is to accept that there is much you won't understand. Let your ignorance be an inspiration to learn, not something to conceal. Wurman recommends standing in front of a mirror and practicing, "Could you repeat that?" or "I'm not sure I understand what you're talking about" instead of pretending to understand what you do not.

Other suggestions include the following:

- Separate what you are really interested in from what you merely think you *should* be interested in.
- Moderate your use of technology.
- Minimize the time you spend reading or watching news that isn't relevant to your life.
- Reduce your pile of office reading.

Source: Richard Saul Wurman, *Information Anxiety*, Doubleday, Garden City, NY; 1989.

Nonverbal Communication

For an extended discussion of technological issues, see "Technology and Communication" in Chapter 2, pp. 39–40.

According to management guru Peter Drucker, "The most important thing in communication is to hear what isn't being said."[3] A nonverbal message is any message that is not written or spoken. The nonverbal message may accompany a verbal message (smiling as you greet a colleague), or it may occur alone (selecting the back seat when entering the conference room for a staff meeting). Nonverbal messages are typically more spontaneous than verbal messages, but that does not mean that they are any less important. One study has shown that only 7% of the meaning communicated by most messages comes from the verbal portion, with the remaining 93% being conveyed nonverbally.[4]

Nonverbal messages are unwritten and unspoken.

The six most common types of nonverbal communication in business are discussed in the following sections.

Even your office space sends nonverbal messages about you. Software designer Sean Selitrennikoff describes his space as "not the office of your average accountant."

Body Movement By far, the most expressive part of your body is your face—especially your eyes. Research shows that receivers tend to be quite consistent in their reading of facial expressions. In fact, many of these expressions have the same meaning across different cultures.[5] Eye contact and eye movements tell you a lot about a person, although—as we shall see later—maintaining eye contact with the person to whom you're speaking is not perceived as important (or even polite) in some cultures.

Cultures differ in the importance they attach to eye contact.

Gestures are hand and upper-body movements that add important information to face-to-face interactions. As the game of charades proves, you can communicate quite a bit without using oral or written signals. More typically, gestures are used to help illustrate and reinforce your verbal message.

Body stance (posture, placement of arms and legs, distribution of weight, and the like) is another form of nonverbal communication. For example, leaning slightly toward the person you're communicating with would probably be taken as a sign of interest and involvement in the interaction. On the other hand, leaning back with arms folded across the chest might be taken (and intended) as a sign of boredom or defiance.

For more on nonverbal communication, see the supplemental lecture/discussion notes in the *Instructor's Resource Manual*, beginning on p. 5.

Physical Appearance Our culture places great value on physical appearance. Television, newspapers, and magazines are filled with advertisements for personal-care products, and the ads typically feature attractive users of these products. Attractive people tend to be seen as more intelligent, more likable, and more persuasive than unattractive people; in addition, they earn more money.[6]

Your appearance is particularly important for making a good first impression. Although you may not be able to change some of your physical features, understanding the importance of good grooming and physical appearance can help you to emphasize your strong points. Also, your clothing, jewelry, office and home furnishings, and automobile provide

Gestures that are routine in the United States may have a very different significance in other cultures. In *Blunders in International Business*, David A. Ricks reports that an American worker inadvertently offended his Korean boss when he beckoned him with a crooked finger, a gesture Koreans consider quite rude.

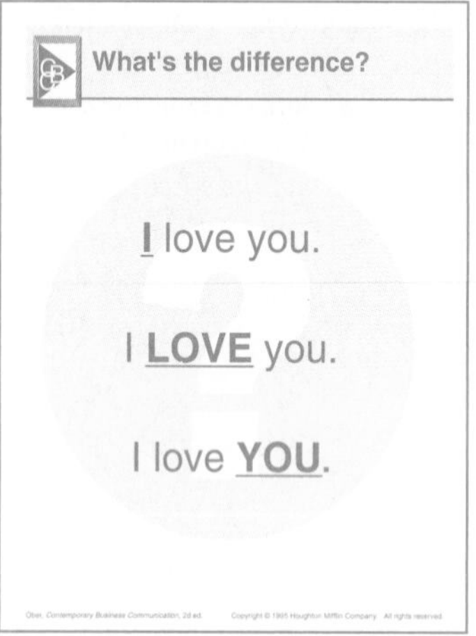
What's the difference?
I love you.
I LOVE you.
I love YOU.

See Transparency 1.3, Voice Qualities.

information about your values, taste, heritage, conformity, status, age, sexuality, and group identification.

Voice Qualities No one speaks in a monotone. To illustrate, read the following sentence aloud, each time emphasizing the italicized word. Note how the meaning changes with each reading.

- *You* were late. (*Answers the question, "Who was late?"*)
- You *were* late. (*Responds to the other person's denial of being late.*)
- You were *late*. (*Emphasizes how late the person was.*)

Voice qualities such as volume, speed, pitch, tone, and accent carry both intentional and unintentional messages. For example, when you're nervous, you tend to speak faster and in a higher pitch than normal. People who constantly speak too softly risk being interrupted or ignored, whereas people who constantly speak too loudly are often seen as being pushy or insecure.

The meaning we attach to time depends upon our status, the specific situation, and our culture.

Time How do you feel when you're late for an appointment? when others are late? The meaning given to time varies greatly by culture, with North American cultures being much more time conscious than South American or Middle Eastern cultures.

Time is related not only to culture but also to one's status within the organization. You would be much less likely to keep a superior waiting for an appointment than a subordinate. Time is also situation-specific. Although you normally might not worry about being five minutes late for a staff meeting, you would probably arrive early if you were the first presenter.

Common facial indications of anxiety or fear include tight or raised eyebrows, narrowed or squinting eyes, a deep frown, and a wrinkled forehead, notes Leon Fletcher in *Speaking to Succeed—In Business, Industry, Professions.*

Touch Touch is the first sense we develop, acquired even before birth. Some touches, such as those made by a physician during an examination, are purely physical; others, such as a handshake, are a friendly sign of willingness to communicate; and still others indicate intimacy. Although touching is a very important form of business communication, it is one that most people do not know how to use appropriately and effectively. The person who never touches anyone in a business setting may be seen as cold and standoffish, whereas the person who touches too frequently may cause the receiver to feel apprehensive and uncomfortable.

Space and Territory When you are on a crowded elevator, you probably look at the floor indicator, at advertisements, at your feet, or just straight ahead. Most people in our culture are uncomfortable in such close proximity to strangers. Psychologists have identified four zones within which people in our culture interact:[7]

Different types of communication occur at different distances.

1. *Intimate Zone:* From physical contact to about 18 inches is where all your body movements occur; this is the area in which you move throughout the day. It is an area normally reserved for close, intimate interactions. Business associates typically enter this space infrequently and only briefly—perhaps to shake hands or pat someone on the back.

2. *Personal Zone:* This zone, extending from 18 inches to about 4 feet, is where conversation with close friends and colleagues takes place. Unlike in the intimate zone, normal talking is frequent in the personal zone. Some, but not a great deal of, business interaction occurs here; for example, business lunches typically occur in this zone.
3. *Social Zone:* From 4 feet to 12 feet, the social zone is where most business exchanges occur. Informal business conferences and staff meetings occur within this space.
4. *Public Zone:* The public zone extends from 12 feet to as far as the eye can see and the ear can hear. This is the most formal zone, and the least significant interactions occur here. Because of the great distance, communication in the public zone is often one way, as from a speaker to a large audience.

Competent communicators recognize their own personal space needs and the needs of others. When communicating with people who prefer more or less space, the competent communicator makes the adjustments necessary to facilitate reaching his or her objective.

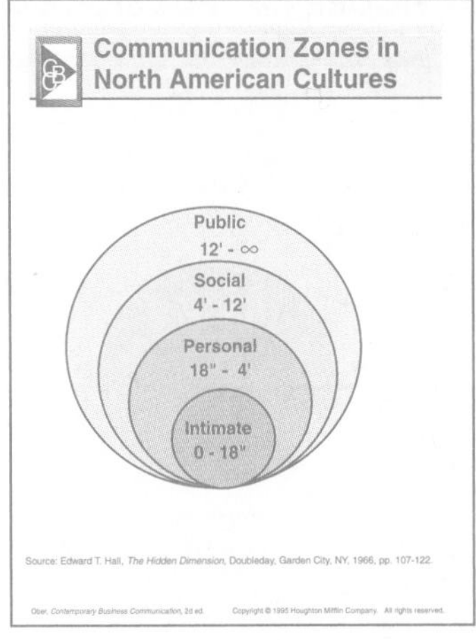

See Transparency 1.4, Communication Zones in North America.

DIRECTIONS OF COMMUNICATION

For an organization to be successful, communications must flow freely through formal and informal channels.

The Formal Communication Network

Within the organization, information may be transmitted from superiors to subordinates (downward communication), from subordinates to superiors (upward communication), among people at the same level on the organizational chart (horizontal communication), and among people in different departments within the organization (cross-channel communication). These four types of communication make up the organization's **formal communication network.** We'll use part of Urban Systems' organizational chart, shown in Figure 1.4, to illustrate the directions of communication. (See the Appendix to Chapter 1 for the complete chart.)

Downward Communication In most organizations the largest number of vertical communications move downward—from someone of higher authority to someone of lower authority. For example, at Urban Systems (Figure 1.4), Dave Kaplan sends a memo to Neelima Shrikhande about a computer report; she, in turn, confers with Eric Fox. Through written and oral channels, information regarding job performance, policies and procedures, day-to-day operations, and other organizational information is communicated.

Higher-level management communicates with lower-level employees through such means as memorandums, conferences, telephone conversations, company newsletters, policy manuals, bulletin-board announcements, and videotapes. One of the problems with written downward

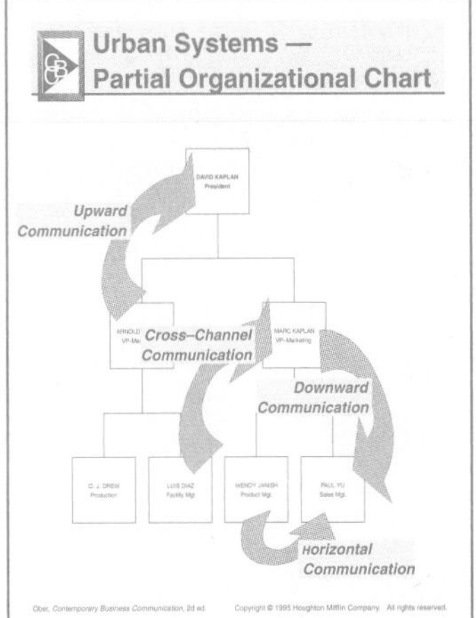

See Transparency 1.5, Directions of Communication.

FIGURE 1.4 Part of the Formal Communication Network at Urban Systems

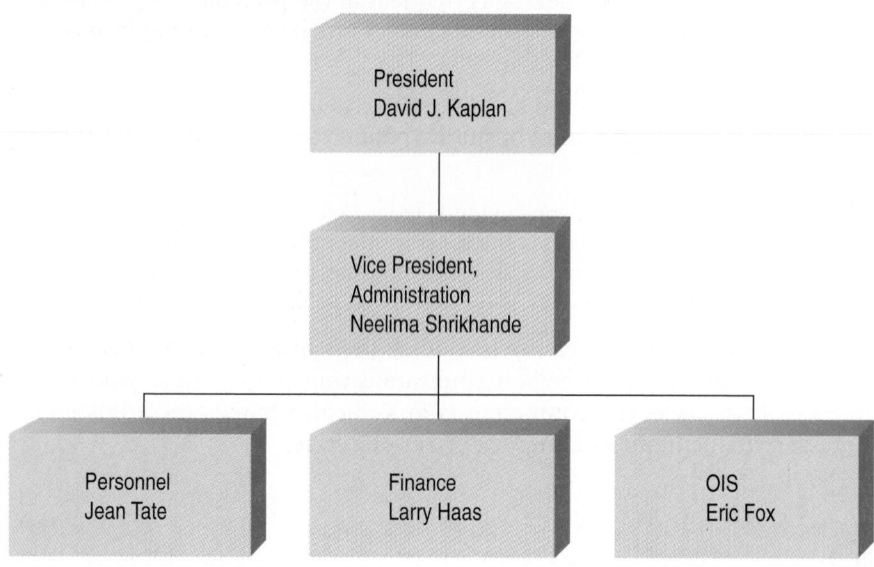

communication is that management assumes that what is sent downward is received and understood. Unfortunately, that is not always the case.

Upward Communication Upward communication is the flow of information from lower-level employees to upper-level employees. In Figure 1.4, for example, Jean Tate sends a monthly status report to the president regarding personnel actions for the month, and Neelima responds to Dave's memo regarding the computer report. Upward communication can take the form of memorandums, conferences, reports, suggestion systems, employee surveys, or union publications, among others.

The free flow of communication upward helps prevent management isolation.

Upward communication is important because it provides higher management with the information needed for decision making. It also cultivates employee loyalty by giving employees an opportunity to be heard, to air their grievances, and to offer suggestions. Finally, upward communication provides the feedback necessary to let supervisors know whether subordinates received and understood messages that were sent downward.

Horizontal Communication Horizontal communication is the flow of information among peers within the same work unit. For example, the administration division holds a weekly staff meeting at which the three managers (Jean, Larry, and Eric) exchange information about the status of their operations.

Horizontal communication is important to help coordinate work assignments, share information on plans and activities, negotiate differences, and develop interpersonal support, thereby creating a more cohesive work unit. The more that individuals or departments within an organization must interact with each other to accomplish their objectives, the more frequent and intense will be the horizontal communication.

The most common form of horizontal communication is the committee meeting, where most coordination, sharing of information, and problem solving take place. Intense competition for scarce resources, lack of trust among coworkers, or concerns about job security or promotions can sometimes create barriers to the free flow of horizontal information.

Cross-Channel Communication Cross-channel communication is the exchange of information among employees in different work units who are neither subordinate nor superior to each other. For example, each year a payroll clerk in Jean Tate's department sends out a request to all company employees for updated information about the number of exemptions they claim on their tax forms.

Staff specialists use cross-channel communications frequently because their responsibilities typically involve many departments within the organization. Because they lack line authority to direct those with whom they communicate, they must often rely on their persuasive skills, as for instance, when the personnel department encourages employees to complete a job-satisfaction questionnaire.

The Informal Communication Network

The **informal communication network** (or the *grapevine,* as it is called) is the transmission of information through nonofficial channels within the organization. In the carpool on the way to work, waiting to use the photocopier, jogging at noon, or at a local PTA meeting—whenever workers come together, they are likely to hear and pass on information about possible happenings in the organization. Employees often say that the grapevine is their most frequent source of information on company plans and performance.

The informal communication network (grapevine) transmits information through nonofficial channels within the organization.

These are the common characteristics of the grapevine:[8]

- Most of the information passed along the grapevine (about 80%) is business related, and most of it (75% to 95%) is accurate.
- The grapevine is pervasive. It exists at all levels in the organization—from corporate boardroom to the assembly line.
- Information moves rapidly along the grapevine.
- The grapevine is most active when change is taking place and when one's need to know or level of fear is highest—during layoffs, plant closings, acquisitions, mergers, and the like.
- The grapevine is a normal, often vital, part of every organization.

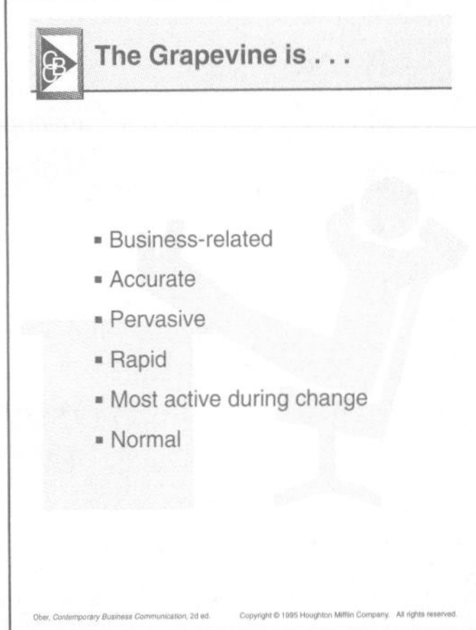

The Grapevine is . . .
Business-related
Accurate
Pervasive
Rapid
Most active during change
Normal

See Transparency 1.6, Characteristics of the Grapevine.

Rather than trying to eliminate the grapevine (a futile effort), wise managers accept its existence and pay attention to it. They act promptly to counteract false rumors. Most of all, they use the formal communication network (including meetings, memos, newsletters, and bulletin boards) to ensure that all news—positive and negative—gets out to employees as quickly and as completely as possible. The free flow of information within the organization not only stops rumors; it's simply good business.

BARRIERS TO COMMUNICATION

Considering the complex nature of the communication process, you should not be surprised that your messages are not always received exactly as you intended. As a matter of fact, sometimes your messages will not be received at all; at other times, they will be received incompletely or inaccurately. Some of the obstacles to effective and efficient communication are verbal; others are nonverbal. As illustrated in Figure 1.5, these barriers can create an impenetrable "brick wall" that makes effective communication impossible.

Verbal Barriers

Verbal barriers are related to what you write or say. They include inadequate knowledge or vocabulary, differences in interpretation, inappropriate use of expressions, overabstraction and ambiguity, and polarization.

FIGURE 1.5 Verbal and Nonverbal Barriers to Communication

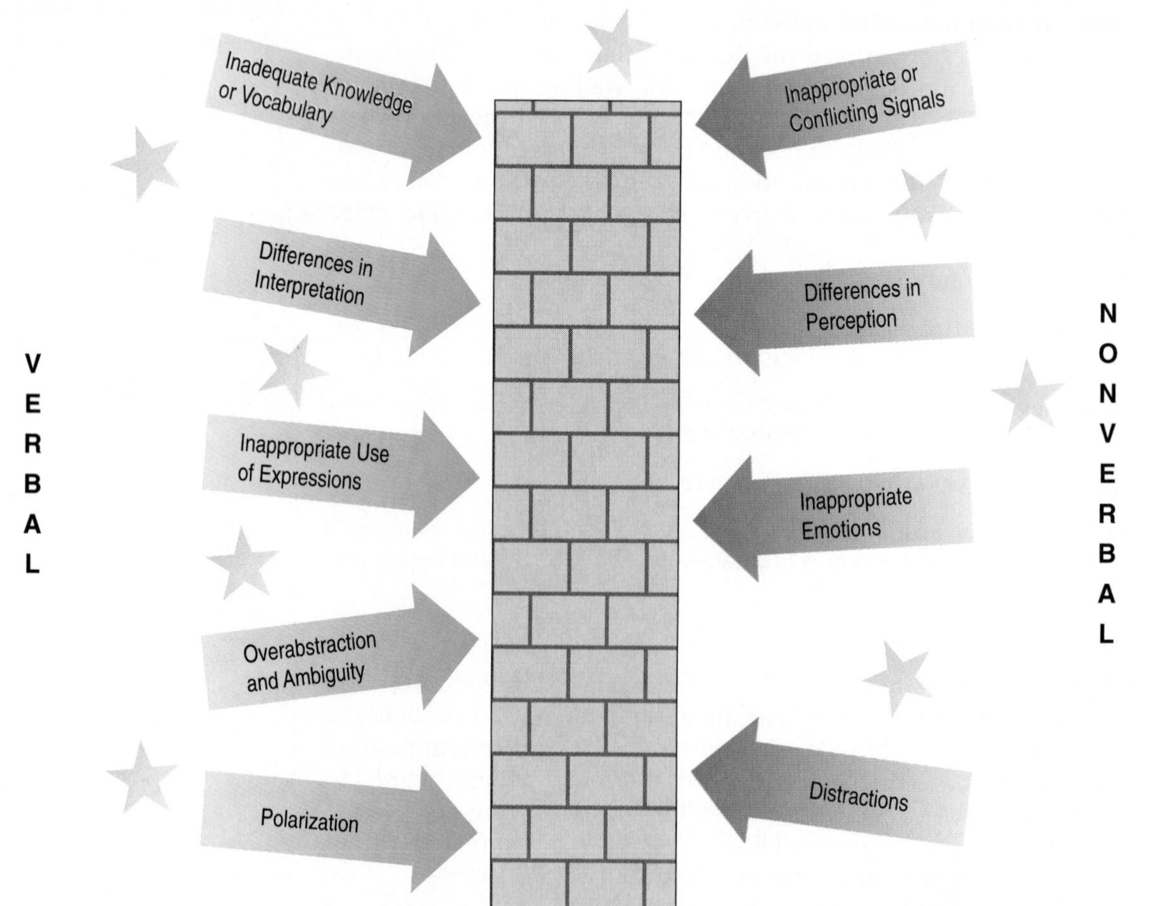

Some may feel that there are communication barriers between a female boss and male subordinates. Theo Schwartzkopf, president of Mid-America Ford Truck Sales, disagrees. She believes that barriers develop when language is not clear, when employees feel no one is listening, and when employees are expected to follow orders without question.

Inadequate Knowledge or Vocabulary Before you can even begin to think about how you will communicate an idea, you must, first of all, *have* the idea; that is, you must have sufficient knowledge about the topic to know what you want to say. Regardless of your level of technical expertise, this may not be as simple as it sounds. Assume, for example, that you are Larry Haas, manager of the finance department at Urban Systems. Dave Kaplan, president of the company, has asked you to evaluate an investment opportunity. You've completed all the necessary research and are now ready to write your report. Or are you?

Have you analyzed your audience? Do you know how much the president knows about the investment so that you'll know how much background information to include? Do you know how familiar he is with investment terminology? Can you safely use abbreviations like *NPV* and *RRR*, or will you have to spell out and perhaps define *net present value* and *required rate of return*? Do you know whether the president would prefer to have your conclusions at the beginning of the report, followed by your analysis, or at the end? What tone should the report take? The answers to such questions will be important if you are to achieve your objective in writing the report.

You must know enough about both your topic and your audience to express yourself precisely and appropriately.

Differences in Interpretation Sometimes senders and receivers attribute different meanings to the same word or attribute the same meaning to different words. When this happens, miscommunication can occur.

Every word has both a denotative and a connotative meaning. **Denotation** refers to the literal, dictionary meaning of a word. **Connotation** refers to the subjective, emotional meaning that you attach to a word. For example, the denotative meaning of the word *plastic* is "a synthetic material that can be easily molded into different forms." For some people, the word also has a negative connotative meaning—"cheap or artificial substitute."

A word's denotation *defines its meaning; its* connotation *indicates our associations with the word.*

Most of the interpretation problems occur because of the personal reactions engendered by the connotative meaning of a word. Do you have a positive, neutral, or negative reaction to the terms *broad, bad, aggressive, hard-hitting, workaholic, corporate raider, head-hunter, gay, golden parachute,* or *wasted?* Are your reactions likely to be the same as everyone else's? The problem with some terms is not only that people assign different meanings to the term but also that the term itself might cause such an emotional reaction that the receiver is "turned off" to any further communication with the sender.

Inappropriate Use of Expressions Expressions are groups of words that have intended meanings that are different from their literal interpretations. Examples include slang, jargon, and euphemisms.

The use of slang, jargon, and euphemisms is sometimes appropriate and sometimes inappropriate.

- **Slang** is an expression, often short-lived, that is identified with a specific group of people. For example, one teenager may say to another, "Yo, G! Why're you frontin' me like that by wearing that fufi pink outfit? Daaagg!" (*Yo, G!:* greeting to a guy or girl; *front:* to embarrass; *fufi:* fussy or pretentious; *Dag:* word for when you want to curse but don't want to use a curse word).

  Teenagers, construction workers, immigrants, computer technology professionals, and just about every other subgroup you can imagine all have their own sets of slang. Using appropriate slang in everyday speech presents no problem; it conveys precise information and may indicate group membership. Problems arise, however, when the sender uses slang that the receiver doesn't understand or that sends a negative nonverbal message about the sender.

- **Jargon** is the technical terminology used within specialized groups; it has sometimes been called "the pros' prose." As with slang, the problem is not in using jargon—jargon provides a very precise and efficient way of communicating with those familiar with it. The problem comes in using jargon either with someone who doesn't understand it or in using jargon in an effort to impress others.

- **Euphemisms** are inoffensive expressions used in place of words that may offend or suggest something unpleasant. Sensitive writers and speakers use euphemisms occasionally, especially to describe bodily functions. How many ways, for example, can you think of to say that someone has died?

Slang, jargon, and euphemisms all have important roles to play in business communication—as long as they're used with appropriate people and in appropriate contexts. They can, however, prove to be barriers to effective communication when used to impress, when used too often, or when used in inappropriate settings.

The word transportation *is abstract; the word* automobile *is concrete.*

Overabstraction and Ambiguity An **abstract word** identifies an idea or feeling instead of a concrete object. For example, *communication* is an abstract word, whereas *memorandum* is a **concrete word,** a word that identifies something that can be perceived by the senses. Abstract words are necessary in order to communicate about things you cannot see or touch. However, communication problems result when you use too many abstract words or when you use too high a level of abstraction. The higher the level of abstraction, the more difficult it is to visualize exactly what the sender has in mind. For example, which sentence communicates more information: "I acquired an asset at the store" or "I purchased a laser printer at ComputerLand"?

Similar communication problems result from the overuse of ambiguous terms such as *a few, some, several,* and *far away,* which have too broad a meaning for use in much business communication. For example, a report contained the following sentence: "The shipping department received a lot of complaints last month." Isn't it important to know exactly how many complaints they received?

Polarization At times, some people act as though every situation is divided into two opposite and distinct poles, with no allowance for a middle ground. Of course, there are some true dichotomies. You are either male or female, and your company either will or will not make a profit this year. But most aspects of life involve more than two alternatives.

For example, you might assume that a speaker either is telling the truth or is lying. In fact, what the speaker actually says may be true, but by selectively omitting some important information, he or she may be giving an inaccurate impression. Is the speaker telling the truth or not? Most likely, the answer lies somewhere in between. Likewise, you are not necessarily either tall or short, rich or poor, smart or dumb. Competent communicators avoid inappropriate *either/or* logic and instead make the effort to search for middle-ground words when such language best describes a situation.

Thinking in terms of all or nothing limits our choices.

Nonverbal Barriers

Not all communication problems are related to what you write or say. Some are related to how you act. Nonverbal barriers to communication include inappropriate or conflicting signals, differences in perception, inappropriate emotions, and distractions.

In his book *Silent Messages,* Albert Mehrabian notes the power of nonverbal communication. When we say one thing—for example, that we are pleased to meet someone—but our actions, posture, or expression suggest something contradictory, others will usually believe what we do rather than what we say.

Inappropriate or Conflicting Signals Suppose a well-qualified applicant for a secretarial position submits a résumé with a typographical error or an accountant's personal office is in such disorder that she could not find the papers she needed for a meeting with the president. When verbal and nonverbal signals conflict, the receiver tends to put more faith in the nonverbal signals because nonverbal messages are more difficult to manipulate than verbal messages.

As has been made clear, many nonverbal signals vary from culture to culture. Remember also that the United States itself is a multicultural country: a banker from Boston, an art shop owner from San Francisco, and a farmer from North Dakota are likely to both use and interpret nonverbal signals in quite different ways. What is appropriate in one context might not be appropriate in another.

Communication competence requires that you communicate nonverbal messages that are consistent with your verbal messages and that are appropriate for the context.

"First impressions are formed in less than five seconds," writes Elayne Snyder in her book *Persuasive Business Speaking*. "They are instant. They are automatic. And they are very hard to change afterwards. Social psychologists call this the Threshold Effect. In business, first impressions are crucial." (Elayne Snyder, *Persuasive Business Speaking,* American Management Association, New York, 1990, pp. 105–106.)

Differences in Perception Even when they hear the same speech or read the same document, people of different ages, socioeconomic backgrounds, cultures, and so forth often form very different perceptions. We discussed earlier the mental filter by which each communication source is interpreted. Because each person is unique, with unique experiences, knowledge, and viewpoints, each person forms different opinions about what he or she reads and hears.

Some people tend automatically to believe certain people and to distrust other people. For example, when reading a memo from the company president, one employee may be so intimidated by the president that he or she accepts everything the president says, whereas another employee may have such negative feelings about the president that he or she believes nothing the president says.

It is generally more effective to depend on logic instead of emotions when communicating.

For an exercise on revising a memo of reprimand that is based on inappropriate emotions, refer students to the *Study Guide*, pp. 67–68.

Inappropriate Emotions In most cases, a moderate level of emotional involvement intensifies the communication and makes it more personal. However, too much emotional involvement can be an obstacle to communication. For example, excessive anger can create such an emotionally charged environment that reasonable discussion is not possible. Likewise, prejudice (automatically rejecting certain people or ideas), stereotyping (placing individuals into categories), and boredom all hinder effective communication. Such emotions tend to create a blocked mind that is closed to ideas, rejecting or ignoring information that is contrary to one's prevailing belief.

Distractions Any environmental or competing element that restricts one's ability to concentrate on the communication task hinders effective communication. Such distractions are called **noise.** Examples of *environmental noise* are poor acoustics, extreme temperature, uncomfortable seating, body odor, poor telephone connections, and illegible photocopies. Examples of *competing noise* are other important business to attend to, too many meetings, and too many reports to read.

Competent communicators make the effort to write and speak clearly and consistently and try to avoid or minimize any verbal or nonverbal barriers that might cause misunderstandings.

SUMMARY

The study of communication is important because communication is such a pervasive part of the organization and because it is so critical for achieving organizational goals. In fact, most managers spend the vast majority of their workday in some form of verbal communication.

The communication process begins with a stimulus. Based on your unique knowledge, experience, and viewpoints, you then filter, or interpret, the stimulus and formulate the message you wish to communicate. The next step is to select a medium of transmission for the message. Finally, the message reaches its destination. If it is successful, the receiver picks it up as a source for communication and provides appropriate feedback to you.

Verbal communication includes oral (speaking and listening) and written (writing and reading) communication. Nonverbal communication includes body movement, physical appearance, voice qualities, time, touch, and space and territory.

The organization's formal communication network consists of downward communication from superiors to subordinates, upward communication from subordinates to superiors, horizontal communication among people at the same level, and cross-channel communication among people in different departments within the organization. The informal communication network (also called the grapevine) consists of information transmitted through nonofficial channels. Rather than try to eliminate it, managers should accept its existence and pay attention to it.

Sometimes barriers are present that interfere with effective communication. Examples of verbal barriers are inadequate knowledge or vocabulary, differences in interpretation, inappropriate use of expressions, overabstraction and ambiguity, and polarization. Examples of nonverbal barriers are inappropriate or conflicting signals, differences in perception, inappropriate emotions, and distractions.

KEY TERMS

For an exercise on matching terms, refer students to the *Study Guide*, p. 65.

Abstract word A word that identifies an idea or feeling as opposed to a concrete object.

Audience The person or persons with whom you're communicating.

Communication The process of sending and receiving messages.

Concrete word A word that identifies something the senses can perceive.

Connotation The subjective or emotional feeling associated with a word.

Denotation The literal, dictionary meaning of a word.

Euphemism An inoffensive expression used in place of an expression that may offend or suggest something unpleasant.

Feedback The receiver's reaction or response to a message.

Filter The mental process of perceiving stimuli based on your knowledge, experience, and viewpoints.

Formal communication network The transmission of prescribed information through downward, upward, horizontal, and cross-channel routes.

Informal communication network The transmission of information through nonofficial channels within the organization; also called the *grapevine*.

Jargon The technical terminology used within specialized groups.

Letter A written message sent to someone outside the organization.

Medium The form of a message—for example, a memo or telephone call.

Memorandum A written message sent to someone within the organization.

Message The information (either verbal or nonverbal) that is communicated.

Noise Environmental or competing elements that distract one's attention during communication.

Nonverbal message A nonwritten and nonspoken message consisting of facial expressions, gestures, voice qualities, and the like.

Report An orderly and objective presentation of information that assists in decision making and problem solving.

Slang An expression, often short-lived, that is identified with a specific group of people.

Stimulus An event that creates within the individual a need to communicate.

Verbal message A message comprised of spoken or written words.

REVIEW AND DISCUSSION

The answers to the review and discussion questions appear in the *Instuctor's Resource Manual*, beginning on p. 6.

1. **Communication at Home Depot Revisited** ▪ Deedy Taylor of The Home Depot understands that communication is essential to the continued success of a company with 25,000 employees in 100 locations across the

country. Although communicating effectively can be exciting, it also involves an element of risk.

a. When Home Depot sends a training videotape to its stores, is the company using verbal or nonverbal communication? Explain your answer.
b. Taylor talks about breaking down boundaries within Home Depot and directing the flow of information in all directions. Is she discussing upward, downward, horizontal, or cross-channel communication?
c. Which nonverbal barriers to communication might prevent the message in a training videotape from being received or understood?

2. What are the five components of the communication process?
3. What is meant by the statement "The stimulus is filtered through your brain"?
4. Give an example of a medium.
5. What are four forms of verbal communication?
6. Give an example of a nonverbal message that reinforces a verbal message and one that contradicts a verbal message.
7. What four directions make up the formal communication network?
8. Why is it difficult to get objective information flowing upward in the organization?
9. What is the difference between horizontal and cross-channel communication?
10. What are the characteristics of the grapevine?
11. Give an example of the denotation and the connotation of a word.
12. What is the difference between slang and jargon? Give an example of each.
13. Compose a sentence containing an overabstraction. Then revise the sentence to make it more concrete.

EXERCISES

Suggestions and sample solutions for exercises appear in the *Instuctor's Resource Manual*, beginning on p. 8.

THE COMPONENTS OF COMMUNICATION

Communication is the process of sending and receiving messages through spoken or written words or through nonverbal means. Communication begins with an internal or external stimulus—an event that creates within you the need to communicate. Your brain receives the stimulus and filters (interprets) it, based upon your unique impression of reality as a result of your experiences, culture, emotions at the moment, personality, knowledge, socioeconomic status, and other variables.

You encode a response by forming a verbal message (composed of written or spoken words), a nonverbal message (composed of facial expressions, gestures, voice qualities, and the like) or a combination of the two. The message is then transmitted through an appropriate medium, such as over the telephone for an oral message, in a memorandum for a written message, or as a nod of the head in a nonverbal message.

The destination is the point at which the transmitted message enters the sensory environment of the receiver. At this point, control passes from sender to receiver, and the transmitted message becomes the source, or stimulus, for the next communication. If the receiver responds by communicating, you receive feedback as to whether and how well your message was received.

Communication is a dynamic process. It does not always proceed orderly from one stage to the next, and it is not always possible to separate senders and receivers.

Ober, *Contemporary Business Communication*, 2d ed.

See Master 1.1, Exercise 3, Collaboration, in the *Instructor's Resource Manual.*

1. **Getting to Know You** ▪ Write a two-page (typed, double-spaced) report introducing yourself to your instructor and to other members of the class. Include such information as the following:

   - *Background:* Your grade level, major, extracurricular activities, work experience, and the like.
   - *Career Objectives:* What type of position would you like immediately upon graduation? With what type of organization and in what part of the country would you like to work? Where do you expect to be in terms of your profession five years from now?
   - *Course Objectives:* Why are you taking this course? What specific skill or skills do you hope to master? What aspects of the course do you expect to find most challenging?
   - *Small-Group Experiences:* What experience have you had in working on group projects? What have you found to be the advantages and disadvantages of such assignments? What type of group would you find most satisfying to work with?

   Include any other information you think would be useful. Edit and proofread your draft and submit it.
2. **Communication Process** ▪ Use an incident from a recent television program to illustrate each of the five components of the communication process. Identify any communication barriers that you observed.

3. **Collaboration** ■ Approximately 1,500 words in this chapter were devoted to the discussion of the components of communication. Working in small groups, write a 250-word abstract (summary) of this discussion. Since this is an informational abstract, you may pick up the exact wording of the original discussion when appropriate. Ensure that all important points are covered, your narrative flows smoothly from one topic to another, and your writing is error-free.
4. **Entrepreneurship** ■ Marty Chernov, owner of a small salvage yard employing 18 people, has an appointment with John Garrison Boyd IV, vice president of Metropolitan Bank, to discuss his application for a $35,000 business loan. What helpful guidelines can you give Marty regarding his nonverbal behavior at the conference?
5. **Communication Directions** ■ Think of an organization to which you belong or a business with which you are familiar. Provide a specific illustration of each of the four directions in the formal communication network. Then develop an organizational chart similar to the one in Figure 1.4.
6. **Grapevine** ■ Read a journal article about the company grapevine. Then write a one-page summary of the article. Proofread for content and language errors and revise as needed. Staple a photocopy of the article to your summary, and submit both to your instructor.
7. **Meanings Are in People** ■ Record your personal connotative meaning of each of the following terms: *tree hugger, profit, stress, conservative, alternative lifestyle, Japanese, affirmative action.*
8. **International** ■ "I'll never understand our people in Pakistan," Eileen said. "I wrote our local agent over there, who's supposedly a financial wizard, this note: 'If your firm wants to play ball with us, we'll need the straight scoop. What's your bottom-line price on the STX model with all the bells and whistles? Also, if you pull out all the stops, can we get delivery by Xmas?' And you know what he did? He wrote me back a long letter, inquiring about my health and my family, but never answering my questions! If they don't get on the ball, I'm going to recommend that we stop doing business with them." From a communication standpoint, what is happening here? What advice can you give Eileen? Rewrite her message to the Pakistani agent to make it more effective.
9. **Technology** ■ Ralph looked up from his computer and remarked, "Fortunately, I do most of my writing on my computer. For example, I send a memo electronically to the other person's computer, where it can be called up and read at his or her convenience. So I don't have to worry about creating any nonverbal barriers." Is Ralph correct? Discuss and give examples of nonverbal barriers that can undermine the effectiveness of Ralph's electronic memos.

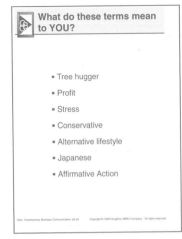

What do these terms mean to YOU?

- Tree hugger
- Profit
- Stress
- Conservative
- Alternative lifestyle
- Japanese
- Affirmative Action

Ober, *Contemporary Business Communication*, 2d ed.

See Master 1.2, Exercise 7, Meanings Are in People, in the *Instructor's Resource Manual.*

CONTINUING CASE 1

Urban Systems Jumps the Gun

Paul, Wendy, and C. B. entered Marc's office ten minutes late for their meeting. Marc immediately came from behind his desk and ushered them to two comfortable sofas positioned around a coffee table. "Can I have my secretary get you a cup of coffee?" he asked. When they all declined, Marc sat down, propped his feet onto the table, and said to C. B., "Now, what seems to be the problem with the advertising schedule?"

A possible solution to the Continuing Case is described in the *Instructor's Resource Manual,* p. 9.

"Just as I explained in my memo to you," C. B. replied, "I've committed $18,500 for a full-page, four-color ad in next month's *Facilities Management* magazine advertising Ultra Light strips for task lighting with modular furniture. Now Wendy tells me that the new strips won't be available for sale until three weeks after *FM* hits the newsstands."

"C. B., I did warn you in December that R & D had run into a minor technical problem that would take a little time to fix," Wendy replied.

"A little time! My goodness, they've been working on 'that little technical problem' for over a month. How was I to know that 'a little time' meant two months?" demanded C. B.

Marc reached over and placed his hand on C. B.'s shoulder and said, "No need to get so upset. How can we fix this problem? Paul, do you have any suggestions?"

Paul replied, "Well, I didn't see a copy of C. B.'s memo to you, so I don't know the details, but it seems to me from reading Wendy's production schedule that C. B. should have known about this problem early enough to hold off on the *FM* advertisement."

"Well, it looks like it's too late to do anything about it this time," said Marc, standing up. "Let's try to have better communication between each group so that we avoid this type of problem in the future. I've got another meeting coming up in 15 minutes that I have to get ready for. Thanks for stopping by."

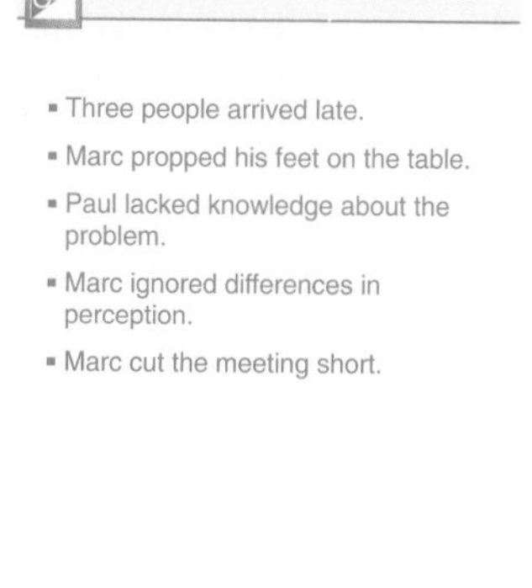

Negative Nonverbal Messages
▪ Three people arrived late.
▪ Marc propped his feet on the table.
▪ Paul lacked knowledge about the problem.
▪ Marc ignored differences in perception.
▪ Marc cut the meeting short.

See Master 1.3, Continuing Case 1, Question 4, in the *Instructor's Resource Manual.*

Critical Thinking

1. From what you know about Marc, were his verbal and nonverbal messages consistent with his personality? Give examples.
2. Using Wendy's remarks about the technical problem and C. B.'s response, illustrate the communication process.
3. How helpful was Marc in this incident? Paul?
4. List five negative nonverbal messages that were communicated in this situation.
5. What communication barriers were present in this situation?

WORDWISE *Word Frequency*

- The average person uses or can decipher 20,000 words; a highly educated person might use up to 50,000.
- About 35 different words make up half of our daily conversation, and about 70 words make up half of our written correspondence.
- The seven most common prefixes and suffixes in U.S. company names are, in order, *Ameri, Nat, Mark, Star, Uni, Lead,* and *Inter.*

URBAN SYSTEMS, INC.

THE COMPANY

Urban Systems, Inc. (US) is a small, "start-up" company whose primary product is Ultra Light, a new, paper-thin light source that promises to revolutionize the illumination industry. The company employs 178 people at its corporate headquarters in Ann Arbor, Michigan, and in a completely automated manufacturing plant in Charlotte, North Carolina. It is incorporated under the laws of the state of Michigan, with all stock privately held by the founders and their families.

Urban Systems has annual sales in the $30 million range, with a net profit last year of $1.4 million. It is considered a progressive company by the investment community, with good management and good earnings potential. The local community considers US to be a good corporate citizen; it is a nonpolluting firm, and its officers are active in the local chamber of commerce and in community affairs.

THE PRODUCT

Ultra Light is a flat, electroluminescent sheet of material that serves as a light source. It is capable of replacing most fluorescent, neon, and incandescent light fixtures. Physically, Ultra Light is a paper-thin sheet of chemically treated material laminated between thin layers of clear plastic. In effect, it is a credit-card thin light fixture that is bendable and that can be produced in a variety of shapes and sizes. Operated either by battery or wall current, it generates a bright white or colored light.

Ultra Light is cost-competitive with other, more conventional lighting, and its life expectancy is measured in years. All of this, combined with the appeal of its very thin profile, battery operation ("use it anywhere"), the evenly distributed light it produces, and the way it can conform to a variety of physical shapes, makes Ultra Light a new product with a lot of potential.

COMPANY HISTORY

US was founded in 1989 by two brothers, David and Marc Kaplan. David was a chemical engineer at Industrial Chemical, Inc., when he developed the basic concept of Ultra Light while working on another project. Because IC was not interested in pursuing the manufacturing and marketing of this product, David bought all rights to Ultra Light from IC and patented it in 1989. Then he and his younger brother Marc, formerly a marketing manager for an advertising agency in Chicago, started Urban Systems in an abandoned warehouse in Midland, Michigan.

The company received start-up funds through personal investments of $50,000 by David Kaplan and $35,000 by Marc and a $68,500 five-year loan from the United States Small Business Administration. Because of Marc's advertising background, the company's five-year business plan focused on marketing Ultra Light initially for advertising purposes—to illuminate signs, point-of-purchase displays, and the like. Later, as the company became better established in the marketplace, plans were to expand into industrial, office, and consumer applications. Hence, a company name—Urban Systems—was selected that was broad enough to encompass a variety of products.

After a somewhat uneven start, US had become profitable by the end of its fourth year of operations and had outgrown its original building. The company recently built an 11,000 square-foot facility in an attractive office park in Ann Arbor, Michigan, to house its administrative, marketing, and R&D functions. The company also moved its manufacturing operations to Charlotte, North Carolina, in a leased facility. The manufacturing facility is completely automated, with state-of-the-art robotics, just-in-time inventory control, and a progressive union-management agreement. The latest three-year labor contract expires next year.

PERSONNEL

The organization chart for Urban Systems is shown in Figure 1. Each corporate position and the person currently occupying that position are described below.

Board of Directors

The board is comprised of David J. Kaplan, chair; Marc Kaplan, vice-chair; Judith Klehr Kaplan (David Kaplan's wife), secretary/treasurer; Thomas V. Robertson, general counsel; and Eileen Jennings (vice president of U.S. National Bank of Michigan). As required by the articles of incorporation, the board meets quarterly at company headquarters.

President

David J. Kaplan

Dave Kaplan, age 46, is a professional engineer-turned-manager. He graduated with honors from the Massachusetts Institute of Technology with a degree in chemical engineering. Upon graduation from MIT, he began working as a chemical engineer in the polymer division at Industrial Chemical, where he worked until 1989 when he started US. During his time at IC, he attended graduate school part-time at Central Michigan University, where he received his MBA degree in 1975. Although he was offered numerous management positions at IC, he elected to continue working as a chemical engineer. His work resulted in numerous profitable patents for IC, and he was considered a highly respected member of the scientific staff.

Dave has published numerous articles in scholarly journals, has presented papers in his area of specialty at several inter-

Case

national conferences, and has served as president of the Michigan Society of Chemical Engineers.

Although he manages his new company effectively, Dave will tell you that some of his happiest times were working in the lab at IC—pursuing some esoteric research project alone and at his own pace. He will also tell you that the aspects of managing Urban Systems that he dislikes the most are the incessant meetings and having to manage and be responsible for the work of others. At US, Dave is considered a perfectionist and a workaholic. Although not an especially warm person, he is highly respected by his staff.

Dave married Judith Klehr immediately upon graduation from college. They have three children (Jonathan, 23, a newspaper reporter in Washington, DC; Michael, 22, a senior at Syracuse University; and Marla, 16, a sophomore in a private school in Ann Arbor). The family lives in Ann Arbor, where Judy is very active in community affairs.

Executive Secretary

Amy Stetsky

Amy Stetsky, or "Stetsky" as she is called by nearly everyone who knows her, was one of the first people hired by Dave Kaplan. She is 32 years old, has an associate's degree in office systems, and recently earned the Certified Professional Secretary (CPS®) designation as a result of passing an intensive two-day exam administered by a division of Professional Secretaries, International. She is highly respected and well-liked by everyone in the organization.

Vice President, Manufacturing

Arnold McNally

Arnie McNally knows the production business from top to bottom. He is 57 years old and has been with the company from the beginning, having been hired away from a similar job at Steelcase Corporation. Although only a high school graduate, McNally has earned the respect of both Dave and his subordinates, including the engineers in the research and development unit.

Arnie gives his staff wide latitude in running their units. He supports them, even when they make mistakes. He does insist, however, on being kept informed at every step of the way. He is a very direct type of person—you always know where you stand with him. If any of his subordinates have some bad news to convey, they know he wants to know immediately and directly—with no beating around the bush.

Although he gets along well with both Dave and his subordinates, he and Marc Kaplan have had several run-ins during the past five years. Privately, he would tell you that he believes Marc is a "lightweight" who is not particularly effective in marketing the firm's products. Arnie is especially upset that Marc has shot down several new product ideas proposed by Arnie's R&D staff.

Vice President, Marketing

Marc Kaplan

People who know both Dave and Marc Kaplan cannot believe they are brothers. Marc, age 42, is the complete opposite of Dave. He is warm and outgoing, with a wide circle of friends both in and out of business. His extensive network of personal and professional contacts has resulted in numerous large and lucrative orders for the firm.

Marc depends heavily on his three managers, especially for in-house operations. He spends a great deal of time away from the office—entertaining customers and prospective customers, attending conventions where US exhibits its products, and making the rounds of golf tournaments and after-hours cocktail parties. Marc is divorced and lives in a high-rise condominium in Ann Arbor, where he has a very active social life.

Marc is aware of Arnie's feelings about him but brushes them aside as normal jealousy. He believes that if he could get Arnie to go on a golf outing with him a few times, things could be patched up. As it is, although their relationship is somewhat strained, it is not affecting either's ability to do his job.

Vice President, Administration

Neelima Shrikhande

Aged 38, Neelima Shrikhande (pronounced *Nee-LEE-ma Shree-KON-dee*) is from India. She has a master of science degree in management information systems from Stanford University. She was promoted to her present position only last year, having served as manager of the Office and Information Systems (OIS) unit at Urban Systems for four years prior to that.

Neelima is single and an ardent feminist. She is also very involved in politics and worked extensively in the unsuccessful campaign of Walter K. Mason, the Liberal Party candidate for governor of Michigan last year.

Neelima manages the division that houses both the personnel function and the office function; the office function employs a large number of clerical and secretarial workers (all of whom are female). When Dave Kaplan offered her the promotion to vice president, Neelima informed him that one of her goals would be to institute policies that would upgrade the role of females within the company. Although she gets along well with Arnie McNally, she resents Marc Kaplan's sometimes condescending attitude toward her and what she considers his chauvinistic attitude toward many of the females on his staff.

FIGURE 1 Urban Systems Organizational Chart

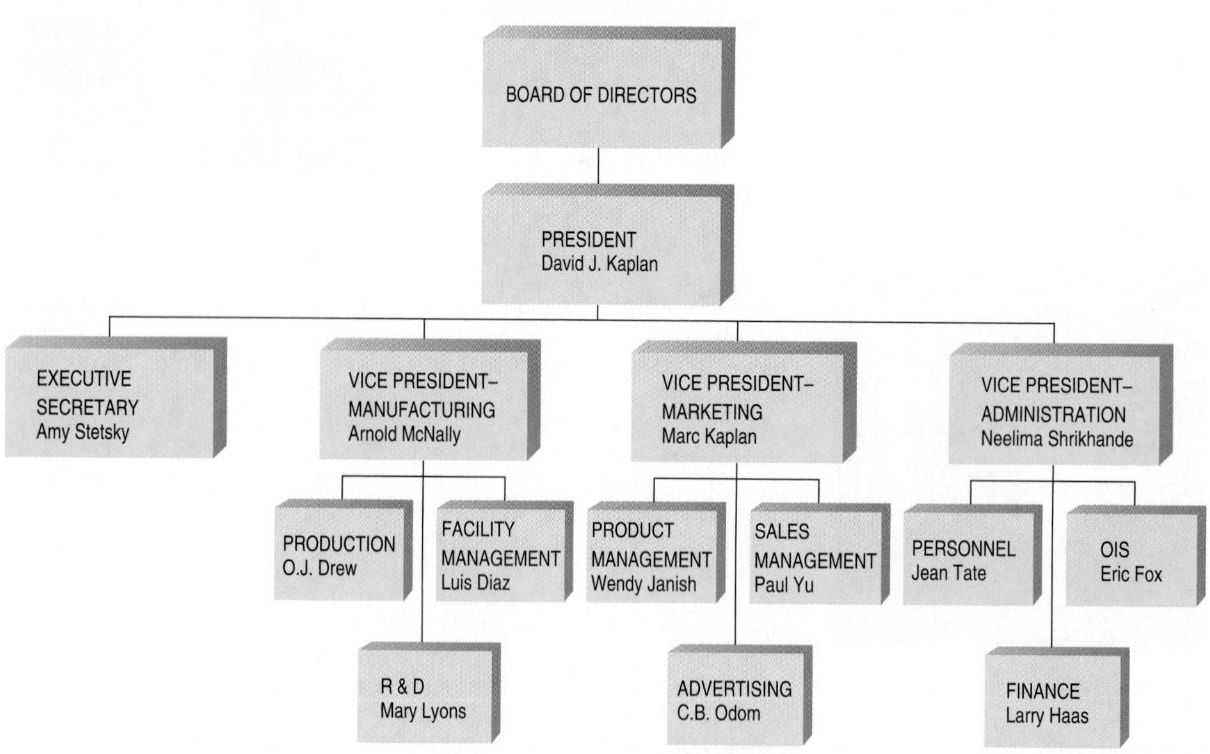

Case

FIGURE 2 Balance Sheet

URBAN SYSTEMS BALANCE SHEET December 31, 19--

Assets	
Current Assets:	
Cash and marketable securities	423,600
Trade receivables	4,942,400
Inventories	5,645,100
Prepaid expenses	307,500
Total Current Assets	11,318,600
Other Assets	5,825,200
Property and Equipment:	
Land	255,300
Buildings and improvements	4,291,600
Machinery and equipment	5,749,500
Furniture and fixtures	347,100
Total	10,643,500
Less allowances for depreciation	4,558,600
Total Property and Equipment	6,084,900
TOTAL ASSETS	23,228,700

Liabilities and Shareholders' Equity	
Current Liabilities:	
Notes payable	3,250,000
Accounts payable	4,971,800
Accrued compensation and taxes	946,100
Other liabilities	952,500
Long-term debt due within one year	205,300
Total Current Liabilities	10,325,700
Long-Term Debt	1,345,600
Deferred Federal Income Taxes	1,800,500
Shareholders' Equity:	
Common stock—par value $1.00 per share	
Authorized shares: 3,000,000	
Outstanding shares: 1,327,500	1,435,800
Additional capital	7,147,900
Retained earnings	1,173,200
Total Shareholders' Equity	9,756,900
TOTAL LIABILITIES AND SHAREHOLDERS' EQUITY	23,228,700

FINANCIAL DATA

By year's end, assets for Urban Systems totaled $23.2 million, with net income of $1.4 million. Earnings per share for the current year were $1.08; and a dividend of $0.64 per share was paid on the 1.3 million outstanding shares (all of which are held by the two Kaplan families). This and other financial information are contained in the most recent financial statements for Urban Systems, shown in Figures 2 and 3.

FIGURE 3 Income Statement

URBAN SYSTEMS
STATEMENT OF OPERATIONS

For the Year Ended December 31, 19--	
Net Sales	29,750,100
Operating Costs and Expenses:	
Cost of Sales	23,026,400
Selling and Administrative Expenses	2,795,200
Interest Income—Net	(289,500)
Other Income—Net	(97,500)
Total Operating Costs and Expenses	27,434,600
Income from Continuing Operations Before Taxes	2,315,500
Provision for Federal Income Taxes:	
Current	689,900
Deferred	195,400
Total Federal Income Taxes	885,300
Net Income	1,430,200
Retained Earnings:	
Retained Earnings—January 1	1,323,600
Dividends per Share—$0.64	849,600
Retained Earnings—December 31	1,173,200
Earnings per Share	1.08

CHAPTER

2 Contemporary Issues in Business Communication

Communication Objectives

After you have finished this chapter, you should be able to

1. Explain the meaning of nonverbal messages communicated in different cultures.
2. Describe the strategies for communicating across cultures.
3. Describe important technological developments that affect business communication.
4. Discuss four implications of technology for communication.
5. Explain the legal and ethical dimensions of communicating.

Every country throughout the world has a different way of doing business. This is why Dorothy Manning founded International Business Protocol, a consulting firm that specializes in helping U.S. companies learn about the nuances and correct approaches to conducting business in foreign lands. Manning is also the co-executive producer of a video series called "The Corporate Diplomat," consisting of several 30-minute videos, each focusing on a different country.

Manning believes that perhaps the most striking difference between American business people and those of other cultures is the American no-nonsense, let's-get-to-it-now approach. "The United States has what we call a monochronic culture, which means that it thinks of time as linear," she explained. "We schedule our time in appointments, in meetings, and in lunches. Those time segments are not supposed to be broken; they're sacred. And so if you have an appointment with your superior, and you have 15 minutes scheduled, you are supposed to have done your homework and to come to the appointment with a prepared, typewritten statement and all the data and information—if you haven't already sent it ahead of time—so you're wasting no time with social pleasantries. And you get right down to business and deal with the issue."

International Business Protocol seminar.

Most other cultures, Manning said, approach business with less intensity and "are offended when Americans jump right into business immediately without having established a personal rapport. Perhaps the Dutch are somewhat like us, and maybe the Germans a little bit, but much, much less so."

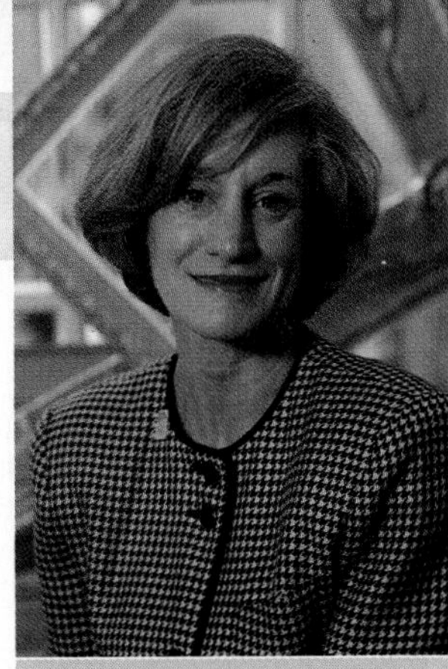

Dorothy Manning

Founder, International Business Protocol, Boston, Massachusetts

Generally speaking, Manning noted that the farther south you go in Europe and the Middle East, "the more it is very important for you to establish a human rapport: a personal, social, and emotional bond" before getting down to business. This relationship, she indicated, does not have to be "embarrassingly deep," but there should be enough of a bond to show "that you enjoy being together and that you have a few things in common."

Moreover, many of these cultures are polychronic, Manning said, "which means that several things happen simultaneously." Therefore, an American with a business appointment in another country can "well expect it to be interrupted by anything from a colleague entering to a secretary entering to a call from home. And the meeting will go on until it's finished, however long it takes." This puts an American in the uncomfortable position of being late for his or her next appointment, Manning said, "but the other person waiting for you expects that, doesn't worry about it if you don't show up on time. That kind of thing drives Americans crazy."

A chapter overview appears in the *Instructor's Resource Manual*, pp. 11–14.

Of course, Americans are not without idiosyncrasies that can make members of other cultures feel uneasy. This is particularly true of the expressiveness of Americans' body language. "In Japan and many other Asian countries, you don't touch people," Manning noted. "You don't shake hands. That's why they bow." Bowing, Manning said, is a way of "showing respect to the soul of the other person." Of course, many Japanese people conducting business in a Western country are familiar enough with our ways not to take offense when an American sticks out his hand. However, Manning indicated it would be prudent to let an Asian business person offer his or her hand first.

There's little doubt that technology—facsimile machines and telephones—has made the world smaller and increased business opportunities for American companies. The danger of technology, Manning indicated, is that it provides little time for Americans "to sit, reflect, and absorb," and to consider what may be the much different point of view of the person receiving the communications. Americans, Manning said, must understand that not all countries think of business so immediately "in terms of the bottom line."

THREE ISSUES AFFECTING COMMUNICATION

Because communication is such a pervasive and strategic part of the organization, almost anything that affects the organization and its employees affects the communication function as well. However, three contemporary issues are having a special impact on business communication:

- *Diversity:* The effects of cultural differences in the workplace—both within the United States and internationally.
- *Technology:* The effects of automation on business communication.
- *Ethics:* The legal and moral implications of communicating in the contemporary business environment.

These three topics are introduced in this chapter on contemporary issues. We will return to them frequently throughout the remainder of this text to discuss their impact on each specific area of business communication.

International business would not be possible without international communication.

DIVERSITY AND COMMUNICATION

When we talk about diversity, we mean cultural differences not only in the American and Canadian work force but also in the worldwide marketplace. The United States is a major participant in international business—both as a buyer and as a seller. This country is the world's largest importer of goods and services and the world's second largest exporter. The dominant role that the United States thus plays in the global economy does not, however, mean that international business matters are handled "the American way." Some years ago a book called *The Ugly American* condemned Americans abroad for their "Let 'em do it our way or not at all" attitude.

Companies Receiving Most of Their Sales from Abroad

Company	% of Sales
Gillette	65
Colgate	65
IBM	59
NCR	59
Coca-Cola	54
Digital Equipment	54
Dow Chemical	54
Xerox	54
Caterpillar	53
Hewlett-Packard	53

Source: *The Business Almanac, 1992*, Hoover Press, Asbury Park, N.J., p. 310.

Ober, *Contemporary Business Communication*, 2d ed.

See Transparency 2.1, International Sales by U.S. Companies.

In Boston, a Digital Equipment Corporation plant's 350-employee work force comes from 44 countries and speaks 19 languages. Written announcements are distributed in English, Chinese, French, Spanish, Portuguese, Vietnamese, and Haitian Creole.

When we talk about culture, we mean the customary traits, attitudes, and behaviors of a group of people. **Ethnocentrism** is the belief that one's own cultural group is superior. Such an attitude hinders communication, understanding, and goodwill between trading partners. An attitude of arrogance is not only counterproductive but also unrealistic, considering the fact that the U.S. population represents less than 5% of the world population. Moreover, of the world's countries, the United States is currently fourth in population and is expected to drop to eighth place by the year 2050.[1]

Another fact of life in international business is that comparatively few Americans speak a foreign language. Although English is the major language for conducting business worldwide, it would be naive to assume that it is the other person's responsibility to learn English. As a matter of fact, only about 8.5% of the world's population speaks English competently (about 450 million out of a world population of 5.3 billion). This means that English-only speakers cannot communicate one-to-one with more than 90% of the people in this world.[2]

Perhaps the (unintended) implication up to this point has been that you must leave the United States and Canada in order to encounter cultures different from your own. Nothing could be further from the truth. In fact, the term *minority,* which traditionally has referred to such groups as blacks, Hispanics, and Asians, is becoming something of a misnomer. To-

FIGURE 2.1 America's Diverse Population

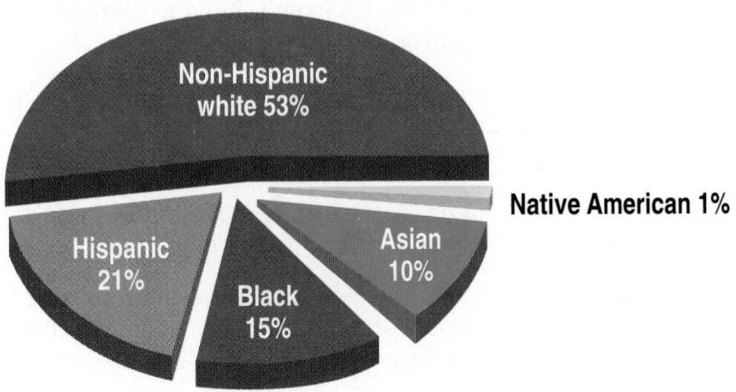

day, minorities make up a majority of the population in one out of six U.S. cities.[3]

The American work force is becoming more diverse.

As illustrated by Figure 2.1, by the year 2050, America's minority groups will make up just under half of the nation's population, and non-Hispanic whites will decrease to 53% of the population, from 75% today. Clearly, the term *global village* that Marshall McLuhan coined applies to our own country as well.

Obviously, diversity will have a profound impact on our lives and will pose a growing challenge for managers. The following discussion provides useful guidance for communicating with people from different cultures—both internationally as well as domestically. Although it is helpful to be aware of cultural differences, competent communicators recognize that each member of a culture is an individual, with individual needs, perceptions, and experiences, and should be treated as such.

Language Differences

In an ideal world, all managers would know the language of each culture with which they deal. An often-quoted saying among international business people is that you can *buy* in your native language anywhere in the world, but that you can *sell* only in the language of the local community. Of course, unless you know you will actually be working in a specific country for an extended period of time, it may not be reasonable or possible for you to learn the host language. However, even if you do not learn the host language, you should try to learn a few common phrases, such as *Good morning, Good afternoon, please,* and *thank you.* Doing so is a form of courtesy that shows personal interest, respect, and acceptance.

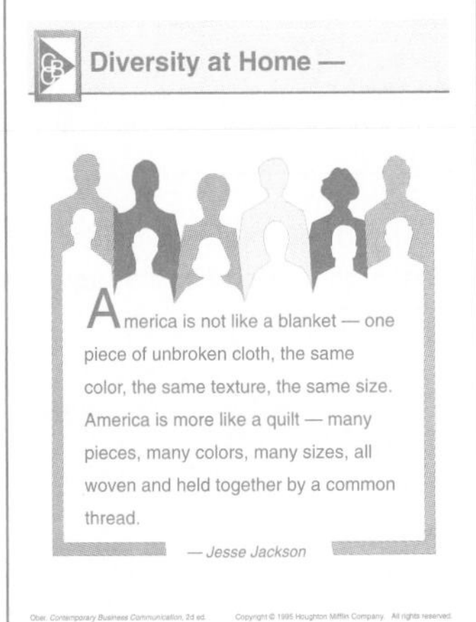

Diversity at Home —
America is not like a blanket — one piece of unbroken cloth, the same color, the same texture, the same size. America is more like a quilt — many pieces, many colors, many sizes, all woven and held together by a common thread.
— Jesse Jackson

See Transparency 2.2, Diversity in America.

Most of the correspondence between American or Canadian firms and foreign firms is in English; in other cases, the services of a qualified interpreter (for oral communication) or translator (for written communication) may be available. But even with such services, problems can occur.

Expressions that make sense in one language often "lose something in the translation."

Consider, for example, the following blunders:[4]

- In Brazil, where Portuguese is spoken, a U.S. airline advertised that its Boeing 747s had "rendezvous lounges," without realizing that *rendezvous* in Portuguese implies prostitution.
- In China, Kentucky Fried Chicken's slogan "Finger-lickin' good" was translated "So good you suck your fingers."
- In Puerto Rico, General Motors had difficulties advertising the Chevrolet's Nova model because the name sounds like the Spanish phrase *No va,* which means "It doesn't go."
- In Thailand, the slogan "Come alive with Pepsi" was translated "Bring your ancestors back from the dead with Pepsi."
- When the CIA used a machine translation system to translate Russian, the Bible verse "The spirit is willing, but the flesh is weak" became "The vodka is good, but the beef is rotten."

To ensure that the intended meaning is not lost during translation, legal, technical, and all other important documents should first be translated into the second language and then retranslated into English. Be aware, however, that communication difficulties can arise even among native English speakers. For example, a British advertisement for Electrolux vacuum cleaners displayed the headline, *Nothing Sucks Like An Electrolux.* In the United States and Canada, we would never use this wording!

Cultural Differences

Cultures differ not only in their verbal language but also in their nonverbal language. Very few nonverbal messages have universal meanings.

Even if both parties are fluent in the same language, differences in interpretations may still occur because of the different cultures. Each person interprets events through his or her mental filter, and that filter is based on the receiver's unique knowledge, experiences, and viewpoints.

For example, the language of time is as different among cultures as the language of words. Americans, Canadians, Germans, and Japanese are very time conscious and very precise about appointments; Latin American and Arab cultures are more casual about time.

For more on cultural difference, see Video Case Study 1, Chiat/Day.

Business people in both Asian and Latin American countries tend to favor long negotiations and slow deliberations. They exchange pleasantries at some length before getting down to business. Likewise, many non-Western cultures use the silent intervals for contemplation, whereas business people from North America tend to have little tolerance for silence in business negotiations. As a result, North Americans may rush in and offer compromises and counterproposals that would have been unnecessary if they had shown more patience.

Body language, especially gestures and eye contact, also varies among cultures. For example, our sign for "okay"—forming a circle with our forefinger and thumb—means "zero" in France, "money" in Japan, and a vulgarity in Brazil. Americans and Canadians consider eye contact important. In Asian and many Latin American countries, however, looking a partner full in the eye is considered an irritating sign of ill breeding.

Touching behavior is very culture-specific. Many Asians do not like to be touched, except for a brief handshake in greeting. However, handshakes

Motorola trains employees all over the world and prepares training materials in many languages. Translating these materials is not a simple, word-for-word job, however. For example, when U.S. course materials are translated for Asian employees, sports metaphors are replaced with stories about families.

in much of Europe tend to last much longer than in the United States and Canada, and Europeans tend to shake hands every time they see each other, perhaps several times a day. Similarly, in much of Europe, men often kiss each other upon greeting; unless an American or Canadian businessman is aware of this custom, he might react inappropriately.

When in doubt about how to act, follow the lead of your host.

Our feelings about space are partly an outgrowth of our culture and partly a result of geography and economics. For example, Americans and Canadians are used to wide-open spaces and tend to move about expansively, using hand and arm motions for emphasis. But in Japan, which has much smaller living and working spaces, such abrupt and extensive body movements are not typical. Likewise, Americans and Canadians tend to sit face to face, so that they can maintain eye contact, whereas the Chinese and Japanese (to whom eye contact is not important) tend to sit side by side during negotiations.

Also, the sense of personal space differs among cultures. In the United States and Canada most business exchanges occur at about five feet. However, in both the Middle East and in Latin American countries, this distance is too far. Business people there tend to stand close enough to feel your breath as you speak. Most Americans and Canadians tend to back away unconsciously from such close contact.

Finally, social behavior is very culture-dependent. For example, in the Japanese culture, the matter of who bows first upon meeting, how deeply the person bows, and how long the bow is held is very dependent upon one's status.

Competent communicators become familiar with such role-related behavior and also learn the customs regarding giving (and accepting) gifts, exchanging business cards, the degree of formality expected, and the accepted means of entertaining and being entertained.

McDonald's offers restaurant management programs and summer corporate internships for minority college students. *Black Enterprise* magazine rated Xerox as one of the best places for blacks to work. Hewlett-Packard lets female applicants know that, as an employer, it was rated highly by *Working Woman* magazine.

Group-Oriented Behavior

The business environment in a capitalistic society such as the United States and Canada places great value on the contributions of the individual toward the success of the organization. Individual effort is often stressed

Expect negotiations to take longer when unanimous agreement rather than majority rule is the norm.

more than group effort, and a competitive atmosphere prevails. In other cultures, however, originality and independence of judgment are not valued as highly as teamwork. The Japanese say, "A nail standing out will be hammered down." Thus, the Japanese go to great lengths to reach decisions through consensus, wherein every participating member, not just a majority, is able to agree.

Closely related to the concept of group-oriented behavior is the notion of saving face. The desire to "save face" simply means that neither party in a given interaction should suffer embarrassment. Human relationships are highly valued in such cultures and are embodied in the concept of *wa*, or the Japanese pursuit of harmony. This concept makes it difficult for the Japanese to say "no" to a request because it would be impolite. They are very reluctant to offend others—even if they unintentionally mislead them instead. Thus, a "yes" to a Japanese might mean "Yes, I understand you" rather than "Yes, I agree." Latin Americans also tend to avoid an outright "no" in their business dealings, preferring instead a milder, less explicit, response. In intercultural communications, one has to read between the lines, because what is left unsaid or unwritten may be just as important as what *is* said or written.

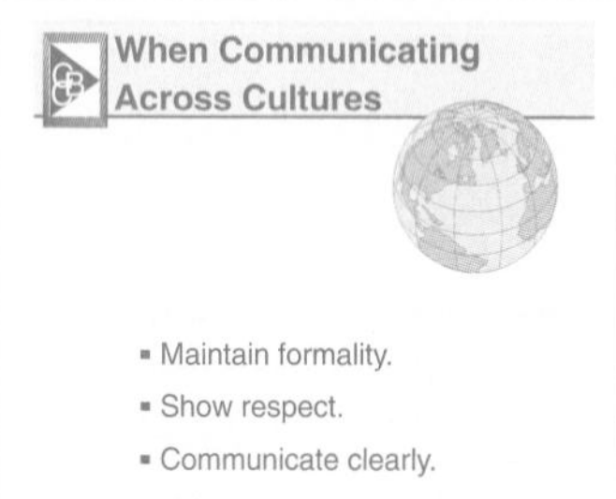
When Communicating Across Cultures
▪ Maintain formality.
▪ Show respect.
▪ Communicate clearly.
▪ Value diversity.

See Transparency 2.3, Strategies for Communicating Across Cultures.

Strategies for Communicating Across Cultures

When communicating with people from different cultures, whether abroad or at home, use the following strategies.

Maintain Formality Compared to the traditional American and Canadian culture, most other cultures value and respect a much more formal approach to business dealings. Call others by their titles and family names unless specifically asked to do otherwise. By both verbal and nonverbal clues, convey an attitude of propriety and decorum. Most other cultures do not equate formality with coldness.

Showing respect is probably the easiest strategy to exhibit—and one of the most important.

Show Respect Withhold judgment, accepting the premise that attitudes held by an entire culture are probably based on sound reasoning. Listen carefully to what is being communicated, trying to understand the other person's feelings. Learn about your host country—its geography, form of government, largest cities, culture, current events, and the like.

Communicate Clearly To ensure that your oral and written messages are understood, follow these guidelines:

- Avoid slang, jargon, and other figures of speech. Expressions such as "They'll eat that up" or "out in left field" are likely to confuse even a fluent English speaker.
- Be specific and illustrate your points with concrete examples.
- Provide and solicit feedback; summarize frequently; provide a written

summary of the points covered in a meeting; ask your counterpart to paraphrase what has been said; encourage questions.

- Use a variety of media: handouts (distributed before the meeting to allow time for reading), audiovisual aids, models, and the like.
- Avoid attempts at humor; humor is likely to be lost on your counterpart.
- Speak plainly and slowly (but not so slowly as to appear condescending), choosing your words carefully.

Value Diversity Those who view diversity among employees as a source of richness and strength for the organization can help bring a wide range of benefits to their organization. Whether you happen to belong to the majority culture or to one of the minority cultures where you work, you will share your work and leisure hours with people different from yourself—people who have values, mannerisms, and speech habits different from your own. This is true today, and it will be even truer in the future. The same strategies apply whether the cultural differences exist at home or abroad.

For more on diversity and communication, see the supplemental lecture/discussion notes in the *Instructor's Resource Manual*, beginning on p. 14.

A person who is knowledgeable about, and comfortable with, different cultures is a more effective manager because he or she can avoid misunderstandings and tap into the greater variety of viewpoints a diverse culture provides. In addition, such understanding provides personal satisfaction.

Cultural diversity provides a rich environment for solving problems and for expanding horizons.

TECHNOLOGY AND COMMUNICATION

In view of the different time zones, physical distances, cultural differences, and varying languages worldwide, the current high level of international business operations would simply not be possible without the increased communication capabilities brought about through technology.

Communication technology makes international commerce possible.

The written language with the longest continuous history is Chinese, which is more than 6,000 years old. However, it was not until Gutenberg's invention of the printing press with movable type in the fifteenth century that mass communication became possible. And it was not until the 1800s—with the invention of the telegraph, the typewriter, the telephone, and the dictating machine—that major technological changes began to have an effect on communications in business.

Other inventions followed in the first half of the twentieth century, culminating with the development of the first electronic computer in 1946. Developed at the University of Pennsylvania, the ENIAC (Electronic Numerical Integrator and Computer) weighed 30 tons and occupied 1,500 square feet of floor space. Today's notebook computers, weighing less than five pounds, offer many times more computing power than this original behemoth.

For more on technology and communication, see Video Case Study 3, Lotus Notes, and Video Case Study 4, Chemical Bank.

Until the advent of word processing, computers were used primarily for large-scale calculations. Word processing was developed in the early 1960s as a means of automating the processing of words, much as computers had automated the processing of numbers.

Ford links employees in Michigan, Germany, and England through videoconferencing.

Word Processing

Word processing is the production of letters, memorandums, reports, and other documents through the use of automated electronic equipment. Most word processing today is done through the use of software programs that operate on microcomputers. The two most popular word processing programs in the business community are WordPerfect® and Microsoft Word®.

Touch keyboarding (typing) skills are critical in the contemporary business environment.

Using word processing, a writer can keyboard a message very quickly, without worrying about format or typographical errors. Then, using the various editing functions built into the software, the writer can revise, delete, add, or reposition words and sentences until the final document is ready to be printed. The document is then stored for later retrieval—most often on a removable floppy disk or on a permanent hard disk.

Sophisticated word processing programs can check spelling, replace a word or phrase throughout a document, automatically insert the current date and page number, generate an index, produce "original" form letters, perform mathematical calculations, copy charts and graphics from other programs (such as spreadsheets), automatically number and position footnotes and endnotes, and arrange text in columns.

Many word processing systems offer additional features designed to improve writing. An electronic thesaurus provides a list of synonyms for words. A grammar and punctuation checker calls attention to simple errors such as repeated words, numbers in incorrect format (for example, "$5,32"), and sentences not started with a capital letter. Other available features include an on-line style manual that you can call to the screen to review rules of grammar, punctuation, and usage; electronic outliners that provide a format the writer can fill in to outline a message; and writing analysis software that can help you analyze the extent to which a document follows the principles of clear writing.

Desktop publishing (DTP) software is a specialized form of word processing that permits users to write, assemble, and design such publications as company newsletters, brochures, and catalogs. Typically, the text is entered (keyboarded) by means of word processing software and then copied into the desktop publishing software, where it can be easily manipulated. After the document has been designed on the computer, it is typically printed out on a laser printer, which produces high-quality output, and then duplicated.

Desktop publishing software provides more advanced graphics features than word processing software, it is faster and cheaper than using a commercial printing company, and it provides users more flexibility and control of their documents. The disadvantage is that not everyone who knows how to keyboard also knows how to design a document so that the result is both effective and attractive.

Desktop presentation software is similar to desktop publishing, except that it is used to produce audiovisual aids for presentations. By means of built-in designs called *templates,* users can create attractive and effective transparencies and slides at a reasonable cost. Transparencies can be made directly from a laser printer (either color or black and white); slides are more often prepared from the computer files by a slide-processing firm. It is likely that the use of desktop presentation software (such as Harvard Graphics®, Aldus Persuasion®, and Freelance Graphics®) will increase greatly in the years ahead.

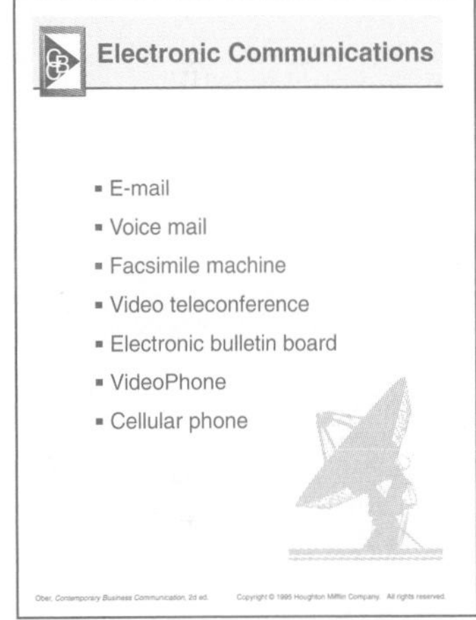

Electronic Communications
▪ E-mail
▪ Voice mail
▪ Facsimile machine
▪ Video teleconference
▪ Electronic bulletin board
▪ VideoPhone
▪ Cellular phone

See Transparency 2.4, Forms of Electronic Communication.

Electronic Communications

Research conducted by AT&T shows that

- 75% of all business calls do not reach the intended party on the first attempt.
- 50% of all business calls are for one-way transfer of information, which requires no feedback or callback.
- 67% of business calls are less important than the work they interrupt.
- 50% of calls take far longer than necessary.[5]

A number of recent advances combine features of the telephone and the mail to produce faster, cheaper ways of sending and receiving messages.

E-mail is cheaper and faster than traditional letters and memos, but less permanent.

In **electronic mail** (or *E-mail*), messages are composed, transmitted, and usually read on computer screens (see Figure 2.2). Messages travel through cables within the company and through telephone lines outside the company. E-mail delivery is almost instantaneous, although the receiver must access the computer system to know that a message is waiting. In many corporations, E-mail has almost completely replaced the traditional interoffice memorandum.

Voice mail, in effect a digital answering machine, allows users to record messages electronically on a computer disk. Voice mail is particularly effective for dealing with *telephone tag,* the annoying cycle of Jane calling John and not reaching him, John returning Jane's call and not reaching her, and so on.

FIGURE 2.2 An Example of Receiving and Answering Electronic Mail

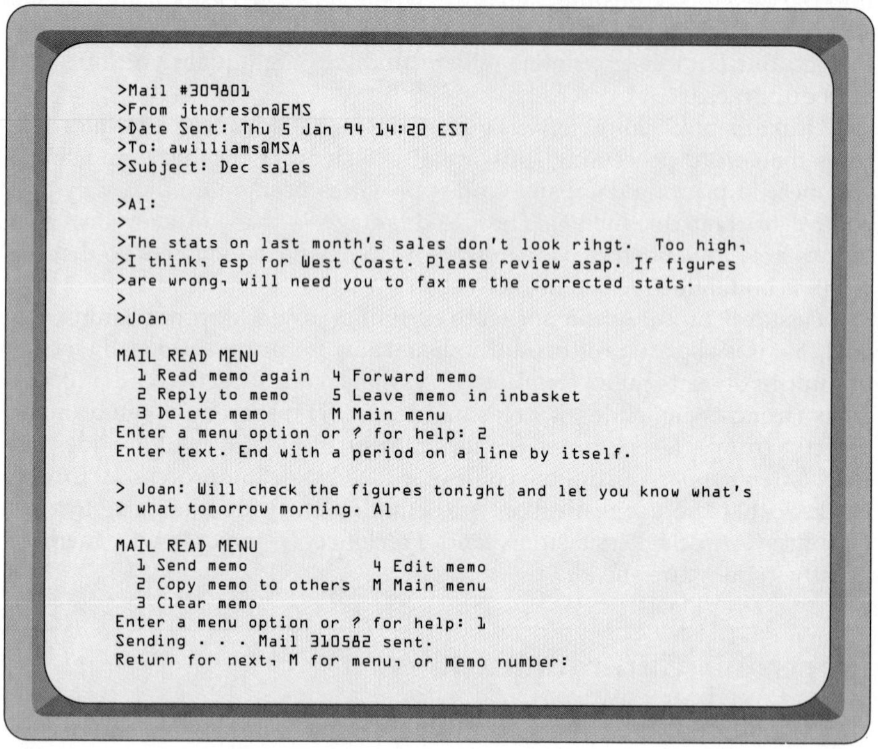

```
>Mail #309801
>From jthoreson@EMS
>Date Sent: Thu 5 Jan 94 14:20 EST
>To: awilliams@MSA
>Subject: Dec sales

>Al:
>
>The stats on last month's sales don't look rihgt.  Too high,
>I think, esp for West Coast. Please review asap. If figures
>are wrong, will need you to fax me the corrected stats.
>
>Joan

MAIL READ MENU
  1 Read memo again   4 Forward memo
  2 Reply to memo     5 Leave memo in inbasket
  3 Delete memo       M Main menu
Enter a menu option or ? for help: 2
Enter text. End with a period on a line by itself.

> Joan: Will check the figures tonight and let you know what's
> what tomorrow morning. Al

MAIL READ MENU
  1 Send memo               4 Edit memo
  2 Copy memo to others     M Main menu
  3 Clear memo
Enter a menu option or ? for help: 1
Sending . . . Mail 310582 sent.
Return for next, M for menu, or memo number:
```

With voice mail, when an incoming call goes unanswered, the voice-mail system is activated, and callers are instructed either how to leave a message or how to reach someone who may be able to help. With both voice mail and electronic mail, users who are away from the office can access their messages via telephone.

A faxed message is cheaper and faster than first-class mail.

A **facsimile** machine (fax, for short) is like a long-distance photocopier: it sends and receives copies of documents over telephone lines. The average Fortune 500 company receives 428 pages a day by fax.[6] Nationwide, about 7 million companies (and a substantial number of individuals) have facsimile machines, and they transmit an average of 25 documents a day. The average transmission is three pages, takes 45 seconds to send, and costs about 20 cents in long-distance tolls.[7] In other words, it is cheaper to send a fax across country than a first-class letter—and the fax document arrives almost instantaneously.

A **videoconference** is a meeting held at different sites linked by cameras and microphones that transmit the live voices and images of the participants. Videoconference popularity has grown tremendously in recent years, spurred by the increasing cost of travel, lower phone rates, and more effective hardware systems.

Electronic bulletin boards are systems that connect computers by telephone to a service for posting messages. Nationwide, many companies are beginning to set up these bulletin boards as inexpensive, speedy message centers for their staff and customers. In addition to private bulletin boards, many commercial bulletin boards are available by subscription, allowing customers to obtain information, buy and sell stocks, read newspaper and magazine articles, order plane tickets, and so on.

Internet is a federally subsidized communication service that provides free worldwide E-mail, bulletin boards, conferencing, and data retrieval. Most college students can obtain a free account on Internet.

Finally, the telephone itself is changing. AT&T's VideoPhone permits users to see and hear the person with whom they're speaking. However, instead of showing continuous motion, the unit produces what amounts to a series of snapshots, or a slide show, with the picture changing every few seconds. VideoPhone works over regular phone lines and video calls cost the same as regular voice-only calls.

In addition, **cellular phones** have become a common accessory in many automobiles, not to mention the hand-held units carried in briefcases, purses, and coat pockets. With an estimated 20 million subscribers in 1995, the cellular phone uses radio waves instead of telephone lines to connect callers almost anywhere in the United States.[8]

Implications of Technology for Communications

Paper will continue to be used for temporary storage because it is so convenient and portable.

We begin our discussion of the implications of technology for communications by refuting one common misconception. Technology will *not* lead to a "paperless office." The prediction of such a phenomenon was based on the belief that companies would eventually store all information on some type of magnetic medium that could then be filed, retrieved, and disseminated at will. Electronic storage, retrieval, and dissemination is faster and cheaper than manual paper methods.

Nevertheless, the paperless office has not come about, and probably never will. The reason, of course, is that paper is so convenient and portable. It is extremely tiring to read a long document on a computer monitor; it is much easier to print out and then read the "hard copy." Also, paper documents can be taken and used anywhere—whether a computer is accessible or not.

In addition to making it easier to create, edit, and disseminate information, technology is having the following effects on business communication.

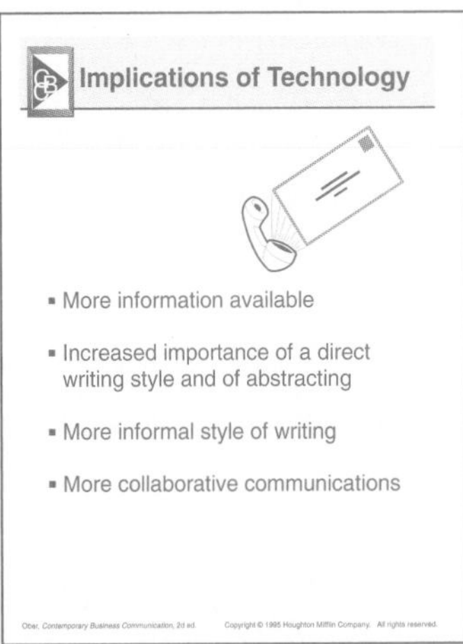
Implications of Technology
More information available
Increased importance of a direct writing style and of abstracting
More informal style of writing
More collaborative communications

See Transparency 2.5, Implications of Technology.

More Information Available Technology has increased dramatically the amount of information instantly available to the manager. Because of the ease with which company data bases can be created, accessed, and manipulated, managers are receiving more computer-generated reports than ever before. In addition, the availability of commercial data bases means the manager can easily obtain industry and financial information from a variety of externally published sources. Finally, because sending copies of documents is so easy with electronic mail and high-speed photocopiers, people tend to send each memo or report to more people than in the past. Without careful management, information overload—in which people receive more information than they can handle—can occur (see the Spotlight, "Overcoming Information Anxiety" on page 12).

Kroger managers can find out how any given product or product line is selling in any store (or stores) during any time period. Computerized scanning machines at the checkout counters provide daily sales figures for each of the 21,000 products in an average store. Another computerized system compiles the data into usable information.

In such a situation, critical thinking becomes an especially important skill in business communication. Being able to sort through information and determine what is important becomes crucial for effective communication.

Competent communicators carefully assess who legitimately needs the information contained in their messages, and they critically evaluate the information in the messages they receive.

Busy executives want the important points summarized up front.

Increased Importance of a Direct Writing Style and of Abstracting News reporters have always known the importance of "front-loading"—putting the most important information up front, where it receives the most attention. Because of the increased pressures on managers to consume more information (with no increase in time available for reading), they are seeking ways to get to the main point of each document as quickly as possible.

Thus, the ability to analyze a mass of data and condense it to a manageable length is becoming more important. Executive summaries, placed at the front of long reports, are now a required part of the reporting process in many organizations. Also, many executives prefer a direct style of writing from their subordinates—with the major ideas presented first, followed by supporting details.

Competent communicators carefully analyze their audience and tailor the content and organization of their messages for that specific audience.

More Informal Style of Writing In yesterday's office, the executive dictated a letter, the secretary transcribed it (perhaps doing some minor editing in the process), the executive revised it, and the letter was retyped and mailed. Today, however, many executives do their own keyboarding and often use electronic mail to send the memo directly to the receiver's computer.

This "writing on the fly" is often done in a very abbreviated style, much as someone would jot notes down on a notepad. Typographical errors may not be corrected (see, for example, the E-mail messages in Figure 2.2), nor are the formalities of traditional correspondence observed. And because many of these messages are never printed on paper, they lack the polished format and appearance of typewritten letters or memos on letterhead stationery. People accustomed to reading such informally written messages tend to overlook the minor errors.

Competent communicators carefully analyze each writing situation to determine what level of formality is expected and desirable. In addition, they always keep their audience and their purpose firmly in mind, regardless of the degree of formality used.

More Collaborative Communications The increasing quantity and complexity of the information available makes it difficult for any one person to have either the time or the expertise to be able to analyze all the data adequately. The differing skills of several individuals are often needed in a joint effort to analyze a given situation and generate proposals or recommendations. Thus, collaborative writing and collaborative oral presentations are becoming quite prevalent in organizations. (As a matter of fact, collaborative communications have always been much more common in organizations than many people realized.)

Competent communicators learn how to work effectively in small groups to gather and analyze data and then to write and revise a written report or prepare an oral presentation. (These topics are discussed further in Chapter 14.)

ETHICS AND COMMUNICATION

Each of us has our own code of **ethics,** or rules of conduct, that might go beyond legal rules to tell us how to act when the law is silent. When composing a business proposal, drafting a sales letter, writing a personnel policy, or recruiting a candidate for a job, we make conscious decisions regarding what information to include and what information to exclude from our messages. For the information that *is* included, we make conscious decisions about how to phrase the language, how much to emphasize each point, and how to organize the message. Such decisions have legal and moral dimensions—both for you as the writer and for the organization.

These companies are actively taking positive steps to raise the ethical consciousness of their employees: Alcoa, Pacific Bell, Pitney Bowes, Hershey Foods, Niagara Mohawk Power, and Nynex.

Defamation

Any false and malicious statement that is communicated to others and that injures a person's good name or reputation may constitute **defamation.** Defamation in a temporary form such as in oral communication is called **slander;** defamation in a permanent form such as in writing or videotape is called **libel.** The three major conditions for defamation are that the statement be false, be communicated to others, and be harmful to a person's good name or reputation. Thus, telling Joe Smith to his face that he is a liar and a crook does not constitute defamation (slander) unless a third person hears the remarks. In addition, truth is generally an acceptable defense to a charge of defamation.

Oral defamation is slander. *Written defamation is* libel.

Competent communicators use objective language and verifiable information when communicating about others. For example, instead of saying, "Mr. Baker is a poor credit risk," they might say, "Mr. Baker was at least ten days late in making his payments to us four times during the past six months."

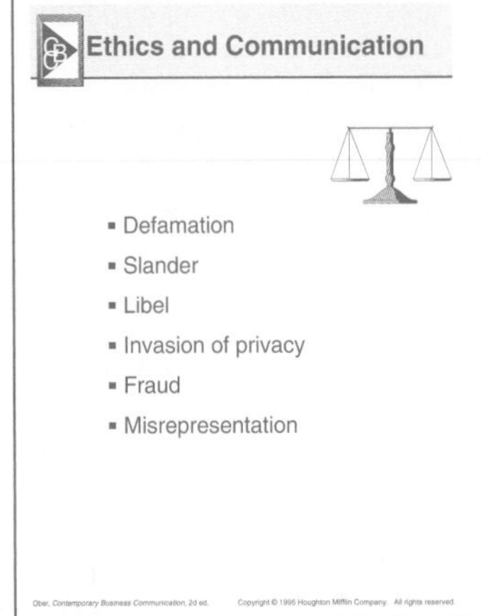

Ethics and Communication
▪ Defamation
▪ Slander
▪ Libel
▪ Invasion of privacy
▪ Fraud
▪ Misrepresentation

See Transparency 2.6, Ethics and Communication.

Invasion of Privacy

Any unreasonable intrusion into the private life of another person or denial of a person's right to be left alone may constitute an **invasion of privacy.** Thus, using someone's name or photograph in a sales promotion without

Customers' perceptions of a company's ethical behavior can affect the bottom line. Consumers upset by the 1989 Valdez oil spill in Alaska's Prince William Sound returned 40,000 Exxon credit cards.

that person's permission may be an invasion of privacy. Of particular concern today are the vast amounts of employee and customer information being maintained in corporate data banks. The proliferation of microcomputers, networks, and electronic mail makes it possible to access large amounts of data about employees and customers very freely.

Various state and federal laws protect the individual's right to privacy. The federal government defines *right to privacy* as "the right of individuals to participate in decisions regarding the collection, use, and disclosure of information personally identifiable to that individual."[9] Thus, someone's right to privacy may be violated if his or her records are read by someone not authorized to examine them.

Competent communicators ensure that they do not misuse information about others in their communications and that their communications are available only to authorized people.

Fraud and Misrepresentation

Investment banker Michael Milken earned as much as $550 million in a single year, but because of his unethical and illegal business practices, his firm, Drexel Burnham Lambert, was heavily fined by the federal government. The company was forced eventually into bankruptcy and Milkin was imprisoned.

A deliberate misrepresentation of the truth for the purpose of inducing someone to give up something of value is called **fraud.** Fraud can occur either when one party actually makes a deliberately false statement (called *active fraud*) or when one party deliberately conceals some information that he or she is required to reveal (*passive fraud*).

To be fraudulent, the statements must involve facts. Opinions and persuasive arguments or exaggerated claims about a product (called *sales puffery*) do not constitute fraud even if they turn out to be false. For example, "The Celeste is the only American-made car that comes with leather seats as standard equipment" is a statement of fact, which, if incorrect, might constitute fraud. However, "The Celeste is the most luxurious car in America" is an opinion; even if most car buyers did not agree with the statement, it would still not be considered fraud.

You should also recognize that a statement of opinion, even if it is not fraudulent, might still be unethical. For example, advertising that "The Celeste is the most luxurious car in America" might not be fraudulent; but it would be highly unethical if, in fact, you did not believe that to be the case.

Misrepresentation is a false statement that is made innocently with no intent to deceive the other party. If misrepresentation is proven, the contract or agreement may be rescinded. If fraud is proven, the contract or agreement may be rescinded, and the offended party may collect monetary compensation.

For more on legal considerations, see the supplemental lecture/discussion notes in the *Instructor's Resource Manual*, beginning on p. 14.

Competent communicators are aware of the relevant laws and ensure that their oral and written messages are accurate, in terms of what is communicated *and* what is left uncommunicated.

Other Ethical Considerations

A message can be true and still be unethical.

Sometimes being legally right is not sufficient justification for our actions (see the Spotlight on Law and Ethics on page 47). Many corporations have developed their own code of ethics to govern employee behavior. For the

SPOTLIGHT ON LAW AND ETHICS

How Would You Respond?

How would you react to each of the following minicases on business ethics developed by Kirk Hanson, a senior lecturer at the Stanford University Graduate School of Business and corporate ethics consultant? Formulate your own responses before reading the suggested solutions.

SITUATIONS

1. You are about to take a job with Almost Perfect, Inc. You like everything you have learned about the company, except the reputation the firm has for long working hours. You have a young family and are committed to spending time with them. What role should the hours have in your decision?
2. You have been on the job for four days. Your boss hands you a report she hasn't had time to complete. "Just copy the numbers off last month's report," she says. "Nobody at headquarters ever really reads these." What do you do?
3. A new engineer who has just joined your group drops by your office and hands you a file stamped with the name of his former employer. "I thought you'd like to have a look at their list of key customers," he says. What do you do?
4. Despite a strongly worded company policy prohibiting gratuities from suppliers, you know your boss in the purchasing department is taking weeklong vacations paid for by a key vendor. What do you do?

SUGGESTED SOLUTIONS

1. Turn down the job or negotiate openly for more reasonable hours. You will never be satisfied if you take a job that sets up a constant value conflict. Be willing to pay the price for a good family life.
2. Offer to collect the real data for the report. Everyone is tested in the first weeks by coworkers who favor short cuts or small ethical compromises. Establish your values; insist on getting the real data if push comes to shove.
3. Give him back the folder unread and tell him, "We don't do things around here like that." Watch him carefully. If he wasn't faithful to his obligations to his former employer, he won't be faithful to you.
4. Report him to a higher authority in the company, but be sure you have some proof before you do. He has violated such a clear standard that it is unlikely he can be persuaded to stop. Ask the higher authority to protect you from retaliation.

Source: The Hanson Group, a corporate-ethics consultancy in Los Altos, California.

business communicator, the matter of ethics governs not only one's behavior but also one's communication of behavior. In other words, how we use language involves ethical choices.

When you have doubts about the ethical propriety of your writing, ask yourself these questions:

1. Is this message true?
2. Does it exaggerate?
3. Does it withhold or obscure information that should be communicated?
4. Does it promise something that cannot be delivered?
5. Does it betray a confidence?
6. Does it play unduly on the fears of the reader?
7. Does it reflect the wishes of the organization?

Competent communicators use their knowledge of communication to achieve their goals while acting in an ethical manner.

The three issues of diversity, technology, and ethics and how they affect our communication efforts have been introduced in this chapter. However, by means of communication Spotlights, these critical topics will be revisited throughout the remainder of the book, as they affect various areas of communication.

SUMMARY

International business depends very heavily on communicating effectively with people of different cultures. Language differences can cause problems, especially in translating slang and jargon. The meanings of nonverbal language also depend on the specific culture, especially the language of time and space, body language, and touching behavior. Finally, cultures differ in terms of the importance attached to group as opposed to individual behavior. Competent communicators maintain formality, show respect, remain flexible, and write and speak clearly when communicating with people of different cultures. They are also aware of the extent to which cultural diversity is a fundamental part of the American and Canadian business organization.

Technology has a major effect on the way we communicate, especially word processing with all its related features for improving the writing process. Other forms of electronic communication include electronic mail, voice mail, electronic bulletin boards, facsimile machines, desktop publishing and presentations, and videoconferencing. As a result of these developments, more information is becoming available to the manager, abstracting and a direct writing style are becoming more important, a more informal style of writing is becoming common in certain situations, and collaborative communications are becoming more prominent.

Regardless of the size of the organization, every business writer faces ethical questions when communicating orally and in writing. Legal questions arise with regard to defamation, invasion of privacy, and fraud or misrepresentation. In choosing what information to convey, and by which words and sentences, we make ethical choices—moral decisions about what is right, even when no question of law is involved.

KEY TERMS

For an exercise on matching terms, refer students to the *Study Guide*, p. 72.

Cellular phone A portable phone that uses radio waves rather than telephone lines to connect callers almost anywhere in the United States.

Culture The customary traits, attitudes, and behaviors of a group of people.

Defamation A false and malicious statement that is communicated to others and that injures a person's good name or reputation.

Desktop presentation The production of audiovisual aids such as transparencies, slides, and handouts by means of a microcomputer.

Desktop publishing (DTP) The writing, assembling, and designing of such publications as company newsletters, brochures, catalogs, and reports on a microcomputer.

Electronic bulletin board An electronic message system accessible by computer connected to a phone line.

Electronic mail Messages that are composed, transmitted, and usually read by means of a computer; also called *E-mail.*

Ethics Rules of conduct that often go beyond legal rules and tell people how to act when the law is silent.

Ethnocentrism The belief that one's own cultural group is superior.

Facsimile machine A machine that scans a document, converts the data into electronic impulses, and then transmits these impulses over phone lines to a receiving machine that reconverts the impulses into a copy of the original document; also called a *fax.*

Fraud A deliberate misrepresentation of the truth that is made to induce someone to give up something of value.

Invasion of privacy Any unreasonable intrusion into the private life of another person or denial of a person's right to be left alone.

Libel Defamation in a permanent form such as in writing or videotape.

Misrepresentation A false statement made innocently with no intent to deceive the other party.

Slander Defamation in a temporary form such as in oral communication.

Videoconference A system using cameras, monitors, and microphones to enable people in different locations to hold meetings that simulate face-to-face meetings.

Voice mail A communication system that allows users to speak into a phone and have their messages recorded electronically on computer disk.

Word processing The production of letters, memorandums, reports, and other documents through the use of automated electronic equipment.

REVIEW AND DISCUSSION

1. **Communication at International Business Protocol Revisited** ▪ As Dorothy Manning knows, today's global marketplace requires that business people understand the nuances of communicating with colleagues, clients, and suppliers in other countries. They should also be aware of the effect that new technology has on communication.
   a. What common U.S. slang phrases relating to time might be misinterpreted by people from other countries? Suggest an alternative for each phrase you identify.
   b. What do you think are the advantages of electronic mail? The disadvantages?
   c. What privacy issues might confront the users of a company-wide electronic mail system?

The answers to the review and discussion questions appear in the *Instructor's Resource Manual*, beginning on p. 15.

2. How do cultures differ in terms of time, body language, touch, and space?
3. What implications does the Japanese emphasis on the group, rather than on the individual, have for communication?
4. What are four strategies for successfully communicating across cultures? Give an example of each.
5. Why is it important for all managers to be knowledgeable about and comfortable with people of different cultures in this country?
6. What components of the word processing environment are available to improve writing?
7. "I don't have to worry about spelling and typing errors because I have a spelling checker on my computer." Discuss the validity of this statement.

8. What is the difference between desktop publishing and desktop presentations?
9. What are four implications of technology for communication?
10. Define *defamation* and describe the two types.
11. What is the difference between fraud and misrepresentation?
12. "Communicating is an ethical act." Discuss this statement.

EXERCISES

Suggestions and sample solutions for exercises appear in the *Instructor's Resource Manual*, beginning on p. 17.

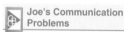

Joe's Communication Problems

- Being late for the appointment
- Making offensive statement about the Japanese
- Using slang expressions
- Making exaggerated movements
- Demanding a quick response
- Sitting facing the manager and maintaining eye contact

See Master 2.1, Exercise 1, International, in the *Instructor's Resource Manual.*

1. **International** ▪ Joe arrived 15 minutes late for his appointment with Itaru Nakamura, sales manager for a small manufacturer to which Joe's firm hoped to sell parts. "Sorry to be late," he apologized, "but you know how the local drivers are. At any rate, since I'm late, let's get right down to brass tacks." Joe began to pace back and forth in the small office. "The way I see it, if you and I can come to some agreement this afternoon, we'll be able to get the rest to agree. After all, who knows more about this than you and I?" Joe sat down opposite his colleague and looked him straight in the eye. "So what do you say? Can we agree on the basics and let our assistants hammer out the details?" His colleague was silent for a few moments, then said, "Yes." Discuss Joe's intercultural skills. Specifically, what did he do wrong? What did Nakamura's response probably mean?
2. **Diversity** ▪ Assume that you are a supervisor in a firm where one-third of the work force is Hispanic, about evenly divided between Mexican American and Cuban American. All are either U.S. citizens or legal residents. Because both groups have Spanish as their native language, can you assume that both groups have similar cultures? Do some research on both groups in terms of their typical educational backgrounds, political beliefs, job experiences, and the like. Organize your findings into a two-page report (typed, double-spaced).
3. **Translations** ▪ Locate two foreign-born people from the same country who speak English as a second language. First, ask one of them to translate literally into his or her native language the ad slogans shown below. Then give the foreign-language translation to the second person, and ask that person to retranslate the slogans into English. Compare the original and the retranslated English versions. What are the implications of any discrepancies?
   - *Twice a day we explain the facts of life* (National Public Radio)
   - *From chips to ships* (Hyundai)
   - *We took a great idea and made it fly* (Samsonite)
   - *Digital has it now* (Digital Equipment)
   - *The heartbeat of America* (Chevrolet)
   - *Satisfy your lust for power and money* (NEC)
4. **Voice-messaging Systems** ▪ You are familiar with voice-messaging systems if you've ever called an organization and received a message like this:

   Welcome to ABC Corporation. To serve you better, we have installed an automatic answering system. If you wish to order a product, press

"1"; if you have a question about one of our products, press "2"; if you wish to speak to a customer representative, stay on the line and an operator will be with you shortly.

What are the advantages and disadvantages of such a system? What kinds of nonverbal signals are associated with their use? If you were in charge of ABC Corporation, would you have installed such a system? Prepare a report on the topic.

5. **Collaboration** ▪ Working in small groups, interview at least three international students or professors, each from a different country. For each country represented, determine the types of written and oral communications common in business, the extent of technological development, problems with the English language, and examples of slang used in their native language. Prepare a written summary of your findings, proofread, revise as necessary, and submit.
6. **Technology** ▪ You are the fleet manager for a magazine distributor. You have been asked to write a report on the feasibility of leasing versus purchasing your fleet of delivery vans. Give a specific example of how you might productively make use of each of these technological innovations in your report: electronic mail, voice mail, electronic bulletin board, facsimile machine, desktop publishing, desktop presentation, and videoconference.
7. **Telecommuting** ▪ Assume that you are an advertising copywriter for a large pharmaceutical firm in Los Angeles, and your first child was born three weeks ago. Now, you wish to work out of your home for the next 12 months, staying in contact with the office through electronic communications. Prepare a list of the equipment you will need and how you will use each piece of equipment. What advantages and disadvantages of this arrangement (called *telecommuting*) do you see for yourself? for your company?
8. **Legal** ▪ Sam was thinking of hiring Olivia Mason for an open sales territory. Knowing she had previously worked at Kentron, he called his friend there, Barry Kelley, to ask about her performance. "She's very smart, but I wouldn't hire her again, Sam," Barry said. "She's a little lazy. Sometimes she wouldn't begin making her calls until late morning or even after lunch. And she was also sloppy with her paperwork. I assume she's honest, but I never could get her to file receipts for all her expenses. Of course, she was going through a messy divorce then, so maybe that affected her job performance." Sam thanked his friend and notified Olivia that she was not being hired for the job. If Olivia learned of Kelley's comments, would she have the basis for a legal suit? If so, what type and on what grounds? How could Kelley have reworded his comments to convey the information in a businesslike, ethical manner?

Barry's Evaluation of Olivia

ORIGINAL: She's very smart, but I wouldn't hire her again, Sam. She's a little lazy. Sometimes she wouldn't begin making her calls until late morning or even after lunch. And she was also sloppy with her paperwork. I assume she's honest, but I never could get her to file receipts for all her expenses. Of course, she was going through a messy divorce then, so maybe that affected her job performance.

IMPROVED: Olivia's college transcript indicates she's a very intelligent individual. However, she received four reprimands from her supervisor for not making her quota of sales calls. On three occasions, she was late in submitting her monthly sales reports, and six times in her three years of employment with us she did not file receipts for all of her expenses. I felt that her job performance was not consistent with her ability.

Ober, *Contemporary Business Communication*, 2d ed.

See Master 2.2, Exercise 8, Legal, in the *Instructor's Resource Manual*.

9. **Ethics** ▪ After testing several new word processing programs, you wrote a memo to your supervisor requesting the purchase of 15 copies of WordPerfect for Windows® so that each member of your staff would have a copy. You just received your memo back from your supervisor with this handwritten note attached to it:

I'm tired of purchasing software and then not have it do what it says it will do. Let's order one copy of the program first and make copies for all your staff. If in two months everyone is still happy with the program, I'll buy 14 more copies to make us legitimate.

How do you respond?

A possible solution to the Continuing Case is described in the *Instructor's Resource Manual*, p. 20.

CONTINUING CASE 2

Urban Systems Sees the Light

Marc Kaplan asked Dave to approve the following draft sales letter, which Marc wanted to mail out next month to the 4,200 members of the Office Furniture Dealers' Association (OFDA) as the kickoff campaign for Urban Systems' Ultra Light Strips. After reading the letter twice, Dave had still not approved it. Something about the tone of the letter bothered him.

Dear Manager:

Would you like us to come visit you in jail?

Now, it's true that you probably won't be put in jail for requiring your computer operators to sit in front of a monitor eight hours a day, but you just might get slapped with a lawsuit from a disgruntled employee who complains of back problems or failing eyesight. One pregnant employee even won damages by blaming her miscarriage on emotional stress caused by too many hours at her word processor! And two studies published this past year that warn of dangers from long periods of working at a computer don't help the situation any.

Before going to your lawyer, come to US—to Urban Systems—for the answer to your problems. We have recently patented a new strip lighting system for modular furniture that will throw precisely the right amount of soft light around the monitor. With Ultra Light Strips, your operators won't have to put up with glare from their monitors, they won't have to position themselves in a certain way just to read the monitor, and they won't have shadows falling on their copy holders.

And if wiring is in place, just about anyone can install Ultra Light Strips. Just order the lengths you need–from 1 foot to 20 feet long. They are completely flexible, so that you can easily bend them around your modular furniture. And because they attach with Velcro strips, you can move them around and reuse them as your needs change.

We're really the only game in town when it comes to flexible task lighting. For example, the Mod Light by GME produces 200 foot-candles—far too much light to provide the needed contrast between the screen and surrounding light; your operators will soon begin to make careless errors from visual fatigue. And the Light Mite from Tedesco has long had a reputation for poor reliability. In addition, both GME and Tedesco produce their light fixtures abroad, while Ultra Light Strips are 100% American-made! With Ultra Light Strips lighting the way, your operators will be more productive, easily paying the cost of these strips

```
within the first six months of use.  Get a jump on the
competition.  And avoid those costly legal battles. Call
us toll-free at 1-800-555-2883 for a free on-site demon-
stration.  We can also show you the many other uses of
Ultra Light that will save your company money.

Sincerely,


Marc Kaplan
Vice President, Marketing
```

Critical Thinking

1. What is your reaction to this letter? Is it effective or not? Is it ethical? Explain.
2. If this letter represented your only knowledge of Urban Systems, what would be your opinion of the company? In other words, what kind of corporate image does the letter portray?
3. Without actually rewriting the letter, what revisions can you suggest for giving Marc's letter a more ethical tone?

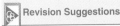

Revision Suggestions

- Use a more positive, less threatening tone.
- Gain the reader's attention with a positive idea.
- Omit the comments about lawsuits.
- Give specific details about the product.
- Omit the comments about the competition.

Ober, *Contemporary Business Communication*, 2d ed.

See Master 2.3, Question 3, in the *Instructor's Resource Manual.*

WORDWISE *Foreign Languages*

- There is no *W* in the Italian alphabet.
- In Iceland, there are no family surnames. A child's name is a possessive form of his or her father's first name.
- When America was founded, English won out over German as our official national language by a single vote.
- The word *taxi* is spelled the same in English, German, French, Swedish, and Portuguese.

PART II

Developing Your Writing Skills

CHAPTER 3

Writing with Style: Individual Elements

CHAPTER 4

Writing with Style: Overall Tone

CHAPTER 5

The Process of Writing

CHAPTER

3 Writing with Style: Individual Elements

Communication Objectives

After you have finished this chapter, you should be able to

1. Write clearly.
2. Prefer short, simple words.
3. Write with vigor.
4. Write concisely.
5. Prefer positive language.
6. Use a variety of sentence types.
7. Use active and passive voice appropriately.
8. Keep paragraphs unified and coherent.
9. Control paragraph length.

Several times a year, George Bolln sits down at his desk and carefully reads final proposals to sell jet engines to Pacific Rim governments. It's no easy task. These proposals, when finished, are often *hundreds* of pages in length, and each can take as long as three months to prepare. The proposals contain a mixture of financial, contractual, and technical language, and Bolln must be sure each aspect of a proposal is examined in painstaking detail in order to avoid complications down the road.

Bolln is manager of Advanced Military Programs for Massachusetts-based General Electric Aircraft Engines—Lynn. He is one of thousands of U.S. executives who are, with increasing frequency, doing business with Korea, Taiwan, Japan, the Philippines, and the People's Republic of China. For G.E. Aircraft Engines, the Pacific Rim business is worth quite a bit; the Korea fighter program is worth $500 million in initial sales alone.

The rules for doing business in the Pacific Rim vary with each country, but there is one constant. The reports must be written in such a way that those who speak English as a second language will not have problems understanding them.

"We obviously avoid using language that's known to only a select group of people in the United States," said Bolln, specifically referring to acronyms that are casually used throughout the military supply business. Bolln must also make sure the language is kept simple, that "flowery" descriptions are simplified. When Bolln spots something in a report, presentation, or proposal that has the slightest chance of being misunderstood, he makes sure the sentence is rewritten.

George Bolln

Manager of Advanced Military Programs, General Electric Aircraft Engines, Lynn, Massachusetts

The need for simple language in these reports is vital. Bolln has learned from his verbal dealings with business people in the Pacific Rim that "the more words you use, the more chance there is for confusion. And language we consider very flowery is sometimes hard [for Pacific Rim business people] to focus on." Bolln has transferred this lesson to the written word, especially since proposals are often translated by customers into summary reports for members of their upper management. Complicated prose, said Bolln, simply doesn't translate well and can lead to costly misinterpretations.

Without a near-perfect report, the company would have a hard time doing business in the Pacific Rim. And since most military programs "don't happen more than once, say, every 15 years in a given country," a misunderstanding or lost competition could cost the company millions of dollars. "Selling aircraft engines," said Bolln, "is not like selling consumer electronics or other commodities."

A chapter overview appears in the *Instructor's Resource Manual*, pp. 22–25.

The entire proposal writing process involves a lot of initial planning; then preliminary proposals are created, followed by the final report and, usually, a number of revisions. Throughout the creation of the proposal, there's plenty of letter writing back and forth—and there, too, the language must be kept simple. Even after the contract is signed, the reporting process still goes on, Bolln said. Progress reports have to be made, and any change in the production schedule has to be noted and approved.

Has the company ever had a deal fall through because of a language slip-up? "No," said Bolln emphatically. And it's clear that he has every intention of keeping it that way.

WHAT DO WE MEAN BY *STYLE?*

If you study the five LAB (Language Arts Basics) exercises in the Reference Manual at the end of this book, you will know how to express yourself *correctly* in most business writing situations; that is, you will know how to avoid major errors in grammar, spelling, punctuation, and word usage. But a technically correct message may still not achieve its objective. For example, consider the following paragraph:

LAB 1 covers commas; LAB 2, other punctuation; LAB 3, grammar; LAB 4, mechanics; and LAB 5, correct word usage.

Not: During the preceding year just past, Oxford Industries operated at a financial deficit. It closed three plants. It laid off many employees. The company's president was recently named Iowa Small Business Executive of the Year. Oxford is now endeavoring to ascertain the causes of its financial exigency. The company president said that . . .

Your writing can be error-free and still lack style, but it cannot have style unless it is error-free.

This paragraph has no grammatical, mechanical, or usage errors. But it is not clear, vigorous, or coherent. For example, consider the phrase "preceding year just past." "Preceding" *means* "just past," so why use both terms? In the second sentence, was closing the three plants the *cause* or the *result* of the financial deficit? What is the point of the sentence about the president? If you were speaking instead of writing, would you really say "endeavoring to ascertain," or would you use simpler language, like "trying to find out"? Finally, there are no transitions, or bridges, between the sentences; as a result, they don't flow smoothly.

Although the paragraph is technically correct, it lacks **style.** By style, we mean the way in which an idea is expressed (not its *substance*). Style consists of the particular words the writer uses and the manner in which those words are combined into sentences, paragraphs, and complete messages.

Now compare the first-draft paragraph above with this revised version:

> *But:* Last year Oxford Industries lost money and, as a result, closed three plants and laid off 200 employees. Now the company is trying to determine the causes of its problems. In explaining the situation to stockholders, Oxford's president, who was recently named Iowa Small Business Executive of the Year, said that . . .

The revised version is more direct and readable. It clarifies relationships among the sentences. It uses concise, familiar language. It presents ideas in logical order. In short, it has style. Chapters 3 and 4 discuss 15 principles of effective writing style for business. Apply these principles of style as you write the letters, memos, and reports that are assigned in later chapters.

Style *refers to the effectiveness of the words, sentences, paragraphs, and overall tone of your message.*

Words

1. Write clearly.
2. Prefer short, simple words.
3. Write with vigor.
4. Write concisely.
5. Prefer positive language.

Sentences

6. Use a variety of sentence types.
7. Use active and passive voice appropriately.

Paragraphs

8. Keep paragraphs unified and coherent.
9. Control paragraph length.

Overall Tone

10. Write confidently.
11. Use a courteous and sincere tone.

FIGURE 3.1 Steps to an Effective Message

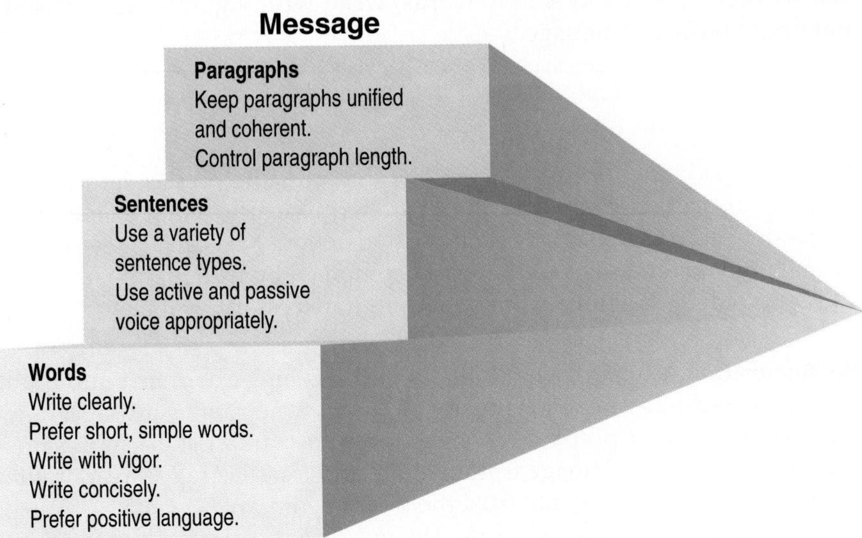

12. Use appropriate emphasis and subordination.
13. Use nondiscriminatory language.
14. Stress the "you" attitude.
15. Write at an appropriate level of difficulty.

Mechanics refers to how an idea is expressed in writing.

While writing the first draft of a message, you should be more concerned with content than with style. Your major objective should be to get your ideas down in some form, without worrying about style and mechanics. (**Mechanics** are elements in communication that show up only in written form, including spelling, punctuation, abbreviations, capitalization, number expression, and word division.)

The more familiar you are with basic stylistic principles, the easier it will be to write your first draft and the less editing you will need to do later. So studying these principles first makes your writing process more efficient. You will then return to these principles when revising your writing to make sure that you have followed each guideline.

Principles 1–9 focus on the *parts* of the message (words, sentences, and paragraphs) and are discussed in this chapter (see Fig. 3.1). Principles 10–15 focus on the tone of the *whole* message and are discussed in the next chapter. At the end of that chapter, a checklist summarizes all 15 writing principles. You should use Checklist 1 in evaluating your own style.

CHOOSING THE RIGHT WORDS

Individual words are our basic units of writing, the bricks with which we build meaningful messages. All writers have access to the same words. The care with which we select and combine words can make the difference between a message that achieves its objective and one that does not. Here are five principles of word choice to help you write more effectively: write clearly, prefer short and simple words, write with vigor, write concisely, and prefer positive language.

1. Write Clearly.

The basic guideline for writing, the one that must be present in order for the other principles to have meaning, is to write clearly—to write messages the reader can understand, depend on, and act on. You can achieve clarity by making your message accurate and complete, by using familiar words, and by avoiding dangling expressions and unnecessary jargon.

Accuracy is the most important attribute in business writing. It involves more than freedom from errors.

Be Accurate A writer's credibility is perhaps his or her most important asset, and credibility depends greatly on the accuracy of the message. If, by carelessness, lack of preparation, or a desire to manipulate, a writer misleads the reader, the damage is immediate and long-lasting. A reader who has been fooled once may not trust the writer again.

Accuracy can take many forms. The most basic is the truth of facts and figures presented. But accuracy involves much more. For example, consider the following sentence from a memo to a firm's financial backers:

> The executive committee of Mitchell Financial Services met on Thursday, May 28, to determine how to resolve the distribution fiasco.

Suppose, on checking, the reader learns that May 28 fell on a Wednesday this year—not on a Thursday. Immediately, the reader may suspect everything else in the message. The reader's thinking might be, "If the writer made this error that I *did* catch, how many other errors that I *didn't* catch are lurking there?"

Now consider more subtle shades of truth. The sentence implies that the committee met, perhaps in an emergency session, for the *sole* purpose of solving the distribution fiasco. But suppose this matter was only one of five agenda items being discussed at a regularly scheduled meeting. Is the statement still accurate? Suppose the actual agenda listed the topic as "Discussion of Recent Distribution Problems." Is *fiasco* the same as *problems?*

Ethical communicators make sure the overall tone of their message is accurate.

The accuracy of a message, then, depends on what is said, how it is said, and what is left unsaid (see, for example, the following section on the importance of completeness). Each writer must assess the ethical dimensions of his or her writing and use integrity, fairness, and good judgment to make sure communication is ethical.

Be Complete Closely related to accuracy is completeness. A message that lacks important information may create inaccurate impressions. A message is complete when it contains all the information the reader needs—no more and no less—to react appropriately.

As a start, answer the five W's; tell the reader *who, what, when, where,* and *why.* Leaving out any of this information may result either in decisions based on incomplete information or in extra follow-up correspondence to gather the needed information. Answering *why* questions is particularly important when you write persuasive and negative messages. For example, if you tell me that I've been promoted, *why* is not uppermost in my mind; however, if you tell me that my promotion was denied, I definitely want to know *why* before I accept the decision. Similarly, if you want to persuade me to do something, you must explain *why*.

Use Familiar Words Your message must be understood in order for someone to act on it. So you must use words that are both familiar to you (so that you will not misuse the word) and familiar to your readers.

Use language that you and your reader understand.

A true story illustrates this point. A young soldier, serving in Vietnam as a typist for a general, received a report he thought the general should see. Believing that "for your edification" meant "for your information" (it actually means "for your *improvement*"), the typist wrote "Sir: For your edification" on the report and sent it to the general. Back came the general's reply: "Private: First, look up the word *edification*. Then see me for *your* edification!"

Don't assume that only long, multisyllabic words cause confusion. Consider the following sentences:

Not: The hexad worked with élan in order to redact their report and eloign their guilt.

But: The six people vigorously edited their report in order to conceal their guilt.

The first version consists entirely of short words, with the longest word having just six letters and two syllables. Probably only a crossword puzzle addict, however, would be able to understand the first version; most readers would understand the second.

Long words are sometimes useful in business communication. Could you use each of the following words correctly in a business-related sentence?

acrimony	halcyon
anomalies	parietal
attenuation	plethora
cognizance	probative
efficacious	remandatory
egress	subrogation

Before you decide that such words are unimportant in business writing, you should know that these words came from a word list based on a computer analysis of actual business letters, memos, and reports.[1] The larger your vocabulary and the more you know about your reader, the better equipped you will be to choose and use correctly those words that are familiar to your reader.

Avoid Dangling Expressions A **dangling expression** is any part of a sentence that doesn't logically fit in with the rest of the sentence. Its relationship with the other parts of the sentence is unclear; it *dangles*. The two most common types of dangling expressions are misplaced modifiers and unclear antecedents.

For an exercise on revising dangling expressions, refer students to the *Study Guide*, pp. 101–102.

Garry Trudeau, a well-known social and political cartoonist, must always choose the right words. His language must be clear, concise, and vigorous. If it's not, Trudeau's message is sure to be lost.

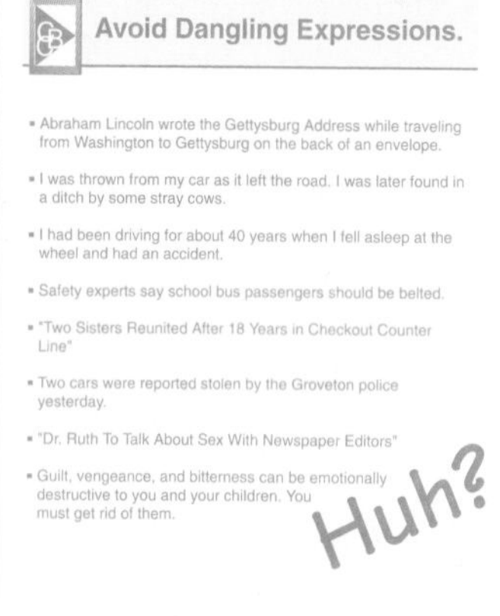

Avoid Dangling Expressions.
▪ Abraham Lincoln wrote the Gettysburg Address while traveling from Washington to Gettysburg on the back of an envelope.
▪ I was thrown from my car as it left the road. I was later found in a ditch by some stray cows.
▪ I had been driving for about 40 years when I fell asleep at the wheel and had an accident.
▪ Safety experts say school bus passengers should be belted.
▪ "Two Sisters Reunited After 18 Years in Checkout Counter Line"
▪ Two cars were reported stolen by the Groveton police yesterday.
▪ "Dr. Ruth To Talk About Sex With Newspaper Editors"
▪ Guilt, vengeance, and bitterness can be emotionally destructive to you and your children. You must get rid of them.
Huh?

See Transparency 3.1, Dangling Expressions.

To correct dangling expressions, (1) make the subject of the sentence the doer of the action expressed in the introductory clause; (2) move the expression closer to the word that it modifies; (3) make sure that the specific word to which a pronoun refers (its *antecedent*) is clear; or (4) otherwise revise the sentence.

Not: After reading the proposal, a few problems occurred to me. (*As written, the sentence implies that "a few problems" read the proposal.*)
But: After reading the proposal, I noted a few problems.

Not: Dr. Ellis gave a presentation on the use of drugs in our auditorium. (*Are drugs being used in the auditorium?*)
But: Dr. Ellis gave a presentation in our auditorium on the use of drugs.

Not: Robin explained the proposal to Joy, but she was not happy with it. (*Who was not happy—Robin or Joy?*)
But: Robin explained the proposal to Joy, but Joy was not happy with it.

Not: You may take your vacation the last week in June or the first week in July, but in that case, you will need to submit your status report early. (*In which case will you have to submit your report early?*)
But: You may take your vacation the last week in June or the first week in July; but if you choose the last week in June, you will need to submit your status report early.

Jargon is sometimes appropriate and sometimes inappropriate.

Avoid Unnecessary Jargon Jargon is technical vocabulary used within a special group. Every field has its own specialized words, and jargon offers a precise and efficient way of communicating with people in the same field. But problems arise when jargon is used to communicate with someone who does not understand it. For example, to a banker the term *CD* means a "certificate of deposit," but to a stereo buff or computer user it means a "compact disk." Even familiar words can be confusing when given a specialized meaning.

Not: Your incorrect bill was caused by a computer virus, which disabled the error-lockout function, resulting in encrypted data.

But: Your incorrect bill was caused by a temporary software problem, which let unreadable data get entered into the computer.

The original sentence might be appropriate when communicating with other information specialists. In this case, a utility company was explaining to a customer why she had received a bill for "$a.00." The explanation was probably as unreadable as the bill had been!

Does the field of business communication have jargon? It does—just look at the Key Terms list at the end of each chapter. The word *jargon* itself might be considered communication jargon. In this text, such terms are first defined and then used to make communication precise and efficient. Competent writers use specialized vocabulary to communicate with specialists who understand it. And they avoid using it when their readers are not specialists.

2. Prefer Short, Simple Words.

Short, simple words are the building blocks of effective business communication.

Short and simple words are more likely to be understood, less likely to be misused, and less likely to distract the reader. Literary authors often write to *impress;* they select words to achieve a specific reader reaction, such as amusement, excitement, or anger. Business writers, on the other hand, write to *express;* they want to achieve *comprehension.* They want their readers to focus on their information, not on how they convey their information. Using short, simple words helps achieve this goal.

Not: To recapitulate, our utilization of adulterated water precipitated the interminable delays.

But: To review, our use of impure water caused the endless delays.

Remind students that big words do not automatically make you sound smart; in fact, they can make you sound pretentious instead. Consider the following sentence: "Walter demonstrates a propensity to utilize a multisyllabic vocabulary, which sometimes obfuscates what he is endeavoring to communicate." The second version, written in a more conversational style, is more direct and easy to understand. "Walter tends to use big words, which can make his meaning unclear."

It is true, of course, that often no short, simple word is available to convey the precise shade of meaning you want. For example, there is no one-syllable replacement for *ethnocentrism* (the belief that one's own cultural group is superior), a concept introduced in Chapter 2. Our guideline is not to use *only* short and simple words but to *prefer* short and simple words. (As Mark Twain, who was paid by the word for his writing, noted, "I never write *metropolis* for seven cents because I can get the same price for *city.* I never write *policeman* because I can get the same money for *cop.*")

Here are some examples of needlessly long words, gleaned from various business documents, with their preferred shorter substitutes shown in parentheses:

ascertain (learn)	initiate (start)
endeavor (try)	modification (change)
enumerate (list)	recapitulate (review)
fabricate (make)	reproduction (copy)
fluctuate (vary)	substantial (large)
illustrate (show)	termination (end)
indispensable (vital)	utilization (use)

You need not strike these long words totally from your written or spoken vocabulary; any one of these words, used in a clear sentence, would be acceptable. The problem is that a writer may tend to fill his or her writing with very long words when simpler ones could be used. Use long words in moderation. Note the following advice from author Richard Lederer:[2]

> When you speak and write, no law says you have to use big words. Short words are as good as long ones, and short, old words like *sun* and *grass* and *home* are best of all. A lot of small words, more than you might think, can meet your needs with a strength, grace, and charm that large words lack.
>
> Big words can make the way dark for those who hear what you say and read what you write. They add fat to your prose. Small words are the ones we seem to have known from birth. They are like the hearth fire that warms the home, and they cast a clear light on big things: night and day, love and hate, war and peace, life and death.
>
> Short words are bright, like sparks that glow in the night; sharp like the blade of a knife; hot like salt tears that scald the cheek; quick like moths that flit from flame to flame; and terse like the dart and sting of a bee.
>
> If a long word says just what you want, do not fear to use it. But know that our tongue is rich in crisp, brisk, swift, short words. Make them the spine and the heart of what you speak and write. Like fast friends, they will not let you down.

Here are more wordy phrases and their one-word substitutes:
Wordy (Concise)
for the reason that (because)
the reason is because (because)
at the present time (now)
at this point in time (now)
despite the fact that (although)

Lederer practices what he preaches. All 223 words in these four paragraphs are one-syllable words!

You've probably heard the advice "Write as you speak." Although not universally true, such advice is pretty close to the mark. Of course, if your conversation is peppered with redundancies, jargon, and clichés, you would not want to put such weaknesses on paper. But typical conversation uses mostly short, simple words—the kind you *do* want on paper. Don't assume that the bigger the words, the bigger the intellect. In fact, you need a large vocabulary and a well-developed word sense to select the best word. And more often than not, that word is short and simple. Write to express—not to impress.

Write to express—not to impress.

For an exercise on revising a wordy memo, refer students to the *Study Guide*, p. 84.

Choosing the Right Word

Avoid These —

× **CLICHÉS.**
Not: As per your request, every effort will be made to fix the problem.
But: As you requested, we will try to fix the problem.

× **REDUNDANCIES.**
Not: Hemingway referred back to our earlier decision not to repeat that mistake again.
But: Hemingway referred to our earlier decision not to repeat that mistake.

× **WORDY EXPRESSIONS.**
Not: Let me know as to whether or not we can start drilling in view of the fact that the problem has been fixed at the present time.
But: Let me know whether we can start drilling because the problem has now been fixed.

× **HIDDEN VERBS.**
Not: We held a meeting to make the arrangements for her visit.
But: We met to arrange her visit.

Ober, *Contemporary Business Communication*, 2d ed.

See Transparency 3.2, Choosing the Right Word.

3. Write with Vigor.

Vigorous language is specific and concrete. Limp language is filled with clichés, slang, and buzz words. Vigorous writing holds your reader's interest. But if your reader isn't even interested enough to read your message, your writing can't possibly achieve its objective. A second reason for writing with vigor has to do with language itself. Vigorous writing tends to lend vigor to the ideas presented. A good idea looks even better dressed in vigorous language, and a weak idea looks even weaker when dressed in limp language.

Use Specific, Concrete Language In Chapter 1, we discussed the communication barriers caused by overabstraction and ambiguity. When possible, choose *specific* words—ones that have a definite, unambiguous meaning. Likewise, choose *concrete* words—ones that bring a definite picture to your reader's mind.

Not: The vehicle broke down several times recently.
But: The delivery van broke down three times last week.

In the first version, what does the reader imagine when he or she reads the word *vehicle*—a golf cart? automobile? boat? space shuttle? Likewise, how many times is *several*—two? three? fifteen? The revised version clarifies what happened.

Sometimes we do not need such specific information. For example, in "The president answered *several* questions from the audience and then adjourned the meeting," the specific number of questions is probably not important. But in most situations, you should watch out for words like *several, recently, a number of, substantial, a few,* and *a lot of.* You may need to be more precise.

Likewise, use the most concrete word that is appropriate; give the reader a specific mental picture of what you mean. Be sure that your terms convey as much meaning as the reader needs in order to react appropriately. Watch out for terms like *emotional meeting* (anger or gratitude?), *bright color* (red or yellow?), *new equipment* (postage meter or cash register?), and *change in price* (increase or decrease?).

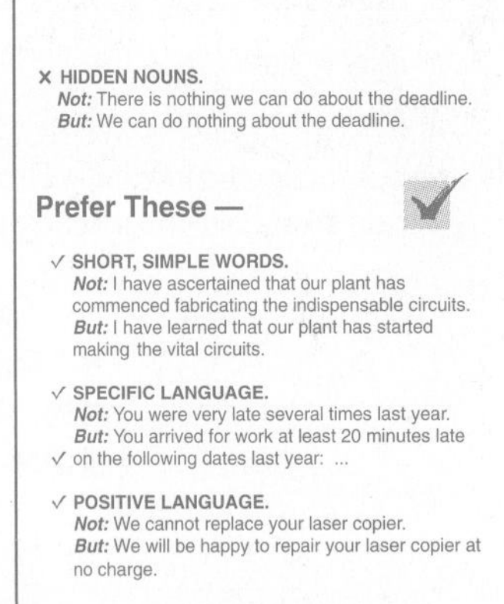

× HIDDEN NOUNS.
Not: There is nothing we can do about the deadline.
But: We can do nothing about the deadline.
Prefer These —
✓ SHORT, SIMPLE WORDS.
Not: I have ascertained that our plant has commenced fabricating the indispensable circuits.
But: I have learned that our plant has started making the vital circuits.
✓ SPECIFIC LANGUAGE.
Not: You were very late several times last year.
But: You arrived for work at least 20 minutes late
✓ on the following dates last year: ...
✓ POSITIVE LANGUAGE.
Not: We cannot replace your laser copier.
But: We will be happy to repair your laser copier at no charge.
Ober, *Contemporary Business Communication*, 2d ed.
Copyright © 1995 Houghton Mifflin Company. All rights reserved.

See Transparency 3.3, Choosing the Right Word (continued).

Concrete words present a vivid picture.

Avoid Clichés, Slang, and Buzz Words A **cliché** (pronounced *klee SHAY*) is an expression that has become monotonous through overuse. It lacks freshness and originality and may also send the unintended message that the writer couldn't be bothered to choose language geared specifically to the reader.

Not: Enclosed please find an application form that you should return at your earliest convenience.
But: Please return the enclosed application form before September 15.

Here are some examples of other expressions that have become overused (even in other countries—see the Spotlight Across Cultures on page 66) and that therefore sound trite and boring. Avoid them in your writing.

According to our records	It goes without saying that
Company policy requires	Needless to say
Do not hesitate to	Our records indicate that
For your information	Please be advised that
If I can be of further help	Take this opportunity to
If you have any other questions	Under separate cover

Picture a person finding "thank you for your letter" in all 15 letters he or she reads that day. How sincere and original does it sound?

As noted earlier, slang is an expression, often short-lived, that is identified with a specific group of people. If you understand each word in an expression but still don't understand what it means in context, chances are you're having trouble with a slang expression. For example, read the following sentence:

> It turns my stomach the way you can break your neck and beat your brains out around here, and they still stab you in the back.

To anyone unfamiliar with American slang (a nonnative speaker, perhaps), this sentence might seem to be about the body, because it refers to

SPOTLIGHT ACROSS CULTURES

Same Rules the World Over

The strategies for writing effective business messages are universal. The passage below, from a business communication text for Chinese business executives, recommends substituting concise phrases for long, empty ones.

"简洁"是有客观标准的。虽然西方国家的作者之间在怎样用词才算"简洁"方面还是有争论的，不过他们的一些看法还是有一定参考价值的。现把他们所做的某些词句的"不简洁"与"简洁"的比较列在下面供参考:

不简洁	简洁
enclosed herewith	enclosed
enclosed you will find	enclosed is
please be advised that	(four wasted words)
please don't hesitate to call upon us	please write us
please feel free to write	please write
prior to	before
this is to advise you	(5 wasted words)
under separate cover	separately
a long period of time	a long time
continuous and uninterrupted	continuous (or: uninterrupted)
during the year of 1971	during 1971
endorse on the back of this check	endorse this check
for a price of $300	for $300

Source: Ge-Lin Zhu, Chief Editor, *Practical Commercial English Handbook* (Beijing, China: Commercial Publishing Company, 1981), p. 49.

For an extended discussion of international issues, see "Diversity and Communication" in Chapter 2, pp. 34–39.

Example of concrete language: Suppose your boss asks you to report on the status of the company's new office site. Instead of "The new office site is a mess," the following statement would be more effective: "The new office will not be complete for several weeks. There's plaster dust everywhere, and the workers are still drilling holes in the walls, installing wiring, and laying carpet."

the stomach, neck, brains, and back. The real meaning, of course, is something like this:

> I am really upset that this company ignores hard work and loyalty when it makes decisions.

Avoid slang in most business writing, for several reasons. First, it is informal, and much business writing, although not formal, is still *businesslike* and calls for standard word usage. Second, slang is short-lived. A slang phrase used today may not be in use—and thus may not be familiar—in three years, when your letter is retrieved from the files for reference. Third, slang is identified with a specific group of people, and others in the general population may not understand the intended meaning. For these reasons, avoid terms such as the following in business writing:

- can of worms
- chew out
- clip joint
- go for broke
- hate one's guts
- knock it off
- once-over
- pay through the nose
- play up to
- security blanket
- sticky fingers
- use your noodle
- wiped out
- zonked out

A **buzz word** is an important-sounding expression used mainly to impress other people. Because buzz words are so often used by government officials and high-ranking business people—people whose comments are "newsworthy"—these expressions get much media attention. They become instant clichés and then go out of fashion just as quickly. At either end of their short life span, they cause communication problems. If an expression is currently being used by everyone, it sounds monotonous, lacking originality. If it is no longer being used by anyone, readers may not understand the intended meaning. Here are examples of recent "in" expressions:

Clichés and buzz words go in and out of style too quickly to serve as effective components of written business communication.

bottom line	paradigm
done deal	parameter
global dimensions	pipeline
impact (verb)	scenario
interface	user-friendly
no-brainer	vision statement

Be especially careful of turning nouns and other types of words into verbs by adding *-ize.* Such words as *agendize, prioritize, strategize, unionize,* and *operationalize* quickly become tiresome.

4. Write Concisely.

Business people are busy people. The information revolution has created more paperwork, giving business people access to more data. Having more paperwork to analyze (but no more time in which to read it), managers want information presented in the fewest possible words. To achieve conciseness, make every word count. Avoid redundancy, wordy expressions, hidden verbs and nouns, and other "space-eaters."

Avoid Redundancy A **redundancy** is the unnecessary repetition of an idea that has already been expressed or intimated. Eliminating the repetition contributes to conciseness. Read these two sets of sentences:

Not: Signing both copies of the lease is a necessary requirement.
But: Signing both copies of the lease is necessary.

Not: Combine the ingredients together.
But: Combine the ingredients.

A *requirement* is by definition *necessary,* so only one of the words is needed. And to *combine* means to bring *together,* so using both words is redundant. Don't confuse redundancy and repetition. Repetition—using the same word more than once—is sometimes effective for emphasis. Redundancy, however, serves no purpose and should always be avoided.

Redundancy and repetition are not the same.

Some redundancies are humorous, as in the classic Samuel Goldwyn comment, "Anybody who goes to a psychiatrist ought to have his head examined," or the sign in a jewelry store window, "Ears pierced while you wait," or the statement in an automobile advertisement, "Open seven days a week plus weekends." Most redundancies, however, are simply *verbiage*—excess words that consume time and space. Avoid them.

Do not use the unnecessary word *together* after such words as *assemble, combine, cooperate, gather, join, merge,* or *mix.* Do not use the unnecessary

Make every word count.

word *new* before such words as *beginner, discovery, fad, innovation,* or *progress.* And do not use the unnecessary word *up* after such words as *connect, divide, eat, lift, mix,* and *rest.* Also avoid the following common redundancies (use the words in parentheses instead):

advance planning (planning)
any and all (any *or* all)
basic fundamentals (basics *or* fundamentals)
but nevertheless (but *or* nevertheless)
consensus of opinion (consensus)
each and every (each *or* every)
free gift (gift)
over again (over)
past history (history)
plan ahead (plan)
repeat again (repeat)
sum total (sum *or* total)
true facts (facts)
when and if (when *or* if)

Use the fewest number of words that will achieve your objective.

Avoid Wordy Expressions Although wordy expressions are not necessarily writing errors (as redundancies are), they do slow the pace of the communication and should be avoided. For example, try substituting one word for a phrase whenever possible.

Not: In view of the fact that the model failed twice during the time that we tested it, we are at this point in time searching for other options.

But: Because the model failed twice when we tested it, we are now searching for other options.

The original sentence contains 28 words; the revised sentence, 16. You've "saved" 12 words. In his delightful book *Revising Business Prose,* Richard Lanham speaks of the "lard factor": the percentage of words saved by "getting rid of the lard" in a sentence. In this case,

$28 - 16 = 12; 12 \div 28 = 43\%$

Thus, 43% of the original sentence was "lard," which fattened the sentence without providing any "nutrition." Lanham suggests, "Think of a lard factor (LF) of ⅓ to ½ as normal and don't stop revising until you've removed it."[3]

Here are examples of other wordy phrases and their preferred one-word substitutes in parentheses:

are of the opinion that (believe)
due to the fact that (because)
for the purpose of (for *or* to)
in order to (to)
in the event that (if)
pertaining to (about)
with regard to (about)

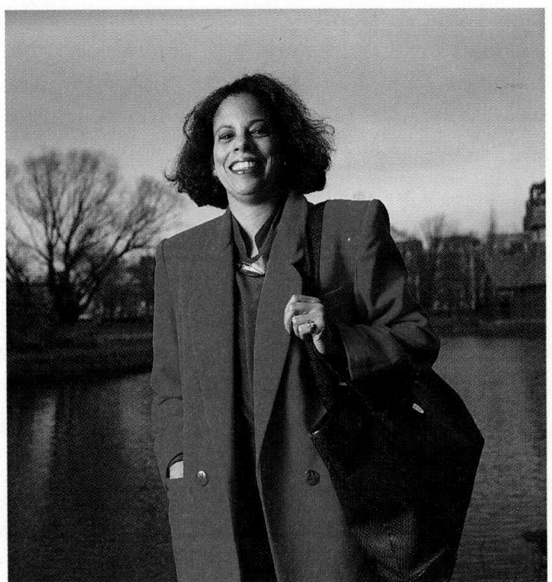

When she first joined the corporate world at Merrill Lynch as vice president of philanthropic programs, Westina Matthews learned that the corporate culture even dictated how to write memos: concisely, with options and recommendations clearly laid out.

Avoid Hidden Verbs A hidden verb is a verb that has been changed into a noun form, weakening the action. Verbs are action words and should convey the main action in the sentence. They provide interest and forward movement. Consider this example:

Changing verbs to nouns produces weak, uninteresting sentences.

Not: Carl made an announcement that he will give consideration to our request.

What is the real action? It is not that Carl *made* something or that he will *give* something. The real action is hiding in the nouns: Carl *announced* and will *consider*. These two verb forms, then, should be the main verbs in the sentence.

But: Carl announced that he will consider our request.

Notice that the revised sentence is much more direct—and four words shorter (LF = 33%). Here are some other actions that should be conveyed by verbs instead of being hidden in nouns:

arrived at the conclusion (concluded)
came to an agreement (agreed)
gave a demonstration of (demonstrated)
gave an explanation (explained)
has a requirement for (requires)
have a need for (need)
held a meeting (met)
made a payment (paid)
performed an analysis of (analyzed)

Here are nine "dull and empty verbs" to avoid, according to business writing consultant and author Donna Freiermuth: make, have, occur, go, move, get, come, do, and be. (Ronnie Gunnerson, "How to Write for Business," *Home-Office Computing*, January 1990, p. 38.)

Avoid Hidden Subjects Like verbs, subjects play a prominent role in a sentence and should stand out, rather than being obscured by an expletive

The pronoun in an expletive does not stand for any other noun.

beginning. An **expletive** is an expression such as *there is* or *it is* that begins a clause or sentence and for which the pronoun has no antecedent. Because the topic of a sentence that begins with an expletive is not immediately clear, you should use such sentences sparingly in business writing. Avoiding expletives also contributes to conciseness.

Not: There was no indication that it is necessary to include John in the meeting.

But: No one indicated that John should be included in the meeting.

Some information need only be implied.

Imply or Condense Sometimes you do not need to explicitly state certain information; you can imply it instead. In other situations, you can use adjectives and adverbs instead of clauses to convey the needed information in a more concise format.

Not: <u>We have received your recent letter</u> and are happy to provide the data you requested.

But: We are happy to provide the data you recently requested.

Not: This brochure, <u>which is available free of charge</u>, will answer your questions.

But: This <u>free</u> brochure will answer your questions.

5. Prefer Positive Language.

Words that create a positive image are more likely to help you achieve your objective than are negative words. For example, you are more likely to persuade someone to do as you ask if you stress the advantages of doing so rather than the disadvantages of not doing so. Positive language also builds goodwill for you and your organization and often gives more information than negative language. Note the differences in tone and amount of information given in the following pairs of sentences:

Not: The briefcase is not made of cheap imitation leather.

But: The briefcase is made of 100% belt leather for years of durable service.

Not: We cannot ship your merchandise until we receive your check.

But: As soon as we receive your check, we will ship your merchandise.

Not: I do not yet have any work experience.

But: My two terms as secretary of the Management Club taught me the importance of accurate recordkeeping and gave me experience in working with others.

Avoid negative-sounding words.

Expressions like *cannot* and *will not* are not the only ones that convey negative messages. Other words, like *mistake, damage, failure, refuse,* and *deny,* also carry negative connotations and should be avoided when possible.

Not: Failure to follow the directions may cause the blender to malfunction.

But: Following the directions will ensure many years of carefree service from your blender.

Not: We apologize for this error.
But: We appreciate your calling this matter to our attention.

Not: We close at 7 p.m. on Fridays.
But: We're open until 7 p.m. on Fridays to give you time to shop after work.

Sometimes you can avoid negative language by switching to the subjunctive mood, which uses words like *wish, if,* and *would* to refer to conditions that are impossible or improbable. Such language softens the impact of the negative message, making it more palatable to the reader. Here are two examples:

The subjunctive mood sounds more hopeful than an outright refusal.

Not: I cannot speak at your November meeting.
But: I wish it were possible for me to speak at your November meeting.

Not: I cannot release the names of our clients.
But: Releasing the names of our clients would violate their right to privacy.

In short, stress what *is* true and what *can* be done rather than what is not true and what cannot be done. This is not to say that negative language has no place in business writing. Negative language is strong and emphatic, and sometimes you may want to use it. But unless the situation clearly calls for negative language, you are more likely to achieve your objective and to build goodwill for yourself and your organization by stressing the positive.

Because words are the building blocks for your message, choose them with care. Using short, simple words; writing with clarity, vigor, and conciseness; and using positive language will help you construct effective sentences and paragraphs.

WRITING EFFECTIVE SENTENCES

The sentence is the basic unit of writing. A sentence has a subject and predicate and expresses at least one complete thought. Beyond these simple attributes, however, sentences vary widely in style, length, and effect. They are also very flexible; writers can move sentence parts around, add and delete information, and substitute words in order to express different ideas and emphasize different points. To build effective sentences, use a variety of sentence types, and use active and passive voice appropriately.

Types of Sentences

SIMPLE:
John listened.
John and Luis listened to the vice president's presentation on cost-cutting methods and decided to try her suggestions sometime during the upcoming quarter.

COMPOUND:
I spoke and Ellie took notes.
Our customers asked for faster service, and we started our same-day shipments.
Our customers asked for faster service; therefore, we started our same-day shipments.

COMPLEX:
When our customers asked for faster service, we started our same-day shipments.

Ober, *Contemporary Business Communication*, 2d ed.

See Transparency 3.4, Sentence Types.

6. Use a Variety of Sentence Types.

There are three basic sentence patterns—simple, compound, and complex—all of which are appropriate for business writing.

Use a simple sentence for emphasis and variety.

Simple Sentence A **simple sentence** contains one independent clause (a clause that can stand alone as a complete thought). Because it presents a single idea and is usually (but not always) short, a simple sentence is often used for emphasis. Although a simple sentence contains only one independent clause, it may have a compound subject or compound verb (or both). All the following are simple sentences:

I quit.

Individual Retirement Accounts are a safe option.

Both Individual Retirement Accounts and Simplified Employee Pension Plans are safe and convenient options as retirement investments for the entrepreneur.

Use a compound sentence to show coordinate (equal) relationships.

Compound Sentence A **compound sentence** contains two or more independent clauses. Because each clause presents a complete idea, each idea receives equal emphasis. (If the two ideas are not closely related, they should be presented in two separate sentences.) Here are three compound sentences:

Stacey listened, but I nodded.

Morris Technologies made a major acquisition last year, and it turned out to be a disaster.

Westmoreland Mines moved its headquarters to Prescott in 1984; however, it stayed there only five years and then moved back to Globe.

Use a complex sentence to express subordinate relationships.

Complex Sentence A **complex sentence** contains one independent clause and at least one dependent clause. For example, notice the first sentence below. "The scanner will save valuable input time" is the independent clause because it makes sense by itself. "Although it cost $2,150" is the dependent clause because it does not make sense by itself.

Although it cost $2,150, the scanner will save valuable input time.

George Bosley, who is the new CEO at Hubbell, made the decision.

I will be moving to Austin when I assume my new position.

The dependent clause provides additional, but subordinate, information related to the independent clause. Sentences that contain two or more independent clauses and one or more dependent clauses are sometimes called *compound-complex sentences.*

Sentence Variety Using a variety of sentence patterns and sentence lengths helps keep your writing interesting. Note how simplistic and choppy too many short sentences can be and how boring and difficult too many long sentences can be.

Too Choppy:

Golden Nugget will not purchase the Claridge Hotel. The hotel is 60 years old. The asking price was $110 million. It was not considered too high. Golden Nugget had wanted some commitments from New Jersey regulators. The regulators were unwilling to provide such commitments. Some observers believe the refusal was not the real reason for the decision. They blame the weak Atlantic City economy for the cancellation. Golden Nugget purchased the Stake House in Las Vegas

> in 1983. It lost money on that purchase. It does not want to repeat its mistake in Atlantic City. *(Average sentence length = 8 words)*
>
> *Too Difficult:*
>
> Golden Nugget will not purchase the Claridge Hotel, which is 60 years old, for an asking price of $110 million, which was not considered too high, because the company had wanted some commitments from New Jersey regulators, and the regulators were unwilling to provide such commitments. Some observers believe the refusal was not the real reason for the decision but rather that the weak Atlantic City economy was responsible for the cancellation; and since Golden Nugget purchased the Stake House in Las Vegas in 1983 and lost money on that purchase, it does not want to repeat its mistake in Atlantic City. *(Average sentence length = 50 words)*

The sentences in these paragraphs should be revised to show relationships more clearly, to keep readers interested, and to improve readability. Use simple sentences for emphasis and variety, compound sentences for coordinate (equal) relationships, and complex sentences for subordinate relationships.

Use a variety of sentence patterns and lengths.

> *More Variety:*
>
> Golden Nugget will not purchase the 60-year-old Claridge Hotel, even though the $110 million asking price was not considered too high. The company had wanted some commitments from New Jersey regulators, which the regulators were unwilling to provide. However, some observers blame the cancellation on the weak Atlantic City economy. Golden Nugget lost money on its 1983 purchase of the Stake House in Las Vegas, and it does not want to repeat its mistake in Atlantic City. *(Average sentence length = 20 words)*

The first two sentences in the revision are complex, the third sentence is simple, and the last sentence is compound. The length of the four sentences ranges from 12 to 27 words. To write effective sentences, use different sentence patterns and lengths. Most sentences in good business writing should probably range from 16 to 22 words.

7. Use Active and Passive Voice Appropriately.

Voice is the aspect of a verb that shows whether the subject of the sentence acts or is acted on. In the **active voice,** the subject does the action expressed by the verb. In the **passive voice,** the subject receives the action expressed by the verb.

> *Active:* Inmac offers a full refund on all orders.
> *Passive:* A full refund on all orders is offered by Inmac.
>
> *Active:* Shoemacher & Doerr audited the books in 1992.
> *Passive:* The books were audited in 1992 by Shoemacher & Doerr.

Passive sentences use some form of the verb *to be* with the main verb, so passive sentences are always somewhat longer than active sentences. In

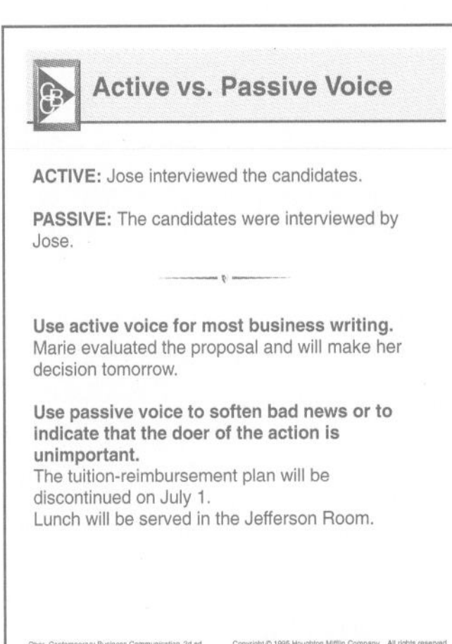

Active vs. Passive Voice
ACTIVE: Jose interviewed the candidates.
PASSIVE: The candidates were interviewed by Jose.
Use active voice for most business writing.
Marie evaluated the proposal and will make her decision tomorrow.
Use passive voice to soften bad news or to indicate that the doer of the action is unimportant.
The tuition-reimbursement plan will be discontinued on July 1.
Lunch will be served in the Jefferson Room.
Ober, Contemporary Business Communication, 2d ed.
Copyright © 1995 Houghton Mifflin Company. All rights reserved.

See Transparency 3.5, Active versus Passive Voice.

the first set of sentences just given, for example, compare *offers* in the active sentence with *is offered by* in the passive sentence.

In active sentences, the subject performs the action; in passive sentences, the subject receives the action.

In active sentences, the subject is the doer of the action; in passive sentences, the subject is the receiver of the action. And because the subject gets more emphasis than other nouns in a sentence, active sentences emphasize the doer, and passive sentences the receiver, of the action. In the second set of sentences, either version could be considered correct, depending on whether the writer wanted to emphasize Shoemacher & Doerr or the books.

Use active sentences most of the time in business writing, just as you naturally use active sentences in most of your conversations. Note that verb *voice* (active or passive) has nothing to do with verb *tense*, which shows the time of the action. As the following sentences show, the action in both active and passive sentences can occur in the past, present, or future.

Not: A very logical argument was presented by Harold. (*Passive voice, past tense*)

But: Harold presented a very logical argument. (*Active voice, past tense*)

Not: An 18% increase will be reported by the eastern region. (*Passive voice, future tense*)

But: The eastern region will report an 18% increase. (*Active voice, future tense*)

Passive sentences are more effective than active sentences for conveying negative information.

Passive sentences are most appropriate when you want to emphasize the receiver of the action, when the person doing the action is either unknown or unimportant, or when you want to be tactful in conveying negative information. All the following sentences are appropriately stated in the passive voice:

Protective legislation was blamed for the drop in imports. (*Emphasizes the receiver of the action*)

Transportation will be provided to the construction site. (*The doer of the action not important*)

Several complaints have been received regarding the new policy. (*Tactfully conveys negative news*)

Words, sentences, and paragraphs are all building blocks of communication. You have seen how using a variety of sentence types and using active and passive voice appropriately can help make your sentences more effective. Now you are ready to combine these sentences to form logical paragraphs.

DEVELOPING LOGICAL PARAGRAPHS

A paragraph is a group of related sentences that focus on one main idea. The main idea is often identified in the first sentence of the paragraph, known as a *topic sentence*. The body of the paragraph supports this main idea by giving more information, analyses, and examples. A paragraph is typically part of a longer message, although one paragraph can hold the entire message, especially in such informal communications as memorandums and electronic mail.

Paragraphs organize the topic into manageable units of information for the reader. Readers need a cue to tell them when they have finished a topic so that they can pause and refocus their attention on the next one. To serve this purpose, paragraphs must be unified and coherent, and they must be of an appropriate length.

Use a new paragraph to signal a change in direction.

8. Keep Paragraphs Unified and Coherent.

Although closely related, unity and coherence are not the same. A paragraph has *unity* when all its parts work together to develop a single idea consistently and logically. A paragraph has *coherence* when each sentence links smoothly to the sentences before and after it.

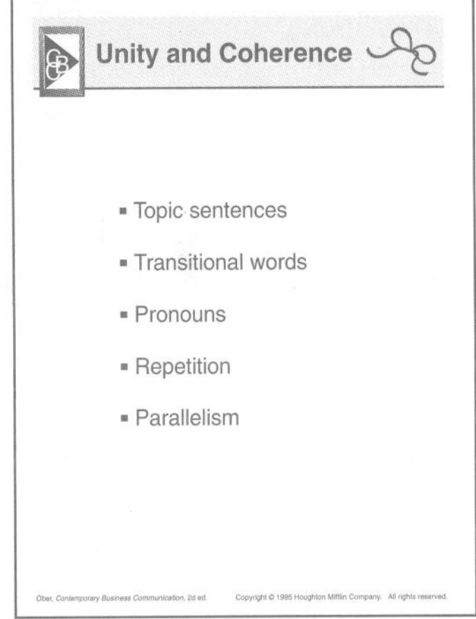

Unity and Coherence
▪ Topic sentences
▪ Transitional words
▪ Pronouns
▪ Repetition
▪ Parallelism

See Transparency 3.6, Paragraph Unity and Coherence.

Unity A unified paragraph gives information that is directly related to the topic, presents this information in a logical order, and leaves out irrelevant details. The following excerpt is a middle paragraph in a memorandum arguing against the proposal that Collins, a baby-food manufacturer, should expand into producing food for adults:

Not: [1] We cannot focus our attention on both ends of the age spectrum. [2] In a recent survey, two-thirds of the under-35 age group named Collins as the first company that came to mind for the category "baby-food products." [3] For more than 50 years we have spent millions of dollars annually to identify our company as the baby-food company, and market research shows that we have been successful. [4] Last year, we introduced Peas 'N Pears, our most successful baby-food introduction ever. [5] To now seek to position ourselves as a producer of food for adults would simply be incongruous. [6] Our well-defined image in the marketplace would make producing food for adults risky.

The paragraph obviously lacks unity. Before reading further, rearrange the sentences to make the sequence of ideas more logical.

You would probably decide that the overall topic of the paragraph is Collins's well-defined image as a baby-food producer. So Sentence 6 would be the best topic sentence. You might also decide that Sentence 4 brings in extra information that weakens paragraph unity and should be left out. The most unified paragraph, then, would be Sentences 6, 3, 2, 5, and 1, as shown here:

But: Our well-defined image in the marketplace would make producing food for adults risky. For more than 50 years we have spent millions of dollars annually to identify our company as the baby-food company, and market research shows that we have been successful. In a recent survey, two-thirds of the under-35 age group named Collins as the first company that came to mind for the category "baby-food products." To now seek to position ourselves as a producer of food for adults would simply be incongruous. We cannot focus our attention on both ends of the age spectrum.

The topic sentence usually goes at the beginning of the paragraph.

A topic sentence is especially helpful in a long paragraph. It usually appears at the beginning of a paragraph. This position helps the writer focus on the topic, so the paragraph will have unity. And it lets the reader know immediately what the topic is.

Sometimes, however, you may want to put the major idea toward the end of the paragraph. For example, if you're communicating negative information, you may want to state your reasons for refusing before you actually make the refusal—which is the topic of the paragraph. Or, if you're trying to persuade someone to do something, you may want to describe the advantages of doing it before you actually make the request.

Coherence is achieved by using transitional words, pronouns, repetition, and parallelism.

Coherence A coherent paragraph weaves sentences together so that the discussion is integrated. The reader never needs to pause to puzzle out the relationships or reread to get the intended meaning. The major ways to achieve coherence are to use transitional words and pronouns, to repeat key words and ideas, and to use parallel structure.

Transitional words help the reader see the relationships between sentences. Such words may be as simple as *first* and other indicators of sequence, as shown by the underlined words in the following paragraph:

> Ten years ago, Collins tried to overcome market resistance to its new line of baby clothes. First, it mounted a multimillion-dollar ad campaign featuring the Mason quintuplets. Next, it sponsored a Collins Baby look-alike contest. Then it sponsored two network specials featuring Dr. Benjamin Spock. Finally, it brought in the Madison Avenue firm of Morgan & Modine to broaden its image.

The words *first, next, then,* and *finally* clearly signal step-by-step movement. Now note the following logical transitions; the underlined words identify the relationships between sentences:

> I recognize, however, that Collins cannot thrive on baby food alone. To begin with, since we already control 73% of the market, further gains will be difficult. What's more, the current baby boom is slowing. Therefore, we must expand our product line.

Transitional words act as road signs, indicating where the message is heading and letting the reader know what to expect. Here are some commonly used transitional expressions grouped by the relationships they express:

Relationship	*Transitional Expressions*
addition	also, besides, furthermore, in addition, moreover, too
cause and effect	as a result, because, consequently, hence, so, therefore, thus
comparison	in the same way, likewise, similarly
contrast	although, but, however, in contrast, nevertheless, on the other hand, still, yet
illustration	for example, for instance, in other words, to illustrate
sequence	first, second, third, then, next, finally
summary/conclusion	at last, finally, in conclusion, to summarize
time	meanwhile, next, since, soon, then

A coherent message is never more important than in a company's mission statement, the document that provides a framework for employees' decision making. Ortho Biotech's statement uses bulleted paragraphs to clearly identify its main points.

A second way to achieve coherence is to use pronouns. Because pronouns stand for words already named, using pronouns binds sentences and ideas together. Pronouns and their antecedents are underlined here:

> If Collins branches out with additional food products, one possibility would be a fruit snack for youngsters. Funny Fruits were tested in Columbus last summer, and they were a big hit. Roger Johnson, national marketing manager, says he hopes to build new food categories into a $200 million business. He is also exploring the possibility of acquiring other established name brands. These acquired brands would let Collins expand faster than if it had to develop a new product of its own.

Purposeful repetition aids coherence; avoid needless repetition.

A third way to achieve coherence is to repeat key words. In a misguided attempt to appear interesting, writers sometimes use different terms for the same idea. For example, in discussing a proposed merger a writer may at different points use *merger, combination, union, association,* and *syndicate.* Or a writer may use the words *administrator, manager, supervisor,* and *executive* all to refer to the same person. Such "elegant variation" only confuses the reader, who has no way of knowing whether the writer is referring to the same concept or to slightly different variations of that concept. Avoid needless repetition, but use purposeful repetition to link ideas and thus to promote paragraph coherence. Here is a good example:

> Collins has taken several steps recently to enhance profits and project a stronger leadership position. One of these steps is streamlining operations. Collins's line of children's clothes was unprofitable, so it discontinued the line. Its four produce farms were likewise unprofitable, so it hired an outside professional team to manage them. This team eventually recommended selling the farms.

Parallelism refers to consistency.

The term **parallelism** means using similar grammatical structure for similar ideas—that is, matching adjectives with adjectives, nouns with nouns, infinitives with infinitives, and so on. Much widely quoted writing uses parallelism: for example, Julius Caesar's "I came, I saw, I conquered" and Abraham Lincoln's "government of the people, by the people, and for the people." Parallel structure smoothly links ideas, thereby enhancing coherence.

Not: The new dispatcher is competent and a fast worker.
But: The new dispatcher is competent and fast.

Not: The new grade of paper is lightweight, nonporous, and it is inexpensive.
But: The new grade of paper is lightweight, nonporous, and inexpensive.

Not: The training program will cover
1. Vacation and sick leaves
2. How to resolve grievances
3. Managing your workstation

But: The training program will cover
1. Vacation and sick leaves
2. Grievance resolution
3. Workstation management

Not: One management consultant recommended either selling the children's-furniture division or its conversion into a children's-toy division.
But: One management consultant recommended either selling the children's-furniture division or converting it into a children's-toy division.

Not: Gladys is not only proficient in word processing but also in desktop publishing.
But: Gladys is proficient not only in word processing but also in desktop publishing.

In the last two sets of sentences above, note that correlative conjunctions (such as *both/and, either/or,* and *not only/but also*) must be followed by words in parallel form. Be especially careful to use parallel structure in report headings that have equal weight and in numbered lists.

Suggest that your students hold their writing at arm's length and look at it with squinted eyes. If their paragraphs are a variety of shapes and sizes, they are not likely to appear too long and boring to the reader. Students should examine massive blocks of text to see if they can be broken down into more manageable units. (Steve Morgenstern, "10 Tips for Writing That Works," *Home Office Computing*, May 1991, p. 28.)

Ensure paragraph unity by developing only one topic per paragraph and by presenting the information in a logical order. Ensure paragraph coherence by using transitional words and pronouns, repeating key words, and using parallel structure.

9. Control Paragraph Length.

How long should a paragraph of business writing be? As with other considerations, the needs of the reader, rather than the convenience of the writer, should determine the answer. Paragraphs should help the reader by signaling a new idea as well as by providing a physical break. Long blocks of unbroken text look boring and needlessly complex. And they may unintentionally obscure an important idea buried in the middle (see Figure 3.2). On the other hand, a series of extremely short paragraphs can weaken coherence by obscuring the underlying relationships.

Excessively long paragraphs look boring and difficult.

Essentially, there are no fixed rules for paragraph length, and occasionally one- or ten-sentence paragraphs might be effective. However, most paragraphs of good business writers fall into the 60- to 80-word range—long enough for a topic sentence and three or four supporting sentences.

FIGURE 3.2 The Effect of Paragraph Length on Readability

THE BOOK MARK
185 SILVER CENTER, BOZEMAN, MT 59715 • Phone: (406) 555-3856

MEMO TO: Max Dillion, Sales Manager
FROM: Richard J. Hayes
DATE: February 25, 19--
SUBJECT: New-Venture Proposal

The purpose of this memorandum is to propose the purchase or lease of a van to be used as a mobile bookstore. We could then use this van to generate sales in the outlying towns and villages throughout the state. We have been aware for quite some time that many small towns around the state do not have adequate bookstore facilities, but the economics of the situation are such that we would not be able to open a comprehensive branch and operate it profitably. However, we could afford to stock a van with books and operate it for a few days at a time in various small towns throughout the state. As you are probably aware, the laws of this state would permit us to acquire a statewide business license fairly easily and inexpensively.With the proper advance advertising, we should be able to generate much interest in this endeavor. It seems to me that this ideas has much merit because of the flexibility it offers us. For example, we could tailor the length of our stay with the size of the town and the amount of business generated. In addition, we could tailor our inventory to the needs and interests of the particular locales. We might spend a day or two at a retirement community, where we would stock books on hobbies, fiction, gardening, and investments. The next week we might visit a town that is celebrating an anniversary, and we would stock books relating to state events and history. In addition, when various organizations are holding conventions in the state, we might make arrangements to park the van at a convenient spot at the convention center and feature books of interest to the particular group attending. The driver of the van would act as the salesperson, and we would, of course, have copies of our complete catalog so that mail orders could be taken as well. Please let me have your reactions to this proposal. If you wish, I can explore the matter further and generate cost and sales estimates.

jmc

THE BOOK MARK
185 SILVER CENTER, BOZEMAN, MT 59715 • Phone: (406) 555-3856

MEMO TO: Max Dillion, Sales Manager
FROM: Richard J. Hayes
DATE: February 25, 19--
SUBJECT: New-Venture Proposal

The purpose of this memorandum is to propose the purchase or lease of a van to be used as a mobile bookstore. We could then use this van to generate sales in the outlying towns and villages throughout the state.

We have been aware for quite some time that many small towns around the state do not have adequate bookstore facilities, but the economics of the situation are such that we would not be able to open a comprehensive branch and operate it profitably. However, we could afford to stock a van with books and operate it for a few days at a time in various small towns throughout the state. As you are probably aware, the laws of this state would permit us to acquire a statewide business license fairly easily and inexpensively.

With the proper advance advertising, we should be able to generate much interest in this endeavor. It seems to me that this ideas has much merit because of the flexibility it offers us. For example, we could tailor the length of our stay with the size of the town and the amount of business generated. In addition, we could tailor our inventory to the needs and interests of the particular locales.

We might spend a day or two at a retirement community, where we would stock books on hobbies, fiction, gardening, and investments. The next week we might visit a town that is celebrating an anniversary, and we would stock books relating to state events and history. In addition, when various organizations are holding conventions in the state, we might make arrangements to park the van at a convenient spot at the convention center and feature books of interest to the particular group attending.

The driver of the van would act as the salesperson, and we would, of course, have copies of our complete catalog so that mail orders could be taken as well. Please let me have your reactions to this proposal. If you wish, I can explore the matter further and generate cost and sales estimates.

jmc

These two memorandums contain identical information. Which is more inviting to read?

Although a single paragraph should never discuss more than one major topic, complex topics often need to be divided into several paragraphs. Your purpose and the needs of your reader should ultimately determine paragraph length.

For an exercise on controlling paragraph length and unity, refer students to the *Study Guide*, p. 85.

SUMMARY

For business writing to achieve its objectives, it must be clear. Use short, simple, specific, and concrete words, and avoid dangling expressions, clichés, slang, buzz words, and unnecessary jargon. Write concisely: avoid redundancies, wordy expressions, and hidden subjects and verbs. Finally, prefer positive language; stress what you can do rather than what you cannot do.

To keep reader interest, use a variety of sentence types, including simple, compound, and complex sentences. Use active voice to emphasize the doer of the action and passive voice to emphasize the receiver of the action.

Your paragraphs should be unified and coherent. Develop only one topic per paragraph, and use transitional words, pronouns, repetition, and parallelism. Although paragraphs of various lengths are desirable, most should range from 60 to 80 words. Help the reader follow your logic by avoiding very long paragraphs and avoiding strings of very short paragraphs.

KEY TERMS

For an exercise on matching terms, refer students to the *Study Guide*, p. 8.

Active voice The sentence form in which the subject performs the action expressed by the verb.

Buzz word An important-sounding term used mainly to impress people.

Cliché An expression that has become monotonous through overuse.

Complex sentence A sentence that has at least one independent clause and at least one dependent clause.

Compound sentence A sentence that has two or more independent clauses.

Dangling expression Any part of a sentence that does not logically connect to the rest of the sentence.

Expletive An expression such as *there is* or *it is* that begins a clause and for which the pronoun has no antecedent.

Mechanics Those elements in communication that show up only in written form, including spelling, punctuation, abbreviations, capitalization, number expression, and word division.

Parallelism Using similar grammatical structure to express similar ideas.

Passive voice The sentence form in which the subject receives the action expressed by the verb.

Redundancy The unnecessary repetition of an idea that has already been expressed or intimated.

Simple sentence A sentence that has one independent clause.

Style The manner in which an idea is expressed (rather than the *substance* of the idea).

REVIEW AND DISCUSSION

The answers to the review and discussion questions appear in the *Instructor's Resource Manual*, beginning on p. 25.

1. **Communication at G.E. Aircraft Revisited** ■ The reports that cross George Bolln's desk may vary in length and complexity, but all must be written in such a way that they can be understood by those who speak English as a second language.
   a. Under what circumstances might a letter to a customer in the Pacific Rim include jargon?
   b. Some of Bolln's reports are sent across the international date line. How can he be sure that readers will understand the timing he intends to convey if he uses the words *today*, *yesterday*, or *tomorrow*?
   c. Why would Bolln prefer positive language when writing to a potential customer?
2. What is meant by the statement "Accuracy involves more than the truthfulness of facts and figures"?
3. Give an original example of each of the following types of expressions:

buzz word	jargon
cliché	redundancy
hidden subject	slang
hidden verb	

4. Substitute a shorter word for each of the following words:

accordingly	consequence	perpetuate
aggregate	finalize	stipulate
analogous	inexhaustible	transmit
characteristic	jurisdiction	verification
commence	materialize	

5. Revise the following phrases, getting rid of the redundancies:

and etc.	exact same	surrounded on all sides
Easter Sunday	good benefits	personal opinion
foreign imports	mutual cooperation	same identical
important essentials	past experience	very unique
component part	refer back	

6. Substitute one word for each of the following wordy expressions:

at the present time	until such time as	it would appear that
in the amount of	few in number	
inasmuch as	in most cases	

7. Why is positive language often more effective than negative language for achieving your objective?
8. What are the three sentence patterns? Under what circumstances should each pattern be used for best effect?
9. In business writing, about how long should the typical sentence and paragraph be? Should all sentences and paragraphs fall within these ranges? Why or why not?
10. Distinguish between active and passive voice, and discuss when each should be used.
11. What is the difference between paragraph unity and paragraph coherence?
12. List four ways to make a paragraph coherent.
13. Write a sentence illustrating parallelism.
14. Why should you avoid extremely long paragraphs?

EXERCISES

Suggestions and sample solutions for exercises appear in the *Instructor's Resource Manual*, beginning on p. 27.

For Exercises 1–7, revise the passages to address the matter of style indicated and to make the passage appropriate for a first-year college student who has never taken a communication or business course. Do not completely rewrite the passages; just correct any style problems.

1. Jargon ▪

```
Regardless of the medium selected, noise may be encoun-
tered after the communication stimulus enters the re-
ceiver's filter.  Such a problem occurs in both the formal
and informal communication networks.  Workers experiencing
ethnocentrism may have special problems with language con-
notations.
```

2. Short and Simple Words ▪

```
The consultant demonstrated how our aggregate remuneration
might be ameliorated by modifications in our propensities
to utilize credit for compensating for services.  She also
endeavored to ascertain which of our characteristics were
analogous to those of other entities for which she had
fabricated solutions.  She recommended we commence to ini-
tiate innumerable modifications in our procedures to in-
crease cash flow, which she considers indispensable for
facilitating increased corporate health.
```

Short and Simple Words

The consultant explained how to increase our total pay by changing our use of credit for paying for services. She also tried to learn how similar we were to other firms for which she had consulted. She thinks it's necessary for us to increase our cash flow in order to improve corporate health.

Ober, *Contemporary Business Communication*, 2d ed.

See Master 3.1, Exercise 2, Short and Simple Words, in the *Instructor's Resource Manual*.

3. Specific and Concrete Words ▪

In an effort to stimulate sales, Mallmart is lowering prices substantially on its line of consumer items. Sometime soon, it will close most of its stores for several days to provide store personnel time to change prices. Markdowns will range from very little on its line of laundry equipment to a great deal on certain sporting equipment. Mallmart plans to rely on advertising to let people know of these price reductions. In particular, it is considering using a popular television star to publicize the new pricing strategy.

4. Clichés, Slang, and Buzz Words ▪

At that point in time the corporate brass were under the gun; they decided to bite the bullet and let the chips fall where they may. They hired a head honcho with some street smarts who would be able to interface with the investment community. Financewise, the new top dog couldn't be beat. He was hard as nails and developed a scenario that would have the company back on its feet within six months. Now it was up to the team players to operationalize his plans.

5. Conciseness ▪

In spite of the fact that Fox Inc. denied wrongdoing, it agreed to a settlement of the patent suit for a price of $6.3 million. Industry sources were surprised at the outcome because the original patent had depreciated in value. In addition to the above, Fox also made an agreement to refrain from the manufacture of similar computers for a period of five years in length. It appears that with the exception of Emerson's new introductions, innovations in workstations will be few in number during the next few years.

6. Positive Language ▪

We cannot issue a full refund at this time because you did not enclose a receipt or an authorized estimate. I'm sorry that we will have to delay your reimbursement. We are not like those insurance companies that promise you anything but then disappear when you have a claim. When we receive your receipt or estimate, we will not hold up your check. Our refusal to issue reimbursement without proper supporting evidence means that we do not have to charge you outlandish premiums for your automobile insurance.

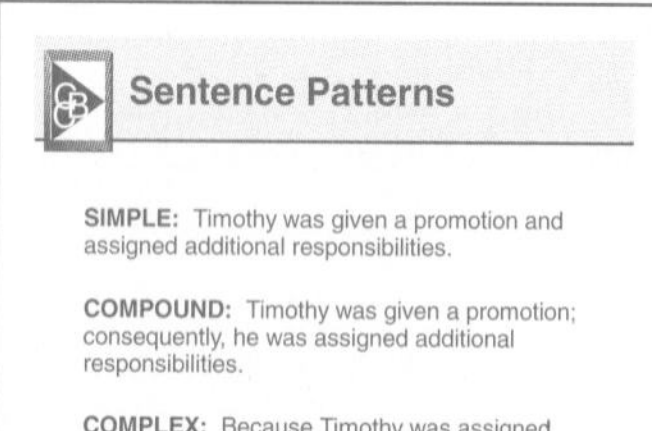

Sentence Patterns
SIMPLE: Timothy was given a promotion and assigned additional responsibilities.
COMPOUND: Timothy was given a promotion; consequently, he was assigned additional responsibilities.
COMPLEX: Because Timothy was assigned additional responsibilities, he was given a promotion.
SIMPLE: Eileen, our corporate counsel, will write the letter on our behalf.
COMPOUND: Eileen is our corporate counsel, and she will write the letter on our behalf.
COMPLEX: Eileen, who is our corporate counsel, will write the letter on our behalf.
Ober, Contemporary Business Communication, 2d ed.
Copyright © 1995 Houghton Mifflin Company. All rights reserved.

See Master 3.2, Exercise 7, Sentence Patterns, in the *Instructor's Resource Manual.*

7. Sentence Patterns ▪ For each of the following lettered items, write a simple, a compound, and a complex sentence that incorporates both items of information. For the complex sentences, emphasize the first idea in each item.

a. Timothy was given a promotion/Timothy was assigned additional responsibilities.

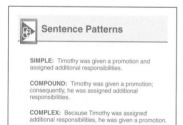

b. Eileen is our corporate counsel/Eileen will write the letter on our behalf.

8. **Sentence Variety** ■ Rewrite the following paragraph by varying sentence patterns and sentence lengths to keep the writing interesting.

Smartfood was founded by Ann Withey, Andrew Martin, and Ken Meyers in 1984. The product was the first snack food to combine white cheddar cheese and popcorn. Ann Withey perfected the Smartfood recipe in her home kitchen after much trial and error. Smartfood sales were reportedly only $35,000 in 1985. During that time, the product was available only in New England. By 1988, sales had soared to $10 million. This attracted the attention of Frito-Lay. The snack-food giant bought Smartfood in 1989 for $15 million. Since the purchase, Frito-Lay has not tampered with the popular Smartfood formula. It has used its marketing expertise to keep sales growing, despite the growing number of challengers crowding the cheesy popcorn market.[4]

9. **Dangling Expressions, Parallel Structure, and Redundancies** ■ Edit the following paragraphs to eliminate grammatical errors. Do not completely rewrite the sentences; just correct any weaknesses.

a. As a young child, his father took him on business trips both to London and Paris. These trips were before the war, when traveling was cheaper and an enjoyable experience.
b. First and foremost, Alan Greenspan is a pragmatist. The favorable advantage of that approach is that he is able to reach a consensus of opinion on most matters. He will announce his latest agreements at a news conference at 3 p.m. in the afternoon.
c. The reason was that business investment fell at a rate of 4% last year and spending for equipment declined. In trying to combat these declines, the Federal Reserve banks maintain excellent relations with the major financial institutions but they are still not doing as much as they had expected.
d. At Hanson we believe that earning stock appreciation for our investors is better than to make temporary profits. In other words, we do not mix up our long and short-term goals; they are not one and the same. This corporate viewpoint has been in effect for many years; it is not a new innovation.

10. **Parallelism** ■ Determine whether the following sentences use parallel structure correctly. Revise sentences as needed to make the structure parallel.

a. The store is planning to install a new cash-register system that is easier to operate, easier to repair, and cheaper to maintain than the current system.
b. According to the survey, most employees prefer either holding the employee cafeteria open later or its hours to be kept the same.

c. The quarterback is expert not only in calling plays but also in throwing passes.
d. Our career-guidance book will cover
   1. Writing résumés
   2. Application letters
   3. Techniques for interviewing

11. **Wordy Expressions** ▪ Revise the following sentences to eliminate wordy phrases by substituting a single word wherever possible.

a. Push the red button in the event that you see any smoke rising from the cooking surface.
b. More than 40% of the people polled are of the opinion that government spending should be reduced.
c. Please send me more information pertaining to your new line of pesticides.
d. Due to the fact that two of the three highway lanes were closed for repairs, I was nearly 20 minutes late for my appointment.

12. **Hidden Verbs** ▪ Revise the following sentences to eliminate hidden verbs and convey the appropriate action.

a. After much deliberation, the group came to a decision about how to respond to the lawsuit.
b. Although Hugh wanted to offer an explanation of his actions, his boss refused to listen.
c. Nationwide Call Systems is performing an analysis of our calling patterns to determine how we can save money on long-distance telephone calls.
d. Our committee will hold a meeting next week to discuss the proposed changes.

13. **Sentence Length** ▪ Write a long sentence (40 to 50 words) that attempts to make sense. Then revise the sentence so that it contains 10 or fewer words. Finally, rewrite the sentence so that it contains 16 to 22 words. Which sentence is the most effective? Why?
14. **Active and Passive Voice** ▪ For each of the following sentences, first identify whether the sentence is active or passive. Then, if necessary, revise the sentence to use the more effective verb voice.

a. An out-of-court settlement of the discrimination suit filed by Marjorie Kramer has been agreed to by Morton Industries. The amount of the settlement was not disclosed.
b. We will begin using the new plant in 1996, and the old plant will be converted into a warehouse.
c. A very effective sales letter was written by Paul Mendleson. The letter will be mailed next week.
d. You failed to verify the figures on the quarterly report. As a result, $5,500 was lost by the company.

15. **Coherence** ▪ Put logical transitions in the blanks to give the following paragraph coherence.

Columbia is widening its lead over Kraft in the computer-magazine war. ________ its revenues increased 27% last

```
year whereas Kraft's increased only 16%. _________ its
audited paid circulation increased to 600,000, compared
to 450,000 for Kraft. _________ Kraft was able to in-
crease both the ad rate and the number of ad pages last
year. One note of worry _________ is Kraft's decision to
shut down its independent testing laboratory. Some indus-
try leaders believe much of Kraft's success has been due
to its reliable product reviews. _________ Columbia has
just announced an agreement whereby Stanford University's
world-famous engineering school will perform product
testing for Columbia.
```

16. **Paragraph Length** ■ Read the following paragraph and determine how it might be divided into two or more shorter paragraphs to help the reader follow the complex topic being discussed.

```
Transforming a manuscript into a published book requires
several steps. After the author submits the manuscript
(in typewritten or computer-generated form), the copy edi-
tor makes any needed grammatical or spelling changes. The
author reviews these changes to be sure that they haven't
altered the meaning of any sentences or sections. Then
the publisher sends the manuscript out for typesetting.
Next, the author proofreads the typeset galleys and gives
the publisher a list of any corrections. These correc-
tions are incorporated into the page proofs, which show
how the pages will look when printed. The author and pub-
lisher review these page proofs for any errors. Only af-
ter all corrections have been made does the book get
published. From start to finish, this process can take as
long as a year.
```

CONTINUING CASE 3

Stetsky Corrects the Boss

A possible solution to the Continuing Case is described in the *Instructor's Resource Manual,* p. 31.

Amy Stetsky opened a new WordPerfect document on her computer and adjusted the headphones of her transcribing unit. She was ready to transcribe some dictation from Dave Kaplan. The dictation was a first draft for part of a speech on the effects of proper lighting that Kaplan is going to deliver next month at a meeting of the Ann Arbor chapter of the Office Systems Research Association. Here's what Stetsky heard:

> Extensive research shows that lighting has a direct affect on worker productivity and job satisfaction. Lighting that is of appropriate quantity and quality provides efficient comfortable illumination and a safe work environment. They also help to develop a feeling of visual comfort and an aesthetically attractive work area. Which increases job satisfaction.
>
> Appropriate lighting makes the task more visible thus increasing both the speed and the accuracy of the work performed. Inadequate amounts of light causes poor workmanship inaccurate work and

lowered production. For example one study conducted by the general industrial corporation showed that when illumination was temporarily reduced by no more than five percent the output of word processing operators decreased by twelve percent. In addition the accuracy of all the operators each of who were paid according to the number of correct lines they produced decreased by eight percentage.

An other study at the interstate national bank showed that errors in processing checks decreased by forty percent when lighting was increased. The productivity of the cash register clerks at a large outlet of united food marts was reduced by twenty eight percent when they were forced to work in reduced lighting for three weeks because of store remodeling. According to the researchers we also spoke with several clerks whom complained about headaches and eyestrain and customers whom complained about slow lines and errors in register receipts.

As a result of such vision research forward looking facilities managers human development personnel and labor unions are all beginning to monitor carefully the quality and quantity of illumination by which employees perform their jobs. Farthermore they are looking to technology to bring more flexibility more efficiency and to provide higher quality illumination for the seeing environment. In short they are looking at light in a new light!

Critical Thinking

1. How effective would this speech section be if it were delivered exactly as written?

Writing Project

2. With Mr. Kaplan's permission, Stetsky routinely edits the dictation as she keyboards it, correcting minor grammar and usage errors. As she transcribes, she also uses correct punctuation, capitalization, spelling, and word division. In short, Stetsky is a professional, and her work reflects it. Assuming the role of Stetsky, transcribe this dictation in double-spaced format (leaving one blank line between each line of type and indenting each paragraph). Make whatever editing changes are needed to correct errors in grammar, mechanics, punctuation, and usage. (If necessary, refer to the LABs in the Reference Manual at the back of the text.)

Edited Draft of Speech

Extensive research shows that lighting has a direct effect on workers' productivity and job satisfaction. Lighting that is of appropriate quantity and quality provides efficient, comfortable illumination and a safe work environment. It also helps develop a feeling of visual comfort; and an attractive work area increases job satisfaction.

Appropriate lighting makes the task more visible, increasing both the speed and the accuracy of work. Inadequate lighting causes poor workmanship and mistakes, and it lowers production. For example, one study conducted by the General Industrial Corporation showed that when illumination was reduced temporarily by no more than 5%, the output of word processing operators decreased by 12%. In addition, the accuracy of all the operators, each of whom was paid according to the number of correct lines produced, decreased by 8%.

Another study at the Interstate National Bank showed that errors in processing checks decreased by 40% when lighting was increased. And the productivity of cash register clerks at a large outlet of United Food Marts was reduced by 28% when the clerks were forced to work in reduced lighting for three weeks because the store was being remodeled. According to the researchers, several clerks also complained about headaches and eyestrain, and customers complained about slow lines and errors in register receipts.

As a result of this kind of research, forward-looking facilities managers, human development personnel, and labor unions are beginning to monitor carefully the quality and quantity of illumination by which employees perform their jobs. Furthermore, they are looking to technology to bring greater flexibility, more efficiency, and higher-quality illumination to the seeing environment. In short, they are looking at light in a new light!

Ober, *Contemporary Business Communication*, 2d ed.

See Master 3.3, Continuing Case 3, Question 3, in the *Instructor's Resource Manual.*

WORDWISE *Oxymorons*

An oxymoron is a combination of contradictory or incongruous words—for example, *jumbo shrimp*. Here are some others, gleaned from recent business journals:

Plastic glasses	Exact estimate
Push-button dial	Unbiased opinion
Fresh frozen	Clearly misunderstood
Working vacation	Oddly appropriate

Writing with Style: Overall Tone

Don't do it right the first time" may sound like a strange piece of advice, but it's exactly what professional writing coach Frank Sanitate tells the lawyers, accountants, and corporate executives who attend his writing seminars. Sanitate thinks that those writers who balk at setting down anything but the perfect word place themselves on the fast track to that dreaded paralysis known as "writer's block." His solution? Write first; think later.

"The way I show people is the *opposite* of what they teach in high school," says Sanitate, who once taught high school English and who worked as an administrator for the American Institute of Certified Public Accountants before he started his consulting company, Sanitate Associates. "I have people just be spontaneous. You can worry about cleaning it up at the editing stage. Self-criticism impedes thinking. It's like having a boss or a teacher looking over your shoulder while you write. That's not conducive to good work."

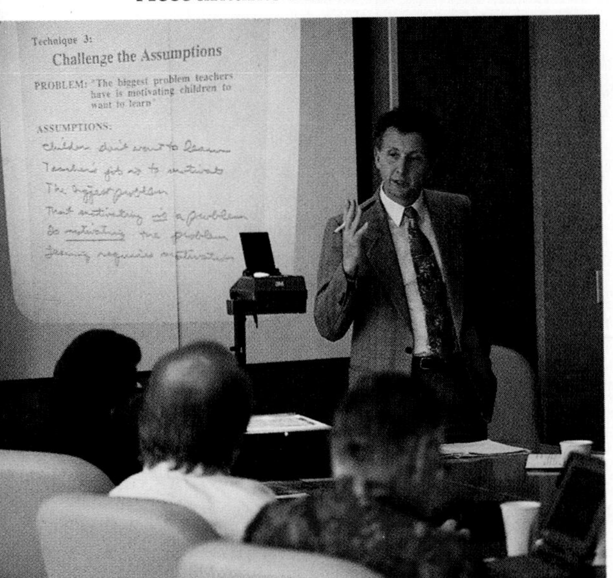

In offering that advice, Sanitate plays a word game with his clients. The "editing stage," during which writers are supposed to clean up their writing, is just Sanitate's term for writing with good style. This trick helps writers get words on paper. After they do, Sanitate then concentrates on fixing word usage. Wrong verb usage, says Sanitate, is particularly common.

"We do a lot of work on verbs. We stress the active rather than the passive voice. There is a problem, particularly in the legal profession, with the

Communication Objectives

After you have finished this chapter, you should be able to

1. Write confidently.
2. Use a courteous and sincere tone.
3. Use appropriate emphasis and subordination.
4. Use nondiscriminatory language.
5. Stress the "you" attitude.
6. Write at an appropriate level of difficulty.

Frank Sanitate

President, Sanitate Associates, Santa Barbara, California

A chapter overview appears in the *Instructor's Resource Manual*, pp. 32–34.

use of jargon and technical writing. The way I deal with that comes under the category of 'simplify.' Because we have three vocabularies—reading, writing, and speaking—I first have them *speak* what they want to say. When they speak it, they use simpler words."

Next, says Sanitate, he encourages his writers to use verbs that, while they may not be as simple as spoken language, are stronger. He reminds writers that the English language offers many words that can be used to say the same thing. "Some of those words have Latin roots," says Sanitate. "Some have Anglo-Saxon roots. I encourage people to use the Anglo-Saxon rather than the Latin."

Then Sanitate tackles another very common problem: long-windedness. For most writers, says Sanitate, the toughest thing to learn is brevity. "They tend to write to impress rather than express," says Sanitate. "They're too wordy, and they're too stuffy. I tell them to get to the point.

"The way I teach unity and coherence is through the concept of accountability. Accountability comes from countability. I tell them to keep track of the ideas. If you have 5 ideas to get across, show your reader all 5 ideas clearly. If you have 25 ideas, show all 25. In order for business writing to be effective, it has to either inform or get some kind of action. The object is not to entertain or to please. You have got to be brief and direct. That in itself is a style."

WHAT DO WE MEAN BY *TONE?*

Having chosen the right words to construct effective sentences and then having combined these sentences into logical paragraphs, we now examine the tone of the complete message—the complete letter, memorandum, report, or the like. **Tone** in writing refers to the writer's attitude toward the reader and the subject of the message. The overall tone of a written message affects the reader just as one's tone of voice affects the listener in everyday exchanges.

The business writer should strive for an overall tone that is confident, courteous, and sincere; that uses emphasis and subordination appropriately; that contains nondiscriminatory language; that stresses the "you" attitude; and that is written at an appropriate level of difficulty. (Style Principles 1–9 were presented in Chapter 3.)

10. Write Confidently.

If you believe in what you have written, write in such a way that your reader does also.

Your message should convey the confident attitude that you have done a competent job of communicating and that your reader will do as you ask or will accept your decision. If you believe that your explanation is complete, that your request is reasonable, or that your decision is based on sound logic, then you are likely to write with confidence. Such confidence has a persuasive effect on your audience. Avoid using language that makes you seem unsure of yourself. Be especially wary of beginning sentences with "I hope," "I trust," "If you agree," and similar self-conscious terms.

Not: If you'd like to take advantage of this offer, call our toll-free number.
But: To take advantage of this offer, call our toll-free number.

Not: I hope that you will agree that my qualifications match your job needs.
But: My qualifications match your job needs in the following respects.

Not: Why not take advantage of our three-month trial subscription?
But: By taking advantage of our three-month trial subscription, you will experience for yourself the practical tips contained in each issue.

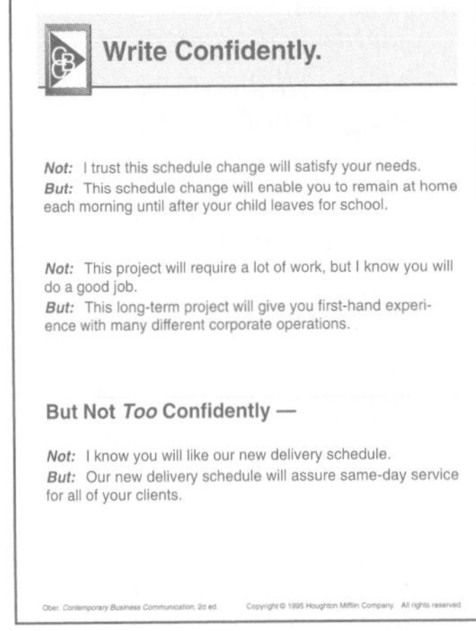

See Transparency 4.1, Writing Confidently.

In some situations, the best strategy is simply to omit information. For example, you should not provide the reader with excuses for denying your request, suggest that something might go wrong, or intimate that the reader might not be satisfied.

Not: I know you are a busy person, but we would really enjoy hearing you speak.
But: The fact that you are involved in so many different enterprises makes your views on small business all the more relevant for our audience.

Other sentence openers that make you sound unsure of yourself include "I believe," "I feel," and "It seems to me."

Not: Let us know if you experience any other problems.
But: Your GrassMaster lawn mower should now give you many years of trouble-free service.

Not: Although some employees have complained that the new uniforms are uncomfortable, most employees like them.
But: Most of our employees like the look and comfort of the new uniforms designed by Bill Blaine.

Modest *confidence is the best tactic.*

A word of caution: Do not appear *overconfident;* that is, avoid sounding presumptuous or arrogant. Be especially wary of using such strong phrases as "I know that," or "I am sure you will agree that."

Not: I'm sure you'll agree our offer is reasonable.
But: This solution should enable you to collect the data you need while still protecting the interests of our clients.

Not: I plan to schedule an interview with you next Thursday to discuss my qualifications further.
But: Please let me know when I may meet with you to discuss my qualifications further.

Competent communicators are *confident* communicators. They write with conviction, yet they avoid appearing to be pushy or presumptuous.

II. Use a Courteous and Sincere Tone.

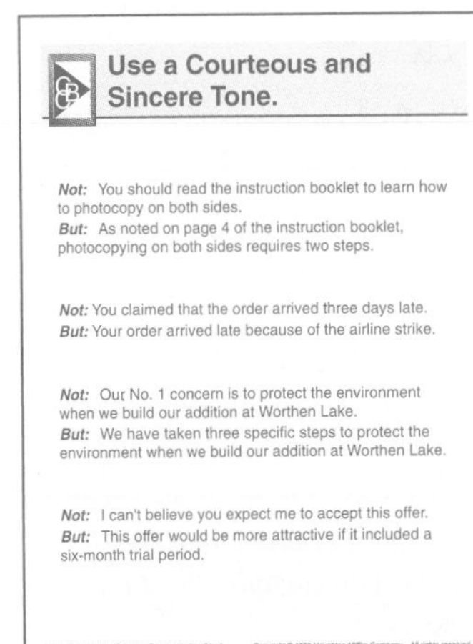

See Transparency 4.2, A Courteous and Sincere Tone.

A tone of courtesy and sincerity builds goodwill for you and your organization and increases the likelihood that your message will achieve its objective. For example, lecturing the reader or filling a letter with **platitudes**

A platitude is a statement so obvious that including it in a message would insult the reader.

(trite, obvious statements) implies a condescending attitude. Likewise, readers are likely to find offensive such expressions as "you failed to," "we find it difficult to believe that," "you surely don't expect," or "your complaint."

Not: Companies like ours cannot survive unless our customers pay their bills on time.

But: By paying your bill before May 30, you will maintain your excellent credit history with our firm.

Not: You sent your complaint to the wrong department. We don't handle shipping problems.

But: We have forwarded your letter to the shipping department. You should be hearing from them within the week.

Not: You must not have read the directions that came with your swing set.

But: As explained on page 13 of the directions that came with your swing set, each swing is designed to support a maximum weight of 150 pounds.

Obvious flattery and exaggeration sound insincere.

Your reader is sophisticated enough to know when you're being sincere. To achieve a sincere tone, avoid exaggeration (especially using too many modifiers or too strong modifiers), obvious flattery, and expressions of surprise or disbelief.

Remind students to avoid sarcasm or irritation in their tone. Readers are likely to be alienated by such comments as: "Of course your new sweater shrank after you washed it. It's supposed to be dry-cleaned only." Prefer the following approach: "As the product label sewn into the sweater indicates, this garment is intended to be dry-cleaned."

Not: Your satisfaction means more to us than making a profit, and we shall work night and day to see that we earn it.

But: We value your goodwill highly and have taken several specific steps to ensure your satisfaction.

Not: Dear Season Ticket Holder: You are quite obviously a highly educated and refined person who appreciates the finer things in life.

But: Dear Season Ticket Holder: Remember how exasperated you were when you had to miss a special concert by the New York Philharmonic because you were away on a business trip?

Not: I'm surprised you would question your raise, considering your overall performance last year.

But: Your raise was based on an objective evaluation of your performance last year.

Competent communicators use both verbal and nonverbal signals to convey courtesy and sincerity (see the Spotlight on Technology on page 91). However, it is difficult to fake these attitudes. The best way to achieve the desired tone is to truly assume a courteous and sincere outlook toward your reader.

Let your reader know which ideas you consider most important.

12. Use Appropriate Emphasis and Subordination.

Not all ideas are created equal. Some are more important and more persuasive than others. Assume, for example, that you have been asked to evaluate and compare the Copy Cat and the Repro 100 photocopiers and then to

SPOTLIGHT ON TECHNOLOGY

Electronic Punctuation Tones Up E-Mail

Although E-mail is technically a form of written communication, sometimes its immediacy and intimacy make it more like a phone conversation than an exchange of letters or memos. But the rich nonverbal cues that are such an important and natural part of conversations (pauses, voice tone, emphasis, and the like) are missing in E-mail exchanges. Without some device to indicate tone of voice, misunderstandings might result. Such problems, called *flaring*, can weaken your ability to accomplish your objective.

In most E-mail systems, it is impossible to use underlining or italics. Instead, you can begin and end a word or phrase you wish to emphasize with underscore characters—for example, "I_must have_this report by Friday." For stronger emphasis, use all capitals ("I MUST HAVE this report by Friday.") Avoid using all capitals for your entire message, however. All capital letters are difficult to read, and they appear to be shouting.

Shortcuts are sometimes used to convey emotions. For example, typing <grin> or just <g> softens the effect of a sarcastic remark and lets the reader know you're joking. Commonly used abbreviations in E-mail include IMHO (in my humble opinion), FWIW (for what it's worth), and BTW (by the way).

Another form of shorthand is the *smiley* or *emoticon*, which is a simple icon used to convey humor and other emotions. Common examples are :-) and :-(. When you tilt your head to left, you can see that the colon represents the eyes and the hyphen represents the nose of a happy or sad face. Here are other examples of smileys (tilt your head to the left to get their meanings):

:'-(I'm crying.
:-X My lips are sealed.
':-) I accidentally shaved off one eyebrow.
0:-) I'm an angel.
}:-> I'm a devil.
*<|:-) I'm Santa Claus.
=:-) I'm a punk rocker.
:-))) I'm overweight.

Although smileys are not appropriate for most business E-mail, occasionally they might lend just the right human touch to a particular message.

Sources: Michael E. Miller, "A Story of the Type That Turns Heads in Computer Circles," *Wall Street Journal*, September 15, 1992, pp. A1, A8; Michael E. Miller, "Sidelong Remarks That May Interest Propellerheads," *Wall Street Journal*, September 15, 1992, p. A8; Daniel Will-Harris, "Electronic Punctuation and Hieroglyphics," *PC Publishing and Presentations*, August–September 1991, p. 40.

write a report recommending one for purchase. Assume that the two brands are alike in all important respects except these:

Feature	*Copy Cat*	*Repro 100*
Speed (copies per minute)	65	58
Cost	$2,750	$2,100
Enlargement/Reduction?	Yes	No

As you can see, Copy Cat has greater speed and more features. Thus, a casual observer might think you should recommend Copy Cat based on its additional advantages. Suppose, however, that most of your photocopying needs involve fewer than five copies of each original, all of them full sized. Therefore, Copy Cat's higher speed and additional features are not as important to you as Repro 100's lower cost; and you decide to recommend purchasing Repro 100. If you want your recommendation to be credible, you must make sure your reader views the relative importance of each feature the same way you do. To do so, use appropriate emphasis and subordination techniques.

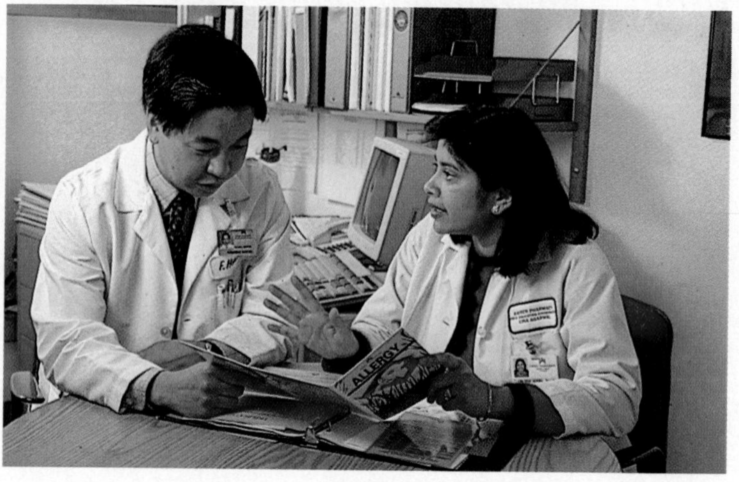

Lina Agarwal, a drug educator for Kaiser, consults with Dr. Frederick Hom about cost-effective medications. In communicating technical information about drugs to a lay audience, emphasis and subordination help show the reader what's important.

To subordinate an idea, put it in the dependent clause.

Techniques of Emphasis To emphasize an idea, use any of the following strategies (to subordinate an idea, simply use the opposite strategy):

1. Put the idea in a short, simple sentence. If you need a complex sentence to convey the needed information, put the more important idea in the independent clause. (The ideas communicated in each independent clause of a *compound* sentence receive equal emphasis.)

   Simple: Repro 100 is the better photocopier for our purposes.
   Complex: Although Copy Cat is faster, 98% of our copying requires fewer than five copies per original. (*Emphasizes the fact that speed is not a crucial consideration for us.*)

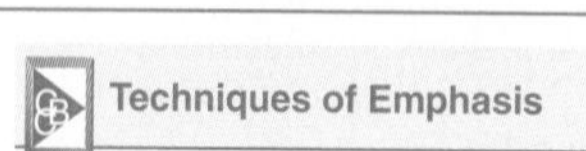
Techniques of Emphasis

- Short, simple sentences
- Major idea first (or last)
- Active voice
- More space
- Language that implies importance
- Repetition
- Mechanical means

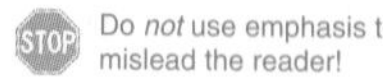

Do *not* use emphasis to mislead the reader!

See Transparency 4.3, Techniques of Emphasis.

2. Place the major idea first or last. The first paragraph of a message receives the most emphasis, the last paragraph receives less emphasis, and the middle paragraphs receive the least emphasis. Similarly, the middle sentences within a paragraph receive less emphasis than the first sentence in a paragraph.

   The first criterion examined was cost. Copy Cat sells for $2,750, and Repro 100 sells for $2,100, or 24% less than the cost of Copy Cat.

3. Use active voice to emphasize the doer of the action and passive voice to emphasize the receiver. In other words, make the noun you want to emphasize the subject of the sentence.

   Active: Repro 100 costs 24% less than Copy Cat. (*Emphasizes Repro 100 rather than Copy Cat.*)
   Passive: The relative costs of the two models were compared first. (*Emphasizes the relative costs rather than the two models.*)

4. Devote more space to the idea.

   The two models were judged on three criteria: cost, speed, and enlargement/reduction capabilities. Total cost is an important consideration for our firm because of the large number of copiers we use and our large volume of copying. Last year our firm used 358 photocopiers and duplicated more than 6.5 million pages. Thus, regardless of the speed or features of a particular model, if it is too expensive to operate, it will not serve our purposes.

5. Use language that directly implies importance, such as "most important," "major," or "primary."

   The most important factor for us is cost.

6. Use repetition (within reason).

   However, Copy Cat is expensive—expensive to purchase and expensive to operate.

7. Use mechanical means (within reason)—enumeration, underscoring, solid capitals, second color, indenting from left and right margins, or other elements of design—to call attention to your ideas.

   But the most important criterion is cost, and Repro 100 costs 24% less than Copy Cat.

Use terms such as "least important" or "a minor point" to subordinate an idea.

The Ethical Dimension In using emphasis and subordination, your goal should be to ensure a common frame of reference between you and your reader; you want your reader to see how important you consider each idea to be. Your goal is *not* to mislead the reader. For example, if you believe that Alternative A is the *slightly* better choice, you would certainly not want to intentionally mislead your reader into concluding that Alternative A is *clearly* the better choice. Such a tactic would be not only unethical but also unwise. Use sound business judgment and a sense of fair play to help you achieve your communication objectives.

Use language that expresses your honest evaluation; do not mislead the reader.

13. Use Nondiscriminatory Language.

Nondiscriminatory language treats everyone equally, making no unwarranted assumptions about any group of people. Using nondiscriminatory language is smart business because (1) it is the ethical thing to do, and because (2) we risk offending others if we do not. Consider the types of bias in this report:

Use language that implies equality.

> The finishing plant was the scene of a confrontation today when two ladies from the morning shift accused a foreman of sexual harassment. Marta Valdez, a Hispanic inspector, and Margaret Sawyer, an assembly-line worker, accused Mr. Engerrand of making suggestive comments. Mr. Engerrand, who is 62 years old and an epileptic, denied the charges and said he thought the girls were trying to gyp the company with their demand for a cash award.

Were you able to identify the following instances of bias or discriminatory language?

- The women were referred to as *ladies* and *girls,* although it is unlikely that the men in the company are referred to as *gentlemen* and *boys.*
- The term *foreman* (and all other *-man* occupational titles) has a sexist connotation.
- The two women were identified by first and last name, without a personal title, whereas the man was identified by a personal title and last name only.

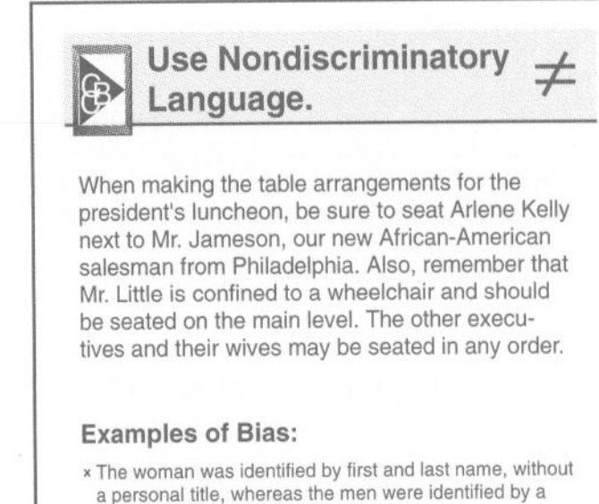

See Transparency 4.4, Nondiscriminatory Language.

- Valdez's ethnicity, Engerrand's age, and Engerrand's disability were identified, although they were irrelevant to the situation.
- The word *gyp,* derived from *gypsy,* is derogatory.

Competent communicators make sure that their writing is free of sexist language and free of bias based on such factors as race, ethnicity, religion, age, sexual orientation, and disability.

Be sensitive to your reader's feelings.

Sexist Language It makes no business sense to exclude or perhaps offend half the population by using sexist language. To avoid sexism in your writing, follow these strategies:

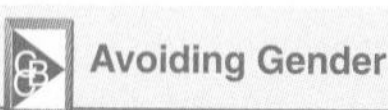

Avoiding Gender Bias
▪ Use neutral job titles.
▪ Avoid language that implies gender.
▪ Avoid demeaning or stereotypical terms.
▪ Use parallel language.
▪ Use appropriate personal titles and salutations.
▪ Consider not using *he* as a generic pronoun.

See Transparency 4.5, Avoiding Gender Bias.

1. Use neutral job titles that do not imply that a job is held by only men or women.

Instead of	*Use*
chairman	chair, chairperson
fireman	firefighter
foreman	supervisor
mailman	mail carrier, letter carrier
salesman	sales representative
stewardess	cabin attendant
woman lawyer	lawyer
workman	worker, employee

2. Avoid words and phrases that unnecessarily imply gender.

Instead of	*Use*
best man for the job	best person for the job
executives and their wives	executives and their spouses
housewife	homemaker
mankind	humanity, people
manmade	artificial, manufactured
manpower	human resources, personnel

3. Avoid demeaning or stereotypical terms.

Males also may be the victims of sexist language.

Instead of	*Use*
My girl will handle it.	My secretary will handle it.
Women don't like football.	Some people don't like football.
Watch your language around the ladies.	Watch your language.
Housewives like our long hours.	Our customers like our long hours.
He was a real jock.	He enjoyed all types of sports.
Each nurse supplies her own uniform.	Nurses supply their own uniforms.

Other sexist terms to avoid are *policeman, clergyman, statesman,* and *handyman.* Instead, use *police officer, member of the clergy, diplomat,* and *janitor* or *custodian.*

4. Use parallel language.

Instead of	*Use*
Joe, a broker, and his wife, a beautiful brunette	Joe, a broker, and his wife, Mary, a lawyer (*or* homemaker).

Ms. Wyllie and William Poe	Ms. Wyllie and Mr. Poe
man and wife	husband and wife

5. Use appropriate personal titles and salutations.

   - If a woman has a professional title, use it.

     Dr. Martha Ralston — the Rev. Deborah Connell

   - Follow a woman's preference in being addressed as *Miss, Mrs.*, or *Ms.*
   - If a woman's marital status or her preference is unknown, use *Ms.*
   - If you do not know the reader's gender, use a nonsexist salutation.

Dear Investor:	Dear Friend:
Dear Customer:	Dear Policyholder:

   - If you cannot tell the reader's gender, you may use the full name in the salutation.

     Dear Chris Andrews: — Dear Terry Brooks:

Follow the reader's preference to be addressed as Ms., Miss, *or* Mrs.

6. Whether it is appropriate to use *he* or *his* as generic pronouns in referring to males or females (e.g., "Each manager must evaluate *his* subordinates annually") is currently a matter of some debate. Proponents argue that its use is based on tradition and on the fact that no genderless alternative pronoun exists. Opponents argue that its use appears to exclude females. Although many business people would not be offended by such use, some would be. The conservative approach is to avoid such usage whenever possible by adopting any of these strategies:

   - Use plural nouns and pronouns.

     All managers must evaluate their subordinates annually.
     But not: Each manager must evaluate <u>their</u> subordinates annually.

   - Use second-person pronouns (*you, your*).

     You must evaluate your subordinates annually.

   - Revise the sentence.

     Each manager must evaluate subordinates annually.

   - Use *his or her* (sparingly).

     Each manager must evaluate his or her subordinates annually.

The generic use of he *and* him *will offend some readers.*

Excessive use of the term he or she *or* his or hers *sounds awkward.*

Other Discriminatory Language We are all members of different groups, each of which may have different customs, values, and attitudes. If you think of your readers as individuals, rather than as stereotypical members of some particular group, you will avoid bias when communicating about race, ethnic background, religion, age, sexual orientation, and disabilities. Group membership should be mentioned only if it is clearly pertinent.

Not: Richard McKenna, noted black legislator, supported our position.
But: Richard McKenna, noted legislator, supported our position.

Not: Because of rising interest rates, he welshed on the deal.
But: Because of rising interest rates, he backed out of the deal.

Not: His Jewish mother always stressed the value of a college education.
But: His mother always stressed the value of a college education.

Not: Anita Voyles performed the job well for her age.
But: Anita Voyles performed the job well.

Not: Patricia Barbour's lesbianism has not affected her job performance.
But: Patricia Barbour's job performance has been exemplary.

Not: The blind consultant made two important recommendations.
But: The consultant made two important recommendations.

Not: Mary, an epileptic, had no trouble passing the medical examination.
But: Mary, who has epilepsy, had no trouble passing the medical examination. (*When the impairment is relevant, separate the impairment from the person.*)

Mention group membership only if it is clearly relevant.

Most of us like to think of ourselves as sensitive, caring people who do not wish to offend others; our writing and speaking should reflect this attitude. Unfortunately, some types of discriminatory language may be so deeply ingrained that using bias-free language may take a concerted effort at first. Bias will not disappear completely from our language until it disappears completely from our lives. Still, competent communicators strive to use language impartially so that readers can focus their attention on *what* is written without being offended by *how* it is written.

14. Stress the "You" Attitude.

Write from the reader's perspective.

Are you more interested in how well *you* perform in your courses or in how well your classmates perform? When you hear a television commercial, are you more interested in how the product will benefit *you* or in how your purchase of the product will benefit the advertiser? If you're like most people reading or hearing a message, your conscious or unconscious reaction is likely to be "What's in it for *me?*" Knowing that this is true provides you with a powerful strategy for structuring your messages to maximize their impact: stress the "you" attitude, not a "me" attitude.

The **"you" attitude** emphasizes what the *receiver* (either the listener or the reader) wants to know and how he or she will be affected by the message. It requires developing **empathy**—the ability to project yourself into another person's position and to understand that person's situation, feelings, motives, and needs. To avoid sounding selfish and uninterested, stress the reader viewpoint—use the "you" attitude.

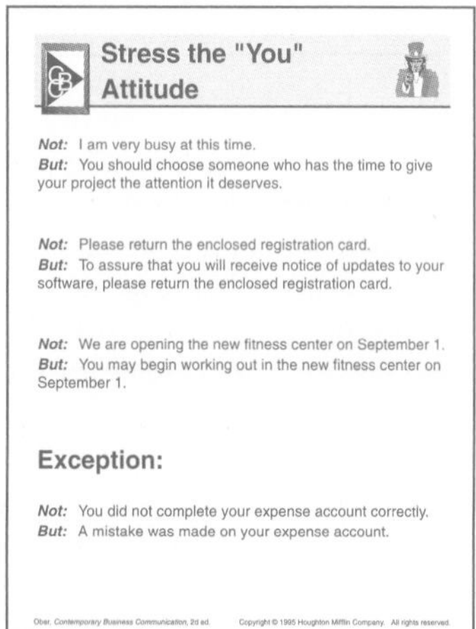

See Transparency 4.6, The "You" Attitude.

Not: I am shipping your order this afternoon.
But: Your order should arrive by Friday.

Not: We will be open on Sundays from 1 to 5 p.m., beginning May 15.
But: You will be able to shop on Sundays from 1 to 5 p.m., beginning May 15.

Not: So that I may begin analyzing my data by May 1, I would like to have the completed questionnaire returned by April 15.
But: So that your views will be included in this study, won't you please return your completed questionnaire by April 15.

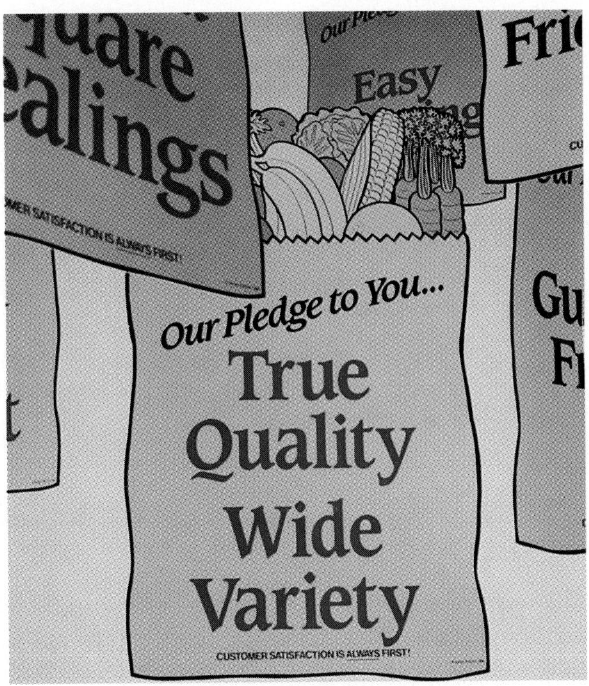

Advertisers are always aware of the need to emphasize customer benefits, but that approach works equally well in other forms of communicating in business, whether it's answering a routine order or persuading someone to accept a major proposal.

Answer the reader's unspoken question, "What's in it for me?"

Reader Benefits An important component of the "you" attitude is the concept of **reader benefits**—emphasizing how the *reader* will benefit from doing as you ask. Sometimes, especially when asking a favor or refusing a request, the best we can do is to show how *someone* (not necessarily the reader) will benefit. But, whenever possible, we should show how someone *other than ourselves* benefits from our request or from our decision.

Not: We cannot afford to purchase an ad in your organization's directory.

But: Advertising exclusively on television allows us to offer consumers like you the lowest prices on their cosmetics.

Not: Our decorative fireplace has an oak mantel and is portable.

But: Whether you're entertaining in your living room or den, you can still enjoy the ambience of a blazing fire because our decorative fireplace is portable. Simply take it with you from room to room.

Note that the revised sentences, which stress reader benefits, are longer than the original sentences—because they contain *more information.* Yet they are not wordy; that is, they do not contain unnecessary words. You can add information and still write concisely.

In some situations you do not *want to focus attention on the reader.*

Exceptions Stressing the "you" attitude focuses the attention on the reader, which is right where the attention should be—most of the time. In some situations, however, you may want to avoid focusing on the reader; these situations all involve conveying negative information. When you refuse someone's request, disagree with someone, or talk about someone's mistakes or shortcomings, avoid connecting the reader too closely with the negative information. In such situations, avoid second-person pronouns (*you* and *your*), and use passive sentences or other subordinating techniques to stress the receiver of the action rather than the doer.

Not: You should have included more supporting evidence in your presentation.
But: Including more supporting evidence would have made the presentation more convincing.

Not: You are mistaken in concluding that San Diego is the best site.
But: Santa Barbara has two advantages over San Diego.

Not: You failed to return the merchandise within the 10-day period.
But: We are happy to give a full refund on all merchandise that is returned within ten days.

Note that none of the revised sentences contains the word *you*. Thus, they help to separate the reader from the negative information, making the message more tactful and palatable.

15. Write at an Appropriate Level of Difficulty.

The term **readability** refers to the ease of understanding a passage based on its style of writing. You should write (and speak) at a level of readability that is appropriate for your specific audience. For example, a toy manufacturer would not use the same language in an advertisement in *Kid's World* (directed primarily to 8-to-10-year-olds) as it would use in an advertisement in *Corporate Wholesaler* (directed primarily to corporate executives).

The Fog Index estimates the amount of "fog" (complexity) in a passage by considering the length of words and sentences.

Various readability formulas are available that estimate the complexity of a passage based on an analysis of such factors as sentence length, number of syllables per word, and word frequency. One of the more commonly used readability formulas is the Fog Index, developed by Robert Gunning (see Figure 4.1).[1] This formula estimates readability based on average sentence length and the percentage of difficult words. The final product is

Of necessity, the writing that these Johnson & Johnson scientists do contains many difficult words. Clear organization helps them make technical messages easy to understand.

FIGURE 4.1 Calculating Readability Using the Fog Index

```
    The attached Wall Street Journal (article) discusses four
large hotel chains that have started frequent-stay plans. |
The purpose of this report is to describe such plans and
(analyze) their costs and (benefits) |Then I will (recommend)
what action, if any, we should take in this regard.|
    To gather the needed data, I studied published reports
prepared by the Hotel and Restaurant Association; |then I
(interviewed) the person in charge of frequent-stay programs
at three hotels.| (Finally,) Dr. Kenneth Lowe, (professor) of
(hospitality) services at Southern Cal, reviewed and commented
on my first draft. |Thus, this (proposal) is based on a large
body of data collected over two months.|
```

1. Select a passage of at least 100 words. Use complete sentences only. (If the passage is long, take several samples and average the results.) Here is an example:
2. Find the average sentence length.
   a. Count the number of words in the passage (count anything with a space before and after as a word). 108
   b. Count the number of sentences (see the tick marks in the above passage). In compound sentences, count each independent clause as a separate sentence. 7
   c. Divide the number of words by the number of sentences. $108 \div 7 = 15.4$
3. Find the percentage of difficult words.
   a. Count the number of difficult words (those containing three or more syllables—see the circled words in the above passage). Do not include the following: 9
      - Compound words—unless one of the individual elements is three or more syllables; for example, *however* and *self-control* are not considered difficult words, but *self-discipline* is considered difficult.
      - Verbs that become three syllables by adding *-ed* or *-es;* for example, *refreshes* is not considered a difficult word, but *refreshing* is considered difficult.
      - Figures or capitalized words.
   b. Divide the number of difficult words by the total number of words in the passage and multiply by 100. $9 \div 108 = .083; .083 \times 100 = 8.3$
4. Add the average sentence length (from Step 2) to the percentage of difficult words (from Step 3). $15.4 + 8.3 = 23.7$
5. Multiply the resulting number by 0.4 to arrive at the reading grade level needed to read and understand the passage. $23.7 \times 0.4 = 9.5$

CHECKLIST I

Writing with Style

WORDS

1. *Write clearly.* Be accurate and complete; use familiar words; avoid dangling expressions and unnecessary jargon.
2. *Prefer short, simple words.* They are less likely to be misused by the writer and more likely to be understood by the reader.
3. *Write with vigor.* Use specific, concrete language; avoid clichés, slang, and buzz words.
4. *Write concisely.* Avoid redundancy, wordy expressions, and hidden subjects and verbs.
5. *Prefer positive language.* Stress what you can do or what is true rather than what you cannot do or what is not true.

SENTENCES

6. *Use a variety of sentence types.* Use simple sentences for emphasis and variety, compound sentences for coordinate relationships, and complex sentences for subordinate relationships. Most sentences should range from 16 to 22 words.
7. *Use active and passive voice appropriately.* Use active voice in general and to emphasize the doer of the action; use passive voice to emphasize the receiver.

PARAGRAPHS

8. *Keep paragraphs unified and coherent.* Develop a single idea consistently and logically; use transitional words and pronouns, repetition, and parallelism.

Encourage students to screen their writing for sentences longer than 22 words; sentences this long are often difficult to understand. They may want to keep the occasional very long sentence—but they should evaluate it to make sure it isn't confusing. If it is, they are probably trying to pack too many ideas into one sentence.

roughly equal to school grade reading level. Thus, a Fog Index of 8 indicates that someone who reads at eighth-grade level can be expected to understand the passage easily.

Independent research has shown that the Fog Index is accurate to within plus or minus one grade level at all levels up to 13.[2] Accuracy at levels higher than 13 is probably irrelevant, because, as Gunning states, any writing with an index higher than 12 (high school senior level) invites misunderstanding.[3] Most business writing should have a Fog Index between 8 and 12. In comparison, *Reader's Digest* has an index of 9 to 10; *Wall Street Journal*, 10 to 11; and *Scientific American*, 11 to 12. Moreover, you should be aware that 25 million Americans read below the fifth-grade level, and 35 to 40 million read between the fifth- and eighth-grade levels.[4]

Although applying the Fog Index (or any other readability formula) is helpful in judging the readability of your message, you should use the results as a guide only. According to Gunning, "The Fog Index is a tool, not a rule. It is a warning system, not a formula for writing."[5]

You could, for example, artificially lower your Fog Index by using shorter sentences and shorter words. But sometimes a longer word is more precise and more familiar than a shorter word. Likewise, lowering the index score by using all short sentences (e.g., all simple sentences) might obscure the relationships among ideas because then all ideas would receive equal emphasis.

A further caution with regard to overreliance on readability measures concerns what they do *not* measure. They do not measure the complexity and organization of the ideas or the design of the document. Perhaps, more

9. *Control paragraph length.* Use a variety of lengths, although most paragraphs should range from 60 to 80 words.

OVERALL TONE

10. *Write confidently.* Avoid sounding self-conscious (by overusing such phrases as "I think" and "I hope"), but also avoid sounding arrogant or presumptuous.
11. *Use a courteous and sincere tone.* Avoid platitudes, exaggeration, obvious flattery, and expressions of surprise or disbelief.
12. *Use appropriate emphasis and subordination.* Emphasize and subordinate through the use of sentence structure, position, verb voice, amount of space, language, repetition, and mechanical means.
13. *Use nondiscriminatory language.* When communicating, avoid bias about gender, race, ethnic background, religion, age, sexual orientation, and disabilities.
14. *Stress the "you" attitude.* Emphasize what the receiver wants to know and how the receiver will be affected by the message; stress reader benefits.
15. *Write at an appropriate level of difficulty.* A Fog Index score of 8 to 12 is generally an appropriate readability level in business writing, although many factors other than syllabic intensity and sentence length affect readability.

important, they do not measure reader interest in the passage. A reader who is intently interested in what you have to say may plow through even the foggiest writing. But if you have reason to expect low reader interest, make your writing especially easy and inviting to read.

Although readability formulas are helpful, other factors are also important.

For an exercise on revising complicated instructions, refer students to the *Study Guide*, p. 92.

EFFECTIVE BUSINESS WRITING

Writing style goes beyond *correctness.* Although a letter that contains many grammatical, mechanical, or usage errors could hardly be considered effective, a letter that contains no such errors might still be ineffective because it lacks style. Style involves choosing the right words, writing effective sentences, developing logical paragraphs, and setting an appropriate overall tone. Checklist 1 summarizes the 15 principles discussed in Chapters 3 and 4.

These principles will help you communicate your ideas clearly and effectively. They provide a solid foundation for the higher-order communication skills you will be developing in the following chapters. At first, you may find it somewhat difficult and time-consuming to constantly assess your writing according to these criteria. Their importance, however, merits the effort. You will find that you are soon beginning to apply these principles automatically as you compose and revise messages.

SUMMARY

Competent communicators achieve their objectives by writing with confidence, courtesy, and sincerity. They recognize that not all ideas are equally important, and they use techniques of emphasis and subordination to develop a common frame of reference between writer and reader. They use nondiscriminatory language in their writing by treating everyone equally and by not making unwarranted assumptions about any group of people.

Effective writing keeps the emphasis on the reader—stressing what the reader needs to know and how the reader will be affected by the message. Effective messages are also written at an appropriate level of difficulty so that the reader can easily understand the passage, based on its style of writing.

KEY TERMS

For an exercise on matching terms, refer students to the *Study Guide*, p. 89.

Empathy The ability to project oneself into another person's position and understand that person's situation, feelings, motives, and needs.

Nondiscriminatory language Language that treats everyone equally, making no unwarranted assumptions about any group of people.

Platitude A trite, obvious statement.

Readability The ease with which a passage can be understood, based on its style of writing.

Reader benefits The advantages a reader would derive from granting the writer's request or from accepting the writer's decision.

Tone The writer's attitude toward the reader and the subject of the message.

"You" attitude A viewpoint that emphasizes what the reader wants to know and how the reader will be affected by the message.

REVIEW AND DISCUSSION

The answers to the review and discussion questions appear in the *Instructor's Resource Manual*, beginning on p. 34.

1. **Communication at Sanitate Associates Revisited** ▪ Writing with style is what Frank Sanitate teaches lawyers, accountants, and corporate executives. Consider the specific writing challenges faced by many of the lawyers in Sanitate's seminars.
   a. Under what circumstances would a lawyer want to be particularly careful to convey an appropriately confident tone in a written document?
   b. Why is nondiscriminatory language important in legal documents?
   c. Would you expect a legal document filed with the U.S. Supreme Court to have a high or low Fog Index? Why?
2. Give an example of a sentence that sounds too confident and one that doesn't sound confident enough. Then revise both sentences to make them more effective.
3. What are three means of achieving a sincere tone in a message?
4. List seven techniques for emphasizing an idea.
5. List seven techniques for subordinating an idea.
6. Why should discriminatory language be avoided in business writing?
7. Do you feel it is appropriate or inappropriate to use the pronoun *he* as a generic pronoun referring to both males and females (e.g., "Each manager

must ensure that *he* submits *his* reports on time"). Write a paragraph defending your position.

8. List six techniques for avoiding sexism in business writing.
9. Construct a sentence illustrating the "you" attitude.
10. Under what circumstances should the reader *not* be the focus of attention in business writing.
11. Which difficulty factors are included and which are not included in the Fog Index. What is an appropriate Fog Index score for most business writing?

EXERCISES

For Exercises 1–4, revise the passages to reflect the writing principle indicated. Do not completely rewrite the passages; just correct any style problems.

Suggestions and sample solutions for exercises appear in the *Instructor's Resource Manual*, beginning on p. 36.

1. Writing Confidently ▪

```
If you believe my proposal has merit, I hope that you will
allocate $50,000 for a pilot study.  It's possible that this
pilot study will bear out my profit estimates so that we can
proceed on a permanent basis.  Even though you have several
other worthwhile projects to consider for funding, I know
you will agree the proposal should be funded prior to Janu-
ary 1.  Please call me before the end of the week to tell me
that you've accepted my proposal.
```

2. Using a Courteous and Sincere Tone ▪

```
You, our loyal and dedicated employees, have always been
the most qualified and the most industrious in the indus-
try.  Because of your faithful and dependable service, I was
quite surprised to learn yesterday that an organizational
meeting for union representation was recently held here.
You must realize that a company like ours cannot survive un-
less we hold labor costs down.  I cannot believe that you
don't appreciate the many benefits of working at Allied.  We
will immediately have to declare bankruptcy if a union is
voted in.  Please don't be fooled by empty rhetoric.
```

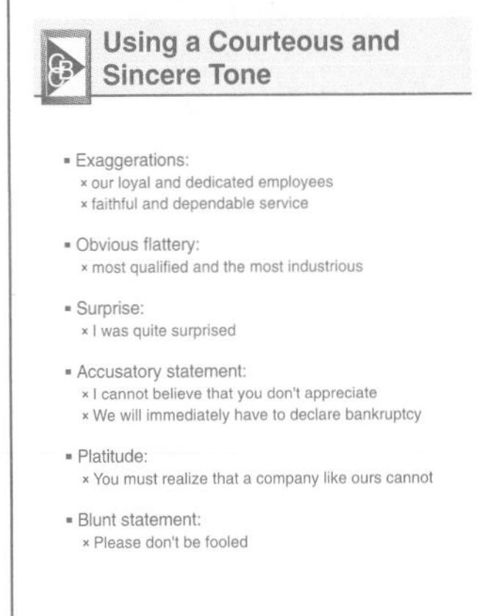

Using a Courteous and Sincere Tone
▪ Exaggerations:
× our loyal and dedicated employees
× faithful and dependable service
▪ Obvious flattery:
× most qualified and the most industrious
▪ Surprise:
× I was quite surprised
▪ Accusatory statement:
× I cannot believe that you don't appreciate
× We will immediately have to declare bankruptcy
▪ Platitude:
× You must realize that a company like ours cannot
▪ Blunt statement:
× Please don't be fooled
Ober, Contemporary Business Communication, 2d ed.
Copyright © 1995 Houghton Mifflin Company. All rights reserved.

See Master 4.1, Exercise 2, Using a Courteous and Sincere Tone, in the *Instructor's Resource Manual*.

3. Using Nondiscriminatory Language ▪

```
Mr. Timmerman argued that the 62-year-old Kathy Beviere
should be replaced because she doesn't dress appropriately
for her receptionist position.  However, the human re-
sources director, who is female, countered that we don't
pay any of the girls in the clerical positions well enough
for them to buy appropriate attire.  Mr. Timmerman did ac-
knowledge that the receptionist, who is a paraplegic, is
well suited for her receptionist job.  He added that he just
wished she would dress more businesslike instead of wearing
the colorful clothes and makeup that reflect her immigrant
background.
```

4. **Stressing the "You" Attitude** ■

```
We are happy to announce that we are offering for sale
an empty parcel of land at the corner of Mission and
High Streets. We will be selling this parcel for $89,500,
with a minimum down payment of $22,500. We have had the
lot rezoned M-2 for student housing. We originally pur-
chased this lot because of its proximity to the univer-
sity and had planned to erect student housing, but our
investment plans have changed. We still feel that our lot
would make a profitable site for up to three 12-unit
buildings.
```

5. **Writing Confidently** ■ Revise the following sentences to convey an appropriately confident attitude.

   a. Can you think of any reason not to buy a wristwatch for dressy occasions?
   b. I hope you agree that my offer provides good value for the money.
   c. Of course, I am confident that my offer provides good value for the money.
   d. You might try to find a few minutes to visit our gallery on your next visit to galleries in this area.

6. **Using Appropriate Emphasis and Subordination** ■ Assume that you have evaluated two candidates for the position of sales assistant. This is what you have learned:

   a. Carl Barteolli has more sales experience.
   b. Elizabeth Larson has more appropriate formal training (college degree in marketing, attendance at several three-week sales seminars, and the like).
   c. Elizabeth Larson's personality appears to mesh more closely with the prevailing corporate attitudes at your firm.

   You must write a memo to Alan Underwood, the vice president, recommending one of these candidates. First, assume that personality is the most important criterion and write a memo recommending Elizabeth Larson. Second, assume that experience is the most important criterion and write a memo recommending Carl Barteolli. Use appropriate emphasis and subordination in each message. You may make up any reasonable information needed to complete the assignment.

7. **Using Nondiscriminatory Language** ■ Revise the following sentences to eliminate discriminatory language.

   a. The mayor opened contract talks with the union representing local policemen.
   b. While the salesmen are at the convention, their wives will be treated to a tour of the city's landmarks.
   c. Our company gives each foreman the day off on his birthday.
   d. Our public relations director, Heather Marshall, will ask her young secretary, Bonita Carwell, to take notes during the president's speech.
   e. Both Dr. Fernandez and his assistant, Andrea McNeill, attended the new-product seminar.

8. **Writing at an Appropriate Level of Difficulty** ■ Select an actual paper that you have written and submitted for a course grade in this or some other course. Compute the Fog Index score of an appropriate passage (or passages) from this paper. What does this score mean? If necessary, revise the passage to adjust the readability level and then recompute your score. Submit both versions and your calculations to your instructor.

9. **Using Techniques of Emphasis** ■ Revise each sentence by applying the indicated technique of emphasis.

   a. Use one complex sentence. In each case, emphasize the problems of cold weather.

      `Outdoor workers in White Butte, North Dakota, have to battle severe winter conditions. However, outdoor workers in Atlanta, Georgia, face mild winter conditions.`

   b. Make the noun you want to emphasize the subject of the sentence.

      `Telephone and utility repair personnel who work outdoors have to cope with dangerous working conditions created by subzero temperatures.`

   c. Use language that directly implies importance.

      `Outdoor workers generally face a range of weather conditions, but frigid temperatures can pose particularly severe problems.`

   d. Use repetition.

      `Utilities in the northern states frequently remind outdoor workers about the cold-weather dangers of frostbite and hypothermia.`

10. **Stressing Reader Benefits** ■ Revise the following sentences to emphasize reader benefits.

    a. `We have been in the business of repairing sewing machines for more than 40 years.`
    b. `We need donations so we can expand the free-food program in this community.`
    c. `Company policy requires us to impose a 2% late charge when customers don't pay their bills on time.`
    d. `Although the refund department is open from 9 a.m. to 5 p.m., it is closed from 1 p.m. and 2 p.m. so our employees can take their lunch breaks.`

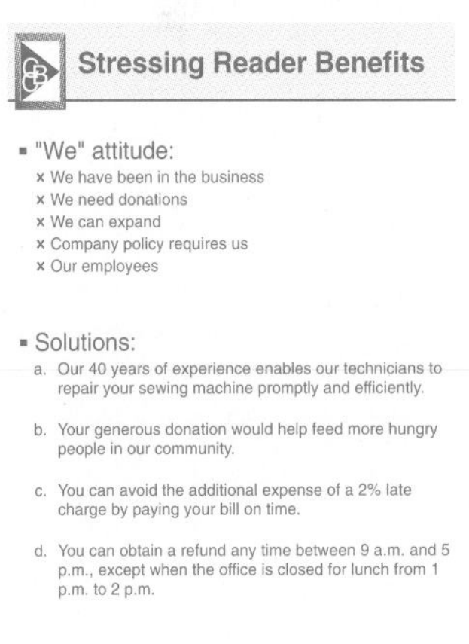

Stressing Reader Benefits
"We" attitude:
× We have been in the business
× We need donations
× We can expand
× Company policy requires us
× Our employees
Solutions:
a. Our 40 years of experience enables our technicians to repair your sewing machine promptly and efficiently.
b. Your generous donation would help feed more hungry people in our community.
c. You can avoid the additional expense of a 2% late charge by paying your bill on time.
d. You can obtain a refund any time between 9 a.m. and 5 p.m., except when the office is closed for lunch from 1 p.m. to 2 p.m.
Ober, *Contemporary Business Communication*, 2d ed.
Copyright © 1995 Houghton Mifflin Company. All rights reserved.

See Master 4.2, Exercise 3, Stressing Reader Benefits, in the *Instructor's Resource Manual.*

11. **Evaluating Writing Style** ■ As a college student with a potentially bright future, you no doubt frequently receive letters from credit-card companies, department stores, insurance firms, and the like, soliciting your business. Select a letter that you or a colleague has received, and analyze it according to each of the 15 principles discussed in Checklist 1. Write a statement of evaluation for each principle.

12. **Exceptions to the "You" Attitude** ■ Revise the following sentences, which convey negative information, to take the focus off the reader.

    a. `Because you paid your bill after the due date, you are being invoiced for an additional 2% late charge.`

b. Your proposal was sent too late for this year's competition.
c. You forgot to include copies of last month's pay stubs with your loan application.
d. Your report was one-sided because it did not provide enough details about the disadvantages of buying directly from the manufacturer.

A possible solution to the Continuing Case is described in the *Instructor's Resource Manual*, pp. 39–40.

CONTINUING CASE 4

Drew Drafts a Drab Memo

Here is a first-draft memo written by O. J. Drew to Arnie McNally:

MEMO TO: Arnold McNally, vice president, manufacturing

FROM: O. J. Drew, production manager

DATE: October 13, 19--

SUBJECT: Charlotte Expansion

As you will remember, when we opened our Charlotte plant, we made plans to increase capacity within three years. We're now approaching the end of our third year, and even though sales are increasing, I suggest we delay any expansion plans for another two years.

To begin with, interest rates are heading up across the board. Last week, North Carolina National Bank and Wachovia Bank both raised their prime rate quite a bit. This is the highest it has been in several years. Other big banks are likely to follow with similar increases. Both NCNB and Wachovia financed our initial efforts in Charlotte—at a lower rate. The Wall Street Journal predicts that interest rates will remain high for at least the next 18 months. A second reason for my suggestion is that present capacity is sufficient to support our present level of sales. If sales continue to grow substantially, we will continue to have sufficient capacity for three more years. We can increase production for minimal plant cost by simply adding a third shift. Adding a third shift will lower per-unit costs and enable us to convert numerous part-time positions to full-time positions, with a corresponding savings in fringe benefits. Finally, our union contract expires next year. Although our plant is automated, we still employ 95 unionized workers. These men's wage demands are high; and unless we are able to jew them down a bit, we will simply not be able to afford an expansion. I predict getting a reasonable union contract this time will be a hard nut to crack. In addition, Neelima believes that

```
if a strike is at all possible, we won't even be using the
capacity we presently have—let alone, expanded capacity.

For these reasons, I recommend we delay any expansion
plans for another two years at least.  I hope you will
agree with me.  Luis Diaz does; and if you desire, we can
produce a formal report of our recommendation for you to
present to the board.  Let me know if you have any ques-
tions.

juv
```

Critical Thinking

1. In terms of what you know about Arnie McNally (see Appendix to Chapter 1), assess the appropriateness of the readability of this memo for its intended audience. What factors not measured by readability formulas affect the readability of this memo?

Writing Projects

2. Analyze each paragraph, using Checklist 1 as the basis for your analysis. What effective and ineffective techniques has Drew used?
3. List each transitional expression that was used in the second paragraph to achieve coherence. Does the paragraph have unity?
4. Revise this memorandum, making whatever changes are necessary to increase its effectiveness. You may make up any needed facts as long as they are reasonable.

Drew's Revised Memo

When we opened our Charlotte plant, we planned to increase capacity within three years. We're now approaching the end of our third year, and even though sales are increasing, I suggest we delay any expansion plans for another two years.

To begin with, interest rates are heading up across the board. Last week, North Carolina National Bank and Wachovia Bank raised their prime rate to 8.375%, their highest rate in nearly four years. Other big banks are likely to follow with similar increases. In fact, The Wall Street Journal predicts that interest rates will remain high for at least the next 18 months.

A second reason for my suggestion is that present capacity is sufficient. If sales continue to grow between 4% and 5% yearly, we will have sufficient capacity for three more years. And if necessary, we could increase production for minimal plant cost by simply adding a third shift. Doing so would lower per-unit costs by 7% and enable us to convert eight part-time positions to full-time positions, with a saving of $24,000 in fringe benefits.

Finally, our union contract expires next year, and I predict getting a reasonable contract this time will be difficult. The wage demands of our 95 unionized workers are high, and unless we are able to get them reduced, we will simply not be able to afford an expansion. In addition, Neelima believes that if a strike does occur, we would not even use the capacity we presently have—let alone, need expanded capacity.

For these reasons, I recommend we delay any expansion plans for another two years at least. If you desire, Luis Diaz and I can produce a formal report of our recommendation for you to present to the Board.

Ober, *Contemporary Business Communication*, 2d ed.

See Master 4.3, Continuing Case 4, Question 4, in the *Instructor's Resource Manual.*

WORDWISE *Writing Style*

- English is the only language to capitalize the first-person singular pronoun *I*.
- Paragraphing was invented by the Greeks. At first, paragraphs were denoted merely by marks in the margin on one long page of unbroken handwriting.
- You and I take spaces between words for granted. Butancientwriting includednospacesbetweenwords.
- Words that have no English-language rhymes include *month, orange,* and *silver*.

CHAPTER

5 The Process of Writing

Communication Objectives

After you have finished this chapter, you should be able to

1. Specify the purpose of your message and analyze your audience.
2. Determine what information to include and in what order to present it.
3. Compose a first draft of your message.
4. Use a variety of strategies to overcome writer's block.
5. Revise for content, style, and correctness.
6. Arrange documents in a standard format.
7. Proofread a document for content, typographical, and format errors.

John Kazzi is the manager of publications at Keep America Beautiful (KAB), a nonprofit educational organization that has been urging Americans since 1953 not to litter and to respect the environment. Today KAB's agenda includes the national issue of handling and disposing of solid waste, and Kazzi's responsibilities include writing newsletters, an annual report, articles for magazines, and educational material. For Kazzi, the writing process boils down to a rewriting process that moves from ideas to organization to words to sentences.

"I start with a big yellow legal pad and write out a list of all the things I want to say," he says. "Then I sit down at my word processor and work up a first draft. After that, I can get into the meat-and-potatoes of revising it two, three, or even four times before someone else sees it. It is very uncommon for me to write something and not make substantial changes to it when I come back to it the next day."

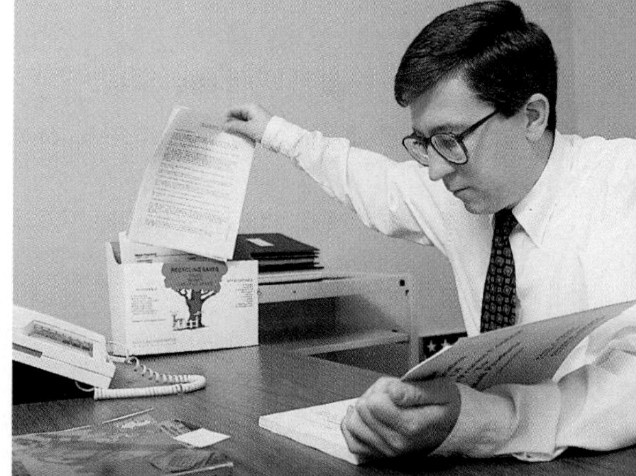

For Kazzi, revision is a process that moves his writing toward greater clarity. His "meat-and-potatoes" effort tightens long sentences and replaces vague language with specific language. And always, *always*, says Kazzi, he strives to stay mindful of two things: who his readers are and what his goals are.

"It's the same for an organization like ours as it is for anyone who is educating the public," says Kazzi. "You identify a concern and then provide an approach that your audience can use to solve the problem. And you can't forget to identify the benefit they derive by participating."

To do that well, says Kazzi, a writer has to choose his words carefully, using language that suits his audience rather than himself. "We are a bit more educated about our topic than some of our audience is because we have to be. But we try not to be overly technical. At the same time we try to give more insight to the reader." Writing about a subject without being to technical, says Kazzi, is part of the honing process. Kazzi has to edit out technical words that might come naturally to him or his colleagues but would confuse his audience. That part of the writing process is, in a sense, a translating process.

When the translating is done, Kazzi can move on to another part of writing: organizing. He must decide where to begin and where to end. "One of the best ways to begin a story is by describing an environmental issue or concern that is shared by many communities. From this national perspective, you can then move right into the local angle by citing an example of what can be done, or is being done, in the reader's own city or town to address the concern. After that, it's a natural transition into what the reader can do as an individual to help. Above all, we try to show people that they CAN make a difference."

All of this may sound like a steady and systematic process, but it isn't. Writing, says Kazzi, is periodically frustrating.

"I've found that outlining the story early in the day and putting the first two or three paragraphs into the computer before lunch is the best way to start. Then, I can eat and go for a walk, knowing that I've gotten over the most difficult part. But, in truth, I'll usually think of a better lead paragraph at lunch, come back, and start to tinker with it all over again.

John Kazzi
Manager of publications, Keep America Beautiful, Inc., Stamford, Connecticut

A chapter overview appears in the *Instructor's Resource Manual*, pp. 41–44.

AN OVERVIEW OF THE WRITING PROCESS

For an exercise in drafting a simple memorandum, as described at the end of this chapter, see Video Case Study 1, Chiat/Day.

When faced with a writing task, some people just start writing. They try to do everything at once, figuring out what to say and how to say it, visualizing an audience and a goal, keeping watch on spelling and grammar, and choosing their words and building sentences—all at the same time. It's not easy to keep switching back and forth from one of these distinct writing tasks to another and still make headway. In fact, unless you're an expert writer, it's harder and slower than breaking the job up into steps and completing each step in turn.

The idea of writing step by step may at first sound as if it will prolong the job, but it won't. The step of planning, for example, gives you a sense of where you want to go and that, in turn, makes getting there faster and easier. The clearer you are about your goals, the more likely your writing will accomplish those goals. And if you save a separate step for proofreading, that job will also go more smoothly and efficiently. After all, it's difficult to spot a typo while you're still trying to think up the "big ending" for your report.

There is no single "best" writing process. In fact, all good writers develop their own process that suits their own ways of tackling a problem.

But one way or another, competent communicators typically perform the following five steps when faced with a business situation that calls for a written response (see Figure 5.1):

The writing process consists of planning, drafting, revising, formatting, and proofreading.

1. *Planning:* Determine what the purpose of the message is, who the reader will be, what information you need to give the reader to achieve your purpose, and in what order to present the information.
2. *Drafting:* Compose a first draft of the message.
3. *Revising:* Revise for content, style, and correctness.
4. *Formatting:* Arrange the document in an appropriate format.
5. *Proofreading:* Review the document to check for content, typographical, and format errors.

FIGURE 5.1 The Five Steps in the Writing Process

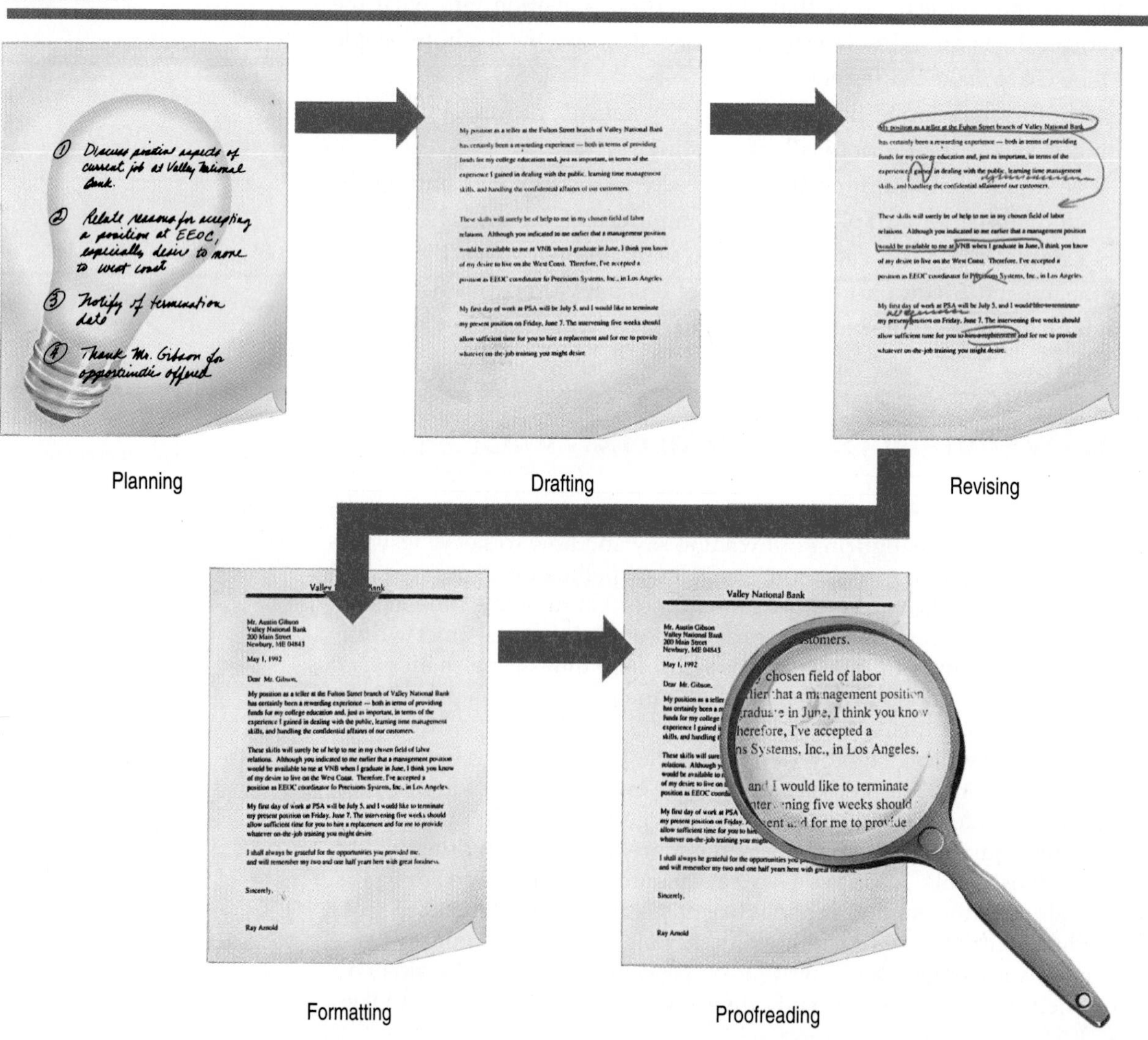

The amount of time you will devote to each step depends on the complexity, length, and importance of the document. Not all steps may be needed for all writing tasks. For example, you may go through all the steps if you are writing a business plan to get funding for a small business from a bank but not if you are answering an electronic mail message inviting you to a meeting. Nevertheless, these steps are a good starting point for completing a writing assignment—either in class or on the job.

Many businesspeople don't write because they think they have no talent, they're afraid of failure, or they fear writer's block. The real problem, say writing consultants, is that businesspeople don't realize what successful writers know: writing is a multistep process, and each step involves different activities. (Judith Yellen and Barret J. Mandel, "Business Writing—Without Blood, Sweat, and Tears," *Working Woman*, June 1990, p. 64.)

PLANNING

Planning, the first step in writing, involves making conscious decisions about the purpose, audience, content, and organization of the message.

Purpose

The first decision relates to the purpose of the message. If you don't know why you're writing the message (that is, if you don't know what you hope to accomplish), then later you'll have no way of knowing whether or not you've achieved your goal. In the end, what matters is not how well-crafted your message was or how attractive it looked on the page; what matters is whether you achieved your communication objective. If you did, your communication was successful; if you did not, it was not.

The purpose should be specific enough to serve as a yardstick for judging the success of the message.

Most writers find it easier to start with a general purpose and then refine the general purpose into a specific one. The specific purpose should indicate the response desired from the reader.

Assume, for example, that you are a marketing manager at Seaside Resorts, a chain of hotels along the California, Oregon, and Washington coasts. You have noted that many of the larger hotel chains have instituted "frequent-stay" plans, which, like the frequent-flier programs they are modeled after, reward repeat customers with free lodging, travel, or merchandise. You want to write a message recommending a similar plan for Seaside Resorts. Your general purpose might be this:

General Purpose: To describe the benefits of a frequent-stay plan at Seaside Resorts.

Such a goal is a good starting point, but it is not specific enough. To begin with, it doesn't identify the intended audience. Are you writing a memo to the vice president of marketing recommending this plan, or are you writing a letter to frequent business travelers recommending that they enroll in this plan? Let's assume, for the moment, that you're writing to the marketing vice president. What is she supposed to *do* as a result of reading your memo? Do you want her to simply understand what you've written? agree with you? commit resources for further research? agree to implement the plan immediately? How will you know if your message achieved its objective? Perhaps you decide that your specific purpose is this:

A clearly stated purpose helps you avoid including irrelevant and distracting information.

Specific Purpose: To persuade the marketing VP to approve the development and implementation of a frequent-stay plan for a 12-month test period in Seaside's three Oregon resorts.

Now you have a purpose that's specific enough to guide you as you write the memo and to permit you to judge, in time, whether your message achieved its goal.

In another situation, your general purpose might be to resolve a problem regarding a shipment of damaged merchandise, and your specific purpose might be to persuade the manufacturer to replace the damaged shipment at no cost to you within ten days. Or your general purpose might be to refuse a customer's claim, and your specific purpose might be to convince the customer that your refusal is reasonable and to maintain the customer's goodwill.

Having a clear-cut statement of purpose lets you focus on the content and organization, eliminating any distracting information and incorporating all relevant information.

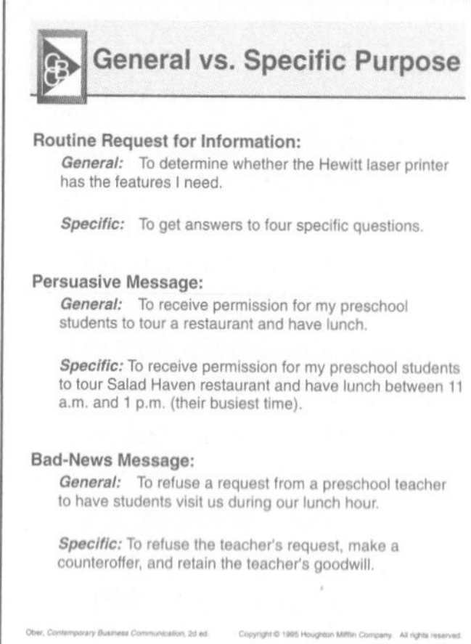

See Transparency 5.1, Purpose of the Message.

Audience Analysis

To maximize the effectiveness of your message, you should perform an **audience analysis;** that is, you should identify the interests, needs, and personality of your receiver. Remember our discussion of mental filters in Chapter 1. Each person perceives a message differently, based on his or her unique mental filter. Thus, we need to determine the level of detail, the language to be used, and the overall tone by answering the pertinent questions about audience discussed below (see Figure 5.2).

Who Is the Primary Audience? For most letters, the audience is one person, which simplifies the writing task immensely. It is much easier to personalize a message addressed to one individual than a message addressed to many individuals. Sometimes, however, you will have more than one audience. In this case, you need to identify your **primary audience** (the person whose cooperation is crucial if your message is to achieve its objectives) and then your **secondary audience** (others who will also read and be affected by your message). If you can satisfy no one else, try to satisfy the needs of the primary decision maker. If possible, also satisfy the needs of any secondary audience.

If, for example, you're presenting a proposal that must be approved by the general manager but that will also require the cooperation of your colleagues in other departments, the general manager is the primary audience and your colleagues are the secondary audience. Gear your message—its content, organization, and tone—first to the needs of the general manager. Most often (but not always), the primary audience will be the highest-level person to whom you're addressing your communication.

Your relationship with the reader determines the tone and content of your message.

What Is Your Relationship with the Audience? Does your audience know you? If not, you will first have to establish your credibility by assuming a reasonable tone and giving enough evidence to support your claims. Are you writing to someone inside or outside the organization? If outside, your message will often be a little more formal and will contain more background information and less jargon than if you are writing to someone inside the organization.

FIGURE 5.2 Questions for Audience Analysis

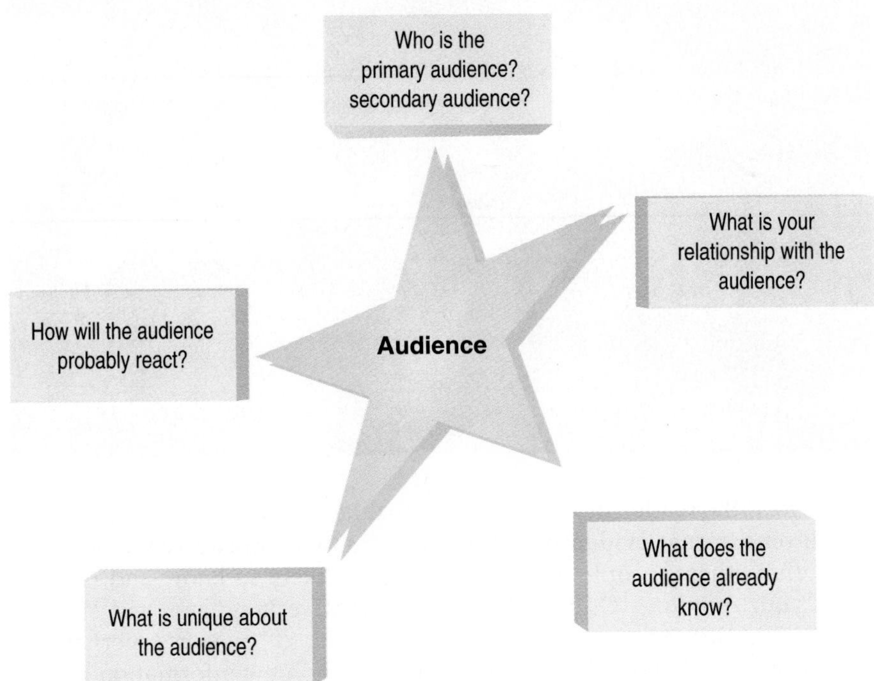

What is your status in the organization in relation to your audience? Communications to your superiors are obviously vital to your success in the organization. Such communications are typically a little more formal, less authoritarian in tone, and more information-filled than communications to peers or subordinates. In addition, such messages are typically "front-loaded"—that is, they use a direct organizational style and present the major idea in the first paragraph. Study your superior's own messages to get a sense of his or her preferred style and diction, and adapt your own message accordingly.

When you communicate with subordinates, be polite but not patronizing. Try to instill a sense of collaboration and of corporate ownership of your proposal. When praising or criticizing, be specific; and criticize the action—not the person. Try to praise in public but criticize in private.

Points to Remember About
Your Audience
▪ Most people are honest and reasonable.
▪ People need specific information.
▪ No one is perfect.
▪ People don't like to be "talked down to."
▪ People want to know what they will gain by taking action.
▪ Most people are likely to react to your message the same way you would if you had received it.

See Transparency 5.2, Audience Analysis.

How Will the Audience React? If the reader's initial reaction to both you and your topic is likely to be *positive,* your job is relatively easy. You can use a direct approach—beginning with the most important information (for example, your conclusions or recommendations) and then supplying the needed details. If the reader's initial reaction is likely to be *neutral,* you may want to use the first few lines of the message to get the reader's attention and convince him or her that what you have to say is important and that your reasoning is sound. Make sure your message is short and easy to read and that any requested action is easy to take.

Suppose, however, that you expect your reader's reaction—either to your topic or to you personally—will be *negative.* Here you have a real sales

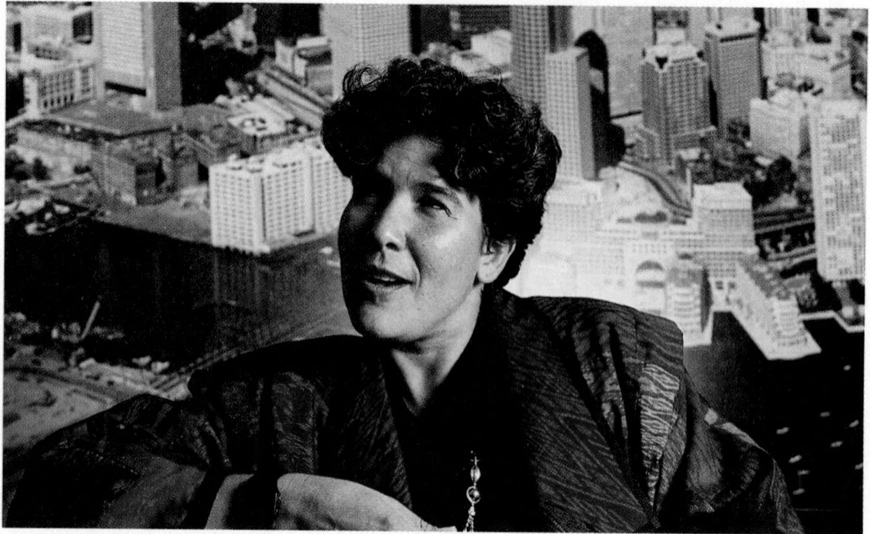

In her role as director of the Boston Redevelopment Authority, Marisa Lago faces many different audiences in the political and business communities. She believes the best approach to all is low key and straightforward.

If the expected reader reaction is negative, present lots of evidence and expert testimony.

job to do. If the reader shows a personal dislike of you, your best strategy is to call on external evidence and expert opinion to bolster your position. Show that others, people whom the reader is likely to know and respect, share your opinions. Use courteous, conservative language, and suggest ways the reader can cooperate without appearing to "give in"—perhaps by reminding the reader that new circumstances and new information call for new strategies.

If you anticipate that your reader will oppose your proposal, your best strategy is to supply extra evidence. Instead of one example, give two or three. Instead of quoting two external sources, quote several. Begin with the areas of agreement, stress reader benefits, and try to anticipate and answer any objections the reader might have. Through logic, evidence, and tone, build your case for the reasonableness of your position.

Determine how much information the reader needs.

What Does the Audience Already Know? Understanding the audience's present grasp of the topic is crucial to making decisions about content and writing style. You must decide how much background information is necessary, whether the use of jargon is called for, and what readability level is appropriate. If you are writing to multiple audiences, gear the amount of detail to the level of understanding of the key decision maker (the primary audience). In general, it is better to provide *too much* rather than too little information.

What Is Unique About the Audience? The success or failure of a message often depends on little things—the extra touches that say to the reader, "You're important, and I've taken the time to learn some things about you."

Make the reader feel important by personalizing the content.

What can you learn about the personal interests or demographic characteristics of your audience that you can build into your message? Is the reader a "take-charge" kind of person who would prefer to have important information up front—regardless of whether the news is good or bad? What level of formality is expected? Would the reader be flattered or be put off by the use of his or her first name in the salutation? Have good things or bad things happened recently at work or at home that may affect the reader's receptivity to your message?

Competent communicators analyze their audience and then use this information to structure the content, organization, and tone of their messages.

Example of Audience Analysis To illustrate the crucial role that audience analysis plays in communication, let's consider three different scenarios for the memo to the marketing vice president requesting a pilot test of a frequent-stay incentive program.

First, assume that Cynthia Haney, vice president of marketing and your immediate superior, will be the only reader of your memo; that is, she has the authority to approve or reject your proposal. Ms. Haney is an old hand in the hotel business, having had 20 years of managerial experience, and she respects your judgment. She has made clear that she likes directness in writing and wants the important information up front—so that she can get the major ideas first and then skim, as necessary, the rest of the communication. The first paragraph of your memo to her might then use a direct approach, as follows:

> The purpose of this memo is to recommend implementing a frequent-stay plan for a 12-month test period in our three Oregon resorts. This recommendation is based on a review of the policies of our competitors and on an analysis of the costs and benefits of instituting such a program. The pertinent data is presented below.

Some readers like a direct approach, regardless of the purpose of the message.

In the next scenario, assume that Haney assumed her position at Seaside Resorts just six months ago and that she is still "learning the ropes" of the hospitality industry. Up to this point, your relationship with her has been cordial, although she is probably not very familiar with your work. That being the case, the first paragraph of your memo might use an indirect approach, in which you discuss your procedures and present the evidence before making a recommendation.

> The attached *Wall Street Journal* article discusses four large hotel chains that have started frequent-stay plans. The purpose of this memo is to describe such plans and analyze their costs and benefits. Then I will recommend what action, if any, we should take in this regard.

In a third scenario, suppose that instead of having confidence in your skills, Haney has given some indication that she *doesn't* yet completely trust your judgment. You might then be wise to add a second paragraph to establish your credibility.

> To gather the needed data, I studied published reports prepared by the Hotel and Restaurant Association. Then, I interviewed the person in charge of frequent-stay programs at three hotels. Finally, Dr. Kenneth Lowe, professor of hospitality services at Southern Cal, reviewed and commented on my first draft. Thus, this proposal is based on a large body of data collected over two months.

Establish credibility by showing the basis for your recommendations.

As can be seen, the type of information you include in your message, the amount, and the organization reflect what you know (or can learn) about your audience.

Content

Mind mapping works because brains usually don't produce ideas in a linear way, says Sonja Sakovich, president of a San Francisco consulting firm. Sakovich has introduced firms such as AT&T and Pacific Bell to mind mapping. At AT&T, systems analysts use mind mapping to clearly illustrate software and information needs. (*Fortune*, November 16, 1992, p. 12.)

Once you have determined the purpose of your message and have identified the needs and interests of your audience, the next step is to decide what information to include. For some letters and simple memos, this step presents few problems. However, many communication tasks require numerous decisions about what to include. How much background information is needed? What statistical data best supports the conclusions? Is expert opinion called for? Would examples, anecdotes, or graphics aid comprehension? Will research be necessary, or do you have what you need at hand?

The trick is to include enough information so that you don't lose the reader, yet to avoid including irrelevant material that wastes the reader's time and obscures the important data. Different writers use different methods for identifying what information is needed. Some simply jot down notes on the points they plan to cover. For all but the simplest communications, the one thing you should *not* do is to start drafting immediately, deciding as you write what information to include. Instead, start with at least a rudimentary outline of your message—whether it's in your head, in a well-developed outline, or in the form of notes on a scratch piece of paper.

One useful strategy is **brainstorming**—jotting down ideas, facts, possible leads, and anything else you think might be helpful in constructing your message. Aim for quantity, not quality. Don't evaluate your output until you've run out of ideas. Then begin to refine, delete, combine, and otherwise revise your ideas to form the basis for your message.

Do not start writing until you have planned what you want to say.

Another possible strategy is **mind mapping** (also called *clustering*), a process that avoids the step-by-step limitations of lists. Instead, you write the purpose of your message in the middle of a page and circle it. Then, as you think of possible points to add, write them down and link them by a line to either the main purpose or to another point. As you think of other details, add them where you think they might fit. This visual outline offers flexibility and encourages free thinking. Figure 5.3 shows an example of mind mapping for our frequent-stay memo.

Organization

The final step in the planning process is to establish the **organization** of the message; that is, to determine in what order to discuss each topic. After you have brainstormed or mapped out your ideas around a main idea, you need to organize them into an outline that you can use to draft your message into its most effective form.

Classification (grouping related ideas) is the first step in organizing your message. Once you've grouped related ideas, you'll then need to differentiate between the major and minor points so that you can line up minor ideas and evidence to support the major ideas.

To maintain good human relations, base your organization on the expected reader reaction.

The most effective sequence for the major ideas often depends on the reaction you expect from your audience. If you expect a positive response, you may want to use a direct approach, in which the conclusion or major idea is presented first, followed by the reasons. If you expect a negative response, you may decide to use an indirect approach, in which the reasons are presented first and the conclusion after.

FIGURE 5.3 A Sample Mind Map

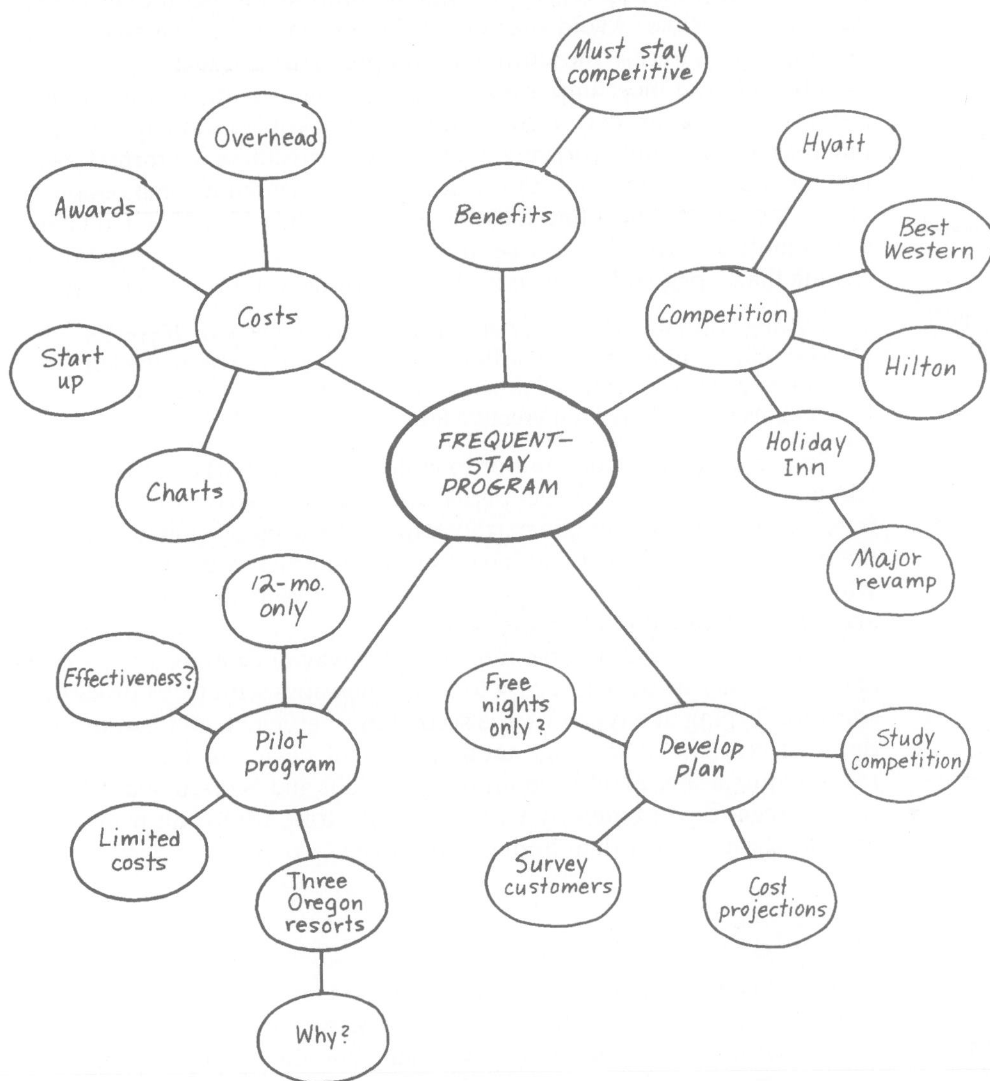

Because of the importance of the sequence in which topics are discussed, the recommended organization of each specific type of communication is discussed in detail in the chapters that follow. (See also Chapter 4's extensive coverage of paragraph unity, coherence, and length—all of which are important elements of organization.)

DRAFTING

Having now finished planning, you are ready to begin **drafting**—that is, composing a preliminary version of a message. The success of this second stage of the process depends on the attention you gave to the first stage.

The warning given earlier bears repeating: don't begin writing too early. Some people believe they have weak writing skills; when faced with a writing task, their first impulse is therefore to jump in and get it over with as quickly as possible. Avoid the rush. Follow each of the five steps of the writing process to ease the journey and improve the product.

Do not combine drafting and revising. They involve two separate skills and two separate mindsets.

Probably the most important thing to remember about drafting is to just let go—let your ideas flow as quickly as possible onto paper or computer screen, without worrying about style, correctness, or format. Separate the drafting stage from the revising stage. Although some people revise as they create, most find it easier to first get their ideas down on paper in rough-draft form, then revise. It's much easier to polish a page full of writing than a page full of *nothing*. As one writing authority has noted,

> Writing is art. Rewriting is craft. Mix the two at your peril. If you let your inner editor (who, according to popular theory, lives in the left side of your brain) into the process too early, it's liable to overpower your artist, blocking your creative flow.[1]

So avoid moving from author to editor too quickly. Your first draft is just that—a *draft*. Don't expect perfection, and don't strive for it. Concentrate, instead, on recording in narrative form all the points you identified in the planning stage. When you have finished and then begin to revise, you will likely discover that a surprising amount of your first draft is usable and will be included in your final draft.

Many writers find that the most efficient way of drafting a message is at the computer because it is easy to revise messages with word processing software. Typing at a typewriter is second most efficient, and handwriting the least efficient. (Dictating, another efficient means of inputting messages, requires special oral communication skills and is discussed in Chapter 15.) Regardless of the way you input your draft, try to edit from typed or printed copy rather than from handwritten copy.

Avoiding Writer's Block

Choose the right environment.
Schedule a reasonable block of time.
State your purpose in writing.
Engage in free writing.
Avoid the perfectionism syndrome.
Think out loud.
Write the easiest parts first.
Writer's Block

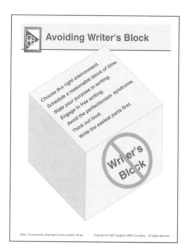

See Transparency 5.3, Avoiding Writer's Block.

Getting Started

If a report is due in five weeks, some managers (and students) spend four weeks worrying about the task and one week (or even one long weekend) actually writing the report. Similarly, when given 45 minutes to write a letter or memo, some people spend 35 minutes anxiously staring at a blank page or blank screen and 10 minutes actually writing. These people are experiencing **writer's block**—the inability to focus on the writing process and to draft a message. The causes of writer's block are typically one or more of the following:

- *Procrastination:* Putting off what we dislike doing.
- *Impatience:* Growing tired of the naturally slow pace of the writing process.
- *Perfectionism:* Believing that our draft must be perfect the first time.

Employ the power of positive thinking: You can write an effective message!

These factors naturally interfere with creativity and concentration. In addition, they lower the writer's self-image and make him or her even more reluctant to tackle the next writing task. The treatment for writer's block lies in the strategies discussed in the following paragraphs.

Even though Neil Simon writes award-winning plays for a living, he probably has experienced writer's block. Choosing the best environment in which to write is one way to avoid writer's block, and although many people prefer a room with no distractions, Simon's writing environment is filled with mementos and framed posters of his plays.

Choose the Right Environment The ability to concentrate on the task at hand is one of the most important components of effective writing. The best environment may *not* be the same desk where you normally do your other work. Even if you can turn off the phones and shut the door to visitors, silent distractions can bother you—a notation on your calendar reminding you of an important upcoming event, notes about a current project, even a photograph of a loved one. Many people write best in a library-type environment, with a low noise level, relative anonymity, and the space to spread out notes and other resources at a large table. Others find a computer room conducive to thinking and writing, with its low level of constant background noise and the presence of other people similarly engaged.

Here are a few more suggestions that may help your students overcome writer's block: try writing at a different time of day than usual, read over your notes before you exercise or go to sleep and let your unconscious work on the piece, dictate your writing task to a tape recorder, or take an exercise break. (Barbara McGarry Peters, "You Can Outwit Writer's Block," *The Writer*, December 1990, pp. 28-29, and Robert Byler, "Ten Tips for Faster and Better Writing," *The Writer*, July 1986, pp. 15-17.)

Schedule a Reasonable Block of Time If the writing task is short, you can block out enough time to plan, draft, and revise the entire message. If the task is long or complex, however, schedule blocks of no more than two hours or so. After all, writing is hard work. When your time is up or your work completed, give yourself a reward—take a break or get a snack.

State Your Purpose in Writing Having identified your specific purpose during the planning phase, write it at the top of your blank page or tack it on the bulletin board in front of you. Keep it visible so that it will be uppermost in your consciousness as you compose.

Engage in Free Writing Review your purpose and your audience; then, as a means of releasing your pent-up ideas and getting past the block, begin **free writing;** that is, write continuously for five to ten minutes, literally without stopping. Although free writing is typically considered a predrafting technique, it can also be quite useful for helping writers "unblock" their ideas.

While free writing, don't look back and don't stop writing. If you cannot think of anything to say, simply keep repeating the last word or keep writing some sentence such as, "I'll think of something soon." Resist the temptation to evaluate what you've written. (If you're composing at a computer, you may want to darken your screen so that you won't be tempted to review what you've written thus far; this is called *invisible writing*.) At the end of five or ten minutes, take a breather, stretch and relax, read what you've written, and then start again, if necessary.

Avoid the Perfectionism Syndrome Remember that the product you're producing now is a *draft*—not a final document. Don't worry about style, coherence, spelling or punctuation errors, and the like. The artist in you must create something before the editor can refine it.

Think Out Loud Some people are more skilled at *speaking* their thoughts than at writing them. Picture telling a colleague about what you're writing, and explain aloud the ideas you're trying to get across. Hearing your ideas will help sharpen and focus them.

You need not write the parts of a message in the order in which they will finally appear. Begin with the easiest parts.

Write the Easiest Parts First The opening paragraph of a letter or memo is often the most difficult one to compose. If that is the case, skip it and begin in the middle. In a report, the procedures section may be easier to write than the recommendations. Getting *something* down on paper will give you a sense of accomplishment, and your writing may generate ideas for other sections.

Try each of these strategies for avoiding writer's block at least once; then build into your writing routine those strategies that work best for you. Just as different athletes and artists use different strategies for accomplishing their goals, so do different writers. There is no one best way, so choose what is effective for you.

REVISING

Revision is the process of modifying a document to increase its effectiveness. Having the raw material—your first draft—available, you can now refine it into the most effective document possible, considering its importance and the time constraints under which you are working. If possible, put your draft away for a period of time—the longer the better. Leaving time between creation and revision helps you distance yourself from your writing. If you revise immediately, the memory of what you "meant to say" rather than what you actually wrote may be so strong that it keeps you from spotting weaknesses in logic or diction.

If you're a typical writer, you will have made numerous minor revisions even as you were composing; however, as noted earlier, you should save the major revisions until later. For important writing projects, you will probably want to solicit comments about your draft from colleagues as part of the revision process.

Although we have discussed revising as the third step of the writing process, in fact it is several steps. Most writers revise first for content, then

The process described in this chapter applies not just to writing but to preparing any form of communication. Project Director Lonnie Bunch (center)—shown here working with curators on an exhibit of American history that will travel to Japan—must consider issues of content, style, and audience to make the exhibit successful.

for style, and finally for correctness. All types of revision are most efficiently done from a typed copy of the draft rather than from a handwritten copy.

Revising for Content

Revise for content, style, and correctness.

After an appropriate time interval, first reread your purpose statement and then the entire draft to get an overview of your message. Ask yourself such questions as these:

- Is the content appropriate for the purpose I've identified?
- Will the purpose of the message be clear to the reader?
- Have I been sensitive to the needs of the reader?
- Is all the information necessary?
- Is any needed information missing?
- Is the order of presentation of the points effective?

Although it is natural to have a certain pride of authorship in your draft document, don't be afraid to make whatever changes you think will strengthen your document—even if it means striking out whole sections and starting again from scratch. The aim is to produce a revised document in which you can have even more pride.

Revising for Style

Next, read each paragraph again (aloud, if possible), using the 15 criteria contained in Checklist 1 on page 100 as the basis for your evaluation. Reading aloud gives you a feel for the rhythm and flow of your writing. Long sentences that made sense as you wrote them may leave you out of breath when you read them aloud.

If time permits and the importance of the document merits it, try reading your message aloud to friends or colleagues, or have them read your revised draft. Ask them what is clear or unclear. Can they identify the purpose of your message? What kind of image do they get of the writer just from reading the message? Making use of Checklist 1 and securing feedback from colleagues will help you identify areas of your message that need revision.

Make sure the readability of your message is appropriate for the intended audience. Calculating the readability of your draft is often a useful first step in the revision process. More important, however, is the analysis that follows the calculation. Considering what you know about the interest level, educational level, and knowledge of your audience, revise the readability of your draft as appropriate.

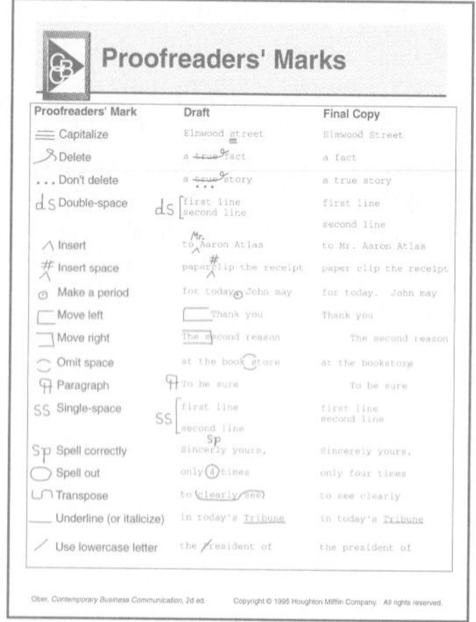

Proofreaders' Marks

Proofreaders' Mark	Draft	Final Copy
Capitalize	Elmwood street	Elmwood Street
Delete	a true fact	a fact
... Don't delete	a true story	a true story
ds Double-space	first line second line	first line second line
Insert	to Aaron Atlas	to Mr. Aaron Atlas
Insert space	paperclip the receipt	paper clip the receipt
Make a period	for today John may	for today. John may
Move left	Thank you	Thank you
Move right	The second reason	The second reason
Omit space	at the book store	at the bookstore
Paragraph	To be sure	To be sure
SS Single-space	first line second line	first line second line
Sp Spell correctly	Sincerly yours,	Sincerely yours,
Spell out	only 4 times	only four times
Transpose	to clearly see	to see clearly
Underline (or italicize)	in today's Tribune	in today's Tribune
Use lowercase letter	the President of	the president of

Ober, *Contemporary Business Communication*, 2d ed.

See Transparency 5.4, Proofreaders' Marks.

Revising for Correctness

The final phase of revising is **editing,** the process of ensuring that writing conforms to standard English. Editing involves checking for correctness, that is, identifying problems with grammar, spelling, punctuation, and word usage. Editing should follow revision, because there is no need to correct minor errors in passages that may later be revised or deleted. Writers who fail to check for grammar, mechanical, and usage errors risk losing credibility with their reader. Such errors may distract the reader, delay comprehension, cause misunderstandings, and reflect negatively on the writer's abilities.

You can write faster and revise much faster on a computer than in longhand.

All three types of revision—for content, style, and correctness—can be accomplished most efficiently on a computer (see the Spotlight on Technology).

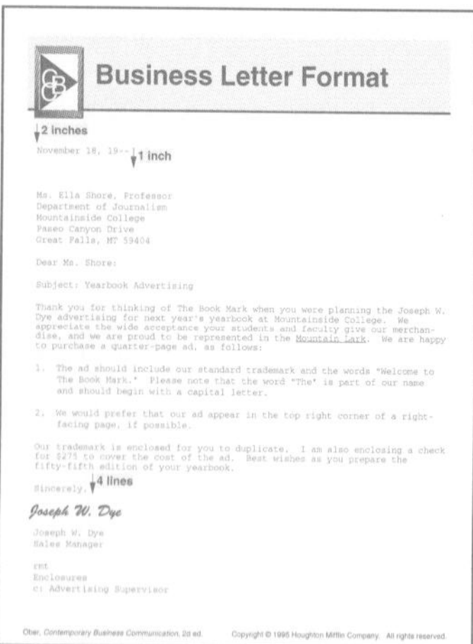

Business Letter Format

2 inches

November 18, 19-- 1 inch

Ms. Ella Shore, Professor
Department of Journalism
Mountainside College
Paseo Canyon Drive
Great Falls, MT 59404

Dear Ms. Shore:

Subject: Yearbook Advertising

Thank you for thinking of The Book Mark when you were planning the Joseph W. Dye advertising for next year's yearbook at Mountainside College. We appreciate the wide acceptance your students and faculty give our merchandise, and we are proud to be represented in the Mountain Lark. We are happy to purchase a quarter-page ad, as follows:

1. The ad should include our standard trademark and the words "Welcome to The Book Mark." Please note that the word "The" is part of our name and should begin with a capital letter.

2. We would prefer that our ad appear in the top right corner of a right-facing page, if possible.

Our trademark is enclosed for you to duplicate. I am also enclosing a check for $275 to cover the cost of the ad. Best wishes as you prepare the fifty-fifth edition of your yearbook.

Sincerely, 4 lines

Joseph W. Dye

Joseph W. Dye
Sales Manager

rmt
Enclosures
c: Advertising Supervisor

Ober, *Contemporary Business Communication*, 2d ed.

See Transparency 5.5, Business Letter Format.

FORMATTING

Letters are external documents that are sent to people outside the organization. Memos are internal documents that are sent to people inside the same organization as the writer. Reports may be either internal or external. No one format for any type of business document is universally accepted as standard; a fair amount of variation is common in industry. Detailed guidelines for the most common formatting standards are presented in the Reference Manual at the back of this text.

To some extent, technology is changing formatting standards. For example, although formatting is traditionally the next-to-last step in the writing process, you may in fact make some formatting decisions at the planning or drafting stages. For example, your word processing program has probably been set with default side margins of 1 inch, which are appropriate for most documents.

SPOTLIGHT ON TECHNOLOGY

Revising on the Computer

Given the pervasive impact of technology and the amount of time contemporary managers spend using computers, every student today should develop touch-keyboarding skills of at least 30 words per minute. Today, keyboarding must be considered a crucial *communication* skill.

Using the computer makes nearly every step of the writing process easier and more effective. Even a mediocre typist (using a hunt-and-peck style) can probably write faster at the keyboard than in longhand. Also, the fact that you can move paragraphs around lets you write the easiest parts first. Or, if you can't think of what to write in one section, you can simply space down a few lines and begin the next topic. But the point at which computers play their most effective role is during revision. For example, in addition to inserting, deleting, and changing wording, with word processing you can easily

- Move paragraphs around to achieve the most logical organization.
- Print drafts quickly (most writers find revising on paper easier than revising on a computer screen).
- Use the search-and-replace function to make a change throughout the document; for example, changing *SEC* to *Securities and Exchange Commission* in a ten-page document can be accomplished in one easy step.
- Use the thesaurus function to produce a list of synonyms for any highlighted word to help you select the word with the precise meaning that is appropriate for the particular context.
- Use the spelling function to help you proofread for typographical and spelling errors. (You should remember, though, that a spelling checker can only *help* you check for errors; words that are misused or errors that form a new word are not identified. Thus, most spelling checkers would not identify any problem with even a sentence as silly as "I mint too meat hem at $5 o'clock four a drinks.")

In addition, grammar and style checkers, which are now standard features of some word processing programs, identify possible examples of awkward writing, clichés, jargon, passive voice, mismatched punctuation marks, and the like (see the following illustration). They then propose alternatives that you can accept, reject, or mark for subsequent fixing. Many of these programs are somewhat slow and nitpicking, and many of the words and phrases they flag are, in fact, used correctly. Nevertheless, for the novice writer they promise an additional aid in improving the style of business documents.

The Original Document...

```
There is a problem of a severe nature in widget production.
It is clear that our current system will not cut the mustard.
We may possibly need to move on this reasonably quickly.  To
start, it would be advantageous to see if a new design is doable.
(This should be looked into at once.
```

RightWriter's Analysis...

```
There is a problem of a severe nature in widget production.
        <<* U12. WORDY. REPLACE   BY severe problem *>>
It is clear that our current system will not cut the mustard.
               ^<<* S14. CONSIDER OMITTING: It is clear that *>>
                      <<* S16. CLICHE: cut the mustard  *>>^
We may possibly need to move on this reasonably quickly.  To
      <<* U13. REDUNDANT. REPLACE may possibly BY may *>>
                <<* S17. WEAK: reasonably quickly *>>^
start, it would be advantageous to see if a new design is doable.
   <<* S13.REPLACE advantageous BY SIMPLER helpful or good? *>>
          <<* U16. NOT A WORD. REPLACE doable BY can be done *>>^
(This should be looked into at once.
^<<* P11. IS THIS PARENTHESIS CLOSED? *>>
                 ^<<* S1. PASSIVE VOICE: be looked *>>

                        <<** SUMMARY **>>

 Overall critique for: C:\WP\test.doc
 Output document name: C:\WP\test.out
 READABILITY INDEX: 5.23
    4th        6th        8th        10th       12th       14th
     |****|*    |    |    |    |    |    |    |    |    |
    SIMPLE     |------ GOOD ------ |                  COMPLEX
    Readers need a 5th grade level of education.
 STRENGTH INDEX:   0.00
    0.0                      0.5                     1.0
     |*   |    |    |    |    |    |    |    |    |    |
    WEAK                                             STRONG
    The writing can be made more direct by using:
                    - the active voice
                    - fewer weak phrases
                    - fewer cliches
                    - more positive wording
 DESCRIPTIVE INDEX:  0.50
    0.1                  0.5                 0.9      1.1
     |****|****|****|****|    |    |    |    |    |    |
    TERSE  | ----------- NORMAL ----------- |    WORDY
    The use of adjectives and adverbs is normal.

 JARGON INDEX: 0.00

 SENTENCE STRUCTURE RECOMMENDATIONS:
    2. Few compound sentences or subordinate
       clauses are being used.
```

Source: RightSoft, Inc., Sarasota, Florida.

CHECKLIST 2

The Writing Process

PLANNING

1. Determine the purpose of the message.
   a. Make it as specific as possible.
   b. Indicate the type of response desired from the reader.
2. Analyze the audience.
   a. Identify the audience and your relationship with this person.
   b. Determine how the audience will probably react.
   c. Determine how much the audience already knows about the topic.
   d. Determine what is unique about the audience—demographic information, interests, desired level of formality, and the like.
3. Determine what information to include in the message, given its purpose and your analysis of the audience.
4. Organize the information.
   a. Prefer a direct approach for routine and good-news messages and for most messages to superiors: present the major idea first, followed by supporting details.
   b. Prefer an indirect approach for persuasive and bad-news messages written to someone other than your superior: present the reasons first, followed by the major idea.

DRAFTING

5. Choose a productive work environment and schedule a reasonable block of time to devote to the drafting phase.

Take personal responsibility for all aspects of a message that goes out under your name.

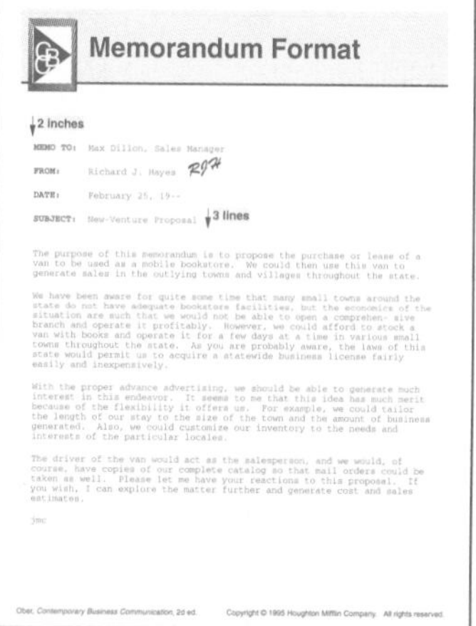
Memorandum Format

2 Inches

MEMO TO: Max Dillon, Sales Manager

FROM: Richard J. Hayes RJH

DATE: February 25, 19--

SUBJECT: New-Venture Proposal

3 lines

The purpose of this memorandum is to propose the purchase or lease of a van to be used as a mobile bookstore. We could then use this van to generate sales in the outlying towns and villages throughout the state.

We have been aware for quite some time that many small towns around the state do not have adequate bookstore facilities, but the economics of the situation are such that we would not be able to open a comprehen- sive branch and operate it profitably. However, we could afford to stock a van with books and operate it for a few days at a time in various small towns throughout the state. As you are probably aware, the laws of this state would permit us to acquire a statewide business license fairly easily and inexpensively.

With the proper advance advertising, we should be able to generate much interest in this endeavor. It seems to me that this idea has much merit because of the flexibility it offers us. For example, we could tailor the length of our stay to the size of the town and the amount of business generated. Also, we could customize our inventory to the needs and interests of the particular locales.

The driver of the van would act as the salesperson, and we would, of course, have copies of our complete catalog so that mail orders could be taken as well. Please let me have your reactions to this proposal. If you wish, I can explore the matter further and generate cost and sales estimates.

jmc

Ober, *Contemporary Business Communication*, 2d ed.

See Transparency 5.6, Memorandum Format.

In addition, E-mail messages all look like memorandums—whether they are sent to someone inside or outside the organization. They typically contain *To:*, *From:*, *Date:*, and *Subject:* lines just as memos do, and they do not contain an inside address or complimentary closing, as is typical in letters. The important point is to use the format that is appropriate for any specific message.

Regardless of who actually types your documents, *you* are the one who signs and submits them, so *you* must accept responsibility for not only the content but also the mechanics, format, and appearance of your documents. In addition, the increasing use of word processing means that executives now keyboard many of their own documents—without the help of an assistant. For example, in 1989 only 42% of top executives used personal computers regularly at work; four years later, in 1993, the number had nearly doubled, to 81%.[2]

Another advantage of standard formatting is simply that it is more efficient. Formatting the documents the same way each time means that you do not need to make layout decisions for each individual document. Thus, a standard format not only saves time but also gives a consistent appearance to the organization's documents. Finally, readers *expect* to find certain information in certain positions in a document. If the information is not there, the reader is unnecessarily distracted. For all these reasons, you should become familiar with the standard conventions for formatting documents.

6. Let your ideas flow as quickly as possible, without worrying about style, correctness, or format. If helpful, write the easiest parts first.
7. Do not expect a perfect first draft; avoid the urge to revise at this stage.
8. If possible, leave a time gap between writing and revising the draft.

REVISING

9. Revise for content: determine whether all information is necessary, whether any needed information has been omitted, and whether the content has been presented in an appropriate sequence.
10. Revise for style: follow the 15 guidelines in Checklist 1.
11. Revise for correctness: use correct grammar, mechanics, punctuation, and word choice (see the Reference Manual).

FORMATTING

12. Format the document according to commonly used standards (see the Reference Manual).

PROOFREADING

13. Proofread for content errors, typographical errors, and format errors.

PROOFREADING

Proofreading is the final quality-control check for your document. Remember that a reader may not know whether an incorrect word resulted from a simple typo or from the writer's ignorance of correct usage. And even one such error can have adverse effects. Being *almost perfect* is not good enough; for example, if your telephone directory were only 99% perfect, each page would contain about four wrong numbers! And imagine the embarrassment of the tax preparer who submitted supporting statements for a client's tax return that contained this direction: "Please reference *Lie 12* on Schedule C." (Would a computer's spelling checker have caught this error?) Or how about the newspaper ad that Continental Airline ran in the May 10, 1993, *Boston Herald,* in which the company advertised one-way fares from Boston to Los Angeles for $48. The actual one-way fare was *$148.* That typographical error cost Continental $4 million, because it sold 20,000 round-trip tickets at a loss of $200 each.[3]

Don't depend on having an assistant catch and correct every mistake; become a "super blooper snooper" yourself. It's your reputation that is at stake. Take responsibility for ensuring the accuracy of your communications, just as you take responsibility for your other managerial tasks. Proofread for content, typographical, and format errors.

- *Content Errors:* First, read through your document quickly, checking for content errors. Was any material omitted unintentionally? Unfortunately, writers who use word processing to move, delete, and insert material, sometimes omit passages unintentionally or duplicate the same passage in two different places in the document. In short, check to be sure that your document *makes sense.*

Typographical errors may send a negative nonverbal message about the writer.

- *Typographical Errors:* Next, read through your document slowly, checking for typographical errors. Watch especially for errors that form a new word; for example, "I took the figures *form* last month's reports." Such errors are difficult to spot. Also be on the lookout for repeated or omitted words. Double-check all proper names and all figures, using the original source if possible. (Don't overlook the possibility that you may have copied the words or figures incorrectly in your notes or first draft.) Professional proofreaders find that writers often overlook errors in the titles and headings of reports, in the opening and closing parts of letters and memos, and in the last paragraph of all types of documents.
- *Format Errors:* Visually inspect the document for appropriate format. Are all the parts included and in the correct position? What will be the receiver's first impression before reading the document? Does the document look attractive on the page? Do not consider the proofreading stage complete until you are able to read through the entire document without making any changes. There is always the possibility that in correcting one error you inadvertently introduced another.

Finally, after planning, drafting, revising, formatting, and proofreading your document, transmit it—with the sure knowledge and satisfaction that you've taken all reasonable steps to ensure that it achieves its objectives. The steps in the writing process are summarized in Checklist 2.

INTRODUCING MICROWRITING ACTIVITIES

For more on Microwriting activities, see the supplemental lecture/discussion notes in the *Instructor's Resource Manual,* beginning on p. 44.

Beginning with this chapter, every chapter concludes with a Microwriting activity designed to illustrate important communication concepts covered in the chapter (see the following section). These short case studies of typical communication assignments include the *problem,* the *process,* and the *product.* The problem defines the situation and discusses the need for a particular communication task. The process is a series of questions that provides step-by-step guidance for accomplishing the specific communication task. Finally, the product is the key—the finished document.

Microwriting activities guide you step-by-step through a typical writing assignment by posing and answering relevant questions about each aspect of the message.

Microwriting provides a practical demonstration of a particular type of communication, shown close up so that you can see the *process of writing,* not just the results. This process helps you focus on one aspect of writing at a time. Use the Microwriting steps regularly in your own writing so that your written communications will be easier to produce and more effective in their results.

Pay particular attention to the questions in the Process section, and ask yourself similar questions as you compose your own messages. Finally, read through the finished document, and note any changes made from the draft sentences composed in the Process section.

A Simple Memo

PROBLEM

Today is December 3, 19—, and you are Alice R. Stengren, president of the Entrepreneurial Association of Reed Northern College. *EARN* is the newest of the six student organizations in the school of business and has 38 members. It was formed two years ago when the department of management instituted a major in entrepreneurship. The purposes of EARN are (1) to provide opportunities for members to learn more about entrepreneurship, primarily through monthly meetings that feature guest speakers; (2) to provide social interactions for future entrepreneurs; and (3) to promote entrepreneurship as a major or minor course of study at the college.

To further the third purpose, the association recently voted to institute a $1,000 EARN scholarship. The scholarship will be awarded on the basis of merit to a junior or senior business student majoring in entrepreneurship at Reed Northern. Funds for the scholarship will be raised by selling coffee and doughnuts each day from 7:30 to 10:30 a.m. in the main lobby of the school of business building. Write a memo to Dean Richard Wilhite, asking permission to start this fund-raising project in January.

PROCESS

1. What is the purpose of your memo?

   Convince the dean to let EARN sell coffee and doughnuts in the main lobby from 7:30 to 10:30 a.m. daily, beginning in January.

2. Describe your primary audience.

   Dean Richard Wilhite:

   - Former president of Wilhite Energy Systems (started the company—an entrepreneur himself)
   - 46 years old; has been business dean at RNC for six years (very familiar with the school and college)
   - Nationally known labor expert
   - Holds tenure in the department of management (same department as entrepreneurship major)
   - Has spoken about the need to increase scholarships
   - Devotes a great deal of time to lobbying the legislature and raising funds (recognizes the need for fund-raising)
   - Doesn't know me personally but is familiar with EARN

3. Is there a secondary audience for your memo? If so, describe.

   No secondary audience.

4. Considering your purpose, what information should you include in the memo? (Either brainstorm and jot down the topics you might cover or construct a mind map.)

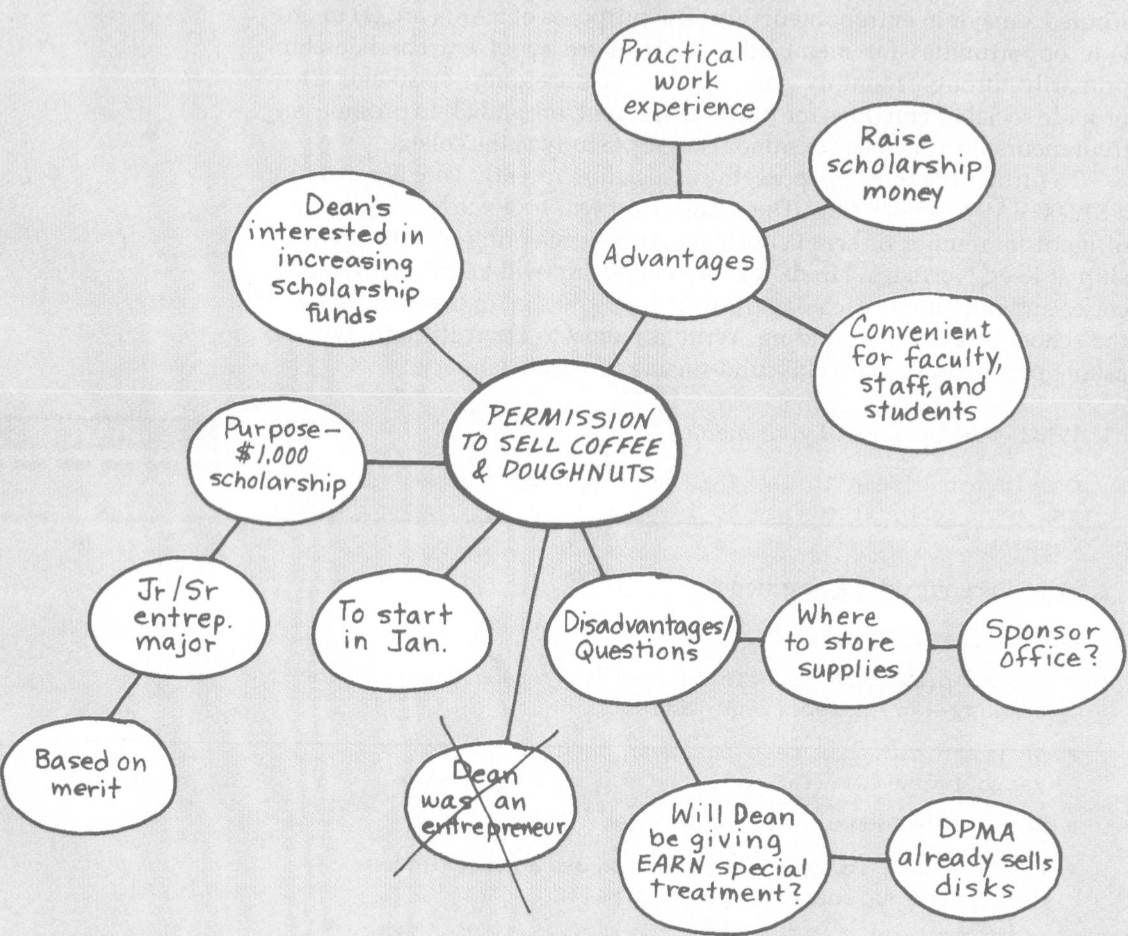

5. Jot down the major topics in the order you'll discuss them.

```
a. Dean's interest in increasing scholarships
b. Introduce scholarship and our fund-raising proposal
c. Practical work experience that members will get
d. Possible drawbacks (where to store supplies; special
   treatment for EARN)
e. Other needed details
f. Close—convenient for faculty, staff, students
```

6. Using the rough outline developed in Step 5, write your first draft. Concentrate on getting the needed information down. Do not worry about grammar, spelling, punctuation, transition, unity, and the like at this stage.

```
    The Entrepreneurial Association of Reed Northern (EARN)
shares your interest in increasing the number of
scholarships available to business majors. We recently
voted to establish an annual $1000 scholarship for a jr. or
sr. student majoring in Entrepreneurship. To fund this
scholarship, we propose selling doughnutsand coffee in the
main lobby from 7:30-10:30 a.m. daily. All of the profits
will be earmarked for the Scholarship fund. A secondary
benifit of this project is that it will provide practical
work experience for our club members. We will purchase out
own supplies and equipment, and keep careful records. When
they are not in use, the supplies and equipment will be
stored in the office of Professor Grant Edwards, our Sponsor.
DPMA follows similar procedures with it's fund raising
project of selling computer disks in the main lobby.
    We need your approval of this scholarship project in
time for us to begin in January.  This project also provides
a convenient service for faculty, staff and students.
```

7. Print out your draft and revise it for content, style, and correctness. (As needed, refer to the Reference Manual at the back of the book for guidance on grammar, mechanics, punctuation, and usage and to Checklist 1 on page 100 for style pointers.)

8. Format your revised draft, using plain paper and a standard memo style. Then proofread.

The Entrepreneurial Association of Reed Northern (EARN) shares your interest in increasing the number of scholarships available to business majors. Toward that end, We recently voted to establish an annual $1,000 scholarship for a (jr.) or (sr.) student majoring in Entrepreneurship. To fund this scholarship, we propose selling doughnuts and coffee in the main lobby from 7:30 to 10:30 a.m. daily. All ~~of the~~ profits will be earmarked for the Scholarship fund. ¶ A secondary benefit of this project is that it will provide practical work experience for our club members. We will purchase ~~out~~ our own supplies and equipment and keep careful records. When ~~they are~~ not in use, the supplies and equipment will be stored in the office of Professor Grant Edwards, our Sponsor. The (DPMA) follows similar procedures with it's fund raising project of selling computer disks in the main lobby.

~~We need~~ We look forward to receiving your approval of this ~~scholarship~~ fund-raising project in time for us to begin in January. ~~This project also provides~~ a convenient service for faculty, staff and students.

In addition to raising new scholarship money and providing work experience for our members, we will also be providing

ENTREPRENEURIAL ASSOCIATION OF REED NORTHERN

102 Waldt Hall
PH: 555–1003

MEMO TO: Dean Richard Wilhite

FROM: Alice R. Stengren, President ARS
Entrepreneurial Association of Reed Northern

DATE: December 3, 19--

SUBJECT: Establishment of EARN Scholarship

The Entrepreneurial Association of Reed Northern (EARN) shares your interest in increasing the number of scholarships available to business majors. Toward that end, we recently voted to establish an annual $1,000 scholarship for a junior or senior student majoring in entrepreneurship. To fund this scholarship, we propose selling doughnuts and coffee in the main lobby from 7:30 to 10:30 a.m. daily. All profits will be earmarked for the scholarship fund.

A secondary benefit of this project is that it will provide practical work experience for our club members. We will purchase our own supplies and equipment and keep careful records. When not in use, the supplies and equipment will be stored in the office of Professor Grant Edwards, our sponsor. The Data Processing Management Association follows similar procedures with its fund-raising project of selling computer disks in the main lobby.

We look forward to receiving your approval of this fund-raising project in time for us to begin in January. In addition to raising new scholarship money and providing work experience for our members, we will also be providing a convenient service for faculty, staff, and students.

EARN your way through college!

SUMMARY

The writing process is a series of steps designed to produce written messages in an effective and efficient manner. These steps—planning, drafting, revising, formatting, and proofreading—are summarized in Checklist 2.

The amount of time devoted to each step depends on the complexity, length, and importance of the document. Not all steps may be needed for each document, the steps don't necessarily have to come in order, and one step doesn't necessarily have to be completed before the next one begins. However, you would be well advised to follow each step consciously and carefully in the beginning. Then, after gaining experience and confidence, you can adapt the process to form a writing routine that is most effective and efficient for you personally.

KEY TERMS

For an exercise on matching terms, refer students to the *Study Guide*, p. 96.

Audience analysis Identification of the needs, interests, and personality of the receiver of a communication.

Brainstorming Jotting down ideas, facts, possible leads, and anything else that might be helpful in constructing a message.

Drafting Composing a preliminary version of a message.

Editing The stage of revision which ensures that writing conforms to standard English.

Free writing Writing continuously for 10 to 15 minutes without stopping as a means of generating a large quantity of material that will be revised later.

Mind mapping Generating ideas for message content by first writing the purpose of the message in the center of a page and circling it, then writing possible points to include, linking each one to either the purpose or to another point; also called *clustering*.

Organization The sequence in which topics are presented in a message.

Primary audience The reader of a message whose cooperation is most crucial if the message is to achieve its objective.

Revising Modifying the content and style of a draft to increase its effectiveness.

Secondary audience Any reader other than the primary audience who will be affected by the message.

Writer's block The inability to focus one's attention on the writing process and to draft a message.

REVIEW AND DISCUSSION

The answers to the review and discussion questions appear in the *Instructor's Resource Manual*, beginning on p. 47.

1. **Communication at Keep America Beautiful Revisited** ▪ Whether John Kazzi of Keep America Beautiful is writing a news release, a newsletter, or an educational article, he never loses sight of two basic elements: who his readers are and what his goals are.
   a. Identify the primary and secondary audiences for one of Kazzi's news releases.
   b. What is Kazzi's purpose in writing a news release?
   c. Describe Kazzi's relationship with the audiences for his news releases.

2. Give an example of a general purpose and a specific purpose for a particular communication task.
3. How does your relationship with the audience affect the content and tone of the message?
4. What strategies should you employ if you expect your audience (a subordinate) to react negatively?
5. Distinguish between a direct and an indirect organization plan.
6. What steps should precede the drafting stage? Why?
7. List eight possible strategies for overcoming writer's block.
8. Why should a time gap be left between writing a first draft and revising the draft?
9. Why is it generally not a good idea to combine the drafting and the revising stages?
10. Why should executives know how to format common business documents in a standard style?
11. Why should touch-keyboarding skill be considered a strategic communication skill today?
12. What three types of errors should you check for when proofreading a document?

EXERCISES

1. Microwriting a Simple Memo ▪

PROBLEM

According to a story you read in the student newspaper this morning (May 25), the president of your university has proposed to the board of trustees that beginning next year, every employee pay the same price for his or her contribution to the university's health-insurance plan—regardless of whether the employee is single, married without children, or married with children.

You are single and do not feel it is fair that single employees will be required to pay the same premium for health insurance as married employees pay for family coverage. As president of the Campus Singles Club, an organization comprised of single staff and faculty members at the university, write to the president objecting to this proposal.

PROCESS

a. What is the purpose of your memo?
b. Describe your primary audience.
c. Is there a secondary audience for your memo? If so, describe.
d. Brainstorm for a few moments, jotting down all the points you might cover in your memo.
e. Review the points you've jotted down and then list all the points you will cover—in the order you will cover them.
f. Using this rough outline, compose a first draft. Don't worry for now about style, grammar, and mechanics.
g. Print out your draft and revise it for content, style, and accuracy.

PRODUCT

Format your revised draft, using plain paper and a standard memo format. Then proofread and submit to your instructor both your memo and your responses to the above questions.

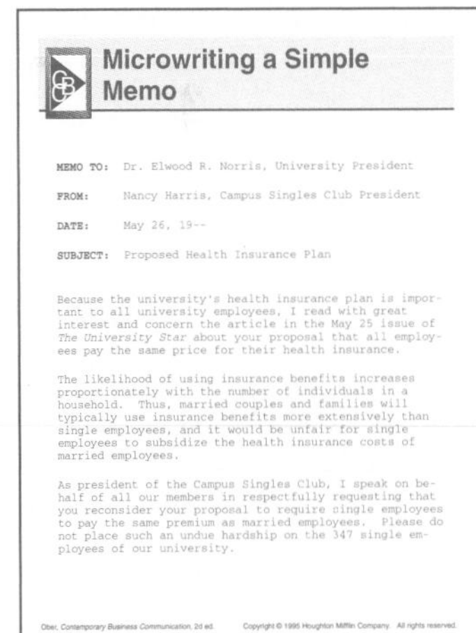
Microwriting a Simple Memo

MEMO TO: Dr. Elwood R. Norris, University President

FROM: Nancy Harris, Campus Singles Club President

DATE: May 26, 19--

SUBJECT: Proposed Health Insurance Plan

Because the university's health insurance plan is important to all university employees, I read with great interest and concern the article in the May 25 issue of *The University Star* about your proposal that all employees pay the same price for their health insurance.

The likelihood of using insurance benefits increases proportionately with the number of individuals in a household. Thus, married couples and families will typically use insurance benefits more extensively than single employees, and it would be unfair for single employees to subsidize the health insurance costs of married employees.

As president of the Campus Singles Club, I speak on behalf of all our members in respectfully requesting that you reconsider your proposal to require single employees to pay the same premium as married employees. Please do not place such an undue hardship on the 347 single employees of our university.

Ober, *Contemporary Business Communication*, 2d ed.

See Master 5.1, Exercise 1, Microwriting a Simple Memo, in the *Instructor's Resource Manual*.

Sample solutions for Exercises 2-16 appear in the *Instructor's Resource Manual*, beginning on p. 51.

2. **Communication Purpose** ▪ Compose a specific goal for each of the following communication tasks:
   a. A memo to a professor asking him to change a grade.
   b. A letter to MasterCard about an incorrect charge.
   c. A letter to the president of a local bank thanking her for speaking at your student organization meeting.
   d. A memo of reprimand to a subordinate for leaving the warehouse unlocked overnight.
3. **Communication Purpose and Reader Response** ▪ For each of the following communication tasks, indicate the specific purpose and the desired response.
   a. A letter to a state senator about a proposed state surcharge on college tuition.
   b. A memo to your payroll department head about an incorrect pay stub.
   c. A letter to the college newspaper discussing the quality of the cafeteria food in recent months.
   d. A memo to your assistant asking about the status of an overdue report.
4. **Audience Analysis** ▪ Assume you must write a letter to your current business communication professor, asking him or her to let you take your final examination one week early so that you can attend your cousin's wedding.
   a. Perform an audience analysis of your professor. List everything you know about this professor that might help you compose a more effective letter.
   b. Write two good opening sentences for this letter, the first one assuming that you are an A student who has missed class only once this term and the second assuming you are a C student who has missed class six times this term.
5. **Audience Analysis Revisited** ▪ Now assume the role of the professor (see Exercise 4) who must reply to the request of the student with the C grade who has missed class six times. You'll tell the student that you are not willing to schedule an early exam.
   a. Perform an audience analysis of yourself (as the student). What do you know about yourself that would help the professor write an effective letter?
   b. Should the professor use a direct or indirect organization? Why?
   c. Write the first sentence of the professor's letter.
6. **Free Writing** ▪ As office manager for a small insurance firm, you want to buy a scanner to use with the three IBM PowerPoint computers in your office. The scanner would let you input graphics (charts and pictures) into your computer documents and enter data without having to rekeyboard. A scanner operates like a photocopier: you feed a copy of a picture or a page of text into the machine, and the picture or text then appears on your computer screen, where it can be used by your word processing or other software programs.

   You must write a memo, the goal of which is to convince the general manager to let you buy a scanner and related software for $1,785. Think for a few moments about ways you could use this equipment. Then free write for 10 to 15 minutes without stopping and without worrying about the quality of what you're writing. (You may first want to reread the discussion of free writing on page 119 of this chapter.)

Now examine what you have written. If you were actually going to write the memo, how much of your output could you use after revision?

7. **Analysis of Primary and Secondary Audiences** ▪ Assume you are a store credit manager who has decided not to approve the credit application of a person who applied at the suggestion of a neighbor working at the store. You'll have to write a letter explaining your decision, which was based on a credit report showing the applicant's tendency to pay bills two or three months late.
   a. Who is the primary audience? List what you know about the primary audience. What does this audience know about credit and about your store? How will the audience probably react to the news in your letter? Should you use a formal or informal tone?
   b. Who is the secondary audience? List what you know about the secondary audience, including the credit manager's relationship with the secondary audience, what that audience knows about credit, and how that audience is likely to react to the message.
   c. Based on your audience analysis, should you use a direct or indirect organization? Why?
   d. Given the purpose of this letter, what information should you include?
8. **Mind Mapping (Clustering)** ▪ Assume you must write a two-page, double-spaced abstract of the important points of this chapter. *Without reviewing the chapter,* prepare a mind map of the points you might want to cover.
9. **Organizing** ▪ Prepare a rough outline for the abstract in Exercise 8, using the mind map as your guide. List the major and minor points you will cover and the order in which you will cover them. (You do not have to follow your mind map precisely; it's only for guidance.)
10. **Brainstorming and Organizing** ▪ Assume that you are going to write a letter to your state senator about a proposed state surcharge on college tuition fees. Determine a specific purpose, then brainstorm at least six facts, ideas, and questions you might want to raise in your letter. Next, decide which are major points and which are minor points. Once you've selected either a direct or an indirect approach, arrange the items on your list in logical order.
11. **Drafting** ▪ Building on the process of brainstorming and organizing in Exercise 10, draft the letter to your legislator.
    a. Write the specific purpose at the top of your blank page.
    b. Write the easiest part of the letter first. Which part did you start with? Why?
    c. Continue to draft the remaining sections of the letter. In what order did you complete your letter? Why?
    d. Did you use every fact, question, or idea on your list? Explain your choices.
12. **Collaboration** ▪ You will work in groups of four for this assignment. Assume that a large shopping center is next to your campus and many day students park there for free while attending classes. The shopping center management is considering closing this lot for student use, citing the need for additional space for customer parking. The four members of your

group represent four student organizations (a sorority, a fraternity, a business student organization, and a campus service organization), which have decided to write a joint letter to the manager of the shopping center, trying to convince him to maintain the status quo.

Following the five-step process outlined in this chapter, compose a one-page letter to the manager. Brainstorm to generate ideas for the content of the letter; have each member of the group call out possible points to include while one person writes down all the ideas. Don't evaluate any of the ideas until you have worked for 10 to 15 minutes. Then discuss each point listed and decide which ones to include and in what order.

Format your letter in block style. Address it to Mr. Martin Uthe, Executive Manager, Fairview Shopping Center, P.O. Box 1083, DeKalb, IL 60115. Type an envelope, sign and fold the letter, and insert it into the envelope before submitting it to your instructor.

13. **Revising** ▪ Revise the following draft of a memo from Tim White to Jack Presley. White is an assistant vice president and Presley is a vice president (and White's superior) at Irving Bank. After revising, format the memo in an appropriate format, using January 4 this year as the current date.

    As you know, I'm required to give numerous speeches each year for the Irving Bank. The purpose of this memo is to request funds and released time to attend the national convention of Toastmasters International, which meets February 3-6 in Honolulu, Hawaii. During the past six months I made 18 presentations to outside groups. I expect to make even more during the next six months. These presentations were to school groups, civic clubs, and professional organizations. Attending this convention will help me to sharpen my speaking skills. Also, since I chair the continuing education committee of Toastmasters International, I have scheduled a meeting of our committee for this convention. Since I'm not ordinarily very busy at this time of the year, my work here at Irving will not suffer during my four day absence. Also, when I assume my new position as assistant loan officer next year, I will be required to make numerous presentations to our board of directors.

14. **Revising** ▪ Bring in a one-page composition you have written in the past—an essay exam item, business letter, or the like. Make sure your name is *not* on the paper. Exchange papers among several colleagues (so that you are not revising the paper of the person who is revising yours) and complete the following revision tasks:

    a. Read the paper once, revising for content. Make sure that *all needed information is included,* no unneeded information is included, and the information is presented in a logical sequence.
    b. Read the paper a second time, revising for style. Make sure that the words, sentences, paragraphs, and overall tone are appropriate.
    c. Read the paper a third time, revising for correctness. Make sure that correct grammar, mechanics, punctuation, and word choice are followed.

    Return the paper to the writer. Then, using the revisions of your paper as a guide only (after all, *you* are the author), prepare a final version of the page. Submit both the marked-up version and the final version of your paper to your instructor.

15. **Proofreading** ■ Assume that you are Michael Land and you wrote and typed the following letter. Proofread the letter, using the line numbers to indicate the position of each error. Proofread for content, typographical errors, and format. For each error, indicate by a *yes* or *no* whether the error would have been identified by using a computer's spelling checker. Assume that the letter is formatted exactly as shown, but on letterhead stationery. (*Hint:* Can you find 30 content, typographical, or format errors?)

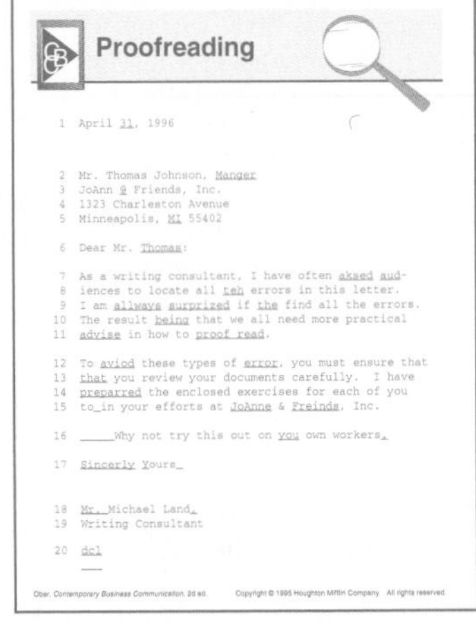

Proofreading

1 April 31, 1996

2 Mr. Thomas Johnson, Manger
3 JoAnn @ Friends, Inc.
4 1323 Charleston Avenue
5 Minneapolis, MI 55402

6 Dear Mr. Thomas:

7 As a writing consultant, I have often aksed aud-
8 iences to locate all teh errors in this letter.
9 I am allways surprized if the find all the errors.
10 The result being that we all need more practical
11 advise in how to proof read.

12 To aviod these types of error, you must ensure that
13 that you review your documents carefully. I have
14 preparred the enclosed exercises for each of you
15 to in your efforts at JoAnne & Freinds, Inc.

16 Why not try this out on you own workers.

17 Sincerly Yours

18 Mr. Michael Land,
19 Writing Consultant

20 dcl

Ober, *Contemporary Business Communication*, 2d ed.

See Master 5.2, Exercise 15, Proofreading, in the *Instructor's Resource Manual.*

1 April 31, 1996

2 Mr. Thomas Johnson, Manger
3 JoAnn @ Friends, Inc.
4 1323 Charleston Avenue
5 Minneapolis, MI 55402

6 Dear Mr. Thomas:

7 As a writing consultant, I have often aksed aud-
8 iences to locate all teh errors in this letter.
9 I am allways surprized if the find all the errors.
10 The result being that we all need more practical
11 advise in how to proof read.

12 To aviod these types of error, you must ensure that
13 that you review your documents carefully. I have
14 preparred the enclosed exercises for each of you
15 to in your efforts at JoAnne & Freinds, Inc.

16 Why not try this out on you own workers.

17 Sincerly Yours

18 Mr. Michael Land,
19 Writing Consultant

20 dcl

16. **Proofreading** ■ Imagine that you wrote and typed the following memo to the head of your college bookstore. Proofread the memo for content, typographical errors, and format using the line numbers to indicate the position of each error. For each of the 14 errors in the memo, indicate by a *yes* or *no* whether the error would have been identified by using a computer's spelling checker. Assume that the memo is formatted exactly as shown, on plain paper.

MEMO TO: Minoru Yamagishi

FROM: Sandy Gorman

DATE: November 20, 19–

SUBJECT: Topics for new Sales Training Program

The prupose of this memo is to suggest two additional topics to be included in the new sales training program. These topics relate directly to the chalenges of calling on supermarkets and chain stores, too markets we will pursue more aggressively next year.

The first topic is how to perform a market analysis. As you know, conducting a market anallysis for a large store is a more complex than conducting the same analysis for a small store. For example, our salesmen should know how to estimate the size of the trading area for both a large and small stores.

The second topic relates to the combined effect of local and and national advertising. Supermarkets in particuler are seeking new and innovative ways of using advertising to boost store traffic. If our salespeople are trained to show how our national product advertising can support the supermarket's own local advertising, we start to build a significant advantage over our competitor's.

Please let me know, if you have any questions about these two topics or if you need more information.

sg

CONTINUING CASE 5

Two Heads Are Better Than One

Last year the OIS Department installed a voice mail system. One of the features of this system is that users can now call over the telephone and dictate their correspondence and reports. All executives below the rank of vice president use the system. Three full-time transcriptionists in the OIS Department then transcribe the dictation using word processing software. Turnaround time is typically less than five hours.

One of the three transcriptionists is a full-time temporary. Yesterday, Angela Harper, one of the other two transcriptionists, told department head Eric Fox that she really wants to be able to spend more time with her three-year-old son. She asked about the possibility of job-sharing. She has a friend, Li Ying Yu, who has had extensive experience as a transcriptionist and who would also like to work half-time. Angela could work from 8 a.m. until noon daily, and Li Ying could work from 1 until 5 p.m. daily. Angela would be willing to stay a few minutes late each day, and Li Ying would be willing to come a few minutes early so that they could coordinate their work. Eric has had difficulty finding a permanent replacement for the temporary worker; he does not want to lose Angela as well.

On the plus side, if he accepts Angela's plan, he will have two highly qualified employees. If one employee is sick the other might be willing to cover for her. Two employees working only half a day would probably be more productive than one employee working the entire day, and any deficiencies in one employee might be compensated for by the other (e.g., if one employee is better at handling technical vocabulary, such dictation could be saved for her). On the negative side is the fact that there might be some coordination problems (especially in the beginning), and fringe benefits will be increased somewhat (he estimates about 15%).

Eric decides to write a memo to Neelima Shrikhande recommending the concept of job-sharing for this one position. Because job-sharing would be a new company policy, he knows that his memo will ultimately be forwarded to David Kaplan for his reaction.

A possible solution to the Continuing Case is described in the *Instructor's Resource Manual*, pp. 55–56.

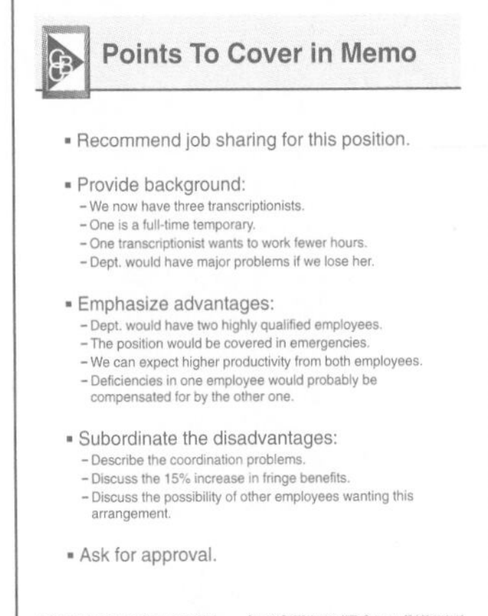

See Master 5.3, Continuing Case 5, Question 3, in the *Instructor's Resource Manual.*

Critical Thinking

1. Assume the role of Eric Fox. What is the specific goal of your memo?
2. Who are the primary and secondary audiences for this memo? What do you know about the primary audience that will help you write a more effective memo?

Writing Projects

3. List the points you should cover in the memo—in order.
4. Write a draft of the memo. (You may make up any needed information, as long as it is reasonable.)
5. Revise the draft.
6. Format the memo, proofread, and submit.

WORDWISE *How's That Again?*

Here are examples of errors that have appeared in newspapers and on student papers (none of these errors, incidentally, would have been flagged by a spelling checker):

- Harper Lee wrote *Tequila Mockingbird.*
- The vice president died of a harder tack.
- *Help Wanted:* Secretary without going personality.
- Michelangelo painted the ceiling of 16 chapels.
- Proteins are composed of a mean old acid.

PART III

BASIC CORRESPONDENCE

CHAPTER

6

Routine Messages

Communication Objectives

After you have finished this chapter, you should be able to

1. Compose a routine request.
2. Compose a routine reply.
3. Compose a routine claim letter.
4. Compose a routine adjustment letter.

In the dynamic, competitive world of stocks and bonds, no request for product information is entirely routine. At the brokerage house of Kidder, Peabody, where the pace never slows, stockbrokers have to consider each family's or company's financial situation and provide factual information while at the same time building a personal relationship. In some cases, the law requires that customers receive product information (such as the prospectus for a mutual fund) before they are allowed to invest, so answering requests for product information is an important part of the daily routine at this leading Wall Street firm.

Writing as many as 25 responses a day is not uncommon for Gwen Salley, investment executive at Kidder, Peabody, and every response has to be both accurate and professional. "My business is primarily conducted over the phone and through the mail. All my letters have to be absolutely correct in terms of spelling, grammar, and punctuation. They cannot reflect sloppiness or a lack of ability to pay attention to detail, because nobody wants to work with a broker who operates that way."

Much of the time, Salley talks with people about their financial needs and goals and then follows up with a letter enclosing the product information they have requested. Because business people get a lot of mail, she strives to capture the reader's attention in the very first sentence. "The first thing I do in my letter is to recollect something from our conversation. This helps clients recognize who is writing," she explained.

Gwen Salley

Investment executive, Kidder, Peabody and Company, Inc., New York City

Knowing that her audience doesn't have the time to read long letters, Salley tries to hold hers to one page. "I quickly get to the point by the second or third sentence. I refer to the enclosed product information and then I relate that product to the person's specific financial needs or concerns," she said. Her business card accompanies each letter, and she invites clients to call her if they have any questions. However, when writing to people who are not Kidder, Peabody clients, Salley will often end her letters by offering to call in the near future to discuss the product.

Although the objective is to provide the requested information, not to make a sale, the stockbroker also wants readers to feel comfortable about doing business with her and with the firm she represents. One way Salley builds goodwill is by briefly repeating some of the needs and goals that readers have mentioned during earlier conversations. "It shows that I listened and that I understood what they asked for. It's also an affirmation of the importance of their concerns."

A chapter overview appears in the *Instructor's Resource Manual*, pp. 58–60.

She customizes every letter, no matter how routine, and works hard to set her correspondence apart from the bulk mail and other items in an investor's mailbox. "Each letter is written specifically for that customer or prospect," Salley noted. "To personalize a letter a little more, I'll sometimes jot a handwritten note at the bottom. This indicates to the reader that the letter is not just a form letter that is sent to everyone. I want readers to see that I've considered their needs and am willing to do the little extra things that will encourage them to start or continue a relationship with me."

PLANNING THE ROUTINE MESSAGE

Most of the typical manager's correspondence consists of communicating about routine matters. For example, a small-business owner asks for a catalog and credit application from a potential supplier; a manager at a large corporation sends a memo notifying employees of a change in policy; a consumer notifies a company that an ordered product arrived in damaged condition; or a government agency responds to a request for a brochure.

Technology is enhancing employee communication, making routine interoffice communication easier and more effective. For example, UNUM Corporation's 7,000 employees use electronic mail to keep in touch, and managers at A. L. Williams insurance company's 1,000 branches use a private television network.

Although routine, such messages are of interest to the reader because the information the message contains is necessary for day-to-day operations. For example, although no company is pleased when a customer is dissatisfied with one of its products, the company *is* interested in learning about such situations so that it can correct the problem and prevent its recurrence.

When the purpose of a message is to convey routine information and our analysis of the audience indicates that the reader will probably be interested in its contents, we use a **direct organizational plan.** The main idea

The direct style presents the major idea first, followed by needed details.

is stated first, followed by any needed explanation, then a friendly closing, as illustrated in the following routine message to employees:

> From Memorial Day through Labor Day, office hours will begin and end one-half hour earlier than usual. Thus, from May 29 through September 1, the hours of operation will be from 7:30 a.m. to 4 p.m. Beginning September 5, we will switch back to our regular schedule of 8 a.m. to 4:30 p.m.
>
> As usual, the main entrance to the building will remain unlocked from one hour before to one hour after office hours. At other times, you must sign in at the security entrance on 42nd Street.
>
> We hope you will enjoy having more free time during summer daylight hours.

A 1988 study suggested that business communication is culture-specific, and business writers should understand the communication principles of the receiver's country. For example, the French organize business letters differently and use a more formal communication style than U.S. businesses. (Iris Varner, "A Comparison of American and French Business Correspondence," *The Journal of Business Communications* 25 (4), pp. 55-65.)

The advantage of using a direct organizational plan for routine correspondence is that it puts the major news first—where it stands out and gets the most attention. This saves the reader time because he or she can quickly see what the message is about by scanning the first sentence or two. The **indirect organizational plan,** in which the reasons are presented before the major idea, is often used for persuasive and bad-news messages and is covered in subsequent chapters.

Much routine information is communicated via an interoffice memorandum (called a *memo,* for short), which is a written message from one member of the organization to another. Memos differ in format from business letters (see the Reference Manual), primarily in their use of a TO:/FROM:/DATE:/SUBJECT: heading rather than the inside address, salutation, and complimentary closing used in letters.

Memos also differ in content. First, because the communication is between people who work in the same environment, the use of technical jargon, abbreviations, and the like is often appropriate because their meaning will be understood and their use saves time. The writer can typically begin a memo by directly addressing the issue at hand without the need for extensive background explanation; in fact, many memos consist of only a few sentences perhaps written in an informal style.

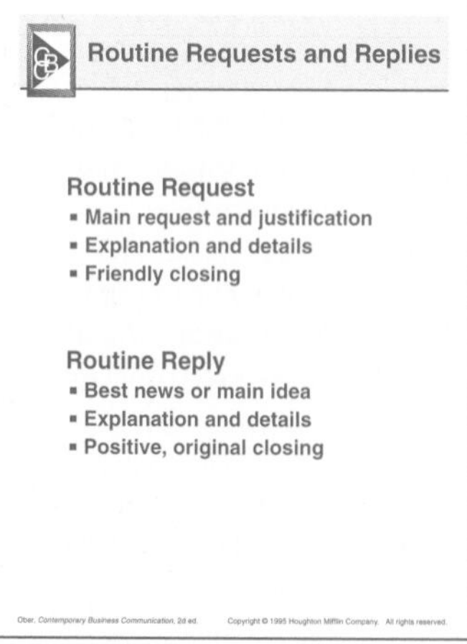

Routine Requests and Replies
Routine Request
▪ Main request and justification
▪ Explanation and details
▪ Friendly closing
Routine Reply
▪ Best news or main idea
▪ Explanation and details
▪ Positive, original closing

See Transparency 6.1, Organization of Routine Requests and Replies.

As we have seen, formal memos and letters differ in both format and content. However, as noted in Chapter 5, with the increasing use of electronic mail, the distinctions between the two are becoming less clear. Still, the principles of effective business writing discussed in Chapters 3–5 apply, regardless of the medium used to transmit the message.

Before learning how to write routine messages, you should know that many times a letter or memo is not the most efficient means of achieving your objective. Often a quick phone call or a walk down the hall to a colleague's office will work faster and at less expense than a letter or memo. However, when you need a permanent record of your message (or of the reader's response to your message) or when the topic requires elaboration, a written message is more effective.

For example, if you want to confirm that the staff meeting starts at 10 a.m. tomorrow, you would probably telephone a colleague. However, if you want to confirm that a colleague has agreed to share the cost of a new advertising campaign, you would probably want to have this information on file in a written memo.

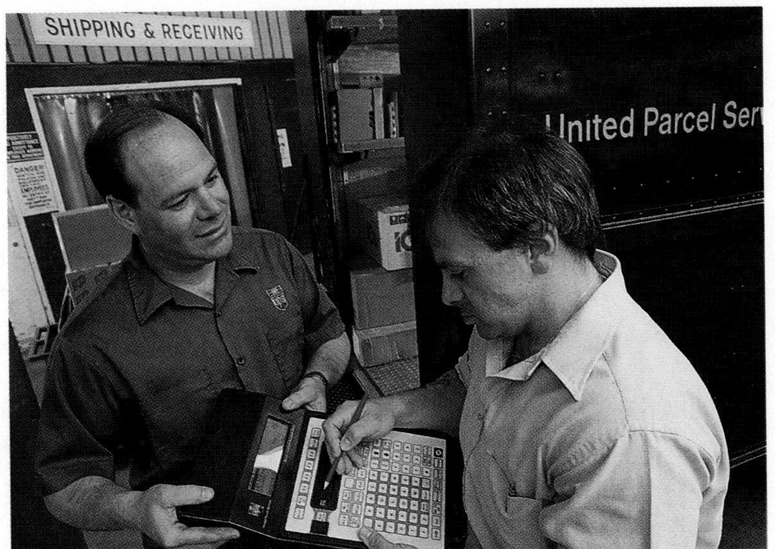

If anyone has a lot of routine information to manage, it's United Parcel Service. UPS has solved their problems by making technology portable and easy to use; here a customer writes his signature directly onto an order-taking computer.

Of course, not all messages are routine, as we will see in the following chapters. Messages that the reader is likely to resist require persuasion and are discussed in Chapter 7, messages that contain bad news are discussed in Chapter 8, and special types of messages are discussed in Chapter 9.

Use an indirect plan for letters that present negative news or anticipate reader resistance.

ROUTINE REQUESTS

A request is routine if you anticipate that the reader will readily do as you ask without having to be persuaded. For example, a request for specific information about an organization's product is routine because all organizations appreciate the opportunity to promote their products. However, a request for free samples of a company's product to distribute at your store's anniversary sale might not be routine because the company might have concluded that such promotion efforts are not cost-effective; thus, you would have to *persuade* the reader to grant the request.

Major Idea First

When making a routine request, present the major idea—your request—clearly and directly in the first sentence or two (see, however, the Spotlight Across Cultures on page 147). You may use a direct question, a statement, or a polite request to present the main idea. A polite request is a statement that is phrased as a question out of courtesy but takes a period instead of a question mark, such as "May I please have your answer by May 3." Use a polite request when you expect the reader to respond by *acting* rather than by actually giving a yes-or-no answer. Always pose your request clearly

Use a direct question, polite request, or statement to present your request.

and politely, and give any background information needed to set the stage. All of the following are effective routine requests:

Explain why you're making the request.

Direct Question: Does Black & Decker offer educational discounts for public institutions making quantity purchases of tools? Blair Junior High School will soon be replacing approximately 50 portable electric drills used by our industrial-arts students.

Statement: I would appreciate your letting me know how I might invest in your deferred money-market fund. As an American currently working in Bangkok, Thailand, I cannot easily take advantage of your automatic monthly deposit plan.

Polite Request: Would you please answer several questions about the work performance of Janice Henry. She has applied for the position of industrial safety officer at Inland Steel and has given your name as a reference.

Decide in advance how much detail you are seeking. If you need only a one-sentence reply, it would be unfair to word your request in such a way as to cause the writer to provide a three-page answer. Define clearly the type of response you want and phrase your request to elicit that response.

Not: Please explain the features of your Interact word processing program.

But: Does your Interact word processing program automatically number lines and paragraphs?

Do not ask more questions than are necessary. Make the questions easy to answer.

Remember that you are imposing on the goodwill of the reader. Ask as few questions as possible—and never for any information that you can reasonably get on your own. If many questions *are* necessary, number them; most readers will answer questions in the order in which you pose them and will thus be less likely to skip one unintentionally. Yes-or-no questions or short-answer questions are easy for the reader to answer; but when you need more information, use open-ended questions.

Arrange your questions in logical order (for example, order of importance, chronological order, or simple-to-complex order), word each question clearly and objectively (to avoid bias), and limit the content to one topic per question. If appropriate, assure the reader that the information provided will be treated confidentially.

Routine Request

Dear Ms. Pearson:

Would you please provide information regarding your banquet facilities.

We are considering holding our annual awards luncheon for 265 of our personnel at your hotel on March 25. Our decision will be based on answers to the following questions:

1. Is your facility available from 9 a.m. until 3 p.m. on that date? Although our luncheon runs from noon until 2 p.m., we need the additional time for setup and takedown.
2. Do you offer free use of audiovisual equipment? We would need an overhead projector and screen and a color display system that would enable us to project computer images. We would supply the portable computer.
3. Do you have a variety of hot lunches that can be served tableside for between $15 and $18, including tax and gratuities?

Thank you for providing this information in time for us to make our site selection by January 15.

Sincerely,

Ober, *Contemporary Business Communication*, 2d ed.

See Transparency 6.2, Routine Request Model.

Explanation and Details

Most of the time you will need to give additional explanation or details about your initial request. Include any needed background information (such as the reason for asking) either immediately before or after making the request. For example, suppose you received the polite request given earlier asking about Janice Henry's job performance. Unless you were also told that the request came from a potential employer and that Janice Henry had given your name as a reference, you might be reluctant to provide such confidential information.

SPOTLIGHT ACROSS CULTURES

When in Rome . . .

The direct organizational style is suggested for each type of message presented in this chapter. This style can be summarized in five words: *Present the major idea immediately*. American business executives have little time and patience for needless formalities and "beating around the bush."

Such is not always the case, however, when writing to someone whose culture and experiences are quite different from your own. Natives of some countries may find letters written in the direct style too harsh and abrupt, lacking in courtesy. You should therefore adapt your writing style to the expectations of the reader.

For example, an American manufacturer sent a form sales letter to many domestic and foreign retail stores, inviting inquiries about stocking its line of fishing tackle. Note the differences in two of the responses the manufacturer received:

The moral is simple. Write as your receiver expects you to write. Take a cue from his or her own writing. If the letters you receive from an international associate are written in a direct style, you may safely respond in a similar style. However, if the letters you receive are similar to the Chinese response below, you might try a more formal, less direct style when responding. Although you would not want to *adopt* the reader's style, you might need to *adapt* your own, based on your analysis of the audience.

```
Would you please send me a sample of the
fishing tackle you advertised in your
October 3 letter, along with price and
shipping information.  As a long-time
retailer of fishing tackle, I would be
especially interested in any items you
might have for fly fishing.

Since the trout season starts in six weeks,
I would appreciate having this information
as soon as possible.
```

American Response

```
It was with great pleasure that we received
your letter dated 3 October.  We send our
deepest respects and wish to inform you
that Yoon Sung Fishing Tackle Company, Ltd.,
has been selling fishing items for 38 years.

We would be pleased to consider your
merchandise.  May we ask you to please send
us samples, price, and shipping information.
It will be a great pleasure to conduct
business with your company.
```

Chinese Response

For an extended discussion of international issues, see "Diversity and Communication" in Chapter 2, pp. 34–39.

Or assume that you're writing to a former employer or professor asking for a letter of recommendation. You might need to give some background about yourself to jog the reader's memory. Or you might need to justify or expand on your request. Put yourself in the reader's position. What information would you need to answer the request accurately and completely?

If possible, show how others benefit from your having the requested information.

A reader will be more likely to cooperate if you can show how he or she will benefit from agreeing to your request. In fact, it is often the communication of such benefits that makes the message routine rather than persuasive.

> Will you please help us serve you better by answering several questions about your banking needs. We're building a branch bank in your neighborhood and would like to make it as convenient for you as possible.

In general, you should identify reader benefits when they may not be obvious to the reader, but you need not belabor the point if such benefits are obvious. For example, a memo asking employees to recycle their paper and plastic trash would probably not need to discuss the value of recycling since most readers would already be familiar with the advantages of recycling.

Friendly Closing

Close on a friendly note.

For more on routine requests, see the supplemental lecture/discussion notes in the *Instructor's Resource Manual*, p. 60.

In your final paragraph, assume a friendly tone. If you are writing to an individual, enclosing a stamped and addressed reply envelope is a courteous gesture; most businesses, on the other hand, would prefer to use their own preprinted envelopes. Close by expressing appreciation for the assistance to be provided (but without seeming to take the recipient's cooperation for granted), by stating and justifying any deadlines, or by offering to reciprocate. Make your ending friendly and positive, as illustrated by the following examples:

> Please let me know if I can return the favor.
>
> We appreciate your providing this information, which will help us make a fairer evaluation of Janice Henry's qualifications for this position.
>
> May I please have the product information by October 1, when I place my Christmas wholesale orders. That way, I will be able to include Kodak products in my holiday sales.

Figure 6.1 illustrates these guidelines for writing a routine request.

If your students need practice punctuating sentences, refer them to LAB 1 for commas or LAB 2 for other punctuation marks.

Routine Replies

Routine replies provide the information requested in the original letter or otherwise comply with the writer's request. Like the original request letters, they are organized in a direct organizational style, putting the "good news"—the fact that you're responding favorably—up front.

Respond promptly so that the information will arrive in time to be used.

For an exercise in writing a routine-reply message, see Video Case Study 1, Chiat/Day.

Probably one of the most important guidelines to follow is to answer promptly. If a potential customer asks for product information, ensure that the information arrives before the customer must make a purchase decision. Otherwise, the time it took you to respond will have been wasted. Also, delaying a response might send the unintentional nonverbal message that you do not want to comply with the writer's request.

Your response should be courteous. If you appear to be acting grudgingly, you will probably lose any goodwill that a gracious response might have earned for you or your organization.

> *Not:* Although we do not like to provide the type of information you requested, we have decided to do so in this case.
>
> *But:* We are happy to provide the information you requested.

Grant the request or give the requested information early in the message. Doing so not only saves the reader's time but also puts him or her in a good state of mind immediately. Although the reader may be pleased to hear that "We have received your letter of June 26," such news is not nearly so eagerly received as telling the reader that "I would be pleased to speak at your Lion's Club meeting on August 8; thanks for thinking of me." Put the good news up front—where it will receive the most emphasis.

FIGURE 6.1 Routine Request

This letter is from a potential customer to a manufacturer.

H S P
Home Security Products
Box 302, Edenton, NC 27932
919-555-4022

September 3, 19--

Mr. Albert Gleason, Sales Manager
Saito Printers, Inc.
4480 Thrush Way
El Paso, TX 79922

Dear Mr. Gleason:

Would you please provide me with information regarding your Saito 150 portable
1 printer. I am interested in purchasing 34 lightweight printers that our
marketing representatives can use with their Toshiba 1200XE notebook computers
when they travel.

Presents the request in the first sentence, followed by the reason for asking.

Specifically, I would like answers to the following four questions:

1. Does the Saito 150 produce letter-quality output?

2. Is it battery-operated? (Since we wish to use the printer for traveling, such a feature is important.)

3. Does the printer have a 15-inch carriage?

4. Does it come with a six-month guarantee?

Enumerates questions for emphasis and clarity; makes questions easy to answer.

2 I would appreciate your faxing me the information I need to make a purchase
(Fax: 919-555-0327). I would also appreciate receiving ordering information.

Expresses appreciation; hints at a reader benefit.

Sincerely,

Carolyn J. Ryerson

Carolyn J. Ryerson
Purchasing Director

ref
3 By Fax

Grammar and Mechanics Notes

1 *Your Saito 150 portable printer.*: Use a period after a polite request. 2 *appreciate your faxing:* Use the possessive form of a pronoun (*your*) before a gerund (*faxing*). 3 Type a delivery notation (such as *By Fax* or *By Federal Express*) below the reference initials (or below any enclosure or copy notation). One advantage of facsimile (fax) messages over E-mail is that fax messages can be prepared on the organization's letterhead stationery.

Routine Reply

Dear Mr. Olson:

We would enjoy hosting your awards luncheon for 265 guests on March 25. Our 29th floor L'Enfant Room, which seats 300 banquet-style and has a lovely view of the Cleveland skyline, is available until 4:30 p.m. that day.

To provide round-the-clock expert service for our business and convention guests, we have contracted with an outside firm to provide all audiovisual equipment services for a nominal charge. You may make arrangements directly with GuestServ by calling them at 555-1086.

For the health-conscious guest, we offer a variety of soup-and-salad lunches for between $12 and $18, including beverage, tax, and gratuity. We also offer a hot buffet line with your choice of two main dishes for between $16 and $20. Hot meals served tableside begin at $19.75 for our popular braised chicken with currant sauce.

No matter what your choice, you will find that our facilities, food, and service live up to the "Cleveland's finest" label recently awarded to us by *Cleveland Monthly* magazine. Please call me on my direct line at 555-3288 to let me know how the Berkshire might serve your organization.

Sincerely,

Ober, *Contemporary Business Communication*, 2d ed.

See Transparency 6.3, Routine Reply Model.

Be sure to answer all the questions asked or implied, using objective and clearly understood language. Although it is often helpful to provide additional information or suggestions, you should never fail to at least address all the questions asked—even if your answer is not what the reader hopes to hear. Questions are usually answered in the order in which they were asked, but consider rearranging them if a different order makes more sense. Determining what your reader already knows about the topic should help you decide what information to include and how to phrase it.

The reader will probably be in a positive mood as the result of your letter, and you may consider either including some sales promotion if appropriate or building goodwill by implying such characteristics about your organization as public spiritedness, quality products, social responsibility, or concern for employees. To be effective, sales promotion and goodwill appeals should be subtle; avoid exaggeration and do not devote too much space to such efforts.

Often the writer's questions have been asked by others many times before; in such a situation, a form letter may be the most appropriate way to respond. A **form letter** is a letter with standardized wording that is sent to different people. With word processing, it is often difficult to tell the difference between a form letter and a personal letter. If a stockholder wrote asking why your company conducted business in South Africa, a personal reply would probably be called for. However, if a potential stockholder wrote asking for a copy of your latest annual report, you might simply send an annual report, along with a form letter such as the following:

Consider using form letters for answering frequent requests.

> We are happy to send you our latest annual report. Also enclosed is a copy of a recent profile of Dennison Industries contained in the June issue of *Fortune* magazine.
>
> As you study our annual report, note the diversity of our product offerings—from men's clothing to massive earth movers. This diversity is one of the reasons we have shown a profit for each of the past 57 years. Our 5-, 10-, and 15-year income statements are shown on page 8 of the enclosed report.
>
> Dennison Industries stock is traded on the New York Stock Exchange, listed under "DenIn." Simply call your local broker to join the 275,000 other satisfied investors in Dennison Industries common stock.

Refer to any enclosures in your letter to make sure they are read.

In the body of your message, refer to any enclosure and then add an enclosure notation at the bottom of the letter. Referring to a specific page of an enclosed brochure or to a particular paragraph of an enclosed document helps ensure that such enclosures will be read.

Close your letter on a positive, friendly note. Avoid such clichés as "If you have additional questions, please don't hesitate to let me know." Use original wording, personalized especially for the reader. After all, the reader might receive many letters like yours, and if he or she has already encountered "Thank you for your interest in our products" five times that day, the expression will sound trite and insincere.

Use positive language to create a positive impression.

Figure 6.2 is a routine reply to the request shown in Figure 6.1. The original request asked four questions about the printer, and the answers are as follows: (1) No, the printer does not produce true letter-quality output;

FIGURE 6.2 Routine Reply

This letter responds to the request in Figure 6.1.

SAITO
PRINTERS
4480 Thrush Way ▪ El Paso, TX 79922 ▪ Telephone: 915-555-9335

September 12, 19--

Ms. Carolyn J. Ryerson
Purchasing Director
Home Security Products
Box 302
Edenton, NC 27932

Dear Ms. Ryerson:

Yes, our popular Saito 150 portable printer does come with a 15-inch carriage. This wider carriage will enable your representatives to print out even your most complex spreadsheets while on the road. Of course, the pinstops also adjust easily to fit standard 8½-by-11-inch paper. .

Begins by answering the "yes" question first.

1 For quiet operation late at night in your hotel room, the Saito uses ink-jet
printing. This technology provides nearly the same quality output as a laser
2 printer at less than half the cost. Either plain paper or specially coated
paper may be used.

Answers all questions, using positive language and pointing out the benefits of each feature.

Although many travelers use their laptop computers on a plane or in their
automobiles, our research shows that they typically wait until reaching their
destination to print out their documents. Thus, the Saito uses AC power only,
3 thereby reducing its weight by nearly a pound. The extra-long 12-foot power
cord will let you power-up your printer easily no matter where the electrical
outlet is hidden. And our 30-day warranty, standard in the computer industry,
ensures the reliability and trouble-free service that our customers have come
to expect of all Saito products.

Uses paragraphs instead of enumeration to answer each question because each answer requires elaboration.

4 To order or take the Saito 150 for a test drive, call your local Computerland
(Phone: 800-555-2188). They will show you how to increase your productivity
while increasing your luggage weight by less than 4 pounds.

Gives important purchase information; closes on a forward-looking note.

Sincerely yours,

Albert Gleason

Albert Gleason
Sales Manager

juc
By Fax

Grammar and Mechanics Notes

1 *ink-jet printing:* Hyphenate a compound adjective before a noun. 2 *specially coated paper:* Do not hyphenate a compound adjective if the first word ends in *-ly*. 3 *its:* Do not confuse *its* (the possessive pronoun) with *it's* (the contraction for *it is*). 4 *a test drive,:* Place a comma after an introductory expression.

CHECKLIST 3

Routine Requests and Replies

ROUTINE REQUESTS

1. Present the major request in the first sentence or two, preceded or followed by reasons for making the request.

2. Provide any needed explanation or details.

3. Phrase each question so that it is clear, is easy to answer, and covers only one topic. Ask as few questions as possible, but if several questions are necessary, number them and arrange them in logical order.

4. If appropriate, incorporate reader benefits and promise confidentiality.

5. Close on a friendly note by expressiong appreciation, justifying any necessary deadlines, offering to reciprocate, or otherwise making your ending personal and original.

For other examples of routine responses, see the *Instructor's Resource Manual*, pp. 82, 83, 84, 85, and 86.

(2), No, it is not battery operated; (3) Yes, it does have a 15-inch carriage; and (4) No, it does not come with a six-month warranty. As you can see, only one of the four questions can be answered with an unqualified "yes," and that is the question the respondent chose to lead off with. Positive language helps soften the impact of the negative responses to the other three questions. Also, reader benefits are stressed throughout the letter. Instead of just describing the features, the writer shows how the features can benefit the reader.

Checklist 3 summarizes the points you should consider when writing and responding to routine requests. Use this checklist as a guide in structuring your message and in evaluating the effectiveness of your first draft.

ROUTINE CLAIM LETTERS

Routine Claim and Adjustment Letters

Routine Claim Letter

- Identify the problem.
- Provide necessary details using objective, courteous language.
- Ask confidently for action.

Routine Adjustment Letter

- Respond promptly.
- Give the good news up front.
- Briefly explain what went wrong and how you fixed the problem.
- Reestablish the customer's confidence.
- Close on a confident, forward-looking note.

Ober, *Contemporary Business Communication*, 2d ed.

See Transparency 6.4, Organization of Routine Claim and Adjustment Letters.

A **claim letter** is written by the buyer to the seller, seeking some type of action to correct a problem with the seller's product or service. The purchaser may be an individual or an organization. A claim letter differs from a simple complaint letter in that it requests some type of adjustment (such as repairing or replacing the product). As a matter of fact, many complaint letters would probably be more successful if they carried an implied claim that the writer wanted some adjustment to be made as a result of poor service, unfair practices, or the like. The desired adjustment might be nothing more than an explanation or apology, but the mere fact that you request some direct action will increase your chances of getting a satisfactory response.

A claim letter can be considered routine if you can reasonably anticipate that the reader will comply with your request. If, for example, you ordered a shipment of shoes for your store that were advertised at $23.50 each and the wholesaler charged you $32.50 instead, you would write a routine claim letter, asking the seller to correct the error. But suppose the wholesaler marked the price down to $19.50 two days after you placed your order. Then instead of writing a routine claim letter, you might want

6. If writing to an individual or nonprofit organization, enclose an addressed and stamped envelope for reply.

ROUTINE REPLIES

1. Answer promptly and graciously.
2. Grant the request or begin giving the requested information in the first sentence or two.
3. Address all questions asked or implied; include additional information or suggestions if helpful.
4. Include subtle sales promotion if appropriate.
5. Consider developing a form letter for frequent requests.
6. Refer to any items you enclose with the letter, and insert an enclosure notation at the bottom.
7. Close on a positive and friendly note, use original wording, and avoid such clichés as "If you have any further questions, please let me know."

to write a persuasive letter, trying to convince the wholesaler to give you the lower price. (Persuasive letters are discussed in the next chapter.)

Contemporary corporate culture places a premium on quality, and most companies make a genuine effort to settle claims from customers. They want to know if their customers are dissatisfied with their products so that they can correct the situation. A dissatisfied customer may not only refuse to purchase additional products from the offending company but may also tell others about the bad experience. One study of consumers showed that the typical dissatisfied customer tells nine or ten other people about the incident and that each of them, in turn, tells four or five more people. The typical satisfied customer, on the other hand, recommends the product or service to four or five other people.[1]

Write your claim letter promptly—as soon as you've identified a problem. Delaying unnecessarily might not only push you past the warranty date but might also raise suspicions about the validity of your claim; the more recent the purchase, the more valid your claim will appear.

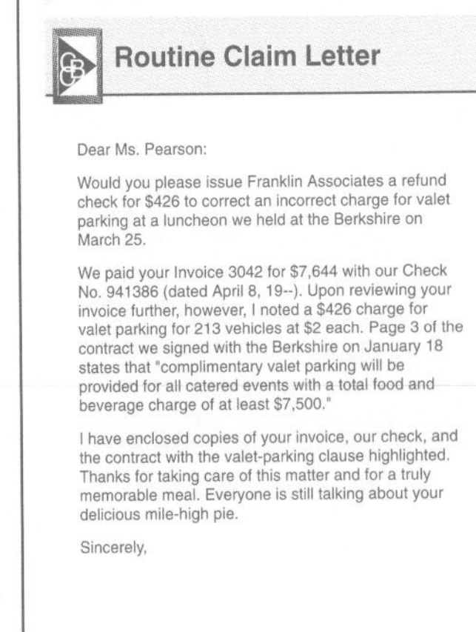
Routine Claim Letter

Dear Ms. Pearson:

Would you please issue Franklin Associates a refund check for $426 to correct an incorrect charge for valet parking at a luncheon we held at the Berkshire on March 25.

We paid your Invoice 3042 for $7,644 with our Check No. 941386 (dated April 8, 19--). Upon reviewing your invoice further, however, I noted a $426 charge for valet parking for 213 vehicles at $2 each. Page 3 of the contract we signed with the Berkshire on January 18 states that "complimentary valet parking will be provided for all catered events with a total food and beverage charge of at least $7,500."

I have enclosed copies of your invoice, our check, and the contract with the valet-parking clause highlighted. Thanks for taking care of this matter and for a truly memorable meal. Everyone is still talking about your delicious mile-high pie.

Sincerely,

Ober, *Contemporary Business Communication*, 2d ed.

See Transparency 6.5, Routine Claim Model.

Although some consumer advocates suggest addressing your claim letter to the company president, business courtesy argues for first giving the company's order department or customer relations department an opportunity to solve the problem. Such departments are designed to handle these problems most efficiently; and their employees are the most knowledgeable about specific company policies and procedures, product history, warranty information, decisions in similar cases, and the like. Only if your claim is not settled satisfactorily at this level should you then appeal to a higher level of management in the company.

Assume a courteous tone; avoid emotionalism.

Although you may be frustrated or angry as a result of the situation, remember that the person to whom you're writing was not *personally* responsible for your problem. Be courteous and avoid emotional language. Assume that the company is reasonable and will do as you reasonably ask. Avoid any hint of anger, sarcasm, threat, or exaggeration. A reader who becomes angry as a result of the strong language in your claim letter will be less likely to do as you ask. Instead, using factual and unemotional language, begin your routine claim letter directly, telling exactly what the problem is.

McDonald's, USAir, Federal Express, and Clairol are just a few of the many companies that see customers' complaints as a way to improve service. Their policies are to respond positively to customers' claims by answering their letters and offering gift certificates or replacement merchandise. (Bill Kelley, "Reality Check," *Sales & Marketing Management*, January 1993, pp. 50-53.)

Not: You should be ashamed at your dishonest advertising for the videotape *Safety Is Job One.*

But: The videotape *Safety Is Job One* that I rented for $125 from your company last week lived up to our expectations in every way but one.

Not: I am disgusted at the way United Express cheated me out of $12.50 last week. What a rip-off!

But: An overnight letter that I mailed on December 3 did not arrive the next day, as promised by United Express.

After you have identified the problem, begin your explanation. Provide as much background information as necessary—dates, model numbers, amounts, photocopies of canceled checks or correspondence, and the like. Use a confident tone and logic (rather than emotion) to present your case. Write in an impersonal style, avoiding the use of *you* pronouns so as not to link your reader too closely to the negative news.

Provide needed details.

Not: I delivered this letter to *you* sometime in the early afternoon on December 3. Although *you* promised to deliver it by 3 p.m. the next day, *you* failed to do so.

But: As shown on the enclosed copy of my receipt, I delivered this letter to United Express at 3:30 p.m. on December 3. According to the sign prominently displayed in the office, any package received by 4 p.m. is guaranteed to arrive by 3 p.m. the following business day.

If possible, mention something positive about the product.

Tell exactly what went wrong and how you were inconvenienced. If it is true and relevant, mention something positive about the company or its products to make your letter appear reasonable.

> According to the enclosed receipt, my letter was not delivered until 8:30 a.m. on December 5. Because the letter contained material needed for a dinner meeting on December 4, it arrived too late to be of any use. This is not the type of on-time service I've routinely received from United Express during the eight years I've been using your delivery system.

Finally, tell what type of adjustment you expect. Do you want the company to replace the product, repair it, issue a refund, simply apologize, or what? End the letter on a confident note.

> I would appreciate your refunding my $12.50, thereby reestablishing my confidence in United Express.

In some situations, you may not know what type of adjustment is reasonable; then, you would leave it up to the reader to suggest an appropriate course of action. This might be the situation when you suffered no monetary loss but simply wish to avoid an unpleasant situation in the future (such as discourteous service, long lines, or ordering the wrong model because of having received incomplete or misleading information).

> Please let me know how I might avoid this problem in the future.

Figure 6.3 illustrates a routine claim letter about a defective product, asking for a specific remedy. Figure 6.4 illustrates a routine claim letter about poor service, leaving the type of adjustment up to the reader.

FIGURE 6.3 Routine Claim—Remedy Specified

This claim letter is about a defective product.

AH

April 15, 19--

Customer Relations Representative
Color-Vu Graphics
P.O. Box 210742
Dallas, TX 75211

1 Dear Customer Relations Representative:

Subject: Poor Quality of Slides from Invoice 4073

The poor quality of the 13 color slides you processed for me on April 8 made them unsuitable for use in my recent presentation to 200 marketing representatives. As a result, I had to use black-and-white transparencies instead.

Identifies the problem immediately and tells how the writer was inconvenienced.

The enclosed slide is typical of all 13 slides from this order. As you can
2 see, the colors often run together and the type is fuzzy. The slides are not
equivalent in quality to those illustrated in the Color-Vu advertisement on
3 page 154 of the April Business Management.

Provides the needed details in a non-emotional, businesslike manner.

I have already given the presentation for which these slides were made, so redeveloping them would not solve the problem. Because I have not yet paid your Invoice 4073 for $176.50, dated April 12, would you please cancel this charge. If you would like me to return the other 12 slides, I shall be happy to do so.

Identifies and justifies the specific remedy requested.

4 I know that despite one's best efforts, mistakes will occasionally happen, and I am confident that you will correct the problem promptly.

Closes on a confident note.

Sincerely,

Claire D. Scriven

Claire D. Scriven
Marketing Manager

ric
Enclosure

AMERICAN HOMES
642 Poplar Street ▪ Denver, CO 80220
303-555-2118

Grammar and Mechanics Notes

1 If an addressee's name is unknown, you may use a title in both the inside address and the salutation. 2 *run together and:* Do not insert any punctuation before the *and* separating the two independent clauses because the second clause, "the type is fuzzy," is so short. 3 *April Business Management:* Underline or italicize magazine titles. 4 *occasionally* has two *c*'s and one *s*.

FIGURE 6.4 Routine Claim—Remedy Not Specified

This claim letter is about poor service.

AH

April 15, 19--

Mr. Philip Williams
General Manager
Ambassador Hotel
101 Grant Street
Denver, CO 80203

Dear Mr. Williams:

Presents a balanced view of the problem.

I feel sure you will want to know about our recent experience at your hotel. Although our sales representatives who stayed there last week thought your deluxe rooms were beautiful, they also thought the housekeeping service was substandard.

Provides the needed details.

We rented 218 single rooms on April 10-12 for our annual marketing managers' 1
conference. When a few representatives complained about the housekeeping
service, I explored the matter further. Here's what I learned: 2

Enumerates specific examples—for credibility—and tells how the guests were inconvenienced.

1. Six people commented that at least one lamp in their room had a burned-out light bulb. Because they worked on projects late each night, the lack of adequate lighting was an inconvenience.

2. Twelve people commented that their rooms sometimes were not cleaned until 3
after 5 p.m., even though they were out of the room all day. They were then disturbed during their evening working hours when the housekeepers showed up to clean the rooms.

3. Others spoke about the general uncleanliness of their rooms.

Appears reasonable by also presenting positive comments; leaves the specific remedy to the reader; implies a possible future reader benefit.

Because our 200 representatives have enjoyed meeting at the Ambassador in the past, won't you please let me know how I can be assured that the housekeeping service will be up to your usual high standards in the future.

Sincerely,

Claire D. Scriven

Claire D. Scriven
Marketing Manager

ric

AMERICAN HOMES
642 Poplar Street ■ Denver, CO 80220
303-555-2118

Grammar and Mechanics Notes

1 *April 10-12:* Do not space before or after the hyphen. 2 Do not confuse *further* (to a greater degree) with *farther* (distance). 3 *Twelve people:* Spell out a number that begins a sentence.

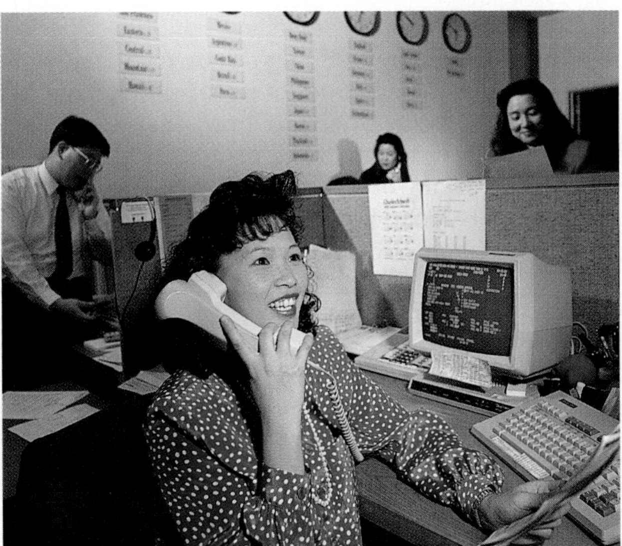

Because communication is "routine" doesn't mean it's in English. Charles Schwab's San Francisco office is equipped to take stock orders in several Asian languages.

ROUTINE ADJUSTMENT LETTERS

An **adjustment letter** is written to inform a customer of the action taken in response to the customer's claim letter. Few people bother to write a claim letter unless they have a real problem, so most claims companies receive are legitimate and are adjusted according to the individual situation. If the action taken is what the customer asked for or expected, a routine adjustment letter using the direct organizational plan would be written.

An adjustment letter responds to a claim letter.

You should note that *anyone* in an organization may be called upon to write claim and adjustment letters—not just those working in purchasing or sales or customer service. For example, an accounting manager may send (and receive) a letter complaining of poor service from an employee.

Overall Tone

A claim represents a possible loss of goodwill and confidence in your company or its products. Because the customer is upset, the overall tone of your adjustment letter is crucial. Since you have already decided to honor the claim, your best strategy is to adopt a gracious, trusting tone. Give your customer the benefit of the doubt. It does not make sense to adopt a grudging or resentful tone and risk losing whatever goodwill you might have gained from granting the adjustment.

Adopt a gracious, confident tone for your adjustment letters.

Not: Although our engineers do not understand how this problem could have occurred if the directions had been followed, we are nevertheless willing to repair your generator free of charge.

But: We are happy to repair your generator free of charge. Within ten days, a factory representative will call you to schedule a convenient time to make the repair.

Avoid using negative language when describing the basis for the claim.

Your overall tone should show confidence both in the reader's honesty and in the essential worth of your own company and its products. To the extent possible, use neutral or positive language in referring to the claim (for example, write "the situation" instead of "your complaint"). Also avoid appearing to doubt the reader. Instead of saying "you claim that," use more neutral wording, such as "you state that."

Finally, respond promptly. Your customer is already upset; the longer this anger remains, the more difficult it will be to overcome.

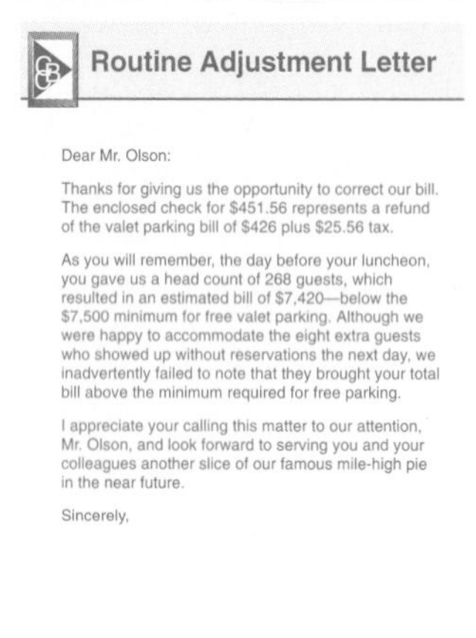

Routine Adjustment Letter

Dear Mr. Olson:

Thanks for giving us the opportunity to correct our bill. The enclosed check for $451.56 represents a refund of the valet parking bill of $426 plus $25.56 tax.

As you will remember, the day before your luncheon, you gave us a head count of 268 guests, which resulted in an estimated bill of $7,420—below the $7,500 minimum for free valet parking. Although we were happy to accommodate the eight extra guests who showed up without reservations the next day, we inadvertently failed to note that they brought your total bill above the minimum required for free parking.

I appreciate your calling this matter to our attention, Mr. Olson, and look forward to serving you and your colleagues another slice of our famous mile-high pie in the near future.

Sincerely,

Ober, *Contemporary Business Communication*, 2d ed.

See Transparency 6.6, Routine Adjustment Letter Model.

Good News First

Nothing that you are likely to tell the reader will be more welcomed than the fact that you are granting the claim, so put this news up front—in the very first sentence if possible. The details and background information will come later.

> A new copy of the *American World Dictionary* is on its way to your office, and I assure you that no pages are missing from this copy. I checked it myself!
>
> The enclosed $12.50 check reimburses you for your company's delayed overnight letter. Thank you for bringing this matter to my attention.
>
> Thanks to you, we have undertaken a new training program for our housekeeping staff. Please use the enclosed coupon for two nights' free stay at the Ambassador to see for yourself the difference your letter has made.

It is appropriate to apologize for serious problems.

It is often appropriate to thank the reader for giving you an opportunity to resolve the situation, but what about apologizing? An apology, which tends to emphasize the negative aspects of the situation, is probably not necessary for small, routine claims that are promptly resolved to the customer's satisfaction. Instead, emphasize the positive aspects and look forward to future transactions. If, however, the customer has been severely inconvenienced or embarrassed and the company is clearly at fault, a sincere apology would be in order. In such a situation, first give the good news and then apologize in a businesslike manner; avoid repeating the apology in the closing lines.

> I have contracted with a local mason to rebuild your home's brick walkway, which our driver mistakenly damaged on February 23. I am truly sorry for the inconvenience this situation has caused you and am grateful for your understanding.

Explanation

After presenting the "good news," you must educate your reader as to why the problem occurred and, if appropriate, what steps you've taken to make sure it doesn't recur. Explain the situation in sufficient detail to be believable, but don't belabor the reason for the problem. Emphasize the fact that

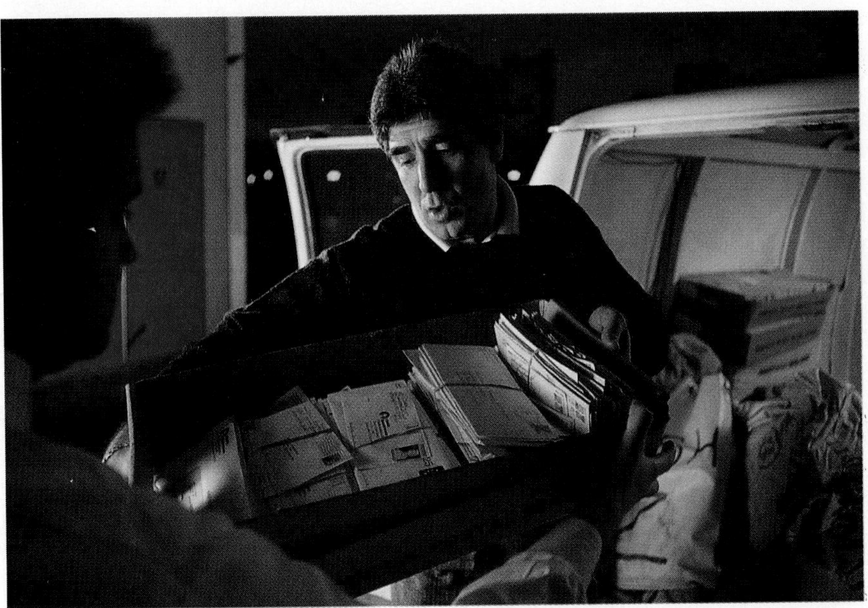

Fidelity Investments routes so many messages through its mail room (53 million pieces of mail were dispatched by the company last year) that the U.S. Postal Service feels Fidelity could have as many as 21 different Zip Codes of its own!

you stand behind your products. Avoid using negative language, don't pass the buck, and don't hide behind a "mistakes-will-happen" attitude.

Explain specifically, but briefly, what went wrong.

> Let me explain what happened. On December 4, the plane that had your letter in its cargo bay could not land at O'Hare Airport because of a snowstorm and was diverted to Detroit. Although our Detroit personnel worked overtime to reload the mail onto a delivery truck, which was then driven to Chicago, it did not arrive until early on December 5.

Because the reader's faith in your products has been shaken, you also have a sales job to do. You must build into your letter **resale**—that is, information that reestablishes the customer's confidence in the product purchased or in the company that sells the product. In order to be believable, do *not* promise that the problem will never happen again; that's unrealistic. Do, however, use specific language, including facts and figures when possible.

Use resale to reassure the customer of the worth of your products.

> *Not:* We have taken steps to ensure that this situation will not happen again.
>
> *But:* Fortunately, such incidents are rare. For example, even considering bad weather, airline strikes, and the like, United Express has maintained an on-time delivery record of 97.6% during the past 12 months. No other delivery service even comes close to this record.

Sometimes you may decide to honor a claim even when the customer is at fault—perhaps because the writer has been a good customer for many years or represents important potential business. In such situations, your beginning paragraph should still convey the good news that you're honoring the claim, but you might temper the enthusiasm a bit. And in the explanatory paragraphs, you would tactfully communicate to the reader the

If the customer is at fault, explain in tactful, impersonal language how to avoid such problems in the future.

Responding positively to a customer's complaint can turn anger into brand loyalty, according to Technical Assistance Research Programs, Inc. (TARP). TARP suggests that a customer whose complaints have been satisfied will more likely purchase products in the future than a customer who never complained. (Michael Abrams and Matthew Pease, "Wining and Dining the Whiners," *Sales & Marketing Management*, February 1993, pp. 73-75.)

facts surrounding the case—that the reader is at fault, the product was misused, the warranty has expired, or whatever the situation requires.

On the one hand, it is necessary to inform the reader of the circumstances so that he or she won't keep repeating the problem. On the other hand, if you do so in an insulting manner, you will lose the reader's goodwill. Instead, use impersonal, tactful language, taking special pains not to lecture the reader or sound condescending. For example, in the second paragraph that follows, note that the pronoun *you* is not used at all when explaining the misuse of the equipment.

> Because we value your friendship, we are pleased to repair your Braniff 250 copier free of charge. Our maintenance technician tells me that she took care of the problem on September 15.
>
> Your machine's register indicated that 9,832 copies had been made since the copier was installed on July 18. The Braniff 250 is designed for low-level office use—fewer than 1,500 copies per month. If you find that you will continue to experience high-volume usage, may I suggest trading up to the Braniff 300, which will easily handle your needs. We will gladly offer you $1,300 as a trade-in allowance.

Positive, Forward-Looking Closing

Do not mention the claim in the closing. Instead, look to the future.

End your letter on a positive note. Do not refer to the problem again, do not apologize again, do not suggest the possibility of future problems, and do not imply that the reader might still be upset. Instead, use strategies that imply a continuing relationship with the customer, such as including additional resale, a comment about the satisfaction the reader will receive from the repaired product or improved service, or appreciation for the reader's interest in your products.

Include sales promotion only if you are confident that your adjustment has restored the customer's confidence in your product or service; otherwise, it might backfire. If used, sales promotion should be subtle and should involve a new product or accessory rather than promoting a new or improved model of what the reader has already bought.

For other examples of adjustment letters, see the *Instructor's Resource Manual*, pp. 91, 92, 93, 94, 95, and 96.

Not: Again, I apologize for the delay in delivering your letter. If you experience such problems again, please don't hesitate to write.

But: We have enjoyed serving your delivery needs for the past eight years, Ms. Clarke, and look forward to many more years of service.

Or: If you're the type of person who has frequent crash deadlines, Ms. Clarke, you will probably be interested in our eight-hour delivery service. It is described in the enclosed brochure.

Figures 6.5 and 6.6 show two versions of an adjustment letter for the claim letter presented in Figure 6.3. Figure 6.5 assumes the company was at fault; Figure 6.6 assumes the reader was at fault but that management decided to grant the request for a refund anyway. Although both letters grant the refund, note the more subdued tone and the "we-are-not-to-blame" attitude in the second letter. Finally, Checklist 4 summarizes the guidelines for writing routine claim and adjustment letters.

FIGURE 6.5 Adjustment Letter—Company at Fault

This adjustment letter responds to the claim letter in Figure 6.3.

COLOR - VU GRAPHICS
The Media Specialists

April 22, 19--

Ms. Claire D. Scriven
1 Marketing Manager
American Homes
642 Poplar Street
Denver, CO 80220

Dear Ms. Scriven:

Color-Vu Graphics is, of course, happy to cancel the $176.50 charge for
2 Invoice 4073. I appreciate your taking the time to write and send us a sample
3 slide (you may simply discard the other slides).

Upon receiving your letter, I immediately sent your slide to our quality-
4 control personnel for closer examination. They agreed with you that the slide
should have been redeveloped before it left our processing lab. We have now
revised our procedures to ensure that before each slide leaves our lab, it is
inspected by someone other than the person preparing it.

To better serve the media needs of our corporate customers, we are installing the Kodak 1120 processor, the most sophisticated development system available. Thus, when you send us your next order, you'll see that your slides are of even higher quality than those in the Business Management advertisement that impressed you.

Sincerely yours,

David Foster

David Foster
Customer Relations

ied

P.O. BOX 210742 ▪ DALLAS, TX 75211 ▪ 214-555-0932

Tells immediately that the adjustment is being made; thanks the reader.

Explains briefly, but specifically, what happened.

Looks forward to a continuing relationship with the customer; does not mention the problem again.

Grammar and Mechanics Notes

1 Type the position title either on the same line as the person's name or, as here, on a line by itself. 2 *Invoice 4073:* Capitalize a noun that precedes a number. 3 *slides).:* Place the period outside the closing parenthesis unless the entire sentence is in parentheses. 4 *personnel:* Do not confuse *personnel* (employees) with *personal* (private).

FIGURE 6.6 Adjustment Letter—Customer at Fault

This adjustment letter responds to the claim letter in Figure 6.3.

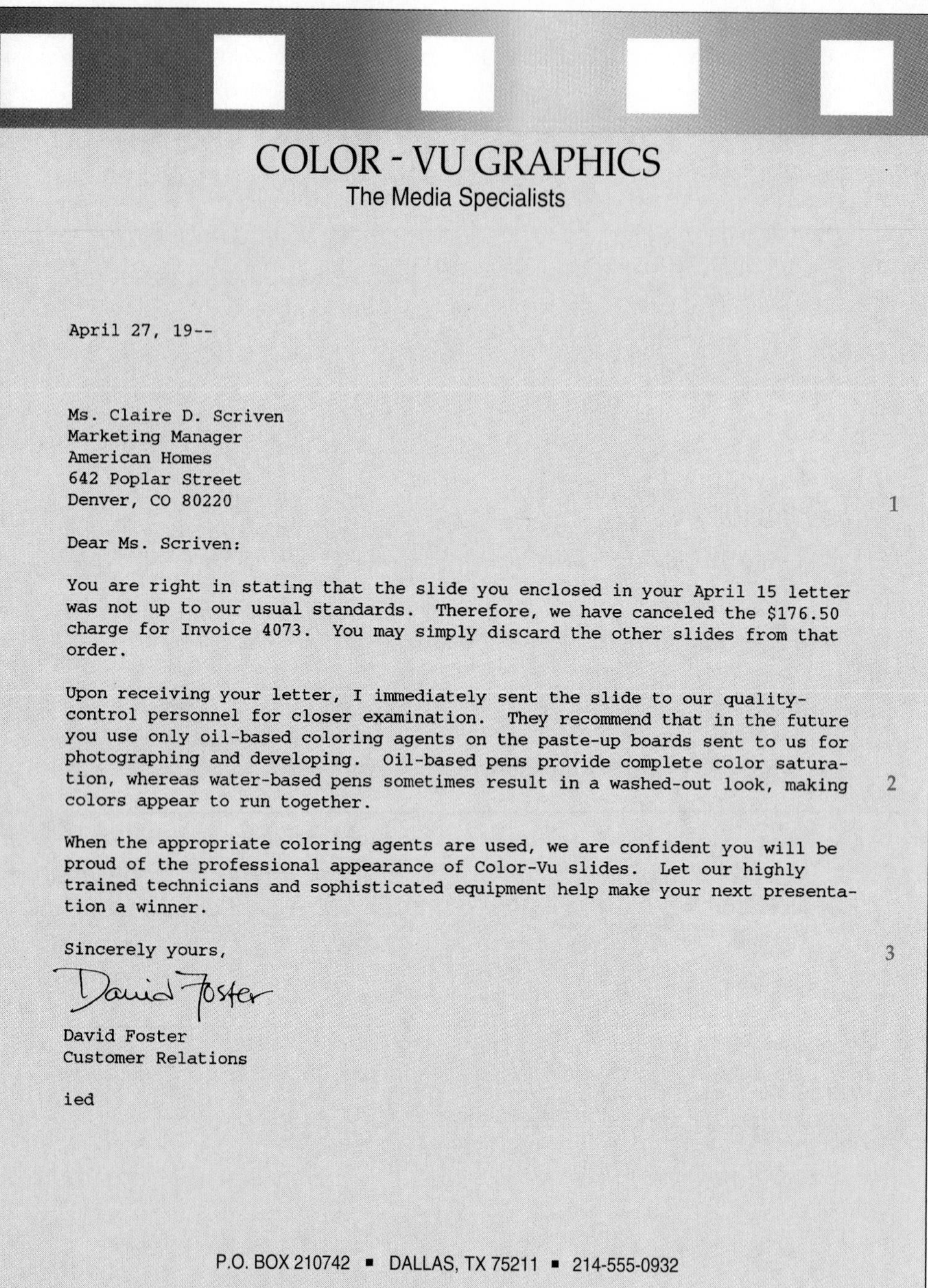

COLOR - VU GRAPHICS
The Media Specialists

April 27, 19--

Ms. Claire D. Scriven
Marketing Manager
American Homes
642 Poplar Street
Denver, CO 80220 1

Dear Ms. Scriven:

Uses subdued language to tell that the adjustment is being made.

You are right in stating that the slide you enclosed in your April 15 letter was not up to our usual standards. Therefore, we have canceled the $176.50 charge for Invoice 4073. You may simply discard the other slides from that order.

In a tactful tone, explains how the problem was caused by the customer.

Upon receiving your letter, I immediately sent the slide to our quality-control personnel for closer examination. They recommend that in the future you use only oil-based coloring agents on the paste-up boards sent to us for photographing and developing. Oil-based pens provide complete color saturation, whereas water-based pens sometimes result in a washed-out look, making 2
colors appear to run together.

Includes resale to close on a confident, forward-looking note.

When the appropriate coloring agents are used, we are confident you will be proud of the professional appearance of Color-Vu slides. Let our highly trained technicians and sophisticated equipment help make your next presentation a winner.

Sincerely yours, 3

David Foster
Customer Relations

ied

P.O. BOX 210742 ▪ DALLAS, TX 75211 ▪ 214-555-0932

Grammar and Mechanics Notes

1 Use the capitalized two-letter Postal Service abbreviation for state names in addresses.
2 *whereas* is one word. 3 *Sincerely yours,*: Capitalize only the first word in a complimentary closing.

CHECKLIST 4

Routine Claim and Adjustment Letters

ROUTINE CLAIM LETTERS

1. Write your claim letter promptly—as soon as you've identified a problem. Try to determine the name of the appropriate individual to whom to write; if that is not possible, address your letter to the customer relations department.
2. Strive for an overall tone of courtesy and confidence; avoid anger, sarcasm, threats, and exaggeration. If true and relevant, mention something positive about the company or its products somewhere in the letter.
3. Begin the letter directly, identifying the problem immediately.
4. Provide as much detail as necessary. Using impersonal language, tell specifically what went wrong and how you were inconvenienced.
5. If appropriate, tell what type of adjustment you expect—replacement, repair, refund, or apology. End on a confident note.

ROUTINE ADJUSTMENT LETTERS

1. Respond promptly; your customer is already upset.
2. Begin the letter directly, telling the reader immediately what adjustment is being made.
3. Adopt a courteous tone. Use neutral or positive language throughout.
4. If appropriate, somewhere in the letter thank the reader for writing, and apologize if the customer has been severely inconvenienced or embarrassed because of your company's actions.
5. In a forthright manner, explain the reason for the problem in sufficient detail to be believable, but don't belabor the point. If appropriate, tell what steps you've taken to prevent a recurrence of the problem.
6. Provide information that reestablishes your customer's confidence in the product or your company. Be specific enough to be believable.
7. If the customer was at fault, explain in impersonal and tactful language the facts surrounding the case.
8. Close on a positive note. Include additional resale, subtle sales promotion, appreciation for the reader's interest in your products, or some other strategy that implies customer satisfaction and the expectation of a continuing relationship.

MICROWRITING

A Routine Adjustment Letter

PROBLEM

You are Kathryn Smith, a correspondent in the customer service department of Exciting Interiors, a large home-furnishings store. This morning (May 25, 19—), you received the following letter from Mrs. Henrietta Daniels, an angry customer:

> Dear Customer Service Manager:
>
> I am really upset at the poor-quality shades that you sell. Two months ago I purchased two pairs of your pleated fabric shades in Wedgewood Blue at $35.99 each for my two bathroom windows. A copy of my $74.32 bill is enclosed.
>
> The color has already begun to fade from these shades. I couldn't believe it when I checked and found that they now look tie-dyed! That is not the look I wish for my home.
>
> Since these shades did not provide the type of wear that I paid for, please refund my $74.32.
>
> Sincerely,

You take Mrs. Daniels's itemized bill down to the sales floor and find the model of shades she purchased. You can only conclude that Mrs. Daniels's home has large bathroom windows because the only size this particular shade comes in is 64 inches long by 32 inches wide. And printed right on the tag attached to the shade is this caution: "Warning: The imported fabric in this shade makes them unsuitable for use in areas of high humidity." Clearly, these shades were not made for bathroom use. You call up Mrs. Daniels's account on your computer and find that she has been a loyal customer for many years. You decide, therefore, to refund her $74.32, even though she misused the product. Write the adjustment letter (Mrs. Henrietta Daniels, 117 Hanley Drive, Grass Valley, CA 95949).

PROCESS

1. What is the purpose of your letter?

   To refund Mrs. Daniels's money, tactfully explain that you were not at fault, and retain her goodwill.

2. Describe your audience.

   - An important customer
   - Angry at you at the present time
   - Now believes your product isn't of high quality
   - May be the type of person who doesn't read instructions carefully

3. List in the appropriate order the topics you'll discuss.

   a. Give the refund.
   b. Explain that the shades weren't intended for bathroom use.
   c. Promote your cotton and polyester bathroom curtains.

4. Write a gracious opening sentence for your letter that tells Mrs. Daniels you're refunding the $74.32. Be warm and positive in granting her request. Remember, however, that she was at fault; therefore, do not be overly enthusiastic.

   You have been a valued and faithful customer of ours for several years, Mrs. Daniels, and we are therefore refunding your $74.32.

5. Write the sentence that explains how the shades were misused. Use tactful, neutral, and impersonal language, avoiding the use of second-person pronouns (*you* and *your*).

   As the tag attached to the shades explains, the fine imported woven material used in these shades reflects sunlight without fading but will not withstand the high humidity typical of bathrooms.

6. Now write your closing paragraph, in which you promote your cotton and polyester bathroom curtains.

   For the elegant look and durable service you want in your bathroom, please consider the cotton and polyester bathroom curtains shown in the enclosed brochure. They come in Wedgewood Blue and can be custom-ordered in the exact size you desire.

EXCITING
INTERIORS

May 25, 19--

Mrs. Henrietta Daniels
117 Hanley Drive
Grass Valley, CA 95949

Dear Mrs. Daniels:

You have been a valued customer of ours for several years, and we are, therefore, refunding your $74.32. A check for that amount is enclosed. You can simply return the blue shades to our customer service window the next time you stop by Exciting Interiors.

As the tag attached to the shades explains, the fine imported woven material used in these shades reflects sunlight without fading but will not withstand the high humidity typically found in bathrooms. However, when these shades are used on windows in living rooms, dining rooms, and bedrooms, they will provide many years of beautiful and carefree service.

For the elegant look and durable service you want in your bathroom, please consider the cotton and polyester bathroom curtains shown on the enclosed brochure. They come in Wedgewood Blue and can be custom-ordered in the exact size you require. Please come in and let us show them to you.

Sincerely,

Kathryn Smith

Kathryn Smith
Customer Service Department

jmr
Enclosure

177 Walnut Street Boston, MA 02108 617-555-7777

SUMMARY

Most business writing tasks involve routine matters in which the writer conveys either positive or routine information that is of interest to the reader. Such situations call for a direct organizational plan in which the major purpose of the message is presented first. The major idea is followed by any needed background information or additional explanation, and the message ends on a friendly, forward-looking note.

Guidelines for writing routine requests and routine replies are summarized in Checklist 3. Guidelines for writing routine claim letters and routine adjustment letters are summarized in Checklist 4. Use both checklists in composing such messages and in revising your drafts.

KEY TERMS

For an exercise on matching terms, refer students to the *Study Guide*, p. 105.

Adjustment letter A letter written to inform a customer of the action taken in response to the customer's claim letter.

Claim letter A letter from the buyer to the seller, seeking some type of action to correct a problem with the seller's product or service.

Direct organizational plan A plan in which the major purpose of the message is communicated first, followed by any needed explanation.

Form letter A letter with standardized wording that is sent to different people.

Indirect organizational plan A plan in which the reasons or rationale are presented first, followed by the major idea.

Resale Information that reestablishes a customer's confidence in the product purchased or in the company that sold the product.

REVIEW AND DISCUSSION

The answers to the review and discussion questions appear in the *Instructor's Resource Manual*, beginning on p. 62.

1. **Communication at Kidder, Peabody Revisited** ▪ The 25 letters Gwen Salley writes every day are routine messages answering questions about products and services offered by Kidder, Peabody. However, each letter has to be carefully tailored to the needs and interests of the reader.
   a. When Salley writes in response to routine requests for information, which organizational plan is more appropriate for her letters—direct or indirect?
   b. Should Salley provide product information to a long-time customer in a letter or a memo? Why?
   c. Is a form letter an appropriate way for Salley to answer requests from people who are not yet her clients?
2. Explain the basic parts of the direct organizational plan. For what types of messages is this plan appropriate?
3. Assume you need information from a bank about interest rates for a 90-day loan for your small business. Write three versions of the first sentence of your letter, using (a) a direct question, (b) a polite request, and (c) a statement.
4. What guidelines should you follow when asking questions in a routine request?
5. Why should routine requests be answered promptly?

6. Critique each of the following first sentences of a routine reply:

```
a. Your letter of November 23 has been referred to me for
   reply.
b. Although we will not be able to help you with remodel-
   ing your factory, we can provide expert remodeling
   service for your office area.
c. Our trained architects and interior designers can pro-
   vide a complete remodeling plan for your office area.
d. Thank you for inquiring about our comprehensive remod-
   eling services.
```

7. Compose an appropriate last sentence for your routine reply for the situation referred to in 6 above.
8. Under what circumstances is a form letter desirable for answering routine inquiries?
9. How does a claim letter differ from a complaint letter?
10. Why should claim letters be written promptly? Why should they be answered promptly?
11. What should be the overall tone of the claim letter? of the adjustment letter?
12. Under what circumstances would the direct organizational plan *not* be appropriate for a claim letter? for an adjustment letter?
13. Under what circumstances should you apologize in an adjustment letter?
14. How does an adjustment letter in which the company is at fault differ from an adjustment letter in which the customer is at fault?
15. What is the difference between *resale* and *sales promotion?*
16. Assume you've agreed to replace a customer's broken CD player that has been sent to you for inspection. Compose an appropriate last sentence for this adjustment letter.

EXERCISES

Exercise 1 is linked with Exercise 12 of Chapter 7. A sample solution for Exercise 1 appears in the *Instructor's Resource Manual*, p. 64. A formatted solution appears on *IRM* p. 78. An exercise on microwriting a routine message appears on *IRM* pp. 302–304.

1. Microwriting a Claim Letter for a Defective Product ■

PROBLEM

You are J. R. McCord, purchasing agent for People's Energy Company. On February 3 you ordered a box of 12 multistrike printer ribbons for your Sampson Model 25 printers at $9.35 each, plus $6.85 shipping and handling—total price of $119.05. The catalog description for this ribbon (Part No. 02-8R01656) stated, "Fits Epson and Xerox printers and most compatibles." Since the Sampson is advertised as a Xerox clone printer, you assumed the ribbons would fit. When the order arrived, you discovered that the ribbons didn't fit your Sampson. Although the ribbon cartridge is the same shape, it is about ¼ inch thicker and won't seat properly on the spindles.

You believe that your supplier's misleading advertising caused you to order the wrong model ribbon. You'd like the company to either refund the $119.05 you paid on its Invoice 95-076 or replace the ribbons with ones that do work with your printers. You'll be happy to return the entire case of ribbons if the company will give you instructions for doing so.

Write your routine claim letter.

PROCESS

a. What is the purpose of your letter?
b. Describe your audience.
c. Write the first sentence of your letter, in which you identify the problem. Strive for an overall tone of courtesy and confidence.
d. Using impersonal language, write the middle section of the letter, in which you tell specifically what went wrong and how you were inconvenienced by the problem.
e. Write the last paragraph of the letter, in which you identify the type of adjustment you expect and also perhaps mention some positive aspect about the company or its products.

PRODUCT

Revise, format, and proofread your letter, which should be addressed to the Customer Service Department of Nationwide Office Supply, located at 2640 Kerper Boulevard in Dubuque, IA 52001. Submit to your instructor both your responses to the process questions and your final letter.

2. **Routine Request—Product Information** ■ Luis St. Jean is a famous design house in France with annual sales of $1.2 billion in clothing, perfume, scarves, and other designer items. Each year it prepares more than 150 original designs for its seasonal collection. As head buyer for Cindy's, an upscale women's clothing store at Mall of America in Minneapolis, you think you might like to begin offering LSJ's line of perfume. You need to know more about pricing, types of perfume offered, minimum ordering quantities, marketing assistance provided by LSJ, and the like. You'd also like to know if you can have exclusive marketing rights to LSJ perfumes in the Minneapolis area and whether you would have to carry LSJ's complete line (you don't think the most expensive perfumes would be big sellers).

   Write to Mr. Henri Vixier, License Supervisor, Luis St. Jean, 90513 Cergy, Pointoise Cedex, France, seeking answers to your questions.

You may wish to link Exercises 2-10 with Exercise 9 in Chapter 15. Sample solutions for these exercises appear in the *Instructor's Resource Manual*, beginning on p. 65. Formatted solutions appear in the *IRM*, beginning on p. 79.

3. **Routine Request—Membership Information** ■ Although your job as training assistant at Glenco Services is only part-time while you finish college, your boss wants you to gain more experience in public speaking and has suggested that you join Podium International. Podium is devoted to helping members perfect their public-speaking skills. You don't know whether your town has a local chapter, so you write to the group's regional headquarters (at PO Box 4909A, Louisville, KY 40202). You want to request membership information and the location of the nearest local chapter. Direct your letter to the membership director.

4. **Routine Request—Letter of Recommendation** ■ As part of your application papers for a one-semester internship at American Express, you are asked to include a letter of recommendation from one of your business professors. You made a good grade in MGT 382: Wage and Salary Administration, which you took three semesters ago from Dr. Dennis Thavinet in the Management Department at your university. You liked the course well enough that you missed class only twice (for good reasons). Although you were not one of the most vocal members in class, Dr. Thavinet did commend you for your group project. American Express (at 1850 East Camelback Road, Phoenix, AZ 85017) wants to know especially about your ability to work well with others.

   Write to Dr. Thavinet, asking for a letter of recommendation. You would like him to respond within one week.

Routine Request

Dear Dr. Thavinet:

As part of my application for a one-semester internship, American Express has requested that I include a letter of recommendation from one of my management professors. Will you please write that recommendation for me.

I took MGT 382, Wage and Salary Administration, from you Fall 19--. I received my best grade that semester (A-) in your course and missed only two days of class due to an illness.

American Express is particularly interested in people who can work well with others. As you may recall, you commended my group for a project that developed a comprehensive compensation program for Duffey's Ice Cream Parlor. I have also been involved in several other successful group projects while in school. My enclosed résumé provides more information about my qualifications.

A letter of recommendation from you would certainly increase my chances of receiving this internship. I would be most grateful if you will write to the personnel department at American Express, 1850 East Camelback Road, Phoenix, AZ 85017, before April 15, because interns are going to be selected at the end of this month.

Sincerely,

Ober, *Contemporary Business Communication*, 2d ed.

See Master 6.1, Exercise 4, Request for Letter of Recommendation, in the *Instructor's Resource Manual*.

5. **Routine Request—Product Information** ■ Choose an advertisement from a newspaper or magazine for a product or service about which you

have some interest. The ad probably does not have sufficient space to provide all the information you need to make an intelligent purchase decision. Write to the company (if necessary, locate its address using one of the directories available in your library), asking at least three questions about the product. Be sure to mention where you learned about the product. Try to encourage a prompt response.

Attach a copy of the ad to your letter and submit both to your instructor. Your instructor may ask you to mail the letter so that the class can later compare the types of responses received for different products.

6. **Routine Response—Membership Information** ■ Assume you're the membership director for Podium International (see Exercise 3). You receive a letter from Jonathan Grillo, a college student working part-time as a training assistant at Glenco Services. He asks for membership information and the location of the nearest local chapter. You believe public speaking is a valuable skill for people in any profession, and you have found it to be personally rewarding as well. At the same time, you know that many people find public speaking a difficult, nerve-racking experience.

   Write Grillo (6201 Great Ring Boulevard, Dallas, TX 75231) a letter that promotes the benefits of public speaking and, at the same time, responds to his requests. Refer to the membership brochure that you are including with your letter. Also let him know that the nearest chapter meets monthly in Fort Worth; you will ask that chapter president to contact him with information about upcoming meetings.

7. **Routine Response—Student Information** ■ As the dean of admissions for Eastern State University, you have received a letter from Linda O'Kelly, a first-year student at the State University of New York, 665 Catskill Hall, Oswego, NY 13126. She is interested in transferring to your school, but she has a number of questions about the courses and the transfer requirements. Here are her questions and the answers:

   a. *Does the school offer an undergraduate degree in environmental engineering?* Yes, the school initiated this program two years ago.
   b. *What are the requirements for transfer students?* Transfer students must have at least a 2.75 first-year GPA to be considered for admission as sophomores.
   c. *Can all courses taken at another school be transferred for credit?* No, only courses for which Eastern State has an equivalent offering are accepted for credit.

   Your school accepts only a few transfer students each semester, but you don't want to discourage Ms. O'Kelly (who may be among the few accepted). Respond to her letter and mention that you are sending additional information (such as a course catalog) in a separate package.

Dear Ms. Shearing:

I am happy to provide the information you requested about our restaurant on January 27, 19--. You will be pleased to know that we purchase only top-quality government-inspected meat, fish, and fowl.

The U.S. Department of Agriculture provides strict guidelines for meat producers. Most cattle today are raised in specially designed lots that are cleaned daily to ensure animal and human health. Also, to ensure healthy animals and promote faster growth, antibiotics and hormones that have been approved safe for both animals and humans by the U.S. Department of Agriculture are fed to the animals. The highest quality beef, in demand by beef consumers in stores as well as in top restaurants such as ours, is produced this way.

The trout that we serve in our restaurant is grown on a farm, where careful monitoring of water and conditions results in less disease. This process provides a safer, higher-quality product for our customers.

I am pleased to answer your questions about the food we serve and look forward to seeing you soon at Maison Richard.

Sincerely,

Ober, *Contemporary Business Communication*, 2d ed.

See Master 6.2, Exercise 8, Routine Response, in the *Instructor's Resource Manual*.

8. **Routine Response—Product Information** ■ As the business manager for Maison Richard, a 200-seat restaurant in Seattle, you received an inquiry from Chris Shearing, 1926 Second Avenue, Seattle, WA 98101. She had several questions about the type of meat you serve in your restaurant. Here are her questions and the answers:

   a. *Are the cattle from which your beef comes allowed to roam freely on an open range instead of being fattened in cramped feedlots?* No, allowing free-roaming would increase the muscle tissue in the beef, making it less tender.
   b. *Are the cattle fed antibiotics and hormones?* Yes, to ensure a healthy animal and to promote faster growth.
   c. *Does your trout come from lakes and streams?* No, they're farm-grown, which is more economical and results in less disease.

Ms. Shearing is a well-known animal-rights activist, and you want to present your case as positively as possible to avoid the loss of her goodwill and any negative publicity that might result. Respond to her letter, supplying whatever other appropriate information you feel is reasonable.

9. **Routine Response—Form Letter** ■ Assume the role of assistant to the secretary at Sparkle Cola. Your office receives dozens of letters every day requesting a copy of Sparkle Cola's annual report. Demand has been particularly strong this year because of the company's aggressive international growth plans, which have captured the attention of investors around the world. As a result, you no longer have any copies from the first printing of the current annual report. You don't want to make potential investors wait two weeks until the second printing is complete. In the interim, you are sending out black-and-white photocopies of the report to anyone who requests a copy.

   Prepare a form letter explaining the situation. Mention that you will send a full-color copy as soon as the second printing becomes available and that you will put each person on the list to receive next year's copy automatically (it will be released in April). Also offer to send quarterly reports on request.

10. **Routine Response—Form Letter** ■ You are the executive producer for "The Sherry Show," a popular syndicated morning talk show featuring Sherry Baker as host. The show features interviews and panel discussions on a wide variety of current topics.

    Because Sherry takes questions and comments from the audience, it is important to have a full house each day. When the show started two years ago, you had trouble filling the 150-seat studio. Now, however, you get more ticket requests than you can accommodate. Anyone wanting a ticket must write at least four months ahead and can request no more than four tickets (which are free). The show tapes from 9:30 until 11 a.m. Monday through Friday each week. Tickets are for reserved seats, but any seats not occupied by 9 a.m. are released on a first-come, first-served basis. Studio doors close promptly at 9:15 each morning and do not reopen until the show ends at 11 a.m. Children under age 12 are not admitted.

    Write a form letter telling people how to order tickets and conveying other needed information. The letter will be sent to anyone who requests ticket information.

11. **Collaborative Routine Response—Project Information** ■ You are a member of the President's Council, an organization made up of the presidents of each student organization on campus. You just received a memorandum from Dr. Robin H. Hill, dean of students, wanting to know what types of social projects the student organizations on campus have been engaged in during the past year. The dean must report to the board of trustees on the important role played by student organizations—both in the life of the university and community and in the development of student leadership and social skills. She wants to include such information as student-run programs on drug and alcohol abuse, community service, and fund-raising.

    Working in groups of four, identify and summarize the types of social projects that student organizations at your institution have completed this year. Then organize and synthesize your findings into a one-page memo to Dr. Hill. After writing your first draft, have each member review and comment on the draft. Then revise as needed and submit. Use only factual data for this assignment.

Sample solution for Exercise 11 appears in the *Instructor's Resource Manual*, p. 71.

Sample solution for Exercise 12 appears in the *Instructor's Resource Manual*, pp. 71–72. Formatted solution appears on *IRM* p. 87.

12. Claim Letter—Incorrectly Personalized Product ■ You are the marketing manager for Statewide Telemarketing, a company that conducts telemarketing campaigns on behalf of local banks, department stores, and insurance agencies. To advertise your company, you recently ordered 500 dark blue personalized pens from Midwest Stationery, a local stationery store. In turn, the store sent the order to a Chicago manufacturer, which stamped your firm's name on the pens and shipped the order directly to your office. However, when the pens arrived, the personalization was incorrectly spelled "Statwide Telemarketing." When you called the stationery store, the salesperson instructed you to write directly to the manufacturer and to include your original order along with one of the pens.

Write to the manufacturer, Prairie Pens, at 7140 Rush Street, Chicago, IL 60611, to request a replacement order. You are willing to return the pens but not to pay the postage; you think the manufacturer should pay for any return postage. You plan to distribute these pens at a convention next month, so you would like the replacement order to arrive within two weeks.

Exercise 13 is linked with Exercise 10 of Chapter 7. Sample solution for Exercise 13 appears in the *Instructor's Resource Manual*, pp. 72–73. Formatted solution appears on *IRM* p. 88.

13. Claim Letter—Inaccurate Reporting ■ As the chief programmer for ReSolve®, a basic computer spreadsheet program for Windows, you were pleased that your product was reviewed in the current issue of *Computing Trends*. The review praised your product for its "lightning-fast speed and convenient user interface." You were not pleased, however, that your product was downgraded because it lacked graphics capability. The reviewer compared ReSolve with full-featured spreadsheet programs costing, on average, $200 more than your program. No wonder, then, that your program rated a 6.6 out of 10, coming in third out of the five programs reviewed. If your program had been compared with similar low-level programs, you feel certain that ReSolve would have easily come out on top.

Although you do not want to get the magazine upset with your company (Software Entrepreneurs, Inc.), you do feel that it should compare apples with apples and should conduct another review of your program. Write to Roberta J. Horton, their review editor, at 200 Public Square in Cleveland, OH 44114, and tell her so.

Sample solution for Exercise 14 appears in the *Instructor's Resource Manual*, p. 73. Formatted solution appears on *IRM* p. 89.

14. Claim Letter—Poor Service ■ As the owner of Parker Central, a small plumbing business, you try to instill in all your employees a *customer-first* attitude. Therefore, you were quite put off by your own treatment yesterday (July 13) at the hands of the receptionist at Englehard Investment Service (231 East 50 Street, Indianapolis, IN 46205). You showed up 20 minutes early for your 2:30 p.m. appointment with Jack Nutley, an investment counselor with the firm. You were meeting with him for the first time to discuss setting up a Simplified Employee Pension (SEP) plan for your 20 employees.

To begin with, the receptionist ignored you for at least five minutes until she finished the last paragraph of a document she was typing. Then, after finding out whom you wanted to see, she did not even call Jack's office to announce your arrival until 2:30 p.m. Finally, you learned that Jack had just become ill and had to go to the doctor. So you wasted half an afternoon and were also insulted by the receptionist's rude treatment.

You decide to write to Jack Nutley about the receptionist's office behavior. Your *claim* is for better service in the future. You want him to know that if you are going to continue to be treated in such a manner, you have no interest in doing business with his firm. Write the claim letter.

15. Claim Letter—Hidden Damage ■ Your company, Pocket Clocks, makes pocket-sized clocks for travelers. As the head of quality assurance, you spot-check every shipment of parts your firm receives so that you can uncover any problems before the components go to the assembly line. This morning, while checking a new shipment of plastic clock cases, you discovered that the cases in the top layer had been crushed. The value of the damaged parts is $75. You called the manufacturer, which confirmed that the cases were insured for any damage that occurred in transit.

The carrier, Rapid Cargo, requires that claims for hidden damage (damage not apparent from the condition of the shipping carton) be accompanied by the original of the receipt signed upon delivery. The carrier also requires that the carton and the damaged goods be made available for inspection by its insurance adjuster.

Write a letter to Eric Sorenson, who heads Rapid Cargo's claims department (at 82110 Grosvenor Lane, Bethesda, MD 20814-2199). Explain your claim, ask for reimbursement of $75 for the damaged goods, and mention that you are holding the goods and carton aside until the adjuster can examine them. Contrary to the carrier's instructions, you are not going to enclose the original delivery receipt with your letter; you are sending a photocopy with your letter, and the insurance adjuster can examine the original during the inspection visit.

Sample solution for Exercise 15 appears in the *Instructor's Resource Manual*, pp. 73–74. Formatted solution appears on *IRM* p. 90.

16. **Adjustment Letter—Company at Fault** ▪ Assume the role of customer service representative at Nationwide Office Supply (see Exercise 1). You've received Mr. McCord's letter (People's Energy Company, Wheatley Road, Old Westbury, NY 11568). You've done some background investigation and have learned that what the customer said is true—the Sampson Model 25 *is* a Xerox clone and your catalog *does* state that this ribbon fits Xerox printers and most compatibles. The problem came about because the Model 25, Sampson's newest model, was introduced shortly after your catalog went to press. This model uses a slightly shorter spindle than previous Sampson models.

    Unfortunately, you do not carry in your inventory a ribbon that will fit the Sampson Model 25. The customer should return the case of ribbons COD, marking on the address label "Return Authorization 95-076R." In the meantime, you've authorized a refund of $119.05; Mr. McCord should receive the check within ten days. Convey this information to Mr. McCord.

Exercise 16 is linked with Exercise 12 of Chapter 7. Sample solution for Exercise 16 appears in the *Instructor's Resource Manual*, pp. 74–75. Formatted solution appears on *IRM* p. 91.

17. **Adjustment Letter—Company at Fault** ▪ Assume that you are the customer service representative at Prairie Pens who receives the claim letter from Ann Marie Thompson of Statewide Telemarketing, 25830 West Oaklawn Drive, Springdale, AR 72764 (see Exercise 12). You track down the original production order and discover that the person responsible for setting type for the screen made an error. Although you can screen another 500 pens and ship them in one day, your warehouse is out of dark blue pens. You do have royal blue pens, so you decide to substitute these and charge Statewide 25% less than they were billed for their first-choice color. You plan to cancel the first invoice and prepare a new invoice with the lower price, which should go a long way toward softening the error.

    Although the customer offered to return the faulty shipment, you have no use for these personalized pens. However, you can turn these unwanted pens into a gesture of goodwill. When you write to Statewide, note that you will not bill the customer for these pens and suggest that the customer keep the pens for office use. Let Ms. Thompson know—in a letter you will send by fax—what you are doing to solve her problem, and assure her that the new pens will be shipped tomorrow.

Sample solution for Exercise 17 appears in the *Instructor's Resource Manual*, p. 75. Formatted solution appears on *IRM* p. 92.

Sample solution for Exercise 18 appears in the *Instructor's Resource Manual*, p. 75. Formatted solution appears on *IRM* p. 93.

18. Adjustment Letter—Customer at Fault ■ Assume the role of customer service representative at Nationwide Office Supply (see Exercises 1 and 16). You've done some background investigation and have learned that Mr. McCord was somewhat mistaken in stating that the Sampson Model 25 is a Xerox clone. What Sampson advertises instead is that the Model 25 uses the same character set as Xerox printers; this means that all fonts available from Xerox can also be downloaded to the Model 25. Sampson neither states nor implies that Xerox-compatible ribbons or other supplies will fit its machines.

Because the customer made an innocent mistake and you will be able to resell the unused ribbons, you decide to honor his claim anyway. He should return the case of ribbons prepaid, marking on the address label "Return Authorization 95-076R." In the meantime, you're shipping him a dozen ribbons (Part No. 02-9R32732) that *will* work on the Model 25; he can expect to receive them within ten days. You're also enclosing your summer catalog.

Sample solution for Exercise 19 appears in the *Instructor's Resource Manual*, p. 76. Formatted solution appears on *IRM* p. 94.

19. Adjustment Letter—Customer at Fault ■ You are the customer service representative for Rapid Cargo, the carrier involved in the hidden damage claim made by Pocket Clocks in Exercise 15. Your insurance adjuster has visited Pocket Clocks, which is located at 3900 Colonial Parkway, Stoughton, MA 02072. After checking the damage, inspecting the packaging, and looking around the customer's warehouse, the adjuster has concluded that the goods were not damaged in transit but instead because of improper handling in the warehouse. The adjuster observed cartons stacked 25 high in the Pocket Clocks warehouse, despite instructions on each carton that warned against stacking them more than 10 high.

Because you personally know Donna Reid, the head of quality assurance at Pocket Clocks, you decide to reimburse the $75 as requested. Write to Paul Hwang, the warehouse manager for Pocket Clocks, and let him know your decision. Offer to help him analyze his firm's procedures for storing goods and suggest ways of using the available warehouse space more efficiently. This should eliminate the need to stack cartons higher than recommended.

Exercise 20 is linked with Exercise 10 of Chapter 7. Sample solution for Exercise 20 appears in the *Instructor's Resource Manual*, p. 76. Formatted solution appears on *IRM* p. 95.

20. Adjustment Letter—Form Letter ■ As the new review editor at *Computing Trends* (see Exercise 13), you've already come to expect that whenever products are panned in your magazine, you can expect a negative reaction from the developers. You're happy to hear from them, however, because they sometimes bring to light additional information that your readers will find helpful. Unless the review contained a factual error, your policy is to publish the letters in the "Feedback" column in a future issue. (In this particular instance, you compared ReSolve with the full-featured spreadsheets because that is exactly how Software Entrepreneurs, Inc., advertises the program.)

You review most major software products once yearly in your state-of-the-art computer labs, using criteria established by your readers. Write a form letter that you can send to product developers who write to complain about the review of their products, giving them this information.

Exercise 21 is linked with Exercise 10 of Chapter 8. Sample solution for Exercise 21 appears on the *Instructor's Resource Manual*, pp. 76–77. Formatted solution appears on *IRM* p. 96.

21. Adjustment Letter—Form Letter ■ Assume the role of fulfillment representative at Paperbacks by Post, a book club that automatically mails members a selected paperback every month unless he or she sends back a postcard declining the shipment. Although the system works well most of the time, occasionally a member receives a book even after returning the refusal postcard. In such cases, your company asks the member to take the parcel to the post office, which will return it at company expense. You also cancel the invoice and send the member a discount coupon toward future selections.

Write a form letter that you can send to members who complain about receiving an unwanted shipment. Advise them to act promptly, posting returns no later than two weeks after receipt.

CONTINUING CASE 6

The Case of the Briefcase

A possible solution to the Continuing Case is described in the *Instructor's Resource Manual*, p. 77.

It was Friday afternoon and Paul Yu was determined to take care of all pending correspondence before leaving for the weekend. On Tuesday, he had received a memo from Maurice Potts, an Urban Systems sales representative, that said in part:

> Last week I made a sales presentation to Albany Electronics and carried two briefcases with me—my regular case plus a second case filled with handouts and brochures. At the conclusion of my presentation, I distributed the handouts and brochures, picked up my regular briefcase and left—completely forgetting about my second case. When I discovered what had happened the following morning, I immediately called Albany Electronics, but they have been unable to locate the missing case.
>
> This leather briefcase was two months old and cost $287.50 (see the attached sales slip). Since the Urban Systems policy manual states that employees will be reimbursed for all reasonable costs of carrying out their assigned duties, may I please be reimbursed for the $287.50 lost briefcase.

Paul had been thinking about this situation all week; he had even discussed it with Marc, but Marc told him to make whatever decision he thought reasonable. On the one hand, Maurice is a good sales representative. And the policy manual does contain the exact sentence Maurice quoted. On the other hand, Paul does not feel that US should be responsible for such obvious mistakes as this; assuming responsibility for such mistakes would not only be expensive but also might encourage padded expense accounts.

Finally, Paul decides to do two things. First, he'll write a memo to the sales staff, interpreting more fully company policy. Policy 14.2 is entitled *Reimbursement of Expenses,* and Paragraph 14.2.b states, "With the approval of their supervisors, employees will be reimbursed for all reasonable costs of carrying out their assigned duties." Paul wants the sales staff to know that in the future he intends to interpret this policy to mean that any personal property that is stolen will be reimbursed at its present value (not its replacement value) if reasonable care has been taken to secure such property, if the incident is reported within three days, and if the value of the property can be determined. Lost or damaged personal property will normally not be reimbursed, no matter what the reason. Any sales representative may, of course, appeal Paul's decisions to the vice president of marketing.

Second, because the present policy may not have been sufficiently clear, Paul will write a memo to Maurice and agree to reimburse him $287.50 for the briefcase. He'll also enclose a copy of the new policy memo he is sending out to the sales staff.

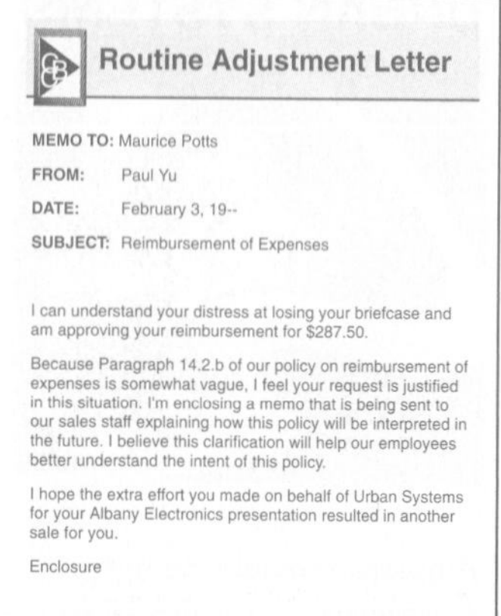

Routine Adjustment Letter

MEMO TO: Maurice Potts
FROM: Paul Yu
DATE: February 3, 19--
SUBJECT: Reimbursement of Expenses

I can understand your distress at losing your briefcase and am approving your reimbursement for $287.50.

Because Paragraph 14.2.b of our policy on reimbursement of expenses is somewhat vague, I feel your request is justified in this situation. I'm enclosing a memo that is being sent to our sales staff explaining how this policy will be interpreted in the future. I believe this clarification will help our employees better understand the intent of this policy.

I hope the extra effort you made on behalf of Urban Systems for your Albany Electronics presentation resulted in another sale for you.

Enclosure

See Master 6.3, Continuing Case 6, Memo to Maurice Potts, in the *Instructor's Resource Manual.*

Critical Thinking

1. How reasonable was Maurice Potts's claim? Was the intent of the policy clear? Should Paul have reimbursed him? Why or why not?
2. How reasonable is Paul's interpretation of the company policy?

Writing Projects

3. Compose the two documents that Paul intends to write: the memo to the sales staff and the memo to Maurice Potts. Format them in an appropriate style.

WORDWISE *Focus on Letters*

- *Uncopyrightable* is a 15-letter word that has no repeated letters.
- There are three words in the English language in which one letter is repeated six times: *degenerescence* (six *e*'s), *indivisibility* (six *i*'s), and *nonannouncement* (six *n*'s).
- A *mirror word* is a word with letters that look the same when viewed both upside down and wrong side out (that is, by turning the page upside down and viewing it in a mirror). There are nine such letters: B, C, D, E, H, I, K, O, and X. *CHOICE* is a mirror word; *OHIO* is a mirror state.

CHAPTER

7

Persuasive Messages

The welfare of thousands of cats, dogs, and other animals depends on how persuasive Joanne Lawson and her staff can be. Lawson is senior director of direct marketing for the American Society for the Prevention of Cruelty to Animals (better known as the ASPCA). Her department sends out 14 million appeal letters every year, raising nearly $9 million annually to aid animals across the country.

Writing such persuasive letters is a time-consuming but rewarding process, and Lawson and her staff start by analyzing the audience. "The ASPCA has seven different direct-mail programs, and we view each as having its own distinct audience," she explained. For example, she distinguishes between *joiners*—people who want to be involved as members of an organization—and *nonjoiners*. "Membership means a conscious decision to support an organization mentally and financially," she noted. "However, some people like to donate to an organization without the responsibility of membership. Nonjoiners get the benefit of helping animals without the perceived responsibility of becoming a member."

The ASPCA's letters are carefully tailored to each audience's particular needs and interests. Lawson stresses that knowing how people feel about the organization's work is an important ingredient in planning a persuasive message. "Donors and members are devout animal lovers. They don't just care about animals, they love them. Members want the satisfaction of knowing that when we write about cats and dogs that need help, these stories have a happy ending."

Communication Objectives

After you have finished this chapter, you should be able to

1. Decide when to use a direct and indirect organizational plan for persuasive messages.
2. Compose a persuasive message promoting an idea.
3. Compose a persuasive message requesting a favor.
4. Compose a persuasive claim.
5. Compose a sales letter.

Joanne Lawson

Senior director of direct marketing, ASPCA, New York City

A chapter overview appears in the *Instructor's Resource Manual*, pp. 97–100.

In addition to using an emotional appeal, Lawson has found that one of the most powerful ways to persuade people to give generously is to describe specifically how contributions are used. "In our renewal letters, which are sent to people whose memberships are about to expire, we emphasize the number of animals we have been able to help in the past year," she said. "We indicate the number of cats and dogs who were adopted by loving, caring families, we describe our legislative efforts on the state and national levels, and we discuss some of the other activities that are supported by membership dollars."

When Lawson writes a letter appealing for donations to address a specific issue or problem, she uses as much space as needed to explain the subject fully. "The rule of thumb is a letter should be only as long as it has to be to effectively convey the message," she explained. Some letters may be four pages long, others two pages long. To attract the reader's attention, the appeal letters often open with a startling fact, then show how the reader can help. Using confident language, the letters address the reader as someone who would certainly want to save an animal's life or stop needless suffering. All fund-raising letters are signed by ASPCA President Roger Caras, who gained a national reputation as a broadcaster and has written some 40 books on animals and wildlife.

The need for money is mentioned at the end of the first page but the actual request for a donation doesn't come until the final page, after the letter has presented specific evidence of the need. According to Lawson, "We give a few examples showing why donations are needed now, and then show what we can do with the donations. The request comes near the end. We create a sense of urgency by telling readers that their support is needed *now*." And readers do respond, giving generously to help America's animals.

PLANNING THE PERSUASIVE MESSAGE

For an exercise in writing a persuasive message, see Video Case Study 2, Ronald McDonald Children's Charities.

Persuasion is the process of motivating someone to take a specific action or to support a particular idea. Persuasion motivates someone to believe something or to do something that he or she would not have otherwise done. Every day many people try to persuade you to do certain things or to believe certain ideas. Likewise, you have many opportunities to persuade others each day.

As an executive, you will also need to persuade others to do as you want. You may need to persuade a superior to adopt a certain proposal, a supplier to refund the purchase price of a defective product, or a potential customer to buy your product or service. In a sense, *all* business communication involves persuasion. Even if your primary purpose is to inform, you still want your reader to accept your perspective and to believe the information you present.

The essence of persuasion is overcoming initial resistance. The reader may resist your efforts for any number of reasons. Your proposal may require the reader to spend time or money—at the very least, you're asking for his or her time to *read* your message. Or the reader may have had bad experiences in the past with similar requests or may hold opinions that predispose him or her against your request.

Persuasion is necessary when the other person initially resists your efforts.

Your job in writing a persuasive message, then, is to talk your readers into something, to convince them that your point of view is the most appropriate one. You'll have the best chance of succeeding if you tailor your message to your audience, provide your readers with reasons they will find convincing, and anticipate their objections. Such tailor-made writing requires careful planning; you need to define your purpose clearly, analyze your audience, and determine the type of appeal to use.

Purpose

The purpose of a persuasive message is to motivate the reader to agree with you or to do as you ask. Unless you are clear about the specific results you wish to achieve, you won't be able to plan an effective strategy that will achieve your goals.

Decide specifically what you want the reader to do as a result of your message.

Suppose, for example, you want to convince your superior to adopt a complex proposal. The purpose of your memo might be to persuade your superior to (a) adopt your proposal, (b) approve a pilot test of the proposal, or (c) schedule a meeting where you can present your proposal in person and answer any questions. Achieving any one of these three goals may require a different strategy. Similarly, if you're writing a sales letter, you must determine whether your purpose is to actually make a sale, to get the reader to request more information, or to schedule a sales call. Again, your specific goal determines your strategy.

Knowing your purpose lets you know what kind of information to include in your persuasive message. "Knowledge is power" and never is this saying truer than when writing persuasive messages. In order to write effectively about an idea or product, you must know the idea or product intimately. If you're promoting an idea, consider all the ramifications of your proposal.

- Are there competing proposals that should be considered?
- What are the implications for the organization if your proposal is adopted and it *fails?*
- How does your proposal fit in with the existing plans and direction of the organization?

If you're promoting a product, how is the product made, marketed, operated, and maintained? You will also need to learn this same information about your competition's products to help you determine the major differences between yours and theirs.

Nikon is spending big money persuading consumers that they need a "wardrobe" of sunglasses—different sunglasses for different activities such as skiing, driving, hiking, flying, and water sports. The ads use athletes such as Todd Skinner and Kristen Ulmer to urge sunglass-buyers to spend from $89 to $275 for the specialized lenses. (Suzanne L. Jennings, "Niches Within a Niche," *Forbes*, April 25, 1994, p. 122.)

Audience Analysis

The more you're able to promote the features of your idea or product as satisfying a *specific* need of your audience, the more persuasive your message will be. Suppose, for example, you're promoting a line of men's shoes; you would stress different features, depending upon your audience.

Young executive:	stylish . . . comes in various shades of black and brown . . . a perfect accessory to your business wardrobe
Mid-career executive:	perfect detailing . . . 12-hour comfort . . . stays sharp looking through days of travel
Retired executive:	economical . . . comfortable . . . a no-nonsense type of shoe

The point to remember is to know your audience and to personalize your message to best meet their needs and interests. Use the *you* attitude to achieve the results you want. When sending a form letter to perhaps thousands of readers, your approach cannot, of necessity, be as personal. Nevertheless, you should still strive to make the approach as personal as possible (see the Spotlight on Technology).

For an extended discussion of technological issues, see "Technology and Communication" in Chapter 2, pp. 39–45.

Knowledge and Attitude of the Reader What does the reader already know about the topic? Determining this will tell you how much background information you should include. What is the reader's predisposition toward the topic? If it is negative, then where one or two reasons might ordinarily suffice, you will need to give more. Initial resistance also calls for more objective, verifiable evidence than if the reader were initially neutral. You also need to learn *why* the reader is resistant so that you can tailor your arguments to overcome those specific objections.

Show how your reader will be affected by your proposal.

Effect on the Reader How will your proposal affect the reader? If the reader is being asked to commit resources (time or money), discuss the rewards for doing so. If the reader is being asked to endorse some proposal, provide enough specific information to enable the reader to make an informed decision. The reader wants to know "What's in it for me?" *You* are already convinced of the wisdom of your proposal. Your job is to let the reader know the benefits of doing as you ask.

To be persuasive, you must present *specific, believable* evidence. However, one of the worst mistakes you could make would be simply to describe the features of the product or to list the advantages of doing as you ask. Instead, put yourself in the reader's place. Discuss how the reader will benefit from your proposal. Emphasize the *reader* rather than the product or idea you're promoting.

Not: The San Diego Accounting Society would like you to speak to us on the topic of expensing versus capitalizing 401-C assets.

But: Speaking to the San Diego Accounting Society would enable you to present your firm's views on the controversial topic of expensing versus capitalizing 401-C assets.

Sometimes your readers won't benefit *directly* from doing as you ask. If you are trying to entice your employees to contribute to the United Way,

SPOTLIGHT ON TECHNOLOGY

A Personal Letter to 5,000 People?

Personalizing a form letter is easy using the merge feature of word processing. The software automatically merges the variable data in the secondary file with the stored paragraphs in the primary file. The example below shows how this is done using WordPerfect for Windows. The inside address, the salutation, and the name and phone number of the local dealer are different in each final printout.

```
Mr. Leon Ellis, Manager
Stephen Wyse Wholesalers
1800 East 26 Street
Little Rock, AR 73206 {END FIELD}
Mr. Ellis  {END FIELD}
Comstock Computer Center {END FIELD}
555-2188 {END FIELD}
{END RECORD}

Mr. Carlos Uriegas-Torres
2400 South Hillcrest
Springfield, MO 65807 {END FIELD}
Mr. Torres  {END FIELD}
Springfield Office Machines {END FIELD}
555-3143 {END FIELD}
{END RECORD}

Ms. Elizabeth Vance, Controller
Econometrics International
466 Owen Avenue
Ypsilanti, MI 48302 {END FIELD}
Ms. Vance  {END FIELD}
Eastern Automation Center {END FIELD}
555-9059 {END FIELD}
{END RECORD}
```

Secondary File

```
{DATE}


{FIELD}1~

Dear {FIELD}2~:

Thank you for requesting information about our Hoskins 9600-baud modem and
software.  More than 70 of the Fortune 100 companies now use the Hoskins modem
to move information between their field staff and headquarters.

To take a no-risk 30-day test drive, simply call your local dealer, {FIELD}3~
at {FIELD}4~.  They will have a Hoskins 9600-baud modem delivered to your
office within the week.  Happy telecommunicating.

Sincerely,


Mary Zimmerman
Sales Manager

eic
```

Primary File

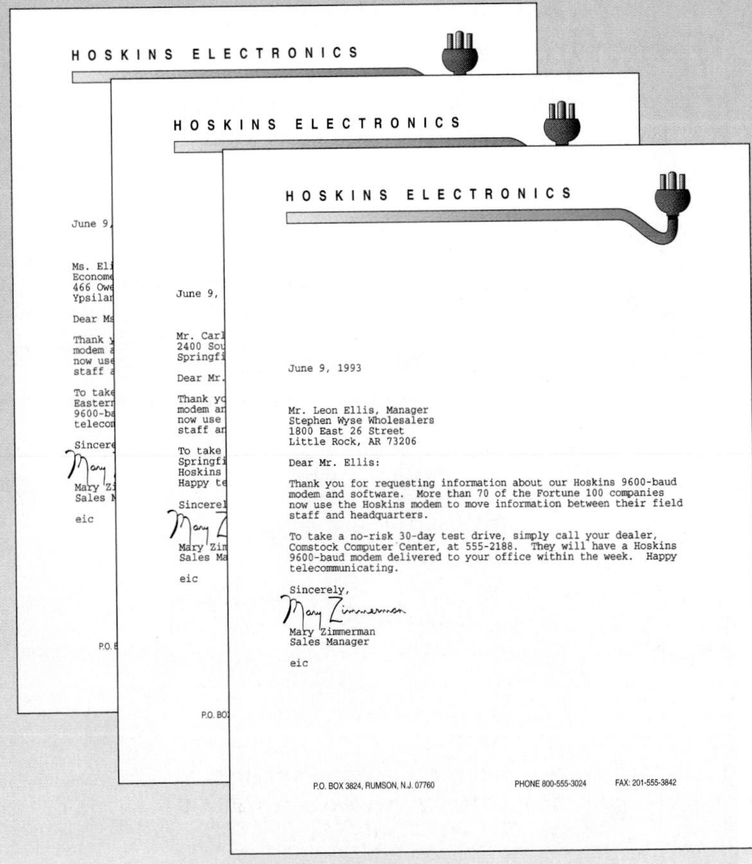

HOSKINS ELECTRONICS

June 9, 1993

Mr. Leon Ellis, Manager
Stephen Wyse Wholesalers
1800 East 26 Street
Little Rock, AR 73206

Dear Mr. Ellis:

Thank you for requesting information about our Hoskins 9600-baud modem and software. More than 70 of the Fortune 100 companies now use the Hoskins modem to move information between their field staff and headquarters.

To take a no-risk 30-day test drive, simply call your dealer, Comstock Computer Center, at 555-2188. They will have a Hoskins 9600-baud modem delivered to your office within the week. Happy telecommunicating.

Sincerely,

Mary Zimmerman
Sales Manager

eic

P.O. BOX 3824, RUMSON, N.J. 07760 PHONE 800-555-3024 FAX: 201-555-3842

Final Printouts

Discussing indirect benefits prevents your request from sounding selfish.

for example, it would be difficult to discuss direct reader benefits. In such situations, discuss the *indirect* benefits of reader participation; for example, show how someone other than you, the solicitor of the funds, will benefit.

> Your contribution will enable inner-city youngsters, many of whom have never even been outside the city of Columbus, to see pandas living and thriving in their natural habitat.

A reader who trusts you is more likely to trust your message.

Writer Credibility What is your credibility with the reader? The more trustworthy you are, the more trustworthy your message will appear. Credibility comes from many sources. You may be perceived as being credible by virtue of the position you hold or by virtue of being a well-known authority. Or you may achieve credibility for your proposal by supplying convincing evidence, such as facts and statistics that can be verified.

Suppose, for example, you have worked in an advertising production department and have extensive experience with color reproduction. If you are writing a memo to a colleague suggesting that certain photos will not reproduce clearly and should therefore be replaced, you probably don't need to explain your expertise. Your colleague is likely to believe you. But if you are writing a letter to the photographer, who does not know you, you would probably want to discuss past incidents that lead you to conclude the photos should be replaced.

Types of Appeals

For an exercise in identifying types of appeals, see Video Case Study 1, Chiat/Day.

Based on your reader's knowledge about the topic, the effect your proposal will have on the reader, and the reader's predisposition toward you and

Lobbyists, like these waiting outside a senate committee room at the Texas state capitol, spend a great deal of time writing persuasive messages to convince legislators to pass laws. Their credibility—their reputation for getting the facts right—is important to their success.

your topic, you must decide what information to include in your message and what type of appeal to emphasize. A variety of appeals are available.

Logical appeals relate to one's reasoning ability; emotional appeals relate to one's feelings.

Logical Versus Emotional *Logical* appeals are directed toward rational perceptions and involve such practical concepts as durability, economy, convenience, safety, and efficiency. *Emotional* appeals are directed toward feelings and involve such concepts as excitement, glamour, prestige, belonging, and feeling good about oneself.

Logical: Our stationery's 25% rag content means that your correspondence will remain legible even after ten years in the file cabinet.

Emotional: Our stationery's 25% rag content means that your correspondence will make an important statement about you to your colleagues.

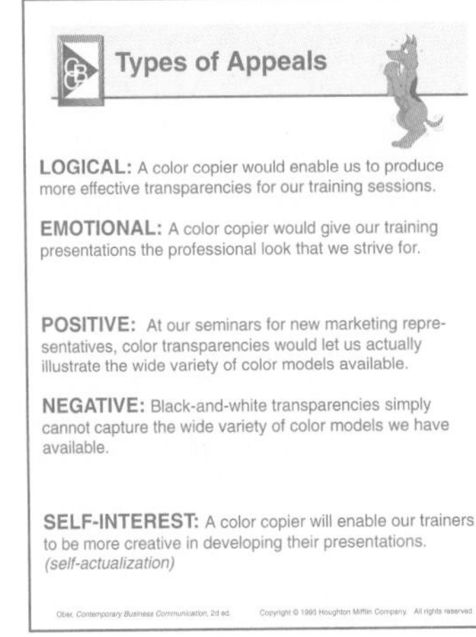

See Transparency 7.1, Types of Appeals in Persuasive Messages.

Sales letters for consumer goods often emphasize emotional appeals, whereas sales letters for industrial goods often emphasize logical appeals. Likewise, inexpensive or nonessential products often emphasize emotional appeals, whereas expensive or essential products often emphasize logical appeals. Non-sales persuasive messages may use either logical or emotional appeals, depending on the individual circumstances.

Logical: Adopting this proposal will increase our market share by 1.5% within six months.

Emotional: Adopting this proposal will give our company an international reputation as the leader in Pacific Rim marketing.

Positive Versus Negative Most persuasive appeals are positive, stressing the benefits to the reader of accepting the writer's proposal. Negative appeals, in contrast, stress the drawbacks of *not* accepting the writer's proposal—for example, buying life insurance to avoid leaving one's family destitute. Negative appeals are used mostly for health and safety issues, such as for antismoking and drug-abuse campaigns. Some products lend themselves to either positive or negative appeals; for example, driving within the legal speed limit can be promoted as either saving gas (positive appeal) or deterring accidents (negative appeal).

Positive appeals stress the advantages of doing as one asks; negative appeals stress the disadvantages of not doing as one asks.

Positive: By donating a pint of blood next Thursday, you will help ensure a continued supply of plasma for Clifford County residents.

Negative: To avoid the possibility of your facing emergency surgery with an inadequate supply of blood available, please do your part next Thursday.

Unless you have reason to expect that a negative appeal will be effective for your particular audience, it is generally better to stress the positive aspects of accepting your suggestion.

Self-Interest The most effective appeals focus on the reader's self-interest and satisfy a need of the reader. Although a persuasive message cannot *create* a need, it can make the reader aware of an existing need. Abraham

A self-interest appeal stresses an existing need of the reader.

Maslow has hypothesized that people generally act in order to satisfy certain needs. He identified the following five levels of needs:[1]

Level	*Need*	*Examples*
1	Physiological	Air, water, food, sleep, and shelter
2	Safety and security	Personal security, financial security, stability, and protection
3	Social	Love, friendship, and group membership
4	Esteem and status	Self-worth, recognition, and respect
5	Self-actualization	Fulfillment and creativity

According to Maslow, people generally satisfy their needs in order, from lowest (physiological) to highest (self-actualization), although he recognized that people are sometimes motivated by more than one category of need at a time.

One strategy for writing an effective persuasive letter, then, is to decide which level of need your reader is currently trying to satisfy and then appeal to that specific need. In large measure, the nature of the product or idea determines the type of need it meets. However, you can sometimes position the same product to meet different needs.

Assume, for example, that you wanted to persuade your reader to purchase the Elimistress, an isometric exercise device designed to release tension and reduce stress. You might promote the product in a number of ways, depending on the level of need you wished to satisfy.

Physiological: Using the Elimistress a half-hour a day will help your body recover from the stress of the modern executive's typical day.

Social: Don't let the stress of the day's problems affect your leisure-time enjoyment. Use the Elimistress a half-hour a day and enjoy life again.

Self-actualization: Is undue stress and anxiety affecting your ability to fulfill your potential? If so, use the Elimistress a half-hour a day to help unleash your pent-up creativity.

ORGANIZING A PERSUASIVE REQUEST

A persuasive request seeks to motivate the reader to accept your idea (rather than to buy your product). The purpose of your message, your knowledge of the reader, and the type of appeal you choose will help determine the content of your message and the sequence in which you discuss each topic.

Determining How to Start the Message

In the past, it was common practice to organize *all* persuasive messages using an indirect organizational plan—presenting the rationale first, followed by the major idea (the request for action)—and this plan is still used for the majority of persuasive messages. However, writers today should determine which organizational plan (direct or indirect) will help them better achieve their objectives.

Direct Plan—Present the Major Idea First Most superiors prefer to have memos from their subordinates organized in the direct style introduced in Chapter 6. Thus, when writing persuasive memos that travel up the organization, you should generally present the main idea (your recommendation) first, followed by the supporting evidence. The direct organizational plan saves time and immediately satisfies the reader's curiosity about your purpose. To get readers to accept your proposal when using the direct plan, present your recommendation along with the criteria or brief rationale in the first paragraph.

Prefer the direct plan when writing persuasive messages to your superior.

Not: I recommend we hold our Pittsburgh sales meeting at the Mark-Congress Hotel.

But: I have evaluated three hotels as possible meeting sites for our Pittsburgh sales conference and recommend we meet at the Mark-Congress Hotel. As discussed below, the Mark-Congress is centrally located, has the best meeting facilities, and is moderately priced.

In general, you should use the direct organizational plan for persuasive messages when

- Writing to superiors within the organization.
- Your audience is predisposed to listen objectively to your request.
- The proposal does not require strong persuasion (that is, when there are no major obstacles present).
- The proposal is long or complex (a reader may become impatient if your main point is buried in a long report).
- You know that your reader prefers the direct approach.

Indirect Plan—Gain the Reader's Attention First Unfortunately, many times your readers will initially resist your suggestions. Your job then is to explain the merits of your proposal and show how the reader will benefit from doing as you ask. Because a reluctant reader is more likely to agree to an idea *after* he or she understands its merits, your plan of organization is to convince the reader before asking for action.

Thus, you should use the indirect organizational plan when writing to subordinates, when strong persuasion is needed, or when you know that your reader prefers the indirect plan. When using the indirect plan, you delay asking for action until after you've presented your reasons. A subject line is therefore not generally used in persuasive letters. If a subject line is a standard part of the heading for your organization's memorandums, make it neutral. Don't announce your purpose immediately but rather lead up to it gradually.

Not: SUBJECT: Proposal to Sell the Roper Division

But: SUBJECT: Analysis of Roper Division Profitability

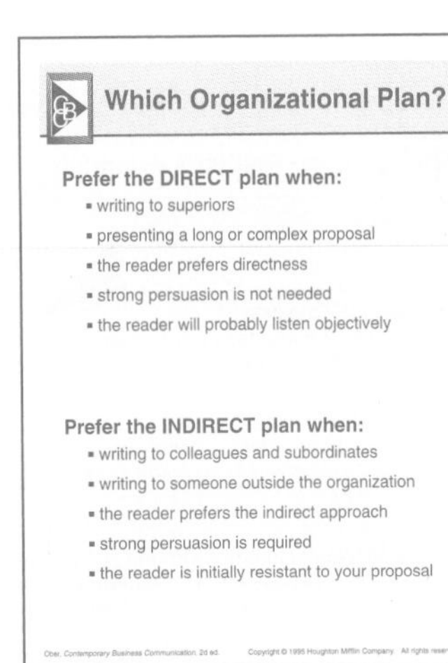

Which Organizational Plan?
Prefer the DIRECT plan when:
• writing to superiors
• presenting a long or complex proposal
• the reader prefers directness
• strong persuasion is not needed
• the reader will probably listen objectively
Prefer the INDIRECT plan when:
• writing to colleagues and subordinates
• writing to someone outside the organization
• the reader prefers the indirect approach
• strong persuasion is required
• the reader is initially resistant to your proposal

See Transparency 7.2, Organizational Plans for Persuasive Messages.

Advertisers often use emotional appeals. What emotions do you think this ad from the Caesars Palace resort hotel in Las Vegas is trying to evoke?

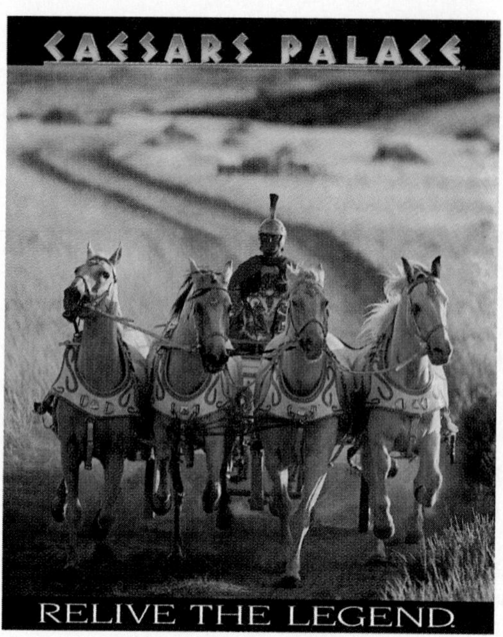

The first test of a good opening sentence in a persuasive request is whether it is interesting enough to catch and keep the reader's attention. It won't matter how much evidence you have marshaled to support your case if the recipient does not bother to continue reading carefully after the first sentence.

A **rhetorical question** is often effective as an opening sentence. A rhetorical question is asked strictly to get the reader thinking about the topic of your message; a literal answer is not expected. Of course, obvious questions are not effective motivators for further reading and, in fact, may insult the reader's intelligence. Similarly, yes-or-no questions rarely make good lead-ins because pondering an answer doesn't require much thought.

Not: How would you like to save our department $7,500 yearly?
But: What do you think the labor costs are for changing just one light bulb? $2? $5? More?

Not: Did you know that the Hartford Community Fund is more than 50 years old?
But: What do Tina Turner and the Hartford Community Fund have in common?

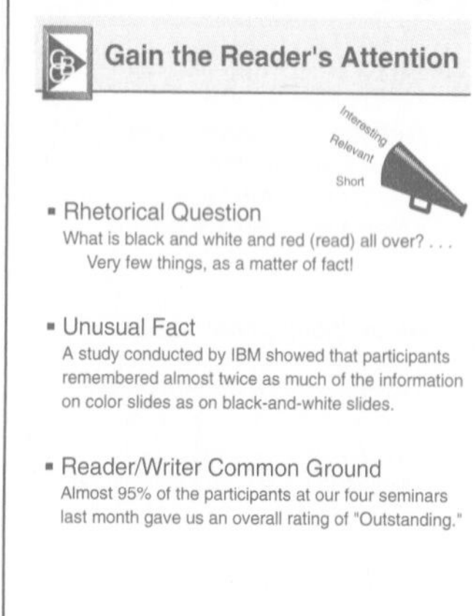

Gain the Reader's Attention
Interesting
Relevant
Short
▪ Rhetorical Question
What is black and white and red (read) all over? . . . Very few things, as a matter of fact!
▪ Unusual Fact
A study conducted by IBM showed that participants remembered almost twice as much of the information on color slides as on black-and-white slides.
▪ Reader/Writer Common Ground
Almost 95% of the participants at our four seminars last month gave us an overall rating of "Outstanding."
Ober, Contemporary Business Communication, 2d ed.
Copyright © 1995 Houghton Mifflin Company. All rights reserved.

See Transparency 7.3, Gaining the Reader's Attention.

Sometimes an unusual fact or unexpected statement will draw the reader into the message. At other times, you might want to select some statement about which the reader and writer will agree—to immediately establish some common ground.

Our company spent more money on janitorial service last year than on research and development.

A five-year-old boy taught me an important lesson last week.

Automotive News calls your 6-year/60,000 mile warranty the best in the business. *(opening for a claim letter)*

Your opening statement must also be relevant to the purpose of your message. If it is too far off the topic or misleads the reader, you risk losing goodwill, and the reader may simply stop reading. At the very least, the reader will feel confused or deceived, making persuasion more difficult.

The opening statement must be relevant.

Keep your opening statement short. Often an opening paragraph of just one sentence will make the message inviting to read. Few readers have the patience to wade through a long introduction to figure out the purpose of the message. In summary, make the opening for a persuasive message written in the indirect organizational plan interesting, relevant, and short. The purpose is to make sure your reader gets to the body of your message.

Creating Interest and Justifying Your Request

Regardless of whether your opening is written in a direct or indirect style, you must now begin the process of convincing the reader that your request is reasonable. This process may require several paragraphs of discussion, depending on how much evidence you think will be needed to convince the reader. Because it takes more space to state *why* something should be done than simply to state *that* it should be done, persuasive requests are typically longer than other types of messages.

To convince your readers, you must be objective, specific, logical, and reasonable. Avoid emotionalism, obvious flattery, insincerity, and exaggeration. Let your evidence carry the weight of your argument.

Provide convincing evidence and use a reasonable tone.

Not: Locating our plant in Suffolk instead of in Norfolk would result in considerable savings.

But: Locating our plant in Suffolk instead of in Norfolk would result in annual savings of nearly $175,000, as shown in Table 3.

Not: Why should it take a thousand phone calls to convince your computer to credit my account for $38.50?

But: Even after five phone calls over the past three weeks, I find that $38.50 has still not been credited to my account.

The type of evidence you present depends, of course, on the circumstances. The usual types of evidence are these:

- *Facts and statistics: Facts* are objective statements whose truth can be verified; *statistics* are facts consisting of numbers. Both must be relevant and accurate. For example, statistics that were accurate five years ago may no longer be accurate today.
- *Expert opinion:* Testimony from authorities on the topic might be presented if their input is relevant and, if necessary, you can supply the experts' credentials.
- *Examples:* Specific cases or incidents used to illustrate the point under discussion should be relevant, representative, and complete.

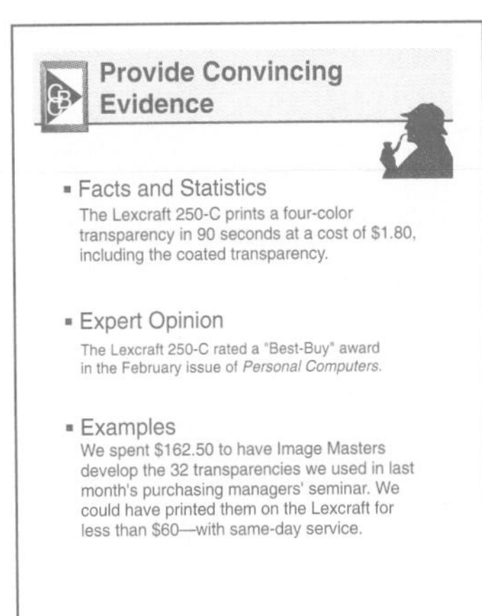

Provide Convincing Evidence
▪ Facts and Statistics
The Lexcraft 250-C prints a four-color transparency in 90 seconds at a cost of $1.80, including the coated transparency.
▪ Expert Opinion
The Lexcraft 250-C rated a "Best-Buy" award in the February issue of *Personal Computers*.
▪ Examples
We spent $162.50 to have Image Masters develop the 32 transparencies we used in last month's purchasing managers' seminar. We could have printed them on the Lexcraft for less than $60—with same-day service.
Ober, *Contemporary Business Communication*, 2d ed.
Copyright © 1995 Houghton Mifflin Company. All rights reserved.

See Transparency 7.4, Providing Convincing Evidence.

Present the benefits (either direct or indirect) that will accompany the adoption of your proposal, and provide enough background and objective evidence to enable the reader to make an informed decision.

Dealing with Obstacles

Ignoring any obvious obstacles to granting your request would provide the reader a ready excuse to refuse your request. Assume, for example, that you're trying to persuade a supplier to provide an in-store demonstrator of the firm's products—even though you know it's against their company policy to do so. If you ignore this factor, you're simply inviting the reader to respond that company policy prohibits granting your request. Instead, your strategy should be to show that *even considering such an obstacle*, your request is still reasonable, perhaps as follows:

Note the reader benefits in the last sentence.

> Last year we sold 356 of your Golden Microwave ovens. We believe the extensive publicity our sale will generate (as well as our previous sales performance) justifies your temporarily setting aside your policy and providing an in-store demonstrator. The ease of use and the actual cooked results that your representative will be able to display are sure to increase the sales of your microwaves.

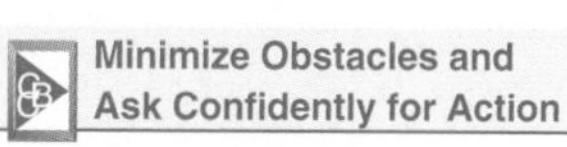
Minimize Obstacles and
Ask Confidently for Action

- **Minimize Obstacles:**
Although the vice president has asked for a moratorium on equipment expenditures until June, if we purchase the $2,100 Lexcraft 250-C printer before December 31, we will actually save that amount in printing costs by April—before our quarterly budget is due.

- **Ask Confidently for Action:**
So that we can have this copier installed in time for us to use at our January sales meetings, may I order this copier for $2,350 (including taxes and shipping) by December 1. Being able to update our charts right up to an hour before our presentation will mean that our figures are the latest available.

Ober, *Contemporary Business Communication*, 2d ed.

See Transparency 7.5, Minimizing Obstacles.

If you're asking someone to speak to a professional organization but are unable to provide an honorarium, emphasize the free publicity the speaker will receive and the impact that the speaker's remarks will have on the audience. If you're asking for confidential information, discuss how you will treat it as such. If you're asking for a large donation, explain how payment can be made on the installment plan or by payroll deduction and point out the tax-deductible aspects of the donation.

Even though you must address the major obstacles, do *not* emphasize them. Subordinate this discussion by devoting relatively little space to it, by dealing with obstacles in the same sentence as a reader benefit, or by putting the discussion in the middle of a paragraph. Regardless of how you do it, show the reader that you're aware of the obvious obstacles and that, despite them, your proposal still has merit.

Motivating Action

Although your request has been stated (direct organizational plan) or implied (indirect organizational plan) earlier, give a direct statement of the request late in the message—after most of the background information and reader benefits have been thoroughly covered. Make the specific action that you want clear and easy to take. For example, if the reader agrees to do as you ask, how is he or she to let you know? Will a phone call suffice, or is a written reply necessary? If a phone call is adequate, have you provided a phone number? If you're asking for a favor that requires a written response, have you included a stamped, addressed envelope?

Ask for the desired action in a confident tone. If your request or proposal is reasonable, there is no need to apologize, and you surely do not want to supply the reader with excuses for refusing. Take whatever steps you can to ensure a prompt reply.

Note the indirect benefit implied.

Not: I know you're a busy person, but I would appreciate your completing this questionnaire.

But: So that this information will be available for the financial managers

CHECKLIST 5

Persuasive Requests

DETERMINE HOW TO START THE MESSAGE

1. **Direct Plan**—Use a direct organizational plan when writing to superiors, when your audience is predisposed to listen objectively to your request, when the proposal does not require strong persuasion, when the proposal is long or complex, or when you know your reader prefers the direct approach. Present the recommendation, along with the criteria or brief rationale, in the first paragraph.

   Indirect Plan—Use an indirect organizational plan when writing to subordinates, when strong persuasion is needed, or when you know your reader prefers the indirect approach. Start by gaining the reader's attention.

   a. Make the first sentence interesting enough to motivate the reader to continue reading. Use, for example, a rhetorical question, unusual fact, unexpected statement, or common-ground statement.
   b. Keep the opening paragraph short (often just one sentence), relevant to the main topic of the message, and, when appropriate, related to a reader benefit.

CREATE INTEREST AND JUSTIFY YOUR REQUEST

2. Devote the major part of your message to justifying your request. Give enough background and evidence to enable the reader to make an informed decision.
3. Use facts and statistics, expert opinion, and examples to support your proposal. Ensure that the evidence is accurate, relevant, representative, and complete.
4. Use an objective, logical, reasonable, and sincere tone. Avoid obvious flattery, emotionalism, and exaggeration.
5. Present the evidence in terms of either direct or indirect reader benefits.

MINIMIZE OBSTACLES

6. Do not ignore obstacles or any negative aspects of your request. Instead, show that even considering them, your request is still reasonable.
7. Subordinate the discussion of obstacles by position and amount of space devoted to the topic.

ASK CONFIDENTLY FOR ACTION

8. State (or restate) the specific request late in the message—after most of the benefits have been discussed.
9. Make the desired action clear and easy for the reader to take, use a confident tone, do not apologize, and do not supply excuses.
10. End on a forward-looking note, continuing to stress reader benefits.

attending our fall conference, I would appreciate your returning the questionnaire by May 15.

Not: If you agree this proposal is worthwhile, please let me know by June 1.

But: To enable us to have this plan in place before the opening of our new branch on June 1, simply initial this memo and return it to me.

Note the motivation for a prompt reply.

Checklist 5 summarizes guidelines to use in writing persuasive requests. Although you will not be able to use all these suggestions in each persuasive request, you should use them as an overall framework for structuring your persuasive message.

"You've got to find the decision maker's hot button," says Brenda Brimmer, director of sales for American Express Travel Related Services. "If you're trying to sell an idea that has ten benefits, but only one of those ten really concerns the person who's making the decision, then you'll just be spinning wheels by spending a lot of time on the nine other points." (From Diane Cole, "Putting Words to Work," *Savvy*, July 1985, pp. 32–33.)

For other examples of selling an idea, see the *Instructor's Resource Manual*, pp. 117, 118, 119, 120, and 121.

COMMON TYPES OF PERSUASIVE REQUESTS

In many ways, writing a persuasive request is more difficult than writing a sales letter because reader benefits are not always so obvious in persuasive requests. This section provides specific strategies and examples for selling an idea, requesting a favor, and writing a persuasive claim letter.

Selling an Idea

You will have many opportunities to use your education and experience to help solve problems faced by your organization. On the job you will frequently write letters or memorandums proposing one alternative over another, suggesting a new procedure, or in some other way recommending some course of action. Organize such messages logically, showing what the problem is, how you intend to solve the problem, and why your solution is sound. Write in an objective style and provide evidence to support your claims.

The memo in Figure 7.1 illustrates the selling of an idea. In this case, a marketing supervisor for an auto-parts supplier is asking the vice president to reassign parking spaces to give preference to those employees driving American-made cars. Because the memo is written to his superior, the writer uses a direct organizational style.

Requesting a Favor

Favors require persuasion because the reader gets nothing tangible in return.

It has been said that the wheels of industry are greased with favors. The giving and receiving of favors makes success more likely and makes life in general more agreeable.

A request for a favor differs from a routine request in that routine requests are granted almost automatically, whereas favors require persuasion. For example, asking a colleague to trade places with you on the program for the monthly managers' meeting might be considered a routine request. Asking the same colleague to prepare and give your presentation for you would more likely be a favor, requiring some persuasion.

Although friends and close colleagues often do each other favors as a matter of course, many times in business the granting of a favor might not be so automatic—especially if you don't know the person to whom you're writing. In such situations, you will want to begin your request with an attention-getter and stress the reader benefits from granting the favor.

For a sincere tone, make any flattering comments unique to the reader.

Discuss at least one reader benefit before making your request. Explain why the favor is being asked and continue to show how the reader (or someone else) will benefit from granting the favor. Keep a positive, confident tone throughout, and make the action clear and easy to take.

Often the favor is requested because the reader is an expert on some topic. If that is the case, you may legitimately make a complimentary remark about the reader. Make sure, however, that your compliment sounds sincere. Readers are rightfully suspicious, for example, when they read in a

FIGURE 7.1 Selling an Idea—Direct Plan

This persuasive memo uses the direct plan because the memo travels up the organization.

+ Timkin
+ Electrical
+ Systems

1 MEMO TO: Elliott Lamborn, Vice President

FROM: Jenson Peterson, Marketing Supervisor *JP*

DATE: October 3, 19--

SUBJECT: Proposal to Reassign Parking Lots

As one means of emphasizing our support for the American auto industry, I propose that the close-in parking lots around our headquarters be restricted to use by American-made cars.

Begins by introducing the recommendation, along with a brief rationale.

Whenever customers from the auto industry visit our headquarters, they must either drive by or walk through Parking Lots A and B, those nearest the building. When they do, they will see, as our staff did during a recent
2 inspection, that approximately 30% of our employees drive foreign-made cars—despite the fact that nearly all our business comes from the American auto industry.

I recognize, of course, that many factors go into the decision to purchase a particular car. However, as a purchasing agent from Embassy told me last week, "How can you expect us to support you when you don't support us?" This executive was not asking us specifically to promote Embassy cars—just American-made cars.

Provides a smooth transition to the necessary background information. Cites statistics and external testimony for credibility.

The purpose of this memo, then, is to seek approval to have Parking Lots A and B and Rows 1-5 of the Executive Parking Lot restricted to use by American-made cars. The Maintenance Department estimates that it will need four weeks and about $500 to make the needed signs.

Repeats the recommendation after presenting most of the rationale.

Our labor contract requires union approval of any changes in working conditions. However, Sally Merritt, our shop steward, has told me that she would be willing to discuss this matter—especially if a similar restriction is made for the Executive Parking Lot.

Neutralizes an obvious obstacle.

3 Since our quarterly marketing managers' meeting will be held on November 8-10, I look forward to being able to announce the new plan to them then. By approving this change, you will be sending a powerful positive message to headquarters visitors: our employees believe in the products we sell.

Closes on a positive, confident note; motivates prompt action.

urs

– 1034 York Road
– Baltimore, MD 21204
– Phone: 301-555-1086

Grammar and Mechanics Notes

1 If you need the space for a long one-page memo, begin typing the heading lines 1 inch from the top (instead of 2 inches) or begin 2 or 3 lines below the letterhead. 2 *30%:* Use figures and the % sign in business correspondence. 3 *managers' meeting:* Place the apostrophe *after* the *s* to form the possessive of a plural noun (*managers*).

For a discussion on persuading someone to give charity and persuading someone to grant credit, see the supplemental lecture/discussion notes in the *Instructor's Resource Manual*, p. 100.

For other examples of requesting a favor, see the *Instructor's Resource Manual*, pp. 122, 123, and 124.

If your students need practice in writing pronouns correctly, refer them to "Apostrophes: Pronoun" in LAB 2, p. 599.

form letter that they have been specifically chosen to participate in some project. ("Me and how many thousands of others" they might wonder.) On the other hand, such a compliment in a letter that is obviously personally typed and signed has much more credibility.

The most important factor to remember in asking for a favor has to do with the favor itself rather than with the writing process. Keep your request reasonable. Don't ask someone else to do something that you can or should do for yourself.

Figure 7.2 illustrates a persuasive request, asking for a favor. The reader and writer do not know each other, which makes persuasion a little more challenging and which calls for an indirect organizational plan. Reader benefits (the opportunity to promote the reader's firm and the flattering prospect of being the center of attention) are included.

Writing a Persuasive Claim

As discussed in Chapter 6, most claim letters are routine letters and should be written using a direct plan of organization—stating the problem early in the letter. Because it is to the company's benefit to keep its clientele happy, most reasonable claims are settled to the customer's satisfaction. Therefore, persuasion is not ordinarily necessary.

Suppose, however, that you wrote a routine claim letter and the company, for some reason, denied your claim. If you still feel that your original claim is legitimate, you might then write a *persuasive* claim letter—using all the techniques discussed earlier in this chapter for writing persuasive requests. Or assume that your new photocopier broke three days after the warranty period expired. The company is not legally obligated to honor your claim, but you may decide to try to persuade them to do so anyway.

Avoid showing anger.

Showing anger in your persuasive claim letter would be counterproductive, even if the company turned down your original claim. The goal of your letter is not to vent your anger but to solve a problem. And that is more likely to happen when a calm atmosphere prevails.

As in a routine claim letter, you will need to explain in sufficient detail precisely what the problem is, how it came about, and how you want the reader to solve the problem. Use a calm, objective, courteous tone, avoiding anger and exaggeration. Although similar in some respects to a routine claim letter, the persuasive claim differs in two important ways: it has an attention-getting opening and it presents more evidence.

Research shows that 95% of dissatisfied customers don't bother to complain to the company in question, which makes the 5% who do complain a valuable source of information about what the company can do to improve its product or service. A reasonable complaint letter, then, is likely to elicit a reasonable response from any company interested in its customers' satisfaction. (Adapted from Michael Abrams and Matthew Pease, "Wining and Dining the Whiners," *Sales and Marketing Management*, February 1993, pp. 73–75.)

Attention-Getting Opening Recall that you begin a routine claim letter by stating the problem. This type of opening would not be wise for a persuasive claim, because the reader may conclude the claim is unreasonable until he or she gets to your rationale.

Not: Would you please repair my Marlow 203 copier without charge, even though the 90-day warranty expired last week.

But: We took a chance and lost! We bet that the Marlow 203 we purchased from you 96 days ago would prove to be as reliable as the other ten Marlows our firm uses.

The original opening is counterproductive, providing a ready excuse for denying the claim. The revised version holds off making the request

FIGURE 7.2 Requesting a Favor—Indirect Plan

This persuasive request uses the indirect plan because the writer does not personally know the reader and thus cannot expect the favor to be granted automatically.

BALTIMORE IBM
USER'S GROUP

B

January 15, 19--

Ms. Tanya Porratt, President
The Office Training Group
1800 Ten Hills Road, Suite B
Boston, MA 02145

Dear Ms. Porratt:

"Desktop publishing has been around for 100 years."

1 This comment of yours in a recent interview published in the *Boston Globe*
certainly made me sit up and think. After all,the first desktop publishing
software was introduced only in 1986—certainly not 100 years ago.

Opens by quoting the reader, thus complimenting her.

Members of the Baltimore IBM User's Group would enjoy and benefit from hearing
a respected DTP professional who has been actively involved in the field since
2 its inception. As the speaker at our annual banquet at the Baltimore Park
Plaza Hotel on April 25, you would be able to present your ideas on DTP to our
200 members. You would, of course, be our guest for the banquet, which begins
at 7 p.m. Your 45-minute presentation would begin at 8:30 p.m.

Intimates the request; provides the necessary background information.

We will reimburse you for air travel and hotel accommodations. Although our nonprofit association is unable to offer an honorarium, we do offer you an opportunity to introduce your firm and to present your ideas to representatives of every major company in the Baltimore metropolitan area.

Subordinates a potential obstacle by putting it in the dependent clause of a sentence.

We would like to announce your speech as the lead article in our next
newsletter, which goes to press on March 23. Won't you please use the
3 enclosed postal card to let us know that you can come. We will have a large,
enthusiastic audience of decision-makers waiting to hear you.

Closes with a restatement of a reader benefit.

Cordially,

Magda D. Lyon

Magda D. Lyon
Banquet Chairperson

jrk
Enclosure

P.O. Box 1038 ▪ Baltimore, MD 21204 ▪ 301-555-9879

Grammar and Mechanics Notes

1 *Boston Globe:* Either italicize or underline the titles of complete works, such as newspapers, magazines, or books. 2 *its:* Use no apostrophe when the pronoun is used to show possession. 3 *that you can come.:* Use a period after a courteous request.

until enough background information has been provided. Note also the personal relationship the writer is beginning to establish with the reader in the revised version—discussing not only that the company owns ten other Marlow copiers but also that the other copiers have all been very reliable. Such an understanding tone will make the reader more likely to grant the request.

In a courteous manner, provide complete details.

More Evidence Because your claim either is nonroutine or has been rejected once, you will need to present as much convincing evidence as possible. Explain fully the basis for your claim; then request a specific adjustment.

Figure 7.3 illustrates these guidelines for writing a persuasive claim letter.

For other examples of persuasive claims, see the *Instructor's Resource Manual*, pp. 125, 126, 127, and 128.

WRITING A SALES LETTER

The heart of most business is sales—selling a product or service. Much of a company's sales effort is accomplished through the writing of effective sales letters—either individual letters for individual sales or form letters for large-scale sales.

In large companies, the writing of sales letters is centered in the marketing or advertising department and is a highly specialized task performed by advertising copywriters and marketing consultants. Within a few years after graduation, however, a growing number of college students opt to own their own businesses. These start-up companies are typically quite small, with only a few employees.

Small-business owners often write their own sales letters.

In such a situation, the company must mount an aggressive sales effort in order to develop business, but the company is often too small to hire a full-time copywriter or marketing consultant. Thus, the owner usually ends up writing these sales letters, which are vital to the ongoing health of the firm. So no matter where you intend to work, the chances are that at some point you will need to write sales letters.

The indirect organizational plan is used for sales letters. It is sometimes called the *AIDA* plan, because you first gain the reader's *attention*, then create *interest* in and *desire* for the benefits of your product, and finally motivate *action*.

Selecting a Central Selling Theme

Companies are quickly learning the connection between customer service and ease of making sales. Closing the sale is a lot easier when a salesperson can say to a customer, "If you are not satisfied, we will give you your money back."

Your first step is to become thoroughly familiar with your product, its competition, and your intended audience. Then, you must select a **central selling theme** for your letter. Most products have numerous features that you will want to introduce and discuss. For your letter to make a real impact, however, you need to have a single theme running through your letter—a major reader benefit that you introduce early and emphasize throughout the letter. One noted copywriting consultant calls this principle a basic law of direct-mail advertising and labels it $E^2 = 0$, meaning that when you try to emphasize *everything*, you end up emphasizing *nothing*.[2]

FIGURE 7.3 Making a Persuasive Claim—Indirect Plan

This persuasive claim uses the indirect plan because the writer does not personally know the reader and because strong persuasion is needed.

June 18, 19--

Customer Services Supervisor
Northern Airlines, Inc.
P.O. Box 6001
Denver, CO 80240

Dear Customer Services Supervisor:

I think you will agree that a relaxing 90-minute flight on Northern Airlines is more enjoyable than a grueling six-hour automobile trip.

Begins on a warm and relevant note.

1 Yet, on June 2, my wife and I found ourselves doing just that—driving from
Saginaw, Michigan, to Indianapolis—in the middle of the night and in the
company of three tired children.

Provides a smooth transition from the opening sentence.

We had made reservations on Northern Flight 126 a month earlier. To obtain
2 the cheapest fare ($136 per ticket), we had purchased nonrefundable tickets.
When we arrived at the airport, we were told that Flight 126, scheduled to
depart at 8 p.m., had been canceled. Your gate agent (Ms. Nixon) had
graciously rebooked us in complimentary first-class seats on the next
available flight, leaving at 9:45 the following morning.

Provides the necessary background information.

Since the purpose of our trip was to attend a family wedding on June 3, we had no choice but to cancel our rebooked flight and to drive to Indianapolis instead. When we tried to turn in our tickets for a refund, Ms. Nixon informed us that because the flight had been canceled due to inclement weather, she would be unable to credit my American Express charge card.

Tells exactly what the problem is in a neutral, courteous tone.

As a frequent flier on Northern, I've experienced firsthand the "Welcome
Aboard!" feeling that is the basis for your current advertising campaign; and
3 I believe you will want to extend that same taken-care-of feeling to your
ticket operations as well. Please credit my American Express charge card
(Account No. 4102 817 171) for the $680 cost of the five tickets, thus putting
out the welcome mat again for my family.

Provides a rationale for granting the claim; asks confidently for specific action; mentions the reader benefit of keeping a satisfied customer.

Sincerely,

Oliver J. Arbin

Oliver J. Arbin
4 518 Thompson Street
Saginaw, MI 48607

Grammar and Mechanics Notes

1 *just that—driving:* If your keyboard doesn't have a dash, type two hyphens (--) with no space before or after. 2 *nonrefundable:* Write most *non-* words solid—without a hyphen.
3 taken-care-of feeling: Hyphenate a compound adjective that comes before a noun.
4 For personal business letters on plain paper, type your address below your name.

It would be unrealistic to expect your reader to remember five different features that you mention about your product. In any case, you have only a short time to make a lasting impression on your reader. Use that time wisely to emphasize what you think is the most compelling benefit from owning your product. Two means of achieving this emphasis are *position* and *repetition.* Introduce your central selling theme early (in the opening sentence if possible), and keep repeating it throughout the letter.

Gaining the Reader's Attention

Review the earlier section on gaining the reader's attention when writing persuasive requests.

A reply to a request for product information from a potential customer is called a **solicited sales letter.** An **unsolicited sales letter,** on the other hand, is a letter promoting a firm's products that is mailed to potential customers who have not expressed any interest in the product. (Unsolicited sales letters are also called *prospecting letters.*)

Because most sales letters are unsolicited, you have only a line or two in which to grab the reader's attention. Unless a sales letter is addressed to the reader personally and is obviously not a form letter, the reader is likely to just skim it—either out of curiosity or because the opening sentence got the reader's attention.

Most readers will scan the opening even of a form letter, perhaps just to learn what product is being promoted. If you can capture their attention in these first few lines, they may continue reading. Otherwise, all your efforts will have been wasted. The following types of opening sentences have proven effective for sales letters.

Technique	*Example*
Rhetorical question	What is the difference between extravagance and luxury? (*promoting a luxury car*)
Thought-provoking statement	Most of what we had to say about business this morning was unprintable! (*promoting early-morning television news program*)
Unusual fact	If your family is typical, you will wash one ton of laundry this year. (*promoting a laundry detergent*)
Current event	The new Arrow assembly plant will bring 1,700 new families to White Rock within three years. (*promoting a real-estate company*)
Anecdote	During six years of college, the one experience that helped me the most did not even occur in the classroom. (*promoting a weekly business magazine*)
Direct challenge	Drop the enclosed Pointer pen on the floor, writing tip first, and then sign your name with it. (*promoting a no-blot ball-point pen*)

In introducing the purple dinosaur Barney, Sheryl Leach focused on her ultimate audience, the child. She gave potential buyers copies of the Barney tape for their own kids. When they saw how much their children liked Barney, many ordered the tapes for their stores.

As in persuasive requests, the opening to a sales letter should be interesting, short, and original. When possible, incorporate the central selling theme into your opening; and avoid irrelevant, obvious, or timeworn statements.

Many attention-getting openings consist of a one-sentence paragraph.

If you have received an inquiry from a potential customer about your product, you know that the person is already at least mildly interested in the product. Therefore, when you write solicited sales letters, an attention-getting opening is not as crucial. In such a situation, you might begin by expressing appreciation for the customer's inquiry and then start introducing the central selling theme.

Creating Interest and Building Desire

If your opening sentence is directly related to your product, the transition to the discussion of features and reader benefits will be smooth and logical. Make sure that the first sentence of the following paragraph relates directly to the idea introduced in your opening sentence. Unrelated ideas will make the reader pause and feel puzzled.

Interpreting Features The major part of your letter (typically, several paragraphs) will probably be devoted to creating interest and building desire for your product. You should not only describe the product and its features but, more important, *interpret* these features by showing specifically how each will benefit the reader. Make the reader—not the product—the subject of most of your sentences.

Devote several paragraphs to interpreting the product's features.

Marketers refer to the benefit a user receives from a product or service as the **derived benefit.** As Charles Revson, founder of Revlon Cosmetics, once said, "In our factory we make lipstick; in our advertising we sell hope."[3]

Not: The JT Laser II prints at the speed of eight pages per minute.

But: After pressing the print key, you'll barely have time to reach over and retrieve the page from the bin. The JT Laser II's print speed of eight pages per minute is five times faster than that of the typical dot-matrix printer.

Not: Masco binoculars zoom from 3 to 12 power.

But: With Masco binoculars, you can look a ruby-throated hummingbird squarely in the eye at 300 feet and see it blink.

Interpret — Don't Just Describe

Not: The Comfy Lap Desk is 13" by 31".

But: The Comfy Lap Desk's 13" by 31" surface provides enough room to hold an open encyclopedia and still have room to take notes.

Not: This portable desk weighs only 12 ounces.

But: You don't have to be afraid to rest this lap desk on your knees for hours at a time. It weighs just 12 ounces — about the same as your favorite can of soft drink.

See Transparency 7.6., Interpreting Features.

Although emphasizing the derived benefit rather than product features is generally the preferred strategy, there are two situations that call for emphasizing product features instead: when promoting a product to experts and when promoting expensive equipment. For example, if the car you're promoting to sports car enthusiasts achieves a maximum torque of 138 ft.-lbs. at 3,000 rpm or produces 145 hp at 5,500 rpm, tell the reader that. You would sound condescending trying to interpret what this means to such experts.

Using Vivid Language Use action-packed verbs when talking about the product's features and benefits. Within reason, use colorful adjectives and adverbs, being careful to avoid a hard-sell approach. Finally, to convey a dynamic image, use positive language, stressing what your product *is*, rather than what it is *not*.

Not: The paper tray is designed to hold 200 sheets.
But: The paper tray holds 200 sheets—enough to last the busy executive a full week without reloading.

Not: The Terminator snowblower is not one of those lightweight models.
But: The Terminator's 4.5 hp engine is 50% more powerful than the standard 3.0 hp engine used in most snowblowers.

Maintain credibility by providing specific facts and figures.

Using Objective, Ethical Language To be convincing, you must present specific, objective evidence. Simply saying that a product is great is not enough. You must provide evidence to show *why* or *how* it is great. Here is where you'll use all the data you gathered about your product before you started to write. Avoid generalities, unsupported superlatives and claims, and too many or too strong adjectives and adverbs.

Positive statements by independent agencies lend powerful support.

Not: At $395, the Sherwood moped is the best buy on the market.
But: The May 1995 *Independent Consumer* rated the $395 Sherwood moped as the year's best buy.

Not: We are sure you will enjoy the convenience of our Bread Bakery.
But: Our Bread Bakery comes with one feature we don't think you'll ever use: a 30-day, no-questions-asked return policy.

For an extended discussion of legal and ethical issues, see "Ethics and Communication" in Chapter 2, pp. 45–48.

Although the law allows you to promote your product aggressively, there are certain legal and ethical constraints under which you will want to operate. The guidelines provided in the Spotlight on Law and Ethics apply to American law and customs. When operating in the international environment, you should follow local laws and customs.

Focusing on the Central Selling Theme The recurring theme of your letter should be the one feature that sets your product apart from the competition. If your reader remembers nothing else about your product, this one feature is what you want him or her to remember. Whenever possible, unify the features under one umbrella theme—whether the theme is convenience, ease of use, flexibility, price, or some other distinguishing characteristic around which you can build your case.

An encyclopedia called *Rezide* offers a wealth of demographic information organized by Zip Code. In book form or CD-ROM, it provides 122 statistics—such as income and number of bedrooms—for each of the 42,496 U.S. Zip Codes. Companies like Spiegel use *Rezide* for target marketing and direct mail campaigns. ("42,496 Secrets Are Bared," *Fortune*, January 24, 1994.)

Discussing and fully interpreting these features may take a considerable amount of space; and some readers may be unwilling to read through a long sales letter. However, those who do will be more motivated to respond favorably. The test of an effective sales letter is the number of sales it generates—*not* the number of people who read the letter.

Mentioning Price If price is your central selling theme, introduce it early and emphasize it often. In most cases, however, price is not the central sell-

SPOTLIGHT ON LAW AND ETHICS

What May You Say in a Sales Letter?

May I say that our product is the best on the market? Yes. You may legally express an opinion about your product; this is called *puffery*. You may not, however, make a claim that can be proven false, such as saying that your product is cheaper than a competing product when, in fact, it is not.

The typist mistakenly typed the price of our product as $19.95, instead of the correct price of $29.95. Do I have to sell it for $19.95?
No. You are not legally responsible for an honest mistake, as long as your intent was not to deceive the buyer.

May I include a sample of my product with my letter and require the reader to either send payment or return the product at my expense?
No. Readers do not have to pay for or return any unordered goods. They may legally treat them as a gift from you.

I want to send a sales letter promoting our rock music to high school students. May I legally accept orders from minors?
Yes. You may accept their orders, and if you do, you are legally bound to honor the contract. However, until they reach the age of adulthood (18 years in some states and 21 in others), minors may legally cancel a contract and return the merchandise to you.

I want to sell the furniture in my showroom that has small knicks and scratches on it. If I state in my sales letter that all sales are final and sale items are marked "as is," do I have to issue refunds to anyone who complains?
No. By using the term "as is," you tell the consumer that you are not promising new merchandise.

Without my knowledge, my assistant wrote a letter in which she promised a customer a 10% price break; such a price reduction is clearly against store policy. Do we have to honor my assistant's price?
Yes. Your assistant was acting as your agent, and her promise is legally binding on your firm.

Sources: Ronald A. Anderson, Ivan Fox, and David P. Twomey, *Business Law and the Legal Environment*, 14th ed. South-Western, Cincinnati, OH, 1990; Gordon W. Brown, Edward E. Byers, and Mary Ann Lawlor, *Business Law: With UCC Applications*, 7th ed. McGraw-Hill, New York, 1989; Neil Story and Lynn Ward, *American Business Law and the Regulatory Environment*, South-Western, Cincinnati, OH, 1989.

ing theme and should therefore be subordinated. Introduce the price late in the message, after most of the advantages of owning the product have been discussed. To subordinate price, state it in a long, complex, or compound sentence, perhaps in a sentence that also mentions a reader benefit.

> You'll consider the $250 cost of this spreadsheet seminar repaid in full the very next time your boss asks you to revise the quarterly sales budget—on a Friday afternoon!

Use techniques of subordination when mentioning price.

Sometimes it is helpful to present the price in terms of small units, for example, showing how subscribing to a weekly magazine costs less than $1 per week, rather than $50 a year. Or compare the price to a familiar object—about what you'd pay for your morning newspaper or cup of coffee.

Referring to Enclosures Sometimes, some of the features of a product or service are best displayed in a brochure that you can enclose with the sales letter. Subordinate your reference to the enclosure, and refer to some specific item in the enclosure to increase the likelihood of its being read.

Note the porcelain robin's detailed coloring on the actual-size photograph on page 2 of the enclosed brochure.

Use the enclosed order blank to send us your order today. Within three weeks, you will be enjoying this museum-quality sculpture in your own home.

Motivating Action

For an exercise on microwriting a persuasive request, see the *Instructor's Resource Manual*, pp. 305–307.

Although the purpose of your letter should be apparent right from the start, delay making your specific request until late in the letter—after you have created interest and built desire for the product. Then state the specific action you want.

If the desired action is an actual sale, make the action easy to take by including a toll-free number, enclosing an order blank, accepting credit cards, and the like. For high-priced items, it would be unreasonable to expect to make an actual sale by mail. Probably no one has read a sales letter promoting a new automobile and then phoned in an order for the car. For such items, your goal is to get the reader to make just a small step toward purchasing—sending for more information, stopping by the dealer for a demonstration, or asking a sales representative to call. Again, make the step easy for the reader to take.

Provide an incentive for prompt action by, for example, offering a gift to the first 100 people who respond or stressing the need to buy early while there is still a good selection, before the holiday rush, or during the three-day sale. Make your push for action *gently,* however. Any tactic that smacks of high-pressure selling at this point is likely to increase reader resistance.

Use confident language when asking for action, avoiding such hesitant phrases as "If you want to save money" or "I hope you agree that this product will save you time." When asking the reader to part with money, it is always a good idea to mention a reader benefit in the same sentence.

Push confidently, but gently, for prompt action.

Not: Hurry! Hurry! Hurry! These sale prices won't be in effect long.

Not: If you agree that this ice cream maker will make your summers more enjoyable, you can place your order by telephone.

But: To have your Jiffy Ice Cream Maker available for use during the upcoming July 4 weekend, simply call our toll-free number today.

Consider putting an important marketing point in a postscript (P.S.). Some marketing studies have shown that a postscript notation is the most often read part of a sales letter.[4] It can be as long or as short as needed, but it should contain new and interesting information.

P.S. If you stop in for a demonstration before May 1, you'll walk out with a free box of color transparencies (retail value $21.95)—just for trying Up Front, the new presentation software program by Acme Products.

For an exercise on revising a promotional sales letter, refer students to the *Study Guide*, pp. 118–119.

The above guidelines for writing an effective sales letter are illustrated in Figure 7.4 and summarized in Checklist 6. As always, the test of the effectiveness of a message is whether it achieves its goal. Use whatever information you have available (especially in terms of audience analysis) to help your letter achieve its goal.

If your students need practice using commas, refer them to LAB 1, beginning on p. 594.

FIGURE 7.4 Sales Letter

H S P
Home Security Products
Box 302, Edenton, NC 27932
919-555-4022

1

2 Dear Homeowner:

Do you view your home as an investment or as your castle? Is it primarily a tax write-off or a place of refuge—a place where you can find comfort and respite from workday stress?

Most of us view our homes as places where we can feel safe from outside intrusions. Thus, we feel threatened by government statistics showing that 5.3% of all U.S. households were burglarized last year. How can we protect ourselves?

Today, there's a simple and dependable alarm that protects up to 2,500 square feet of your home. Just plug in the Safescan Home Alarm System, adjust the sensitivity to the size of your home, and turn the key. You then have 30 seconds to leave and 15 seconds to switch off the alarm once you return.

Worried that your dog might trigger the alarm? You needn't be, because
3 Safescan's microprocessor screens out normal sounds like crying babies, outside traffic, and rain. But hostile noises like breaking glass and splintering wood trigger the alarm. The 105-decibel siren is loud enough to alert neighbors and to drive away even the most determined burglar.

What if a smart burglar disconnects the electricity to your home or pulls the plug? No problem, because built-in batteries assure that Safescan operates through power failures up to 24 hours, and the batteries recharge automatically. Best of all, installation couldn't be easier. Simply mount the 4-pound unit on a wall (we supply the four screws), and plug it in. Nothing could be faster.

Finally, there is a $259 home alarm that you can trust; and the one-year warranty and 30-day return policy ensure your complete satisfaction.

Last year, 3.2 million burglaries occurred in the United States, but you can now tip the odds back in your favor. To order the Safescan Home Alarm System, use your credit card and call our operator toll-free at 800-555-2934. Within ten days, Safescan will be guarding your home, giving you peace of mind.

Sincerely,

Jeffrey Parret

Jeffrey Parret
National Sales Manager

Starts with a rhetorical question.

Uses Maslow's Level 2 need (safety and security) as the central selling theme.

Presents specific evidence and discusses it in terms of reader benefits.

Emphasizes *you* instead of the product in most sentences.

Subordinates price in a long sentence that also discusses benefits.

Makes the desired action clear and easy to take; ends with a reader benefit.

Grammar and Mechanics Notes

1 In general, omit the date and inside address in form sales letters. 2 *Dear Homeowner:* Note the generic salutation. 3 *crying babies, outside traffic, and:* Separate items in a series by commas.

CHECKLIST 6

Sales Letters

PREPARE

1. Learn as much as possible about the product, the competition, and the audience.
2. Select a central selling theme—your product's most distinguishing feature.

GAIN THE READER'S ATTENTION

3. Make your opening brief, interesting, and original. Avoid obvious, misleading, and irrelevant statements.
4. Use any of the following types of openings: rhetorical question, thought-provoking statement, unusual fact, current event, anecdote, direct challenge, or some similar attention-getting device.
5. Introduce (or at least lead up to) the central selling theme in the opening.
6. If the letter is in response to a customer inquiry, begin by expressing appreciation for the inquiry and introduce the central selling theme.

CREATE INTEREST AND BUILD DESIRE

7. Make the introduction of the product follow naturally from the attention-getter.
8. *Interpret* the features of the product; instead of just describing the features, show how the reader will benefit from each feature. Let the reader picture owning, using, and enjoying the product.
9. Use action-packed, positive, and objective language. Provide convincing evidence to support your claims—specific facts and figures, independent product reviews, endorsements, and so on.
10. Continue to stress the central selling theme throughout.
11. Subordinate price (unless price is the central selling theme). State price in small terms, in a long sentence, or in a sentence that talks about benefits.

MOTIVATE ACTION

12. Make the desired action clear and easy to take.
13. Ask confidently, avoiding the hesitant "if you'd like to" or "I hope you agree that."
14. Encourage prompt action (but avoid a hard-sell approach).
15. End your letter with a reminder of a reader benefit.

MICROWRITING

A Sales Letter

PROBLEM

You are the proprietor of Lee's Consumer Products, a small retail store located in the Fiesta Mall, 1200 Dobson Road, Mesa, AZ 85201. You are the exclusive dealer for Voice Note, a recorder that allows you to record messages to yourself rather than scribbling them on scraps of paper.

The recorder is 2½ × 1 × ½ inches, weighs 3 ounces, and is made in Japan from sturdy plastic. It records messages up to 30 seconds long and holds 10 minutes of dictation. A lock button prevents recording over a message. After the message has been played back, the loop-to-loop tape automatically resets for use the next time. The Voice Note is operated by pressing the record button and speaking. It runs on two AAA batteries that are included and comes with a 90-day warranty and a 30-day full-refund policy.

To promote this product, you decide to try a direct-mail campaign directed at the business community. You purchase a mailing list containing the names and addresses of the 800 members of the Phoenix Athletic Club, a downtown facility used by business people for lunch, after-work drinks, exercise, and social affairs. The club has racquetball and tennis courts, an indoor pool, and exercise rooms. Its yearly membership fee is $1,500. You decide to send these 800 members a form letter promoting the Voice Note for $29. You'll include your local phone number (555-2394) for placing credit-card orders by phone, or the readers may stop by the store to purchase the recorder in person.

PROCESS

1. Describe your audience.

   - Business men and women
   - Active (sports and exercise facilities)
   - Upscale (can afford $1,500 annual membership)
   - Probably very busy professionally and socially

2. What will be your central selling theme?

   Convenience/portability is the unique benefit of Voice Note.

3. Write an attention-getter that is original, interesting, and short; that is reader-oriented; that relates to the product; and, if possible, that introduces the central selling theme.

   You're driving home on the freeway in bumper-to-bumper traffic when the solution to a nagging problem facing you at work suddenly pops into your head. But by the time you get home 30 minutes later, your good idea has vanished.

4. Jot down the features you might discuss and the reader benefits associated with each feature.

    Size is $2\frac{1}{2} \times 1 \times \frac{1}{2}$ inches, weighs 3 oz.: *Smaller and lighter than a microcassette recorder; fits in shirt pocket or purse; easy to use on the go.*

    Records 30-second messages—up to 10 minutes' worth: *Room enough for most "to-do" messages—20 different ones.*

    Press record button and then speak; lock function prevents overrecording: *Easy to use, even in car; not a lot of buttons to fiddle with.*

    Powered by two AAA batteries (included): *Real portability.*

5. Write the sentence that mentions price. (Since price is not the central selling theme, it should be subordinated.)

    The Voice Note's price of $29 is less than you'd pay for a bulky microcassette recorder that is much less convenient for on-the-go use.

6. What action are you seeking from the reader?

    To purchase the Voice Note.

7. How can you motivate prompt action?

    Make the action easy to take; offer warranty and guarantee satisfaction; stress the sooner you buy, the sooner you'll enjoy using it.

A Sales Letter, continued

PRODUCT

LEE'S

CONSUMER

PRODUCTS

Dear Club Member:

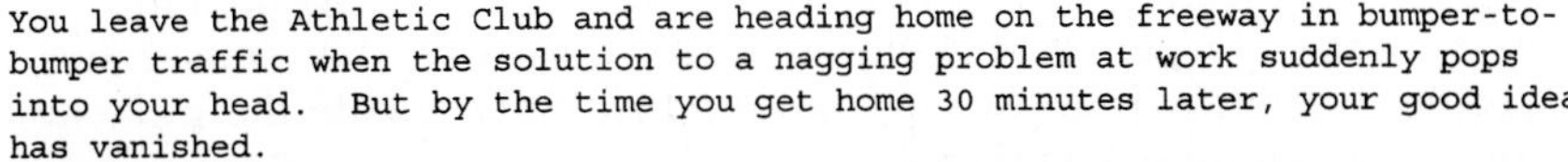

You leave the Athletic Club and are heading home on the freeway in bumper-to-bumper traffic when the solution to a nagging problem at work suddenly pops into your head. But by the time you get home 30 minutes later, your good idea has vanished.

Next time, carry Voice Note, the 3-ounce recorder that allows you to record reminders to yourself on the go. Now you can "jot" down your ideas as soon as they occur: while jogging, waiting at the bank, or lying in bed at 3 a.m. As you know, inspiration often strikes far from a pad and pencil!

Much smaller than a microcassette (2½ x 1 x ½ inches), Voice Note slips into your shirt pocket or purse. And there aren't a lot of buttons to fiddle with. Just press Record and speak. A lock button prevents overrecording your earlier messages.

You can record up to 20 different messages of 30 seconds each—"to-do" messages like "Call Richard about the Hewlett contract" or "Place order for 200 shares of SRP stock" or even "Pick up Jenny from soccer practice at 5:30." After playback, the tape automatically resets for immediate reuse.

For true portability, the Voice Note is powered by two AAA batteries (included). Your satisfaction is guaranteed by our 90-day warranty and 30-day full-refund policy.

The Voice Note's price of $29 is less than you'd pay for a bulky microcassette recorder that is much less convenient for on-the-go use. For credit-card orders, simply call us at 555-2394. Or stop by our retail store at Fiesta Mall for a personal demonstration. The next time you need to pick up a quart of milk on the way home, make a Voice Note. You won't come home empty-handed.

Sincerely,

Richard E. Lee

Richard E. Lee
Proprietor

cd

Fiesta Mall ▪ 1200 Dobson Road ▪ Mesa, AZ 85201 ▪ 602-555-6372

SUMMARY

The ability to write persuasively is crucial for success in business. In order to write persuasively, you must overcome the reader's initial resistance, establish your own credibility, and develop an appeal that meets a need of the reader. You must also become thoroughly familiar with your reader so that you can translate the advantages of your idea or the features of your product into specific reader benefits.

When writing to superiors, use a direct writing style, giving the proposal or recommendation, along with the criteria or brief rationale, in the first paragraph. For most other persuasive messages, prefer an indirect writing style. First gain the reader's attention by using an opening paragraph that is relevant, interesting, and short.

For persuasive requests, devote the majority of the message to discussing the merits of your proposal and showing specifically how your proposal meets some need of the reader. Provide evidence that is accurate, relevant, representative, and complete. Discuss and minimize any obstacles to your proposal. For sales letters, introduce a central selling theme early and build on it throughout the message. Devote most of the message to showing how the reader will specifically benefit from owning the product. Subordinate the price, unless price is the central selling theme.

For all types of persuasive messages, end on a confident, positive note, making sure the reader knows what action is desired and making the action easy to take. Persuasive messages are often longer than other types of messages because of the need to present convincing evidence. By taking the space needed to support your statements with specific facts and figures, you'll increase your ability to persuade your readers.

KEY TERMS

For an exercise on matching terms, refer students to the *Study Guide*, p. 115.

Central selling theme The major reader benefit that is introduced early and emphasized throughout a sales letter.

Derived benefit The benefit a potential customer would receive from using a product or service.

Persuasion The process of motivating someone to take a specific action or to support a particular idea.

Rhetorical question A question asked strictly to get the reader thinking about the topic; a literal answer is not expected.

Solicited sales letter A reply to a request for product information from a potential customer.

Unsolicited sales letter A letter promoting a firm's products mailed to a potential customer who has not expressed any prior interest in the product; also called a *prospecting letter*.

REVIEW AND DISCUSSION

1. **Communication at ASPCA Revisited** ▪ The 14 million letters sent by the ASPCA every year are successful because Joanne Lawson and her staff think about their audiences, plan their messages carefully, and take the time to consider objections that might arise.

a. Would a direct or an indirect organizational plan be more appropriate when writing to people who have never received a letter from the ASPCA?
b. How can the ASPCA establish credibility with an audience that has not been involved with the organization in the past?
c. What obstacles do you think the ASPCA might have to overcome when writing to ask for a donation?

The answers to the review and discussion questions appear in the *Instructor's Resource Manual*, beginning on p. 101.

2. What is meant by the term *persuasion?*
3. Why might the reader initially resist your persuasive efforts?
4. What are the sources of writer credibility?
5. What is the difference between a logical appeal and an emotional appeal? When should each be used?
6. Give an example of a direct reader benefit and an indirect benefit.
7. What should you know about your reader before beginning to write a persuasive letter?
8. Under what circumstances should a direct organizational plan be used for a persuasive request?
9. What are some characteristics of an effective attention-getter?
10. How should the writer deal with obstacles to his or her proposal?
11. Why are persuasive messages often longer than other types of messages?
12. Why is showing anger a poor strategy in a persuasive claim letter?
13. What is a central selling theme? Why is it important in a sales letter?
14. Why should the reader instead of the product be the focus of attention in a sales letter?
15. What are some techniques for subordinating the price in a sales letter?

EXERCISES

1. Microwriting a Persuasive Message—Selling an Idea ▪

Exercise 1 is linked with Exercise 2 of Chapter 8. A sample solution for Exercise 1 appears in the *Instructor's Resource Manual*, p. 103. A formatted solution appears on *IRM* p. 117. An exercise on microwriting a persuasive request appears on *IRM* pp. 305–307.

PROBLEM

You are O. B. Presley, a sales representative for Midland Medical Supplies. Like most of the other 38 Midland reps, you are on the road three or four days a week, promoting your products to hospitals, clinics, and physicians in private practice. Three years ago, Midland purchased 8-pound laptop computers for all sales reps. These computers simplified your job immensely, especially in terms of filing call reports. Each evening in your hotel room you keyboard the report, showing to whom you spoke, their experiences with your products, what they'd like to see changed, and the like. You then submit these reports, along with actual orders, electronically to headquarters via the computer's built-in modem.

It occurs to you that you could be more productive by replacing your bulky laptop (which doesn't even have a hard drive) with a notebook computer and built-in portable printer. That way, whenever a customer wanted a specification sheet for a new product, you could electronically send for the information from the company's mainframe computer and print it out on the spot for the customer. You're sure you'd get additional sales as a result.

The specific system you're interested in is the Canon NoteJet, a 486-based notebook computer that has a built-in modem and ink-jet printer. The entire system weighs just 7.7 pounds and sells for $2,499 with 4MB of RAM and a 100MB hard disk. The only problem is that you don't know what to do with your present laptop computer. There's not much demand for used laptops, especially for three-year-old eight-pounders. Still, you feel notebooks would be a good investment for all sales reps. Send a memo to Charles J. Redding, national sales manager, trying to sell him on the idea.

Selling an Idea — Direct Pattern

As a means of increasing my sales productivity, I propose the purchase of a notebook computer with built-in printer. Maintaining a competitive edge is critical to increasing our sales today.

Several times during the past six months I have lost sales because I could not provide customers with the information they needed immediately. With a notebook computer with built-in printer, I could electronically send for information from the company's mainframe computer and print a specification sheet for any product immediately. Since the customer would have the needed information right on the spot, the sale could be completed while I'm still with the customer.

The Canon NoteJet is a 486-based notebook computer with built-in modem and ink-jet printer. It weighs 7.7 pounds and comes with 4MB of RAM and a 100MB hard drive (my current computer doesn't even have a hard drive).

I estimate that the $2,499 cost of the Canon NoteJet would pay for itself in increased sales within eight months. My present three-year-old computer would then serve as a valuable back-up computer for me or for my district manager when she is visiting my sales territory.

May I please have approval to purchase the Canon NoteJet. If I can get the computer by the end of the month, I can begin increasing sales during the second quarter of the year.

Ober, *Contemporary Business Communication*, 2d ed.

See Master 7.1, Exercise 1, Microwriting a Persuasive Message, in the *Instructor's Resource Manual.*

PROCESS

a. Describe your audience.
b. Should you use a direct or indirect organizational plan? Why?
c. Write the opening sentence of your memo.
d. List the reasons you might discuss for your proposal—including any reader benefits associated with each reason.
e. What is an obstacle that might prevent you from achieving your objective?
f. Write a sentence that addresses this obstacle (subordinate this discussion).
g. Write the last paragraph of your memo, in which you state (or restate) your request. Make the action easy for the reader to take, ask confidently, and end on a forward-looking note.

PRODUCT

Draft, revise, format, and proofread your memo. Then submit both your responses to the process questions and your revised memo to your instructor.

Sample solutions for Exercises 2-4 appear in the *Instructor's Resource Manual*, pp. 103–105. Formatted solutions appear on *IRM* pp. 118-120.

2. **Selling an Idea—Indirect Organizational Plan** ▪ Refer to Exercise 1. Assume that you (O. B. Presley) are relatively new on the job and have not yet earned the trust of the national sales manager. In addition, you know that Redding is not a big fan of technology. Therefore, you decide to write your memo using an indirect organizational plan.
3. **Selling an Idea—Direct Organizational Plan** ▪ You are the night manager for White Mountain Gas, a 24-hour, self-service gasoline station on a New Hampshire highway. The station owner, Adam Bream, has asked you to survey customers about the new credit-card-activated pumps that he is considering installing. This pump would authorize a sale and release the gasoline hose when the customer inserted a credit card; after the customer finished using the hose, the pump would automatically shut off and print a receipt. Bream wants to know what customers think before he goes ahead.

   You have talked with 300 customers over the course of two weeks, and more than three-quarters of them liked the idea: they *don't* like having to walk to the office to pay, and the new pump sounds as if it would be faster. But at least 35 people expressed concern over learning how to use the pump, and another 20 or so said they never pay by credit card. These people were worried that attendants might not be available for assistance and cash transactions after the new pumps were installed.

   Based on your research, you want to recommend that the station install the new pumps. To help reluctant customers, you think that extra attendants should be on hand for the first two months. You also want your boss to be aware that some people were worried about not being able to pay cash for their gas. Using a direct organizational plan, write a persuasive memo to Bream about your recommendations.
4. **Selling an Idea—Indirect Organizational Plan** ▪ Reconsider the problem of persuading Adam Bream to accept your recommendations (see Exercise 3). Assume that your customer survey indicated that more than one-third of your customers were apprehensive about the change. Some

went so far as to say that they would switch gas stations rather than be forced to use the new pumps. You assured these customers that the gas station would always have an attendant on duty to help, but you know your boss will be worried by this negative reaction. Despite the potential problems, you believe that the new pumps will be accepted, and in time preferred, once customers learn how to use them. Write a memo, using the indirect organizational plan, to persuade Bream that this idea is a good one.

5. **Selling an Idea—Oversized Dressing Rooms** ■ You are Robert Kilcline, a merchandising manager at Lordstrom, Inc., a women's clothing store in Seattle. Your firm has decided to open a new store in Fashion Square Mall, an upscale department store on the north side. Retail space is quite expensive in this mall (nearly 50% more expensive than at your other locations), so Lordstrom facility engineers are trying to make every inch of space count.

   Despite the costs, you feel that to be competitive in this mall, you will have to offer superior customer service. You already offer a no-questions-asked return policy, abundant inventory to ensure a complete selection of sizes and colors, and a harpist who performs on the main floor from 11 a.m. until 2 p.m. daily. But you think that the new store should also have oversized dressing rooms—ones large enough to hold a comfortable chair, garment rack, and adjustable three-sided mirrors. You want your customers to be able to make their selections in comfort.

   You estimate that adding the furnishings and additional 20 square feet per dressing room in the new store will add $18,500 to the construction costs, plus $155 to the monthly lease. Present your ideas in a memo to your boss, Rebecca Lordstrom, executive vice president.

Exercise 5 is linked with Exercise 5 of Chapter 8. Sample solutions for Exercises 5–6 appear in the *Instructor's Resource Manual*, pp. 106–107. Formatted solutions appear on *IRM* pp. 121–122.

6. **Requesting a Favor—Change in Timing** ■ As the bookkeeper for Crosslanes Pharmacies, you have to provide the owners with a full set of financial statements every quarter. Part of your work involves reporting bank balances at the end of each month. However, the company's bank sends its statement in the middle of each month, so you always have to call for the figures before you can start your work. Most of the time, the people at the bank do not seem to mind your calls, but sometimes they sound rushed and annoyed. To solve this problem, you want the bank to change its procedure and send your statement at the end of each month. You would get the information when you need it, and you would not have to bother the bank's employees. Write to Len Goddard (Branch Manager, Forest Island Bank, 700 Founder's Highway, Kansas City, MO 64101) to request this procedural change.

Exercise 6 is linked with Exercise 7 of Chapter 8.

7. **Requesting a Favor—Field Trip** ■ You are David Pearson, owner and manager of Jack 'n Jill Preschool. During the next few weeks, you will be discussing food and nutrition with the youngsters; and you want to end the unit by having the children walk to the nearby Salad Haven, take a tour of the kitchens, and then make their own salads for lunch from the restaurant's popular salad bar. Of course, each family would pay for their child's meal. In fact, to help make the visit easier, you'll collect the money beforehand and pay the cashier for everyone at once. You will ask several parents to come with you to help supervise the 23 children, ages three through five, although they will probably need some extra help from the salad-bar attendants. You can come any day during the week of October 10–14. State regulations require that the children eat lunch between 11 a.m. and 12:30 p.m.

   Write to Donna Jo Luse (Manager, Salad Haven, 28 Grenvale Road, Westminster, MD 21157) asking for permission to make the field trip.

Requesting a Favor — Indirect Pattern

We believe it's never too early to begin teaching students the value of good nutrition, of eating the very kinds of foods you serve at Salad Haven Restaurant.

Over the next few weeks the children at Jack 'n Jill Preschool will be discussing food and nutrition. At the end of the unit we would like to bring the students on a field trip to your restaurant. Would it be possible for the students to tour your kitchens and then make their own salads for lunch at your popular salad bar?

We would arrange to have several parents present to supervise the 23 children (ages three to five) in our group, and I would collect the money from each person in advance. Because state law requires that the children eat lunch between 11 a.m. and 12:30 p.m., I suggest that we bring the children early. They could first tour your kitchens and then eat at 11 a.m., thus allowing us to finish in time for you to accommodate your regular customers during the noon rush hour.

Can we count on you to help us arrange this educational experience for our students so they can learn more about good nutrition? We could come in any day from October 10 to 14. I would appreciate hearing from you by next week so that we can arrange for parental supervision. We will all enjoy eating in your fine restaurant.

Ober, *Contemporary Business Communication*, 2d ed.

See Master 7.2, Exercise 7, Requesting a Favor—Field Trip, in the *Instructor's Resource Manual*.

Sample solutions for Exercises 8–22 appear in the *Instructor's Resource Manual*, pp. 108–116. Formatted solutions appear on *IRM* pp. 124–136.

8. **Requesting a Favor—Celebrity Donation** ▪ Coming out of the movie theater after watching the Academy Award–winning movie *Rocky Mountain Adventure,* starring Robert Forte, you suddenly have an idea. As executive director of the Wilderness Fund, you've been searching for an unusual raffle prize for your upcoming fund-raiser. You wonder whether you could persuade Robert Forte to donate some item used in this popular movie (perhaps a stage prop or costume item) for the raffle. The Wilderness Fund is an 8,000-member nonprofit agency dedicated to preserving forest lands—the very type of lands photographed so beautifully in Forte's latest movie. Write to the actor at Century Studios, 590 North Vermont Avenue, Los Angeles, CA 90004.

Exercise 9 is linked with Exercise 11 of Chapter 8.

9. **Writing a Persuasive Claim—Azaleas** ▪ You are Vera Malcolm, the facilities manager for Public Service Company of Arkansas. In preparation for the recent dedication of your new hydroelectric plant, you spruced up the grounds near the viewing stand. As part of the stage decorations, you ordered ten potted azaleas at $28.50 each (plus $10.50 shipping) from Jackson-Parsons Nurseries (410 Wick Avenue, Youngstown, OH 44555) on February 3. The bushes were guaranteed to arrive in show condition—ready to burst into bloom within three days—or your money would be cheerfully refunded.

   The plants arrived in healthy condition but were in their final days (perhaps hours) of flowering—certainly in no shape to display at the dedication. You decided, instead, to plant the azaleas as part of your permanent landscaping. Because the plants arrived only three days before the dedication, you had to purchase substitute azaleas from the local florist—at a much higher price. In fact, you ended up paying $436 for the florist plants—$140.50 more than the Jackson-Parsons price. You feel that the nursery was responsible for your having to incur the additional expenditure. Write a letter asking Jackson-Parsons to reimburse your company for the $140.50.

Exercise 10 is linked with Exercises 13 and 20 of Chapter 6 and Exercise 4 of Chapter 8.

10. **Writing a Persuasive Claim—Inaccurate Reporting** ▪ As the CEO of Software Entrepreneurs, Inc., you just received a memo from the chief programmer for your ReSolve spreadsheet program. The programmer had written to the review editor at *Computing Trends* protesting inaccurate reporting; the reply (from Hal Burk) was a form letter describing the magazine's policy on product reviews (see Exercises 13 and 20 of Chapter 6). Although you are glad to know that your product will be included in the yearly software review, you agree with your programmer that the editor made an error in downgrading your program. Apparently the reviewer worked with the original version of ReSolve and not with the improved version that was released one month before the review appeared. The new version is so powerful that it outperforms the competition on nearly every test used by the reviewer to determine product rankings.

    Because magazine deadlines require that articles be completed well in advance of the printing date, you realize that the magazine could not possibly have included the improved version in their tests. However, you would like the review editor to print a small item noting the availability of the improved ReSolve in an upcoming issue. Write to Burk with this request.

11. **Writing a Persuasive Claim—Ripped Suit** ▪ After a hurried taxi ride from LaGuardia Airport to the Marriott Marquis Hotel on May 15, you barely made it to your 2 p.m. appointment. You did not realize until you sat down at the conference table that you had ripped the pants of your $450 suit on an exposed spring in the taxi seat. The next day, your tailor tells you

there is no way to repair the rip attractively, so the suit is, in effect, now useless. Since you've owned the suit for a year, you don't expect the taxi company to reimburse you for $450, but you do think reimbursement of $200 is reasonable. From your taxi receipt, you learn that you took Taxi 1145 belonging to Empire State Taxi (50 West 77 Street, New York, NY 10024). Since this is a personal claim, write your letter on plain paper, using your own return address.

12. **Writing a Persuasive Claim—Defective Product** ▪ Assume the role of J. R. McCord again, purchasing agent at People's Energy Company (see Exercises 1 and 16 of Chapter 6). Because Nationwide Office Supply believes you were at fault, it refused your initial routine claim. However, you've been a good customer for many years; last year, in fact, you purchased $5,800 worth of office supplies from Nationwide. In addition, since you've not used the ribbons, they could be resold easily. Thus, you've decided to write Nationwide again, this time adding persuasion to your claim letter.

Exercise 12 is linked with Exercises 1 and 16 of Chapter 6.

13. **Selling a Product—Letter Critique** ▪ Select a sales letter that you or a friend has received. Critique the letter, noting the specific ways that it does and does not follow the guidelines discussed in this chapter (see especially Checklists 5 and 6). Then revise the letter to remedy any weaknesses. Submit the original letter and your revised version to your instructor, along with a memo explaining the rationale for your revisions.
14. **Selling a Product—Limited Time Offer** ▪ As the sales manager for Shop-At-Home Appliances, you maintain a mailing list of customers who have bought from you in the past. You are overstocked on several items and want to convince previous customers that they should call to place an order when you put these models on sale for a limited time—from August 14 until September 1. Select a major appliance such as a dishwasher, range, or refrigerator, and write a sales letter to an audience familiar with your store's service and selection reminding them of your exceptionally low sale prices. Consult the appliance ads in your local paper to come up with any details you need about the product itself, including the features, price, warranty, delivery, and other information your readers should know. Use a suitable salutation for your form letter, but omit the date and inside address. Let customers know they can order by calling you toll-free at 800-555-8755.
15. **Selling a Product—Work Boots** ▪ As sales manager for Industrial Footwear, Inc., send a form sales letter advertising your Durham work boot to 3,000 members of Local 147 of the Building Trades Union. Local 147 is made up primarily of construction workers on high-rise buildings in Houston, Texas.

    The Durham is an 8-inch, waterproof insulated boot, made of oil-tanned cowhide. It exceeds the guidelines for steel-toe protection issued by the American National Standards Institute (ANSI). The Durham has an all-rubber heel that provides firm footing, and its steel shanks provide additional support for arches and heels. It comes in whole sizes 7–13 in black or brown at a price of $79, plus 4.50 shipping. The price is guaranteed for the next 30 days. There is a one-year, no-questions-asked warranty.

    Select a suitable salutation for your form letter and omit the date and inside address. The purpose of the letter is to motivate readers to order the shoe by using the enclosed order blank or by calling your toll-free order number, 800-555-2993.
16. **Writing a Solicited Sales Letter—Real Estate** ▪ As a realtor in the local franchise of National Home Sales, you receive a letter from Ms. Edith Willis (667 Rising Hills Drive, Xenia, OH 45385). Her letter states, in part,

```
I am a single mother of two young children who is being
transferred to your town and wish to purchase a three-bed-
room condominium in a nice area in the price range of
$85,000-$110,000.  I would be able to make a down payment
of up to $20,000.  Would you please write me, letting me
know whether you have any property available that would
fit my needs.
```

Although the housing market in your small town is tight, you do have a condominium available that might suit her needs. It has three bedrooms plus a finished basement, is air-conditioned (important in your part of the country), and is four years old. The neighborhood elementary school is considered the best in town; the only drawback is that the condominium is next door to a large but attractive apartment building. The home is listed for $119,900, although you think the owners would accept $110,000–$115,000.

Send Ms. Willis a photograph and fact sheet on the listing. The purpose of your letter is to encourage her to phone you at 602-555-3459 to make an appointment to visit your office so that you can personally show her this and perhaps other properties you have available.

17. **Writing a Solicited Sales Letter—Training Programs** ▪ Assume that you are the marketing manager for Train the Trainer, Inc., a company that offers instructional seminars for leaders of employee training programs. As a result of a favorable article in an industry magazine, you receive several letters asking for more information. Rather than send a form letter with your sales brochure, you decide to tailor your letters to the needs of the individual prospects. The first letter you receive is from Benjamin Nadir, vice president of human resources for Consolidated Southwest Industries (located at 8800 Medallion Drive, Las Cruces, NM 88001). Nadir's firm manufactures glass containers for juices and other beverages. Nadir wants to know whether you offer a seminar on improving product quality in a manufacturing environment. He wants to prepare his trainers to work with the company's 650 employees to reduce the number of defects per thousand containers produced.

    Your firm recently developed a quality-assurance seminar that you could adapt to meet Nadir's specific needs. You are equipped to train up to 20 participants in a day-long seminar, held either on site or at your own or neutral facilities, for a flat fee of $4,500. The fee includes training materials that can be customized and duplicated for the client's employees. Write a sales letter that will convince Nadir to hire your firm.
18. **Writing an Unsolicited Sales Letter—Form Letter** ▪ Refer to Exercise 17, in which you assumed the role of marketing manager for Train the Trainer, Inc. Now that you have developed and tested a quality-improvement seminar suitable for the manufacturing environment, you're ready to offer it to other manufacturers. Draft a form letter to be mailed to executives who head personnel training departments at 100 leading manufacturers. Select a suitable salutation for the form letter, omit the date and inside address, and include your toll-free number—800-555-3455—for response. Also mention that you are enclosing a postpaid postcard that the executives can return if they want to receive a free packet of material you've prepared about reducing defects and improving quality in manufacturing.
19. **Collaborative Writing—Selling a Product** ▪ Select an ad from a newspaper or journal published within the past month. Working in groups of three or four, write an unsolicited form sales letter for the advertised product, to be signed by the sales manager. (You may need to gather additional information about the product.) The audience for your letter will be either the students or the faculty at your institution (you decide which). Include

only actual data about the product and about the audience. Submit a copy of both the advertisement and your letter.

20. **Selling a Service—Small Business** ▪ While studying for your bar exams, you decide to start a part-time business delivering singing telegrams throughout the Atlanta metropolitan area. For a flat fee of $50, you'll personally deliver a greeting card and sing any song (in good taste) of the customer's choice—using either the actual wording of the song or special lyrics composed by the customer. You promote your company (Musical Messages) for birthdays, anniversaries, graduations, promotions, and other special occasions. Send a form letter to a random sample of Atlanta's residents, promoting your service. The purpose of your letter is to persuade the reader to call you at 404-555-9831 to order a singing telegram. Orders must be prepaid (no credit cards), and you require seven days' notice.
21. **Selling a Service—Film Developing** ▪ You operate Quik Snap, a one-hour film developing laboratory. After three years in business, you want to branch out by offering your services through independent drugstores and convenience stores in your area. Any film dropped off before 11 a.m. will be processed and back at the store no later than 5 p.m. the same day. If Quik Snap misses the deadline, the film is developed free. You will provide the stores with envelopes for the rolls of film, preprinted forms for customers to fill out, a drop box, and a window sign promoting the service. Your van will pick up every day between 11 a.m. and 12 noon, and will make deliveries between 4 and 5 p.m. You will charge only $5.95 for developing a 36-print color roll, a price that's competitive with the photo chains in the neighborhood, and you will pay participating retailers a fee of 50 cents for every roll they send for processing. Send a form letter to selected stores in your area, asking them to call you toll-free at 800-555-1170 to sign up for the service.
22. **Form Letter—Selling for Charity** ▪ As the director of fund-raising for the Buckeye Bread Basket, a Cleveland, Ohio, charity that buys food for people in need, you are starting a new program. You plan to sell holiday greeting cards to raise money for your annual Thanksgiving Day dinner. This year, more than 400 needy people (including singles and families) are expected to attend the dinner. An Ohio artist created the original watercolor scene on the cards, which come in boxes of 10, with green envelopes. People who buy the cards are able to take a tax deduction for their donations; the money from the sale of a single box can feed a hungry family of four on Thanksgiving.

    Write a form letter that will persuade people to order your cards. The price is $12 per box, plus $1 postage and handling, and orders can be placed using the enclosed form and return envelope.

CONTINUING CASE 7

Flying High at Urban Systems

Neelima, Jean, and Larry were analyzing the quarterly expense report. "Look at line item 415," Neelima said. "Air-travel expenses have increased 28% from last year. Is there any room for savings there?"

"Jean and I were discussing that earlier," Larry said. "I think we should begin requiring our people to join all the frequent-flyer programs so that after they fly 20,000 to 30,000 miles on any one airline, they get a

A possible solution to the Continuing Case is described in the *Instructor's Resource Manual*, p. 116.

free ticket. Then we should require them to use that free ticket the next time they have to take a business trip for us."

"I disagree," Jean said. "To begin with, there's no easy way to enforce the requirement. Who's going to keep track of how many miles each person flies on each airline and when a free flight coupon is due that person? It would make us appear to be Big Brother, looking over their shoulders all the time.

"In addition, our people put in long hours on the road. If they can get a free ticket and occasionally are able to take their spouses along with them, what's the big deal? They're happier and probably end up doing a better job for us."

"Still," Larry countered, "company resources were used to purchase the original tickets, so logically the free tickets belong to the company. And why should our people who travel get free tickets, compliments of the company, when those who don't travel do not get free tickets?"

Jean was ready with a counterargument, but Neelima put an end to the discussion: "Both of you think about the matter some more and let me have a memo by next week giving me your position. Then I'll decide."

Critical Thinking

FOR Larry's proposal:

- Using free tickets from frequent-flyer programs would save the company money.
- All employees should be entitled to the same fringe benefits.
- Nontraveling employees might experience lowered morale.
- Company money was used to buy the tickets, so logically the free tickets belong to the company.

AGAINST Larry's proposal:

- There is no easy way to enforce the requirement.
- Additional personnel would be needed to monitor the process, which would be expensive in itself.
- The morale of employees who do travel is improved if occasionally they can travel with family members.
- Employees who are happy with their job benefits are more highly motivated.

Ober, *Contemporary Business Communication*, 2d ed.

See Master 7.3, Continuing Case 7, in the *Instructor's Resource Manual*.

Critical Thinking

1. Jot down all the reasons you can think of for and against Larry's proposition—including any reasons that might not have been discussed at the meeting. What are the benefits associated with each reason?

Writing Projects

2. Assume the role of Larry. Write a memo to Neelima trying to persuade her to begin requiring employees to use their frequent-flyer miles toward business travel. Knowing that Jean will be writing a memo arguing the opposing viewpoint—that employees should be able to use their free airline tickets for personal use—try to counteract her possible arguments.
3. Now assume the role of Jean. Write a memo to Neelima arguing for the status quo. Try to anticipate and counteract Larry's likely arguments.

WORDWISE *Vowels*

- *Facetious* uses all the vowels in alphabetical order. The vowels appear in reverse order in *uncomplimentary*.
- The dot over the letter *i* is called a *tittle*.
- There are three words in the English language with two consecutive *u*'s: *vacuum*, *residuum*, and *continuum*.

CHAPTER

8

Bad-News Messages

In 1990, after 30 years of growth, Digital Equipment Corporation felt the pain of a slow economy and an industry-wide slump. When the computer giant found itself in the unfamiliar position of having to report a quarterly loss, it did what it could to soften the news. But to soften the news, Digital's media relations people had to first control it. That meant that they had to get the news out in their own terms before it got out in some other form. In the endless dance with the press, corporate media experts always try to lead, never to follow.

"Any time you start reacting to news, you're playing catch-up," says Alan Pike, one of a team responsible for presenting Digital's information to the media. "It's a no-win situation. Of course, we all get caught flat-footed at some point. Anyone in this business who says he doesn't is not telling the truth, but the best defense is a good offense."

Perhaps because the Digital Equipment Corporation is in the computer business, management is keenly aware of the power of information. Digital goes to great lengths to control information about itself, employing groups of public relations workers who disseminate information to different countries. Like most public relations professionals, the Digital team communicates with the media with several forms of communication: straight news releases, backgrounders, fact sheets, and white papers. In deciding which to use, Pike considers three criteria: the amount of influence he wants to exert, the nature of the information, and the nature of the recipient.

Communication Objectives

After you have finished this chapter, you should be able to

1. Decide when to use a direct and indirect organizational plan for bad-news messages.
2. Compose a message that rejects an idea.
3. Compose a message that refuses a favor.
4. Compose a message that refuses a claim.
5. Compose an announcement that conveys bad news.

Alan Pike

Manager of corporate public relations, Center for Expertise, Digital Equipment Corporation, Maynard, Massachusetts

A chapter overview appears in the *Instructor's Resource Manual*, pp. 137–140.

"A press release is formula," says Pike. "But it is a formula on purpose. The idea behind the press release is that the news is timely. The white paper, on the other hand, is research driven, and the fact sheet is just a straightforward list. The backgrounder, though, is almost a narrative. It paints a larger picture of an issue. It is very helpful to news reporters or when we are dealing with a new product."

When the news is bad, Digital's team looks hard for a positive aspect, particularly a positive aspect with staying power. "You can't blanch the numbers," says Pike. "A bad quarter is a bad quarter. So what you have to do is position the report as the beginning of the recovery or the end of the bad times. It's not just to make it palatable, but it's to put it in a greater context, to make the bad news relative. Then it's not as horrendous."

Unfortunately, says Pike, as hard as he looks for a positive aspect, newspapers look for the horrendous. After all, bad news sells papers. So Pike and his team are customarily braced for the worst. What happens then when negative news does leak out?

"Before we get carried away, we get the facts," says Pike. "We can't ignore it or slow it up in bureaucratic red tape. One of the real problems is a tendency for denial. But these things very seldom go away. [For bad news to simply disappear] you have to be the kind of guy who wins the lottery. Usually it just festers. What we are dealing with here is low control and high credibility."

PLANNING THE BAD-NEWS MESSAGE

For an exercise in writing a bad-news message, see Video Case Study 2, Ronald McDonald Children's Charities.

At some point in our lives we have all probably been both the bearers and the recipients of bad news. And just as most people find it difficult to accept bad news, they also find it difficult to convey bad news. Therefore, like persuasive messages, bad-news messages require careful planning. How you write your messages won't change the news you have to convey, but it may determine whether your reader accepts your decision as reasonable—or goes away mad.

Your objectives are to convey the bad news and retain the reader's goodwill.

Your purpose in writing a bad-news message is twofold: first, to say "no" or to convey bad news; and second, to retain the reader's goodwill. To accomplish these goals, you must communicate your message politely, clearly, and firmly. And you must show the reader that you've seriously considered the request and that, as a matter of fairness and good business practice, you must deny the request.

Sometimes you can achieve your purpose better with a phone call or personal visit than with a written message. A phone call is often appropriate when the reader will not be personally disappointed in the outcome, and a personal visit is often called for when you are giving a subordinate negative news of considerable consequence. Frequently, though, a written message is most appropriate because it lets you more carefully control the wording, sequence, and pace of the ideas presented. In addition, it provides a permanent record of what was communicated.

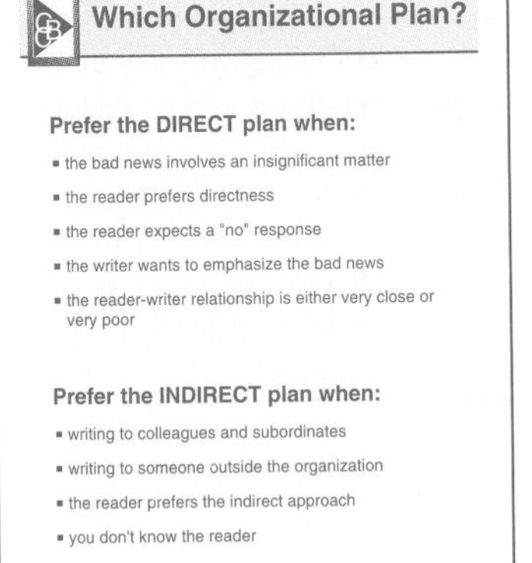

See Transparency 8.1, Organizational Plan for Bad-News Messages.

Organizing to Suit Your Audience

The reader's needs, expectations, and personality—as well as the writer's relationship with the reader—will largely determine the content and organization of a bad-news message. Thus you need to put yourself in the place of the reader.

To decide whether to use the direct or indirect plan for refusing a request, check the sender's original message. If the original message was written in the direct style, the sender may have considered it a routine request, and you would be safe in answering in the direct style. If the original message was written in the indirect style, the sender probably considered it a persuasive request, and you should consider answering in the indirect style. (As indicated below, however, memorandums written to one's superior are typically written in the direct style, regardless of whether the reader considers the message routine or persuasive.)

For example, a memo telling employees that the company cafeteria will be closed for one day to permit installation of new equipment can be told directly and in a paragraph or two. A memo telling employees that from now on the company cafeteria will be reserved for management and that other employees will have to go outside for lunch (and pay higher prices) would require more explanation and should probably be written in the indirect style.

Prefer the direct organizational plan for communicating bad news to your superior.

Direct Plan—Present the Bad News Immediately As discussed in Chapter 6, many requests are routine; the writer simply wants a yes-or-no decision and wants to hear it in a direct manner. Similarly, if an announcement of bad news is not likely to generate an emotional response from readers, you should use a direct approach. The direct plan for bad-news messages is basically the same plan used for routine messages discussed in Chapter 6: present the major idea (the bad news) up front. To help readers accept your decision when using the direct plan, present a brief rationale along with the bad news in the first paragraph.

Not: The annual company picnic originally scheduled for August 3 at Riverside Park has been canceled.

But: Because on-going construction at Riverside Park might present safety hazards to our employees and their families, the annual company picnic originally scheduled for August 3 has been canceled.

The two most common sources of organizational bad news are falling short of budget projections and problems with employees, according to business communication experts. (Walter Kiechel III, "Breaking Bad News to the Boss," *Fortune*, April 9, 1990, pp. 111-112.)

As usual, state the message in language as positive as possible, while still maintaining honesty.

Not: Our departmental compliance report will be late next month.

Not: I am pleased to announce that our departmental compliance report will be submitted on March 15.

But: The extra time required to resolve the Baton Rouge refinery problem means that our departmental compliance report will be submitted on March 15 rather than on March 1.

Then follow with any needed explanation and a friendly closing. The direct organizational plan should be used under the following circumstances:

- The bad news involves a small, insignificant matter and can be considered routine. If the reader is not likely to be emotionally involved and thus not seriously disappointed by the decision, use the direct approach.
- The reader prefers directness. Superiors typically prefer that *all* messages from subordinates be written in the direct style.
- The reader expects a "no" response. For example, mid-career job applicants know that job offers at their level are typically made by phone and job rejections by letter. Thus, upon receiving a letter from the prospective employer, the applicant expects a "no" response; under these circumstances, delaying the inevitable only causes ill will and makes the writer look less than forthright.
- The writer wants to emphasize the negative news. Suppose that you have already refused a request once and the reader writes a second time; under these circumstances, a forceful "no" might be in order. Or, consider the situation where negative information is to be included in a form letter—perhaps as an insert in a monthly statement. Because the reader might otherwise discard or only skim an "unimportant-looking" message, you should consider placing the bad news up front—where it will be noticed.
- The reader-writer relationship is at either extreme—either very close or very poor. Consider using the direct approach if the relationship is either so friendly that you can assume the continued goodwill of the reader or so strained and suspicious that the reader may think he or she is being given the runaround if the bad news is buried in the middle.

In some situations, it is necessary to emphasize the bad news.

A message organized according to a direct plan is not necessarily any shorter than one organized according to an indirect plan. Both types of message may contain the same basic information but simply in a different order. For example, assume that the program chairman of the Downtown Marketing Club has written to ask you to be the luncheon speaker at the March 8 meeting, but because of a prior commitment, you must decline. If you have a close relationship with the reader, you might choose the direct approach, as follows:

Direct messages are not necessarily shorter than indirect messages.

> Except for the fact that I'll be in Mexico on March 8, I would have enjoyed speaking to the Downtown Marketing Club. As you know, Hansdorf Industries is opening an outlet in Nogales, and I'll be there March 7–14 interviewing marketing representatives and setting up sales territories.

If, however, you find yourself in need of a speaker during the summer months, please keep me in mind. My travel schedule thus far is quite light during June, July, and August.

As a long-time member of the Downtown Marketing Club, I've enjoyed and benefited from the luncheon speakers the club sponsors each month. Best wishes, Roger, for a successful year as program chairperson. *(114 words)*

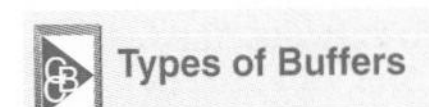

Types of Buffers

- AGREEMENT
  I agree with you that full-color visual aids are more effective and attractive than black-and-white ones.
- APPRECIATION
  Thanks, Tony, for taking the initiative to research the feasibility of purchasing a color printer for our training department.
- COMPLIMENT
  Congratulations, Tony, on the 95% approval rating from our seminar participants. That's a first for our department.
- FACTS
  Last week's approval of our Westinghouse proposal will mean a dramatic increase in the number of technical seminars we'll sponsor next year.

See Transparency 8.2, Types of Buffers.

Now assume the same situation except that you do not know the reader. This time, you might choose the indirect approach, as follows:

As a long-time member of the Downtown Marketing Club, I've enjoyed and benefited from the luncheon speakers the club sponsors each month. Monica Foote's December talk on the pitfalls of international marketing was especially interesting.

As you may have read in the newspaper, Hansdorf Industries is opening an outlet in Nogales, Mexico, and I'll be there March 7–14 interviewing marketing representatives and setting up sales territories. Thus, you will need to select another speaker for your March 8 meeting.

If you find yourself in need of a speaker during the summer months, Mr. Caine, please keep me in mind. My travel schedule thus far is quite light during June, July, and August. *(111 words)*

Direct messages are often shorter than indirect messages only because the direct plan is often used for *simpler* situations, which require less explanation and background information than do indirect messages.

Complex situations typically call for an indirect organizational pattern and require more explanation than simpler situations.

Indirect Plan—Buffer the Bad News Because the preceding conditions are *not* true for many bad-news situations, you will often want to use an indirect plan—especially when giving bad news to

- Subordinates
- Customers
- Readers who prefer the indirect approach
- Readers you don't know.[1]

With the indirect approach, you present the reasons first, then the negative news. This approach emphasizes the *reasons* for the bad news, rather than the bad news itself.

Suppose, for example, a subordinate expects a "yes" answer upon opening your memo. Putting the negative news in the first sentence might be too harsh and emphatic, and your decision might sound unreasonable until the reader has heard the rationale. In such a situation, you should begin with a neutral and relevant statement—one that helps establish or strengthen the reader-writer relationship. Such a statement serves as a **buffer** between the reader and the bad news that will follow.

A buffer lessens the impact of bad news.

Recall the earlier situation, introduced in Chapter 7, in which the owner of an appliance store wrote one of its suppliers, asking them to provide an in-store demonstrator of the firm's products (even though it was

Annual reports of poor-performing companies are less readable than reports of good-performing companies. Good news is reported in short, simple sentences, but bad news is obscured by the passive voice, long sentences (such as a 51-word sentence in a Continental Airlines annual report), and placing the bad news at the end of the letter to stockholders. (R. Subramanian, R. G. Insley, and R. D. Blackwell, "Performance and Readability: A Comparison of Annual Reports of Profitable and Unprofitable Corporations," *Journal of Business Communication,* 30:1, 1993, p. 56.)

against the company's policy to do so) during their anniversary sale. In Chapter 7 we assumed the role of the appliance store owner and wrote a persuasive message. Now let's assume the role of the supplier, who, for good business reasons, must refuse the request. Because we're writing to a good customer, we decide to use an indirect plan. We might start our message by using any of the following types of buffers:

Buffer Type	*Example*
Agreement	We both recognize the promotional possibilities that often accompany big anniversary sales such as yours.
Appreciation	Thanks for letting us know of your success in selling Golden Microwaves. *(However, avoid thanking the reader for asking you to do something that you're going to refuse to do; such expressions of appreciation sound insincere.)*
Compliment	Congratulations on having served the community of Greenville for ten years.
Facts	Three-fourths of the Golden distributors who held anniversary sales last year reported at least a 6% increase in annual sales of our home products.
General principle	We believe in furnishing Golden distributors a wide range of support in promoting our products.
Good news	Golden's upcoming 20%-off sale will be heavily advertised and will certainly provide increased traffic for your February anniversary sale.
Understanding	I wish to assure you of Golden's desire to help make your anniversary sale successful.

Note these characteristics of an effective opening buffer for bad-news messages:

A buffer should be neutral, relevant, supportive, interesting, and short.

1. It is *neutral.* To serve as a true buffer, the opening must not convey the negative news immediately. On the other hand, guard against implying that the request will be *granted,* thus building up the reader for a big letdown.

   Not neutral: Stores like Parker Brothers benefit from Golden's policy of not providing in-store demonstrators for our line of microwave ovens.

   Misleading: Your tenth-anniversary sale would be a great opportunity for Golden to promote its products.

2. It is *relevant.* The danger with starting *too* far from the topic is that the reader might not recognize that the letter is in response to his or her request. In addition, an irrelevant opening seems to avoid the issue, thus sounding insincere or self-serving. To show relevance and to personalize the opening, you might include some reference to the reader's letter in your opening sentence. A relevant opening provides a smooth transition to the reasons that follow.

   Irrelevant: Golden's new apartment-sized microwave oven means that young couples, retirees, and even students can enjoy the convenience of microwave cooking.

3. It is *supportive.* The purpose of the opening is to help establish compatibility between the reader and writer. If the opening is controversial or seems to lecture the reader, it will not achieve its purpose.

   Unsupportive: You must realize how expensive it would be to supply an in-house demonstrator for anniversary sales such as yours.

4. It is *interesting.* Although buffer openings are not substitutes for the strong attention-getters that are used in persuasive messages, they should nevertheless be interesting enough to motivate the recipient to continue reading. Therefore, avoid giving obvious information.

   Obvious: We have received your letter requesting an in-store demonstrator for your upcoming tenth-anniversary sale.

5. Finally, it is *short.* Readers get impatient if they have to wait too long to get to the major point of the message.

   Too long: As you may remember, for many years Golden provided in-store demonstrators for our line of microwave ovens. We were happy to do this because we felt that customers needed to see the spectacular results of our new browning element, which made microwaved food look as if it had just come from a regular oven. We discontinued this practice five years ago because . . .

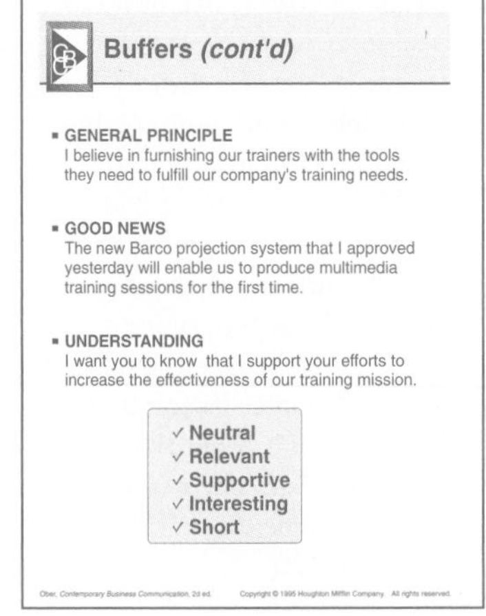

See Transparency 8.3, Types of Buffers (continued).

Ethical communicators use a buffer *not* in an attempt to manipulate or confuse the reader but in a sincere effort to help the reader accept the disappointing information in an objective manner.

Justifying Your Decision

Presumably, you reached your negative decision by analyzing all the relevant information. Whether you began in a direct or indirect manner, explain your analysis to help convince the reader that your decision is reasonable. The major part of your message should thus focus on the reasons rather than on the bad news itself.

For routine bad-news messages (that is, those written in a direct approach), the reasons can probably be stated concisely and matter-of-factly. Indirectly written messages, however, require more careful planning—because the stakes are typically greater.

Relevant buffers provide a smooth transition to the discussion of reasons.

Provide a smooth transition from the opening buffer and present the reasons honestly and convincingly. If possible, explain how the reasons benefit the reader or, at least, benefit someone other than you. Thus, refusing to exchange a worn garment might enable you to offer better-quality merchandise to your customers, raising the price of your product might enable you to switch to nonpolluting energy for manufacturing it, or refusing to provide copies of company documents might protect the confidentiality of customer transactions. Presenting reader benefits keeps your decision from sounding selfish.

Sometimes, however, granting the request is simply not in the company's own best interests. In such situations, don't "manufacture" reader

When delivering bad news to a supervisor, think about where it falls on a "who's responsible" continuum, advises Hendrie Weisinger, author of *The Critical Edge*. If the bad news is the message-bearer's fault, be forthright about that fact. If it's the supervisor's fault, depersonalize the news and use a buffer to soften the blow. (Walter Kiechel III, "Breaking Bad News to the Boss," *Fortune*, April 9, 1990, pp. 111-112.)

benefits; instead, just provide whatever short explanation you can and let it go at that.

> Because this data would be of strategic importance to our competitors, we treat it as confidential. Similar information about our entire industry (SIC Code 1473), however, is collected in the annual *U.S. Census of Manufacturing*. These census reports are available in most public and university libraries.

Show the reader that your decision was a *business* decision, not a personal one. Show that the request was taken seriously, and don't hide behind company policy. If the policy is a sound one, it was established for good reasons; therefore, explain the rationale for the policy.

> *Not:* Company policy prohibits our providing an in-store demonstrator for your tenth-anniversary sale.
>
> *But:* A survey of our dealers three years ago indicated they felt the space taken up by in-store demonstrators and the resulting traffic problems were not worth the effort; they were also concerned about the legal implications of having someone cooking in their stores.

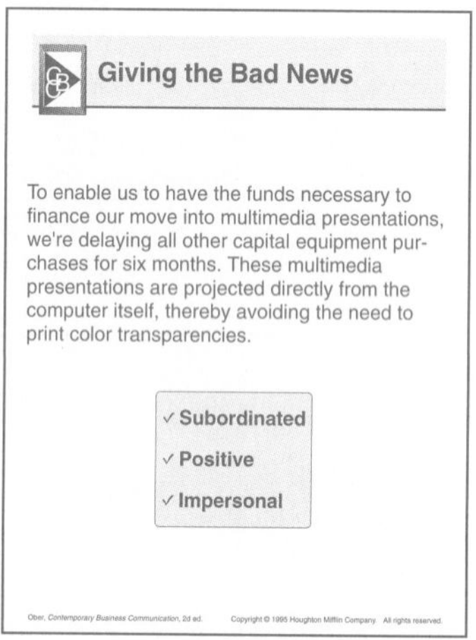

See Transparency 8.4, Giving the Bad News.

The reasons justifying your decision should take up the major part of the message, but be concise or your readers may become impatient. Do not belabor a point and do not provide more background than is necessary. If you have several reasons for refusing a request, present the strongest ones first—where they will receive the most emphasis. If possible, avoid mentioning any weak reasons. If the reader feels he or she can effectively rebut even one of your arguments, you're simply raising false hopes and inviting needless correspondence. Finally, be aware of the ethical and legal aspects of your decisions and your justification of your decisions (see the Spotlight on Law and Ethics).

Giving the Bad News

The reader should be able to infer the bad news before it is presented.

The bad news is communicated up front in directly written messages. And even in an indirectly written message, if you have done a convincing job of explaining the reasons, the bad news itself will come as no surprise; the decision will appear logical and reasonable—indeed the *only* logical and reasonable decision that could have been made under the circumstances.

To retain the reader's goodwill, state the bad news in positive language, stressing what you *are* able to do rather than what you are not able to do. Avoid, for example, such phrases as "cannot," "are not able to," "impossible," "unfortunately," "sorry," and "must refuse." To subordinate the bad news, put it in the middle of a paragraph, and include in the same sentence (or immediately afterward) additional discussion of reasons.

> In response to these dealer concerns, we eliminated in-store demonstrators and now advertise exclusively in the print media. Doing so has enabled us to begin featuring a two-page spread in each major Sunday newspaper, including your local paper, the *Greenville Courier*.

When using the indirect plan, phrase the bad news in impersonal language, avoiding the use of "you" and "your." The objective is to distance

SPOTLIGHT ON LAW AND ETHICS

Ten Reasons to Consult Your Lawyer

Because memos, letters, and corporate communications may be used as evidence against you or your organization in a court of law, it is often wise to check with a lawyer to make sure that what you write doesn't violate state or federal law. You should consult legal counsel when a document that you have written

1. Commits you to a legally binding contract.
2. Commits you to a warranty or guarantee of a product or service.
3. Makes an advertising claim.
4. Amends or modifies corporate policy.
5. Requests documents from an attorney.
6. Makes a statement to an insurance adjuster, the police, or a government agency.
7. Reports an accident involving a product, service, or employee.
8. Concerns the termination of an employee.
9. Concerns workers' compensation or insurance matters.
10. Concerns any product or process that will affect the environment.

the reader from the bad news so that it will not be perceived as a personal rejection. So as not to point out the bad news that lies ahead, avoid using "but" and "however" to introduce the bad news. The fact is, most readers won't remember what was written before the "but"—only what was written after it.

Avoid any temptation to apologize for your decision. You may reasonably assume that if the reader were faced with the same options and had the same information available, he or she would have acted in a similar way. There is no reason to apologize for any reasonable business decision.

You do not need to apologize for making a rational business decision.

In some situations, the refusal can be implied, making a direct statement of refusal unnecessary. But don't be evasive. If you think a positive, subordinated refusal might be misunderstood, go ahead and state it directly. However, even under these circumstances, you should use impersonal language and include reader benefits.

Closing on a Pleasant Note

Any refusal, even when handled skillfully, has negative overtones. Therefore, you need to end your message on a more pleasant note. Make your closing original, friendly, and positive by using any of the following techniques. Avoid referring back to the bad news.

Do not refer to the bad news in the closing.

Technique	*Example*
Best wishes	Best wishes for success with your tenth-anniversary sale. We have certainly enjoyed our ten-year relationship with Parker Brothers and look forward to continuing to serve your needs in the future.

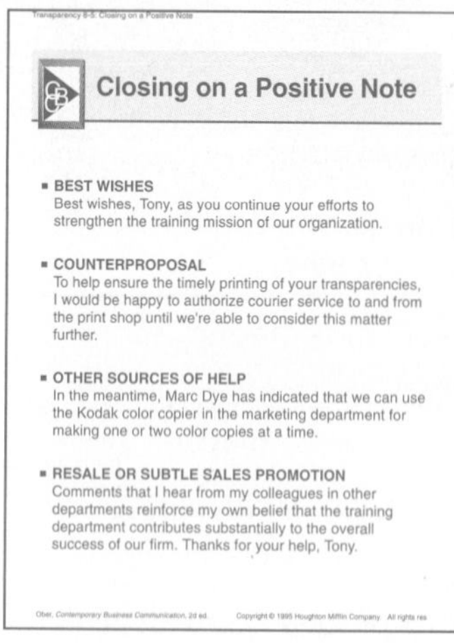

See Transparency 8.5, Closing on a Positive Note.

Counterproposal	To provide increased publicity for your tenth-anniversary sale, we would be happy to include a special 2-by-6-inch boxed notice of your sale in the *Greenville Courier* edition of our ad on Sunday, February 8. Just send us your camera-ready copy by January 26.
Other sources of help	A dealer in South Carolina switched from using in-store demonstrators to showing a video continuously during his microwave sale. He used the 10-minute film *Twenty-Minute Dinners with Pizzazz* (available for $45 from the Microwave Research Institute, P.O. Box 800, Chicago, IL 60625) and reported a very favorable reaction from customers.
Resale or subtle sales promotion	You can be sure that the new Golden Mini-Micro we're introducing in January will draw many customers to your store during your anniversary sale.

Close the letter on a positive, friendly, helpful note.

To sound sincere and helpful, make your ending original. If you provide a counterproposal or offer other sources of help, provide all the information the reader needs to follow through. If you include sales promotion, make it subtle and reader-oriented. Avoid statements such as the following:

Problem to Avoid	*Example of Problem*
Apologizing	Again, I am sorry that we were unable to grant this request.
Anticipating problems	If you run into any problems, please write me directly.
Inviting needless communication	If you have any further questions, please let me know.
Referring back to bad news	Although we are unable to supply an in-store demonstrator, we do wish you much success in your tenth-anniversary sale.
Repeating a cliché	If we can be of any further help, please don't hesitate to call on us.
Revealing doubt	I trust that you now understand why we made this decision.
Sounding selfish	Don't forget to feature Golden microwaves prominently in your anniversary display.

In short, the last idea the reader hears from you should be positive, friendly, and helpful. Checklist 7 summarizes guidelines for writing bad-news letters. The rest of this chapter discusses strategies for writing bad-news replies and bad-news announcements.

CHECKLIST 7

Bad-News Messages

DETERMINE HOW TO START THE MESSAGE

1. **Direct Plan**—Use a direct organizational plan when the bad news is insignificant, the reader prefers directness or expects a "no" response, the writer wants to emphasize the bad news, or the reader-writer relationship is either extremely close or extremely poor. Present the bad news (see Steps 8–11 below), along with a brief rationale, in the first paragraph.

   Indirect Plan—Use an indirect organizational plan when writing to subordinates, customers, readers who prefer the indirect plan, or readers you don't know. Start by buffering the bad news following these guidelines:

   a. Remember the purpose: to establish a common ground with the reader.
   b. Select an opening statement that is neutral, relevant, supportive, interesting, and short.
   c. Consider establishing a point of agreement, expressing appreciation, giving a sincere compliment, presenting a fact or general principle, giving good news, or showing understanding.
   d. Provide a smooth transition from the buffer to the reasons that follow.

JUSTIFY YOUR DECISION

2. If possible, stress reasons that are for the benefit of someone other than yourself.
3. State reasons in positive language.
4. Avoid relying on "company policy"; instead, explain the reason behind the policy.
5. State reasons concisely to avoid reader impatience. Do not overexplain.
6. Present the strongest reasons first; avoid discussing weak reasons.

GIVE THE BAD NEWS

7. If using the indirect plan, subordinate the bad news by putting it in the middle of a paragraph and including additional discussion of reasons.
8. Present the bad news as a logical outcome of the reasons given.
9. State the bad news in positive and impersonal language. Avoid terms such as "cannot" and "your."
10. Do not apologize.
11. Make the refusal definite—by implication if possible; otherwise, by stating it directly.

CLOSE ON A POSITIVE NOTE

12. Make your closing original, friendly, off the topic of the bad news, and positive.
13. Consider expressing best wishes, offering a counterproposal, suggesting other sources of help, or building in resale or subtle sales promotion.
14. Avoid anticipating problems, apologizing, inviting needless communication, referring to the bad news, repeating a cliché, revealing doubt, or sounding selfish.

BAD-NEWS REPLIES

Despite the skill with which a persuasive message is written, circumstances of which the reader is unaware may require a negative response. Your organization's well-being (and your own) may depend on the skill with which you are able to refuse a request and maintain the goodwill of the reader.

Rejecting an Idea

One of the more challenging bad-news messages to write is one that rejects someone's idea or proposal. Put yourself in the role of the person making the suggestion. He or she has probably spent a considerable amount of time in developing the idea, studying its feasibility, perhaps doing some research, and, of course, writing the original persuasive message.

Consider, for example, the persuasive memo presented in Figure 7.1 (see Chapter 7), in which Jenson Peterson tried to persuade Elliott Lamborn to restrict the nearest parking lots to American-built automobiles. Peterson obviously thinks his idea has merit. He went to the trouble of having his staff count the number of foreign-made automobiles in the lots, getting a cost estimate for making the change, and contacting the union representative to get the union's position. Finally, he organized all his information into an effectively written memo.

Having invested that much time and energy into the proposal, Peterson probably feels quite strongly that his proposal is valid, and he likely expects Lamborn to approve it. If—or in this case *when*—his proposal is rejected, Peterson will be surprised, and disappointed.

Because Lamborn is Peterson's superior, he could send Peterson a directly written memo saying in effect, "I have considered your proposal and must reject it." But Peterson is obviously intelligent and enterprising, and Lamborn does not want to discourage future initiatives on his part. As with all such bad-news replies, then, Lamborn's twin objectives are to refuse the proposal and retain Peterson's goodwill.

Rejecting someone's idea requires extreme tact and sound reasons.

To be successful, Lamborn has an educating job to do. He must give Peterson the reasons for the rejection, reasons of which Peterson is probably unaware. He must also show that he recognizes Peterson's proposal as carefully considered and that the rejection is based on business—not personal—considerations.

For other examples of rejecting an idea, see the *Instructor's Resource Manual*, pp. 155 and 158.

Considering the amount of effort Peterson has put into this project, Lamborn's memo will be most effective if written in the indirect pattern. This pattern will let Lamborn move his subordinate gradually into agreeing that the proposal is not in the best interests of the firm.

Lamborn's memo rejecting Peterson's proposal is shown in Figure 8.1. Although we label this memo a bad-news message, actually it is also a *persuasive* message. Like all bad-news messages, the memo seeks to persuade the reader that the writer's position is reasonable.

Refusing a Favor

Many favors are asked and granted almost automatically. Doing routine favors for others in the organization shows a cooperative spirit, and a spirit of reciprocity often prevails—we recognize that the person asking us for a

FIGURE 8.1 Rejecting an Idea—Indirect Plan

This memo responds to the personal request in Figure 7.1.

+ Timkin
+ Electrical
+ Systems

MEMO TO: Jenson Peterson, Marketing Supervisor

FROM: Elliott Lamborn, Vice President *EL*

DATE: October 15, 19--

SUBJECT: Parking Lot Proposal

Uses a neutrally worded subject line.

Your October 3 memo certainly enlightened me regarding the automobile buying
1 habits of our employees. I had no idea that one-third of our workers drive
foreign-made cars.

Starts with a supportive buffer; the second sentence provides a smooth transition to the reason.

The increasing popularity of foreign-made cars recently led Timkin management to conclude that we should extend our promotional thrust to take advantage of this expanding market. President Wrede has appointed a task force to determine how we might enter the Japanese, German, and English auto markets. In fact, our newest long-range plan, which will be presented to the board next week, estimates that within five years, international sales will account for 15% to 18% of Timkin's sales.

Begins discussing the reason.

Our successful entry into the international automotive market will mean that many of the foreign-made automobiles Timkin employees drive will have Timkin electrical systems. Thus, our firm will benefit from the continuing presence of these cars in all our lots.

Presents the refusal in the last sentence of the paragraph, using positive and impersonal language.

2 Your memo got me to thinking, Jenson, that we might be missing an opportunity
to promote our products to headquarters visitors. Would you please develop
some type of awareness campaign (perhaps a bumper sticker for employee cars
that contain a Timkin electrical system or some type of billboard) that shows
our employees support the products we sell. I would appreciate having a memo
from you with your ideas by November 3 so that I might include this project in
3 next year's marketing campaign.

Closes on a forward-looking, off-the-topic note.

amp

– 1034 York Road
– Baltimore, MD 21204
– Phone: 301-555-1086

Grammar and Mechanics Notes

1 *one-third:* Spell out and hyphenate fractions. 2 *thinking, Jenson, that:* Set off nouns of direct address (*Jenson*) with commas. 3 *year's:* Use apostrophe plus *s* to form the possessive of a singular noun (*year*).

favor today may be the person from whom we'll need a favor next week. Sometimes, however, for business or personal reasons, we are not able to accommodate the other person and must decline an invitation or a request for a favor.

The type of message written to refuse a favor depends on the particular circumstances. Occasionally, someone asks a "big" favor—perhaps one involving a major investment of time or resources. In that case, the person has probably written a thoughtful, reasoned message trying to persuade you to do as he or she asked. If you must refuse such a significant request, you should probably present your refusal indirectly, following the guidelines given earlier.

Most requests for favors, however, are routine, and a routine request should receive a routine response; that is, a response written in the direct organizational plan. A colleague asking you to attend a meeting in her place, a superior asking you to serve on a committee, or a business associate inviting you to lunch is not going to be deeply disappointed if you decline. The writer has probably not spent a great deal of energy composing the request; the main thing he or she wants to know from you is "yes" or "no."

When refusing routine requests, give the refusal in the first paragraph.

For other examples of refusing favors as well as examples of refusing applications, requests, business, and invitations, see the *Instructor's Resource Manual*, pp. 156–157, 159–162, and 165–166.

In such situations, give your refusal in the first paragraph, but avoid curtness and coldness. Common courtesy demands that you buffer the bad news somewhat and that you at least give a quick, reasonable rationale for declining. Although the refusal itself might not lose the reader's goodwill, a poorly written refusal message might! The memo in Figure 8.2 declines a request to serve on a corporate committee and is written using a direct plan.

Assume for a moment that Peter Carmichael had decided, instead, that his best strategy would be to write the memo (Figure 8.2) in the indirect pattern, explaining his rationale before refusing. His opening buffer might then have been as follows:

> Like you, I believe our new Executive-in-Residence program will prove to be effective for both Utah State and for the executives who participate.

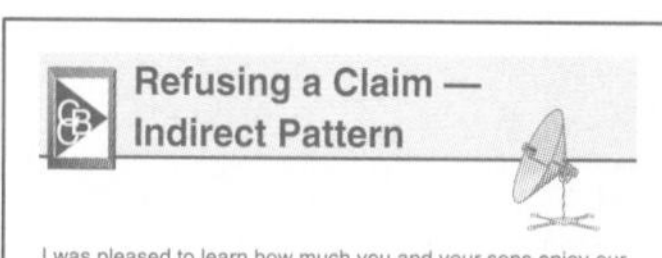

I was pleased to learn how much you and your sons enjoy our cable service and can surely understand your frustration at not having cable available for a four-day period in June.

You and 2,500 cable customers went without service during this period while our workers installed new fiber-optic lines in your area. Because routine maintenance and upgrading, which result in superior service to our customers, are allowed under our license with the city of Plattsburg, all customers are charged their regular monthly bills during these periods. The payoff, of course, is the increased services that will become available within the coming year.

To be more precise, three of the channels that are now priced as premium channels will become part of the basic monthly service, and additional pay-per-view concerts and sports events will become available.

We are confident your sons will agree that the wait was a good investment the first time they are able to watch a first-run movie or a WBA boxing championship bout free, in the comfort of their own home.

Ober, *Contemporary Business Communication*, 2d ed.

See Transparency 8.6, Refusing a Claim—Indirect Pattern.

Refusing a Claim

The indirect plan is almost always used when refusing an adjustment request because the reader (the dissatisfied customer) is emotionally involved in the situation. The customer is already upset by the failure of the product to live up to expectations. If you refuse the claim immediately, you risk losing the customer's goodwill. And, as noted previously, every dissatisfied customer tells nine or ten people about the bad experience and they, in turn, tell four or five others. Clearly, you want to avoid such situations.

The tone of your refusal must convey respect and consideration for the customer—even when the customer is at fault. To separate the reader from the refusal, begin with a buffer, using one of the techniques presented earlier (for example, showing understanding).

FIGURE 8.2 Refusing a Favor—Direct Plan

■●▲ ■●▲ ■●▲ ■●▲ ■●▲ ■●▲ ■●▲ ■●▲ ■●▲ ■●▲

KEMPERER MANUFACTURING

1 May 18, 19--

TO: Wanda K. Berenson
Personnel Department

FROM: Peter R. Carmichael *PRC*
Accounting Department

SUBJECT: Your Memo of May 9, 19--

You did such a good job of explaining the merits of our new Executive-in-Residence program that I've tentatively decided to apply for the program myself. To keep my options open, then, I must ask you to select someone else to serve on the evaluation committee.

Gives a quick reason, immediately followed by the refusal.

Since I may be an applicant myself, I believe it would be inappropriate for me to suggest an alternate committee member.

Provides additional details.

2 I will know by July 1 whether my workload for the fall semester will allow me to apply. If I decide not to apply, I shall be back in touch with you then to see if there is some way I can assist you in getting this important program off to a successful start.

Closes on a helpful note.

iem

3 c: Fay Lee, Director of Accounting

24 South 500 East ■ Salt Lake City, Utah 84102 ■ PHONE: 801-555-3061

Grammar and Mechanics Notes

1 Many different formats for memos are acceptable. 2 *July 1 whether:* Do not use a comma after an incomplete date. 3 Use a copy notation *(c:)* to indicate who else received a copy of the document.

> Frequent travelers like you depend on luggage that "can take it"—luggage that will hold up for many years under normal use.

When explaining the reasons for denying the claim, do not accuse or lecture the reader. At the same time, however, don't appear to accept responsibility for the problem if the customer is at fault. In impersonal, neutral language, explain why the claim is being denied.

> *Not:* The reasons the handles ripped off your Sebastian luggage is that you overloaded it. The tag on the luggage clearly states that you should use the luggage only for clothing, with a maximum of 40 pounds. However, our engineers concluded that you had put at least 65 pounds of items in the luggage.
>
> *But:* On receiving your piece of Sebastian luggage, we sent it to our testing department. The engineers there found stretch marks on the leather and a frayed nylon stitching cord. They concluded that such wear could only have been caused by contents weighing substantially more than the 40 pounds maximum weight that is stated on the luggage tag. Such use is beyond the "normal wear and tear" covered in our warranty.

Use impersonal, neutral language to explain the basis for the refusal.

Note that in the second example, the pronoun "you" is not used at all when discussing the bad news. By using third-person pronouns and the passive voice, the example avoids directly accusing the reader of misusing the product. The actual refusal, given in the last sentence, is conveyed in neutral language.

An offer of a compromise, however small, helps retain the reader's goodwill.

As with other bad-news messages, close on a friendly, forward-looking note. If you can offer a compromise, it will take the sting out of the rejection and show the customer that you are reasonable. It will also help the customer save face. Be careful, however, that your offer does not imply any assumption of responsibility on your part. The compromise can either come before or be a part of the closing. For example,

> Although we replace luggage only when it is damaged in normal use, our repair shop tells me the damaged handle can easily be replaced. We would be happy to do so for $22.50, including return shipping. If you will simply initial this letter and return it to us in the enclosed, addressed envelope, we will return your repaired luggage within four weeks.

Somewhere in your letter you might also include a pitch for resale. The customer has had a negative experience with your product. If you want your reader to continue to be a customer, you might restate some of the benefits that led him or her to buy the product in the first place. But use this technique carefully; a strong pitch may simply annoy an already unhappy customer.

For other examples of refusing a claim, see the *Instructor's Resource Manual*, pp. 154, 163, and 164.

Consider the persuasive request written by Oliver Arbin presented in Figure 7.3. Mr. Arbin, as you may remember, was upset that his family's flight to Indianapolis was canceled and that they were thus forced to make a six-hour drive instead. He wanted a refund of the $680 cost of his five nonrefundable tickets. It appears, on further investigation, that Mr. Arbin was not completely forthright. The letter refusing his claim request is shown in Figure 8.3.

FIGURE 8.3 Refusing a Claim—Indirect Plan

This letter responds to the personal claim in Figure 7.3.

NORTHERN AIRLINES

June 27, 19--

Mr. Oliver J. Arbin
518 Thompson Street
Saginaw, MI 48607

1 Dear Mr. Arbin

We make no money when our customers are forced to take long trips by car rather than by flying Northern Airlines; and when that happens, we want to find out why.

Opens on an agreeable and relevant note.

A review of the June 2 log of the aborted Flight 126 shows that it was scheduled to depart at 8 p.m. and was canceled at 7:10 p.m. because of
2 inclement weather. Passengers were asked to remain in the boarding area; those who did were rebooked on Flight 3321, which departed at 9:15 p.m. Flight 3321 arrived in Indianapolis at 10:40 p.m., just 75 minutes later than the scheduled arrival of Flight 126. Given these circumstances, Ms. Lois Nixon, the ticket agent, was correct in disallowing any refund on nonrefundable tickets.

Begins the explanation; presents the refusal in impersonal language.

Since you indicated that you're a frequent traveler on Northern, I've asked our Scheduling Department to add you to the mailing list to receive a complimentary subscription to our quarterly Saginaw flight schedule. A copy of the current schedule is enclosed. From now on, you'll be sure to know exactly when every Northern flight arrives at and departs from Tri-Cities Airport.

Closes on a helpful note; implies that the reader will continue to fly on Northern.

Sincerely

Madelyn Masarani

Madelyn Masarani
Service Representative

eta
3 Enclosure

P.O. BOX 6001, DENVER, CO 80240 ▪ PHONE: 303-555-3990 ▪ FAX: 303-555-3992

Grammar and Mechanics Notes

1 Insert no punctuation after the salutation and complimentary closing when using open punctuation. 2 *boarding area;*: Use a semicolon to separate two closely related independent clauses not connected by a conjunction. 3 Use an enclosure notation to alert the recipient to look for some inserted material.

BAD-NEWS ANNOUNCEMENTS

Bad-news announcements are not in response to any request.

The previous section discussed strategies for writing negative replies. Often, however, the bad news we have to present involves a new situation; that is, it is not in response to another message. And quite often, these messages go to a large audience, as, for example, when you're announcing a major price increase or new rules and regulations. Such announcements may be either internal (addressed to employees) or external (addressed to customers, news media, stockholders, and the like).

As with other bad-news messages, you must decide whether to use the direct or indirect plan of organization. Be guided by the effect the bad news will have on the recipients and your relationship with them.

Bad News About Normal Operations

If the reader will not be disappointed, present the bad news directly.

Assume that management has decided a price increase of 10% is justified on the Danforth cabin tent you manufacture. This price increase requires that you notify your order department, your wholesalers, and finally, a special retail customer.

To notify the order department of the price change (a routine matter), you would probably send a memo like this, written in the direct pattern:

> Effective March 1, the regular price of our Danforth cabin tent (Item R-885) changes from $149.99 to $164.99, an increase of 10%. Any order postmarked before March 1 should be billed at the lower price, regardless of when the order is actually shipped.
>
> The new price will be shown in our spring catalog, and a notice is being sent immediately to all wholesalers. If you receive orders postmarked after March 1 but showing the old price, please notify the wholesaler before filling the order.

Companies announcing layoffs, such as Digital Equipment Corporation and Tandem Computers, keep lines of co-munication open and dispel rumors promptly to improve employee morale. Companies keep in touch through management-employee meetings as well as technologies like teleconferencing and 800 numbers direct to the CEO. ("Memo to Workers: No More Big Daddy," *Newsweek*, December 16, 1991, p. 46.)

The preceding message reflects the fact that the price increase will have minor negative consequences to the order department. Therefore, the news is given directly—in the first sentence—followed by the details. Because the person receiving this memorandum will not be personally disappointed in the news, you don't need to explain the price increase.

However, you also need to notify your wholesalers of this price increase. What will be their reaction? They will probably not be personally disappointed because price increases are common in business and come as no surprise; thus a direct message is called for. But wholesalers *do* have a choice about where to buy tents for resale, so you need to justify your price increase.

A reason may be presented first—even in a message written in a direct pattern.

> Because of the prolonged strike in South African mines, we now must purchase the chrome used in our Danforth cabin tent elsewhere at a higher cost. Thus, effective March 1, the regular price of the Danforth tent (Item R-885) will change from $149.99 to $164.99.
>
> As a courtesy to our wholesalers, however, we are billing any orders postmarked prior to March 1 at the old price of $149.99. Use the enclosed form or call our toll free number—800-555-9843—to place your order for what *American Camper* calls the "sock-it-to-me" tent.

Note how the bad news is cushioned by (1) presenting the reason first—a reason that is clearly beyond your control; (2) selling at the old price until March 1; and (3) including resale in the closing paragraph.

Finally, you need to write a third message about the price increase. For the past two years, you have had an exclusive marketing agreement with the Association for Backpackers and Campers. They promote the Danforth cabin tent in each issue of *Field News,* their quarterly magazine, at no cost to you in exchange for your offering their members the wholesale price of $149.99 (instead of the retail price, which is about 35% higher).

ABC selected the Danforth tent because of its quality *and* because of its attractive price, and you want to make sure that your price increase does not endanger this agreement. Thus, you write an indirect-pattern letter, in which your major emphasis is on the reasons, not the results.

> The popularity of the Danforth cabin tent that you feature in each issue of *Field News* is based on our exclusive use of a chrome frame. Chrome is twice as strong as aluminum, yet weighs about the same.
>
> Because of the prolonged strike in South African mines, we were faced with the choice of either switching to aluminum or securing the needed chrome elsewhere at a higher cost. We elected to continue using chrome in our tent. This decision to maintain quality has resulted in a change in the wholesale price of the Danforth cabin tent (Item R-885) from $149.99 to $164.99.
>
> The Danforth tent promotion in the spring issue of *Field News* should be changed to reflect this new price. Since the spring issue usually arrives the last week of February, we will bill any orders postmarked before March 1 at the lower price of $149.99.
>
> We have enjoyed the opportunity to serve ABC members and extend best wishes to your organization for another successful year of providing such valuable service to American backpackers and campers.

If the reader must be persuaded of the reasonableness of your decision, use the indirect approach.

For other examples of bad-news announcements, see the *Instructor's Resource Manual,* pp. 167, 168, 169, 170, 171, 172, 173, and 174.

Another situation that calls for indirect organization is one in which a change in organizational policy will adversely affect employees. It is just as important, of course, to retain the goodwill of employees as it is of customers. Acceptance of a new policy depends not only on the reasons for the policy but also on the skill with which the reasons are communicated. An example of such a situation is shown in Figure 8.4.

When dealing with issues that are of such personal interest to the reader, don't hurry your discussion. Take as much space as necessary to show the reader that your decision was not made in haste, that you considered all options, and that the reader's interests were taken into account.

Explain thoroughly the basis for your decision.

Note, especially, the use of personal and impersonal language throughout the memo. When discussing insurance programs that will be retained (third paragraph), "you" and "your" are used extensively. When discussing the program that will be dropped (fourth paragraph), impersonal language is used instead. The purpose is to closely associate the readers with the good news and to separate them from the bad news. Such deliberate use of language does not manipulate the reader; it simply uses good human relations to bring the reader to an understanding and appreciation of the writer's position.

FIGURE 8.4 Bad-News Announcement—Indirect Plan

Danforth Recreational Industries

TO: All Danforth Employees

FROM: Mary Louise Lytle, Vice President *MLL*

DATE: July 8, 19--

Uses a neutral subject line.

RE: Change in Insurance Coverage 1

Begins with a compliment.

Thanks to you, President Adams will announce a 13% increase in sales for the year that ended June 30. Six of the seven divisions met or exceeded their sales quota for the year. What an example of the Danforth spirit! 2

Provides a smooth transition to the explanation; uses figures for believability.

Our pleasure at the 13% increase in sales is somewhat tempered by a corresponding increase in expenditures for the year. In studying the reasons for this increase, we found that fringe benefits, especially insurance, were the largest contributor. Medical insurance costs increased 23% last year and have risen 58% in the past three years.

Uses the overall welfare of all employees as the reader benefit; presents the good news before the bad.

In order to continue providing needed coverage for our employees and their families and still hold costs to a reasonable level, we've analyzed the use and cost of each component of our program. We learned that last year 89% of you used your health insurance at least once, with the average being 12 family-member consultations per year. Clearly, your health insurance is important to you and, therefore, to us. Similarly, although only 6% used your major medical insurance for hospital care last year, protecting our employees from devastating health-care costs remains a top priority for us.

Implies that fairness demands a change; subordinates the bad news in the middle of a long paragraph.

The other major component of our medical insurance program is dental. Here we found that only 9% of our employees used this coverage last year, yet dental insurance represented 19% of our total medical insurance costs. We believe the funds now being used for dental care for a small minority of our employees can better be used to pay the escalating costs of health and major-medical coverage for all our employees. Thus, effective next January 1, all company-paid insurance programs will include only health and major-medical coverage. Although dental coverage will be discontinued at that time, all requests for reimbursement for dental bills submitted on or before December 31 will be paid at the normal rates.

Closes by discussing a different, but related, topic.

The Benefits Office will hold an open forum on July 28 from 2 to 3 p.m. in the 3
second-floor auditorium to solicit your input and views on all areas of employee benefits. Please come prepared with questions and comments on pensions, vacations, medical insurance, stock-option plans, and other areas of interest. Your input will enable us to continue to provide our family of employees the kind of protection and options you deserve.

ada

Grammar and Mechanics Notes

1 You may use *RE:* instead of *SUBJECT:* in the memo heading. 2 *President Adams:* Capitalize a title that is used before a name. 3 *3 p.m.:* Use figures to express time; type the abbreviation *p.m.* in lowercase letters, with no space after the internal period.

Bad News About the Organization

If your organization is experiencing serious problems, your employees, customers, and stockholders should hear the news from you—not from newspaper accounts or rumors. For extremely serious problems that receive widespread attention (for example, product recalls, unexpected operating deficits, or legal problems), the company's public relations department will probably issue a news release.

Often, some type of correspondence is also necessary. For example, owners of recalled products must be notified, customers must be notified if an impending strike will affect delivery dates, and employees must be notified if they will be affected by plant closings or layoffs. To show that these situations are receiving attention from top management, such messages should generally come from a high-level official.

Show that the situation is receiving top-management attention.

If the situation about which you are writing has news value, assume that your communication may find its way to a reporter's desk. Thus, make sure not only that the overall tone of the letter is appropriate but also that individual sentences of the letter cannot be misinterpreted if they are lifted out of context.

Throughout your message, choose each word with care. In general, avoid using words with negative connotations and emphasize those with positive connotations. Effective communication techniques can help you control the emphasis, subordination, and tone of your *own* message; however, you cannot do so for a news item that quotes individual parts of your message. For example, note the following misinterpretation of a sentence from a company president's letter that was contained in a published news item.

Write in such a way as not to be misinterpreted.

News item:	Although other drilling companies in the area erect 8-foot fences around their excavation sites, Owens-Ohio President Robert Leach admitted in a letter to stockholders yesterday that "our company does not require fences around these sites."
President's actual statement:	Unlike several other firms in the area, we have always had a strict policy of not allowing any digging in residential areas. In fact, all our excavation sites are at least 2 miles from any paved road and are well marked by 10-foot signs. Because these sites are so isolated, our company does not require fences around these sites.

The last sentence of the president's statement would have been more effective had it been worded in positive, impersonal language.

> Fences are unnecessary in such isolated sites and, in fact, can cause safety hazards of their own. For example, . . .

If the reader has already learned about the situation from other sources, your best strategy is to use a direct organizational pattern. In a spirit of helpfulness and forthrightness, confirm the bad news quickly and

In an organizational crisis, tell everything and tell it fast, says Frank Corrado in *Media for Managers*. Johnson & Johnson used this approach after the 1982 Tylenol poisonings. Top management sought national exposure on "60 Minutes" and "Donahue," and the public relations department managed thousands of press inquiries and a toll-free line (which received 350,000 calls). (Frank Corrado, *Media for Managers*, Prentice-Hall, Englewood Cliffs, NJ, 1984, pp. 101, 107.)

Companies like Macy's department store chain that are forced to declare Chapter 11 bankruptcy face a real challenge in conveying bad news. They must try to keep creditors, customers, and stockholders content long enough for the company to get back on its feet financially.

begin immediately to provide the necessary information to help the reader understand the situation. For example,

> As you entered the building this morning, you may have seen the evidence of a burglary last night. The purpose of this memo is to let you know exactly what happened and to outline steps we are taking to ensure the continued safety of our employees who work during evening hours.

For an exercise on microwriting a bad-news letter, see the *Instructor's Resource Manual,* pp. 308–310.

If the reader is hearing the news for the first time, your best strategy is to use the indirect pattern, using a buffer opening and stressing the most positive aspects of the situation (in this case, the steps you're taking to prevent a recurrence of the problem).

For an exercise on revising a bad-news memo, refer students to the *Study Guide,* pp. 127–128.

> Employees in our data-entry and maintenance departments who work at night perform a valuable service for Martin Company, and their safety and well-being are of prime concern to us. In that spirit, I would like to discuss with you several steps we are taking as a result of . . .

Figure 8.5 shows a letter written to alert customers about a possible demonstration to be held outside the site of a meeting announcing a new product. By showing a respectful attitude toward the demonstrators and by avoiding emotional language, the writer is able to convey the bad news with a minimum of fuss. And the fact that each customer received a personally typed letter from the president is in itself reassuring.

Being a part of the management team sometimes requires that you support decisions with which you personally disagree.

This letter also illustrates another common aspect of bad-news messages: occasionally, you may have to defend positions with which you personally disagree. Your disagreement may be strategic (it's not a smart move at this time) or philosophical (we shouldn't be selling and promoting this product). The issue, of course, goes much deeper than communicating. If you and your organization's philosophies consistently do not mesh, you might be happier finding employment in a more compatible environment. If you decide to stay, however, you should have no qualms about defending any legal and ethical position the organization decides to take.

FIGURE 8.5 Bad-News Announcement—Personal Letter

A personal letter from the president draws the needed attention.

PACIFIC LABORATORIES
A LIFE-LABS COMPANY

1 November 8, 19--

Ms. Michelle Loftis
Planning Department
Crosslanes Pharmacies
3842 Le Purc Boulevard
El Toro, CA 92630

Dear Ms. Loftis:

The breakthrough in over-the-counter birth control that Pacific Laboratories will announce at 3 p.m. on December 5 at the Park Inn will present a very substantial marketing opportunity for Crosslanes Pharmacies. I'm pleased you can be with us for the announcement.

Uses sales promotion for the opening buffer.

Like many scientific breakthroughs, our new product is generating quite a bit of interest in the media. Already, 12 newspapers and television stations have requested and been granted permission to cover this product announcement. We
2 welcome such coverage and believe that an open discussion of such products will lead to more informed decisions by consumers.

Presents the company in a favorable light by using a reasoned and even-handed approach.

In the same spirit, we have taken no steps to prevent any demonstrations outside the Park Inn on that day. It is likely that some pro-life and anti-abortion groups will march and distribute leaflets. So long as they do so peacefully, they are perfectly within their rights. We also are within our rights to hold a meeting without disruption, and there will be adequate
3 security personnel on hand to ensure that everything runs smoothly. We do ask that you bring your original invitation (or this letter) to identify yourself, and we suggest that you use the Broad Street entrance to the hotel.

Treats the news of the expected demonstrations (the bad news) objectively and unemotionally.

We look forward to showing off the efforts of five years of research by our staff. The safety, convenience, and ease of use of this product will make it a very popular item on your pharmacy shelves.

Closes with additional sales promotion and reader benefits.

Sincerely,

Stephen Lynch

Stephen Lynch
President

jel

924 Ninth Street, Santa Monica, CA 90403 ■ Phone: 415-555-2389

Grammar and Mechanics Notes

1 Begin the date and closing lines at the center point when using a modified block style of letter. 2 *coverage and:* Do not insert a comma before the conjunction (*and*) because what follows is not an independent clause. 3 *runs smoothly:* Use an adverb (*smoothly*) instead of an adjective (*smooth*) to modify a verb.

MICROWRITING

A Bad-News Message

PROBLEM

You are the owner and president of Hudson Research Services. Your firm recently constructed a new headquarters building on a five-acre lot, and you've landscaped the unused four acres with lighted walkways, fountains, and ponds for employees to enjoy during their lunch hours and before and after work. Your lovely campus-like site is one of the few such locations within the city limits.

Joan Bradley, the mayor of your city, is running for reelection. She has written to you asking permission to hold a campaign fund-raiser on your grounds on July 7 from 8 p.m. until midnight. This event will be for "heavy" contributors; up to 150 people, each paying $500, are expected. Her reelection committee will take care of all catering, security, and cleanup.

You do not want to become involved in this event for numerous reasons. Write to the mayor (The Honorable Joan Bradley, Mayor of Hudson, Hudson, OH 44236) and decline her request.

PROCESS

1. Describe your primary audience.

   - Very important person (don't want to offend her)
   - Holds political views different from my own
   - Possibility of her losing the election (don't want to appear to be backing a loser)

2. Describe your secondary audience.

   - The 150 big contributors (What will be their reaction to my refusal?)
   - The other candidates (do not wish to offend anyone who might become the next mayor)

3. Brainstorm: List as many reasons as you can think of as to why you might refuse her request. Then, after you've come up with several, determine which one will be most effective. Underline that reason.

   - Other sites in the city offer a more suitable environment for the event
   - Would have to provide the same favor for every other candidate
   - Possible harm to lawn, plants, and animals
   - Company policy prohibits outside use

4. Write your buffer opening—neutral, relevant, supportive, interesting, and short.

   Thank you for your kind comments about our lovely grounds. With much effort, our staff has been able to create an environment in which plants and animals not normally found in the Midwest are able to thrive here.

5. Now skip to the actual refusal itself. Write the statement in which you refuse the request—making it positive, subordinated, and unselfish.

   ```
   To protect our delicate environment, we now restrict the
   use of these grounds to company employees.
   ```

6. Write the closing for your letter—original, friendly, off the topic of the refusal, and positive. *Suggestions:* best wishes, counterproposal, other sources of help, or subtle resale.

   ```
   As an alternative, may I suggest the beautiful grounds at
   the Ohio Educational Consortium on Lapeer Street.  They
   were designed with an Ohio motif by Larry Miller, the
   designer for our grounds.
   ```

PRODUCT

Hudson Research Services
1836 Great Rd.
Hudson, OH 44236
216-555-0684

May 20, 19--

The Honorable Joan Bradley
Mayor of Hudson
Hudson, OH 44236

Dear Mayor Bradley:

Thank you for your kind comments about our lovely grounds. Our staff has been able to create an environment here in which plants and animals not normally found in the Midwest are able to thrive.

For example, after much effort, we have finally been able to attract a family of Eastern Bluebirds to our site. At this very moment, the female is sitting on three eggs, and various members of our staff unobtrusively check on her progress each day.

Similar efforts have resulted in the successful introduction of beautiful but sensitive flowers, shrubs, and marsh grasses. To protect this delicate environment, we restrict the use of these grounds to company employees, many of whom have contributed ideas, plants, and time in developing the grounds.

As an alternative, may I suggest the beautiful grounds at the Ohio Educational Consortium on Lapeer Street. They were designed with an Ohio motif by Larry Miller, the designer for our grounds. Various public events have been held there without damage to the environment. Susan Siebold, their executive director, can be reached at 555-9832 if you wish to contact her about using their facilities.

Sincerely,

J. W. Hudson

J. W. Hudson
President

tma

SUMMARY

When writing a bad-news message, your goal is to convey the bad news and, at the same time, keep the reader's goodwill. A direct organizational plan is recommended when you are writing to superiors, when the bad news involves a small, insignificant matter, or when you want to emphasize the bad news. When using the direct plan, state the bad news in positive language in the first paragraph, perhaps preceded or followed by a short buffer and/or a reason for the decision. Then present the explanation or reasons, and close on a friendly and positive note.

When writing to subordinates, customers, or people you don't know, you should generally use an indirect plan. This approach begins with a buffer—a neutral and relevant statement that helps establish or strengthen the reader-writer relationship. Then follows the explanation of or reasons for the bad news. The reasons should be logical and, when possible, should identify a reader benefit. The bad news should be subordinated, using positive and impersonal language; apologies are not necessary. The closing should be friendly, positive, and off the topic.

Depending on the individual circumstances, either the direct or indirect pattern may be used to reject an idea, refuse a favor, deny a claim, or present bad news about normal operations or about the organization itself.

KEY TERM

Buffer A neutral and supportive opening statement designed to lessen the impact of negative news.

For an exercise on matching terms, refer students to the *Study Guide*, p. 124.

REVIEW AND DISCUSSION

The answers to the review and discussion questions appear in the *Instructor's Resource Manual*, beginning on p. 140.

1. **Communication at Digital Equipment Corporation Revisited** ▪ Digital's Alan Pike recognizes that business communicators tend to deny the existence of bad news. He fights that tendency and works hard to dig out the facts—good or bad—in a timely manner and to stress the positive aspects of every situation.
   a. Should Pike use the direct or indirect pattern in a memo to employees that announces the bad news of lower-than-expected quarterly earnings?
   b. What opening buffer might Pike use in a bad-news letter about lower quarterly earnings written to securities analysts, whose buy-and-sell recommendations are vital to a publicly traded company like Digital?
   c. Where in the bad-news letter to the securities analysts should Pike include Digital's apology for the disappointing earnings?
2. What are the two objectives of a bad-news message?
3. Under what conditions should a direct plan of organization be used for bad-news messages?
4. Why are direct messages often shorter than indirect messages?

5. Indicate whether a direct or indirect message would be more effective when writing to
   a. A colleague, refusing her offer of a free ride to your upcoming sales conference, because you have to go a day early.
   b. Employees, telling them that for the first time no vacations may be scheduled during July and August.
   c. Your superior, informing him that the quarterly employee newsletter will be three days late because the offset machine broke down.
   d. The sales staff, informing them that their sales quotas will be increased by 8% for the coming year.
   e. Stockholders, informing them of an impending federal investigation of your vice chairperson.
6. Why is the opening sentence called a "buffer"?
7. List the five characteristics of an effective buffer.
8. Critique each of the following buffers; then revise them to correct the weaknesses.

   a. `Thank you so much for asking me to serve on the employee relations committee.`
   b. `You can always depend on Meyers to honor claims for damaged merchandise.`
   c. `I wish I could grant your request to mail your organization's newsletter from our mailroom.`

9. Critique each of the following reasons or explanations for refusing; then revise them to correct the weaknesses.

   a. `Unfortunately, the cost of participating in this project is prohibitive; furthermore, . . .`
   b. `You can surely understand that participating in this project would be prohibitively expensive.`
   c. `That is why company policy prohibits all such endeavors.`

10. You wish to refuse a worker's request to use the microcomputer at her desk after hours to compose a newsletter for a charitable organization to which she belongs. Write the statement in which you actually say "no."
11. What techniques are effective for the closing of a bad-news message? What techniques should you avoid?
12. Write an effective closing sentence for a letter in which you refuse to honor a claim for a damaged dress because it was improperly laundered.

EXERCISES

1. Microwriting a Claims Refusal ▪

A sample solution for Exercise 1 appears in the *Instructor's Resource Manual*, p. 142. A formatted solution appears on *IRM* p. 154. An exercise on microwriting a bad-news letter appears on *IRM* pp. 308–310.

PROBLEM

You have just received a claim letter from John Stodel (306 Hyde Court, Kirkwood, MO 63122-4541). Mr. Stodel purchased a Clipper lawn mower (Model 306-B) from you two years ago. For the third time, he has written a claim letter requesting that you repair his $486 mower for free because its self-propelled mechanism stopped working after 15 months of use. Twice already, you've sent polite adjustment letters, denying the claim on the basis that the Model 306-B comes with a one-year warranty and the repair does not fall within the warranty period. You don't want to be rude, but you wish he would stop writing to you about a matter that you've already decided. Let him know.

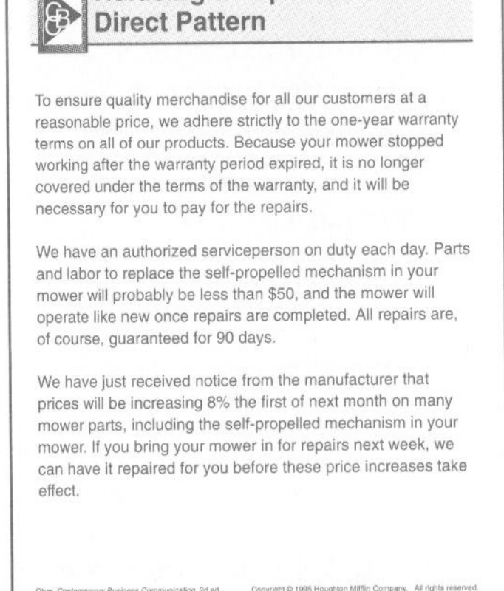

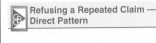

Refusing a Repeated Claim — Direct Pattern

To ensure quality merchandise for all our customers at a reasonable price, we adhere strictly to the one-year warranty terms on all of our products. Because your mower stopped working after the warranty period expired, it is no longer covered under the terms of the warranty, and it will be necessary for you to pay for the repairs.

We have an authorized serviceperson on duty each day. Parts and labor to replace the self-propelled mechanism in your mower will probably be less than $50, and the mower will operate like new once repairs are completed. All repairs are, of course, guaranteed for 90 days.

We have just received notice from the manufacturer that prices will be increasing 8% the first of next month on many mower parts, including the self-propelled mechanism in your mower. If you bring your mower in for repairs next week, we can have it repaired for you before these price increases take effect.

See Master 8.1, Exercise 1, Microwriting a Claims Refusal, in the *Instructor's Resource Manual.*

PROCESS

a. What is the purpose of your message?
b. Describe your audience.
c. Should you use a direct or indirect organizational plan? Why?
d. Write the first sentence of your letter. Be firm and businesslike—but polite and respectful. Remember that you want to retain the customer's goodwill.
e. How much space should you devote to discussing the reasons for your refusal to honor the claim? Why?
f. Write the last sentence of your letter. Again, strive for a firm, businesslike, polite, and respectful tone.

PRODUCT

Draft, revise, format, and proofread your letter. Then submit both your answers to the process questions and your revised letter to your instructor.

2. **Rejecting an Idea—Notebook Computer** ■ You are Charles J. Redding, and you have received the memo written by O. B. Presley (Exercise 1 of Chapter 7). You have, of course, considered all kinds of options to make the sales representatives more productive—notebook computers with built-in printers, cellular telephones for their cars, computerized answering and call-forwarding services, and the like. The fact is that your firm simply cannot afford them for every sales representative. And some of the less energetic representatives clearly do not need them. Instead, your company's philosophy is to pay your representatives top salary and commission and then have them purchase out of their commission earnings whatever "extra" devices or services they deem worthwhile.

   You have, however, checked with your purchasing department and find that your corporate price for the Canon NoteJet is $1,850, instead of the retail price of $2,499 Presley quoted. You would be happy to have the company purchase this machine for Presley and deduct the cost from his commission check. Even though Presley will be disappointed in what you have to say, send him a memo conveying this information.

Exercise 2 is linked with Exercise 1 of Chapter 7. Sample solution for Exercise 2 appears in the *Instructor's Resource Manual*, pp. 142–143. Formatted solution appears on *IRM* p. 155.

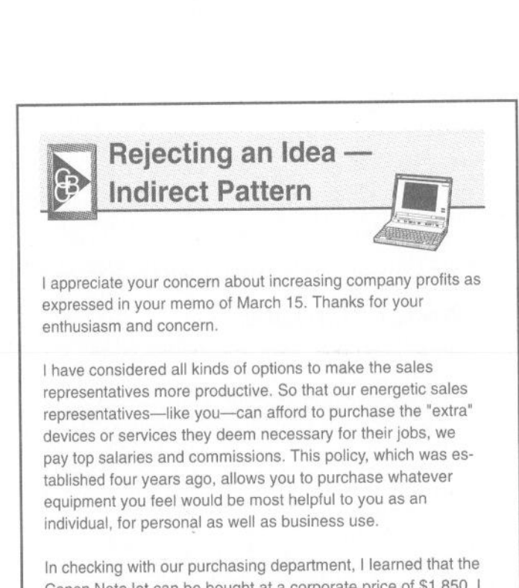

Rejecting an Idea — Indirect Pattern

I appreciate your concern about increasing company profits as expressed in your memo of March 15. Thanks for your enthusiasm and concern.

I have considered all kinds of options to make the sales representatives more productive. So that our energetic sales representatives—like you—can afford to purchase the "extra" devices or services they deem necessary for their jobs, we pay top salaries and commissions. This policy, which was established four years ago, allows you to purchase whatever equipment you feel would be most helpful to you as an individual, for personal as well as business use.

In checking with our purchasing department, I learned that the Canon NoteJet can be bought at a corporate price of $1,850. I would be happy to have the machine purchased through the company, thereby saving you $649. We could simply deduct the cost from your next quarterly commission check so that you wouldn't have to make payment at this time. Please let me know if you would like me to place the order for you.

See Master 8.2, Exercise 2, Rejecting an Idea—Notebook Computer, in the *Instructor's Resource Manual.*

3. **Refusing an Application—McDonald's Franchise** ■ As the director of franchise operations for McDonald's, Inc., you must evaluate the hundreds of applications for franchises you receive each month. Today you received an application from Maxine Denton, who is developing a large shopping center complex in Austin, Texas. Her corporation wants to open a McDonald's restaurant in her shopping center. Of course, they will have no trouble coming up with the initial investment. And they will select a qualified manager who will then go through McDonald's extensive training and orientation course.

   But McDonald's has a policy against granting franchises to corporations, real estate developers, and other absentee owners. They want their owners to manage their stores personally. They prefer high-energy types who will devote their careers to their restaurant and not be involved in numerous other business ventures. Write to Ms. Denton (she's the president of Lone Star Development Corporation, P.O. Box 1086, Houston, TX 77001), turning down her application.

Exercise 4 is linked with Exercise 10 of Chapter 7. Sample solutions for Exercises 4–22 appear in the *Instructor's Resource Manual*, pp. 143–153. Formatted solutions appear on *IRM* pp. 157–174.

4. **Refusing a Request—Product Review** ▪ You are Hal Burk, the product reviewer for *Computing Trends* who received the letter from Heather Lawson, CEO of Software Enterpreneurs, Inc. (see Exercise 10 of Chapter 7). You are accustomed to software firms being upset about product reviews; no matter when you test a product, the improved version is almost certain to be released soon afterward. If you waited for the improved version of every product you want to test, you would never be able to write a review. Instead, you test the version of each product that consumers are able to buy in their local stores at the time the review is conducted.

   You will not test the new ReSolve until you conduct the next scheduled review of spreadsheet programs, in nine months. Space limitations do not permit you to include new product announcements on the review page, but the magazine does have a special feature section for such information. Write a letter to Lawson to convey your position.

Exercise 5 is linked with Exercise 5 of Chapter 7.

5. **Refusing an Idea—Oversized Dressing Rooms** ▪ You are Rebecca Lordstrom (see Exercise 5 of Chapter 7), and you certainly appreciate Robert Kilcline's memo recommending oversized dressing rooms for your new store in Fashion Square Mall. Robert has always been very customer-conscious, a trait you try to instill and nurture in all your employees.

   After checking with the facility planner for the new store, you find that the Fashion Square Mall management has only a certain amount of space available for your store. Thus, any space taken up by the dressing rooms would have to be at the expense of the public store areas.

   Write a memo to Robert, giving him this information. Perhaps he can suggest other ways instead to enhance customer service.

Exercise 6 is linked with Exercise 5 of Chapter 9.

6. **Refusing a Favor—Summer Internship** ▪ Assume the role of vice president of operations for Kolor Kosmetics, a small manufacturer in Biloxi, Mississippi. One of your colleagues from the local chamber of commerce, Dr. Andrea T. Mazzi, has written asking whether your firm can provide a summer internship in your department for her son Peter, a college sophomore who is interested in a manufacturing career. Kolor Kosmetics has no provisions for temporary summer employees and does not currently operate an internship program. Further, the factory shuts down for a two-week vacation every July.

   Write Dr. Mazzi (at 3930 Lyman Turnpike, Biloxi, MS 39530) to let her know this information. Perhaps there are other ways that her son can gain firsthand experience in manufacturing during the summer.

Exercise 7 is linked with Exercise 6 of Chapter 7.

7. **Refusing a Request—New Timing** ▪ As Len Goddard, the branch manager of Forest Island Bank in Kansas City, Missouri (see Exercise 6 of Chapter 7), you need to respond to the letter from Crosslanes Pharmacies' bookkeeper. Although you understand the bookkeeper's problem, your bank's central automated statement rendition system is not set up to allow customers to select their preferred statement dates. Instead, every statement for customers of your branch is printed and mailed on the same day, which happens to be the 15th of the month.

   You can, however, suggest two alternatives. First, you can designate a branch employee to be the regular contact for Crosslanes. Whenever Nancy Lewis, the bookkeeper, needs information about account balances, she may call Herb Tyson, your head teller. Second, Crosslanes can consider switching its account to your nearby branch in Independence. All statements from that branch are printed and mailed at the end of the month, a system better suited to the bookkeeper's needs. Crosslanes can still make deposits and withdrawals at the Kansas City branch. Write to Nancy Lewis and suggest these alternatives.

8. **Refusing a Favor—Field Trip** ▪ You are Donna Jo Luse and you have received the letter written by David Pearson (see Exercise 7 of Chapter 7). Lunch is, of course, your busiest time, and no one has the time then (or the patience) to provide a tour of the kitchens and help 23 youngsters make their salads. Perhaps, instead, they could come for a tour and snack midmorning or midafternoon. Write to Mr. Pearson (Jack 'n Jill Preschool, 113 Grenvale Road, Westminster, MD 21157), refusing his request.

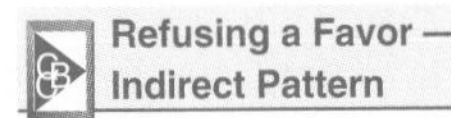

Refusing a Favor — Indirect Pattern

We certainly agree that children should learn the value of good nutrition at a very young age. I compliment you for making this training available to the youngsters at your school.

Lunch is, of course, our busiest time, and many business people choose our restaurant because of the fast service we provide at noon. Therefore, it is necessary for our employees to devote their full attention to their jobs during this hectic period.

If it would be possible for you to bring the children in before 11 a.m. or after 1:30 p.m. during the week of October 10 to 15, we would enjoy providing a tour of our kitchens and a free midmorning or midafternoon snack as well. Our employees would then have the time to answer any questions and to give the youngsters the individual attention they deserve.

Please let me know the date and time you would like to schedule a tour. We look forward to having you with us.

Ober, *Contemporary Business Communication*, 2d ed.

See Master 8.3, Exercise 8, Refusing a Favor—Field Trip, in the *Instructor's Resource Manual.*

9. **Refusing Business—Hotel Reservation** ▪ You are the manager of the Daytona 100, a 100-room hotel in Daytona, Florida, that caters to business people. You've received a reservation from Alpha Kappa Psi fraternity at Ball State University to rent 24 double rooms during their spring break (April 6–13). They have offered to send a $1,000 deposit to guarantee the rooms if necessary.

   As a former AKPsi, you know that these are responsible students who would cause no problems. You also recognize that when these students graduate and assume positions in industry, they are the very type of people you hope will use your hotel. However, because of previous bad experiences, you now have a strict policy against accepting reservations from student groups. Write to the AKPsi treasurer (Scott Rovan, 40 Cypress Grove Court, No. 25, Muncie, IN 47304), conveying this information.

10. **Refusing a Claim—No Refund** ▪ Once again, assume you are the fulfillment representative at Paperbacks by Post (see Exercise 21 of Chapter 6). Roberto Valazquez has written to request that you take back a book he received three months ago. The problem is not the book itself, which he read and enjoyed, but the value for the money. He complains that the book is too short (162 pages) to justify the amount he paid ($3.95). Valazquez wants his money back, and he also wants the book club to refund the cost of shipping the book back.

    This is the fourth time in five months that Valazquez has returned a book. Each time he had a different complaint—once he didn't like the cover illustration, another time he found the language offensive—and you agreed to send him his refunds. At this point, however, you believe that he is simply reading the books and then making up an excuse to avoid paying for them. You decide not to refund his money on this occasion (the number of pages and price of the book were both clearly noted in the announcement Valazquez received before the book was shipped). You also decide to cancel his membership. Write him a letter (at 717 North Walnut Street, Jacksonville, FL 32241) to let him know your decisions.

Exercise 10 is linked with Exercise 2 of Chapter 6.

11. **Refusing a Claim—Azaleas** ▪ You are the customer service representative for Jackson-Parsons Nurseries and have received the letter written by Vera Malcolm (see Exercise 9 of Chapter 7). Jackson-Parsons goes to great expense to use only the highest-quality patented stock and to ship each order packed in dampened sphagnum moss. However, there is no way that any nursery can control the care that plants receive on reaching their destination. Your obligation in this matter clearly ended when Ms. Malcolm did not notify you of the problem immediately. If she had, you would have cheerfully refunded her money. But evidently the azaleas are now thriving where they were planted, and you feel you have no further obligation. Tell this to Ms. Malcolm in a letter (Public Service Company of Arkansas, 189 Blackwood Lane, Little Rock, AR 72207).

Exercise 11 is linked with Exercise 9 of Chapter 7.

12. **Collaborative Writing—AIDS Policy** ▪ Working in groups of three or four, assume the role of the grievance committee of your union. Your small company has its first known case of an employee with AIDS. The employee, an assistant manager (nonunion position), has indicated that she

intends to continue working as long as she is physically able. The company has upheld her right to do so.

You've received a memo signed by six union members who work in her department, objecting to her continued presence at work. They are worried about the risks of contracting the disease from a coworker. Although they have compassion for the assistant manager, they want the union to step in and require that she either resign or be reassigned so that union members do not have to interact with her in the course of completing their own work.

Your committee does some research on the topic and based on your findings decides not to intervene in this matter. Do the research and write a memo to Katherine Kellendorf, chair of the Committee of Concerned Workers, giving her your decision.

13. **Declining an Invitation—Dinner** ▪ You are the purchasing manager at your firm and have received a letter from Barbara Sorrels, one of your firm's major suppliers. She will be in town on October 13 and would like to take you out to dinner that evening. However, you have an early-morning flight on October 14 to Kansas City and will need to pack and make last-minute preparations on the evening of the 13th. Write to Ms. Sorrels (P.O. Box 20, Johnson City, TN 37614), declining her invitation.
14. **Declining an Invitation—Public Speaking** ▪ You are Tanya Porratt, president of The Office Training Group. You just received an invitation from Magda D. Lyon to address a dinner meeting of the Baltimore IBM User's Group (see Figure 7.2). In the past, you frequently accepted such invitations. However, your firm is in the process of being purchased by Triton Technology Corporation, and for the time being you have new rules to follow: you cannot speak in public until the merger has been completed. Because you are unsure of the final date, you are refusing all speaking engagements until October. Tell this to Lyon in a letter.
15. **Bad-News Announcement—Undercharge** ▪ The Wade & Roe law firm is an important customer of your delicatessen. Almost every day you receive a large lunch order from their receptionist, which you deliver to their premises. They pay their bill monthly. In recording their January payment of $348.50, you discover you made an error in billing them. You sent them a bill for $348.50 when, in fact, their charges totaled $438.50. Write them a letter, explaining the matter and requesting payment of the remaining $90 (Fred Walsh, Office Manager, Wade & Roe, Suite 350, North Serrano Place, Los Angeles, CA 90004).

Exercise 16 is linked with Exercise 3 of Chapter 9.

16. **Bad-News Announcement—No Inventory** ▪ Put yourself in the shoes of Alan Teison, the director of distribution for Nu-Shu Sneakers, the best-selling children's sneaker in the United States. Because of this popularity, the company is struggling to keep up with soaring demand. Although you are pleased that sales are so strong, you are concerned that you often lack sufficient inventory to fill every order you receive. Unfortunately, due to temporary stock-outs, some stores will have to wait. One unlucky store is Step Out (212 E. Main Street, Wheat Ridge, CO 80034).

    Write to Lily Greenhill, the store manager, explaining that the three styles she ordered are out of stock but you will fill her order as soon as your inventory is replenished. The next shipment from your factory is due in four weeks, so you expect to deliver back-ordered merchandise within five weeks. That date still allows Greenhill time to promote her (your) products for back-to-school wear.
17. **Bad-News Announcement—No Renewal** ▪ Assume the role of Gene Harley, the leasing manager of Northern Plaza. You have decided not to

renew the lease of T-Shirts Plus, which operates a tiny T-shirt decorating outlet in the mall. Three times in the past 13 months, the store's employees have left their heat-transfer machinery switched on after closing. Each time, the smoke activated the mall's smoke alarms and brought the fire department to the mall during the late-night hours. Although no damage has occurred, your insurance agent warns that the mall's rates will rise if this situation continues.

The lease that T-Shirts Plus signed five years ago specifies that either party can decide not to renew. All that is required is written notification to the other party at least 90 days in advance of the yearly anniversary of the contract date. By writing this week, you will be providing adequate notice. Convey this information to the store's manager, Henry D. Curtis (at Northern Plaza, Brook Parkway North, Cranbrook, British Columbia, V1C 2Z3, Canada).

18. **Bad-News Announcement—Accounting** ▪ As budget specialist, send a memo to all departments telling them that beginning July 1, all unused balances in their departmental budgets will revert to the organization's central fund. Previously, departments were permitted to carry forward unspent funds to the new year. However, this has caused problems in budgeting and forecasting. Any purchase orders processed by June 10 will be charged against this year's budget; those processed after that date will be charged against the new budget.

19. **Bad-News Announcement—No Party** ▪ Nobody likes a party more than Edgar Dunkirk, the president of Rockabilly Enterprises. In the early days, the company's holiday parties were legendary for their splendid food arrangements and outstanding entertainment (featuring the label's popular singing stars). Employees performed elaborate skits and competed for valuable prizes that included color television sets and videocassette recorders. These days, however, sales of the company's country and rockabilly recordings are down. In fact, Dunkirk recently had to lay off 150 of the company's 350 employees, the most severe austerity measure in the company's history.

    Because so many employees had to be let go, including some who had helped Dunkirk found the company a decade ago, the president has decided that a lavish party would be inappropriate. He has therefore cancelled the traditional holiday party. As Dunkirk's vice president of personnel, you must prepare a memo conveying this information to Rockabilly's employees.

20. **Bad-News Announcement—Fringe Benefits** ▪ When your organization moved to its new building in Dallas three years ago, you negotiated a contract with the Universal Self-Parking garage a half-block away to provide free parking to all employees at Grade Level 11 or above. Your rationale was that these managerial employees often work long hours and that convenient, free parking was a justifiable fringe benefit.

    Universal has just notified you that when your contract expires in three months, the monthly fee will increase by 15%. Given the state of the economy and your organization's declining profits, you feel that not only can you not afford the 15% increase but you must, reluctantly, discontinue the free parking altogether.

    Therefore, beginning January 1, all employees must locate and pay for their own parking. Your organization continues to promote ride sharing; and the receptionist has copies of the city bus schedule, which stops a block from your building. Write a memo to these managerial employees giving them the information.

21. **Bad-News Announcement—Product Recall** ■ You have received two reports that users of your ten-stitch portable sewing machine, Sew-Now, have been injured when the needle broke off while sewing. One person was sewing lined denim and the other was sewing drapery fabric—neither of which should have been used on this small machine. Fortunately, neither injury was serious. Although your firm accepts no responsibility for these injuries, you decide to recall all Sew-Now machines to have a stronger needle installed.

    Owners should take their machines to the store where they purchased them. These stores have been notified and already have a supply of the replacement needles. The needle can be replaced while the customer waits. Or, users can ship their machines to you prepaid (Betsy Ross Sewing Machine Company, 168 West 17th Avenue, Columbus, OH 43210). Other than for shipping, there is no cost to the user.

    Prepare a form letter that will go out to the 1,750 Sew-Now purchasers. Customers can call your toll-free number (800-555-9821) if they have questions.
22. **Bad-News Announcement—Charter Canceled** ■ As the head of Galactic Travel & Leisure, you plan summertime charter tours to Europe, South America, and Asia. Twenty-five people signed up for a trip to Tokyo that was scheduled to depart next week. However, a strike by airport personnel has completely shut down the city airport. Although commercial flights are being temporarily transferred to a nearby municipal airport, charter flights are not being handled in the same way. The strike is expected to last all week, so you have no choice but to cancel the charter. You can either provide your customers with refunds (less the nonrefundable deposits) or transfer their reservations to an identical Tokyo trip you are organizing for next month.

    Write a form letter to your customers giving them this information. Ask that customers call you toll-free at 800-584-2863 to give you their decisions by Friday. Your staff will be available until 8 p.m. on Wednesday and Thursday evenings to answer any questions and make alternative travel arrangements. You will automatically send a refund check to any customers who do not respond by Friday.

URBAN SYSTEMS

CONTINUING CASE 8

No Such Thing as a Free Flight

A possible solution to the Continuing Case is described in the *Instructor's Resource Manual*, p. 153.

Neelima has now received the memos she requested from Jean and Larry regarding the frequent-flyer program (see Continuing Case 7 in Chapter 7). She has thought about the issue quite a bit and discussed it with Marc, Arnie, and Dave.

It seems to her that Larry has the more convincing argument: Company funds *were* used to purchase the tickets; therefore, the company logically owns the free tickets its employees earned. In addition, allowing traveling employees to keep their free tickets in effect amounts to an additional fringe benefit that equally hard-working nontraveling employees do not receive. So Neelima decides to begin requiring US employees to use their frequent-flyer free tickets for business travel rather than personal travel.

Now she needs to write to Jean and Larry to communicate her decision. Larry, of course, will be pleased; Jean will be extremely disappointed—not only because she believes her position to be correct but because she will feel threatened by being turned down by her superior. Jean was promoted to her present position only several months ago and is still a little unsure of her abilities.

Neelima also needs to issue a policy memo to all employees outlining the new program. The system will have to operate on trust; she does not intend to act as "Big Brother," policing the program and verifying mileage. Each employee will be required to join the frequent-flyer program for any airline he or she uses in connection with business travel. Employees can use different versions of their name if they also have a frequent-flyer number for their nonbusiness travel.

The expense report form will be revised to include a check-off question that asks if their frequent-flyer mileage for the flight was recorded. The clerk in OIS who makes all flight reservations will be instructed to ask each manager requesting tickets if he or she has accumulated enough miles on any airline to receive a free flight. Other details can be worked out.

Although many employees, especially those in marketing and R & D who travel extensively, will be upset, Neelima is confident her decision is reasonable and in the best interests of Urban Systems.

Critical Thinking

1. Should Neelima send Jean and Larry a joint memo or separate memos? Why?

Writing Projects

2. Write the needed memos: to Jean and Larry (either a joint memo or separate memos, depending on your response to Question 1) and to the staff.
3. Assume that Urban Systems employees do *not* travel extensively and that Neelima's memo outlining the new restrictions will be considered a routine policy announcement. Write a second version of this memo to the staff using the direct pattern.

WORDWISE *Euphemisms*

Politically Incorrect	*Correct*
Cheap	Fiscally retentive
Crooked	Ethically challenged
Old	Chronologically gifted
Drunk	Sobriety deprived
Pet	Animal companion
Bald	Hair disadvantaged
Plastic	Synthetic glass

CHAPTER

9

Special Messages

Communication Objectives

After you have finished this chapter, you should be able to

1. Compose a mixed-news message.
2. Compose a letter of recommendation.
3. Compose a letter that rejects a job applicant.
4. Compose a personnel evaluation.
5. Compose a letter that approves or denies credit.
6. Compose a collection letter.
7. Compose a goodwill message.

Imagine answering 25,000 phone calls and 20,000 letters about credit every day. That's the task facing TRW Information Services, one of the nation's largest credit-reporting services. Representatives at the company's national consumer assistance center in Allen, Texas, must take the time to research and answer each inquiry individually.

But when a consumer asks a newspaper columnist, radio commentator, or television reporter for help with a credit-reporting problem, the media will turn for answers to Janis Lamar, TRW's director of external communications. Lamar's responsibility, as a liaison between the company and the news media, is to explain to the consumer (her primary audience) as well as to the media, the media audience, and elected officials (her secondary audience) the reasoning behind a particular aspect of the credit-reporting process that has received publicity.

Many of these inquiries concern credit denials, so Lamar has to deal not only with bad-news messages themselves but also with their legal ramifications. "When I respond to a consumer's letter sent to me by the media, I have to go beyond merely addressing the specific issue in question," she said. "A major challenge impacting TRW's external communications with consumers, officials, and the media is a lack of understanding about the credit-reporting process. Buffering the bad news isn't nearly as important as clearly communicating why. When bad news is clearly and completely communicated, it can be more readily understood; news that is understood is much easier to accept. While it is important to answer the consumer's specific question, it is equally important to explain it, frame it, and place it in context."

Although letters with legal implications have to follow specific guidelines, they should not be brusque or insensitive. "I may be a company representative, but I am also a consumer, and I try to put myself in the reader's position. I aim to write a letter I would want to receive, one that is personal, caring, informative, and helpful. When people are emotional or angry, we have to try a little harder to get them to understand the facts. For example, when I must use a specific technical or legal term, I define the term and explain its meaning. Generally, I have learned it is better to explain too much than too little."

At the same time, credit reporting is a highly regulated business, operating under specific federal and state guidelines, so Lamar has to keep these rules in mind as she writes. "Since my responses may be published or reported by the media, I ask TRW's law department to review any letter that concerns legal issues," she said. "This ensures that my response reflects current regulations, that I've investigated every possible avenue to assist the consumer, that I am not creating a document that could be used against the company in a lawsuit, and that my business communications are 100% accurate."

Lamar sees every letter she writes as an opportunity for a "teaching moment," an opportunity to educate consumers about the credit-reporting process and legal requirements. "TRW plays a strong role as a consumer educator and adviser, not just a bearer of bad news," she noted. "Although some consumers may view credit-reporting agencies as their adversaries, we try to help people understand the process and how the system works on their behalf."

Janis Lamar
Director of external communications, TRW, Orange, California

A chapter overview appears in the *Instructor's Resource Manual*, pp. 175–178.

PLANNING THE SPECIAL MESSAGE

Up to this point, we have considered strategies for writing routine, persuasive, and bad-news messages. Although the suggested organizational plan differs for each type of message, all three have one feature in common: each type has a single business objective—to convey routine information, to persuade the reader to do as you wish, or to convey bad news.

Suggest to your students that they avoid "no" and "not" in their business writings, says Deborah Dumaine in *Write to the Top: Writing for Corporate Success*. Instead of "Do not waste energy," try "Conserve energy." Instead of "Don't take a negative approach," try "Accentuate the positive." (Random House, New York, 1989, pp. 92–93.)

Mixed-news messages have more than one purpose.

The messages discussed in this chapter are a little more complex. For example, some business messages have more than one objective, as when the same message must convey both good and bad news. Other types of messages require special consideration because they have legal implications that determine in part what you may or may not say. And the primary objective of some messages is simply goodwill, as when conveying sympathy, for example.

No one organizational pattern will serve the needs of each of these special types of messages. Instead, you must first identify your objective and then organize each message in a way that will help you achieve that objective.

MIXED-NEWS MESSAGES

For an exercise in writing a mixed-news message, see Video Case Study 2, Ronald McDonald Children's Charities.

Complex business operations often generate complex writing situations, and many of these writing situations involve more than one objective. You may, for example, need to combine good news with bad news or bad news with persuasion.

Good News and Bad News

For other examples of mixed-news messages, see the *Instructor's Resource Manual*, pp. 192, 193, 194, 195, and 196.

Sometimes you have both good news and bad news to convey. Perhaps an angry customer wrote a claim letter asking you not only to refund the $39.95 she paid for an electric coffee maker but also to reimburse her for the $87.50 damage that occurred when the electrical element came loose and burned her countertop. You might be willing to give a $39.95 refund for the coffee maker (good news) but not an $87.50 reimbursement for the damaged countertop (bad news). As with bad-news messages, your objectives here are to communicate the needed information clearly while at the same time retaining the reader's goodwill.

Emphasize the good news, explain before presenting the bad news, and stress reader benefits.

Messages that convey both good news and bad news should present the good news (the most favorable aspect of the message) first, where it will receive the most attention. Explain the basis of the decision, using neutral and impersonal language; subordinate the bad news, presenting it as positively as possible; and end on a friendly note.

Figure 9.1 shows a mixed-news message. The good news is that the reader has been accepted for graduate study. The bad news is that he will not be admitted for the fall semester but must wait until the spring semester.

Bad News and Persuasion

Suppose a customer orders a product you no longer sell. You might write, giving the bad news that you cannot fill the order and then try to persuade

FIGURE 9.1 Mixed-news Message

This message communicates both good news and bad news.

COASTAL STATE COLLEGE
Graduate School of Business Administration
Berkeley, California 94720

March 3, 19--

Mr. Perry Mack
1048 Continental Way
Belmont, CA 94002

Dear Mr. Mack:

Congratulations on being accepted into Coastal State's Master of Business Administration program. We notified the Graduate Division last week that you have been granted regular admission.

Presents the good news first.

1 The latest Board of Regents figures show that our MBA program has the third
largest enrollment in the state. Students benefit from this large enrollment
because all the major corporations now actively recruit on campus each
semester. And because many of our new enrollees are full-time executives, our
students also develop a wide network of friends and professional contacts
throughout the state.

Begins presenting the reasons for the bad news.

To better manage our increased enrollments and to continue providing the
quality of education that California business has come to expect of our
graduates, we have staggered our enrollments, admitting some students for the
2 fall semester and others for the spring semester. You are scheduled to start
your MBA program in January 19--. If a vacancy opens up for the fall
semester, you will be notified prior to July 1. Otherwise, you should assume
that your classes will begin on January 8. Course registration procedures are
outlined in the enclosed packet of information.

Introduces the bad news in the same sentence as a reader benefit.

We look forward to having you join our program, Mr. Mack. We will benefit
3 from your insights and experiences and feel sure that you will benefit from
and enjoy our unique approach to management education.

Closes on a positive note.

Sincerely,

Georgia E. Grumann

Georgia E. Grumann
Director of Admissions

rah
Enclosure

Grammar and Mechanics Notes

1 *MBA:* Look up the correct format for abbreviations; many, like "MBA," are written solid, without periods. 2 *fall semester:* Do not capitalize the names of seasons. 3 *experiences and:* Do not use a comma between parts of a compound predicate.

More and more middle managers, like these at Yoplait, are being paid by a combination of salary and bonus. This presents companies with a classic mixed-news situation: "We're lowering your salary, but you can more than make it up through a big bonus if you do well."

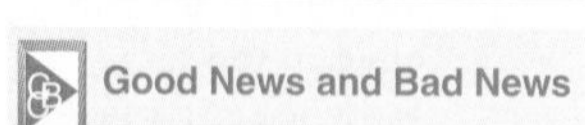

Good News and Bad News

- **Present the good news**

  I am happy to offer you a position as a summer intern in our personnel department from May 15 until August 10.

- **Present the rationale for the bad news and then subordinate the bad news.**

  Because this position was not budgeted for last year, it will be an unpaid internship. We are confident, however, that the experiences we will design for you and the people you will meet will make this assignment a very enjoyable, worthwhile one for you.

- **End on a friendly note.**

  Please call my office at 555-3792 to let me know whether you will be able to accept this internship. We look forward to having you on board next summer.

Ober, *Contemporary Business Communication*, 2d ed.

See Transparency 9.1, Mixed-News Message.

the customer to accept a substitute product that you do sell. In such a situation, organize your message as follows:

Use a Buffer Opening Begin with a neutral, relevant, and supportive opening. If you're trying to persuade the reader to accept a substitute product, for example, your opening might sound like this:

> I was pleased to learn that your Arco cellular telephone has served you so well for the past five years. For someone who travels as much as you do, a cellular telephone provides portable communication at an economical price.

Explain the Situation Explain the reason for the bad news, present the bad news, and discuss why the reader should adopt your alternative suggestion. The first two purposes should be accomplished quickly, with the major discussion centered on the benefits of doing as you suggest. Avoid using the word "substitute," and avoid negative comments about the original idea or product. Instead, concentrate on the positive aspects of the alternative you're proposing, as follows:

> When you purchased your Arco, it was the most technologically advanced cellular telephone available. In the five years since, however, major advances have been made in cellular technology that have not yet been incorporated into the Arco line. Thus, a year ago, we began offering the Zoom cellular telephone exclusively.
>
> The Zoom comes with an exclusive snap-on battery pack that makes it an ideal unit for portable use. For example, no longer will you be tied to your car for emergency communications. Even if your car battery fails, you can still call for help. And despite its smaller size, battery pack, and greater number of features, the Zoom cellular telephone costs only a few dollars more than the Arco—$304.99 for the Zoom compared to $279.99 for the Arco.

Ask for the Desired Action Clearly explain what action you want the reader to take. Write confidently, but avoid making decisions for the reader; for example, do not automatically send the substitute product without first getting the reader's approval. Close with a final reference to a reader benefit.

> Please let us know your wishes by completing the enclosed card and returning it to us. Within three days, you can be enjoying the convenience of true portability that only today's Zoom cellular telephone can provide.

Although the risk is small, a negative reference may trigger a wrongful-termination suit. Settlements range from $5,000 to $60,000; awards average $622,000, but some have been as high as $2 million. (Sharon Geltner, "Reference Checks that Give You the Real Scoop," *Working Woman,* May 1991, p. 22.)

MESSAGES WITH LEGAL IMPLICATIONS

All written messages have certain legal implications. For example, if you knowingly write something false about a company that results in damages to that company's reputation or financial well-being, you are guilty of libel. Three types of messages have special legal implications: messages about personnel matters, credit letters, and collection letters (see the Spotlight on Law and Ethics).

Messages with special legal implications require careful planning.

Letters of Recommendation

Writing a letter of recommendation presents not only legal but also ethical considerations. The overriding guideline is that you must be fair—fair to your own conscience, fair to the prospective employer, and fair to the applicants, including those for whom you are *not* writing a letter of recommendation.

To be fair to yourself, you must act in good faith. If you are satisfied in your own mind that you have written an honest and objective appraisal of the person's qualifications, you should have no concerns about the applicant's ultimate fate. That decision is the responsibility of the prospective employer.

You must also be fair to the employer because he or she is relying on your honest observations to make an appropriate hiring decision. There is also an implied reciprocity at work: if you do not give honest evaluations, how can you expect others to do so when you need their input in making hiring decisions?

Finally, you must be fair to the applicants. You are not doing anyone a favor by helping him or her get a job for which he or she is not qualified. Similarly, if an unqualified person you recommend does get the job, your recommendation may have helped deny the job to a better-qualified candidate. Thus, neither the unqualified person who got the job nor the qualified person who was denied the job was treated fairly.

Letter of Recommendation

- **Opening**

I am happy to write a letter of recommendation for Josephine Sawyer, who has applied for a position as a marketing manager at your firm. Josie worked as a full-time intern in our personnel department last summer and asked that I provide this confidential information.

- **Providing Specific, Job-Related Evidence**

Josie worked on a variety of projects under the direct supervision of our assistant personnel manager. We were particularly impressed with her intimate knowledge of Windows-based computer software. Her familiarity with Microsoft Word, Excel, and Access made her productive from her very first day of work. In addition, she got along well with all members of the department.

Ober, *Contemporary Business Communication,* 2d ed.

See Transparency 9.2, Letter of Recommendation.

Letters of recommendation may be of two types—general or specific. General letters are often requested by students as part of the personnel

SPOTLIGHT ON LAW AND ETHICS

Legal Implications of Personnel Messages

I refused to write a letter of recommendation for a former employee, and he did not get the position. Now he's threatening to sue me. Does he have a legal case against me?

No. You are not required to give a reference for a former employee. In fact, some employers now provide only factual information about former employees (name, starting and stopping work dates, positions, salary, and the like) because of their concern for legal problems.

Our company has no policy allowing my subordinates to see the evaluations I write and place in their personnel files. Do they have such a legal right?

All federal employees have the right to review and photocopy their personnel files. But only a few states have passed laws that allow business employees to review their files.

In my termination letter to an employee, I gave as one reason for his termination the aggravation of always having to rearrange his work schedule to permit him to observe the Sabbath on Saturdays. Was this a legitimate reason?

No. The law requires you to make reasonable accommodations to enable your employees to practice their religious beliefs—including rearranging schedules. You would have to show that doing so created an undue hardship on your firm.

Another department head has asked for my opinion about offering one of my employees a management position. However, I believe she is too old for the position. Should I say so in my recommendation?

No. It is illegal to discriminate on the basis of age. You would have to have evidence that *most* people at that age would not be able to perform the new job competently.

I declined to give a reason for terminating an unsatisfactory worker. Was I within my legal rights?

Yes, in most states. Only a few states require an employer to tell an employee why he or she has been fired. Most employees are classified as "at-will" employees and can be fired for any reason or for no reason at the will of the employer. The exception is that they may not be fired for discriminatory reasons. In addition, union agreements may affect the company's ability to discharge union employees.

I wrote in a letter of recommendation that a former employee was chronically late for work. As a result, he did not get the job and is now threatening to sue me for libel. Will he win?

No, not if you can document that, in fact, the worker *was* chronically late. You may provide the prospective employer any factual evidence that has a direct bearing on job performance as long as such information was solicited.

Sources: Ronald A. Anderson, Ivan Fox, and David P. Twomey, *Business Law and the Legal Environment*, 14th ed., South-Western, Cincinnati, OH, 1990; Gordon W. Brown, Edward E. Byers, and Mary Ann Lawlor, *Business Law: With UCC Applications*, 7th ed., Mc-Graw-Hill, New York, 1989; Neil Story and Lynn Ward, *American Business Law and the Regulatory Environment*, South-Western, Cincinnati, OH, 1989.

For an extended discussion of ethical issues, see "Ethics and Communication" in Chapter 2, pp. 45–48.

record they file with their college placement office. Sometimes a form is provided; otherwise, you should use a generic salutation, such as "Dear Prospective Employer." Specific letters require your evaluation of a candidate's fitness for a specific position. Gear your comments to the specific job, making sure that you answer completely each question that is asked.

Regardless of whether you're writing a general or specific letter, begin by providing certain standard information:

- The full name of the job applicant (may be given in a subject line instead)
- The position the applicant is seeking
- The nature and length of your relationship with the applicant

A good legal safeguard is to label the information "confidential" and to state that you are providing this information at the specific request of either the applicant or the prospective employer. Because state laws differ, assume that whatever you write may, at some time, be seen by the applicant.

> Mr. Chung Kuang Chao, who has applied for the position of systems analyst at your firm, has asked me to write a letter on his behalf, and I am happy to provide this confidential information. Chao worked for me part-time from February 1993 until April 1994 as a computer programmer while he was a full-time undergraduate student. He left when the special project for which he was hired was completed.

Although companies increasingly have policies that forbid giving outside references, most fears of litigation may be unfounded. A 1991 study showed that only a very small number of defamation suits actually go to trial (from 1985 to 1990, only 118 reported cases) and that plaintiffs lose 75% of the cases. (Lauren Picker, "Job References: To Give or Not to Give," *Working Woman*, February 1992, p. 21.)

The major part of your recommendation will, of course, be your comments on the applicant's performance and potential. From the employer's viewpoint, the most helpful comments are those that are reinforced with examples and specific factual information. Include only relevant information—information that will help the prospective employer evaluate the candidate's qualifications. Be especially careful to avoid mentioning any factors that might later become the basis for a discrimination lawsuit, such as age, race, religion, or handicaps.

Include only relevant information, and document each general comment with examples or factual data.

> I would evaluate Chao's programming skills as excellent. He designed, wrote, debugged, and ran four complex computer programs for me, each comprising between 750 and 1,000 lines of code in C+ language. His programs were innovative, efficient, and well documented.

Most people do not ask someone to write a letter of recommendation unless they have had pleasant relations with that person. Thus, most such letters are primarily positive in tone. No one is perfect, however. If the negative trait is either irrelevant to the applicant's performance on the job or if you are unable to document the deficiency, simply avoid mentioning it.

Occasionally you *will* need to include some negative aspect regarding the applicant's qualifications for a particular job. When doing so, avoid value judgments and opinions and simply relate the specific facts.

> *Not:* The one problem I had with Chao was that he was somewhat lazy and undependable.
>
> *But:* Chao was absent from work an average of twice a month. A few of these absences were unexpected in that he did not call to report that he would be unable to come to work.

Because so much of what typically goes into a letter of recommendation is positive, any negative information tends to stand out and receive, perhaps, more attention than it deserves. You are the best judge of how to use emphasis and subordination appropriately to present the negative information fairly. The point is not to downplay the negative information but rather to make sure the reader perceives it with the same degree of importance as you do.

For example, if you believe Chao's attendance problems were fairly unimportant, you might either omit them altogether or subordinate them

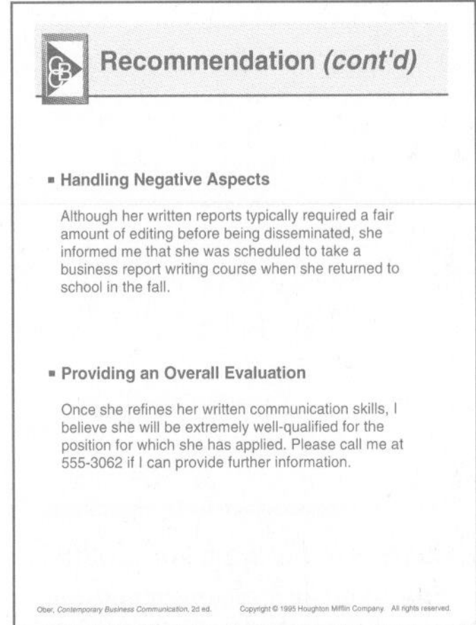

Recommendation (cont'd)
Handling Negative Aspects
Although her written reports typically required a fair amount of editing before being disseminated, she informed me that she was scheduled to take a business report writing course when she returned to school in the fall.
Providing an Overall Evaluation
Once she refines her written communication skills, I believe she will be extremely well-qualified for the position for which she has applied. Please call me at 555-3062 if I can provide further information.
Ober, Contemporary Business Communication, 2d ed.
Copyright © 1995 Houghton Mifflin Company. All rights reserved.

See Transparency 9.3, Letter of Recommendation (continued).

by placing them in the dependent part of a sentence, using the independent part of a sentence to explain the negative aspect or to present more favorable information:

> Although Chao was absent from work an average of twice a month, he was able to complete all his assigned work competently and on schedule. Furthermore, . . .

If possible, provide an overall summary evaluation of the candidate.

End your letter by making some summary, overall evaluation of the candidate. If your evaluation of the candidate has raised some questions about which the prospective employer might need more information, offer to provide more information if necessary. Under such circumstances, offering to answer further questions would be a genuine offer of help, not a cliché.

> Based on my observation of Chao's performance, I recommend him highly for the position of systems analyst. If I can provide additional confidential information, please call me at 571-555-3220.

For other examples of letters of recommendation, including one that an employer is unwilling to write, see the *Instructor's Resource Manual,* pp. 197, 198, and 199.

Figure 9.2 shows a letter of recommendation that contains mostly positive information but that also conveys a minor bit of negative information, which the writer believes to be relatively unimportant.

Letters to the prospective employer declining to write a recommendation are written in the direct pattern.

To protect themselves from possible lawsuits, some companies refuse to provide any personal information about former employees. In fact, one survey of human resources executives indicated that 41% of the companies polled have such a policy.[1] Other companies provide only oral evaluations, preferring not to supply any written record of their comments. A letter to the prospective employer declining to evaluate a job applicant should be straightforward, giving whatever factual information about the applicant you feel is appropriate.

> Ms. Susan Buehler, about whom you inquired on October 4, worked for us as a teller from January 1991 until May 1993. Because of the legal implications, we no longer provide evaluations of former employees. This policy was in existence before Ms. Buehler was hired and should not be taken as a negative reflection on her performance.

If you honestly feel that you should not recommend a candidate, you should decline to do so. Your letter to the applicant, telling him or her of your decision, should be indirect, stating the refusal as tactfully and in as friendly a way as possible. If the reason for not providing a recommendation is related to company policy, explain that the decision had nothing to do with the applicant personally. However, if you simply prefer not to recommend this particular applicant, you need not provide a reason.

Letters to the applicant declining to write a recommendation are written in the indirect pattern.

> Congratulations on your recent marriage and on your move to San Francisco. I am pleased to learn that you have found temporary employment in the Bay area and are now seeking a permanent position.
>
> Because your most recent employer will be able to provide more current and more relevant information about you than I can, I suggest asking him or her to write a letter of recommendation for you instead.
>
> Best wishes as you prepare for the future.

FIGURE 9.2 Letter of Recommendation

This letter evaluates a candidate for a specific position.

Wheaton Products

The Breakfast-Food Company

July 3, 19--

Mr. Foster B. Clark
Human Resources Department
Eastern Englehard
3524 Water Street, N.W.
Washington, DC 20007

1 RECOMMENDATION FOR SHEILA J. HORTON

I am pleased to recommend Sheila Horton for the position of assistant
advertising manager with your company. I was Miss Horton's immediate
supervisor when she worked for Wheaton as an advertising copywriter from
2 September 1990 until March 1994 and am providing this confidential information
at her request.

Starts by giving the applicant's name, position applied for, and nature and length of relationship.

Miss Horton's writing skills are superior. During her employment here, she composed the narrative for all our print ads, sales letters, and radio spots. We credit much of our marketing success to her efforts. One of her sales letters won second place in the statewide Eddy Award competition in 1992. Our public relations department routinely asked her to edit our annual report for clarity, organization, and readability.

Reinforces general comments with specific examples and factual information.

Her position required that she interact extensively with higher management, outside suppliers, and two subordinates. In her dealings with management and outside personnel, she was always tactful, articulate, and cooperative. Although she had some problems in supervising her two assistants (a secretary and a copy editor), I'm confident she will improve in this area with more experience. She always availed herself of every opportunity to attend work-related seminars on a variety of management topics, and she was an active member of several professional associations.

Presents negative news so that it will be perceived as intended.

I have a very high regard for Miss Horton and recommend her to you. You will
3 find that she is an intelligent, experienced, and motivated manager.

Ends by giving an overall evaluation of the candidate.

Anne Bryant

ANNE BRYANT, MARKETING DIRECTOR

abl

600 Grant Avenue ■ Pittsburgh, PA 15219 ■ 412-555-2747

Grammar and Mechanics Notes

1 This letter is written in the Simplified style, with no salutation or complimentary closing.
2 *September 1990:* Do not use a comma in a date if only the month and year are given.
3 *intelligent, experienced, and:* Use a comma before the conjunction connecting items in a series.

Applicant-Rejection Letters

People would not apply for a job with your firm unless they believed your organization would be a good place to work; thus, they flatter your firm by applying. It is only right, then, to treat all applicants with courtesy and respect—even those whom you do not choose.

For an exercise on revising a rejection letter, refer students to the *Study Guide*, p. 136.

The large number of applications received by some firms requires that a form letter be used for rejecting an application. However, regardless of the firm's size, if the applicant survived the initial screening process and was actually interviewed, a personal letter is required.

Keep a job-rejection letter short and friendly.

The most effective pattern for a rejection letter is a modification of the indirect approach: a short buffer, perhaps mentioning some specific incident from the interview; the rejection and explanation, perhaps indicating that someone else was chosen rather than that the reader was *not* chosen; and, finally, a friendly, off-the-topic closing. The rejection letter should be short because the reader is anxious to learn your decision.

For another example of an applicant rejection letter, see the *Instructor's Resource Manual*, p. 200.

> It was a genuine pleasure to meet you on August 15 and to interview you for the position of assistant advertising manager with our firm. I enjoyed hearing your reactions to the recent changes in our industry.
>
> We received nearly 50 high-quality applications for this position and finally filled it with a person from New York who has had extensive experience in supervising a large staff of artists and copywriters.
>
> I appreciate your interest in Eastern Englehard, Ms. Horton, and wish you success in your search for a position in the Washington, DC, area.

Personnel Evaluations

In most organizations, superiors evaluate their subordinates periodically. Such evaluations are typically first reported orally directly to the subordinate and then written for the employee's personnel file. Superiors also evaluate their employees at other times, as when a manager sends a memo to a subordinate discussing a specific problem with the employee's job performance.

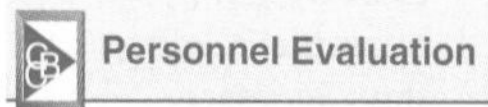

Personnel Evaluation

I enjoyed meeting with you yesterday to discuss your job performance during the past six months.

As we discussed, I consider your general secretarial skills to be excellent. You are proficient in all relevant aspects of computer software and general office duties, and I frequently get positive feedback about your professional treatment of our office visitors. In addition, I truly appreciate the many times you have voluntarily stayed after work to finish a rush assignment. Your help after hours last Tuesday in putting the finishing touches on our five-year plan was especially appreciated.

We also discussed the concern expressed to me by the superiors of two of the other secretaries in this division that they believe a more cooperative attitude on your part would be helpful in scheduling meetings, providing needed documents, and the like. You indicated that you would work on this problem and that we would reevaluate the situation in two months.

Overall, Rene, you are an above-average secretary and are vitally important to the operation of this office. I'm pleased to have you as my assistant and look forward to your professional contributions and continued growth in the years ahead.

Ober, *Contemporary Business Communication*, 2d ed.

See Transparency 9.4, Personnel Evaluation.

In many ways, a personnel evaluation is like a letter of recommendation. You want to be fair both to the employee and to the organization, and you want to document any praise or criticism with specific examples. A personnel evaluation differs, however, in that its emphasis is on *improvement*. Both the employee and the organization have a vested interest in seeing that any weaknesses are understood by the employee and that an improvement plan is developed and implemented.

The message (typically a memo) should end on a friendly, helpful, and forward-looking note. A typical personnel evaluation memo is shown in Figure 9.3. This evaluation discusses both strong and weak points of the employee's performance. Use Checklist 8 as a guide when writing personnel messages.

FIGURE 9.3 Personnel Evaluation

— Memorandum —

DATE: July 15, 19--

TO: Robert Plachta, Mailroom Supervisor

FROM: Sharon Northcutt, Administrative Office Manager SN

SUBJECT: Semiannual Performance Review

The purpose of this memorandum is to review the points we discussed at our July 9 meeting regarding your performance for the first six months of the year.

As shown on the enclosed Personnel Rating Form, I evaluate your technical
skills as excellent. You continue to stay abreast of the latest technology in
mail management, and your recent efforts to further automate the mailroom will
1 likely save the organization $15,000-$20,000 yearly in labor costs. More
important, the organization will benefit from more timely mail delivery.

Documents each general comment.

I discussed with you in some detail the fact that two female managers in other departments have complained to me recently of inappropriate remarks you have made to them. They wished to remain anonymous, so I am not exploring the matter further. We agreed, however, that within the next month, you will schedule a one-hour conference with Ms. Arelia Gomez in Personnel. She will outline for you the types of actions and comments that are and that are not permissible legally or according to company policy. You will write me a memo summarizing the outcome of that conference. I am confident that once you learn the corporate and legal implications of your remarks, no further action will be necessary and we can then simply forget about this matter.

Presents negative information objectively; outlines an improvement plan.

I continue to be highly satisfied with your management skills. Your reports
2 are well written and on schedule, and your subordinates are quite happy with
your supervision. In addition, you maintain a safe and pleasant work
environment—an especially noteworthy achievement, considering the large
amount of equipment and traffic in your department.

Continues with positive comments, which subordinate the earlier negative discussion.

My overall evaluation of your performance, Bob, is that you are an above-average manager. I'm pleased to have you as a member of my staff and look forward to continuing to work with you as you seek to increase the effectiveness and efficiency of our mailroom operations.

Ends with an overall evaluation.

3 ceo
Enclosure
c: Personnel File—Robert Plachta
Arelia Gomez, Personnel

Grammar and Mechanics Notes

1 *$15,000-$20,000:* Do not space before or after a hyphen. 2 *well written:* Do not hyphenate a compound adjective that comes *after* a noun. 3 The correct order for end-of-message notations is (1) reference initials, (2) enclosure notation, and (3) copy notation. These notations may be single- or double-spaced.

CHECKLIST 8

Personnel Messages

Note: For *all* personnel messages, ensure that the information is accurate and that your message follows all federal and state laws regarding employment practices.

WRITING A LETTER OF RECOMMENDATION

1. Be fair—to yourself, to the prospective employer, to the applicant whom you're recommending, and to the other applicants for the same position.
2. Begin by giving the name of the applicant, the position for which the applicant is applying, and the nature and length of your relationship with the applicant.
3. Label the information "confidential," and state that you were asked to provide this information.
4. Discuss only job-related traits and behaviors, be as objective as possible, and support your statements with specific examples.
5. If writing a recommendation for a specific position, answer all questions asked and gear your comments to the applicant's qualifications for the particular job.
6. Present any negative information in such a way that the reader will perceive it with the same degree of importance that you do.
7. Close by giving an overall summary of your evaluation.

REJECTING A JOB APPLICANT

1. Keep the letter short; the candidate is anxious to learn whether your decision is "yes" or "no."
2. Provide a short, supportive buffer, perhaps mentioning some specific positive comment about the candidate's résumé or interview.
3. Indicate that another candidate was chosen (not that the reader was *not* chosen), and briefly explain why.
4. Close on an off-the-topic note, perhaps thanking the reader for applying or extending best wishes.

WRITING A PERSONNEL EVALUATION

1. Be fair—to yourself, to the employee, and to the organization.
2. Discuss only job-related behaviors and traits.
3. Document any praise or criticism with specific examples; avoid exaggeration.
4. Ensure that any negative information receives only the appropriate amount of emphasis.
5. Emphasize the improvement aspect of the evaluation; that is, state specifically what steps should be taken to improve performance.
6. Close with an overall summary of your evaluation or with a friendly, forward-looking comment.

Credit Letters

For more on evaluating credit applicants and the legal aspects of credit, see the supplemental lecture/discussion notes in the *Instructor's Resource Manual*, beginning on p. 178.

Credit represents the confidence that a business has in a customer's ability and intention to pay his or her debts. Allowing customers to buy on credit has become the accepted way of doing business in America.

Typically, requesting credit or checking references does not require writing a letter; however, approving or denying credit does. The customer applies for credit by completing a credit-application form. Most cities have a credit bureau, which is an association of stores, banks, credit unions, and the like, that collects information about customers' borrowing and bill-pay-

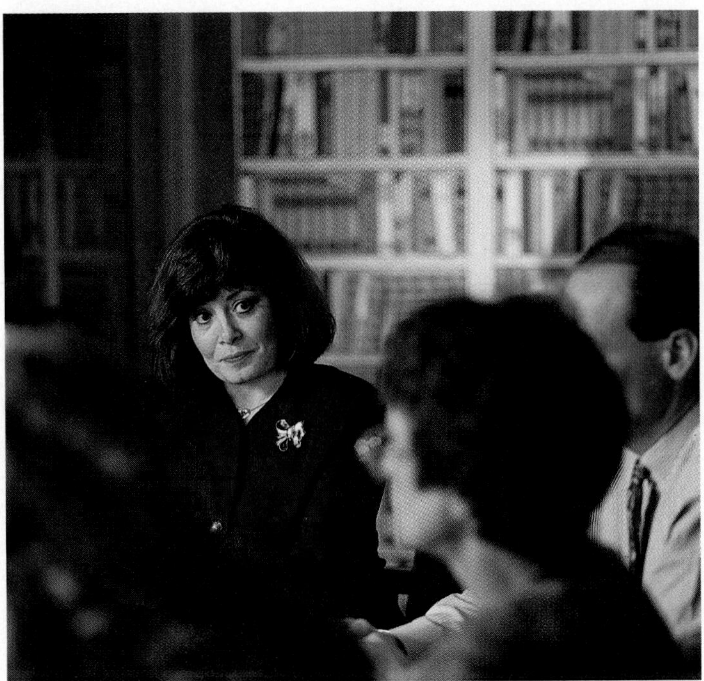

At VCW, Inc., a company selling insurance to independent truckers, founder V. Cheryl Womack has employees write personal mission statements as part of their evaluations. They review their goals annually to check their performance.

ing habits. The bureau provides a credit history, for a fee, to firms requesting such information about an individual or business.

Because an individual's or business's credit reputation is so important, much federal and state legislation has been enacted to ensure that the rights of consumers are protected. For these reasons, as well as for ethical considerations, you must make sure that both your credit decisions and your communication of such decisions are based on an objective and accurate analysis of all relevant data.

Use a direct pattern for approving credit.

Approving Credit Because of the volume of credit requests received, most firms use form letters for approving credit, often personalizing them through the use of word processing. The decision to grant credit is good news, so the use of a form letter is not likely to create ill will.

As with all good-news messages, write the credit-approval letter in the direct pattern. Begin by telling the reader that credit has been approved. Then provide the needed explanation (primarily the credit arrangements); a clear and complete presentation of this information now will help avoid misinterpretation and collection problems later. If the credit arrangements are long and complex, consider putting them in an enclosure to keep the letter itself relatively short.

A full discussion of the credit arrangements sends the message that you take these commitments seriously.

Once you've made the decision to grant the line of credit, avoid a heavy-handed, distrusting approach. Instead, be gracious and use impersonal language when discussing repayment terms.

Not: You are required to pay your bills by the 15th of each month.

But: Payment is due by the 15th of each month.

End your letter on a forward-looking note. Discuss how the customer will benefit from doing business with your firm, and use sales promotion or resale to encourage the customer to make use of his or her new credit. A credit-approval letter is shown in Figure 9.4. Note that the mail-merge feature of word processing permits the use of a personal inside address, salutation, and maximum credit amount, even though this is a form letter.

For another example of a credit-approval letter, see the *Instructor's Resource Manual*, p. 203.

Denying Credit Credit may be denied for any number of legitimate business reasons: insufficient information, excessive obligations, irregular employment record, and poor payment history, among others.

Use an indirect pattern for refusing credit.

Because purchasing on credit has become such a widespread way of conducting both business and personal affairs, a credit denial is especially serious for the applicant. Individual applicants often take it as a personal affront, calling into question the person's character and integrity. For business applicants, a credit denial limits the firm's ability to stock sufficient inventory or supplies. Damage to a person's reputation or to the profit-making ability of a business might result in a lawsuit. For these reasons, you need to use good judgment in refusing credit and in communicating your refusal.

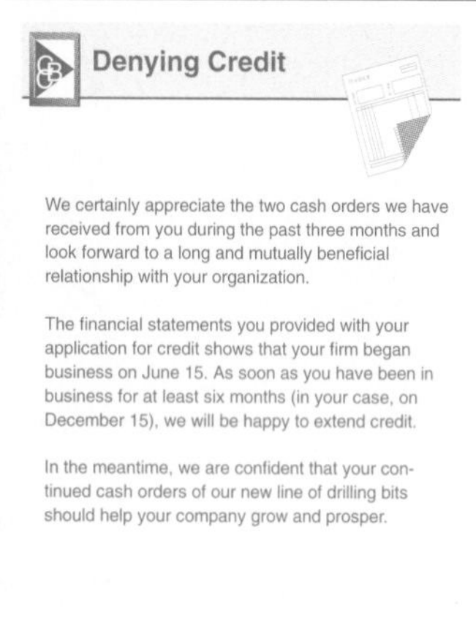

Denying Credit
We certainly appreciate the two cash orders we have received from you during the past three months and look forward to a long and mutually beneficial relationship with your organization.
The financial statements you provided with your application for credit shows that your firm began business on June 15. As soon as you have been in business for at least six months (in your case, on December 15), we will be happy to extend credit.
In the meantime, we are confident that your continued cash orders of our new line of drilling bits should help your company grow and prosper.

See Transparency 9.5, Denying Credit.

Form letters for denying credit are often used by large firms. Although the volume of credit requests may make such a step necessary, it is difficult to personalize such refusal letters and retain goodwill with form letters. Retaining the goodwill of a rejected credit applicant is important because you want to retain the customer's business—on a cash basis for now, but perhaps on a credit basis at some point in the future if the applicant's financial condition improves.

Thus, the overall tone of the refusal letter should be one of respect, thoughtfulness, and helpfulness. Given the serious nature of the refusal, such letters should be written in an indirect pattern, beginning with a buffer opening.

> Your request for a line of credit with Bateman's shows that you appreciate the profit-making potential of our line of fine jewelry and our extensive national advertising efforts.

The buffer should provide a smooth transition to the explanation that follows. Because the Fair Credit Reporting Act permits rejected applicants to request an explanation for the credit refusal, specifying the reasons in your initial letter helps avoid needless future correspondence. Explain the reasons factually and impersonally, taking care not to sound patronizing. State the refusal in neutral or positive language, avoiding terms like "must refuse," "does not meet," and "poor financial position." Because your decision was based on an objective analysis of the evidence, no apology is needed.

Sometimes you may want to omit the reasons for denying credit for human-relations reasons.

> Our experience shows that at least a 2-to-1 ratio of current assets to current liabilities is desirable to enable firms to pay their bills without undue hardship. As soon as your firm is able to meet this ratio, we will be happy to extend credit to you.

After giving the refusal, move quickly to a forward-looking closing. If you can offer a counterproposal, do so. If you can realistically offer hope

FIGURE 9.4 Credit Approval

James River Enterprises

November 8, 19--

Ms. Jill Boyer, Vice President
The Home Builder, Inc.
1001 Main Street
Houston, TX 77002

Dear Ms. Boyer:

1 The Home Builder's fine credit history certainly merits credit privileges with
our firm. Beginning immediately, you may charge purchases up to $3,000. When
2 you mail or phone in your next order, simply say, "Charge it."

Begins by giving the good news.

3 Bills are mailed on the 15th of each month and include all charges for the preceding month. Bills paid by the 25th of each month qualify for a 2% prompt-payment discount. Otherwise, the net amount is due by the 15th of the following month. A monthly finance charge of 1.5% (18% annual rate) is added to any balance unpaid after 30 days.

Explains the credit arrangements.

As one of our valued credit customers, you will not only enjoy credit privileges but also receive our quarterly sales brochures. These brochures describe new products added to our growing inventory of insulation products as well as sale items at discounts of 15% to 35% off our regular low prices.

Includes sales promotion.

Use your new line of credit today, Ms. Boyer, to order some of the specials advertised in our winter sales brochure that is enclosed. As usual, your purchases will reach you within three days and are backed by our unconditional 30-day return policy.

Encourages use of new credit privileges.

Cordially,

L. P. Ewald

L. P. Ewald
Credit Manager

amx
Enclosure

1251 Avenue of the Americas
New York, NY 10020

212-555-1000

Grammar and Mechanics Notes

1 *Builder's:* Add an apostrophe plus *s* to show possession of a singular noun. 2 *"Charge it.":* Type the period *before* the closing quotation mark. 3 *15th of each month:* Use ordinal numbers (*1st, 2d,* and so on) only when the day comes before the month; otherwise use cardinal numbers (for example, *May 15,* not *May 15th*).

FIGURE 9.5 Credit Denial

This letter is a rejection version of the credit-approval letter shown in Figure 9.4.

James River Enterprises

November 8, 19--

Ms. Jill Boyer, Vice President
The Home Builder, Inc.
1001 Main Street
Houston, TX 77002

Dear Ms. Boyer:

Begins with a supportive buffer.

I appreciate both your recent cash order and the confidence you have shown in us by your credit application. I sincerely hope the grand opening of your new home-improvement center was both enjoyable and successful.

First gives the reason for the refusal, then presents the refusal in positive language.

The National Small Business Council estimates that 75% of start-up firms like
yours that achieve profitability within three months will have a secure 1
future. Given the current interest in home remodeling, I feel sure The Home
Builder will reach this milestone, at which time we will be pleased to
reconsider your application for credit.

Discusses advantages of continuing to purchase for cash.

During this critical three-month period, your continued purchases for cash
will enable you to take advantage of our 2% cash discount, thus contributing
to profitability. Also, our overnight delivery system will enable you to 2
maintain smaller inventories.

Closes by making a genuine offer of assistance.

Because we want to do everything we reasonably can to help you succeed, I am
asking Mr. Willard Perkins, our national sales manager, to telephone you. Mr. 3
Perkins has had extensive experience in display management and will be able to
provide some valuable tips that should help you promote all of your
merchandise more effectively.

Cordially,

L. P. Ewald

L. P. Ewald
Credit Manager

amx

1251 Avenue of the Americas
New York, NY 10020

212-555-1000

Grammar and Mechanics Notes

1 *yours:* Do not use an apostrophe to show possession with a personal pronoun.
2 *overnight:* Write as one word. 3 *national sales manager:* Do not capitalize a job title that *follows* a personal name.

CHECKLIST 9

Credit Letters

Note: For *all* credit letters, ensure that the information is accurate and that your message follows all federal and state laws regarding credit practices.

APPROVING CREDIT

1. Use a form letter if necessary.
2. Write in the direct pattern; begin by telling the reader that credit has been approved.
3. In the middle section, provide the needed information about the credit arrangements, using impersonal language and a gracious tone.
4. End on a forward-looking note, perhaps by including resale about your firm or sales promotion to encourage using the new line of credit.

DENYING CREDIT

1. Use a form letter only if necessary.
2. Use an overall tone of respect, thoughtfulness, and helpfulness. Stress the goodwill aspects, because you want to keep the reader as a cash customer.
3. Begin with a relevant, supportive, and neutral buffer, perhaps an expression of appreciation or subtle resale.
4. Use impersonal and objective language in presenting the reasons. Discuss only relevant information, stick to the facts, and don't embarrass the reader.
5. Present the refusal in neutral or positive language; do not apologize.
6. Close on an optimistic, off-the-topic note. Stress the benefits of continuing to buy for cash.

for a positive decision at some point in the near future, do so. At a minimum, discuss the advantages of continuing to do business with your firm on a cash basis. End on an optimistic note, without referring back to the refusal.

Discuss the advantages of cash transactions.

> In the meantime, we look forward to continuing to serve you on a cash basis. And you can look forward to continuing to receive the 2% discount we offer for cash purchases. We expect the new creations featured in our fall advertising campaign to be very popular with the type of clientele your store attracts.

Figure 9.5 shows a credit-denial letter that follows these guidelines; it is a refusal version of the approval letter presented in Figure 9.4. Guidelines for approving and denying credit are summarized in Checklist 9.

For other examples of credit-denial letters, see the *Instructor's Resource Manual*, pp. 204 and 205.

Collection Letters

The primary purpose of collection messages is to collect past-due accounts. The secondary purpose is to retain the debtor's goodwill. Although letters are the most commonly used medium for collection messages, the telephone can be used either instead of or in conjunction with letters. In addition, some firms have been successful in using Express Mail, Mailgrams, and fax (facsimile) messages to emphasize the urgency of the situation.

In addition to various state laws, the federal Fair Debt Collection Practices Act prescribes the types of actions you may and may not take in your efforts to collect legal debts. You may not, for example,

You may not use unreasonable actions or language in trying to collect a debt.

- Use abusive, obscene, or defamatory language.
- Communicate with the debtor's employer, relatives, or friends about the unpaid debt; you may, however, communicate the facts to credit bureaus, collection agencies, and attorneys.
- Harass the debtor or intentionally cause mental distress; for example, you may not telephone the debtor before 8 a.m. or after 9 p.m. unless he or she agrees.
- Misrepresent your messages; for example, you may not send anonymous messages or disguise your message as a letter from the IRS.

In communicating directly with the debtor, you are usually on sound legal ground as long as you stick to the facts. For example, you may tell a debtor that you will sue him or her if payment is not received by a certain date—if that is what you actually intend to do.

Because more than one letter are often needed to collect past-due accounts, most companies use a series of collection letters. The most successful collection series have these four features in common:

1. *Understanding:* Show understanding by adopting a tone of reasonableness and helpfulness. Avoid anger; after all, the reader is your customer—not your enemy.
2. *Timeliness:* Delinquent debtors will take as much time to pay as you allow them. Establish a prompt and systematic procedure for notifying people of delinquent accounts—beginning a few days after the account is due and spaced no more than two weeks apart. This gives enough time in between for debtors to pay without receiving another collection letter but never lets them forget about the debt.
3. *Increasing urgency:* Most people typically pay their bills on time. Therefore, your first letters should be rather routine, increasing in urgency with each message. Poor credit risks tend to pay first those debts that seem the most pressing.
4. *Completeness:* Each letter should contain the reader's account number (often included in a subject line), the amount owed, and a postpaid envelope (to facilitate prompt action).

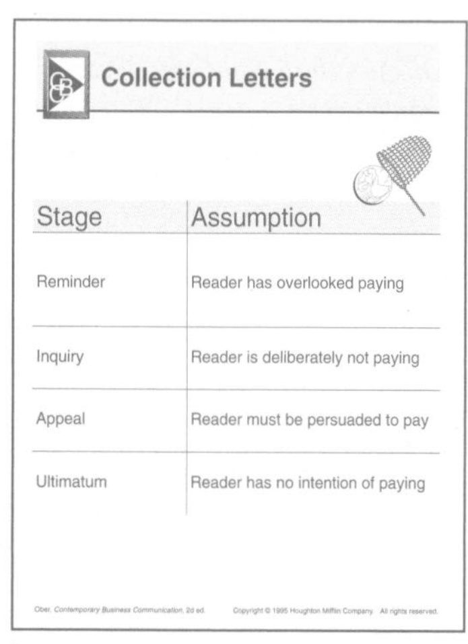

See Transparency 9.6, Collection Letters.

The collection process usually begins with the mailing of the monthly statement, and the vast majority of accounts are paid within the due date. For those that are not, a four-stage series (reminder, inquiry, appeal, and ultimatum) is used, although more than one message may be sent at any one of these stages.

Reminder At the reminder stage, you assume that the reader has simply overlooked paying and will pay when reminded. Some of your best customers will occasionally forget to send in a payment or will be away when bills come due, and you want to avoid insulting or embarrassing them.

Make the reminder appear routine; an individually typed letter would be much too personal at this stage.

Avoid personal letters at the reminder stage.

Often the reminder notification is simply a second copy of the bill, perhaps on colored paper for emphasis or with a sticker or stamp containing the phrase "Friendly Reminder," "Please Remit," or "Second Notice" on it. Or you might use an impersonal computer-generated note, with a short message such as the following:

> This note is a friendly reminder of the balance of $875.26 that was due on your account on October 15. Many thanks in advance for both your payment and your continued patronage. We sincerely appreciate both.

Depending upon your analysis of the situation, you may send more than one reminder notice before moving to the next stage. However, once you can reasonably assume that the customer has not merely *forgotten* to pay, you should move to the next stage.

Inquiry The assumption at this stage is that the customer will still pay eventually but that payment is consciously being withheld because of some unusual circumstance. The purpose of the inquiry letter, then, is to determine why payment hasn't been made and to arrange for either payment or an explanation. These letters are typically short and are considered routine; thus, they are written in the direct pattern. Personalizing the letter at this stage is appropriate.

The goal of the inquiry stage is to get some *response from the debtor.*

> Your October 15 account balance of $875.26 is now two months past due. Since this is the first time that you have been as much as a day late, I wonder whether something unusual has happened. Can I be of help?
>
> Won't you please either pay the full balance immediately or give me a call so that we can arrange a special repayment plan that will suit your particular circumstances.

The tone of this letter is one of understanding and helpfulness. The aim is to get *some* action from the reader—preferably a check for the full amount or a partial payment or at least an explanation and plan for repayment. Don't provide excuses, such as asking whether there was some problem with the product or service. If there were, the delinquent debtor would already have used that as an excuse for deferring payment. Likewise, do not mention that you believe the customer has merely overlooked paying. That was the tactic used in the reminder stage, and it didn't work. In other words, once you leave one stage, do not backtrack.

At the inquiry stage, you can no longer assume the reader has merely overlooked paying. The reader is *consciously withholding payment.*

Send only one inquiry letter. If it doesn't result in payment, move directly to the appeal stage. Some firms skip the inquiry stage altogether for new customers or for those with poor payment records and go immediately to the third stage.

Appeal The appeal stage assumes the reader must now be *persuaded* to pay. Consider the situation: these debtors know they owe you the money, and they are not pleased to receive your letters because they know what the letters are about before reading them. Thus, you have an uphill battle to get them to do as you ask, and that calls for persuasion and an indirect approach.

These letters must not be unduly long if you want the delinquent debtor to read them; you do not have time to develop numerous appeals. So, just as you develop a central selling theme for your persuasive sales letters, you should develop a central appeal for your collection letters at this stage. Emphasize that appeal throughout the letter, beginning with the attention-getter.

Five common types of appeal, in increasing order of forcefulness, are resale, fair play, pride, self-interest, and fear. The first letter in the appeal stage typically uses one of the milder appeals; if that is not successful, subsequent letters use one of the more forceful methods.

Technique	*Example*
Resale	Your Signet fax machine's ability to send and receive documents across the country in seconds is surely a profit-enhancing strategy for construction companies such as yours.
Fair play	When you ordered the Signet fax machine, we were happy to program the ten telephone numbers for you and train you in its use. We even threw in a free 100-foot roll of thermal paper.
Pride	The pride that you have in Ellsworth Construction Company's fine reputation is shared by others. Congratulations on the positive write-up in last Sunday's *Dispatch.*
Self-interest	How many months of having to pay cash for all your purchases did it take for you to secure the A-1 credit rating you have enjoyed up to this point?
Fear	What will be the effect on your profits next quarter if suddenly you are forced to pay cash for all your purchases?

Use negative appeals only when all else fails.

A rhetorical question (as in the self-interest and fear examples above) is often effective in gaining the reader's attention. Your opening statement must introduce the appeal you intend to use, and your subsequent paragraphs should develop this theme further—politely, but clearly and forcefully. In no uncertain language, explain the consequences of not paying, and ask for payment directly, forgoing subtlety. Stress the reader benefits of doing as you ask.

Letters at this stage are typically signed by a high-level official within the firm to stress their urgency. Figure 9.6 shows an appeal letter that uses self-interest as the central appeal. An earlier appeal letter that used resale as its theme was not effective in securing payment.

For other examples of collection letters (at the inquiry, appeal, and ultimatum stages), see the *Instructor's Resource Manual*, pp. 206, 207, and 208.

Ultimatum The final stage, the ultimatum, assumes the reader has no intention of paying. In effect, this letter tells the reader to pay or you will use every legal means at your disposal to secure payment. In a polite and

FIGURE 9.6 Collection Letter

This persuasive letter with self-interest as the central theme is written during the appeal stage.

DISCOUNT OFFICE PRODUCTS

Office of the Vice President

Ms. Kathryn Wheeler, Controller
Ellsworth Construction Company
P.O. Box 3085
Memphis, TN 38194

Dear Ms. Wheeler:

1 Subject: Account 207-362

Uses a subject line to identify the account.

What business can afford to trade in the privilege of five months of buying on credit for just $875.26?

Begins with a rhetorical question.

According to the A-1 credit report we received on you from the Volunteer State
Credit Bureau last August, your firm opened for business in January and was
not able to purchase on credit until June. Thus, it took you five months to
earn this privilege. But your ability to continue purchasing on credit can be
2 maintained only by paying the $875.26 that is now six months past due on your
account.

Buying on credit enables you to stock sufficient inventory and supplies without experiencing the cash-flow problems that sometimes plague less creditworthy customers who must pay cash. And our ten-days-same-as-cash policy means that you do not pay extra for this convenience. Bills paid within ten days of billing do not accrue interest.

Presents the advantages of continued credit privileges.

Please use the enclosed postpaid envelope to mail us your check for $875.26 today. That way, we can put your account back in our "Prompt-Payment" category—right where it belongs!

Closes with a direct request for payment, coupled with another reader benefit.

Sincerely,

Gordon J. Green

Gordon J. Green
3 Vice President

Is signed by a high-level official.

sue
Enclosure

2005 Corporate Avenue ▪ Memphis, TN 38194 ▪ Phone 901-555-2005

Grammar and Mechanics Notes

1 Type a subject line immediately below the salutation, with double spacing above and below. 2 *six months:* Spell out numbers one through ten. 3 *Vice President:* Unless the individual company uses a different style, spell "vice president" as two words, without a hyphen.

CHECKLIST 10

Collection Letters

FOR ALL COLLECTION LETTERS

1. Ensure that the information is accurate and that your message follows all federal and state laws regarding collection practices.
2. Adopt a tone of reasonableness and helpfulness; avoid anger.
3. Send letters promptly and—if payment doesn't result—at systematic intervals, so that the debt is never out of the reader's mind.
4. In every letter include the reader's account number, the amount owed, and a postpaid envelope.

REMINDER STAGE

1. Assume the reader has simply overlooked paying.
2. Avoid embarrassing the customer by sending a personal letter. Instead, send a second copy of the bill or an impersonal form letter.

INQUIRY STAGE

1. Assume the reader is deliberately not paying because of some unusual circumstance.
2. Send a short, personalized letter, written in the direct pattern.
3. Remind the reader that payment is late, ask why the account hasn't been paid, and solicit either payment or a plan for payment.
4. Don't provide excuses and don't suggest that the reader has merely overlooked payment.

APPEAL STAGE

1. Assume the reader must be persuaded to pay.
2. Write a persuasive letter—in the indirect pattern.
3. Select one central appeal to use and stress it throughout the letter. The most effective appeals (in increasing order of forcefulness) are resale, fair play, pride, self-interest, and fear.
4. Make the opening attention-getter interesting, short, and related to the central appeal.
5. In the middle section, continue to stress the central appeal, using reader benefits and positive language to motivate payment.
6. Close by directly asking for payment, combining your request with another reader benefit.

ULTIMATUM STAGE

1. Assume the reader has no intention of paying.
2. Write in a direct pattern; at this point, maintaining goodwill is less important than securing payment.
3. In a polite and businesslike manner, explain exactly what you intend to do if the bill is not paid. Review the efforts you've already made to collect.
4. Give the reader one last opportunity to pay, setting a specific deadline.

businesslike manner, discuss the steps you've taken thus far and the steps you intend to take if payment is not forthcoming. Do not issue idle threats, do not get angry, and do not defame the reader.

The ultimatum letter gives the reader one last chance to pay before you take action.

At this point, maintaining the goodwill of the reader is of less importance than securing payment. Give the reader one last opportunity to pay, setting a specific deadline for receipt of payment. Get to the point immediately in the ultimatum stage by using the direct pattern.

Despite eight letters and four phone calls, we have been unable to secure payment of the $945.63 ($875.26 balance plus interest of $70.37) that you owe us. Your failure to pay leaves us no choice but to turn this matter over to our attorneys to institute legal proceedings against your firm.

This is a drastic step that we'd sincerely like to avoid. The embarrassment that your firm would suffer, the almost certain loss of all credit privileges, and the legal and court costs you would have to pay would have a serious negative effect on your firm's ability to remain profitable. Surely, refusing to pay a legal debt of $945.63 is not worth such dire consequences.

If we have not received a check from you for $945.63 by 5 p.m. on June 23, we will have our attorney institute legal proceedings against your firm immediately. Please do not make this action necessary.

Use Checklist 10 as a guide to writing collection letters.

GOODWILL MESSAGES

A **goodwill message** is one that is sent strictly out of a sense of kindness and friendliness. Examples include messages conveying congratulations, appreciation, and sympathy. These messages achieve their goodwill objective precisely because they have no true business objective. To include even subtle sales promotion in such messages would defeat their purpose. Recipients are quick to see through such efforts. Letters that include sales promotion or resale are *sales* letters, as might be expected, and are covered elsewhere in this text.

That is not to say, however, that business advantages do not accrue from such efforts. People naturally like to deal with businesses and with people who are friendly and who take the time to comment on noteworthy occasions. The point is that such business advantages are strictly incidental to the real purpose of extending a friendly gesture.

Often the gesture could be accomplished by telephoning instead of by writing—especially for minor occasions. But a written message, either in place of or in addition to the phone call, is more thoughtful, more appreciated, and more permanent. And because it requires extra effort and the recipient will receive fewer of them, a written message is much more meaningful than a telephone message.

When writing letters to people or businesses in other countries, business writers must be aware that different cultures attach different meanings to the same words. For example, a 1982 study suggests that Japanese and U.S. firms may have difficulty communicating because they assign different meanings to the word *profit.* (J.J. Sullivan and N. Kameda, "The Concept of Profit and Japanese–American Business Communication Problems," *The Journal of Business Communication,* 19 (1), pp. 33–39.)

General Guidelines

To ensure that your goodwill messages achieve their desired effect, follow these five guidelines:

1. *Be prompt.* Too often, people consider writing a goodwill message but then put it off until it is too late. The most meaningful messages are those received while the reason for them is still fresh in the reader's mind.

Five guidelines for goodwill messages: be prompt, sincere, specific, brief, and direct.

2. *Be sincere.* Avoid language that is too flowery or too strong. Use a conversational tone, as if you were speaking to the person directly, and focus on the reader—not on yourself. Take special care to spell names correctly and to make sure your facts are accurate.
3. *Be specific.* If you're thanking or complimenting someone, mention a specific incident or anecdote. Personalize your message to avoid having it sound like a form letter.
4. *Be brief.* You don't need two pages (or, likely, even one full page) to get your point across. Often a personal note card is more appropriate than full-sized business stationery.
5. *Be direct.* State the major idea in the first sentence or two, even for sympathy notes; since the reader already knows the bad news, you don't need to shelter him or her from it.

Congratulatory Messages

Congratulatory notes should be sent for major business achievements—receiving a promotion, announcing a retirement, winning an award, opening a new branch, celebrating an anniversary, and the like. Such notes are also appropriate for personal milestones—engagements, weddings, births, graduations, and other noteworthy occasions. Congratulatory notes should be written both to employees within the company and to customers, suppliers, and others outside the firm with whom you have a relationship.

> Congratulations, Tom, on your election to the presidency of the United Way of Alberta County. I was happy to see the announcement in this morning's newspaper and to learn of your plans for the upcoming campaign.
>
> Best wishes for a successful fund drive. This important community effort surely deserves everyone's full support.

Thank-You Notes

Thank-you notes are expected in some situations; they are unexpected (and therefore much appreciated) in others.

A note of thanks or appreciation is often valued more than a monetary reward. A handwritten thank-you note is especially appreciated today, when people routinely receive so many "personalized" computer-generated messages. A handwritten note assures the reader that you are offering sincere and genuine thanks, rather than simply sending out a form letter. The more personal approach of a handwritten note must, however, be weighed against the advantage of being able to send a copy of a typed note to the person's supervisor, meaning the recipient is twice blessed.

Thank-you notes (either typed or handwritten) should be sent whenever someone does you a favor—gives you a gift, writes a letter of recommendation for you, comes to your support unexpectedly, gives a speech or appears on a panel, and so on. Don't forget that customers and suppliers like to be recognized as well. Unexpected thank-you notes are often the

Motorola runs an annual quality competition to reward high performance, a contest that draws almost 4,000 entries from employees. Whether aimed at an individual or a group (like the Motorola purchasing team shown here), timely congratulations can be a strong motivating force.

most appreciated—to the salesperson, instructor, secretary, copy center operator, waiter or waitress, receptionist, or anyone else who provided service beyond the call of duty.

> Thank you so much, Alice, for serving on the panel of suppliers for our new-employee orientation program. Your comments on scheduling problems and your suggestions for alleviating them were especially helpful. They were the kind of information that only an old pro like yourself could give.
>
> I think you could tell from the comments and many questions that your remarks were well received by our new employees. Thanks again for your professional contributions.

Sympathy Notes

Expressions of sympathy or condolence to a person who has experienced pain, grief, or misfortune are especially difficult to write but are also especially appreciated. People who have experienced serious health problems, a severe business setback, or the death of a loved one need to know that others are thinking of them and that they are not alone.

For another example of a goodwill letter (a congratulatory letter on a promotion), see the *Instructor's Resource Manual*, p. 209.

The most difficult messages to write are those expressing sympathy over the death of someone. These notes should be handwritten, when possible. They should not avoid mentioning the death, but they need not dwell on it. Most sympathy notes are short. Begin with an expression of sympathy, mention some specific quality or personal reminiscence about the deceased, and then close with an expression of comfort and affection. An offer to help, if genuine, would be appropriate (See Figure 9.7).

Begin by expressing sympathy, offer some personal memory of the deceased, and close by offering comfort.

FIGURE 9.7 Sympathy Note

Robert B. Meyers Executive Vice President

Dear Ralph,

Begins with an expression of sympathy.

I was deeply saddened to learn of Jane's 1
sudden death. It was certainly a great shock
to her many friends and colleagues.

Mentions some specific quality or personal reminiscence.

Jane had a well-earned reputation here 2
for her top-notch negotiating skills and for
her endearing sense of humor. She was an
accomplished manager and a good friend, and
I shall miss her greatly.

Closes with a genuine offer of help.

If I can help smooth the way in your 3
dealings with our personnel office, I would be
honored to help. Please call me on my
private line (555-1036) if there is anything I
can do.

Affectionately,
Bob

Grammar and Mechanics Notes

1 Use either company letterhead or personal stationery for sympathy notes. 2 Insert a comma (instead of a colon) after the salutation of a personal letter. 3 Handwrite the sympathy note, if possible.

A Letter of Recommendation

PROBLEM

Roger Brannen worked as your secretary for three years before quitting to return to college to finish his degree. His secretarial skills were only adequate (he had some trouble adjusting to any new computer program). However, his organizational skills were top-notch; thus, he was always able to complete his work in a timely and competent manner.

Roger had an engaging personality and got along well with his coworkers and with people at higher levels of management with whom he had to deal. Twenty-four and single, he also had somewhat of a playboy reputation among the female staff at your company. However, he always behaved appropriately to everyone during working hours.

Roger is graduating this spring with a degree in business education and has, with your permission, used your name as a reference. Today you received the following letter from Susan Archie, assistant superintendent for personnel for the Atlanta, Georgia, public school system.

> Would you please provide some information on Roger Brannen. Mr. Brannen has applied for the position of cooperative office educator with one of our inner-city schools and has given your name as a work reference.
>
> Since this position requires supervising student interns in clerical and secretarial positions, the person holding this position must have excellent technical skills. How would you rate Mr. Brannen's technical skills? This position also requires frequent and close contact with members of the business community. How successful do you think Mr. Brannen would be in interacting with business executives?
>
> I appreciate your providing this confidential information, which will help us evaluate Mr. Brannen's qualifications for this position.

You sit down to plan and write the requested letter of recommendation to Ms. Archie.

PROCESS

1. Describe your primary audience.
   - Assistant superintendent for personnel for a large school system in a major metropolitan area
   - No vested interest in the outcome
   - Will make hiring decision based partly on the written evaluation you provide
2. Who (if anyone) is your secondary audience?
   - Roger Brannen
   - Other applicants for the same position
   - The student interns
   - The business executives hiring the interns

3. Write the first paragraph of your letter. (Give the applicant's name, the position for which he is applying, and the nature and length of your relationship with him.)

   I am happy to provide the confidential information you requested on Mr. Roger Brannen, who has applied for the position of cooperative office educator with the Atlanta public school system. Roger worked as my full-time secretary from 1990 until 1993.

4. Should you discuss Roger's difficulties in adjusting to new computer programs?

   Yes, these skills are relevant to success in this position. However, they should be placed in appropriate context—he was able to compensate, and overall job performance is what counts.

5. Write the paragraph in which you discuss this aspect of Roger's performance.

   Although it took Roger longer than most other secretaries to learn new software programs, he eventually developed competence in each new program. And his top-level organizational skills enabled him to handle all tasks assigned to him in an efficient and competent manner.

6. Should you discuss Roger's playboy image?

   No, it is not relevant to his job performance, and there are too many legal implications.

7. Write the last paragraph of your letter, in which you provide some type of overall assessment of Roger's capabilities.

   I enjoyed knowing Roger, appreciated the competent work he did for me, and would, if I had the opportunity, rehire him. Please call me if I can provide additional information to help you in the evaluation process.

C H A P M A N

A I R C O N D I T I O N I N G A N D H E A T I N G

March 15, 19--

Ms. Susan Archie
Assistant Superintendent for Personnel
Atlanta Public Schools
10355 Peachtree Street
Atlanta, GA 30303

Dear Ms. Archie:

I am happy to provide the information you requested on Mr. Roger Brannen, who has applied for the position of cooperative office educator with the Atlanta public school system. Roger worked as my full-time secretary from 1990 until 1993 and left to return to college full-time to complete his degree.

Roger's overall technical skills were competent. Although it took him longer than most other secretaries to learn new software programs, he eventually mastered each new program. More important, his top-level organizational skills enabled him to handle all tasks assigned to him in an efficient and competent manner.

Roger's human relations skills were superb. He had an outgoing personality and cooperative attitude. He got along well with everyone, including high-level executives similar to those with whom your student interns work. If he had stayed with us for another year, I expect he would have been promoted to the position of administrative assistant for the executive vice president.

I enjoyed knowing Roger; I appreciated the competent work he did for me; and if I had the opportunity, I would gladly rehire him. Please call me if I can provide additional confidential information to help you in the evaluation process.

Sincerely,

Alden Klahr

Alden Klahr
Vice President

ga

P.O. Box 1076 Charleston, SC 29409 803-555-7084

SUMMARY

When writing a message containing both good news and bad news, present the good news first, explain the rationale for the bad news, present the bad news, and then close on a positive and friendly note. When writing a message that contains both bad news and persuasion, use an indirect approach: start with a buffer opening, explain the reason for the bad news, present the bad news, and present reasons for adopting your alternative suggestion; then close by asking for the desired action.

Letters of recommendation should be fair to all concerned, should discuss and illustrate only job-related behaviors and traits, and should use appropriate emphasis and subordination in presenting negative traits. Job-rejection letters should be short, be written in the indirect pattern, and contain a brief explanation of why another person was chosen. All comments on a personnel evaluation should be fair, job-related, and documented with specific examples. The emphasis should be on job improvement.

When approving a request for credit, give the good news in the first sentence, follow it with the needed details about credit arrangements, and close with resale or sales promotion. When denying a request for credit, begin with a buffer, use impersonal and objective language to present the reasons, give the refusal in neutral or positive language, and end on an optimistic, off-the-topic note.

The series of collection letters should show understanding, timeliness, increasing urgency, and completeness. The reminder stage is very routine and impersonal—often simply a second copy of the bill. The inquiry stage requires a direct-pattern letter that seeks to determine why payment hasn't been made and to arrange for either payment or an explanation. The appeal stage requires a persuasive, indirect-pattern letter, using as a central appeal either resale, fair play, pride, self-interest, or fear. The final stage (ultimatum) is a direct-pattern letter that tells the reader that unless payment is received by a specified date, certain serious actions will be taken immediately.

Goodwill messages include congratulatory messages, thank-you notes, and sympathy notes. The important points to remember for all of these are to write promptly, using a direct pattern, and to be sincere, specific, and brief. Rather than serving an overt business purpose, these notes are written out of a sense of kindness and friendliness.

KEY TERMS

For an exercise on matching terms, refer students to the *Study Guide*, p. 132.

Credit The confidence that a business has in a customer's ability and intention to pay his or her debts.

Goodwill message A message such as a congratulatory, thank-you, or sympathy note that is sent strictly out of a sense of kindness and friendliness.

REVIEW AND DISCUSSION

The answers to the review and discussion questions appear in the *Instructor's Resource Manual*, beginning on p. 179.

1. **Communication at TRW Revisited** ▪ The letters Janis Lamar writes on behalf of TRW are generally complex. They often have legal implications, and because they may be reported in the media, they are usually directed to more than one audience.

a. When Lamar refers to particular legislation in a letter, should she enclose a copy of the law? Why or why not?
b. When TRW receives a letter from a consumer that has been forwarded by the media, should Lamar address her answer to the consumer or to the media? Why do you think so?
c. What reader benefit might Lamar mention in the closing of a letter to help build goodwill?

2. In a message that contains both bad news and persuasion, which should come first? Why?
3. In writing a letter of recommendation, to whom should you be fair? Why?
4. Give three pieces of information about yourself that would be irrelevant to a prospective employer and that should, therefore, not be included in anyone's letter of recommendation.
5. Give three pieces of information about yourself that would be relevant to a prospective employer and that should, therefore, be included in a letter of recommendation.
6. Should negative traits of a candidate always be subordinated? Why or why not?
7. Assume you want to decline to write a letter of recommendation for someone. Should your letter conveying this decision to the prospective employer be written in the direct or indirect pattern? How about your letter conveying this decision to the candidate?
8. What effects do the Equal Credit Opportunity Act, the Truth in Lending Act, and the Fair Credit Reporting Act have on what should and should not be included in letters approving and denying credit?
9. What should go in the first sentence or two of a letter approving credit? of one denying credit?
10. Why is it important to retain the goodwill of those individuals or businesses to whom you deny credit?
11. What are the primary and secondary purposes of collection letters?
12. One of Paul's customers failed to pay a large account on time. As a result, Paul doesn't have enough cash to make his quarterly estimated tax payment to the federal government. May Paul stamp on the envelope of his collection letter "Federal Tax Information Inside" to motivate the debtor to pay more attention to his letter? Why or why not?
13. What are the disadvantages of providing too much or too little time between collection letters?
14. Why is a personal letter inappropriate for the reminder stage?
15. Name the assumption on which each of the four stages of the collection process is based.
16. Which letters in the collection process are written in the direct and which in the indirect pattern?
17. Why is it not appropriate to include sales promotion in goodwill letters?

EXERCISES

1. Microwriting a Mixed-News Message ■

Sample solutions for Exercises 1–22 appear in the *Instructor's Resource Manual*, pp. 181–191. Formatted solutions for most of these exercises appear on *IRM* pp. 192–209.

PROBLEM

You're the editor of a popular management textbook. Previous editions of your textbook have been published in two colors—black and a second color for headings, illustrations, and the like. In order to attract a larger

Good News and Bad News

In order to attract a larger share of the market, we plan to publish the upcoming edition of your textbook in four colors. A four-color format permits eye-catching full-color photographs, charts, and other illustrations.

Four-color books are popular with both students and professors, and our experience has been that sales of four-color books typically increase by about 10% over two-color editions. As a result of the increased production costs of four-color books, we allow 12% author royalty on them rather than the 15% that normally is given for two-color books. However, because sales are expected to increase substantially, we predict that your total royalty check will actually increase under the new arrangements.

Please sign the enclosed copy of this letter, indicating your notification of the change in royalty and in the color format of your next edition, and return it to us in the enclosed envelope. Our sales and marketing staff is eager to begin promoting this new edition.

Ober, *Contemporary Business Communication*, 2d ed.

See Master 9.1, Exercise 1, Microwriting a Mixed-News Message, in the *Instructor's Resource Manual.*

share of the market, you would like to publish the upcoming edition in four colors. A four-color book permits full-color photographs, charts, and other illustrations. You believe such an added feature will dramatically increase sales and increase student interest.

But four-color books are quite expensive. To help defray the cost of four-color printing, you must ask the author to take a smaller royalty percentage—going from 15% on the present edition to 12% on the upcoming edition. The author's contract permits such an arrangement. Write the author (Dr. Judith J. Kondler, College of Business, University of Minnesota, St. Paul, MN 55108) and announce this news.

PROCESS

a. Describe your audience.
b. What are the two purposes of this message? What will be the reader's likely reaction to each purpose?
c. Will you communicate the good news or bad news first? Why?
d. Write the sentence of your letter in which you communicate the good news.
e. For the bad-news part of the letter (that the author will get a reduced royalty percentage), will you use a direct or indirect organizational plan? Why?
f. What reader benefits can you discuss with the rationale for the bad news?
g. Where will you actually give the bad news?
h. Write the sentence that presents the bad news (neutral or positive language, impersonal tone, subordinated).
i. Write the last sentence of your letter (off the topic of the bad news, forward-looking, confident).

PRODUCT

Draft, revise, format, and proofread your letter. Then submit both your responses to the process questions and your revised letter to your instructor.

2. **Mixed-News Message—Good News and Persuasion** ■ Pieter Van Waes, the assistant director of branch operations for Wolverine National Bank, has written you (the director of branch operations) a persuasive memo, proposing that the bank open a new branch in Altoona. Although you had not previously considered Altoona as the site of a new branch, you find Pieter's reasoning compelling and decide to approve the new branch. Not only that, you feel that Pieter would be just the person to manage this new branch, which could be operational in eight months.

   The only problem is that Pieter has three children in high school, and you know he does not wish to relocate the family at this time, even though the job would be a promotion with a substantial increase in salary. Send Pieter a memo, giving him the good news that you have approved his recommendation for the new branch and trying to persuade him to accept the promotion to branch manager of the Altoona office.

Exercise 3 is linked with Exercise 16 of Chapter 8.

3. **Mixed-News Message—Bad News and Persuasion** ■ Resume the role of Alan Teison, the director of distribution for Nu-Shu Sneakers (see Exercise 16 of Chapter 8). One of the three styles ordered by Lily Greenhill, Step Out's store manager, was recently discontinued. In its place, Nu-Shu now offers a sneaker with velcro fastenings and a reinforced ankle cuff. According to your research, these features make the new model sturdier as well as more convenient than the model it replaces. Of course, the new model, NS-125, carries a higher wholesale cost than the previous model ($23.50 versus $20.50) and its suggested retail price is, therefore, higher ($47 ver-

sus $41). Despite the higher price, you believe that parents will be attracted by the extra benefits of the new model.

Like the other styles Greenhill ordered, the NS-125 is out of stock but will be available in about four weeks. Write the store manager and try to convince her to accept the NS-125 and the other two styles, even though the entire shipment will be delayed.

4. **Mixed-News Message—Bad News and Persuasion** ■ You are the director of resurfacing for the Wyoming Department of Transportation. Jim Wycliff, one of your engineers, has requested permission to attend a two-week seminar offered by the University of Wyoming entitled "Load Constraints and Surface Technology." The course costs $1,350 and would require Jim's absence from work for two weeks.

   Although continuing education is an important part of your engineers' schedule, you believe your department would benefit more from having Jim attend a one-week course entitled "Grading Innovations for Erosion Control." Even though this course, also taught at the University of Wyoming, is offered the same week that Jim usually schedules his summer vacation (the second week in July), you are convinced that this is the course he should take. Send Jim a memo, denying his request to attend the load-constraint seminar and trying to persuade him to attend the grading seminar instead. Your department will, of course, pay all expenses associated with the seminar.

5. **Mixed-News Message—Good News and Bad News** ■ Once again, you're the vice president of operations for Kolor Kosmetics in Biloxi, Mississippi (see Exercise 6 of Chapter 8). When Dr. Mazzi wrote you last month asking for a summer internship for her son Peter, you reluctantly turned her down. In the meantime, you have discussed the issue with your executive vice president, who suggests that Peter Mazzi might serve as an unpaid intern during August. This would give him a chance to see how your factory operates. At the same time, the factory would benefit from his input on how to design an internship program for college students. Because the internship would be unpaid, you would not have to increase the payroll or cut another employee's hours to compensate.

   Exercise 5 is linked with Exercise 6 of Chapter 8.

   Although Peter Mazzi would gain valuable experience during the one-month internship, you know that the lack of pay is one major stumbling block. Another is that the internship would last for August only; this means Peter would need to look for a July-only job, not an easy task in your area.

   a. Write to Peter Mazzi (at 10-A Gulf Hall, De Soto College, Hernando, MS 38632) and try to persuade him to accept your offer.
   b. Write to Dr. Mazzi, telling her of your offer to her son.

6. **Letter of Recommendation—Willingness to Write** ■ Frances Kinchelow worked for your medium-priced restaurant for two years as the sous chef. The customers raved about her soup creations; she revised your somewhat bland soup menu and operated a clean and safe kitchen. When she decided to seek employment as a sous chef at a well-known restaurant in a nearby resort, you were surprised and also disappointed.

   Frances's only fault was that you never could get her to watch expenses. If the recipe called for fresh ingredients, she was unwilling to use the cheaper canned or frozen substitutes. Often the leftover ingredients spoiled because they could not be used in other recipes. Whenever you spoke to her about this, she promised to do better but soon reverted to her old ways. You finally decided that these were her personal standards, and you reluctantly raised the soup prices to accommodate her.

The hotel manager where Frances has applied has written, asking you for a recommendation for Frances. Write the requested letter of recommendation (Mr. Jean Lefiere, Manager, Twin Oaks, 111 East Madison Street, Tampa, FL 33602).

7. **Letter of Recommendation—Willingness to Write** ▪ Return to Exercise 5 above. You offered Peter Mazzi an unpaid, monthlong internship with Kolor Kosmetics. He accepted your offer and reported for work on August 1. After rotating through the assembly and quality-assurance departments, Mazzi joined your staff for three days, then went on to work with purchasing and shipping. He was helpful and enthusiastic, coming in early and staying late every day in order to make the most of the internship.

   At the start of his third week, Mazzi told the human-resources director that a conflict had arisen concerning his final week of work. Originally, Mazzi's classes had been scheduled to start on August 29, but the chairperson of the management department invited Mazzi to join a graduate seminar starting on August 25. Although Mazzi had agreed to work until August 27, your company allowed him to leave on August 25.

   Yesterday you received a letter from Mazzi, asking you to provide a general letter of recommendation for his file with the campus placement office. Although Mazzi did not finish out the month as you had planned, his performance was above average, so you decide to do what he asks. No form was enclosed with the letter; when you write, use the salutation "Dear Prospective Employer."

8. **Letter of Recommendation—Unwillingness to Write** ▪ Despite your letter, Frances Kinchelow (187 Second Street, Tampa, FL 33620-5650) didn't get the sous chef job (see Exercise 6 above). She then quit her position with you suddenly, without giving any advance notice, and, according to your other workers, began drinking heavily. Three months later, you receive a letter from Frances, indicating that she has been on extended vacation for the past three months and is now ready to return to work. She requests that you send a letter of recommendation for her to the Luau Ladle (165 South King Street, Honolulu, HI 96813). She has sent a copy of her letter to you to Akio Imoto, general manager of the Luau Ladle. You decide *not* to write the letter of recommendation.

   a. Write to Mr. Imoto, declining to give any subjective evaluation; you may provide a brief factual summary of Frances's employment history with you.
   b. Write to Frances, telling her of your decision.

9. **Letter of Recommendation—Unwillingness to Write** ▪ As the media director for Metro Associates, a small advertising agency in Philadelphia, you hired Bob Henrichsen to assist you in scheduling television commercials for your clients. Although his background was in newspaper advertising, from his very first day (January 17) Henrichsen enthusiastically pitched in to learn the basics of buying time on broadcast and cable television. Soon, however, you began to notice small discrepancies between the media schedules you prepared and the time Henrichsen actually booked on each station. At first you thought you were mistaken. But each time you brought up a change you'd discovered, Henrichsen claimed that he had found a better buy or a more appropriate slot for the commercial.

   Of course, media schedules must be approved by the clients before any time can be purchased, so you had a lot of explaining to do once you uncovered these "improvements." After the third such incident, you were preparing to give Henrichsen a written warning when he announced that he was leaving to join WAPP, a local television station. On September 30, his last day, Henrichsen asked you to send a letter of recommendation to Matilda Wanamaker, WAPP's station manager. You do write Wanamaker (at Station WAPP, 90 Franklin Boulevard West, Philadelphia, PA 19101), but given your experience with Henrichsen, you decide to provide only the facts of his employment.

10. **Rejecting a Job Applicant—Collaborative Writing** ▪ You are the proprietor of Knight Galleries, a major Manhattan gallery dealing in the purchase and sale of fine contemporary art. Traditionally, most of your sales have been to private collectors and museums. However, noting the trend for business firms to purchase fine art for display and investment purposes, you've decided to expand into this market. You advertised in two gallery magazines for an art-marketing consultant, who would serve as your primary contact with such firms. Your ad stated qualifications as five years of art-consulting experience and a college degree in fine arts. Much to your surprise, you received nearly 100 applications. By studying the résumés and checking references, you narrowed the list to five candidates, whom you brought to New York for interviews.

    After the five interviews, you had much difficulty choosing between Ryan McNeil and Marie Durmond. Ryan has a degree in art history and has served as an art-marketing representative for a small Santa Fe gallery for seven years. Marie has a BFA degree in art from Simmons College, has worked as art curator for First National Bank in Manhattan for three years, and has been a working painter for the past three years. You finally chose Ryan and he accepted the position. Working in groups of three or four, do the following:

    a. Write a form letter that will go to the 93 rejected candidates, telling them that they were not selected.
    b. Write to Marie, giving her the news (Apt. 14-C, 226 Avenue of the Americas, New York, NY 10020).

11. **Rejecting a Job Applicant—Position Eliminated** ▪ Assume the role of Gloria Sibley, the director of student affairs for Pawtucket Community College in Pawtucket, Rhode Island. The budget you submitted two months ago requested funding for a new position, that of activities coordinator. You prepared a job description, which your boss approved, and when you advertised, you received 42 replies. Because the job requires a background in recreation and facilities management, you quickly weeded out the 37 candidates who didn't have the right qualifications. After interviewing the remaining five, you settled on one candidate, Thomas Chonowsky, who has seven years of experience and impressive references (which you checked).

    Before you were able to write to Chonowsky with an employment offer, the college's board of directors ordered an immediate reduction in all departmental expenditures to make up for an expected shortfall in funding. As a result of these cuts, your activities coordinator position has been eliminated. Write to Chonowsky (at 29 Raynham Road, Taunton, MA 02780) to explain why he is not being hired.

Rejecting a Job Applicant

It was a pleasure to meet with you on November 3 and to discuss your background and impressive qualifications for the position of activities coordinator at Pawtucket Community College. I was particularly impressed with your research into recreation programs offered at colleges in Australia, which may have important implications for administrators in North America.

When we originally advertised this position, we anticipated that we would receive full funding for the coming year's budget. Based on an expected shortfall in state funding, however, Pawtucket's board of directors has just ordered a reduction in all departmental expenditures. As a result, the position of activities coordinator will not be filled at this time.

I sincerely appreciate your interest in Pawtucket Community College. We would have enjoyed having you on staff, and I wish you every success as you continue your search for a new position.

Ober, *Contemporary Business Communication*, 2d ed.

See Master 9.2, Exercise 11, Rejecting a Job Applicant, in the *Instructor's Resource Manual.*

12. **Personnel Evaluation** ▪ As chief of the three-person legal staff of a manufacturing concern, you prepare for the semiannual performance evaluation of Arthur Rodin, a legal assistant on your staff. As you reflect on his performance, you note these items:

    a. He is a good researcher.
    b. His writing skills are excellent; his oral skills are satisfactory, especially considering the fact that he has a slight lisp.

c. He gets along well with everyone on the staff.
d. He sometimes volunteers for more work than he can handle; as a result, he occasionally misses an important deadline.
e. He's quite computer literate, using word processing and such on-line computerized legal data bases as Lexus and Dialog®.
f. The other two attorneys have told you they often can use entire paragraphs that Art has written for their legal briefs, without changing a word.

Although you will present this information to Art in a face-to-face meeting, company policy requires that a written memorandum be placed in each employee's personnel file. Write the memo to Art, adding whatever other reasonable information you feel is appropriate.

13. **Personnel Evaluation** ▪ As the sales manager for Superior Trucking, you supervise five salespeople who call on large agricultural producers around the country. Every year you sit down with each salesperson to review his or her performance and to agree on improvements to be made in the coming year. You are reviewing the following notes on the performance of Leo Michaels, a long-time employee.

a. He consistently meets or exceeds sales quotas for his region.
b. Although he makes a point of being punctual when meeting with customers and prospects, he rarely files his monthly sales reports on time. Until he files these reports, you have no way of knowing the status of a particular account.
c. He missed two consecutive quarterly sales meetings because of conflicting appointments with key clients. During the week after each meeting, you had to meet with Michaels for several hours to explain the new policies, company procedures, and other details he missed.
d. Michaels is a good team player. When he gets a lead about a potential customer in someone else's region, he immediately calls or sends a memo to that salesperson.

In addition to discussing these items with Michaels, and coming up with an improvement plan, you have to document the evaluation by preparing a memo for his personnel file. Compose this memo and include any additional details you feel are appropriate.

The following information applies to Exercises 14–19.

You are the credit manager for Reginald's, an exclusive men's clothing store on Rodeo Drive. Your line of merchandise ranges from $80 ties to $1,250 silk suits. Your most popular items (and those with the biggest markup) are Alex Henry sports jackets, which average $400 each. These back-pleated jackets are carried by only ten stores in the entire country; they've received much publicity lately because the president of the United States, who golfs frequently in Palm Springs, often wears jackets with the distinctive AH pocket crest.

You sell on credit exclusively through the use of the Reginald Card. There is no interest charge on any outstanding balance paid within ten days of the statement date. After ten days, interest accrues at the rate of 18% annually.

14. **Credit Letter—Approval** ▪ Pat Brody, a film editor (8025 Briar Summit Drive, Los Angeles, CA 90046), has applied to you for credit. You checked out his credit history with the local credit bureau and found that he has a solid history of paying his bills on time. You hear from industry sources that he is very proud of his good reputation within the financial community. You approve him for a Reginald Card. Write him a letter, giving the needed information.

15. **Credit Letter—Denial** ■ The Prop Shop is a specialty store that supplies props to the television and movie industry. They have been in business for two years and have made several cash purchases of various items of clothing from you during that period. When they applied for credit, you made your usual inquiry to the local credit bureau and found that their history of payment has been erratic. Some months (when they were under contract to supply props for a production), they paid all bills immediately; at other times, they were as much as six months late in paying bills; and two rather substantial bills were finally written off as uncollectible.

    You decide that Reginald's should not offer credit to the Prop Shop at this time. However, because you would like to see the AH label featured in more movie and television scenes, you wish to retain them as a cash customer. In fact, as soon as their credit history improves, you would be happy to issue them a Reginald Card. Write them (515 South Flower Street, Los Angeles, CA 90071), and deny the owners a card for now.
16. **Credit Letter—Denial** ■ Dean Grant, a self-employed costume designer, has mailed in an application for the Reginald Card. Over the past few months he has become a regular in Reginald's. In fact, the salespeople now make it a point to call him when a new shipment of Alex Henry jackets arrives. He has never used a credit card in your store; instead, he pays by check for each purchase. When a salesperson suggested that Grant apply for the Reginald Card, he took home the application, filled it out, and sent it back, asking for a $2,000 credit line.

    According to his application, Grant has been self-employed for 4 months; he was out of work for 7 months before starting his own costume-design business. Previously, he worked for 9 months at Golden Studios and, before that, for 14 months at Down-Home Productions. Because of this employment background, you decide to deny Grant's application at this time. If his self-employment income remains steady for a year, however, you will reconsider his application at that time. Write Grant (at 1468 Melrose Avenue, Apartment 6G, Los Angeles, CA 90071) and let him know your decision.
17. **Collection Letter—Inquiry Stage** ■ Dean Grant's self-employment income rose steadily over the course of a year, and when he reapplied four months ago, you approved the application. He paid his first two credit bills promptly but has not yet paid his third. You received no response to the reminder notice you sent two weeks ago, which included a duplicate copy of his $479.36 statement. The salespeople tell you that Grant has not been seen in the store for several weeks. Write an inquiry letter asking for either the full amount or a partial payment of 50% of the balance, with the remainder due at the end of next month.
18. **Collection Letter—Appeal Stage** ■ It was just your luck—the Prop Shop is prospering; meanwhile Pat Brody has had a run of bad luck and cannot find steady work. As a result, his account is now $1,863.45 in arrears and has been for four months. You have already sent him three reminder letters and one inquiry letter—to no avail. Write the first letter in the appeal stage of the collection process.
19. **Collection Letter—Ultimatum Stage** ■ Despite your two well-written appeal letters, Pat Brody (see Exercise 18) has still not paid his bill; in fact, you've not heard from him at all. With interest, the unpaid balance is now $2,030.67 and is six months past due. If you do not receive his check for this amount within two weeks, you will institute a lawsuit and report the incident to the Greater Los Angeles Credit Bureau. Write him, giving him one final chance to pay before you take him to court.

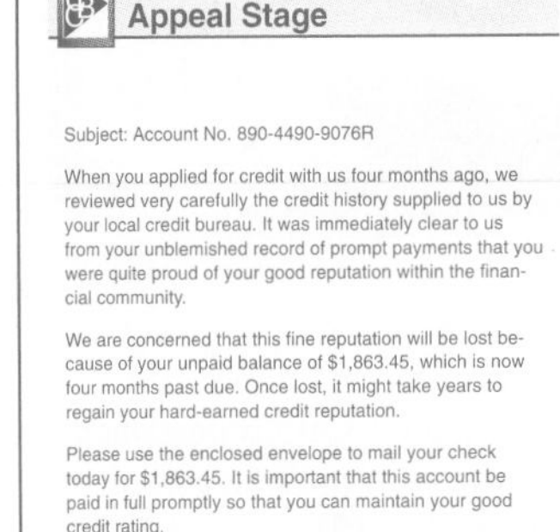
Collection Letter — Appeal Stage

Subject: Account No. 890-4490-9076R

When you applied for credit with us four months ago, we reviewed very carefully the credit history supplied to us by your local credit bureau. It was immediately clear to us from your unblemished record of prompt payments that you were quite proud of your good reputation within the financial community.

We are concerned that this fine reputation will be lost because of your unpaid balance of $1,863.45, which is now four months past due. Once lost, it might take years to regain your hard-earned credit reputation.

Please use the enclosed envelope to mail your check today for $1,863.45. It is important that this account be paid in full promptly so that you can maintain your good credit rating.

Ober, *Contemporary Business Communication*, 2d ed.

See Master 9.3, Exercise 18, Collection Letter—Appeal Stage, in the *Instructor's Resource Manual*.

20. **Goodwill Letter—Appreciation** ■ Think of a recent speech you heard and enjoyed—perhaps a speaker at a student organization meeting, a speaker sponsored by your university, a guest speaker in class, or some similar presentation. If necessary, do some research to locate a correct mailing address for this person. Then write this person a letter of appreciation, letting him or her know how much you enjoyed and benefited from his or her remarks. (If you have not heard a speech you enjoyed lately, write a former professor, expressing appreciation for what you learned in class). Use only actual data for this assignment.
21. **Congratulatory Letter—Promotion** ■ You have been doing business with Elinor Padawer of Eastern Temporary Services for the past four years. Whenever you needed a temporary secretary, Padawer sent you someone capable and enthusiastic. Padawer called you yesterday with the news that she has been promoted to branch manager of the office in Hartford, Connecticut, effective May 1. You will miss Padawer's personal touch and sense of humor; however, you know that she has been hoping for this promotion because her only brother lives in Hartford. Write Padawer a handwritten note of congratulations.
22. **Goodwill Letter—Sympathy** ■ You are the national marketing manager of your organization. You've just learned that the mother of John Statler, your West Coast manager, died this morning. Although you did not know her personally, you learn that she was 87 years of age and died instantly of a massive stroke. She was a widow and had lived alone in apparent good health, tending her small garden and enjoying life. Since John has already left for his mother's home and you cannot reach him by phone, send him a handwritten sympathy note.

CONTINUING CASE 9

The Good, The Bad, and the Persuaded

A possible solution to the Continuing Case is described in the *Instructor's Resource Manual*, p. 191.

Neelima Shrikhande has received a three-page memo from Eric Fox on the topic of word processing software. From the start, Urban Systems has taken a laissez-faire approach to the purchase of most software—letting each department decide which programs to purchase and support. As a result, at least five different word processing programs are presently being used at US.

Eric feels that having to support so many different programs is inefficient, time-consuming, and costly. He wants Neelima to standardize on one word processing program—namely, Version 6.0 of SuperDoc. SuperDoc is the best-selling Windows word processing program in the country. About half of the word processing users at the company presently use Version 5.2 of SuperDoc. The upcoming Version 6.0, although requiring a major relearning effort, promises to be even more useful.

Eric feels that now is an especially appropriate time to standardize on one program because three of the five word processing programs now in use at Urban Systems are being revised within the coming year. Because users will have to relearn a program anyway, Eric believes they might as well all learn the same package.

Neelima has thought over the advantages and disadvantages of standardizing on one package for the manufacturing, marketing, and administration units and for Amy Stetsky. She has concluded that standardizing on one program is a good idea. However, she has decided that the one package Urban Systems will approve for purchase and support is Version 3 of AutoMate. Although no one at US presently uses AutoMate, it is a powerful, easy-to-use software program that integrates word processing, data base, spreadsheet, graphics, communication, and E-mail functions.

Because the cost of each $275 AutoMate program will have to come from individual departmental budgets, Neelima will not require an immediate switchover. However, she hopes to persuade users to move to AutoMate as soon as possible. And in the future, she will not approve any purchases of additional copies of present software programs (current or new versions), except on a case-by-case basis.

Critical Thinking

1. What are the specific advantages of requiring all users at Urban Systems to use the same software program? Should Neelima include any of these advantages in her memo to the staff announcing this new policy?
2. What are the disadvantages of standardization? How can Neelima neutralize these disadvantages (or at least the most serious ones) when communicating her decision to the staff?

Writing Projects

3. Write the memo from Neelima to Eric in which she agrees with him on standardization but not on which software to adopt.
4. Considering the advantages and disadvantages of this decision, write the memo from Neelima to the staff in which she tells them of her decision and tries to persuade them to purchase copies of AutoMate for their staff as quickly as possible.

WORDWISE *Meanings*

- It's an age of paradox when we have mobile homes that don't move, sports clothes to work in and sweatshirts to loaf in, and junk food that costs more than real food.
- Is there a difference between *fat chance* and *slim chance*? between *loosen* and *unloosen*? between *flammable* and *inflammable*?
- Do you know the difference between *burn down* and *burn up?* Things that are fixed to the ground, like houses, *burn down;* things that are not fixed to the ground, like brush piles, *burn up.*

PART IV

REPORT WRITING

CHAPTER

10

Planning the Report

Communication Objectives

After you have finished this chapter, you should be able to

1. Describe four common characteristics of business reports.
2. Describe four common types of business reports.
3. Identify the three major purposes of business reports.
4. Analyze the audience for business reports.
5. Discuss the need for managing reports in the organization.

Associate publisher Richard Perkins faces 10 sales deadlines every year. As one of three associate publishers at *Worth*, a magazine geared toward the financial and lifestyle interests of upper-income consumers, Perkins supervises a team of salespeople who are responsible for convincing financial services firms and automotive marketers in Detroit and in the Northeast to buy advertising space. One of the reports he and his sales team use often is the proposal.

Why use proposals? "The ultimate purpose of a proposal is to sell," Perkins says. A proposal must be persuasive, but it can't substitute for a sales call even though it may pave the way for one. "When people can't meet with us, they may ask for a proposal," he explains. "Our proposal has to put the magazine's heart and soul on paper, because the proposal is representing the magazine at that moment to the readers."

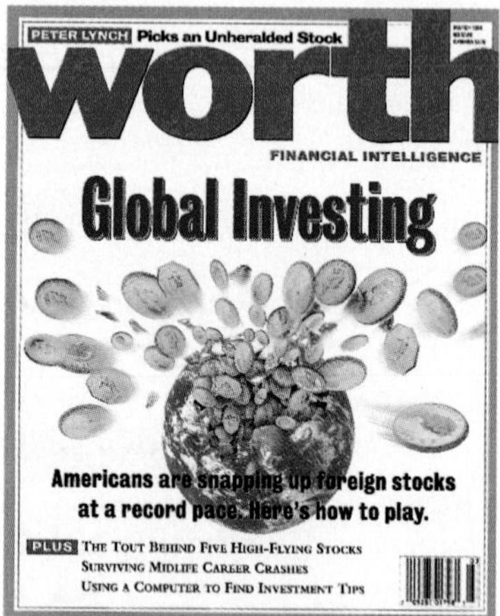

Perkins tailors each report to the reader's needs. "It's critical that the information in the proposal shows how the magazine is going to help the company solve a particular problem or achieve a particular goal," he says. For example, simply saying that an ad will be positioned next to an article doesn't show how the marketer will benefit. The *Worth* proposals explain that an ad works better when it's next to an editorial, because readers are likely to spend more time reading an editorial and will therefore be exposed to the ad for a longer period.

Perkins stresses that no two reports, especially proposals, are exactly alike. "Most marketers have different needs, so a generic approach does not work," he notes. "The customized approach is the key to success. We research each marketer's needs and show what we can do for that company."

Richard Perkins
Associate publisher,
Worth magazine,
New York City

At the end of a meeting with a potential customer, Perkins may leave behind a one- or two-page proposal that summarizes why that company should advertise in the pages of *Worth*. Even when a marketer is not initially considering *Worth*, Perkins may submit a brief report if he believes that advertising in a particular issue fits with that firm's goals. "This unsolicited proposal may be in the form of a letter that says,'Here are three reasons why you should consider *Worth*,' " he says. If his proposal is persuasive, it can open the door to a subsequent meeting, a potential sale, and ultimately an advertising schedule.

Like the other reports that Perkins writes, proposals have to be accurate, and they have to include sufficient evidence to support the conclusions. *Worth* proposals cite evidence based on syndicated research into the magazine's readership and reader purchasing patterns. The magazine also sponsors an in-depth study of subscribers, which gives advertisers and their agencies the chance to learn more about the magazine's audience. When Perkins includes this information in a report, he indicates the source so readers can have confidence in the data.

A chapter overview appears in the *Instructor's Resource Manual*, pp. 212–214.

Although the proposals Perkins prepares are not contracts, they have to reflect the magazine's integrity. "Proposals have to be written in the spirit of good business and with every intention to provide what you say you're going to provide," he says. "But the goodwill stops when you can't perform as promised. Companies aren't going to do business with you now, and they're not going to talk with you a second time, unless there's a good reason why you could not perform."

A wide variety of reports helps managers solve problems.

WHO READS AND WRITES REPORTS?

Consider the following routine informational needs of management and other personnel in a large, complex, and perhaps multinational organization:

- A sales manager at headquarters uses information provided by the field representatives to make sales projections.
- A busy vice president asks subordinates to gather and analyze information needed to make an operational decision.
- A personnel supervisor relies on the firm's legal staff to interpret government requirements for completing a compliance report.
- A manager prepares a proposal for the company to bid on a government project.
- An administrator informs all subordinates about a new company policy on hiring temporary personnel.

"If I see something that's only one page, I read it right away," admits Susan Bergan, vice president in the North American Investment Center at Citibank. "But if it's ten pages, it seems too long or weighty to read right away. It gets postponed." (From Diane Cole, "Putting Words to Work," *Savvy*, July 1985, pp. 32-33.)

Don't let reports substitute for face-to-face communication. If a misunderstanding arises or a problem needs to be addressed, talking to your colleague is usually much more effective than writing. (Adapted from Owen Edwards, "Send Me A Memo—or Better Yet, Don't," *Across the Board*, November 1992, pp. 12–13.)

These common situations show why a wide variety of reports have become such a basic part of the typical management information system (MIS). Because constraints are imposed by geographical separation, lack of time, and lack of technical expertise, managers must rely on others to provide the information, analysis, and recommendations they need for making decisions and solving problems. Because reports travel upward, downward, and laterally within the organization, both reading and writing reports are a typical part of nearly every manager's duties.

Reports can range from a fill-in form to a one-page letter or memo to a multivolume manuscript. For our purposes, we define a business report as an orderly and objective presentation of information that helps in decision making and problem solving. Note the different parts of our definition.

- The report must be *orderly* so that the reader can locate the needed information quickly.
- It must be *objective* because the reader will use the report to make decisions that affect the health and welfare of the organization.
- It must present *information*—facts, data. Where subjective judgments are required, as in drawing conclusions and making recommendations, they must be presented ethically and be based squarely on the information presented in the report.
- Finally, the report must aid in *decision making* and *problem solving*. There is a practical, "need-to-know" dimension in business reports that is sometimes missing in scientific and academic reports. Business reports must provide the specific information that management and other personnel need to make a decision or solve a problem. This goal should be uppermost in the writer's mind during all phases of the reporting process.

CHARACTERISTICS OF BUSINESS REPORTS

To better understand your role as a reporter of business information, consider the four following characteristics of business reports:

1. Reports vary widely—in length, complexity, formality, and format.
2. The quality of the report process affects the quality of the final product.
3. Reports are often a collaborative effort.
4. Accuracy is the most important trait of a report.

Let's examine each of these characteristics further.

Reports Vary Widely

There is no such document as a standard report—in length, complexity, formality, or format. The sales representative who spends five minutes completing a half-page call report showing which customers were contacted has completed a report. Likewise, the team of designers, engineers, and marketing personnel who spend six months preparing a six-volume proposal to submit to the U.S. Department of Defense has completed a report. The typical report lies somewhere in between. One analysis of 383 actual business reports found that 36% were one page, 37% were two to three pages, and 27% were four or more pages long.[1]

The typical business report is 1–3 pages long and written in narrative format.

Most reports are written using a standard narrative (manuscript) format, but reports may also be in the form of letters, memos, or preprinted forms. In addition to the body, a report may include such preliminary (prefatory) parts as a cover letter, title page, table of contents, and executive summary. Supplemental parts may include a list of references, appendixes, and index.

Although reports may be either oral or written, most important reports are written; even most oral reports are written initially. In other words, many reports are first written and then presented orally. Having the report available in written format is important for several reasons: (1) the written report provides a permanent record, (2) it can be read and reread as needed, and (3) the reader can control the pace—rereading the complex parts, marking the important points, and skipping some sections.

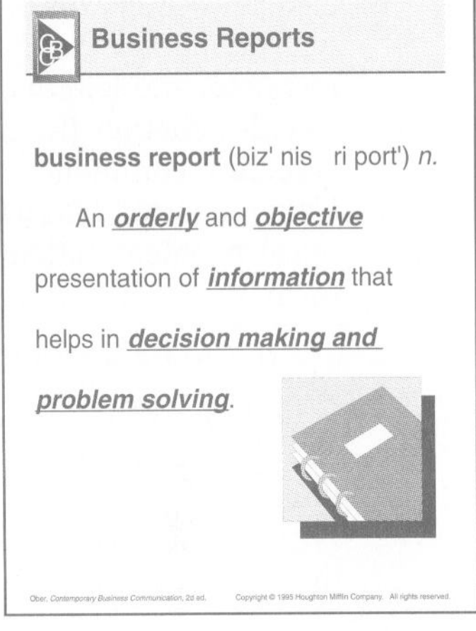
Business Reports
business report (biz' nis ri port') n.
An orderly and objective presentation of information that helps in decision making and problem solving.

See Transparency 10.1, Definition of a Business Report.

The Quality of the Process Affects the Quality of the Product

Writing a report involves much more than "writing a report." As contradictory as this statement might seem, consider a fairly routine report assignment—determining whether to recommend the purchase of Brand A, B, or C overhead projector for your organization's conference room. Before you can begin to write your recommendation, you must do your homework. At a minimum, you must (1) determine what technical features are most important to the users of the machines; (2) evaluate each brand in terms of these features; (3) compare the brands on such characteristics as cost, maintenance, reliability, and ease of use; and (4) draw a conclusion about which brand to recommend.

A report may be well written and still contain faulty data.

If at any step you make a mistake, your report will be worse than useless; it will contain errors that the reader will in turn rely on to make a decision. Suppose you interviewed only 2 of the 50 managers who will be using the new projector. The needs of these 2 managers may not be typical of the needs of the other 48. For example, both of these managers may need color projection, whereas the other 48 may need only black and white. Or suppose you failed to consider the amount of down time required by each brand. Regardless of its features, no machine can meet the needs of its users when it is inoperable.

As such situations show, your report itself (the end product of your efforts) can be well written and well designed, with appropriate charts and tables; yet, if the process by which the information was assembled and analyzed was defective, erroneous, or incomplete, the report will be also. The final product can be only as good as the weakest link in the chain of events leading up to the report.

Lego Group spent approximately $2 million gathering data on theme parks worldwide. Based on the findings, it decided to spend $100 million for a Lego theme park near San Diego. Lego Group hopes to attract 1.8 million visitors and is targeting its park toward children ages 3 to 13 and their parents. The opening is planned for 1999. (Richard C. Morais, "Babes in Toyland?" *Forbes*, January 3, 1994, pp. 70–71.)

CHECKLIST 11

The Reporting Process

PLANNING

1. Define the purpose of the report.
   a. Determine why the issue is important; what use will be made of the report; and what the time, resource, and length constraints are.
   b. Decide whether the purpose is to inform, analyze, or recommend.
   c. Using neutral language, construct a one-sentence problem statement, perhaps in question form.

2. Define the audience for the report.
   a. Is the report for an internal or external reader?
   b. Did the reader authorize the report or is it voluntary?
   c. What is the level of knowledge and interest of the reader?

DATA GATHERING

3. Determine what data will be required.
   a. Factor the problem statement into its components parts, perhaps stating each subproblem as a question.
   b. Determine what data will be needed to answer each subproblem.

4. Decide which methods to use to collect the needed data.
   a. Ensure that any secondary data used is current, accurate, complete, free from bias and misinterpretation, and relevant.
   b. If secondary data is not available, determine whether to collect primary data through survey, observation, or experimentation.
   c. Determine the most efficient means of collecting the needed data.

5. Collect the data.
   a. Ensure that all informational needs have been identified.
   b. Allot sufficient time to gather the needed data.
   c. Ensure that the collection methods will produce valid and reliable data.

ANALYSIS

6. Compile the data in a systemic and logical form, organizing it according to the subproblems.

7. Analyze each bit of data individually at first and then in conjunction with each other bit of data. Finally, look at all the data together to try to discern trends, contradictions, unexpected findings, areas for further investigation, and the like.

8. Construct appropriate visual aids.

WRITING

9. Draft the report.
   a. Consider the needs of the reader and the nature of the problem.
   b. Determine the organization, length, formality, and format of the report.
   c. Make sure the report is clear, complete, objective, and credible.

10. Revise the report for content, style, and correctness.

11. Use generally accepted formatting conventions to format the report in an attractive, efficient, and effective style.

12. Proofread to ensure that the report reflects the highest standards of scholarship, critical thinking, and care.

As indicated in Checklist 11, the reporting process involves planning, data gathering, analysis, and writing. We will cover the two major components of the planning stage—defining the purpose of the report and analyzing the audience—later in this chapter. The other three steps are discussed in the following chapters.

At Motorola's Communication (or Comm) Sector, employees and managers brainstorm to develop improvements for two-way radios. This scene is typical in business where a combination of talents joins to produce a collaborative report.

Reports Are Often a Collaborative Effort

Complex reports require the talents of many people.

Short, informal reports are usually a one-person effort. But many recurring reports in an organization are multiperson efforts. It is not likely, for example, that general management would ask a single person to study the feasibility of entering the generic-product market. Instead, a combination of talents would be needed—marketing, manufacturing, personnel, and the like.

Such joint efforts require well-defined organizational skills, time management, close coordination, and a real spirit of cooperation. Although more difficult to manage than individually written reports, collaborative reports offer these advantages:

- They draw on the diverse experiences and talents of many members.
- They increase each manager's awareness of other viewpoints.
- They typically result in higher-quality output than might be the case if a single person worked alone on a complex assignment.
- They can produce a final product in less time than would be possible otherwise.
- They help develop important networking contacts.
- They provide valuable experience in working with small groups.

Characteristics of Reports
▪ They vary widely in —
- length
- complexity
- formality
- format
▪ The quality of the process affects the quality of the product.
▪ They are often a collaborative effort.
▪ Accuracy is their most important trait.

See Transparency 10.2, Characteristics of Reports.

Accuracy Is the Most Important Trait

No report weakness—including making major grammatical mistakes, misspelling the name of the report reader, or missing the deadline for submitting the report—is as serious as communicating inaccurate information. It's a basic tenet of management that bad information leads to bad decisions.

Your most important job is to ensure that the information you transmit is correct.

And in such situations, the bearer of the "bad" news will surely suffer the consequences.

Suppose while conducting the research for the overhead projector report, you inadvertently noted that the bulbs for Brand A had a 100-hour life when, in fact, they have a 300-hour life. If operating costs were a major criterion, your final recommendation might be incorrect based on this simple careless error. It doesn't even matter how the error occurred—whether you made it or the typist made it. You are responsible for the project, and the praise or criticism of the results of your efforts will fall on you.

To achieve accuracy, follow these guidelines:

1. *Report all the relevant facts.* Errors of *omission* are just as serious as errors of *commission.* Don't mislead the reader by reporting just those facts that tend to support your position.

   Not: During the two-year period of 1993–1994, our return on investment averaged 13%.

   But: Our return on investment was 34% in 1993 but −8% in 1994, for an average of 13%.

2. *Use emphasis and subordination appropriately.* Your goal is to help the reader see the relative importance of the points you discuss. If you honestly think a certain idea is of minor importance, subordinate it—regardless of whether it reinforces or weakens your ultimate conclusion. Don't emphasize a point simply because it reinforces your position, and don't subordinate a point simply because it weakens your position.

Achieving Accuracy

- Report all the relevant facts.
- Use emphasis and subordination appropriately.
- Give enough evidence to support your conclusions.
- Avoid letting personal biases and unfounded opinions influence your interpretation and presentation of the data.

Ober, *Contemporary Business Communication*, 2d ed.

See Transparency 10.3, Achieving Accuracy.

3. *Give enough evidence to support your conclusions.* Make sure that your sources are accurate, reliable, and objective and that there is enough evidence to support your position. Sometimes your evidence (the data you gather) may be so sparse or of such questionable quality that you are unable to draw a valid conclusion. If so, simply present the findings and don't draw a conclusion. To give the reader confidence in your statements, discuss your procedures thoroughly and cite all your sources.

4. *Avoid letting personal biases and unfounded opinions influence your interpretation and presentation of the data.* Sometimes you will be asked to draw conclusions and to make recommendations, and such judgments inherently involve a certain amount of subjectivity. But you must make a special effort to look at the data objectively and to base your conclusions solely on the data. Avoid letting your personal feelings influence the outcomes. Sometimes the use of a single word can unintentionally convey bias.

   Not: The accounting supervisor *claimed* the error was unintentional.

   But: The accounting supervisor *stated* the error was unintentional.

COMMON TYPES OF REPORTS

Management needs comprehensive, up-to-date, accurate, and understandable information to achieve the organization's goals. Much of this information is communicated in the form of reports. The most common types of business reports are periodic reports, proposals, policies and procedures, and situational reports. Each of these types is discussed and illustrated below.

Periodic Reports

Periodic reports are recurring routine reports submitted at regular intervals.

Three common types of periodic reports are routine management reports, compliance reports, and progress reports.

Routine Management Reports Every organization requires its own set of recurring reports to provide the knowledge base from which decisions are made and problems are solved. Some of these routine management reports are statistical, consisting sometimes of just computer printouts; other management reports are primarily narrative. Routine management reports range from accounting, financial, and sales updates to various personnel and equipment reports.

Compliance Reports Many state and federal government agencies require companies doing business with them to file reports showing that they are complying with regulations in such areas as affirmative action, contacts with foreign firms, labor relations, occupational safety, and financial dealings. Completing these compliance reports is often mostly a matter of gathering the needed data and reporting it honestly and completely. Typically, very little analysis of the data is required.

Progress Reports Interim progress reports are often used to report the status of long-term projects. These reports are submitted periodically to management for internal projects, to the customer for external projects, and to the investor for an accounting of venture capital expenditures. Typically, these narrative reports (1) tell what work has been accomplished since the last progress report, (2) document how well the project is adhering to the schedule and budget, (3) describe any problems encountered and how they were solved, and (4) outline future plans (see Figure 10.1).

Proposals are persuasive reports written to an external audience.

Proposals

A **proposal** is a written report that seeks to persuade a reader from outside the organization to do as the writer wishes (internal proposals are a form of situational report and are discussed in a following section). For example, a manager may write a proposal that seeks to persuade a potential customer to purchase goods or services from the writer's firm, persuade the federal government to locate a new research facility in the headquarters city of the writer's firm, or persuade a foundation to fund a project to be undertaken by the writer's firm.

Proposals may be solicited or unsolicited. Government agencies and many large commercial firms routinely solicit proposals from potential suppliers. For example, the government might publish an RFP (request for proposal) stating its intention to purchase 5,000 microcomputers, giving detailed specifications regarding the features it needs on these computers,

FIGURE 10.1 Periodic Report

This progress report is submitted in letter format.

Davenport Construction Company

May 9, 19--

Mr. Ellis Shepherd, Chief
Manufacturing Department
Columbia-Collins, Inc.
680 Fourth Avenue
Louisville, KY 40202

Dear Mr. Shepherd:

Begins by giving the purpose and an overall summary.

This letter brings you up to date on the status of the construction of your new warehouse on Lafayette Street. As you will see, construction is on schedule and within budget, with no major problems foreseen.

Provides a brief background of the project.

<u>Background</u>: On January 3, 19--, Columbia-Collins contracted with Davenport Construction Company to construct a 48' x 96' frame warehouse at 136 Lafayette Street. Turn-key price was $96,500, with construction to begin on March 10 and to be completed no later than July 20. We agreed to provide interim progress reports on April 10, May 10, and June 10.

<u>Work Completed to Date</u>: We have now completed the following jobs:

Identifies the work completed, in progress, and still to be done.

1. By February 20, all of the plans had been approved by the appropriate regulatory agencies.

2. The foundation was poured on March 27.

3. The exterior of the building, including asphalt roofing and aluminum 1
siding, was completed on April 23.

<u>Work in Progress</u>: The following work has been started but has not yet been 2
completed:

Uses enumerations to make the items stand out.

1. The dry-wallers are installing the interior walls and partitions; they should be finished by the end of next week.

2. The electricians are installing the lighting, alarm system, outlets, and other electrical requirements.

3. The plumbers have installed the necessary fixtures in the washrooms and are installing the Amana high-energy-efficient heating/cooling unit.

3

144 North Limestone
Lexington, KY 40507
Phone: 606-555-9935

Grammar and Mechanics Notes

1 *exterior . . . was:* Ignore intervening words when establishing subject/verb agreement.
2 *been started but:* Do not insert a comma between parts of a compound predicate. 3 Leave at least a 1-inch bottom margin (most word processing programs do this automatically).

FIGURE 10.1 ***(Continued)***

4 Mr. Ellis Shepherd
Page 2
May 9, 19--

5 Work to Be Completed: From now until July 20, we will be completing these tasks:

1. The vinyl flooring will be installed by June 23.
2. The painters are scheduled to paint the interior on July 1-3.
3. The modular rack storage system is scheduled to be installed by July 15.
4. The landscaper will install all landscaping by July 15, including exterior lighting and an underground sprinkler system.
5. The city inspector and fire marshal will perform a final inspection on July 17.

Anticipated Problems or Decisions to Be Made: Listed below are a minor problem regarding a shipment delay and a decision that we need from you:

1. The modular rack storage system was ordered on April 3 and should have been delivered two weeks ago. I've spoken with our supplier and she assures me that the system will be delivered by May 12. If so, we should have no problems installing it on schedule.
2. By June 25, you will need to make a final color selection for the interior walls. The plan calls for one color. In making your selection, you might want to remember that the exterior of the warehouse is Colonial Blue (a pale blue), and the metal storage system is putty.

We appreciate the opportunity to build this facility for you and are sure you will enjoy using it. I will provide you another update in June.

Sincerely,

Mark Handorf

Mark Handorf
Project Supervisor

jit

Uses first- and second-person pronouns (appropriate in a letter or memo report).

Identifies problems and needed decisions.

Closes on a goodwill note.

Grammar and Mechanics Notes

4 Type the second page on plain paper, with a 1-inch top margin and a heading that identifies the recipient, page number, and date. 5 *Work to be Completed:* When underlining a phrase, underline the spaces between the words, but do not underline the punctuation that follows (for example, the colon).

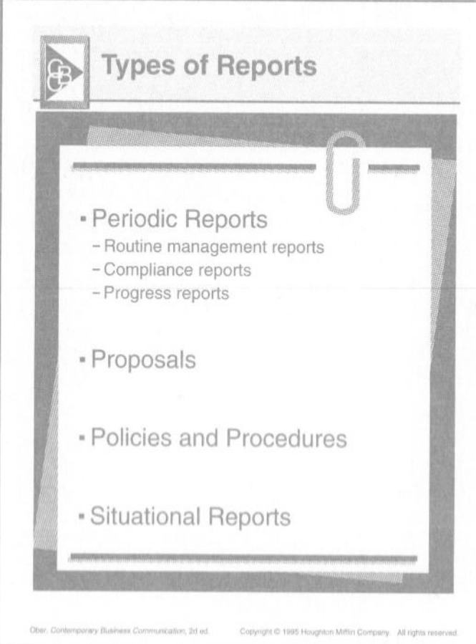

See Transparency 10.4, Types of Reports.

and inviting prospective suppliers to bid on the project. Similarly, the computer manufacturer that submits the successful bid might itself publish an RFP to invite a parts manufacturer to bid on supplying some component the manufacturer needs for these computers.

The unsolicited proposal differs from the solicited proposal in that it typically requires more background information and more persuasion. Because the reader may not be familiar with the project, the writer must present more evidence to convince the reader of the merits of the proposal.

The proposal reader is typically outside the organization. The format for these external documents may be a letter report, a manuscript report, or even a form report, with the form supplied by the soliciting organization. If the soliciting organization does not supply a form, it will likely specify in detailed language the format required for the proposal. Obviously, the reader's instructions should be followed explicitly. Despite the merits of a proposal, failure to follow such guidelines may be sufficient reason for the evaluator to reject it.

When writing a proposal, the writer must keep in mind that the proposal may become legally binding on the writer and his or her organization. In spelling out exactly what the writer's organization will provide, when, under what circumstances, and at what price, the proposal report writer creates the *offer* part of a contract which, if accepted, becomes binding on his or her firm.

Both solicited and unsolicited proposals require persuasion.

Proposals are persuasive documents, and all the techniques you learned about persuasion in letter and memo writing apply equally here.

- Give ample, credible evidence for all statements.
- Do not exaggerate.
- Provide examples, expert testimony, and specific facts and figures to support your statements.
- Use simple, straightforward, and direct language, preferring simple sentences and the active voice.
- Stress reader benefits. Remember that you are asking for something, usually a commitment of money; let the reader know what he or she will get in return.

As can be seen, having a good idea is not enough. You must be able to present that idea clearly and convincingly so that it will be accepted. The benefits of clear and persuasive writing go far beyond the immediate goal of securing approval for your current project. A well-written proposal increases both your visibility and your credibility with the reader and with the company on whose behalf you wrote the proposal.

Although proposals vary in length, organization, complexity, and format, the following sections are common:

1. *Background:* Introduce the problem you're addressing and discuss why it merits the reader's consideration. Provide enough background information to show that a problem exists and that you have a viable solution.
2. *Objectives:* Provide specific information about what the outcomes of the project will be. Be specific and honest in discussing what the reader will get for his or her commitment of resources.

The city of Atlanta's successful proposal to the International Olympic Committee to host the 1996 Games was elaborate and detailed, laying out plans for the numerous events that will take place in 11 separate sports sites.

3. *Procedures:* Discuss in detail exactly how you will achieve these objectives. Include a step-by-step discussion of what will be done, when, and exactly how much each component will cost.

Provide all the objective information the reader needs to make a decision.

4. *Qualifications:* Show how you, your organization, and any others who would be involved in conducting this project are qualified to do so. If appropriate, include testimonials or other external evidence to support your claims.
5. *Request for approval:* Directly ask for approval of your proposal. Depending on the reader's needs, this request could come either at the beginning or at the end of the proposal.
6. *Supporting data:* Include as an appendix to your proposal any relevant but supplementary information that might bolster your arguments.

As with all persuasive writing, the use of clear and objective language, ample evidence, and logical organization will help you achieve your goals. An example of a proposal for a small project is shown in Figure 10.2.

Policies and Procedures

Policies are broad operating guidelines that govern the general direction and activities of an organization; **procedures** are the recommended methods or sequential steps to follow when performing a specific activity. Thus, an organization's attitude toward promoting from within the firm would constitute a *policy,* and the steps to be taken to apply for a promotion

FIGURE 10.2 Proposal

THE WRITING DOCTOR 

Anne Skarzinski, President

September 16, 19--

Ms. Carolyn Soule, Employee Manager
Everglades National Corporation
1407 Lincoln Road, Suite 15
Miami, FL 33139

Dear Ms. Soule:

Begins by identifying the purpose of the letter.

Subject: Proposal for an In-House Workshop on Business Writing 1

I enjoyed discussing with you the business writing workshops you intend to sponsor for the engineering staff at Everglades National Corporation. As you requested, I am submitting this proposal to conduct a two-day workshop.

Background

Provides specific examples to show that a need exists.

On September 4-5, I interviewed four engineers at your organization and analyzed samples of their writing. My research indicates that your engineers
are typical of many highly trained specialists who know exactly what they want 2
to say but sometimes do not structure their communications in the most effective manner. Problems with audience analysis, organization, and overall writing style were especially apparent when they were communicating with nonspecialists either inside or outside the organization.

Suggests a reasonable solution.

Because your engineers devote much of their time to written communications, a workshop that teaches writing as a process should prove especially helpful. Thus, I propose that you sponsor a two-day writing workshop that I will
develop entitled "The Process of Business Writing." The workshop could be 3
held during any two days between November 26 and December 10; the two dates need not be consecutive.

Objectives

Tells exactly what the proposal should accomplish.

The workshop would help your engineers achieve these objectives:

1. Specify the purpose of a message and perform an audience analysis.

2. Determine what information to include and in what order to present it.

3. Choose the right words for a message and construct effective sentences and logical paragraphs.

4. Set an appropriate overall tone by using confident, courteous, and sincere
language; using appropriate emphasis and subordination; and stressing the 4
"you" attitude.

P.O. Box 1036 • West Palm Beach, FL 33402 • Phone (813) 555-1036

Grammar and Mechanics Notes

1 Leave one blank line before and after a subject line. 2 *highly trained specialists:* Do not hyphenate a compound modifier when the first word (an adverb) ends in -ly. 3 *"Business Writing."* Place the period inside the closing quotation mark. 4 *language; using:* Separate these items in a series with semicolons because the first item contains internal commas; note that all three items are in parallel form.

Ms. Carolyn Soule
Page 2
September 16, 19--

5. Revise a draft for content, style, correctness, and readability.

6. Format written communications in an efficient standard format.

Procedures

The enclosed outline shows the coverage of the course. The workshop would require a meeting room with participants seated at tables, an overhead projector, and a chalkboard or some other writing surface. The program would be divided into four half-day segments, each lasting three hours. The first two hours would be devoted to discussing the topics listed, followed by a 15-minute break. The final hour would consist of group and individual writing assignments, with appropriate guidance, discussion, and feedback provided.

Provides enough details to enable the reader to understand what is planned.

5 My fee for teaching the two-day workshop would be $2,000, plus expenses (including photocopying handouts, automobile mileage, and lunch on the workshop days). Your organization would be responsible for arranging and providing the morning and afternoon refreshments and lunch for the participants.

Discusses costs in an open and confident manner.

Qualifications

I would be responsible for planning and conducting the workshop. As you can see from the enclosed data sheet, I've had 15 years of consulting experience in business communications and have spoken and written widely on the topic. You may contact any of the individuals listed in the consulting section of the data sheet to learn their reactions to my previous presentations.

Highlights only the most relevant information from the enclosed data sheet.

Summary

6 My experience in working with professionals such as your engineers has taught me that they recognize the value of effective business communications and are motivated to improve their writing skills. The course should help your engineers become more effective communicators and more effective managers for Everglades National Corporation.

Shows how the reader will benefit from doing as asked.

I wish you much success in your efforts to upgrade the writing skills of your professional staff. Please call me at 555-1036 to let me know your reactions to this proposal.

Closes on a friendly, confident note.

7 Sincerely yours,

Anne Skarzinski

Anne Skarzinski, President

mje
Enclosures

Grammar and Mechanics Notes

5 *$2,000:* Omit the decimal point and zeroes for even amounts of money. Use a comma in all numerals of four or more digits except years. 6 *engineers has:* Use the singular verb (*has*) because the subject is *experience,* not *engineers.* 7 *Sincerely yours,:* Capitalize only the first word of a complimentary closing.

would constitute a *procedure.* Policy statements are typically written by top management; procedures are typically written by the managers and supervisors who are involved in the day-to-day operation of the organization.

Avoid making policies so general that they are of little practical help.

Begin a policy statement by setting the stage; that is, justify the need for a policy. Your justification should be general enough that the policy covers a broad range of situations but not so general that it has no real "teeth." Ensure that the reader knows exactly who is covered by the policy, what is required, and any other needed information. Finally, show how the reader, the organization, or *someone* benefits from this policy.

Write procedures in a businesslike, step-by-step format.

Write procedures in a businesslike but not formal manner, using the active voice. Imagine that you are explaining the procedure orally to someone. Go step by step through the process, explaining, when necessary, what should *not* be done as well as what should be done. Try to put yourself in the reader's shoes. How much background information is needed; how much jargon can safely be used; what reading level is appropriate? Anticipate questions and problems. Show and tell; that is, use pictures and diagrams as appropriate.

Don't assume that the reader knows anything about the process, but likewise don't assume that the reader is completely ignorant. Since it would be impossible to answer every conceivable question, concentrate on the high-risk components—those tasks that are difficult to perform or that have serious safety or financial implications if performed incorrectly.

Minimize the amount of conceptual information included, concentrating instead on the practical information. (Remember that a person can learn to drive a car safely without needing to learn how the engine actually propels the car forward.) Usually, numbered steps are appropriate, but use a narrative approach if it seems more effective.

Have typical users review and edit drafts of policies and procedures.

After you have written a draft, have several employees (who are typical of those who will use the document) read and comment on it. If the document is a policy, ask them questions to see if they really understand the policy. If it is a procedure, have them follow the steps to see if they work. Revise as necessary.

An example of a policy is given in Figure 10.3 and a procedure in Figure 10.4. Could you follow this procedure and get the desired results?

Situational Reports

Situational reports are one-of-a-kind reports.

In any organization, unique problems and opportunities appear that require one-time-only reports. Many of these situations call for information to be gathered and analyzed and for recommendations to be made. These so-called *situational reports* are perhaps the most challenging for the report writer. Because they involve a unique event, the writer has no previous reports to use as a guide; he or she must decide what types of information and how much information is needed and how best to organize and present the findings.

A sample situational report is shown in Figure 10.5. The guidelines presented in the upcoming report chapters are especially applicable to situational reports because of the many decisions that surround these one-of-a-kind reporting projects.

FIGURE 10.3 Policy

STANDARD PRACTICE GUIDE	SUBJECT: Alcohol	
	EFFECTIVE DATE: May 1, 1989	
CENTRAL MICHIGAN UNIVERSITY	NUMBER: U-803	PAGE 1 OF 1

SUBJECT: Alcohol

APPLIES TO: All Faculty, Staff, and Student Employees

Central Michigan University (CMU) is committed to providing a workplace which is free from the unauthorized or unlawful manufacture, distribution, dispensation, or possession of beverage alcohol.

It is the intent of CMU to provide a healthful, safe, and secure work environment. No employee will report to work evidencing any effects of alcohol consumption. Use of beverage alcohol is limited to those locations approved by CMU policy or licensed by the State of Michigan. Violations of this policy will result in disciplinary action, up to and including dismissal pursuant to university procedures relating to employee discipline.

All university employees will, as a condition of employment, abide by the terms of this policy.

CMU supports programs aimed at the prevention of alcohol abuse by its employees. CMU's Employee Assistance Program provides preventative programs, counseling for employees experiencing alcohol dependency problems, and assistance for problems related to alcohol abuse. Such counseling is confidential and unrelated to performance evaluations. Leaves of absence to obtain treatment may be obtained under the medical leave provision of the appropriate labor agreement, employee handbook, or policy.

Provides in the heading the necessary background information for filing and locating the policy.

Tells who is affected by the policy.

Introduces the topic and provides a setting.

Uses an appropriate balance between general and specific language to describe the policy.

Shows a caring attitude by closing with a discussion of reader benefits.

Grammar and Mechanics Note

Each organization usually has its own specific style for formatting policy statements. This university uses a preprinted form.

FIGURE 10.4 Procedure

Uses a descriptive title.

Begins with the act that starts the process and ends with the final result.

Contains only essential information.

Details, clearly and concisely, what steps are necessary and in what order.

Maintains parallel structure (complete sentences are not necessary).

PROCEDURE FOR HIRING A TEMPORARY EMPLOYEE

Actor	*Action*
Requester	1. Requests a temporary employee with specific, specialized skills by filling out Form 722, "Request for a Temporary Employee." 2. Secures manager's approval. 3. Sends four copies of Form 722 to buyer of special services in the Purchasing Department.
Buyer of Special Services	4. Sends all four copies to the labor analyst in the Budget Control Department.
Labor Analyst	5. Checks overtime figures of regular employees in the department or section. 6. If a question, contacts manager to learn of any upcoming increased workload. 7. If satisfied that the specific people and skills are necessary, checks budget. 8. If funds are available, approves Form 722, returns three copies to buyer, files the fourth copy.
Buyer of Special Services	9. Notifies outside temporary help contractor by telephone and follows up the same day with a confirming letter. 10. Negotiates a mutually agreeable effective date. 11. Contacts both Personnel and Furniture/Equipment sections by phone, telling them of the number of people, the effective dates, and the equipment requirements.
Personnel	12. Notifies Security, Badges, and Gate Guards. 13. Returns one copy of Form 722 to the requester. 14. Provides a temporary ID.
Contractor of Temporary Help Services	15. Furnishes assigned employee or employees with information on the job description, effective date, and the individual to whom to report.
Temporary Employee	16. Reports to receptionist one half-hour early on effective day.

Grammar and Mechanics Note

The format used is optional. This procedure uses a *playscript* format that clearly specifies what role each person plays in the process.

FIGURE 10.5 Situational Report

This situational report is shown in manuscript format.

THE FEASIBILITY OF A MIXED-USE DEVELOPMENT IN PHOENIX

David M. Beall

Mixed-use development (MXD) is a form of real estate that integrates three or more land uses (e.g., office, retail, hotel, residential, and recreation) in a high-density configuration with uninterrupted circulation
1 from one component to another. Interviews with seven local real estate developers and bankers and documents available from the Greater Phoenix Chamber of Commerce provided information on the feasibility of constructing a mixed-use development in Phoenix.

Begins by introducing the topic and discussing the procedures used. This report uses the indirect pattern, saving the recommendations until the end.

Low Land Prices and Low-Density Population Weaken MXD Potential

Land prices are a key economic factor in real estate development. High prices force developers to develop land with highly intensive uses to justify land costs. The much more expensive cost of an MXD makes economic sense only when high land prices justify the investment. Land prices in Phoenix, however, are relatively low compared to prices in other major U.S. cities.

The Galleria in Houston (a mixed-use development) and the Metrocenter in Phoenix (a large Phoenix shopping center) are similar-sized developments that offer an excellent comparison of how land prices dictate development
2 intensity. The Galleria site cost $85,000 per acre in 1964; six years later, the Metrocenter site cost only $10,000 per acre (Rogers, 1975, p. 148)

Successful MXDs tend to be located in high-density urban cores, where sufficient traffic is generated. The Phoenix market, on the other hand, is a low-density environment, as reflected by its horizontal urban form. Approximately 67% of the Phoenix housing stock is single-family homes, and relatively few commercial buildings reach over six stories high ("Inside Phoenix," 1992).

Is organized according to the criteria used to solve the problem.

3 **Financing Would Be Difficult**

The area bankers interviewed are reluctant to become involved with a new type of large-scale commercial development. Instead, they prefer to sponsor projects with which they have had experience. According to one banker, "A bank is only as successful as its last loan" (Weiss, 1994, p. 36). The bankers believe the economic risks associated with developing an MXD outweigh the rewards. They cite such adverse factors as high development costs, complexity, and lack of expertise (Allen, 1994; Gorman, 1994; Oaks, 1994).

Uses the author-date format for citing references (see Reference Manual).

Davenport Should Delay MXD Project

Because of Phoenix's relatively low land costs and low-density population and the difficulty of securing financing, Davenport should not pursue a mixed-use development in the Phoenix area now. However, because the Southwest is growing so rapidly, Davenport should reevaluate the Phoenix market in three years.

Closes by making a recommendation based on the findings presented.

Grammar and Mechanics Notes

1 *real estate developers:* Do not hyphenate a compound noun (*real estate*) that comes before another noun (*developers*). 2 *site:* location (*cite:* "to quote"; *sight:* "to view"). 3 Be consistent in formatting report side headings; there is no one standard format (other than consistency). This report uses "talking" headings, which identify both the topic and the major conclusion of each section.

PURPOSES OF REPORTS

At the outset, you need to determine why you are writing the report. Business reports generally aim to either inform, analyze, or recommend.

Informational reports present information without analyzing it.

Informing Informational reports relate objectively the facts and events surrounding a particular situation. No attempt is made to analyze and interpret the data, draw conclusions, or recommend a course of action. Most periodic reports, as well as policies and procedures, are examples of informational reports. In most cases, these types of reports are the easiest to complete. The report writer's major interest is in presenting all of the relevant information objectively, accurately, and clearly, while refraining from including unsolicited analysis and recommendations.

Analytical reports interpret the information.

Analyzing One step in complexity above the informational report is the analytical report, which not only presents the information but also analyzes it. Data by itself may be meaningless; it must be put into some context before readers can make use of it. As social forecaster John Naisbitt has remarked, "We are drowning in information, but starved for knowledge."[2]

Consider, for example, this informational statement: "Sales for the quarter ending June 30 were $780,000." Was this performance good or bad? We cannot possibly know unless the writer *analyzes* the information for us. Here are two possible interpretations of this statement:

For an exercise on the purposes of reports and audience analysis, see Video Case Study 3, Lotus Notes.

> Sales for the quarter ending June 30 were $780,000, up 7% from the previous quarter. This strong showing was achieved despite an industry-wide slump and may be attributed to the new "Tell One—Sell One" campaign we introduced in January.

> Sales for the quarter ending June 30 were $780,000, a decline of 5.5% from the same quarter last year. All regions experienced a 3 to 5% *increase* except for the western region, which experienced an 18% decrease in sales. John Manilow, western regional manager, attributes his area's sharp drop in sales to the budgetary problems now being experienced by the state governments in California and Arizona.

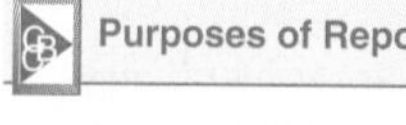

Purposes of Reports

✓ **Informing —**
Nearly 2,400 viewers and organizations pledged a total of $213,000 during our recent drive.

✓ **Analyzing —**
This amount represented an increase of 11% from last year's total.

✓ **Recommending —**
As a result of the success of this effort, I recommend we delay our fall drive for two months.

See Transparency 10.5, Purposes of Reports.

The report writer must be careful that any conclusions drawn are reasonable, valid, and fully supported by the data presented. Although the writer must attempt to avoid inserting his or her own biases or preexisting opinions into the report, analysis and interpretation can never be completely objective. The report writer makes numerous decisions that call for subjective evaluations. Note the difference in effect of the following two statements, which contain the same information but in reversed order:

Original: Although it is too early to determine the effectiveness of Mundrake's efforts, he believes the steps he is taking will bring Limerick's absentee rate down to the industry average of 3.6% by December.

Reversed: Although Mundrake believes the steps he is taking will bring Limerick's absentee rate down to the industry average of 3.6% by December, it is too early to determine the effectiveness of his efforts.

The original order leaves a confident impression of the probable success of the steps taken, whereas the reversed order leaves a much more negative impression.

Recommending Recommendation reports add the element of endorsing a specific course of action (see, for example, the situational report in Figure 10.5). The writer presents the relevant information, interprets it, and then suggests a plan of attack. The important point is that you must let the data be the basis for any conclusions you draw and any recommendations you make. You want to analyze and present your data so that the truth, the whole truth, and nothing but the truth emerges. In other words, avoid the temptation of beginning with a preconceived idea and then marshaling and manipulating data to support it.

Recommendation reports propose a course of action.

For an exercise on revising an analyst's report, refer students to the *Study Guide*, pp. 145–147.

In a sense, your final recommendation is only the tip of the iceberg, but it is a very visible tip. The reasonableness, clarity, and strength of your recommendation can have major implications for your career and for your organization's well-being.

AUDIENCE ANALYSIS

The audience for a report—the reader or readers—is typically homogeneous. Many times, of course, the audience is one person; but even when it is not, the audience usually consists of people with similar levels of expertise, background knowledge, and the like. Thus, you can, and should, develop your report to take into account the needs of your reader. In doing so, you will need to consider the following elements.

Audience Analysis

- Internal or External Audience
- Authorized or Voluntary Report
- Level of Knowledge and Interest

Ober, Contemporary Business Communication, 2d ed. Copyright © 1995 Houghton Mifflin Company. All rights reserved.

See Transparency 10.6, Audience Analysis.

Internal Versus External Audiences

Internal reports are written for readers within the organization and are usually less formal than external reports, for which the reader might be a customer, potential customer, or government agency. Internal reports also typically require less background information and can safely use more technical vocabulary than external reports, which are often more sensitive to public relations issues.

Internal reports are also directional and are aimed at the writer's superiors, peers, or subordinates. The strategy used must be appropriate for the audience's position. For example, reports often have a costs-and-profits tone when directed to superiors, a conversational tone when directed to peers, and an emphatic tone when directed to subordinates.

Authorized Versus Voluntary Reports

Authorized reports are written at the specific request of some higher authority. Thus, the reader has an inherent interest in the report. Voluntary reports, on the other hand, are prepared on the writer's own initiative. Therefore, the reader needs more background information and frequently more persuasive evidence than do readers of authorized reports.

Internal reports are generally less formal and contain less background information than external reports.

SPOTLIGHT ACROSS CULTURES

Context in International Reports

Most business reports are written for a relatively homogeneous audience. However, in the international arena the reader and writer often have different cultural viewpoints. The greater the amount of knowledge, perceptions, and attitudes the reader and writer share (that is, the higher the *context* of the communication exchange), the less important it is for report writers to directly express *everything* they wish to communicate. Conversely, the less the reader and writer have in common, the more they need to convey every nuance of their meaning explicitly through words—that is, the less they can assume to be implicitly understood.

Contexting can be categorized as either high or low. When report writers have considerable knowledge and experience in common with their readers, their reports are generally *highly contexted.* In highly contexted reports, what the writer chooses *not* to put into words is still essential to understanding the actual message intended. But the writer assumes that what is not said is actually *already understood.*

When report writers rely relatively little on shared knowledge and experience, their report is *low contexted.* As a result, in low-context exchanges more information must be explicitly stated than in high-context ones. Thus, low-context cultures tend to rely on *direct* communication; they often consider the indirect pattern a waste of time or a strain on the receiver's patience. High-context cultures, on the other hand, tend to rely on *indirect* communication to smooth over interpersonal differences and to keep from losing face in a conflict situation. They often consider directness rude and offensive.

To a large extent, contexting is a culturally learned behavior, with the degree of context varying from culture to culture. As shown below, Germans and German-speaking Swiss tend to be low-context cultures (all important information is explicitly stated) whereas the Japanese, Arabic, and Latin American people tend to be high-context cultures (much important information is implicitly assumed).

As Stella Ting-Toomey has noted, "In the HCC [high-context culture] system, what is not said is sometimes more important than what is said. In contrast, in the LCC [low-context culture] system, words represent truth and power." Competent communicators ensure that the degree of explicitness, the amount of detail, and the assumptions

Importance of Context in Different Cultures

Authorized reports may be either periodic or special. Periodic reports are submitted on a recurring, systematic basis. Very often they are form reports, with space provided for specific items of information. Readers of periodic reports need little introductory or background information because of the report's recurring nature. Readers of special, one-time reports, on the other hand, need more explanatory material because of the uniqueness of the report.

Voluntary reports require more background information and more persuasion than authorized reports.

Level of Knowledge and Interest

Is the reader already familiar with your topic? Will he or she understand the terms used, or will you need to define them? If you have a heterogeneous audience for your report, striking an appropriate balance in level of detail given will require careful planning.

Gear the amount of information presented and the order in which it is presented to the needs of the reader.

Most reports are written in the direct pattern, with the major conclusions and recommendations given up front (but see, however, the Spotlight Across Cultures). This is especially true when you know the reader is interested in your project or will likely agree with your opinions and judgments. Reports that make a recommendation with which the reader may disagree are often written in the indirect pattern because you want the reader to study the reasons first. The reader will be more likely to accept or at least consider the recommendation if he or she has first had an opportunity to study its rationale.

For an extended discussion of international issues, see "Diversity and Communication" in Chapter 2, pp. 34–39.

MANAGING REPORTS

Throughout this chapter, a strong case has been made for the increasingly important role that business reports play in the successful management of the contemporary organization. However, too much of a good thing is a bad thing. Without proper management, reports, especially computer printouts, can backfire, becoming a nuisance and contributing to information overload.

In an effort to reduce information overload at AT&T, Victor A. Pelson, president of AT&T's General Markets Group, has banned thick, bound reports from offices and fancy slide shows from presentations. Because employees can digest only a limited amount of information, he wants to be sure that they are exposed only to information that is relevant to their jobs.

With the increasing availability of data and the ease with which that data can be manipulated, copied, and distributed, managers sometimes tend to generate every type of report possible and then submit them all to higher-level management. Some managers seem to devote more energy to generating reports than to analyzing and making use of their contents.

Thus, someone in the organization—preferably someone in higher management—should be assigned the task of controlling reports. Periodically (typically, annually) this individual should make an inventory of all recurring reports and determine the continuing usefulness of each one. Some reports may be eliminated altogether, some modified, others merged, and, where justified, new reports authorized.

This review process will guarantee that business reports continue to serve management rather than vice versa. With or without such controls, all managers should ensure that the reports they write serve some actual purpose, stick to that purpose, and avoid including extraneous computer data just because it's easily available.

Ensure that all reports serve a specific purpose, that only needed information is included, and that all recipients actually need the report.

MICROWRITING

A Proposal

PROBLEM

You and your colleagues who teach business communication at Valley State College are interested in setting up a business writer's hotline—a telephone service that will provide answers to grammar, mechanics, and format questions from people who call in. You see this as a way of providing a much-needed service to local business people, as well as a way of providing positive public relations for your institution.

Each faculty member is willing to donate time to answer the phones, but you will need funds for telephone lines, answering machines, reference books, advertising, and the like. You decide to apply for a grant from the A. C. Reynolds Foundation to fund the project for one year. After that, if the hotline is successful, you will either reapply for funds or ask the Valley State College administration to fund the continuing costs. For requests less than $3,000, the foundation requires a simple narrative report explaining and justifying the request.

PROCESS

1. What is the background of the problem?

   Every writer has occasional questions about writing style but may not have a reference book or style manual available to answer the question. We know there is a need for such a service because we frequently get calls from people on campus with these questions. Although several grammar hotlines operate nationally, none is available within a 200-mile radius of Portland.

2. What will be the outcome of the project?

   A telephone service that will be available free of charge 24 hours a day to answer any question regarding business writing.

3. Describe the audience for this report and the implications for structuring your report.

   The A. C. Reynolds Foundation makes grants to nonprofit organizations in the Portland area, mostly for small projects of less than $10,000 each. Because of the foundation's small size and personal orientation, a direct and personal (rather than scholarly) writing style will be used. Since there is no reason to expect that the foundation holds a negative attitude toward this project, the proposal will be written in a direct pattern—the request for funds will be made at the beginning of the report.

4. Describe how the hotline will work.

    a. A faculty member will answer phoned-in questions each weekday from 10 a.m. until 2 p.m. Questions phoned in at other times will be recorded on an answering machine.
    b. A phone line with a call-forwarding feature will be installed.
    c. The faculty will agree on which books should serve as the standards of reference.
    d. The faculty will attempt to answer any reasonable question about grammar, mechanics, format, and the like but will not review or edit anyone's writing and will not answer questions requiring extensive research.

5. What are the advantages of this project?

    a. Enhancing the college's reputation as an asset to the community.
    b. Providing a genuine service to business writers.
    c. Aiding business productivity by decreasing communication problems.
    d. Helping the business communication faculty stay abreast of their fields.

6. What will the project cost?

    The faculty members will donate their time. Two copies of each of the reference books needed will cost $123.50. The telephone line will cost $61.30 monthly, and the long-distance charges for returning calls are estimated at $55 monthly. An answering machine costs $119.50. Monthly advertisements in the campus newspaper and in the local newspaper are estimated at $62.50.

7. What are the qualifications of those involved in this project?

    Each of the 12 faculty members has a doctoral degree, with an average of eight years of teaching business communication and related courses.

PRODUCT

THE BUSINESS WRITER'S HOTLINE

A Proposal Submitted by Professor Steve Harland
Valley State College of Portland, Oregon
March 15, 19--

All business writers have occasional questions about writing style. Indeed, the business communication faculty at Valley State College frequently receives calls asking questions about punctuation, subject-verb agreement, the correct format for business correspondence, and the like. Although several grammar hotlines operate nationwide to answer such questions, none is presently available within a 200-mile radius of Portland.

Thus, the business communication faculty of Valley State College requests that a grant for $2,388.60 be awarded for the purpose of establishing and operating a Business Writer's Hotline for one year to benefit the Portland community and Valley State College students, faculty, and staff.

Outcome of the Project

The project will fund the establishment and operation of a Business Writer's Hotline in which qualified faculty members answer telephone inquiries from business writers on the subject of grammar, mechanics, and format. The service will operate at no cost to users and will be available each day that Valley State College is in session. This hotline will

1. Increase business productivity by lessening the chance that an error in writing will cause communication problems, needless delays, or even incorrect decisions.

2. Provide a service to business writers (including college students, faculty, staff, business people, and the general community) who presently have no convenient way of getting their questions answered.

3. Enhance the college's reputation as an asset to the local community.

4. Help the faculty consultants keep abreast of the kinds of writing decisions that are causing problems for the university and business community.

Procedures

When school is in session, a faculty member will be available to answer any phoned-in questions every weekday from 10 a.m. until 2 p.m. Questions phoned in at other times will be recorded on an answering machine, with a telephone response provided by the end of the next working day.

A dedicated telephone line with a call-forwarding feature will be installed. Faculty members on duty can simply have the calls forwarded to their offices so that they can work on other matters when no phone calls are being received.

Faculty consultants will attempt to answer any reasonable question regarding grammar, mechanics (including punctuation and spelling), document format, and the like. They will not review or edit anyone's writing and will not be available to answer questions that will require extensive research. Three books will serve as the standard references: *The Chicago Manual of Style, The Associated Press Stylebook and Libel Manual,* and *The American Heritage Dictionary.* Other reference works will be consulted as needed.

The hotline will begin operating the first day of the school year after the award of the grant and will continue for one year. A small ad announcing the availability of this service will be placed monthly in the *Valley State Voice* and in the *Portland Herald.*

A detailed log will be maintained showing the amount of use and types of questions answered. These records will show whether the service is fulfilling a need and whether a need exists for additional collegiate education or industry training in business writing.

Budget

The following budget is projected for the Business Writer's Hotline for the first year of operation:

Purchase of two copies each of the three standard reference books	$ 123.50
Purchase of one telephone-answering machine	119.50
Rental of one telephone line (12 mo. @ $61.30)	735.60
Long-distance charges (12 mo. estimated @ $55)	660.00
Newspaper advertisements (12 mo. @ 62.50)	750.00
Total	$2,388.60

Note: The faculty consultants will provide their time at no cost to the project.

Personnel Qualifications

Each of the 12 faculty members who will act as a voluntary consultant has a doctoral degree and an average of eight years of experience teaching business communication and related courses. Thus, the faculty members have had much experience in answering the types of questions likely to be encountered.

The curriculum vitae of each instructor is provided in Appendix A.

Summary

The establishment of a Business Writer's Hotline will increase the communication skills and the quality of writing of the local community. The recurring cost of $2,145.60 is less than $10 per day and 40 cents per hour for the 45 weeks of 24-hour service. This cost is a small amount to pay for the benefits that will be provided to area business writers, the college, and the faculty volunteers.

SUMMARY

Reading and writing reports are a typical part of nearly every manager's duties. Reports vary greatly in length, complexity, formality, and format, and many are collaborative efforts. Accuracy is the most important trait of all reports, and the quality of the process affects the quality of the final product.

The most common types of reports are periodic reports (including routine management, compliance, and progress reports), proposals, policies and procedures, and situational reports. The purpose of each type of report may be either to inform, to analyze, or to recommend. Because the audience for a specific report is typically homogeneous, you should develop your report to take into account the reader's needs—in terms of level of knowledge and interest, internal versus external readers, and authorized versus voluntary reports.

Reports can become a drain on the organization's resources if they are not controlled. Management should therefore periodically inventory and review all reports to ensure that only needed reports are being generated and distributed and that they contain the information needed to help solve problems and make decisions.

KEY TERMS

For an exercise on matching terms, refer students to the *Study Guide*, p. 142.

Policy A broad operating guideline that governs the general direction or activities of an organization.

Procedure The recommended methods or sequential steps to be followed when performing a specific activity.

Proposal A written report that seeks to persuade a reader outside the organization to do as the writer wants.

REVIEW AND DISCUSSION

The answers to the review and discussion questions appear in the *Instructor's Resource Manual*, beginning on p. 215.

1. **Communication at *Worth* Magazine Revisited** ▪ Proposals help Richard Perkins and his salespeople persuade companies to buy advertising space in *Worth*. Each report is geared to the specific needs and interests of the company being addressed, so no two are exactly alike.
   a. Why would marketers want to know the source of any evidence included in Perkins's reports?
   b. What supporting information might Perkins include in the appendix of a proposal to sell advertising space to a bank?
   c. What background information might Perkins include in an unsolicited proposal to a company that has never advertised in *Worth*?
2. Why do business reports play such an important role in the contemporary organization?
3. Define and give an example of each of the four types of common business reports.
4. What is meant by the statement, "There is no such document as a standard report."
5. What is meant by the statement, "Writing a report involves much more than writing a report"?

6. What are the advantages of collaboratively written reports?
7. Give four guidelines for achieving accuracy in a report.
8. Describe three types of situational reports.
9. Give an example of a solicited proposal and an unsolicited proposal.
10. What sections are typical in a proposal?
11. Give an example of a policy and a related procedure.
12. How much detail should be given in a procedure?
13. Why should reports be controlled?

EXERCISES

1. Microwriting a Proposal—Starting a Student-Run Business ■

Exercise 1 is linked with Exercise 1 of Chapter 14. Sample solutions for Exercises 1–12 appear in the *Instructor's Resource Manual*, pp. 216–220.

PROBLEM

You are the president of the Hospitality Services Association, a campus organization made up of students planning careers in hotel and motel management, tourism, and the like. You've just received a copy of a memo from the provost at your university addressed to the presidents of all campus organizations. The university is seeking proposals from student organizations to run a part-time business, tentatively named University Hosts, which would provide local services and organize various events for campus visitors.

For example, when the admissions office lets University Hosts know that a prospective student and his or her family will be visiting the campus, UH would immediately contact the family and offer to provide any reasonable service to help campus visitors enjoy their stay and receive a favorable impression of the institution. The service would be aimed at potential students and their families, alumni, donors, prospective faculty and staff members, and visiting legislators.

You feel that HSA would be the most logical organization to run this enterprise for the university. Your executive council has authorized you to submit a proposal to the provost. Personnel time (to be supplied by student members of HSA) would be billed at $10 per hour; a 10% surcharge would be added to the actual cost of all services provided (for example, tickets to campus or local events); automobile expenses would be billed at 22 cents per mile; and other charges would be billed at actual cost. Depending on the purpose of the campus visits, costs of the services would be billed either to the university or to the actual clients.

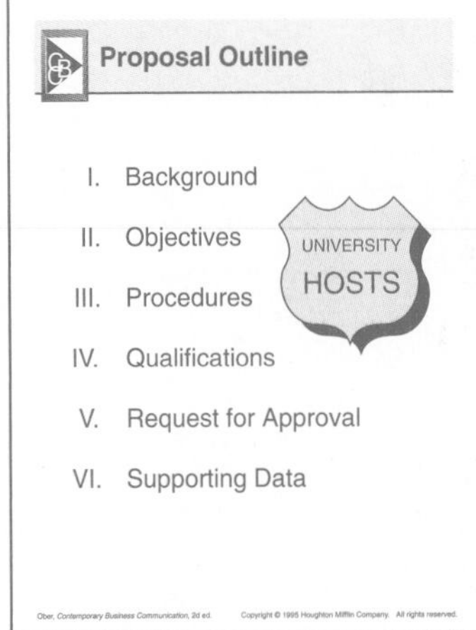

Proposal Outline
I. Background
II. Objectives
III. Procedures
IV. Qualifications
V. Request for Approval
VI. Supporting Data
UNIVERSITY
HOSTS

See Master 10.1, Exercise 1, Microwriting a Proposal, in the *Instructor's Resource Manual*.

PROCESS

a. What is the purpose of your report?
b. Describe your audience.
c. Is this a solicited or unsolicited proposal?
d. List the major advantages of this project and indicate how someone other than HSA will benefit from each advantage.
e. What costs are involved?
f. How are HSA members qualified to operate this business?
g. Will you request approval for this project at the beginning or end of your proposal? Why?
h. Compose an effective first sentence for your proposal.
i. What topics will you cover and in what order? Compose the specific headings for each topic.

PRODUCT

Prepare a three- to five-page typed proposal in memorandum format and submit it, along with your answers to the process questions, to your instructor. (You may invent any reasonable data needed.)

2. **Small Business—Reporting Needs** ▪ Interview the owner/operator of a small business (10 to 50 employees) in your area. Determine the extent and types of reports written and received by employees in this firm. Write a memo report to your instructor summarizing your findings.
3. **Progress Report—Market Analysis** ▪ Your market research firm, National Collegiate Solutions, Inc. (NCSI), was recently hired by Archway Publications, a publisher of teen magazines. Edgar Martin, Archway's vice president of marketing, wants you to analyze the market for a proposed monthly magazine geared toward college students. As director of research for NCSI, you agreed to submit a progress report at the end of each month. It's April 30 (you started the project on April 5), so it's time to tell Martin what your firm has accomplished so far.

   First, you developed a survey questionnaire to gather data on what college students like and dislike about the magazines currently available. After testing this questionnaire on 35 students to be sure the questions were correctly phrased, you made appropriate revisions and obtained Archway's approval of the final instrument. Then you began the lengthy process of conducting 50 face-to-face interviews on each of 12 campuses across the country. By April 29, you had scheduled and completed the 50 interviews on three campuses; you expect to schedule and complete the remainder of the interviews by June 1. All interviews are going according to schedule. You plan to submit a brief synopsis of your findings by June 6, and by June 20 you will submit a full report including conclusions and recommendations.

   Using a letter format, write a progress report to Martin, whose company is located at 15097 Dana Avenue, Cincinnati, OH 45207.
4. **Collaborative Writing—Common Report Types** ▪ Four types of business reports were identified in this chapter. Working in a group of three to five students, obtain a sample of three report types, perhaps from someone at the university or where you work. Analyze these reports for such factors as the following:

   a. Purpose (to inform, analyze, or recommend)
   b. Target audience
   c. Length, format, and degree of formality
   d. Clarity, completeness, and accuracy of the information
   e. Authorship (individual or collaborative)

   Write a two-page memo report to your instructor summarizing your findings.
5. **Situational Report—Library Hours** ▪ You are one member of a four-student team that has volunteered to look into the advantages and disadvantages of extending the college library's hours the week before each long break and the final week of each term or semester. You have heard some students complain that the evening hours are too short; they would especially like to see the library open later during periods when most students are working on research papers, examinations, and projects. Of course, longer hours would have an effect on payroll, staff scheduling, and other aspects of the library's operation. Your team will examine the issues, report your findings, and suggest how the administration might proceed.

   Team up with three other students to plan a situational report for your school's head of administrative services. Prepare a one- to two-page memo to your instructor indicating the purpose of your report, the audience, and the data that you will gather. Also list the issues you expect to examine. Will this situational report include recommendations? Why or why not?

6. **Procedure—Giving Directions** ■ As director of the student union at your institution, you frequently receive calls from for-profit and nonprofit organizations inquiring about reserving a room for special meetings. Sometimes these organizations want food service such as a meal or refreshments, sometimes they want a cash bar, and at other times they simply want an attractive meeting room. Of course, they're also interested in the cost, availability of parking, use of audiovisual equipment, deadlines, forms that need to be completed, and the like.

   Prepare a procedure that can be distributed to inquirers that will answer their most frequent questions and that will take them through the procedure from initial inquiry through paying the final bill (if there is one). Use the actual practices in effect at your institution. Decide on an effective format for the written procedure report.

7. **Policy—Using University Facilities** ■ Refer to Exercise 6. Assume that your institution is establishing a policy that only nonprofit organizations may reserve meeting rooms on campus and that reservations by any on-campus groups take precedence over those from off-campus groups. The reason for this policy is to avoid competing with local commercial establishments and to prevent overcrowding of campus facilities. Prepare a policy statement (University Policy No. 403) for the board of trustees to consider at its next meeting.

8. **Audience Analysis—Curriculum** ■ The dean of your school of business has asked you, as president of the leading business honorary society on campus, to write a report evaluating the advantages and disadvantages of adding another required English course to the curriculum for all business majors.

   Write out what you know (or can learn) about the dean that will help make your report more effective. Include such considerations as internal versus external audience, authorized versus voluntary report, and level of knowledge and interest of the reader. Discuss specifically how each item of information will influence your decisions about content, format, organization, and the like.

Audience Analysis
1. Report is internal, so less background information is needed, and a memo format is appropriate.
2. Report is authorized, so the reader has some inherent interest in the topic; a direct organizational plan is appropriate.
3. Reader is knowledgeable about the subject.
4. Because the report is for a university administrator, a more formal style is appropriate.
5. Because university administrators are busy, conciseness is important.
6. Because the information is being used for making a decision, it must be accurate.
7. Because an evaluation of the advantages and disadvantages has been asked for, analysis is necessary.
Ober, *Contemporary Business Communication*, 2d ed. Copyright © 1995 Houghton Mifflin Company. All rights reserved.

See Master 10.2, Exercise 8, Audience Analysis, in the *Instructor's Resource Manual.*

9. **Audience Analysis—Market Research** ■ Resume the role of director of research for National Collegiate Solutions, Inc. (see Exercise 3 above). Now that all the student interviews have been completed and the data analyzed, you are planning the final report of your findings, conclusions, and recommendations. Analyze your audience for this report. Is the audience internal or external? Is this a solicited or unsolicited report? What is the level of interest of the reader? Should you use a formal or informal style? Will you use a memo, letter, or manuscript format for this report? What organizational plan is appropriate? Prepare a one- to two-page summary of your answers to these questions.

10. **Report Management—Large Business** ■ Interview the records manager at a large business in your area (personally or by phone). Determine what policies the organization follows to control reports, especially recurring reports, in terms of need, frequency, length, distribution, and the like. Write a memo to your instructor summarizing your findings.

11. **Managing Reports—Control Policy** ■ Assume the role of the records manager you interviewed in Exercise 10 above. Your new boss, Cathy Saunders, has been reviewing the various recurring reports generated by managers in the organization. Although you have successfully controlled

these reports in the past, Saunders believes that as the company grows, more reports (both needed and unneeded) will inevitably emerge. She asks you to prepare a policy statement to govern the addition of new reports. Using what you learned from your interview and from this chapter, write a policy statement directed to all company managers. Supply any reasonable information to complete this assignment.

12. **Managing Reports—Procedures** ▪ Your policy statement about new reports (see Exercise 11 above) prompts several inquiries from managers who are uncertain about how to go about discontinuing a recurring report that doesn't seem to be needed any more. When does a report become obsolete? For example, several departments or managers at several levels may be simply accustomed to seeing a given report, even if they no longer need it, but there may be one manager who actually needs and uses the information in the report. You decide to prepare a procedure that describes the steps to take before discontinuing a recurring report. Consider both the writer's and the readers' needs for information. What can you do before distributing your procedure statement to determine whether it is reasonable and appropriate?

A possible solution to the Continuing Case is described in the *Instructor's Resource Manual*, pp. 220–221.

CONTINUING CASE 10

The Copy Cat

Larry Haas has been surprised to learn when examining the quarterly departmental statements that photocopying costs have more than doubled from the previous quarter. In talking over the problem with others, he has learned that some workers photocopy nearly everything on their small departmental photocopier (there are five of these convenient, but relatively inefficient, copiers at headquarters) and other workers copy only small jobs on the departmental copiers and send larger jobs to the copy center, one of the departments managed by Eric Fox.

Jobs that are too big or too complicated for even the copy center to manage are sent to a local print shop. Some departments do this on their own; others rely on the copy center to do it. Regardless of where the copying is done, the individual department is charged for the job. From a company point of view, however, Larry is interested in ensuring that each job is completed in the most cost-effective way possible.

An additional problem Larry discovered is that the company's lax attitude about using the departmental photocopiers has perhaps given the erroneous impression that employees have permission to photocopy personal documents. He has heard of numerous instances regarding the copying of personal insurance forms, recipes, sports stories, even kids' homework.

In speaking with the manager of the copy center, Larry learns that departmental copiers are designed for small jobs—no more than 30 copies of an original and no more than 20 originals per job. Any larger job should be sent to the copy center, which will decide whether to do the job in-house or send it outside. Generally, the in-house center handles one-color jobs on 8½-by-11-inch paper and up to 2,000 copies. Any job requiring more copies, more than one color, special binding, photographs, or the like is sent to the print shop.

Larry decides that a policy is needed on photocopying. And several specific procedures need to be established to accomplish the legitimate photocopying efficiently.

Critical Thinking

1. Taking into account the absence of any formal organizational policy, what are the ethical implications of employees copying personal insurance forms, recipes, sports stories, and the like on the office copier?

Writing Projects

2. Write a policy statement (General Guideline 72) on the topic of photocopying. You may assume any reasonable information needed.
3. Once a job is submitted to the copy center, a procedure must be in place for deciding whether it's an in-house or outside job. Write a procedure that covers the situation from when the job reaches the copy center until it is returned to the requester.

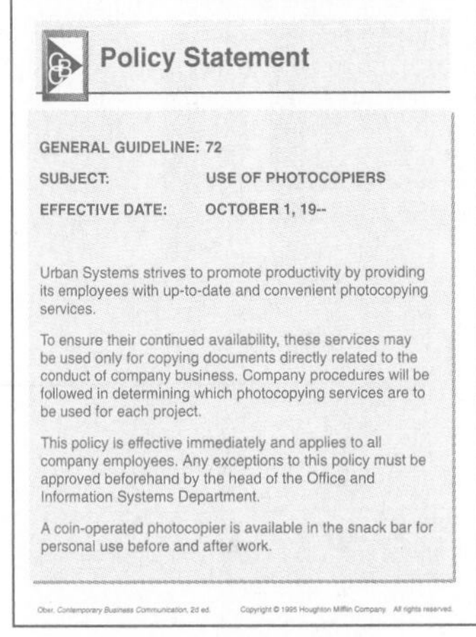

Policy Statement

GENERAL GUIDELINE: 72
SUBJECT: USE OF PHOTOCOPIERS
EFFECTIVE DATE: OCTOBER 1, 19--

Urban Systems strives to promote productivity by providing its employees with up-to-date and convenient photocopying services.

To ensure their continued availability, these services may be used only for copying documents directly related to the conduct of company business. Company procedures will be followed in determining which photocopying services are to be used for each project.

This policy is effective immediately and applies to all company employees. Any exceptions to this policy must be approved beforehand by the head of the Office and Information Systems Department.

A coin-operated photocopier is available in the snack bar for personal use before and after work.

Ober, *Contemporary Business Communication*, 2d ed.

See Master 10.3, Continuing Case 10, in the *Instructor's Resource Manual.*

WORDWISE *The United States*

- Maine is the only state in the United States that has only one syllable.
- The only letter not used in the spelling of any of the 50 states in the United States is *q*.
- You probably know that French nouns are either masculine or feminine. But did you know that in French, *Texas* and *Montana* are masculine, but *Florida* and *California* are feminine?

CHAPTER

11

Collecting the Data

Communication Objectives

After you have finished this chapter, you should be able to

1. Evaluate the quality of secondary data.
2. Develop an efficient search strategy.
3. Use print and computerized indexes and directories efficiently.
4. Take notes in an accurate and efficient manner.
5. Develop an effective questionnaire and cover letter.
6. Select an appropriate sample for a survey.
7. Conduct a data-gathering interview.
8. Discuss the appropriate use of observation, telephone inquiries, and experimentation.

Mary Hall oversees research at the New York–based advertising agency Della Femina McNamee. Her research helps determine who is likely to buy a product, what kind of advertising will sell it, and whether or not the advertising has been effective. When Hall sees an advertisement on television that appeals to her, she knows that before the commercial appeared on the air, someone did a lot of research and collected a lot of data to persuade her—and other consumers like her—to buy the product.

Hall, who has 17 years of marketing experience, noted that the first step in creating advertising is to research the product category "so that you're very well educated about what's going on, what the product's about, what the trends are, what the regulatory situation is, and what the advertising history is." It's important, she added, "to understand what marketers in that category have been through already, what they're familiar with and not familiar with."

The New York City Columbus Quincentennial Commission used the services of Della Femina McNamee.

Say, for example, the agency has been asked to sell a new cookie. Hall's staff would use several on-line data bases, which can retrieve major newspaper and magazine articles about virtually anything, including cookies and the companies that make them. The information will tell the agency what types of advertising campaigns have worked with what kinds of cookies in the past and which have failed. In addition to on-line data base services, the agency can also rely on its library of periodicals and books.

Mary Hall

Senior vice president, director of research, Della Femina McNamee, New York City

But, Hall cautioned, the information she gathers is a tool that helps shape a campaign—not an answer to what will *absolutely* work or fail. Common sense should also play a role; for instance, it probably would not be a good idea to run perfume commercials during a football game.

Once a product category's history is understood, Hall indicated, "You need to discover who your target audience is. You want to know what the various segments of the target are." If the product is not new to the market but is a new account for the agency, Hall needs to find out if people "use it and like it, or use it occasionally, or if they have used it and rejected it, or if they've ever heard of it at all, or if they've heard of it and haven't tried it."

But that, she said speaking quickly, is still just the beginning: "Then you need to know the demographic characteristics of [each of] these groups." To gather this information, questionnaires are developed and given to focus groups. One basic rule of questionnaires, Hall said, is that they begin with the general and end with the specific, which helps the advertiser determine who is likely to buy a product. The questionnaires are designed to teach the agency about a person's lifestyle and the products people use, and to indicate whether they're likely to spend money in a given category. "You need that [information] to design any kind of primary research, to make it pertinent and relevant, and also to make it efficient, because you may decide that some of those segments aren't going to be useful, and you don't want to waste time and money selling to people who are least likely to buy a product."

Hall indicated that the most important part of her research is based on one question: "Who am I going to talk to?"

PLANNING THE DATA COLLECTION

As noted in Chapter 10, collecting the data is by no means the first step in the reporting process. Before collecting any data, you must define the report purpose and analyze the intended audience. Then you must determine what data is needed to solve the problem. (*Note:* The term *data* is technically the plural form of *datum* and therefore requires a plural noun when referring to the individual items of data. In most cases in this text, however, the term is used in the sense of a collective noun and therefore takes a singular verb.) Sometimes the data you need will be in your mind or in documents you already have at hand, sometimes it will be in documents located elsewhere, and sometimes the data is not available at all but must be generated by you.

Types of Data
Secondary
– Published
Journals
Magazines
Newspapers
Books
Brochures
Pamphlets
Technical reports
– Unpublished
Company records
Legal documents
Personal records
Medical records
Primary
– Surveys
Questionnaires
Interviews
Telephone inquiries
– Observation
– Experimentation

See Transparency 11.1, Types of Data.

Start the data-collection phase by **factoring** your problem, that is, by breaking it down into its component parts so that you will know what data

Determine what questions must be answered in order to solve your report problem.

For more on data collection, including taking notes and collecting primary data through interviews, see Video Case Study 3, Lotus Notes.

you need to collect. The easiest way to do this is to think about what questions you need to answer before you can solve the problem. The answers to these questions will ultimately provide the answer to the overall problem you're trying to solve, and the question topics may, in fact, ultimately serve as the major divisions of your report.

Research and report writing are a cost, just like other corporate expenses. Thus, you should use data-collection methods that will provide the needed data with the least expenditure of time and money but at the level of completeness, accuracy, and precision needed to solve your problem. In other words, there is a break-even point to data collection. You do not want to provide a $100 answer to a $5 question, but neither do you want to provide a $5 answer to a $100 question.

The two major types of data you will collect are secondary and primary data. **Secondary data** is data collected by someone else for some other purpose; it may be published or unpublished. Published data includes any material that is widely disseminated, including the following:

- Journal, magazine, and newspaper articles (*Note:* Technically, a *journal* is a scholarly periodical published by a professional association or university, and a *magazine* is a commercial periodical published by a for-profit organization. Although the distinction is sometimes useful in evaluating secondary sources, the two terms are used interchangeably in this chapter to refer to any periodical publication.)
- Books
- Brochures and pamphlets
- Technical reports

Helping businesses sort through the multitude of demographic data, TIGER software uses 1990 Census data to produce census tabulation by small geographic area.

Unpublished secondary data includes any material that is not widely disseminated, including the following:

- Company records (such as financial records, personnel data, and previous correspondence and reports)
- Legal documents (such as court records, regulatory hearings, and legislative acts)
- Personal records (such as diaries, receipts, and checkbook registers)
- Medical records

Primary data is collected by the researcher to solve the specific problem at hand. Because you are collecting the data yourself, you have more control over its accuracy, completeness, objectivity, and relevance. The three main methods of primary data collection are surveys (questionnaires, interviews, and telephone inquiries), observation, and experimentation.

Nearly all reporting tasks use secondary data.

Although secondary and primary data are both important sources for business reports, we usually start our data collection by reviewing the data that is already available. Not all report situations require collecting new (primary) data, but it would be unusual to write a report that did not use some type of secondary data.

Studying what is already known about a topic and what remains to be learned makes the reporting process more efficient because the report

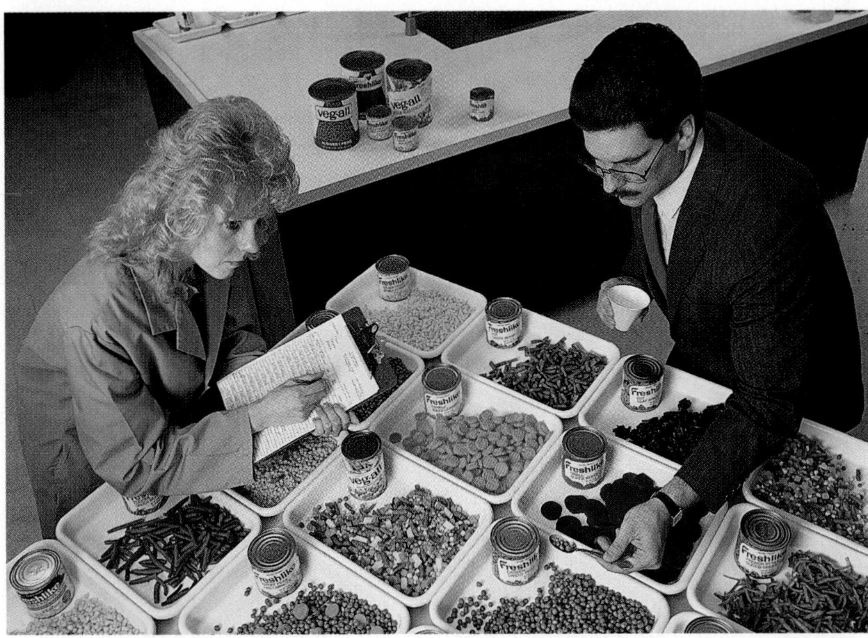

Workers at Wisconsin-based Larsen's research lab (shown here) prepare primary data from a comparative product test. Direct observation can be an expensive way to collect data, but sometimes it is the most effective.

writer can then concentrate scarce resources on generating new information rather than rediscovering existing information. Also, studying secondary data can provide sources for additional information, suggest methods of primary research, or give clues for questionnaire items—that is, provide guidance for primary research. For these reasons, our discussion of data collection begins with secondary sources.

COLLECTING SECONDARY DATA

Secondary and primary data are of equal importance.

Secondary data is neither better nor worse than primary data; it's simply *different*. The source of the data is not as important as its quality and its relevance for your particular purpose. The major advantages of using secondary data are economic: using secondary data is less costly and less time-consuming than collecting primary data. The disadvantages relate not only to the availability of sufficient secondary data but also to the quality of the data that is available. Never use any data before you have evaluated its appropriateness for the intended purpose.

Evaluating Secondary Data

By definition, secondary data was gathered for some purpose other than your own. Therefore, the categories used, the population sampled, and the analyses reported might not be appropriate for your use. Ask yourself the following questions about any secondary sources you're thinking about incorporating into your report.

What Was the Purpose of the Study? If the study was undertaken to genuinely find the answer to a question or problem, you can have more confidence about the accuracy and objectivity of the results than if, for example, the study was undertaken merely to prove a point. People seeking honest answers to honest questions are more likely to select their samples carefully, to ask clear and unbiased questions, and to analyze the data appropriately.

Avoid using biased data in your report.

Be wary of secondary data if the researcher had a vested interest in the outcome of the study. For example, you would probably have more faith in a study extolling the merits of the Hubbard automobile that had been conducted by *Consumer Reports* than one conducted by Hubbard Motors, Inc.

How Was the Data Collected? Were appropriate procedures used? Although you may not be an experienced researcher yourself, your reading of secondary data (including this chapter of your textbook) will likely alert you to certain standard research procedures that should be followed. For example, common sense should tell you that if you are interested in learning the reactions of all factory workers in your organization to a particular proposal, you would not gather data from just the newly hired workers. Likewise, if a questionnaire were sent to all the factory workers and only 10% responded, you would probably not be able to conclude that the opinions of these few respondents represent the views of all the workers.

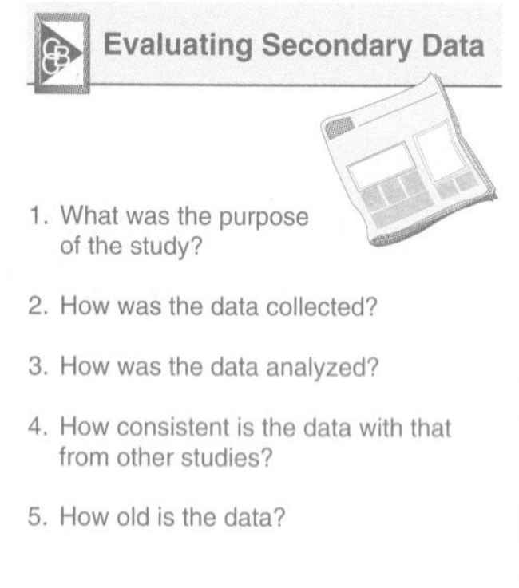
Evaluating Secondary Data
1. What was the purpose of the study?
2. How was the data collected?
3. How was the data analyzed?
4. How consistent is the data with that from other studies?
5. How old is the data?

See Transparency 11.2, Evaluating Secondary Data.

How Was the Data Analyzed? As we shall see in Chapter 12, different types of data lend themselves to different types of analyses. Survey data, for example, is analyzed differently from experimental data. Sometimes the low number of responses to a particular question or ambiguity in the question itself prevents us from drawing any valid conclusions.

In some situations, even though the analysis was appropriate for the original study, it may not be appropriate for your particular purposes. For example, suppose you're interested in the reactions of teenagers and the only available secondary data used the category "under 21 years of age." You would not know whether the responses came mostly from those younger than 13 years old, those 13 to 19 years old (your target group), or those older than 19 years old.

How Consistent Is the Data with That from Other Studies? When you find the same general conclusions in several independent sources, you can have greater confidence in the data. On the other hand, if four studies of a particular topic reached one conclusion and a fifth study reached an opposite conclusion, you would need to scrutinize the fifth study carefully before accepting its findings.

Generally, the more consensus you find in secondary data, the more trustworthy the data.

Avoid accepting something as true simply because you read it in print. Because the reader of your report will be making decisions based on the data you present, take care that the data in your report is accurate.

How Old Is the Data? Data that was true at the time it was collected might or might not be true today. A job-satisfaction study completed at your organization last year may have yielded accurate data then. But if in the meantime your organization has merged with another company, moved its headquarters, or been torn by a strike, the job-satisfaction data may have no relevance today. On the other hand, some data may still be accurate years after its collection. For example, a thorough study of the origins of the labor movement in the United States may have almost permanent validity.

Your data must pass these five tests, whether it comes from company records or published sources. Data that fails even one of these tests should probably be discarded and not used in your report. At the very least, such data requires extra scrutiny and perhaps extra explanation in the report itself if it is used.

Planning the Search Strategy

In the business world, most of the secondary data you use in your reports will probably come from company records—financial records, personnel data, correspondence, reports, and the like. Increasingly, however, business decisions are affected by factors outside the organization for which internal data may not be sufficient. Government regulation, the international business climate, technological developments, and other factors often affect organizational decisions. Because these factors change so rapidly, the smart report writer will ensure that his or her report sources are comprehensive and up to date.

For beginning a research project, some other useful general indexes include the *Business Periodicals Index, Index of Economic Articles, Accountants' Index, New York Times Index, Public Affairs Information Service*, and the *Wall Street Journal Index.*

Consider the negative consequences, for example, of recommending that your firm market a certain product when, in fact, the government has just banned trade with the only country that makes a key component of the product. Only a thorough search for the relevant secondary data would reveal such information.

Your search for published secondary data may take place at your company library or at a city or university library using traditional print resources, or it may take place at your own desk using a computer and modem or compact disk drive. Wherever you choose to seek information, you will save yourself time and get better results if you spend some time at the start planning what to look for.

You locate secondary sources by using key terms, or subject headings.

Develop a List of Key Terms Begin your search for secondary data by developing a list of key terms to be used when you search the directories and indexes for secondary sources. At this stage, your list of key terms should be long and quite general. Don't just select the obvious terms; try to think of related topics that might be of interest to you. As you continue your search, undoubtedly other terms will come to mind.

Consult Directories and Indexes Begin your search with the major directories and indexes for business, government, education, and the like. Each of these sources contains an alphabetized list of subject headings, which you will search using your list of key terms.

Three good listings of government sources are *The American Statistics Index*, the *Monthly Catalog of U.S. Government Publications*, and the *United States Government Publications Index*.

Under each subject heading is one or more **citations** (references to relevant books, journal articles, newspaper articles, or similar sources). A citation for a book identifies the author or editor, book title, name and location of the publisher, and the year of publication. A citation for a journal article identifies the author, title of the article, title of the journal, date, and page numbers of the specific issue in which the article appeared.

If your topic relates primarily to business, the *Business Periodicals Index* is a good starting point; if it relates primarily to education, try the *Education Index*. And for any topic, the *Monthly Catalog* is the basic source for locating data compiled by the federal government.

Do not neglect government sources in your search for secondary data.

Some report writers neglect searching for government data, perhaps because government data is typically not cataloged like other books or periodicals and the writers are not sure how to locate government sources. This neglect is a serious mistake because the U.S. government is the world's largest collector and publisher of information, and the quality of the data it gathers is excellent.

Be sure to consult the card catalog (either manually or via computer). Someone somewhere has probably written a book that is related to your topic. Whereas journal articles often contain the most current statistics, books and monographs often provide more detailed background information and sources for additional research.

If you're having trouble locating sources, you may be using inappropriate headings.

The terms you use to identify your topic might not be the ones used by the indexes and directories you use to locate source documents. If you cannot locate any citations using your term, try a related term or synonym. Some indexes come with a thesaurus that identifies the headings used in the index.

Because so many library collections and all government documents use the Library of Congress classifications, start by using the terms identified in the reference work *Library of Congress Subject Headings* (or *LCSH*). Suppose, for example, that you've been asked to write a report on the feasibility of opening a frozen yogurt store in Akron, Ohio. If you look under the subject heading "yogurt" in the *LCSH*, you will find the following:

Yogurt, Frozen
Use Frozen Yogurt

The notation "Use" (also called "See" in some indexes) tells you that this topic is cataloged under "Frozen" instead of under "Yogurt." If you look up "Frozen Yogurt" in the *LCSH*, you will find the following:

Frozen Yogurt
UF Yogurt, Frozen
BT Frozen Desserts
Yogurt

Learn the meanings of commonly used abbreviations.

"UF" stands for "Used For" and tells you that you are now looking under the correct heading. "BT" stands for "Broader Term" and tells you that if you wish to expand your search, you might use the headings "Frozen Desserts" or "Yogurt." Other *LCSH* abbreviations are "NT"—Narrower Term (to narrow your search) and "RT"—Related Term (to broaden your search). A "See" notation tells you that you're looking under the wrong heading, and "See Also" leads to related topics.

If you were to look up "Frozen Yogurt" in one of the editions of *Business Periodicals Index,* you would find the following citations:

> **Frozen yogurt**
> *See also*
> Frozen yogurt stores
> Market segment report: premium ice cream. J. W. Kochak. graphs il tabs *Restaur Bus* 86:241-2+Jl 1 '87
> A yogurt named Zack's [S. Holt and H. Watts] D. Marth. pors *Nations Bus* 75:52 Ag '87

You can see that the first article listed, "Market Segment Report: Premium Ice Cream," was written by J. W. Kochak and published in the July 1, 1987, issue of *Restaurant Business* and that it contains graphs, illustrations, and tables. Then, if you look up "Frozen Yogurt Stores" as directed by the "See also" reference, you would find three additional headings to search:

> **Frozen yogurt stores**
> *See also*
> Penguin's Place Frozen Yogurt
> Zack's Famous Frozen Yogurt, Inc.
>
> **Chain and franchise operations**
> The frozen yogurt race is red-hot. T. Carson. il tab *Bus Week* p. 67 Mr 7 '88.

Other directories and indexes are read similarly. The front matter or appendix in each directory explains the meaning of any abbreviations used in the citations and provides additional information about the publications listed. (Don't just guess about the meaning of abbreviated titles—look them up!) Most printed directories and indexes are compiled annually. Depending on how fast changes occur in your subject area, you will have to decide how many years' worth of literature you need to search.

Evaluate your sources for their appropriateness for your specific purposes.

Compile and Review the Literature Some report writers like to locate sources, scan them quickly to determine if they are relevant for their purposes, and photocopy promising articles for later study. Other report writers prefer to make their notes immediately. Regardless of your work habits, once you've gathered your initial data, you should review it with the following questions in mind:

- How relevant is each source for my specific needs?
- Does each source meet the five requirements discussed earlier?
- Are there some areas for which I have not gathered sufficient data? (*If so, continue collecting data.*)
- Do any of the articles contain bibliographies and reference lists that might provide leads for additional sources?

You may decide at this point that you need to expand your search by revising or adding to your list of key terms or by searching a few more years' worth of directories and indexes. If you have trouble locating sources, the *Encyclopedia of Business Information Sources* is an excellent refer-

Directories can provide useful facts about financial organizations. Some popular ones are *Moody's Manuals, Thomas' Register of American Manufacturers, Dun & Bradstreet's Million Dollar Directory,* and *Poor's Register of Corporations, Directors, and Executives.*

ence for identifying sources of information on approximately 1,000 different business topics. When necessary, consult a reference librarian.

If, after exhaustive search, you have not been able to locate sufficient sources, you have several options. You can collect the data yourself through primary research; you can write the report using the sources that are available, ensuring that your conclusions are appropriate given the limited amount of data; or you can consult with the person who requested the report for additional direction.

TAKING NOTES

Once you've identified a relevant source, you're ready to take notes. If you're working from a photocopy, quickly read through the article, highlighting the information that is relevant for your purposes. Doing this will enable you to take notes efficiently.

The specific method for recording notes is an individual matter. Whether you record your notes on index cards or sheets of paper or whether you handwrite them or compose them at a keyboard is not important. The point that *is* important is that you must record notes somewhere. Do not stop after the initial step of highlighting relevant material on the photocopy.

Take notes on one side of the paper only.

Writing out your notes serves several purposes. First, the act of rereading the article and putting the information in your own words fixes the information more firmly in your mind, making the later task of writing the report easier. Second, it is much more efficient to work from your notes, which contain only information that is relevant to your needs, than to have to constantly scan an entire document, searching for what you need. Third, you can rearrange your notes so that they follow the organization of your report, making the drafting phase easier.

The traditional suggestion for note taking has been to use index cards, placing one major point on each card. The advantage of this system is that you can easily shuffle your cards to fit your final outline. However, the same flexibility can be achieved when using a full sheet of paper if you write on one side of the paper only. You can later cut each note and assemble the notes in whatever "piles" are appropriate.

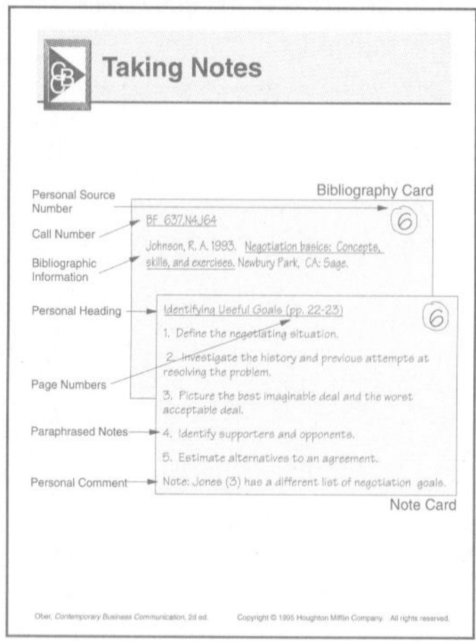

See Transparency 11.3, Taking Notes.

On a computer you can easily use a word processing program to arrange and rearrange your notes on the page or use an outline feature to expand your notes into narrative copy and assemble the final report without having to retype the notes. Figure 11.1 shows a journal article with the relevant points underlined and examples of notes on the article taken manually and on a computer.

Information to Include

Regardless of the format you use for taking notes, include the following information from each source.

Call Number Recording the library call number will save you time if you need to locate the document again later.

FIGURE 11.1 Note Taking

TCBY's frozen yogurt is low-fat, but its stock price could give you a heart attack.

A fatty stock

TO JUDGE FROM the action in TCBY Enterprises, the stock is getting a little ripe around the edges. Based in Little Rock, Ark, TCBY is the nation's largest chain of franchised frozen yogurt shops. (TCBY stands for The Country's Best Yogurt.) As Americans look for low-calorie, low-fat alternatives to ice cream, a lot in investors have jumped on the TCBY bandwagon. As a result, the chain's shares have shot up 150% this year. The recent price is 26¹ valuing the company at nearly $700 million. To put that figure in perspective, TCBY's shareholders' equity is $72 million, sales last year were $98 million, and profits were $20 million. So the stock sells at 7 times sales, almost 10 times book value and 35 times earnings. The yogurt may be low-fat, but the stock looks downright obese.

The stock, incidentally, trades on the NewYork—not Vancouver — Stock Exchange.

You have to hand it to Frank Hickingbotham, TCBY's 52-year old founder and chairman. He has performed something close to a miracle. A born salesman and former lay Baptist minister, Hickingbotham opened the first TCBY store in 1981, after selling a deep-dish pie business. Today he and his son Herren preside over more than 1,300 stores, all bu[...] [...]nchised. Sys[...]

But, as far as the stock market is concerned, Forbes would bet that TCBY has done more than scratch the surface; it has dug a hole for itself. The stock has gotten so rich that is growth falters even for a moment the market will likely seek revenge. In 1986 the company lost one-third of its market value in a single day. Today, the company is not as overvalued as it was then. Still, TCBY again looks like an accident waiting to happen.

Like a farmer expanding onto less productive soil, Hickingbothamwill have to work much harder for future growth. The yogurt market continues to expand. But TCBY's competitors are multiplying.

TCBY is strongest in the Southeast and Midwest; there are 75 TCBY stores in Chicago alone. In other regions, however, things aren't going as well.

In California, for example, the big name is Penguin's, with its snazzy black-and-white stores. Penguin's was acquired last summer by Bongrain, a multibillion-dollar French food outfit that also owns Columbo yogurt. Penguin's already has 125 stores and systemwide 1988 sales of $35 million. With the new Bongrain's backing, Penguin's is eyeing Florida, one of TCBY's biggest markets.

Another strong regional chain is Everything Yogurt, which has 220 stores and projects systemwide sales of $43 million this year. In the New York area, where TC[...] [...]t 37 stores,

growth. The ice cream chains could become tough competition. Already, 1,000 of Baskin Robbins' franchises have gone so far as to add "& Yogurt" to their signs. Dairy Queen, with 5,000 franchised stores, is considering rolling out frozen yogurt nationwide.

There are other weaknesses in the TCBY story. The company grew by keeping the cost of opening a new TCBY store low. Even now, opening a new TCBY store costs about $140,000 depending on location, as compared with around $200,000 for the typical Everything Yogurt and Penguin's stores. To keep costs low, Hickingbotham often allows TCBY stores to open in areas with relatively light traffic. And the construction and design of a basic TCBY outlet looks chintzy compared with some other chains' stores. Sniffs competitor Stephen Beninati, presidnet of Everything Yogurt: "Those stores wouldn't survive ten years of heavy traffic."

In the past, much of TCBY's profits came from selling franchises. But now, the bulk of its business is selling yogurt to franchisees. TCBY's franchises pay about $7 a gallon for their yogurt, versus $5 a gallon for Penguin's franchises, according to one Penguin Franchisee. Should TCBY's franchises demand more favorable prices—a classic conflict in the franchising industry—TCBY's margins would suffer ac[...]ngly.

[...]Whyte, an a[...]

Original marked-up journal article

Eric Schumuckler, *Forbes* (June 26, 1989), p. 133.

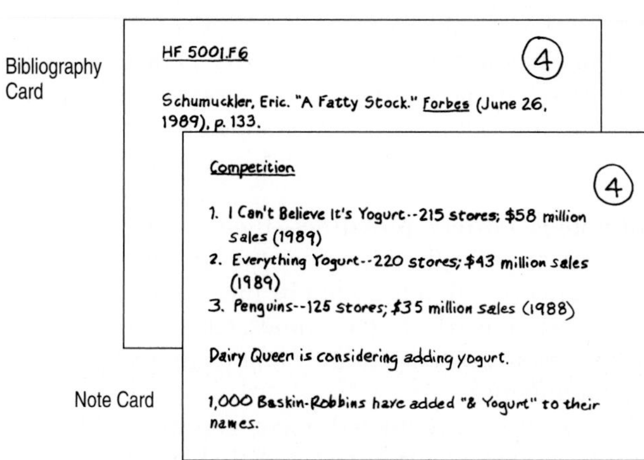

Bibliography Card

HF 5001.F6 (4)

Schumuckler, Eric. "A Fatty Stock." Forbes (June 26, 1989), p. 133.

Note Card

Competition (4)

1. I Can't Believe It's Yogurt--215 stores; $58 million sales (1989)
2. Everything Yogurt--220 stores; $43 million sales (1989)
3. Penguins--125 stores; $35 million sales (1988)

Dairy Queen is considering adding yogurt.

1,000 Baskin-Robbins have added "& Yogurt" to their names.

Handwritten notes

4. HF 5001.56
Schumuckler, Eric. "A Fatty Stock." Forbes (June 26, 1989), p. 133.

(4) OVERVIEW OF FIRM:
TCBY (The Country's Best Yogurt) is the largest chain of franchised frozen yogurt stores, with more than 1,300 stores. All but 125 are franchised.
Net profit for the firm was $20 million in 1988, with systemwide sales of $210 million; $300 million in sales are expected in 1989.

(4) COMPETITION:
Strongest competitor is I Can't Believe It's Yogurt, with 215 stores and $58 million sales in 1989.
Everything Yogurt had 220 stores and $43 million sales in 1989; Penguin's had 125 stores and $35 million sales in 1988.

(4) NOTE:
Forbes believes TCBY stock is overvalued: "The yogurt may be low-fat, but the stock looks downright obese" (p. 133). However, USA Today (June 23, 1989, p. 3B) recommends the stock to investors.

Computer notes

Include all needed bibliographic information in your notes.

Bibliographic Information Record the complete bibliographic information—either on a separate bibliographic card or at the top of the sheet of paper if you're taking notes on paper or via computer. Record the information in the order and style you'll use in your bibliography so that you can later assemble your bibliography directly from these notes. (See the Reference Manual at the back of this text for different methods of documenting your sources.)

Source Number It is not necessary to arrange your sources in alphabetical order, but you should number each source sequentially as you locate it. Then make sure that each note you take from that source is labeled with its corresponding number (see Figure 11.1 for examples). That way, you avoid having to write out the complete citation on each note but can always easily identify the source of each note later.

Headings Assign a topic heading to each note. If you've already scanned the entire article, you should be able to organize the important points into groups. Note, for example, in the computer notes shown in Figure 11.1 that even though the article itself does not contain any headings, the reader grouped the relevant information under separate headings.

Page Numbers Unless the source document is only one page in length, record the page number for every note you take, whether the notes are in your own words or in the words of the original author. You may need the page numbers for each note later for documenting your sources.

Paraphrase Versus Direct Quotation

Paraphrase most data; use direct quotations sparingly.

Paraphrase and quote appropriately. Avoid the temptation to become lazy and simply copy everything in the author's exact words. It is unlikely that the problem you're trying to solve and the problem discussed by the author mesh exactly. More than likely, you'll need to take bits and pieces of information from numerous sources and integrate them into a context appropriate for your own purposes.

Your notes can be of two types—paraphrases or direct quotations—and each should be readily identifiable in your notes. A **paraphrase** is a summary or restatement of a passage in your own words. Paraphrasing involves more than just rearranging the words or leaving out a word or two. It requires, instead, that you understand the writer's idea and then restate it in your own language. Most of your notes should be paraphrases from the original document.

The second type of note is a **direct quotation**—the exact words of another. Use direct quotations only for definitions or for text that is so precise, clear, or otherwise noteworthy that it cannot be improved on. Enclose all direct quotations in quotation marks in your notes. Check immediately that you've written the quotation down accurately and completely, including the appropriate page number(s).

With either paraphrases or directly quoted notes, you may add a personal comment—a note that you make to yourself to help later in analyzing the data and writing the report. Label your personal comments in some distinctive manner. For example, the last item in the computer notes in Figure 11.1 labels a personal comment with the heading "Note" and indicates that another source presents an opposing viewpoint. As you're reading and making notes of a secondary source, don't risk forgetting any insights that come to mind—write them down immediately. But make sure they are clearly labeled as your own ideas to avoid confusing them later with your published sources.

Write down personal comments, questions, and the like as they occur to you.

USING THE COMPUTER TO COLLECT SECONDARY DATA

Today, in most libraries you can perform computer-assisted data searches. An entire knowledge industry has evolved in which organizations store huge amounts of statistical, financial, and bibliographic information in the memory banks of their mainframe computers or on compact disks and then make this information available to users nationwide for a fee.

An electronic **data base** is a computer-searchable collection of information on a general subject area, such as business, education, or psychology. Electronic data bases are fast; you can typically collect more data electronically in an hour or two than would be possible in an entire day of traditional library research.

You can conduct a comprehensive search for secondary data without ever leaving your office via on-line computer searching.

In addition, electronic data bases are typically more current than printed data bases; most are updated weekly or monthly. Also, each contains several years' worth of citations, whereas manual indexes require searching through individual annual volumes and supplements. Finally, electronic data bases are extremely flexible. You can use different search terms, combine them, and modify your search at every step.

Although you may never write another academic report after graduating from college, you *will* continue to need to locate information—for business, political, or personal reasons. Computer-assisted information retrieval has now become so widely available, economical, and easy to use that it has become a powerful new tool helping managers solve problems and make decisions.

Types of Data Bases

Data bases can be of three types—bibliographic, numeric, or full-text. Most data bases provide only bibliographic information and sometimes a brief abstract of documents. Some data bases, such as Disclosure®, are numeric and contain comprehensive financial and other statistical information. And some data bases provide the full text of the documents they contain; for example, the Dow Jones News/Retrieval Service® contains the complete contents of each issue of the *Wall Street Journal*. These data bases are available either as on-line or as CD-ROM data bases.

Unlike CD-ROM data bases, on-line data bases require that you be electronically connected to a remote mainframe computer.

On-Line Data Bases An **on-line data base** is a collection of information stored in a mainframe computer that is accessible by a microcomputer or terminal and a telephone hookup. A user in Bangor, Maine, for example, could use his or her computer and modem to access the ABI/Inform® data base by dialing up the DIALOG® Information Services mainframe computer in Palo Alto, California. The user could then instruct the computer to print out a list of articles on a particular topic from its data base of citations from more than 800 business and management journals.

The main advantage of using an on-line data base is that it can be accessed anywhere a microcomputer, modem, and telephone line are available—from your office, hotel room, or even your automobile. The user can print out citations, abstracts, and sometimes even the full text of the articles. If the full text is not available on-line, information is provided for ordering photocopies of the articles. The user pays a fee for each search. DIALOG, one of the major data base vendors, estimates that a typical search during normal business hours lasts about 10 minutes and costs from $10 to $20.[1]

CD-ROM Data Bases The second major type of computer collection is the **CD-ROM data base,** a collection of information stored on a high-capacity disk that is accessible by a microcomputer with a CD drive. One CD-ROM (compact disk—read-only memory) can hold up to 250,000 pages of text—the equivalent of 1,500 floppy disks. The advantage of using a CD-ROM data base is that the collection is stored on a disk connected directly to the computer you're using. Rather than pay for a telephone hookup to the remote mainframe computer, the library purchases the CD-ROM collection and periodic updates; individual computer searches are typically free to the user. Most of the directories and indexes available in print format are also available in computer format, although sometimes under a different name.

Accessing On-Line and CD-ROM Data Bases

Both on-line and CD-ROM data bases are accessed similarly. Each citation in the data base contains a list of *descriptors*—subject headings that describe the contents of the document stored in the computer. For example, an article on purchasing a TCBY yogurt franchise might have as descriptors "franchising," "frozen desserts," "frozen yogurt," and "TCBY." The user enters relevant key words, and the computer then identifies all citations in its collection that contain those key words.

The search terms used in a computer search correspond to the key words used in a manual search.

The success of your search will depend on how skillfully you choose these key words (or *search terms*). The principles that guide your choice are similar to those we discussed earlier for searches of card catalogs, indexes, and directories, but there's one important difference. The computer makes a very literal search; it will find exactly what you ask for—and nothing more.

If you use the search term "secretaries," the computer will not find citations for the words "secretary" or "secretarial." Most data bases have a feature known as *truncation*, which allows you to search for the root of a term. Thus, a search for "secre/" or "secre*" would retrieve "secret," "secretarial," "secretaries," "secretary," "secretion," and so on. You then choose the entries that are appropriate for your purpose.

The Spotlight on Technology shows the interactive nature of computer-assisted data collection, which allows you to combine categories in order to narrow your topic appropriately. The topic in this case was female managers in the banking industry.

COLLECTING PRIMARY DATA THROUGH QUESTIONNAIRES

Despite your best efforts, you will sometimes find that not enough high-quality secondary data is available to solve your problem. In such a situation, you will probably need to collect primary data. The main methods of primary data collection are surveys, observation, and experimentation.

Don't confuse the terms survey *and* questionnaire: *You* conduct *a survey by* administering *a questionnaire.*

A **survey** is a data-collection method that gathers information through questionnaires, telephone inquiries, or interviews. The **questionnaire** (a written instrument containing questions designed to obtain information from the individual being surveyed) is the most frequently used method in business research. The researcher can economically get a representative sampling over a large geographical area. After all, it costs no more to mail a questionnaire across the country than across the street.

Also, the anonymity of a questionnaire increases the validity of some responses. Certain personal and economic data may be given more completely and honestly when the respondent remains unidentified. In addition, no interviewer is present to possibly bias the results. Finally, respondents can answer at a time convenient for them, which is not always the case with telephone or interview studies.

The main disadvantage of surveys is a low response rate.

The big disadvantage of mail questionnaires is the low response rate, and those who do respond may not be representative (typical) of the population. Indeed, extensive research has shown that respondents tend to be better educated, have higher social status, be more intelligent, have higher need for social approval, and be more sociable than those who choose not to respond.[2] Thus, mail questionnaires should be used only under certain conditions:

- *When the desired information can be answered easily and quickly.* Questionnaires should contain mostly yes-or-no questions, check-off alternatives, or one- to two-word fill-in responses. People tend not to return questionnaires that call for lengthy or complex responses.

- *When the target audience is homogeneous.* To ensure a high response rate, your study must interest the respondents and you must use language they understand. It is difficult to construct a questionnaire that would be clearly and uniformly understood by people with widely differing interests, education, and socioeconomic backgrounds.

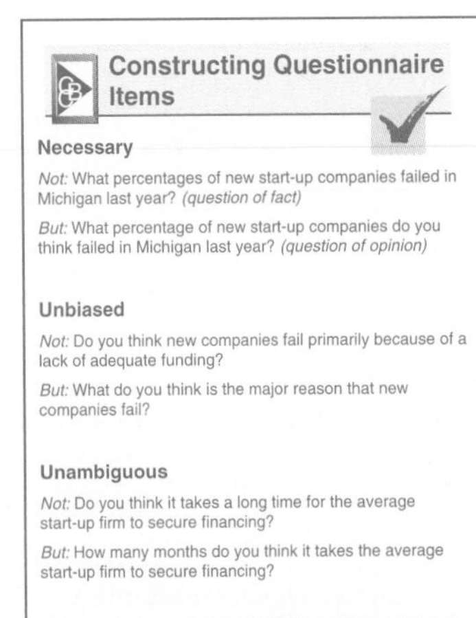
Constructing Questionnaire Items

Necessary

Not: What percentages of new start-up companies failed in Michigan last year? *(question of fact)*

But: What percentage of new start-up companies do you think failed in Michigan last year? *(question of opinion)*

Unbiased

Not: Do you think new companies fail primarily because of a lack of adequate funding?

But: What do you think is the major reason that new companies fail?

Unambiguous

Not: Do you think it takes a long time for the average start-up firm to secure financing?

But: How many months do you think it takes the average start-up firm to secure financing?

Ober, *Contemporary Business Communication*, 2d ed.

See Transparency 11.4, Constructing Questionnaires.

SPOTLIGHT ON TECHNOLOGY

Sample On-Line Search Session

User dials an information retrieval service and is connected to the data base.

```
SIGN ON              7:18:23        07/02/94
(1/74-3/91)
SEARCH MODE-ENTER QUERY

No.   Request                 Documents
```

Steps 1–3: User asks the computer to search for three terms. Computer responds by telling how many documents contain that term as a descriptor.

```
1     banking-industry.de     8394

2     management.de           61847

3     women.de                2994
```

Step 4: User asks for all documents containing all three terms; computer locates 21 such documents.

```
4     1 and 2 and 3           21
```

Step 5: User asks computer to print (p) the first document (1/1) from the 4th search (4). Computer lists author (AU), title (TI), source (SO), descriptors (DE), abstract (AB), service that sells a photocopy of the document (AV), and the accession number (AC)—the number used to identify the document.

```
5     p 4 1/1
AU:   Shinar-Eva-H.
TI:   Sexual Stereotypes of Occupations
SO:   J. Voc. Behavior.  VOL:  v20n8.  PAG: 102-110,
      9 pages.  Aug 1988.
DE:   Role-stereotypes.  Personnel-management.  Women.
      Banking-industry.  Manufacturing-industry.  Retail-
      industry.
AB:   The strength of sexual stereotypes attached to 129 oc-
      cupations was measured by having 60 male and 60 female
      subjects rank these jobs as masculine, feminine, or
      neutral.  An extremely high correlation between male
      and female subjects' mean ratings of the sex appropri-
      ateness of the given occupations indicates that sex
      labeling of occupations is a deeply ingrained feature
      in attitudes toward the world of work.  The results
      showed that those occupations stereotypically associ-
      ated with high levels of competence, rationality, and
      assertion are viewed as masculine while those asso-
      ciated with dependency, passivity, nurturance, and
      interpersonal warmth are perceived as feminine occu-
      pations.  For example, bank tellers, elementary
      school teachers, and librarians had high feminine
      ratings whereas bankers, doctors, politicians, and
      professional athletes had high masculine ratings.
      The notion that males continue to stereotype while
      females have more liberated views is not supported.
AV:   ABI/INFORM
AC:   0120-5582

END OF REQUEST
```

User signs off. Computer shows search took 8 minutes and 26 seconds, or 0.141 hour.

```
SEARCH MODE-ENTER QUERY
       bye

*CONNECT TIME: 0:08:26 HH:MM:SS  0.141 DEC HRS
SESSION 17208
```

- *When sufficient time is available.* Three to four weeks is generally required from questionnaire mailing to final returns—including follow-ups of the nonrespondents. A telephone survey, on the other hand, can often be completed in one day.

Constructing the Questionnaire

Because the target audience's time is valuable, make sure that every question you ask is necessary—that it is essential to help you solve your problem and that you cannot acquire the information from other sources (such as through library research). Guidelines for constructing a questionnaire are provided in Checklist 12. Some of the more important points are illustrated in the following paragraphs.

Your language must be clear, precise, and understandable so that the questionnaire yields valid and reliable data. **Validity** is the extent to which the questionnaire measures what it is supposed to measure. Suppose your questionnaire on consumer buying habits is written at a readability level of Grade 14 but the respondents have an average reading level of Grade 10. Your questionnaire might actually be measuring reading ability and would thus be an invalid measure of consumer buying habits.

A questionnaire can be reliable and still not be valid—it can consistently yield incorrect results.

Reliability refers to the extent to which the questionnaire yields consistent results. Suppose, for instance, your questionnaire asked the respondent to rank 15 criteria for selecting a particular brand, from 1 (most important) to 15 (least important). Because it is nearly impossible to differentiate 15 levels of importance, if the same respondents answered this question on two different occasions, their answers would probably vary somewhat; that is, their responses would be inconsistent and, therefore, unreliable.

Doug Carlson, CEO of Brøderbund, with some customers. Collecting data on customer response at a tradeshow demonstration led to a change in Brøderbund's CD-ROM version of The Tortoise and the Hare. *The software showed the hare crumpling a newspaper and throwing it to the ground. A teacher's comment resulted in addition of the tortoise's scolding the hare for littering.*

CHECKLIST 12

Questionnaires

CONTENT

1. Do not ask for information that is easily available elsewhere.
2. Have a purpose for each question. Make sure that all questions directly help you to solve your problem. Avoid asking for unimportant or merely "interesting" information.
3. Use precise wording so that no question can possibly be misunderstood. Use clear, simple language, and define any term that may be unfamiliar to the respondent or that you are using in a special way.
4. Use neutrally worded questions and deal with only one topic per question. Avoid loaded, leading, or multifaceted questions.
5. Ensure that the response choices are both exhaustive and mutually exclusive (that is, that there is an appropriate response for every one and that there are no overlapping categories).
6. Be especially careful about asking sensitive questions, such as information about age, salary, or morals. Consider using broad categories for such questions (instead of narrow, more specific categories).
7. Pilot-test your questionnaire on a few people to ensure that all questions function as intended. Revise as needed.

ORGANIZATION

8. Arrange the questions in some logical order. Group together all questions that deal with a par-

The question should not yield clues to the "correct" answer.

Each question must also be neutral (unbiased). Consider the following question:

> Do you think our company should open an on-site child-care center as a means of ensuring the welfare of our employees' small children?
>
> ___ yes
> ___ no

This wording of the question obviously favors the "pro" side, thereby biasing the responses toward "yes." A more neutral question is needed if valid responses are to result.

> Which one of the following possible additional fringe benefits would you most prefer?
>
> ___ a dental insurance plan
> ___ an on-site child-care center
> ___ three personal-leave days annually
> ___ other (please specify: ________________________________)

Note several things about this question. First, it is more neutral than the original version; no "right" answer is apparent. Second, the alternatives are arranged in alphabetical order. To avoid possibly biasing the responses, always arrange the alternatives in some logical order—alphabetical, numeric, chronological, or the like.

Finally, note that an "other" category is provided; it always goes last and is accompanied by the request to "please specify." Suppose the one fringe benefit that the vast majority of employees really wanted most was for the company to increase its pension contributions. If the "other" cate-

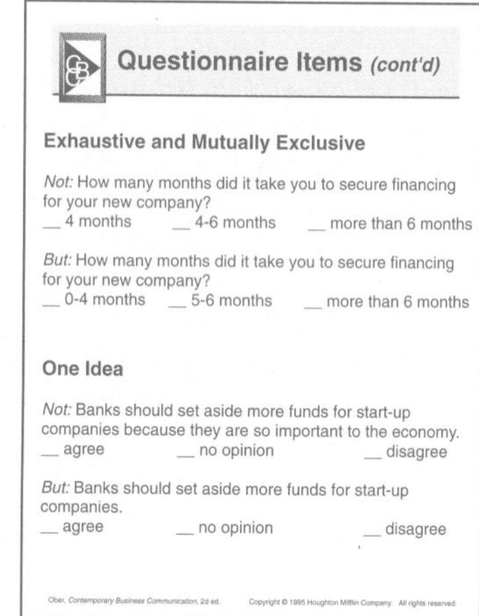

See Transparency 11.5, Constructing Questionnaires (continued).

ticular topic. If your questionnaire is long, divide it into sections.

9. Arrange the alternatives for each question in some logical order—such as numeric, chronological, or alphabetical.

10. Give the questionnaire a descriptive title, provide whatever directions are necessary, and include your name and return address somewhere on the questionnaire.

FORMAT

11. Use an easy-to-answer format. Check-off questions draw the most responses and are easiest to answer and tabulate. Use free-response items only when absolutely necessary.

12. To increase the likelihood that your target audience will cooperate and take your study seriously, ensure that your questionnaire has a professional appearance.

- Use a simple and attractive format, allowing for plenty of white (blank) space.
- Ensure that the questionnaire is free from errors in grammar, spelling, and style.
- Use a good-quality printer or typewriter and make good-quality photocopies.

gory were missing, the researcher would never learn that important information.

Ask only one question in each item.

Ensure that your categories are *exhaustive* (that is, that they include all possible alternatives), by including an "other" category if necessary. Also be certain that each question contains a single idea. Note the following question:

> Our company should spend less money on advertising and more money on research and development.
>
> ____ agree
> ____ disagree

Suppose the respondent believes that the company should spend more (or less) money on advertising *and* on research and development? How is he or she supposed to answer? The solution is to put the two ideas into two questions.

Finally, ensure that your categories are *mutually exclusive;* that is, that there are no overlapping categories.

> In your opinion, what is the major cause of high employee turnover?
>
> ____ lack of air-conditioning
> ____ noncompetitive financial package
> ____ poor fringe benefits
> ____ poor working conditions
> ____ weak management

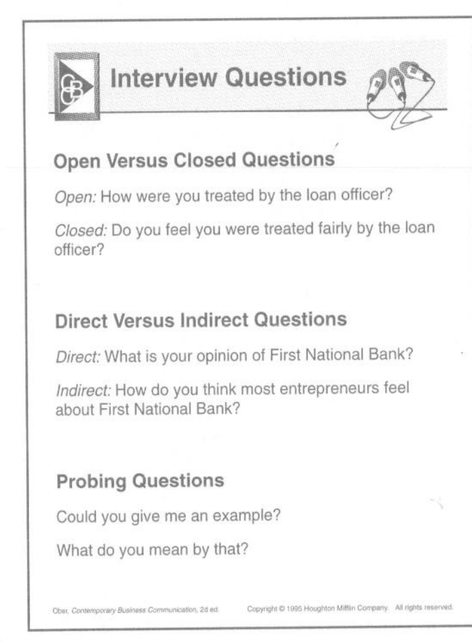

Interview Questions
Open Versus Closed Questions
Open: How were you treated by the loan officer?
Closed: Do you feel you were treated fairly by the loan officer?
Direct Versus Indirect Questions
Direct: What is your opinion of First National Bank?
Indirect: How do you think most entrepreneurs feel about First National Bank?
Probing Questions
Could you give me an example?
What do you mean by that?

See Transparency 11.6, Interview Questions.

The problem with this item is that the "lack of air-conditioning" category overlaps with the "poor working conditions" category and "noncompetitive financial package" overlaps "poor fringe benefits." And all four of these probably overlap with "weak management." Such intermingling of categories will thoroughly confuse the respondent and yield unreliable survey results.

Recognize that respondents may be hesitant to answer sensitive questions (regarding age, salary, morals, and the like). Even worse, they may deliberately provide *inaccurate* responses. When it is necessary to gather such data, ensure that the respondent understands that the questionnaire is anonymous (by prominently discussing that fact in the cover letter). Respondents tend to be more cooperative in answering such questions when broad categories are used. Accurate estimates provided by broad categories are preferable to precise data that is incorrect.

Simply checking a broad range of figures might be less threatening than having to write in an exact figure.

Not: What is your annual gross salary? $______________

But: Please check the category that best describes your annual salary:

____ Less than $15,000
____ $15,000-$25,000
____ $25,001-$50,000
____ More than $50,000

Note that the use of the number "25,001" in the third category is necessary to avoid overlap with the figure "$25,000" in the second category; remember that the categories must be mutually exclusive.

Even experienced researchers find it difficult to spot ambiguities or other problems in their own questionnaires. If time permits, administer the draft questionnaire to a small sample of potential respondents and then revise it as necessary. At a minimum, ask a colleague to edit your instrument with a critical eye. The sample questionnaire shown in Figure 11.2 illustrates a variety of question types, clear directions, and efficient format.

Writing the Cover Letter

Unless you intend to distribute the questionnaires personally (in which case, you would be able to explain the purpose and procedures in person), include a cover letter like the one shown in Figure 11.3 with your questionnaire. The cover letter should be written as a regular persuasive letter (see Chapter 7). Your job is to convince the reader that it's worth taking the time to complete the questionnaire.

Selecting a Sample

The **population** of a study is every member of a group about whom you're trying to find information. The population for our sample questionnaire in Figure 11.2 would be all the students at Central Metropolitan University. But it isn't necessary to survey all 15,000 students at the university in order to be able to predict their views. When a cook takes a single sip from the kettle and decides the soup needs more salt, he or she makes a judgment based on a sample; the cook does not need to consume the entire pot of soup to determine its flavor. Similarly, we can select a **sample** of students—the part of the population that will actually participate in the study.

Types of Samples For a sample to be accurate, it must reflect the makeup of the entire population. One way to achieve this is to select a **random sample**—a sample drawn in such a way that each individual in the population has an equal and independent chance of being selected. You might draw a random sample by putting the names of all members of the population on a slip of paper and then randomly selecting the number of participants needed for the study.

Although only simple random and stratified samples are discussed here, there are many variations to each.

Or, if the names of the members of the population are available on a list, you might select every *n*th person; if you wanted to select a sample of 300 from a population of 1,500, you would select every 5th name (this is called a *systematic random sample*).

Sometimes the business researcher believes that responses from people in different subgroups may differ. In such situations, stratifying the sample will yield more accurate estimates than will using a simple random sample. In a **stratified sample,** subgroups are represented in the sample in proportion to their numbers in the total population. If you are conducting a consumer survey, for example, you might divide your population into high, medium, and low incomes in order to be able to tell whether groups with different buying power hold different views.

Avoid using a **convenience sample**—a sample that uses whatever subjects happen to be available. Since you cannot be sure that the respondents are typical of the population, you cannot draw any valid conclusions about the population from such data. At best, projects using convenience samples should be considered preliminary research.

Sample Size Despite widespread belief, large samples are not needed in order to draw valid conclusions. Small samples can be very precise if they are representative of the population. The needed sample size is determined through applying a statistical formula; and as shown in Figure 11.4, the size of the population has only a small bearing on the needed sample size. For example, if your population size is 10,000, you need a sample size of 370; however, if your population size increases to 1 million, the sample size increases by only 14 (to 384).

The percentage of people responding to your survey (called the *response rate*) typically has more effect on the accuracy of your findings than does the initial size of your sample. It is much better to get a 90% response from a random sample of 350 than it is to get a 50% response from a sample of 5,000—even though the smaller study yields only 315 responses whereas the larger study yields 2,500 responses. The reason is that with a 90% response rate, you can have more assurance that your respondents are typical of the population. Thus, using follow-up postcards, telephone calls, and the like to persuade people to respond to your initial mailing is a better use of your resources than is sending out an excessively large number of questionnaires initially.

The response rate is usually more important than the sample size.

FIGURE 11.2 Questionnaire

Uses a descriptive title.

Provides clear directions; gives name and address of the researcher.

Uses check-off responses for Questions 1–3.

Uses fill-in-the-blank responses for Question 4.

Uses ranking responses for Question 8.

STUDENT USE OF COMPUTERS AT CMU 1

This survey is being conducted as part of a research project for ADS 360 (Business Communication). Please complete this questionnaire only if you (a) are a full-time junior or senior student at CMU, (b) attended CMU last semester, and (c) have declared a major. Please return the completed questionnaire in the enclosed campus envelope to Pat Jones, 105 Woldt Hall.

A. DESCRIPTIVE INFORMATION

1. Grade level:
   ___ junior
   ___ senior

2. Gender:
   ___ female
   ___ male

3. Age: 2
   ___ 20 or younger
   ___ 21-24
   ___ 25 or older

4. Are you pursuing a teaching or nonteaching major?
   ___ teaching *(Please write in name of major:* ______________________)
   ___ nonteaching *(Please write in name of major:* ______________________)

5. College where major is located:
   ___ Arts and Sciences
   ___ Business
   ___ Education
   ___ Other *(Please specify* ______________________)

6. Did you use a microcomputer at CMU last semester either as a course requirement or for personal use?
   ___ yes *(Please continue with Question 7.)*
   ___ no *(Please disregard the following questions and return the questionnaire to the researcher.)*

B. TYPE AND EXTENT OF COMPUTER USE 3

7. During the last semester, which type of microcomputer did you use <u>most frequently</u>?
   ___ IBM or compatible
   ___ Macintosh
   ___ other *(Please specify* ______________________)

8. Which on-campus computer labs were most convenient for completing your out-of-class computer assignments? *[Please rank from 1 (most) to 4 (least) the convenience of each lab; write in the appropriate number in each blank.]*
   ___ business lab
   ___ dormitory lab
   ___ library lab
   ___ student center lab

9. Listed on the next page are different types of computer software. For each, first check the type of use you made of this software at any time during the previous semester. You may check both *Required* and *Personal* if appropriate. An example of personal use would be typing a term paper using 4

Grammar and Mechanics Notes

1 Make the title and section headings stand out through the use of bold type and perhaps a larger type size. 2 If space is at a premium, group shorter questions on the same line (as in Questions 1–3). 3 Leave as much white (empty) space as possible. 4 Although not always possible (as illustrated here), try to avoid splitting a question between two pages.

word processing software—if such use were not required. Then, for each type of software used, check the total number of hours of use during the semester, including both in-class and out-of-class use.

TYPE OF SOFTWARE	TYPE OF USE			AMOUNT OF USE		
	None	Required	Personal	<5 hrs	5-10 hrs	>10 hrs
EXAMPLE: Games	___	___	✓	___	✓	___
Accounting/Financial	___	___	___	___	___	___
Data base	___	___	___	___	___	___
Educational (tutorial)	___	___	___	___	___	___
Graphics/Presentation	___	___	___	___	___	___
Programming	___	___	___	___	___	___
Spreadsheet	___	___	___	___	___	___
Word processing	___	___	___	___	___	___
Other *(please specify)* ________________.	___	___	___	___	___	___

Provides clear directions and an example for the complex check-off responses in Question 9.

Lists alternatives in alphabetical (or some other logical) order.

5 C. STUDENT OPINIONS

Please check whether you agree with, have no opinion about, or disagree with each of the following statements.

	Agree	No Opinion	Disagree
10. Considering my major, I am receiving adequate training in the use of computers.	___	___	___
11. The computer equipment at CMU is not up to date.	___	___	___
12. I have to wait an unreasonable length of time to get onto a computer in the lab.	___	___	___
13. I enjoy working with computers.	___	___	___
14. Most instructors provide adequate instruction in the use of the software they require.	___	___	___
15. Lab attendants are not as helpful as they should be.	___	___	___

Uses attitude-scale responses for Questions 10–15; this section contains a combination of positive and negative statements.

D. IMPROVEMENTS NEEDED

16. If you could make <u>one</u> suggestion to the university administration to improve computer services at CMU, what would that suggestion be?

6 ____

____

____

____

Saves the open-ended question for last.

Grammar and Mechanics Notes

5 Label different sections if the questionnaire is more than one or two pages long.
6 Provide sufficient space for the respondent to answer open-ended questions.

FIGURE 11.3 Questionnaire Cover Letter

This cover letter would accompany the questionnaire shown in Figure 11.2.

CENTRAL METROPOLITAN UNIVERSITY

PO BOX 0049 • FAIRBANKS, ALASKA 99701

February 8, 19--

Dear Fellow Student: 1

Begins with a short attention-getter.

"Oh no—not another computer project!"

Provides a smooth transition to the purpose of the letter.

Have you ever felt this way during the first day of class when the instructor makes the course assignments? Or, instead, do you sometimes wonder, "Why is the instructor making us do this project manually when it would be so much easier to do on a computer?" 2

Provides reasons for cooperating.

Either way, here is your chance to provide the CMU administration with your views on student computer use at Central Metropolitan University. This research project is a class project for ADS 360 (Business Communication), and the results will be shared with Dr. Dan Rulong, vice president for academic computing.

Makes the requested action easy to take.

If you are a full-time junior or senior student, attended CMU last semester, and have declared a major, please take five minutes to complete this question- 3
naire. Then simply return it by February 19 in the enclosed envelope. You'll be doing yourself and your fellow students a big favor.

Sincerely,

Pat Jones

Pat Jones, Project Leader
105 Woldt Hall

Enclosures

CMU
1879

Grammar and Mechanics Notes

1 *Dear Fellow Student:* Use a generic salutation for form letters that are not individually prepared. 2 *on a computer?":* Position the question mark *inside* the closing quotation mark if the entire quoted matter is a question. 3 *questionnaire* contains two *n*'s and one *r*.

FIGURE 11.4 Maximum Sample Size Needed for a Given Population Size
(With a 95% probability that the sample statistics will be within ±5% of the population parameters)

Population	Sample
100[a]	80
150	108
200	132
250	152
300	169
500	217
750	260
1,000	285
1,500	306
2,000	322
3,000	341
5,000	357
10,000	370
15,000	375
30,000	379
50,000	381
75,000	382
1,000,000	384

Interpretation: 95 times out of 100, the findings based on this sample study would vary by no more than 5 percentage points—plus or minus—from the results that would have been obtained if every member of the population had been studied.

[a]When the population is less than 100, the entire population should be studied.

COLLECTING PRIMARY DATA THROUGH INTERVIEWS

Personal interviews are generally considered to be the most valid method of survey research. In a personal interview, the interviewer can probe, ask for clarification, clear up any misunderstandings immediately, ensure that all questions are answered completely, and pursue unexpected avenues. Thus, data resulting from an interview is often of a higher quality than data resulting from a questionnaire.

Although expensive to conduct, personal interviews are most appropriate for gathering in-depth or complex data.

Personal interviews are most appropriate when in-depth information is desired. The interview permits open-ended questions and gives the respondent free rein to answer as he or she desires. Respondents are likely to *say* more than they will write. Research into topics such as motives, deeply

Rubbermaid conducts interviews with consumers in malls like this one, gathering information on their response to new products.

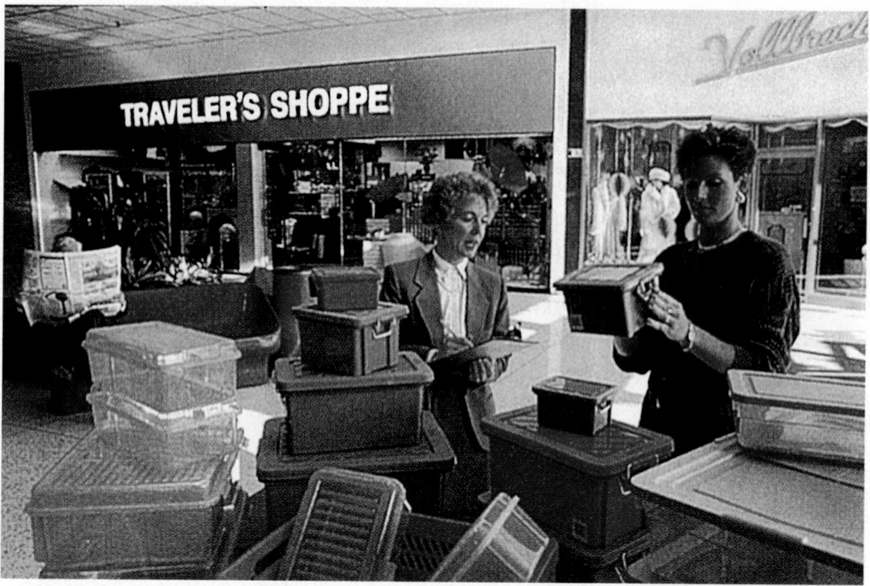

Advise students conducting interviews to give their subjects time to answer. Toby Fulwiler and Alan R. Hayakawa note in *The Blair Handbook* that while a brief silence might mean your question needs clarification, your interviewee might just be thinking over the question, considering a careful response.

held feelings, and complex issues simply does not lend itself to the objective questions found in most questionnaires.

There are, however, several problems with interviews. Interview research is expensive; it is time-consuming to schedule the interviews, conduct them, and analyze the subjective data that flows from them. Also, in-depth interviewing requires specially trained and experienced interviewer.

Second, the interviewer can consciously or unconsciously bias the results—by not recording the answers exactly, for instance, or showing a favorable or unfavorable reaction to a response, or hurrying through parts of the interview. Different interviewers may experience the same situation and "see" different things. Thus, analyzing interview data is often more difficult than analyzing questionnaire data. The subjective nature of the data given and of the data received affects the validity of the research.

Finally, a personal interview is not appropriate for eliciting information of a sensitive nature. Questions about age, salary, personal beliefs, and the like should not be used in face-to-face questioning where anonymity is not possible. (The alert interviewer can, however, sometimes get an estimate of these variables by carefully observing the interviewee and his or her environment.)

In most situations, the sample for a questionnaire study is selected so that each member is typical of the population. However, interviewees are often selected for just the opposite reason: they may have *unique* expertise or experiences to share, and the data they provide will serve as "expert testimony" and not be tabulated and generalized to the population.

Types of Questions

In most ways, your interview questions should follow the guidelines given in Checklist 12 for questionnaire items; they should be clear and unbiased and deal with only one topic per question. However, because of the increased complexity of many interview topics, you now have other choices to make.

Open Versus Closed Questions Open-ended questions allow the interviewee flexibility in responding, whereas closed questions limit the subject matter of the response:

Use both open-ended and closed questions.

Open: What is your opinion of the NAFTA trade treaty?
Closed: How much of your firm's business is attributable to international sales?

Open questions expose the interviewee's priorities and frame of reference and may uncover information that the interviewer may never have thought to ask about. Interviewees like open questions because they are easy to answer (there is no wrong answer), and they give recognition to the interviewee—by letting him or her talk through ideas while the interviewer listens intently. The drawbacks to open questions are that they are time-consuming and the responses may be rambling, difficult to record, and difficult to tabulate later.

Closed questions save time and are very useful when you know exactly what type of information you want, when you intend to tabulate the responses, and when the responses don't require elaborate explanation by the interviewee. The amount of interview information that can be obtained by closed questions, however, is fairly restricted; if all your questions lend themselves to the closed format, a questionnaire would probably yield just as valid results for much less expense.

In actual practice, the interviewer usually uses both open and closed questions, often following up a closed question with an open one.

Closed: Do you agree or disagree with the proposal?
Open: Why?

Closed: Will it have any effect on your own firm?
Open: In what way?

Direct Versus Indirect Questions Most questions may be asked directly. In threatening or sensitive situations, however, you may want to resort to indirect questions, which are less threatening because they let the interviewee camouflage his or her response.

Direct: How would you evaluate your boss's people skills?
Indirect: How do you think most people in this department would evaluate the boss's people skills?

Conducting the Interview

As an interviewer, you must wear two hats—that of an observer and that of a participant. You participate by asking questions, but you must also analyze the responses to ensure that the interviewee is indeed answering the

Listening in an interview involves much more than simply hearing what is being said.

question asked and to determine if follow-up questions are needed. Fulfilling this dual role requires concentration, preparation, and flexibility.

To secure the greatest cooperation from interviewees, you should make them feel comfortable and important (They are!). The first few minutes of the interview are crucial for establishing rapport. Begin with a warm greeting; reintroduce yourself; and explain again the purpose of the interview, how the information will be used, and how much time will be required.

It is difficult to listen actively if you are busy taking notes.

One of the barriers to effective listening during an interview is the need for note taking. Keep note taking to a minimum by using a small portable cassette recorder when possible. Always get permission first, assuring the interviewee that the purpose is to make certain that he or she is not misquoted and to let you give his or her responses your full attention. Keep the recorder out of sight (perhaps on the floor beside you) so that the interviewee is not constantly reminded that his or her remarks are being recorded. Test the recording level beforehand to ensure that the responses will be audible.

Always use an **interview guide**—a list of questions to ask, with suggested wording and possible follow-up questions. Mark off each question as it is asked *and* answered (don't assume that just because a question was asked, it was answered). Nothing is more embarrassing than repeating a question that has already been answered, and nothing is more frustrating than learning after the interview is over that you failed to ask an important question.

Provide smooth transitions when moving from topic to topic by using periodic summaries of what has been covered and previews of what will be covered next; for example,

> We've covered the start-up and initial funding for your firm. Next, I'd like to investigate any problems your firm experienced during its early years.

Follow up a point if the interviewee's response is inadequate in some way; for example, the interviewee may have consciously or unconsciously failed to answer all or part of a question, given inaccurate information, or given a response you did not understand completely. When the response needs amplification, you can probe by asking for more information, by asking for clarification, or by simply repeating the question.

Indicate when the interview is over—either by a direct statement or by such nonverbal gestures as putting your papers away or standing up. Experienced interviewers often end an interview by asking these two questions:

> Is there some question you think I should have asked that I didn't ask? (*to uncover unexpected information*)
>
> May I call you back if I need to verify some information? (*to enable the checking of some fact or spelling or to ask a quick follow-up question*)

Leave the interviewee with a sense of accomplishment by quickly summarizing the important points you've gathered (to show that you've listened) or by restating how the information will be used. Finally, express appreciation once more for the time granted.

COLLECTING PRIMARY DATA THROUGH OTHER METHODS

Although mail surveys and interviews are the major means for collecting primary information for business purposes, the executive has many other research methods at his or her disposal, including observation, telephone inquiries, and experiments.

Observation is often used in market research. For example, the researcher might measure the amount of display space devoted to the firm's product in a sample of retail stores, record people's facial expressions as they watch a sample television commercial, or count the number of coupons redeemed for a company's product.

Observations can be either personal (visual) or mechanical (for example, using a counter).

Telephone inquiries are an increasingly popular way to obtain information quickly and inexpensively. The information desired must be simple and short. Questions should be answerable with "yes" or "no" or in a few words, and the entire call should require no more than two or three minutes of the respondent's time. There is, however, an increasing public resistance to this form of data gathering. Some people view it as an invasion of privacy; and some view it with distrust, suspecting that the questions are merely a prelude to a sales pitch.

Experimental studies are extremely useful for determining cause-and-effect outcomes. Assume, for example, that you wish to find out whether production workers would produce more when working in a brightly lit as opposed to a moderately lit factory. You might randomly select 200 of your production workers and randomly assign 100 of them to the brightly lit workroom and 100 to the moderately lit workroom.

During the experiment, all other conditions should be held constant—the employees should be exposed to similar working conditions, similar levels of management, and the like. The only factor that should be allowed to vary is the level of lighting. At the end of the experiment, you would compare the average production of each group and then determine which type of lighting caused the higher productivity. Because experiments require very careful planning and control, organizations typically call on the services of research professionals to conduct formal experiments.

The major advantage of experiments is that they enable you to conclude that one event caused *a certain outcome.*

MICROWRITING

A Questionnaire

PROBLEM

You are Martha Halpern, assistant store manager for Just Pool Supplies, a small firm in San Antonio, Texas. You have been asked by Joe Cox, store owner, to determine the feasibility of expanding into the spa supply business. To help you determine whether there is a sufficient demand for spa (hot tub) supplies, you decide to develop and administer a short questionnaire to potential customers.

PROCESS

1. What is the purpose of your questionnaire?

   To determine whether there are enough potential customers to make it profitable for us to expand into the spa supply business.

2. Who is your audience?

   The theoretical population for my study would be all spa owners in the San Antonio area. However, because our major business will still be pool supplies, I'll assume that most of my spa supply business would come from my present pool supply customers.

   Thus, the real population for my survey will be the approximately 1,500 present customers that I have on my mailing list. Figure 11.4 tells me that I should select 306 of these for my sample. Thus, I'll have my data base program generate address labels for every fifth customer.

3. What information do you need from these customers?

   a. Whether they presently own a spa or intend to purchase one in the near future
   b. Where they typically purchase their spa supplies
   c. How much money they typically spend on spa supplies each year
   d. How satisfied they are with their suppliers
   e. What the likelihood is that they'd switch their spa supply business to us
   f. How many spa supply firms are located in the area

4. Is all this information necessary? Can any of it be secured elsewhere?

   I can probably determine the number of spa supply firms and their volume of business from secondary data or from the local chamber of commerce, so I won't need to address that question in my survey. All of the other information is needed and none of it can be obtained elsewhere.

5. Do any of these questions ask for sensitive information, or are any of them difficult to answer?

   No. The question asking about the amount of money spent on spa supplies depends a little on memory; but since most people buy spa supplies only four or five times a year, respondents should be able to provide a fairly accurate estimate.

6. Is there any logical order to the questions in Item 3?

   The question about spa ownership must come first, because respondents cannot answer the other questions unless they own a spa. In reviewing the other questions, I think the logical order appears to be a, c, b, d, and e.

7. Will the questionnaire require a cover letter?

   Yes, because it will be mailed to the respondents, instead of being administered personally. I'll use my word processing program to generate personalized form letters to each of the customers selected.

PRODUCT

Cover Letter

JUST POOL SUPPLIES

P.O Box 2277
San Antonio, TX 78298
Phone: 512-555-0083
Fax: 512-555-2994

February 22, 19--

Mr. Frederic J. Diehl
Rio Rancho Estates
1876 Anderson Road
San Antonio, TX 79299

Dear Mr. Diehl:

We miss you during the winter!

Although you're a frequent shopper at Just Pool Supplies during the summer months when you're using your pool, we miss having the opportunity to serve you during the rest of the year. Therefore, we're considering adding a complete line of spa supplies to our inventory.

Would you please help us make this decision by answering the enclosed five questions and then returning this form to us in the enclosed stamped envelope.

Thanks for sharing your views with us. We look forward to seeing you during our traditional Pool Party Sale in March.

Sincerely,

Martha Halpern

Martha Halpern
Assistant Manager

swm
Enclosure

Questionnaire

SPA SUPPLIES

---

1. Do you presently own a spa?
   ___ yes
   ___ no (Please skip the remaining questions and return this form to us in the enclosed envelope.)

2. Considering the number of times you purchased spa supplies last year and the average amount of each purchase, how much do you estimate you spent on spa supplies last year (include all types of purchases—chemicals, accessories, decorative items, and the like).
   ___ less than $100
   ___ $100-$300
   ___ $301-$500
   ___ more than $500

3. Where did you purchase <u>most</u> of your spa supplies last year? (Please check only one.)
   ___ at a general-merchandise store (e.g., Kmart or Sears)
   ___ at a pool- or spa-supply store
   ___ from a mail-order firm
   ___ other (please specify: ________________________________)

4. How satisfied were you with each of these factors at the store where you purchased most of your spa supplies?

Factor	Very Satisfied	Satisfied	Very Dissatisfied
Customer service	___	___	___
Hours of operation	___	___	___
Location of store	___	___	___
Prices	___	___	___
Quality of products	___	___	___
Quantity of products	___	___	___

5. If Just Pool Supplies were to sell spa supplies, how likely would you be to purchase most of your spa supplies there, assuming that the quality, selection, and pricing would be similar to those for their pool supplies.
   ___ very likely
   ___ somewhat likely
   ___ don't know
   ___ somewhat unlikely
   ___ very unlikely

Thanks for your cooperation. Please return the completed questionnaire in the enclosed enveloped to Martha Halpern, Just Pool Supplies, P.O. Box 10634, San Antonio, TX 78291.

SUMMARY

Secondary data is data collected by others for their own specific purposes. Therefore, the researcher who wants to use secondary data for his or her own study must first evaluate it in terms of why and how the data was collected, how it was analyzed, how consistent the data is with that found in other studies, and how old the data is.

The strategy to use for locating relevant secondary sources consists of developing a list of key terms, consulting directories and indexes, and then compiling and reviewing the literature. Sources can be searched either by using traditional print indexes and directories or by making a computer search using either on-line or CD-ROM data bases. The format of these computer data bases is either bibliographic, numeric, or full-text.

Notes should be taken of each relevant article, using either index cards or full sheets of paper. Record the call numbers, bibliographic information, source numbers, headings, and page numbers for your notes. Most notes should be in the form of paraphrases, with direct quotations used sparingly.

Mail questionnaires are an economical and convenient way to gather primary data when the desired information can be supplied easily and quickly. Care should be taken to ensure that all questions are necessary, clearly worded, complete, and unbiased. The questions and their alternatives should be organized in a logical order, the directions should be clear, and the overall format should be attractive and efficient. The cover letter should be a persuasive letter explaining why it is in the reader's interest to answer the survey.

Some type of random or stratified sample should be used for most survey research. Even small sample sizes can yield valid results if most people respond to the questionnaire.

Personal interviews are preferable to questionnaires when the information desired is complex or requires extensive explanation or elaboration. The interviewer must determine whether to use open or closed questions and whether to use direct or indirect questions. The use of a cassette recorder will enable the interviewer to minimize note taking, thereby enabling him or her to listen more attentively.

Other types of primary data collection sometimes used in business include personal observation, telephone inquiries, and experimental studies.

KEY TERMS

For an exercise on matching terms, refer students to the *Study Guide*, pp. 152–153.

CD-ROM (compact disk—read-only memory) data base A collection of information stored on a high-capacity disk that is accessible by a microcomputer with a CD drive.

Citation A reference to a relevant book, journal article, newspaper article, or similar source.

Convenience sample A nonrepresentative sample that uses whatever subjects happen to be available.

Data base A computer-searchable collection of information on a general subject area, such as business, education, or psychology.

Direct quotation The use of the exact words of another.

Factoring Dividing a report problem into its component subparts as an aid in data gathering and analysis.

Interview guide A list of questions to ask during an interview, with suggested wording and possible follow-up questions.

On-line data base A collection of information stored in a mainframe computer that is accessible by a microcomputer or terminal and telephone hookup.

Paraphrase A summary or restatement of a passage in another form.

Population Every member of a group about whom information is being sought.

Primary data Data that is collected by the researcher to solve the specific problem at hand.

Questionnaire An instrument that contains questions designed to obtain information from the individual being surveyed.

Random sample A sample drawn in such a way that each individual in the population has an equal and independent chance of being selected.

Reliability The extent to which an instrument yields consistent results.

Sample The part of the population chosen to participate in a study.

Secondary data Data that is collected by someone else for some other purpose.

Stratified sample A sample drawn in such a way that certain subgroups are represented in the sample in proportion to their numbers in the population.

Survey A data-collection method that gathers information through questionnaires, telephone inquiries, or interviews.

Validity The extent to which a research instrument measures what it is supposed to measure.

REVIEW AND DISCUSSION

1. **Communication at Della Femina McNamee Revisited** ■ Mary Hall and her research staff at Della Femina McNamee use both secondary and primary research. Whether they're tapping on-line data bases or conducting focus group interviews, the researchers are collecting the data the agency must have to create effective advertising.
   a. What sources of secondary data might Hall check to find information about the market trends and the advertising campaigns for low-fat cookies?
   b. What key terms could she use for her search?
   c. Would Hall get more in-depth information about consumers' reactions to a new low-fat cookie by using open-ended or closed questions?

The answers to the review and discussion questions appear in the *Instructor's Resource Manual*, beginning on p. 226.

2. Why is secondary data an important part of most research?
3. What criteria should be used to evaluate the quality of secondary data?
4. How can government literature be searched? Why is it important to do so?
5. Consult the *Library of Congress Subject Headings*. Locate one or more headings that include these terms: "Use," "See," "See Also," "UF," "BT," "NT," and "RT." What does each of these terms mean?
6. List at least two print indexes or directories and at least two computerized data bases that would be appropriate for researching the following topics:
   a. The use of robots in the automotive industry
   b. The need for elementary school students to learn touch keyboarding
   c. Managing intercultural diversity among workers

7. For each of the three topics in Item 6 above, develop a list of key words to use as descriptors. Make sure your terms are compatible with the *Library of Congress Subject Headings*.
8. Describe your own system for taking notes from secondary sources. Provide an example.
9. Under what circumstances should you use a direct quotation instead of a paraphrase?
10. Compose a questionnaire item using each of the following formats:
    a. Check-off response
    b. Fill-in-the-blank
    c. Ranking
    d. Attitude-scale
    e. Open-ended
11. Assume that you want to survey local rental-unit owners regarding the market for student housing. Compose the first sentence of the cover letter that will accompany your questionnaire.
12. "The larger the sample, the more valid the data." Is this statement true or false? Explain.
13. Under what circumstances is it better to use a personal interview instead of a questionnaire?
14. Assume you wish to interview the vice president for student affairs at your college regarding the adequacy of student housing on campus. Compose an appropriate interview question in each of the following formats:
    a. Open
    b. Closed
    c. Direct
    d. Indirect
15. Why is probing sometimes necessary during an interview? How can it be accomplished?
16. Assume you want to determine whether living on campus is more or less expensive than living off campus. Briefly describe how you might gather the needed information through the use of observation, telephone inquiries, and experimentation.

EXERCISES

Sample solutions for Exercises 1-10 appear in the *Instructor's Resource Manual*, pp. 228–232.

1. Microwriting a Questionnaire ■

PROBLEM

The dean of your school of business has asked you, as director of the Bureau of Business Research at your college, to survey typical businesses in your state that have hired your business graduates within the past five years. The purpose of the survey is to determine whether your business graduates have competent communication skills.

PROCESS

a. Brainstorm for 10 minutes. List every possible question you might ask these businesses; don't worry at this point about the wording of the questions or their sequence.
b. Review your questions. Are all of them necessary? Can any of the information be secured elsewhere?

c. Edit your questions to ensure that they are clear and unbiased.
d. Arrange the questions in some logical order.
e. Where possible, format each question with check-off responses, arranging the responses in some logical order.
f. Do any of the questions ask for sensitive information, or are any of them difficult to answer? If so, how will you handle these questions?
g. What information other than the questions themselves should you include on the questionnaire?
h. Should you add a questionnaire cover letter?

PRODUCT

Draft, revise, format, and proofread your questionnaire. Submit both your questionnaire and your answers to the process questions to your instructor.

Note: For each of the following exercises, assume that you have been asked to write a report on the feasibility of opening a frozen yogurt store in Akron, Ohio. (Your instructor may substitute a different product and/or different city for these assignments.)

2. **Secondary Data—Planning and Search** ■ As you prepare to research the feasibility of opening the frozen yogurt store, you will need a search strategy. Look at the questions in Exercise 4 below. For each question (a through h), select two or more key terms you could use to start the search; then think of at least one key term per question that would broaden your research. Next, list the major directories or indexes you would use to find answers to each question. Finally, check with your college or public librarian to determine which of the directories and indexes (if any) are available on CD-ROM or on-line data bases accessible through the library.

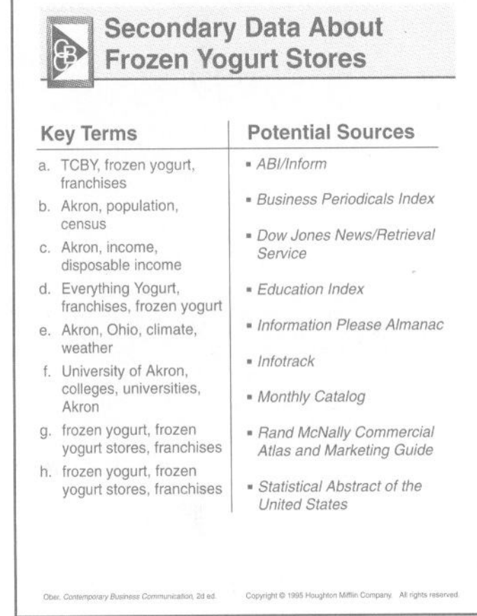

Secondary Data About Frozen Yogurt Stores

Key Terms

a. TCBY, frozen yogurt, franchises
b. Akron, population, census
c. Akron, income, disposable income
d. Everything Yogurt, franchises, frozen yogurt
e. Akron, Ohio, climate, weather
f. University of Akron, colleges, universities, Akron
g. frozen yogurt, frozen yogurt stores, franchises
h. frozen yogurt, frozen yogurt stores, franchises

Potential Sources

- *ABI/Inform*
- *Business Periodicals Index*
- *Dow Jones News/Retrieval Service*
- *Education Index*
- *Information Please Almanac*
- *Infotrack*
- *Monthly Catalog*
- *Rand McNally Commercial Atlas and Marketing Guide*
- *Statistical Abstract of the United States*

Ober, *Contemporary Business Communication*, 2d ed.

See Master 11.1, Exercise 2, Secondary Data, in the *Instructor's Resource Manual.*

3. **Secondary Data—Note Taking** ■ Using whatever indexes would be appropriate, locate and photocopy three journal articles related to this topic. Make notes of each article. Submit photocopies of the articles and your notes to your instructor.
4. **Secondary Data—Locating Specific Information** ■ Answer the following questions, using the latest figures available. Provide a citation for each source.
   a. What were the number of establishments and total sales last year for TCBY, a frozen yogurt franchise?
   b. What is the population of Akron, Ohio? What percentage of this population is between the ages of 18 and 24?
   c. What is the per capita income of residents of Akron?
   d. Who is the chief executive officer of Everything Yogurt, a frozen yogurt franchise? What is his or her address?
   e. What is the climate of Akron, Ohio?
   f. How many students are enrolled at the University of Akron?
   g. What is the market outlook for frozen yogurt stores nationwide?
   h. What is the most current journal or newspaper article you can find on this topic?
5. **Secondary Data—Computer Search** ■ Assume that you have funds to conduct a search using a computer data base. Select the data base that you think would be most helpful and determine which search terms to use. If feasible, conduct the computer search and report the results of your research in a memo to your instructor.
6. **Collaborative Writing—Questionnaire** ■ Since the student body at the University of Akron would provide a major source of potential customers for your yogurt store, you decide to survey the students to gather relevant

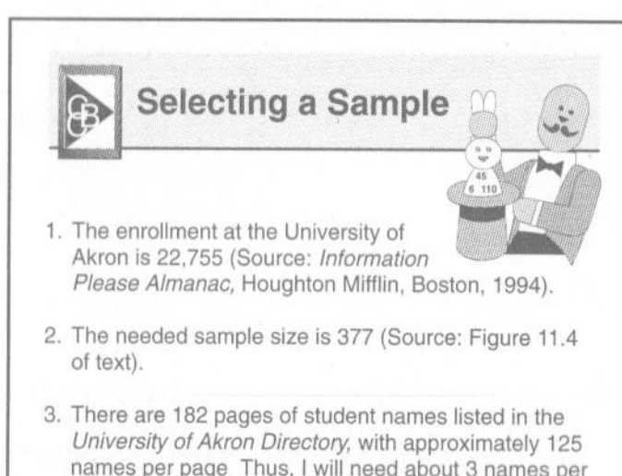

Selecting a Sample
45
6 110
1. The enrollment at the University of Akron is 22,755 (Source: *Information Please Almanac,* Houghton Mifflin, Boston, 1994).
2. The needed sample size is 377 (Source: Figure 11.4 of text).
3. There are 182 pages of student names listed in the *University of Akron Directory,* with approximately 125 names per page Thus, I will need about 3 names per page (377 ÷ 125).
4. Starting at any point in a table of random numbers, I will select the first 3 numbers between 1 and 125. Assume that the random numbers selected are 6, 45, and 110.
5. On every page, I will select the 6th, 45th, and 110th student listed on the page to become a part of my sample.
Ober, *Contemporary Business Communication,* 2d ed.
Copyright © 1995 Houghton Mifflin Company. All rights reserved.

Master 11.2, Exercise 8, Selecting a Sample, in the *Instructor's Resource Manual.*

data. Working in a group of four or five, develop a two-page questionnaire and a cover letter that you will mail to a sample of these students.

Ensure that the content and appearance of the questionnaire follow the guidelines given in Checklist 12. Pilot-test your questionnaire and cover letter on a small sample of students; then revise as necessary and submit to your instructor.

7. **Survey Research—Selecting a Sample** ■ Assume that you wish to send the questionnaire you developed in Exercise 6 to a sample of University of Akron students. Determine from secondary data the current size of the student body, determine the appropriate sample size, and develop a plan for identifying a simple random sample of these students.
8. **Primary Data—Interview** ■ You decide to get some firsthand information from the owner-manager of a premium ice cream or frozen yogurt store in your area (such as Dairy Queen, Baskin-Robbins, TCBY, or I Can't Believe It's Yogurt). Think of the type of information he or she might be able to provide that would help you solve your research problem. Then prepare an interview guide, listing questions in a logical order and noting possible follow-up questions.

   Schedule an interview with the owner-manager and conduct the interview, recording it on tape. Write up your findings in a one- or two-page memo report to your instructor. Retain your tape of the interview until after this assignment has been returned to you.
9. **Primary Data—Observing Customers** ■ One question you haven't yet answered is which toppings a successful frozen yogurt store should offer. Consider how you might use observation to gather the primary data you need to answer this question. Then draft a memo to your instructor in which you describe the methodology you would use; point out the advantages and limitations of using observation in this situation. If you believe that another method of collecting primary data would be more appropriate, explain why.
10. **Primary Data—Other Methods** ■ Assume your anticipated yogurt distributor has eight flavors of frozen yogurt available, but your store will have only four dispensers. Describe how you might conduct an experiment to determine which flavors to stock. How could you get the needed information using other methods of primary data collection?

URBAN SYSTEMS

CONTINUING CASE 11

The Keyboard Strikes Back

A possible solution to the Continuing Case is described in the *Instructor's Resource Manual,* pp. 232–233.

The manufacturing facility in Charlotte employs three data-entry operators who work full-time keyboarding production, personnel, and inventory data into a terminal. This data is then sent over telephone lines to the Urban Systems minicomputer, where it becomes part of the corporate data base for financial, production, and personnel management.

As required by the labor agreement, in addition to a one-hour lunch period, these three operators receive two 15-minute breaks daily; they may take them at any convenient time, once in the morning and once in the afternoon. Otherwise, they generally work at their keyboards all day.

Last year, Arlene Berkowitz, one of the operators, was absent from work for two weeks for a condition diagnosed as carpal tunnel syndrome, a neuromuscular disorder of the tendons and tissue in the wrists caused by repeated hand motions. Her symptoms included a dull ache in the wrist and excruciating pain in the shoulder and neck. Her doctor treated her with anti-inflammatory medicine and a cortisone injection, and she has had no further problems. However, just last week a second data-entry operator experienced similar symptoms; her doctor diagnosed her ailment as "repeated-motion illness" or RSI (repetitive stress injury) and referred to it informally as the "VDT (video display terminal) disease."

Because the company anticipates further automation in the future, with more data-entry operators to be hired, Jean Tate asked her assistant, Pat Robbins, to gather additional information on this condition. In fact, Jean wants Pat to survey all workers at US who use a computer to determine the type and degree of their use and to identify any related health problems. Once the extent of the problem is known, she wants Pat to make any appropriate recommendations regarding the work environment—posture, furniture, work habits, rest breaks, and the like—that will alleviate this problem.

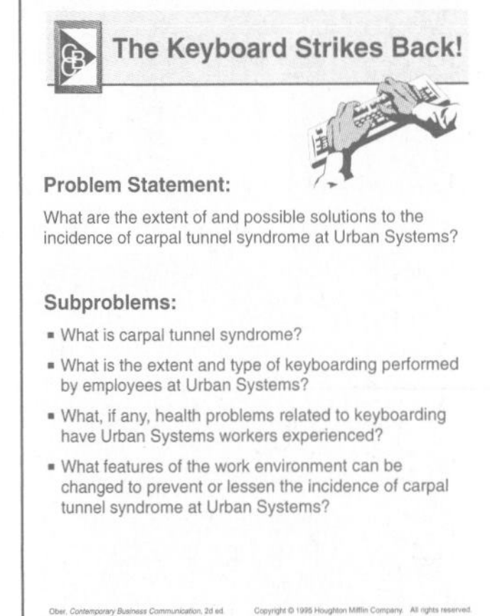

See Master 11.3, Continuing Case 11, Item 3, in the *Instructor's Resource Manual.*

Critical Thinking

1. Assume the role of Pat Robbins. Define the problem of the report and then identify the component subparts (that is, *factor* the problem).
2. Develop a list of key terms to be used for searching for secondary sources.
3. What are the ethical implications of this case?

Writing Projects

4. Search the appropriate indexes and identify five relevant journal articles on this topic. Photocopy each article and save them for a future assignment. Evaluate each article using the criteria given in this chapter; write a one-paragraph summary of your *evaluation* of each article. Using the guidelines given in this chapter, make notes of these articles.
5. Develop an employee questionnaire that elicits the information Jean asked for, plus whatever additional information you believe would be helpful, based on your reading of the journal articles you located. In lieu of a cover letter, include a short introductory paragraph at the top of the questionnaire explaining the purpose of the study and giving any needed directions.

WORDWISE *Word Books*

- The 1993 edition of *Bartlett's Familiar Quotations* contains these new quotations:
  "Me want cookie!" —Cookie Monster (*Sesame Street*)
  "May the force be with you." —Obi-wan Kenobi (*Star Wars*)

- The Vatican has published an updated lexicon for Latin that includes such new terms as
  sphaeriludium electricum nomismate actum (slot machine)
  exterioris paginae puella (cover girl)

- The *Scrabble Dictionary* lists 86 two-letter words.

CHAPTER

12 Analyzing the Data and Preparing Visual Aids

Communication Objectives

After you have finished this chapter, you should be able to

1. Perform a preliminary analysis to edit and evaluate the data collected.
2. Construct clear, concise, and accurate tables.
3. Determine the most effective chart form and construct any charts needed.
4. Interpret the data for the report reader.
5. Avoid misrepresentation when presenting and analyzing data.

How data is presented in a report can have an influence on the direction a company takes. Just ask Jim Solum, manager of Business Systems Development for Wisconsin-based Oshkosh B'Gosh, a company that specializes in children's clothing.

"Resources are often committed to certain areas of a corporation based upon those that represent the highest percentage contribution to total revenue," Solum said.

Reports full of charts and graphs dividing each segment of the company's business into percentages may not tell the whole story. "You have to take a look at the other aspect: How many dollars does it represent? This is where your numbers come in." Twenty percent of a $300+ million business, Solum noted, actually translates into $60 million of revenues. How data is presented affects how it is interpreted, and it is important to choose the type of presentation that best suits the problem. That $60 million figure can be overlooked when shown merely as a percentage of company business.

Oshkosh B'Gosh customers.

"If you start talking percentages, that's one thing, but you have to know when to use percentages and when to use raw data." When a company is looking at a $60 million segment of business, Solum noted, the people dedicated to preserving that market share should be given the tools needed to expand and maintain it. Further digging may show that the overhead costs of maintaining the line may be small in comparison to the line's returns.

Jim Solum
Manager, business systems development, Oshkosh B'Gosh, Oshkosh, Wisconsin

"In that particular case, graphics wouldn't give you an accurate representation. If you start talking to people about $60 million, that's a big hunk of change, with a much bigger impact than the figure *20%*." In fact, this $60 million "is almost as big as our company used to be just six years ago.

"The thing is, it's always been a *percentage* throughout the years. And the percentage usually stays about the same. The idea, if the percentage stays the same, is to look at the dollars involved. In a company such as ours, constant percentages still represent a growing dollar revenue."

Too often, a small, successful segment of a company can be overlooked, especially if it is looked at in the wrong light. "I believe Senator Dirkson said, 'A billion here, a billion there, next thing you know you're talking real dollars.'"

An assistant vice president who prepares colorful bar charts that compare a bank's actual and targeted performance says that top management values the conciseness of the charts because they contain *information*, not just data. "The computer printout doesn't mean much by itself. It doesn't tell you what's relevant in all those numbers." (Christopher O'Malley, "Driving Your Point Home," *Personal Computing*, August 1986, pp. 93–94.)

CONVERTING DATA INTO INFORMATION

At this point in the reporting process, you have presumably gathered enough data from your secondary and primary sources to enable you to solve your problem. (It is always possible, of course, that at any point during data analysis and report writing you may find that you need additional information on a topic.)

Your job at this point, then, is to convert your raw data, which might be represented by your notes, photocopies of journal articles, completed questionnaires, audiotapes of interviews, computer printouts, and the like, into *information*—meaningful facts, statistics, and conclusions—that will help the reader of your report make a decision. In addition to interpreting your findings in narrative form, you will also likely prepare some **visual aids**—tables, charts, photographs, or other graphic materials—to aid comprehension and add interest.

Analysis and interpretation turn data *into* information.

Data analysis is not a step that can be accomplished at one sitting. The more familiar you become with the data and the more you pore over it, the more different things you will see. Data analysis is usually the part of the report process that requires the most time as well as the most skill. The more insight you can provide the reader about the *meaning* of the data you've collected and presented, the more helpful your report will be.

A chapter overview appears in the *Instructor's Resource Manual*, pp. 234–238.

PRELIMINARY DATA ANALYSIS

Preliminary analysis involves editing the data for accuracy and completeness and then evaluating the data to see if it solves the problem; that is, does it give the reader the information needed to make a decision?

Many senior managers are still uncomfortable with computers, says David Shpilberg, head of financial services consulting at Ernst & Young, and their careers may suffer if they are not proficient in new technology. He recommends that companies use computer games to first get computerphobes comfortable interacting with the screen. ("Making It All Worker-Friendly," *Fortune*, Autumn 1993, p. 53.)

Editing

In an ideal world, every respondent would do exactly as he or she were asked, and there would be no need to edit raw data. But that's not what happens. For example, you might get a questionnaire response like that shown in Figure 12.1.

This respondent has checked two answers for one question and written in the margin the reason for doing so. Or, respondents may record an impossible answer (giving a personal birth date of 1845, for example) or give obviously contradictory responses (checking the age category "less than 25 years old" for one question and the category "Medicare" as the major insurance provider in another question, for example). Because of such problems, you should never send your completed questionnaires directly to the computer center for analysis before editing them. Even if you find no errors to correct, you will often find other tidbits of information or insight that you would have missed had your data "never been touched by human hands."

Editing sometimes requires that you guess *the respondent's intentions.*

Data editing is the process of reviewing the data for accuracy and completeness before data analysis. Sometimes you must try to determine the respondent's intentions or predict how the respondent *would have* answered the question. Doing so might occasionally require that you change a respondent's response or fill in a blank response. This is not a step to be taken lightly, however. Good judgment, honest intentions, and high ethical standards should be the hallmarks of editing.

Today, most survey data is tabulated by microcomputer. The survey is *coded*—that is, numbers or symbols are assigned to each question—and responses are fed into the computer with those codes. Numerous microcomputer software programs are available for entering and analyzing data and printing tables and charts of the results. The researcher can edit the data as it's entered into the computer, correcting respondent or keyboarding errors, combining categories, and performing other analysis "on the fly" so to speak. The convenience and flexibility of microcomputer software programs have made computer data analysis a very personalized process.

In addition to performing such specialized statistical analysis, spreadsheet and data base programs can also analyze survey data and produce ta-

FIGURE 12.1 Questionnaire Response That Requires Editing

8. Number of full-time employees in your company:
 X fewer than 500
 ___ 500-1,000
 X more than 1,000

Note: We have 350 employees in our parent organization but more than 1,000 when you include our overseas subsidiaries.

bles and charts, which can then be copied directly into a word processing program for producing the final report.

Evaluating the Data

Determine the meaning of each finding by itself, in conjunction with each other finding, and in conjunction with all other findings.

When analyzing the data, you must first determine whether the data does, in fact, solve your problem. It would make no sense to prepare elaborate tables and other visual aids if your data is irrelevant, incomplete, or inaccurate. To help you make this initial evaluation of your data, assume for the sake of simplicity that you have gathered only three bits of information—a paraphrase from a secondary source, a chart you developed, and a computer printout, labeled Findings A, B, and C, respectively (see Figure 12.2). Now, you are ready to analyze this data.

First, look at each piece of data in isolation (Step 1). If Finding A were the only piece of data you collected, what would it mean in terms of solving the problem? What conclusions, if any, could you draw from this one bit of data? Follow the same process for Findings B and C, examining each in isolation, without considering any other data.

Then look at each piece of data in combination with the other bits (Step 2). For example, by itself Finding A might lead to one conclusion, but when viewed in conjunction with B and C, it might take on a different shade of meaning. In other words, does adding Findings B and C to your data pool *reinforce* your initial conclusion? If so, you can use stronger language in drawing your conclusion. Or does it *weaken* your initial conclusion? If so, you might wish to qualify your conclusion with less certain language or refrain from drawing any conclusion at all.

Finally, synthesize all the information you've collected (Step 3). When you consider all the facts and their relationships together, what do they mean? For example, if Findings A, B, and C all point in the same direction, you might be able to define a trend. More important, you must determine whether all the data taken together provides an accurate and complete answer to your problem statement. If it does, you're then ready to begin the

FIGURE 12.2 The Three Steps in Data Analysis

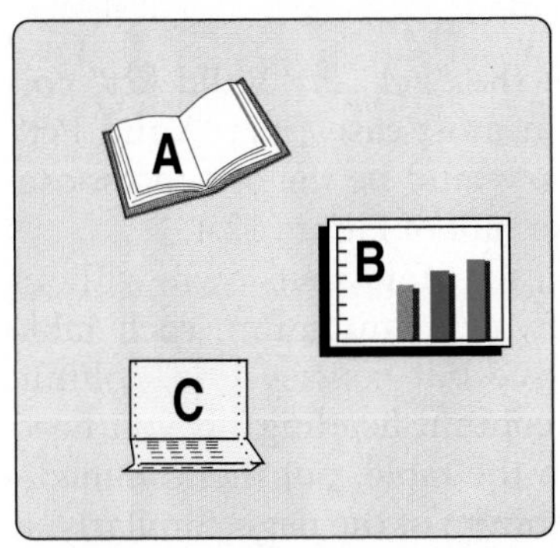

Step 1
Isolation

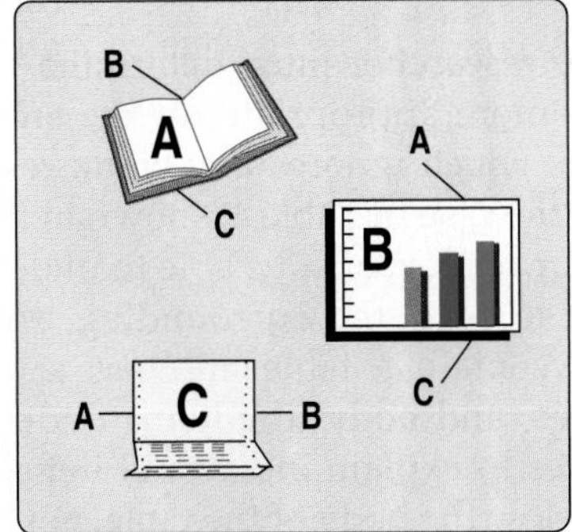

Step 2
Context

Step 3
Synthesis

detailed analysis and presentation that will help the reader understand your findings. If it does not, you must backtrack and start the research process again.

CONSTRUCTING TABLES

Tables are often the most economical way of presenting numerical data.

A **table** is an orderly arrangement of data into columns and rows (see Figure 12.3). It represents the most basic form of statistical analysis and is useful for showing a large amount of numerical data in a small space. A table presents numerical data more efficiently and more interestingly than narrative text and provides more information than a graph, though with less visual impact. Because of its orderly arrangement of information into vertical columns and horizontal rows, a table also permits easy comparison of figures. However, trends are more obvious when presented in graphs.

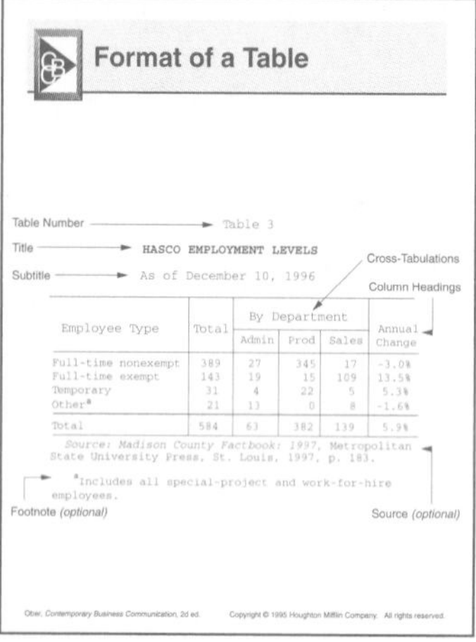

Table 3

HASCO EMPLOYMENT LEVELS

As of December 10, 1996

Employee Type	Total	By Department			Annual Change
		Admin	Prod	Sales	
Full-time nonexempt	389	27	345	17	-3.0%
Full-time exempt	143	19	15	109	13.5%
Temporary	31	4	22	5	5.3%
Other[a]	21	13	0	8	-1.6%
Total	584	63	382	139	5.9%

Source: Madison County Factbook: 1997, Metropolitan State University Press, St. Louis, 1997, p. 183.

[a]Includes all special-project and work-for-hire employees.

See Transparency 12.1, Format of a Table.

Figure 12.4 shows a computer printout of an attitude-scale item (Question 9) on a questionnaire and the corresponding table constructed from this printout. Apex Company, a manufacturer of consumer products headquartered in Des Moines, Iowa, is considering building an addition to its factory there and wants to gauge local opinion before making a commitment.

Consider first the computer printout at the top of Figure 12.4 and the meaning of each column.

- *Value Label:* Shows the five alternatives given on the questionnaire.
- *Value:* Shows the code used to identify each of these five alternatives.
- *Frequency:* Shows the number of respondents who checked each alternative.
- *Pct:* Shows the percentage of each response, based on the total number of respondents ($N = 274$), including those who left this particular item blank.
- *Valid Pct:* Shows the percentage of each response, based on the total number of respondents who actually answered this question ($N = 271$).
- *Cum Pct:* Shows the cumulative percentage—that is, the sum of this response plus those above it (for example, 79.7% of the respondents either agreed or strongly agreed with the statement).

The researcher must determine whether the "Pct" or "Valid Pct" column is more appropriate for the analysis. In most cases, the "Valid Pct" column, which ignores any blank responses, would be the one to choose. That is the case in Table 4, shown in the lower half of Figure 12.4.

The reader should be able to understand the table without having to refer to the text.

Your reader must be able to understand each table on its own, without having to read the surrounding text. Thus, at a minimum, each table should contain a table number, a descriptive but concise title, column headings, and body (the items under each column heading). If you need footnotes to explain individual items within the table, put them immediately below the body of the table, not at the bottom of the page. Similarly, if the table is based on secondary data, type a source note below the body, giving the appropriate citation. Common abbreviations and symbols are acceptable in tables.

FIGURE 12.3 Table

Use tables to present a large amount of numerical data clearly and concisely.

6

for all of 1995. As it has for the past three years, the Eastern

1 Region led the company's sales force, as shown in Table 14.

Table Number

Table 14

Title

1995 APEX SALES LEADERS BY REGION

Subtitle (optional)

As of December 15

Column Headings

Body

	Region	Sales Leader	Sales[a]	Yearly Change
2, 3	Eastern	Ronald Miller	$17.5	13.4%
	Western			
4	Continental	Dorothy Cheung	13.6	-2.1
	Hawaii/Alaska	David Kane	3.2	4.0
	Midwestern	C. J. Peri-Watts	9.7	4.6
	Southern	Rita Rosales	8.2	-5.2
	Plains	B. B. Cody	6.0	15.8
5	Average	----------------	$ 9.7	5.08%

Source (optional)

Source: *Insurance Leaders DataQuest* (New York: Insurance Institute of North America, 1995), 143-179.

Footnote (optional)

[a]In millions.

The sales leaders in two of the regions (Western and Southern) experienced decreased sales, even though they remained the top pro-

Grammar and Mechanics Notes

1 Position the table at the end of the first paragraph that makes reference to the table.
2 Type the dollar sign (at the left-most position) before the first number and before a total or average amount. 3 Unless the column heading clearly indicates that the amounts are percentages, use the percent sign after each amount. 4 Align word columns at the left, number columns at the right. 5 To indicate a blank item in a total or average row, type a row of hyphens the length of the widest item in the column.

FIGURE 12.4 From Computer Printout to Report Table

Computer Printout

Q.9 "APEX COMPANY IS AN ASSET TO OUR COMMUNITY"

VALUE LABEL	VALUE	FREQUENCY	PCT	VALID PCT	CUM PCT
Strongly agree	1	41	15.0	15.1	15.1
Agree	2	175	63.8	64.6	79.7
No opinion	3	34	12.4	12.6	92.3
Disagree	4	15	5.5	5.5	97.8
Strongly disagree	5	6	2.2	2.2	100.0
	•	3	1.1	MISSING	
	-----	-----	------	-----	-----
TOTAL		274	100.0	100.0	100.0

VALID CASES 271 MISSING CASES 3

Corresponding Report Table

TABLE 4. RESPONSE TO STATEMENT "APEX COMPANY IS AN ASSET TO OUR COMMUNITY"

Response	No.	Pct.
Strongly agree	41	15.1
Agree	175	64.6
No opinion	34	12.6
Disagree	15	5.5
Strongly disagree	6	2.2
Total	271	100.0

Cross-Tabulation Analysis

Cross-tabulation analysis enables you to look at two or more groups of data simultaneously.

In some cases, the simple question-by-question tabulation illustrated in Table 4 of Figure 12.4 would be sufficient analysis for the reader's purpose. However, in most cases such simple tabulations would not yield all the "secrets" the data holds. Most data can be further analyzed through **cross-tabulation,** a process by which two or more pieces of data are analyzed together. For example, because of the types of products Apex manufactures, you might suspect that different subgroups of respondents would hold different views of the company. Therefore, you can combine Question 9 with the questions about marital status, gender, and age, as shown in Figure 12.5.

This table shows not only the total responses (both the number and the percentages) but also the percentage responses for the subgroups according to marital status, gender, and age. A quick "eyeballing" of the table shows that there do not seem to be any major differences in the perceptions

FIGURE 12.5 Cross-Tabulation Analysis

TABLE 4. RESPONSE TO STATEMENT "APEX COMPANY IS AN ASSET TO OUR COMMUNITY"

	Total		Marital Status		Gender		Age			
Response	Total	Pct.	Married	Single	Male	Female	Under 21	21-35	36-50	Over 50
Strongly Agree	41	15.1%	14.0%	17.6%	15.7%	10.4%	21.7%	8.4%	12.0%	28.4%
Agree	175	64.6%	67.5%	58.8%	67.6%	46.3%	47.8%	65.1%	69.1%	61.0%
No Opinion	34	12.6%	11.2%	15.4%	11.4%	20.9%	17.5%	13.0%	14.3%	9.2%
Disagree	15	5.5%	5.1%	5.5%	4.0%	13.4%	13.0%	8.4%	4.0%	0.7%
Strongly Disagree	6	2.2%	2.2%	2.7%	1.3%	9.0%	0.0%	5.1%	0.6%	0.7%
Total	271	100.0%	100.0%	100.0%	100.0%	100.0%	100.0%	100.0%	100.0%	100.0%

of married versus single respondents. However, there does seem to be a fairly sizable difference between male and female respondents: males have a much more positive view of the company than do females.

If the table in Figure 12.5 were one of only a few tables in your report, it would be just fine the way it is shown. However, suppose the statement "Apex Company is an asset to our community" is one of a dozen attitude items, each of which requires a similar table. It is probably too much to expect the reader to study a dozen similar tables; in such a situation, you should consider simplifying the table.

Sometimes tabular data needs to be condensed for easier and faster comprehension.

There are a number of ways to simplify a table. You should recognize right from the start, however, that whenever you simplify a table (that is, whenever you merge rows or columns or simply delete data), your table loses some of its detail. The goal in simplifying is to gain more in comprehensibility than you lose in specificity. Your knowledge of the reader and his or her needs will help you determine how much detail to present.

With that in mind, consider the simplified version of this table shown in Figure 12.6. The two positive responses ("strongly agree" and "agree") have been combined into one "agree" row, as have the two negative responses. Combining not only simplifies the table but also prevents some possible interpretation problems. Given the original table in Figure 12.5, for example, would you consider the following statement to be accurate: "Less than half of the females agree that Apex Company is an asset to their

FIGURE 12.6 Simplified Table

TABLE 4. RESPONSE TO STATEMENT "APEX COMPANY IS AN ASSET TO OUR COMMUNITY"

	Total		Marital Status		Gender		Age		
Response	Total	Pct.	Married	Single	Male	Female	Under 21	21-50	Over 50
Agree	216	79.7%	81.5%	76.4%	83.3%	56.7%	69.5%	77.3%	89.4%
No Opinion	34	12.6%	11.2%	15.4%	11.4%	20.9%	17.5%	13.7%	9.2%
Disagree	21	7.7%	7.3%	8.2%	5.3%	22.4%	13.0%	9.0%	1.4%
Total	271	100.0%	100.0%	100.0%	100.0%	100.0%	100.0%	100.0%	100.0%

Arlene DeCandia, founder of the Minneapolis conference center Riverwood Metro Business Resort, uses spreadsheets to back up her loan proposals. She tracks not only her business but also the business she has to turn away. Presenting this data in spreadsheets gives the bank hard data to support her plans for expansion.

community"? Technically, the statement is accurate, since the 46.3% who "agree" is *less* than half. However, the statement leaves an incorrect impression because more than half of the females (57%—those who "agree" *and* who "strongly agree") believe Apex Company is an asset to their community. This conclusion is made clear in Figure 12.6.

Note also that the two middle-age groups ("21–35" and "36–50") have been combined into one age group ("21–50"). Because the company's products are geared mainly to this large middle group, the company wanted to compare the responses of this important group with the responses of the less important younger and older groups.

More data is not always better than less data.

This simplification deleted one of the ten columns and two of the five rows—for a net decrease of 46% in the number of individual bits of data presented. When this reduction is multiplied by the number of similar tables, the net effect is rather dramatic. The simplification could even have been taken a step further by rounding each percentage to the nearest whole—a tactic that would have made each table "appear" much simpler, with little loss of precision.

An alternative method of presenting this and similar attitude scale data would be to use a *weighted average.* The weighted average for the question shown in the original computer printout (Figure 12.4) would be calculated as follows:

Response	*Freq.* ×	*Weight* =	*Total*	
Strongly agree	41	5	205	
Agree	175	4	700	
No opinion	34	3	102	
Disagree	15	2	30	
Strongly disagree	6	1	6	
	271		1,043	1,043/271 = 3.8

FIGURE 12.7 Table Using Weighted-Average Analysis

TABLE 4. RESPONSE TO STATEMENT "APEX COMPANY IS AN ASSET TO OUR COMMUNITY"

Total	3.8
Sex:	
Male	3.9
Female	3.8
Marital Status:	
Married	3.9
Single	3.4
Age:	
Under 21	3.8
21-50	3.9
Over 50	4.2

5 = strongly agree; 4 = agree;
3 = no opinion; 2 = disagree;
1 = strongly disagree

As shown in Figure 12.7, the resulting weighted average of 3.8 for the total response would be interpreted this way:

> On a scale of 1 to 5 (where 5 = "strongly agree" and 1 = "strongly disagree"), the average response to this question was 3.8.

The other weighted averages would be interpreted similarly. Because the weighted averages, by themselves, do not tell a lot, weighted averages are most appropriate when the important information is how much one group varies from another (for example, married versus single). The advantage of using weighted averages is that you can condense a mass of data into just a few numbers. The disadvantage is that some readers may not know how to interpret the results.

Arranging Data in Tables

Arrange the data in logical format—usually from high to low.

As discussed earlier, the check-off alternatives in your questionnaire items should be arranged in some logical order, most often either numerical or alphabetical, to avoid possibly biasing the responses. Once you have the data in hand, however, it is often helpful to the reader if you rearrange the data from high to low.

In Figure 12.8, for example, the categories have been rearranged from their original *alphabetical* order in the questionnaire to *descending* order in the report table. Note also that the four smallest categories have been com-

FIGURE 12.8 Arranging Data in Tables

From This:

6. In which of the following categories of clerical workers do you expect to hire additional workers within the next three years? (Check all that apply.)

 211 bookkeepers and accounting clerks
 31 computer operators
 30 data-entry keyers
 24 file clerks
 247 general office clerks
 78 receptionists and information clerks
 323 secretaries
 7 statistical clerks
 107 typists and word processors

To This:

TABLE 2. COMPANIES PLANNING TO HIRE ADDITIONAL CLERICAL WORKERS (BY CATEGORY)

Category	No. of Co's	Pct.[a]
Secretaries	323	99.1
General office clerks	247	75.8
Bookkeepers and accounting clerks	211	64.7
Typists and word processors	107	32.8
Receptionists and information clerks	78	23.9
Miscellaneous	92	28.2
Total	326	

[a]Answers total more than 100% because of multiple responses.

bined into a miscellaneous category, which always goes last, regardless of its size. Finally, note the position and format of the table footnote, which is used to explain an entry in the table.

PREPARING CHARTS

The appropriate use of well-designed charts and graphs (technically, *graphs* are shown on graph paper; however, the two terms are used interchangeably) can aid in reader comprehension, emphasize certain data, create interest, and save time and space because the reader can perceive immediately the essential meaning of large masses of statistical data.

Because of their visual impact, charts receive more emphasis than tables or narrative text. Therefore, you should save them for presenting in-

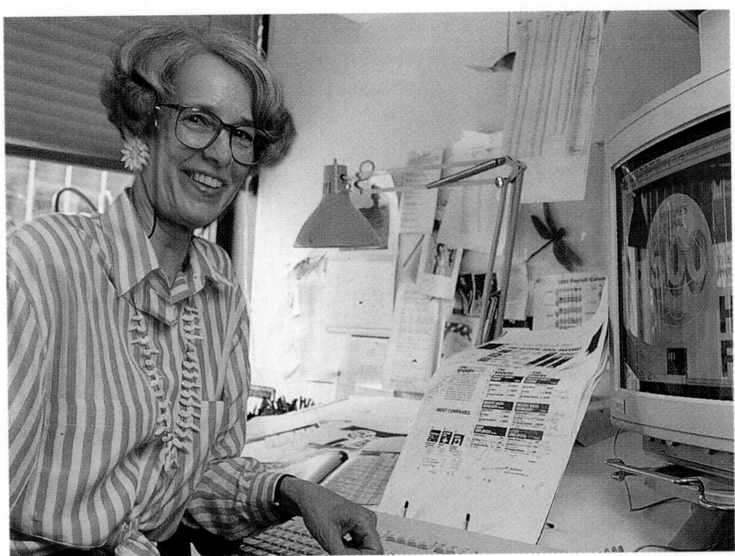

Designer Jean Held makes a living designing infographics—charts and diagrams that shape information to make it immediately accessible to readers—for Fortune *magazine.*

formation that is important and that can best be grasped visually—for example, when the overall picture is more important than the individual numbers. Also recognize that the more charts your report contains, the less impact each individual chart will have.

Keep charts simple. Immediate comprehension is the goal.

The cardinal rule for designing charts is to keep them simple. Trying to cram too much information into one chart will only confuse the reader and lessen the impact of the graphic. Well-designed charts have only one interpretation, and that interpretation should be clear immediately; the reader shouldn't have to study the chart at length or refer to the surrounding text.

Regardless of their type, label all your charts as *figures,* and assign them consecutive numbers, separate from table numbers. Although tables are captioned at the top, charts may be captioned at the top or bottom. Charts used alone (for example, as an overhead transparency or slide) are typically captioned at the top. Charts preceded or followed by text or that contain an explanatory paragraph are typically captioned at the bottom. As with tables, you may use commonly understood abbreviations.

Today, many microcomputer software programs are able to generate special charts automatically from data already contained in spreadsheets or from data entered at the keyboard. The professional appearance and ready availability of such charts often make up for the loss of flexibility in designing graphics precisely to your wishes.

The main types of charts used in business reports and presentations are line charts, bar charts, pie charts, and pictorial charts.

Line Charts

A **line chart** is a graph based on a grid of uniformly spaced horizontal and vertical lines. The vertical dimension represents values; the horizontal dimension represents time. Line charts are useful for showing changes in data over long periods of time and for emphasizing the movement of the data—the trends. Both axes should be marked off at equal intervals and

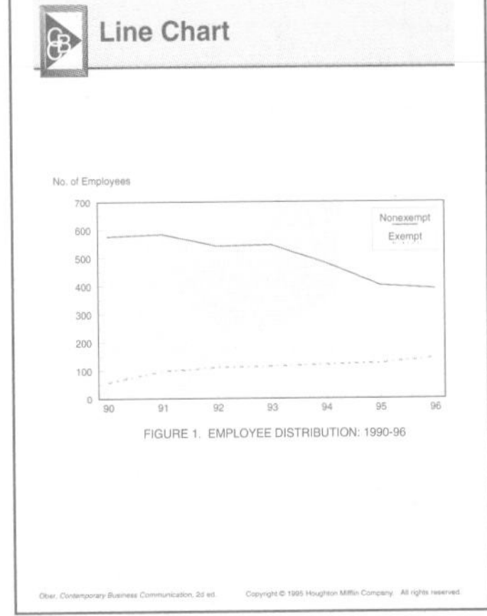

See Transparency 12.2, Line Chart.

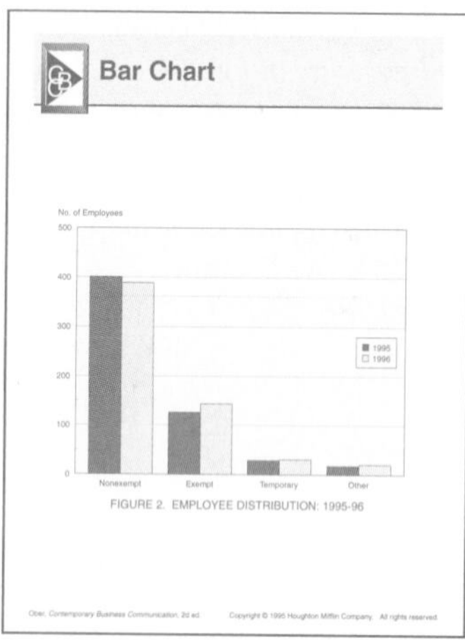

See Transparency 12.3, Bar Chart.

clearly labeled. The vertical axis should begin with zero, even when all the amounts are quite large. In some situations, it may be desirable to show a break in the intervals, as illustrated in Figure 12.9B. Fluctuations of the line over time indicate variations in the trend; the distance of the line from the horizontal axis indicates quantity.

More than one variable may be plotted on the same chart (see Figure 12.9A). For example, both sales and net profits can be plotted on one chart, using either different-colored lines or different types of lines (solid, dotted, and dashed, for example) to avoid confusion. Each line should be labeled clearly.

A variation of the line chart is the area (or surface) chart, which uses shading to emphasize the overall picture of the trend (see Figure 12.9B). A second variation is the segmented area chart, which contains several bands that depict the components of the total trend (see Figure 12.9C). Because the individual components cannot be read accurately, the segmented area chart should be used only to give an overall picture.

Bar Charts

Bar charts compare the magnitude of items. Use vertical bars for comparing items over time.

A **bar chart** is a graph with horizontal or vertical bars representing values. Bar charts are one of the most useful, simple, and popular graphic techniques. They are particularly appropriate for comparing the magnitude or size of items, either at a specified time or over a period of time. The vertical bar chart (sometimes called a *column chart*) is typically used for portraying a time series when the emphasis is on the individual amounts rather than on the trends (see Figure 12.10A).

The bars should all be the same width, with the length changing to reflect the value of each item. The spacing between the bars should generally be about half the width of the bars themselves. Bars may be grouped to compare several variables over a period of time (see Figure 12.10B) or may be stacked to show component parts of several variables (see Figure 12.10C). As with tables, the bars should be arranged in some logical order. If space permits, include the actual value of each bar for quicker comprehension.

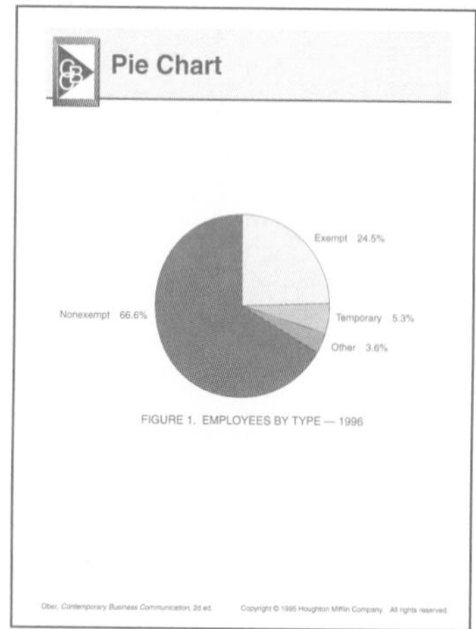

See Transparency 12.4, Pie Chart.

Miscellaneous Charts

Among other frequently used business charts are pie charts, pictographs, map charts, and informal charts.

Pie Charts A **pie chart** is a circle graph whose area is divided into component wedges (see Figure 12.11A). It compares the relative parts that make up a whole. Some software charting programs permit you to "drag out" a particular wedge of the pie chart for special emphasis.

Although pie charts rank very high in popular appeal, graphics specialists hold them in somewhat lower esteem because of their lack of precision and because of the difficulty in differentiating more than a few categories, and in comparing component values across several pie charts.

FIGURE 12.9 Line Charts

A. Simple Line Chart

Figure 1. Apex Sales by Division
1970–1995

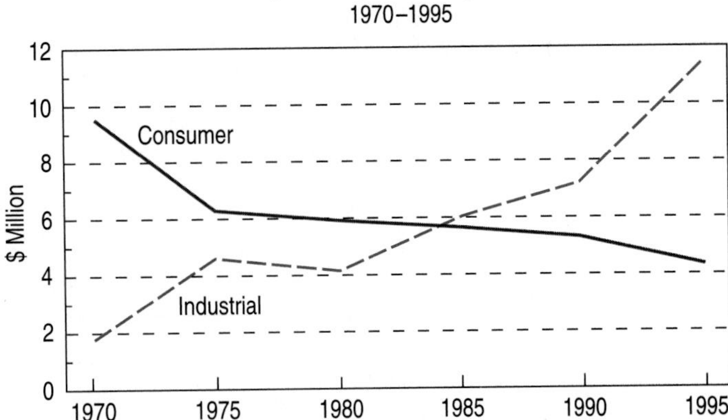

1

B. Area Chart

Figure 2. Average Age of Apex Customer
1970–1995

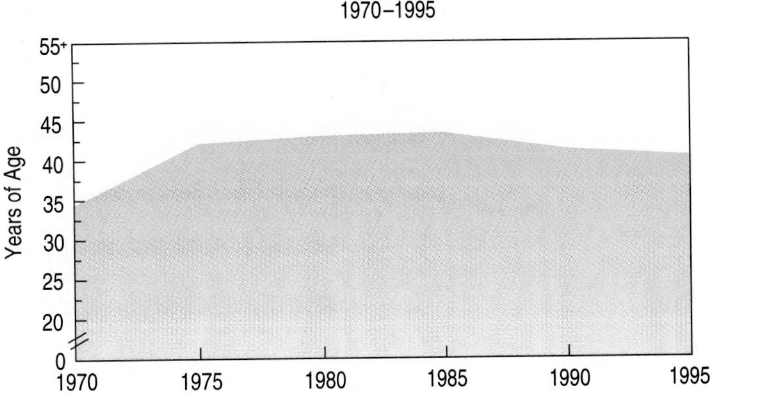

2

C. Segmented Area Chart

Figure 3. Apex Sales by Division
1970–1995

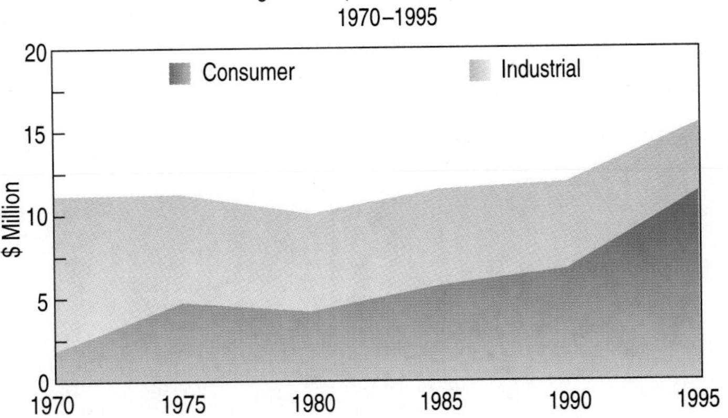

3

Grammar and Mechanics Notes

1 Start the vertical axis at the zero point. 2 Use slash marks if necessary to indicate a break in an interval. 3 Clearly differentiate between two trend lines, and label each.

FIGURE 12.10 Bar Charts

A. Vertical Bar Chart, or Column Chart

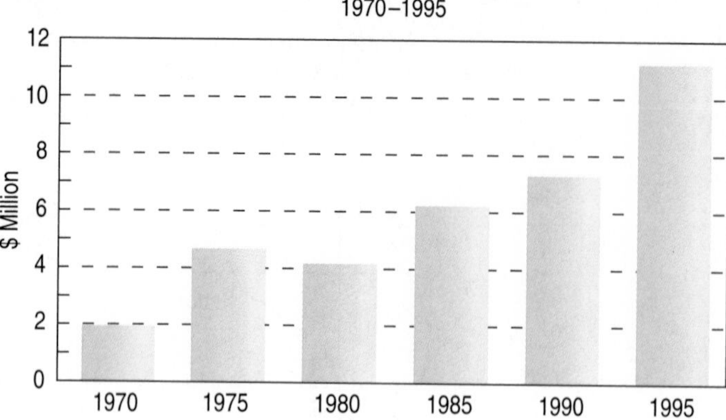 1

B. Horizontal Bar Chart

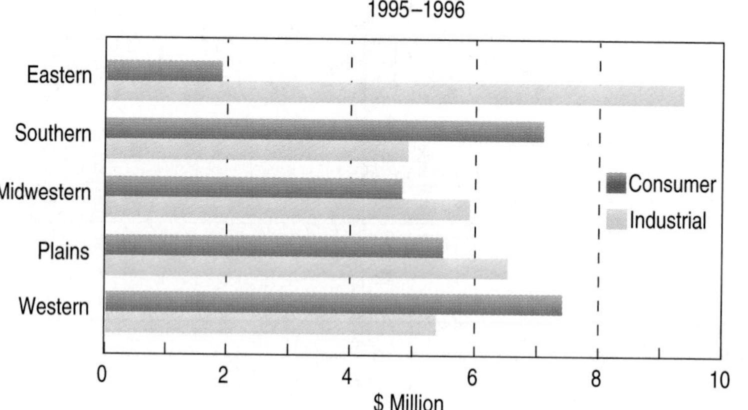 2

C. Stacked Bar Chart

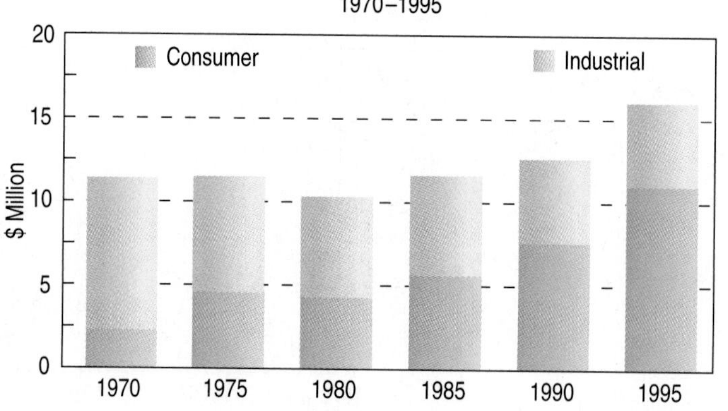 3

Grammar and Mechanics Notes

1 Make all bars the same width; show value differences by varying the length or height. 2 Position the bars either vertically or horizontally. 3 Label all charts (regardless of type) as "Figures"; place the figure number and title either above or below the chart.

FIGURE 12.11 Miscellaneous Charts

A. Pie Chart

Figure 7. 1995 Sales by Region 1

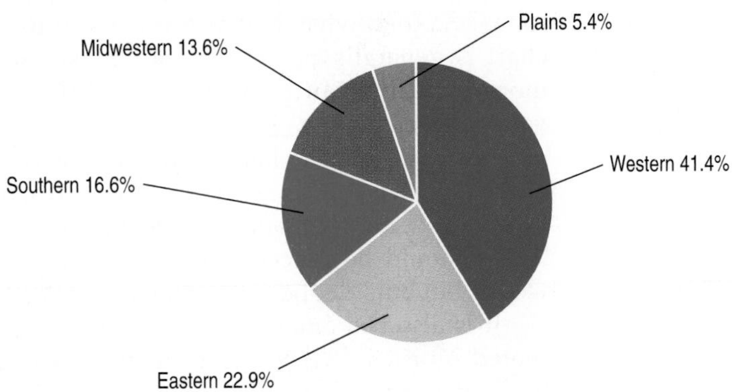

B. Pictograph

Figure 8. Apex Work Force — 1995
(Each symbol represents 5 employees) 2

Production	80
Sales/Marketing	43
Office	30
Management	17
Miscellaneous	24

C. Map Chart

Figure 9. Apex Sales Regions 3

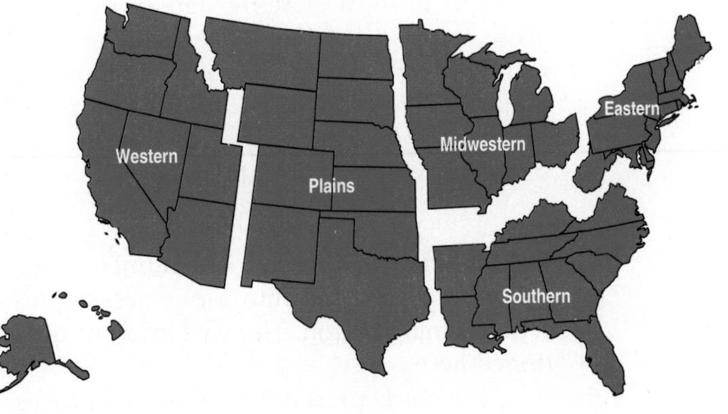

Grammar and Mechanics Notes

1 Begin slicing the pie at the 12 o'clock position and move clockwise in a logical order. 2 Make every symbol in a pictograph the same size. 3 Exclude any irrelevant information on a map chart.

Using desktop publishing, report writers can import charts created by graphics software into their documents. The desktop publishing program will automatically "wrap" the text around the charts.

However, pie charts are useful for showing how component parts add up to make a total when between three and five component parts are used. A chart is generally not needed for presenting only two component parts; more than five can present visual difficulties in perceiving the relative value of each wedge.

It is customary to begin "slicing" the pie at the 12 o'clock position and move clockwise in some logical order (often in order of descending size). When used, a miscellaneous category goes last, regardless of its size. The labels should be placed either inside each wedge, directly opposite the wedge but outside the pie, or in a legend or key.

It is also customary to include the percentages or other values represented by each wedge and to distinguish each wedge by shading, cross-hatched lines, different colors, or some similar device. If you must construct a pie chart manually, use a protractor. Each percentage point would equal 3.6 degrees (out of a 360-degree circle).

Pictorial charts add interest to mass-audience communications.

Pictographs A **pictograph** is a graph with relevant symbols representing the values. For the chart to be effective, the symbol used must have a close and immediate association with the data being presented. Each symbol (called a *pictogram* or *icon*) represents one unit of measure; for example, in Figure 12.11B, each symbolic person represents five employees. The value of each variable should be shown by the *number* of symbols used rather than by the relative size of the symbol. The symbols are stacked either vertically or horizontally, similar to a bar chart. Sometimes symbols cut in half must be used to give an accurate impression.

Map Charts A **map chart** is a visual representation of data based on geography. The type of chart shown in Figure 12.11C is an *outline map,* which shows just the outline of a geographical entity (such as county, state, or country). Outline maps can be used to show the locations of business operations or to show state-by-state or other geographical comparisons. *Guide maps,* on the other hand, are used for giving directions—for example, directing people to a specific office within a building or to a specific street address. Unlike road maps, map charts should contain the minimum geographical information needed. Exclude such information as the names of unneeded cities, rivers, and routes.

Many types of visual aids can be productively used in business communications.

Other Types of Charts The number of different types of visual aids that can be incorporated into a business report is limited only by the report writer's imagination. The vast array of devices available can only be mentioned here.

Flow charts present the steps in a process or the progress of events; the PERT (Program Evaluation and Review Technique) chart is a specialized type of flow chart that shows the management of a project. *Organizational charts* show the overall structural plan of a group or organization. *Diagrams* can be used to show the component parts of an item, to illustrate a process (for example, the data-analysis model shown in Figure 12.2, page 365). *Pho-*

tographs or *drawings* illustrate and clarify the meaning of many business concepts.

Informal Charts A variety of informal business charts are available to generate interest in a topic (see Figure 12.12). Although such publications as *USA Today* and other popular newspapers and magazines make extensive use of three-dimensional graphics and elaborate, illustrated charts (often called "chartoons") to show statistical information, their use in business should be limited to general-interest audiences.

For example, three-dimensional graphics, although attention grabbing, are difficult to interpret because they are often used to display only two-dimensional data (horizontal and vertical), with the third dimension (depth) having no significance. Similarly, three-dimensional pie charts (such as Figure 12.12), which are shown slanted away from the viewer rather than vertically, can be misleading because of perspective—the slices farthest away appear smaller than they actually are. Such graphics are quite effective for gaining attention and providing a general impression but are less effective for conveying the precise meanings needed in business communications.

Checklist 13 summarizes the most important points to consider when constructing tables and charts.

A Word of Caution

Do not overuse visual aids; they will detract from your message.

As the name *visual aids* implies, charts act as a *help*—not a substitute—for the narrative presentation and interpretation. Never use visual aids simply to make your report "look prettier."

Recent research indicates that the format of the data (tables versus graphs) has little effect on the quality of the decisions made when the task requires a thorough analysis of financial data; both formats are judged to be equally effective. Managers appear to have more confidence in their decisions when such decisions are based on data from tables alone as opposed to data from graphs alone, but managers have the most confidence when both formats are used.[1]

These research findings indicate that graphic devices should be used as an *adjunct* to textual and tabular presentations. Although most numerical data can be presented more efficiently in tables, the competent business communicator uses charts to call attention to particular findings. Rarely should the same data be presented in both tabular and graphic formats.

In *The Visual Display of Quantitative Information,* Edward Tufte warns against *chartjunk*—charts that call attention to themselves instead of to the information they contain.[2] With the ready availability and ease of use of computer graphics, the temptation might be to "overvisualize" your report. Avoid using too many, too large, too garish, or too complicated charts. If the impact is not immediate or if interpretations vary, the chart loses its effectiveness. As with all other aspects of the report project, the visual aids must contribute directly to telling your story more effectively. Avoid chartjunk; strive to *express*—not to *impress.*

FIGURE 12.12 Informal Charts

A. 3-Dimensional Pie Chart

Figure 10. 1995 Sales by Region 1

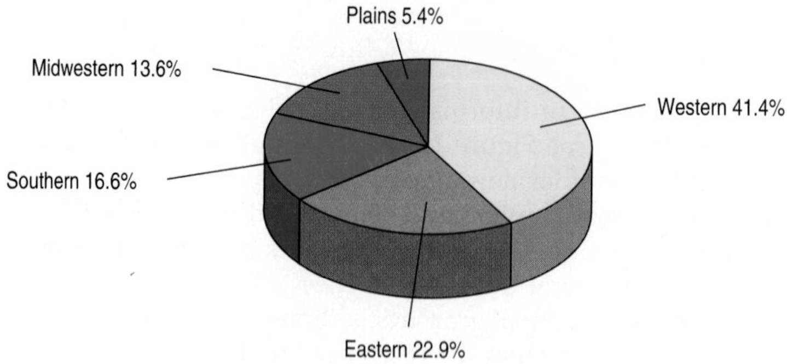

B. Pictorial Bar Chart

Figure 11. Card-Game Revenues—1994 2

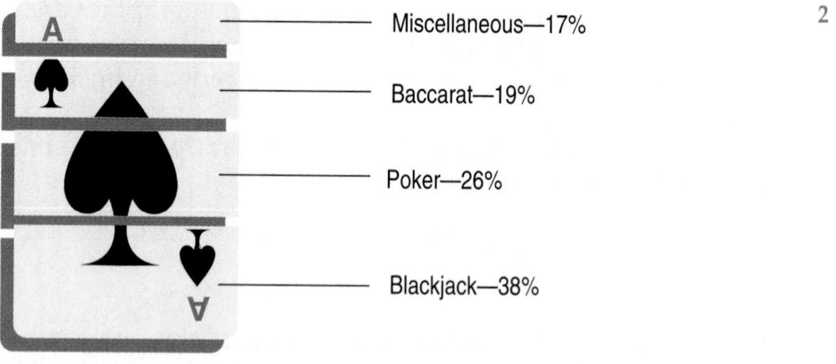

Source: Carl Toller, *1994 Annual Gaming Report*, American Gaming Commission, Atlantic City, NJ, 1994.

C. Pictorial Line Chart

Figure 12. Apex Retained Earnings—1970–1995 3

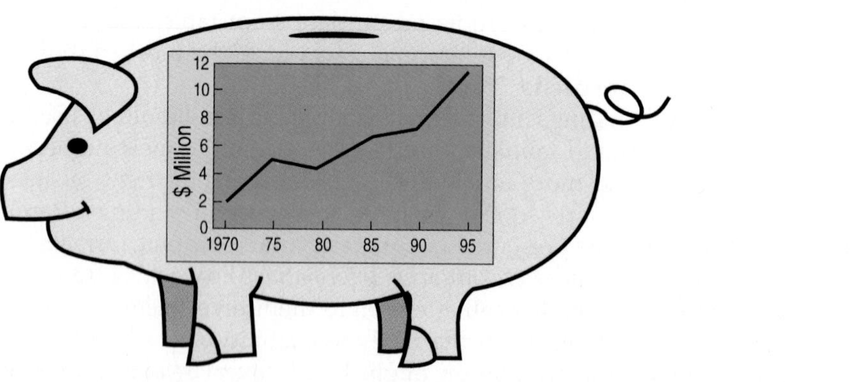

Grammar and Mechanics Notes

1 To avoid distortion, avoid tilting a three-dimensional chart too much.
2 Clearly label the title and amount of each segment. 3 Ensure that any picture used in a chart relates directly and immediately to the subject of the data.

INTERPRETING DATA

In some situations, the numerical data is so simple or the reader is so attuned to the problem that merely presenting the percentages in tabular form may be all that is needed. Such might be the case for a recurring report, where the same quantitative data is presented in the same format month after month. The more typical situation, however, requires the report writer to perform a more in-depth analysis of the quantitative data.

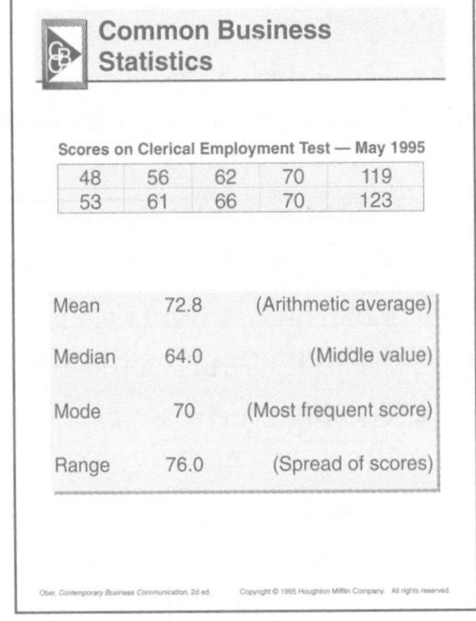
Common Business Statistics

Scores on Clerical Employment Test — May 1995

48	56	62	70	119
53	61	66	70	123

Mean	72.8	(Arithmetic average)
Median	64.0	(Middle value)
Mode	70	(Most frequent score)
Range	76.0	(Spread of scores)

See Transparency 12.5, Common Business Statistics.

Selecting and Calculating Statistics

Statistics is the branch of mathematics dealing with the collection, organization, and interpretation of numerical data. We use statistics every day, as illustrated by the following comments:

> "My GPA last semester was 3.2."
> "We outsold DeVry last month 3 to 2."
> "Our typical customer is a married female in her early twenties."
> "Sales picked up 9% when we offered consumers a $2 rebate."

Even when statistics are not mentioned in a statement, they are often implied. For example, the statement "The Phoenix Suns are going to kill the Chicago Bulls in the playoffs" is probably based on a knowledge of such team statistics as player heights, percentage of shots made, and percentage of games won. (And, as is sometimes the case, even statistically based predictions can prove incorrect—at least they did in 1993!)

Although the study of statistics is beyond the scope of this text, we can usefully review some elementary statistical concepts to help us analyze the data we collect. The most common descriptive statistics used to summarize a mass of data are the mean, median, mode, and range.

Use the mean to describe a group of numbers unless there are one or two extreme values.

Mean The **mean** is the arithmetic average of a group of numbers; it is computed by dividing the sum of the figures by the number of figures in the group. Assume that the ages of the ten respondents to your survey are as follows:

24	28	30	33	60
26	30	33	35	63

The mean age of your respondents is 362/10, or 36.2 years. The mean is the value we usually mean when we talk about an average. It is generally the most important descriptive statistic because it takes into account the numerical value of all the scores in a group. Because the mean is strongly affected by extreme values, however, it should not be used when one or two of the figures are so dramatically different from the others that including them might result in an inaccurate representation of the data.

Median The **median** is the middle value (or midpoint) in a group of numbers arranged from low to high (or vice versa). The median divides the

CHECKLIST 13

Visual Aids

TABLES

1. Use tables to present a large amount of numerical data in a small space and to permit easy comparisons of figures.
2. Number tables consecutively and use concise but descriptive table titles and column headings.
3. Ensure that the table is understandable by itself—without reference to the accompanying narrative.
4. Arrange the rows of the table in some logical order (most often, in descending order).
5. Combine smaller, less important categories into a miscellaneous category and put it last.
6. Use cross-tabulation analysis to compare different subgroups.
7. Use only as much detail as necessary; for example, rounding figures off to the nearest whole increases comprehension. If decimals are used, align them vertically on the period.
8. Use abbreviations and symbols as needed.
9. Ensure that the units (dollars, percentages, or tons, for example) are identified clearly.

CHARTS

1. Use charts only when they will help the reader interpret the data better—never just to make the report "look prettier."
2. Label all charts as *figures*, and assign them consecutive numbers (separate from table numbers).
3. Keep charts simple. Strive for a single, immediate, correct interpretation, and keep the reader's atten-

group into two equal groups. Assume that your ten respondents purchased the following volume of products from you last year:

$5,600	$22,500	$25,800	$31,000	$95,000
$17,800	$24,700	$26,000	$34,000	$175,000

The median sales volume of your ten respondents is half-way between the fifth and sixth responses, or $25,900 (computing the midpoint is not necessary if there is an odd number of figures). In this example, the median of $25,900 is a more accurate representation of the group of figures than would be the mean value of $43,270, because of the effect on the mean of the one extreme value of $175,000 (in fact, only one other respondent purchased as much as the mean value).

Use the median or mode if the mean would not give an accurate representation.

Mode The **mode** is the value in a group of numbers that occurs most frequently. Assume you surveyed ten users regarding their favorite container size of the cheese spread you manufacture, with the following responses:

4 oz.	4 oz.	8 oz.	12 oz.	16 oz.
4 oz.	4 oz.	8 oz.	16 oz.	32 oz.

The mode of this distribution is 4 ounces; that is, the 4-ounce size is the most popular size with the respondents. The chief advantages of using the mode to describe a group of figures are that it is easy to obtain, simple to interpret, and not affected by extreme values in the group of figures. Sometimes it is also the only logical choice. For instance, it would not have made sense in this example to say that the most popular sized container for tion on the *data* in the chart rather than on the chart itself.

4. Prefer two-dimensional charts; use three-dimensional charts only when generating interest is more important than precision.

5. Use the most appropriate type of chart to achieve your objectives. Three of the most popular types of business charts are line, bar, and pie charts.

Line Charts: Use line charts to show changes in data over a period of time and to emphasize the movement of the data—the trends.

- Use the vertical axis to represent amount and the horizontal axis to represent time.
- Mark off both axes at equal intervals and clearly label them.
- Begin the vertical axis at zero; if necessary, use slash marks (//) to show a break in the interval.
- If you plot more than one variable on a chart, clearly distinguish between the lines and label each clearly.

Bar Charts: Use bar charts to compare the magnitude or relative size of items (rather than the *trend* over time), either at a specified time or over a period of time.

- Make all bars the same width; the length varies to reflect the value of each item.
- Arrange the bars in a logical order and clearly label each.

Pie Charts: Use pie charts to compare the relative parts that make up a whole.

- Begin slicing the pie at the 12 o'clock position, moving clockwise in a logical order.
- Label each wedge of the pie, indicate its value, and clearly differentiate the wedges.

cheese spread was 10.8 ounces (the mean), because you don't manufacture that size. (How could a container that doesn't even exist be the most popular choice?)

However, because the mode is based on only part of the data, it is often not representative of the entire group. Suppose in a group of 12 people there are 10 adults, each of a different age, and two children each of whom is a year old. The mode of one year (the most common age) would not be an accurate way to describe this group.

Use the range to indicate how scores differ.

Range Whereas the mean, median, and mode tell how the scores tend to be similar (and are called measures of *central tendency*), the **range** is a measure of *variability* and tells how the scores tend to be different. It is computed by subtracting the highest and lowest figures in a group and then adding 1 (in order to include both the highest and lowest figure). Thus, the respondents shown in the example of mean earlier had an age range of 40 years (63 −24 + 1); or, to put it another way, the respondents ranged in age from 24 to 63 years.

The range, easily computed and easily understood, is quite helpful in presenting a general interpretation of the data. But because it includes only two figures in the group (the highest and the lowest), it is a fairly crude measure and is greatly affected by extreme values. (The computation for a more precise measure of variability, the *standard deviation,* is covered in any standard statistics textbook.) The range *and* one of the measures of central tendency (mean, median, or mode) taken together often provide a clear interpretation of a group of figures.

As should be evident, each of these statistics is useful in its own way in helping the reader understand a mass of data. Other methods of statistical analysis (especially correlation, trend analysis, and tests of inference) are often applied in interpreting the raw data but are beyond the scope of this course and may be beyond the comprehension of some general business readers. The competent communicator selects those statistics that are most helpful to the specific audience and that provide the most accurate picture of the raw data.

Making Sense of the Data

Don't just present tables and figures. Interpret their important points.

As a report writer, you cannot simply present the raw data without interpreting it. The data in your tables and charts helps to solve a problem, and the report writer must make the connection between that data and the solution to the problem. In the report narrative, you need not discuss *all* the data in the tables and charts; that would be boring and insulting to the reader. But you must determine what you think the important implications of your data are, and then you must identify and discuss them for the reader.

What types of important points do you look for? Almost always, the most important finding is the overall response to a question (rather than the responses of the cross-tabulation subgroups). And almost always the category within the question that receives the largest response is the most important point. So discuss this question and this category first. Let's take another look at Apex's Table 4 presented earlier in Figure 12.6 and repeated below in Figure 12.13.

In Table 4, the major finding is this: four-fifths of the respondents believe that Apex Company is an asset to their community. Note that if you give the exact figure given in the table (here, 79.7%), you can use less precise language in the narrative—"four-fifths" in this case, or "one in four," "a slight majority," and the like. Doing so helps you avoid presenting facts and figures too quickly. Pace your analysis because the reader will not be able to comprehend data that is presented too quickly or in too concentrated a format.

At a minimum, discuss the overall response and any important cross-tab findings.

Once you've discussed the overall finding, begin discussing the cross-tabulation data as necessary. Look for trends, unexpected findings, data that reinforces or contradicts other tables, extreme values, data that raises questions, and the like. If these are important, discuss them. In our example, there were no major differences in the responses by marital status, so you would probably not need to discuss them. However, you would need to discuss the big difference in responses between males and females. If possible, present data or draw any valid conclusions regarding the *reasons* for these differences.

Finally, point out the trend that is evident with regard to age: the older the respondent, the more positive the response. If it's important enough, you might display this trend in a graph for more visual effect.

Sometimes you will want to include descriptive statistics (such as the mean, median, range, and standard deviation). At other times, the nature of your data will necessitate the use of inference testing—to determine whether the differences found in your sample data are also likely to exist in the population. By now, you probably know more about the topic on which

FIGURE 12.13 Table to Be Analyzed

TABLE 4. RESPONSE TO STATEMENT "APEX COMPANY IS AN ASSET TO OUR COMMUNITY"

	Total		Marital Status		Gender		Age		
Response	Total	Pct.	Married	Single	Male	Female	Under 21	21-50	Over 50
Agree	216	79.7%	81.5%	76.4%	83.3%	56.7%	69.5%	77.3%	89.4%
No Opinion	34	12.6%	11.2%	15.4%	11.4%	20.9%	17.5%	13.7%	9.2%
Disagree	21	7.7%	7.3%	8.2%	5.3%	22.4%	13.0%	9.0%	1.4%
Total	271	100.0%	100.0%	100.0%	100.0%	100.0%	100.0%	100.0%	100.0%

you're writing than the reader knows. Assist the reader, then, by pointing out the important implications, findings, and relationships of your data. Help your reader reach the same conclusions you have reached.

AVOIDING MISREPRESENTATION

Consider the following situation:

> In preparation for selecting the next sales manager, Roger Davis sent his three assistant sales managers to an intensive, one-week seminar sponsored by the National Sales Management Association. He needed a fast learner for the job and figured the test results from this seminar would tell him who had the most growth potential. Roger asked you, his assistant, to analyze the test results and write a memo report recommending one of the three for the promotion, on the basis of his or her growth potential. (Before reading the discussion that follows, study these test scores and decide whom you will recommend.)

	Pretest Score	*Posttest Score*
Marilyn Driskill	30	50
Donald Malone	50	70
Carlos Sanchez	70	90

Marilyn argues that she should be selected. After all, she improved from a beginning score of 30 to an ending score of 50; her 20-point improvement represents a 67% increase, whereas Donald increased only 40% and Carlos, only 29%.

Donald argues that he should be selected. Because all three candidates showed the same growth (20 points), he believes the decision should be based on other factors—such as the fact that he's the most experienced of the three candidates.

Carlos argues that he should be selected. Because the maximum score on the test was 100 points, he began with only 30 possible points that he could improve; and he actually improved 20 points—or 67% of the maximum. Marilyn, on the other hand, improved only 29% of the points available to her, and Donald improved only 40% of the points available to him.

Whom will you recommend?

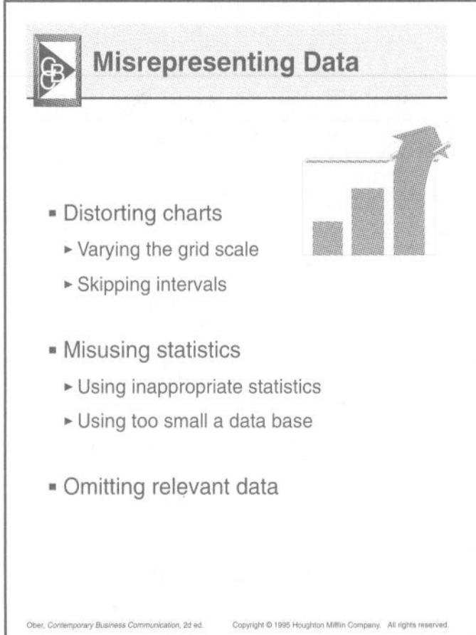

Misrepresenting Data
Distorting charts
Varying the grid scale
Skipping intervals
Misusing statistics
Using inappropriate statistics
Using too small a data base
Omitting relevant data

See Transparency 12.6, Misrepresenting Data.

Misrepresentation includes not only making factual misstatements but also leaving incorrect impressions.

As this vignette makes clear, during the analysis and subsequent write-up of your data, you will have many decisions to make. How much data should you present in the report? In most cases, you will not be able to present all the data you gather. Do you have enough data on which to base a conclusion? If so or if not, how definite should you make that conclusion? Which of your findings should you emphasize and which should you subordinate?

Unfortunately (as in the preceding example), in many cases there is no one right answer. Instead, the answer depends on the purpose of your report and the needs of your reader. Having acknowledged that, however, we can productively discuss some of the more common dilemmas the report writer faces.

Distortion in Charts

There are numerous ways to consciously or unconsciously distort graphic data, or to engage in "cheating by charting."[3] First, consider the different visual impact that can result from simply varying the scale of the grid. The three charts shown in the first row of Figure 12.14 all reflect the same numbers, but notice the different visual impact of each.

Charts can also be distorted by skipping intervals. As noted earlier, all charts should begin at the zero point. In the second row of Figure 12.14, note how the first bar in the distorted chart (the chart on the right) appears to be less than half as large as the second bar, when in actuality it is only slightly smaller.

Distortion in Statistics

Use statistics to help you communicate your story more effectively—not to support a biased viewpoint.

Assume that XYZ Company has 27 employees. The president of the company earns $200,000 yearly, the vice president earns $150,000, and each of the 25 factory workers earns $20,000, for a total annual payroll of $850,000. Would it be accurate for the president to brag that the average employee at XYZ earns $31,481 a year ($850,000/27)? Of course not. In this case, the mean does not give an accurate portrayal for *any* of the employees—not for the president, the vice president, or the factory workers. Either the mode ($20,000) or the median ($20,000) would have been a more accurate figure.

A similar problem exists with statistics taken from too small a data base. If a department of 30 people experienced only one sick day last month and had two sick days this month, reporting that the department's sick days doubled in one month, although technically correct, would give an incorrect impression. The one additional sick day could have been an aberration. In any case, such a statement would disguise the fact that even two sick days a month is a very commendable record indeed.

The situation is similar to the apocryphal report of a basketball game in which the United States team soundly defeated Cuba. The Cuban press proudly proclaimed, "Cuba comes in second in international athletic meet while the United States team was next to last!" Beware of using statistics inappropriately.

FIGURE 12.14 Cheating by Charting

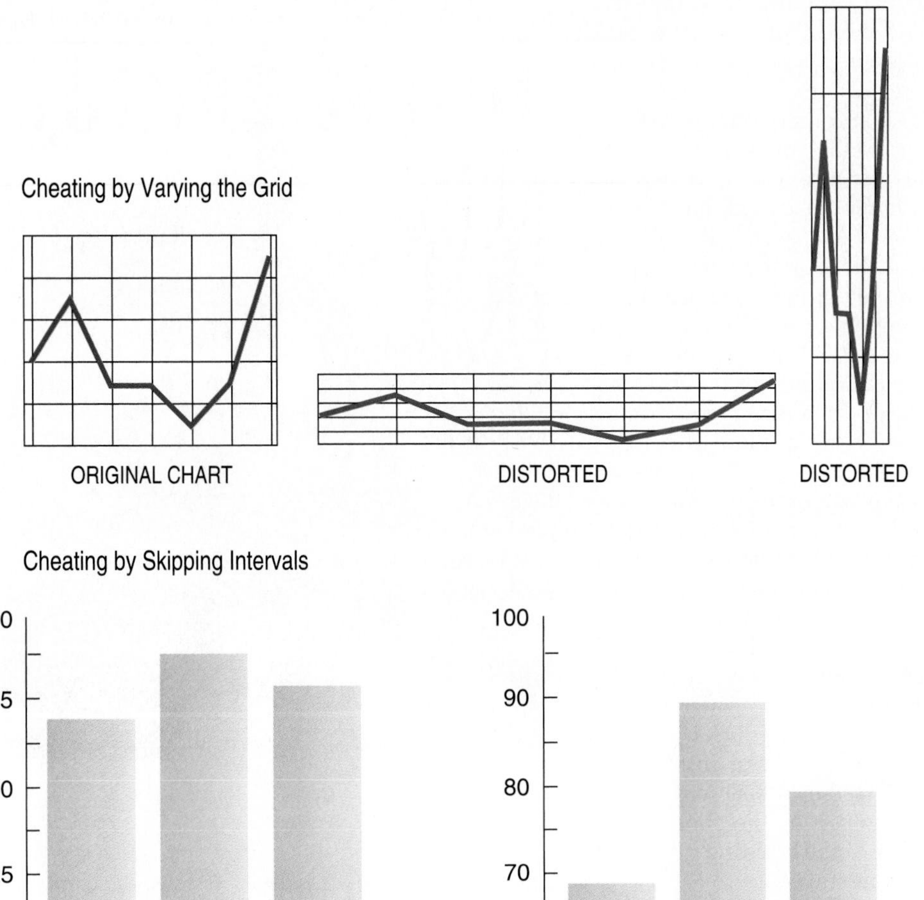

Distortion by Omission

It would be unethical to leave an inaccurate impression, even when what you do report is true. Sins of omission are as serious as sins of commission. Distortion by omission can occur when using quotations out of context, when omitting certain relevant background information, or when including only the most extreme or most interesting data.

It would be inappropriate, for example, to quote extensively from a survey that was conducted 15 years ago without first establishing for the reader that the findings are still valid. Likewise, it would be inappropriate to quote a finding from one study and not discuss the fact that four similar studies reached opposite conclusions.

SPOTLIGHT ON LAW AND ETHICS

A Picture Not *Worth a Thousand Words*

"Seeing is believing" may no longer be the case. Granted, commercial photographers have long used the airbrush to touch up portraits, wedding scenes, and advertising layouts, but only recently has the technology to manipulate photos come to the desktop computer. Today, any computer user, with the appropriate software, can electronically alter photographs—even to the extent that they no longer reflect reality.

As an indication of the extent to which photographs can be manipulated, the cover of a recent *Texas Monthly* magazine showed Texas governor Ann Richards in a computer-altered photograph.

Satan in West Texas ★ Dueling Catfish ★ The Sakowitz Feud
WHITE
HOT
MAMA
Ann Richards Is Riding High. Can She Be the First Woman President?

It does not take a wide stretch of the imagination to ponder the ethical dilemmas report writers may soon face. Suppose, as an adjunct to your report on the status of a building project, you use a digital camera to take a photo of the partially completed building. The digital camera stores the image directly on a compact disk rather than on film. You pop the CD into your personal computer and view the image on the screen. You notice that a worker is standing next to the building, providing a distraction. So you use your software to digitally remove the worker from the image. Then you notice that the sign on the building, which contained a typographical error, had not been fixed when you took the photo (it has since been corrected). Should you digitally correct it on the photo? How about changing the color of the building's exterior, which you plan to paint next week?

By allowing us to capture, store, and manipulate photographs, emerging computer technology is going to have an enormous impact on business communications.

Sources: Sean Callahan, "Eye Tech," *Forbes ASAP,* Spring 1993, pp. 57–67; Jane Hundertmark, "When Enhancement Is Deception," *Publish,* October 1991, pp. 51–55; Jim Meade, "Graphics That Tell the Truth," *Personal Computing,* January 1989, pp. 79–84; Daryl Moen, "Misinformation Graphics," *Aldus Magazine,* January/February 1990, pp. 62–63.

Do not use quotations out of context.

Be especially careful to quote and paraphrase accurately from interview sources. Provide enough information to ensure that the passage reflects the interviewee's *intention.* Here is an example of possible distortions:

Original Quotation:	"I think the Lancelot is an excellent car for anyone who does not need to worry about fuel economy."
Distortion:	Johnson stated that the Lancelot "is an excellent car."
Worse Distortion:	Johnson stated that the Lancelot "is an excellent car for anyone."
Worst Distortion:	Johnson stated that the Lancelot "is an excellent car <u>for anyone</u>!"

The Ethical Dimension

Everyone involved in the reporting situation has a responsibility to act in an ethical manner.

In gathering, analyzing, reporting, and disseminating data, everyone involved has both rights and obligations. For example, the researcher (1) has the right to expect that respondents will be truthful in their responses and (2) has an obligation not to deceive the respondent. Similarly, the organization that is paying for the research (1) has the right to expect that the researcher will provide valid and reliable information and (2) has an obligation not to misuse that data.

Emerging technology will no doubt provide even greater ethical dilemmas (see the Spotlight on Law and Ethics). If your research and corresponding report are to help solve problems and aid in decision making, all parties involved must use common sense, good judgment, and goodwill to make the project successful.

Analyzing Data

PROBLEM

You are a manager at a software-development house that publishes communication software for the HAL and Pear® microcomputers. Together, these two computers comprise about 90% of the business market. In 1995, you were asked to survey users of communication software—a repeat of a similar study you undertook in 1990.

You conducted the survey using the same questionnaire and same procedures from the 1990 study. Now you've gathered the data, along with the comparable data collected in 1990, and have organized it roughly into draft tables, one of which is shown in Figure 12.15. You're now ready to put this table into final report format and analyze its contents.

FIGURE 12.15 Draft Table

Q. From what source did you obtain your last software program?

Source	1990						1995					
	Total		HAL		Pear		Total		HAL		Pear	
	N	%	*N*	%	*N*	%	*N*	%	*N*	%	*N*	%
Mail-order company	28	21.2	24	26.1	4	10.0	60	41.1	25	30.9	35	53.9
On-line bulletin board	3	2.3	2	2.2	1	2.5	4	2.7	2	2.5	2	3.1
Retail outlet	70	53.0	46	50.0	24	60.0	63	43.2	44	54.3	19	29.2
Software publisher	9	6.8	4	4.3	5	12.5	10	6.8	4	4.9	6	9.2
Unauthorized copy	21	15.9	15	16.3	6	15.0	6	4.1	3	3.7	3	4.6
Other	1	.8	1	1.1	0	0.0	3	2.1	3	3.7	0	0.0
Total	132	100.0	92	100.0	40	100.0	146	100.0	81	100.0	65	100.0

PROCESS

1. TABLE FORMAT

a. Examine the format of your draft table—the arrangement of columns and rows. Should you change anything for the final table?

First, the year columns (1990 and 1995) should be reversed. The new data is more important than the old data, so putting it first will emphasize it.

Second, the rows need to be rearranged. They're now in alphabetical order but should be rearranged in descending order according to the first amount column–the 1995 total column. Doing this will put the most important data first in the table.

b. Assuming that you will have many tables in your final report, is there some way to condense the information in this table without undue loss of precision or detail?

Although the number of respondents is important, the readers of my report will be much more interested in the percentages. Therefore, I'll give only the total number of respondents for each column and put that figure immediately under each column heading.

Also, I see immediately that very few people obtained their software from on-line bulletin boards either in 1990 or 1995, so I'll combine that category with the "other" category.

These changes are shown in Figure 12.16.

FIGURE 12.16 Report Table

TABLE 8. SOURCE OF LAST SOFTWARE PROGRAM
(In percentages)

	1995			1990		
Source	Total (N = 146)	HAL (N = 81)	Pear (N = 65)	Total (N = 132)	HAL (N = 92)	Pear (N = 40)
Retail outlet	43.2	54.3	29.2	53.0	50.0	60.0
Mail-order company	41.1	30.9	53.9	21.2	26.1	10.0
Software publisher	6.8	4.9	9.2	6.8	4.3	12.5
Unauthorized copy	4.1	3.7	4.6	15.9	16.3	15.0
Other	4.8	6.2	3.1	3.1	3.3	2.5
Total	100.0	100.0	100.0	100.0	100.0	100.0

2. TABLE INTERPRETATION

a. Study the table in Figure 12.16. If you had space to make only one statement about this table, what would it be?

Retail outlets and mail-order companies are equally important sources for obtaining software, together accounting for more than four-fifths of all sources.

b. What other 1995 data should you discuss in your narrative?

HAL and Pear users obtain their software in different ways: the majority of HAL users obtain theirs from retail outlets whereas the majority of Pear users obtain theirs from mail-order firms.

c. What should you point out in comparing 1995 data with 1990 data?

The market share for retail outlets decreased by almost 20% from 1990 to 1995 while the market share for mail-order companies almost doubled, increasing by 95%.

Also, the use of unauthorized copies appears to be decreasing (although the actual figure is probably somewhat higher than these self-reported figures).

3. VISUAL AIDS

If you wanted to show graphically the change in the popularity of retail outlets versus mail-order companies, what type of chart would you use?

Two years' worth of data would not be enough data points for a line chart, and it would be difficult to compare the relative sizes of wedges between two pie charts. Therefore, a bar chart would be best because the relative sizes of the bars would emphasize the magnitude of the differences that have occurred since 1990 (see Figure 12.17).

PRODUCT

FIGURE 12.17 Bar Chart

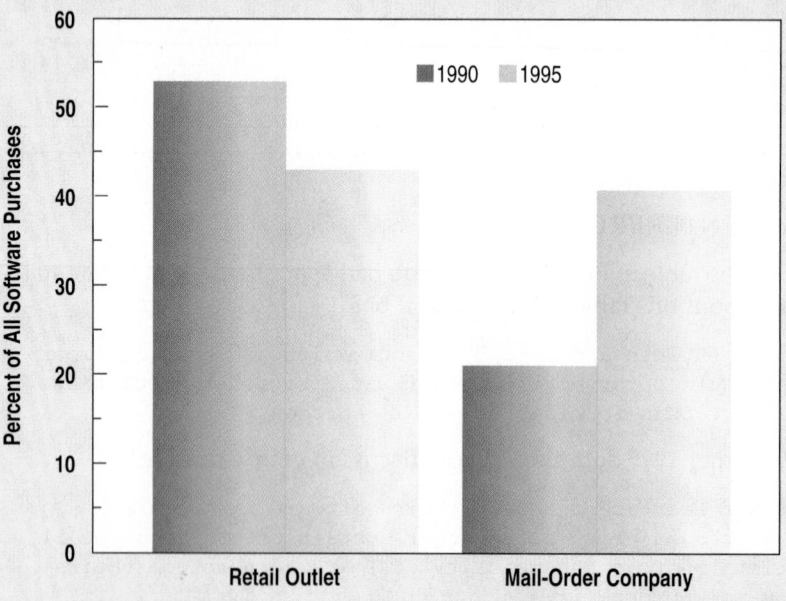

Figure 3. The market share for retail outlets decreased by almost 20% from 1990 to 1995 while the market share for mail-order companies almost doubled, increasing by 95%.

SUMMARY

Raw data becomes *information* only after it has been organized, analyzed, and interpreted so as to point out meaningful facts, statistics, and conclusions that help solve a problem. The first step in the process is to perform a preliminary analysis by editing the data for accuracy and completeness and by evaluating the data to see if it solves the report problem.

Each table you construct from the data should be interpretable by itself, without reference to the text. Often you will want to analyze two or more fields of data together in the same table to help identify relationships. Include only as much data in a table as is helpful, keeping the table as simple as possible. Arrange the data in logical order, most often in order of descending value. Do not analyze every figure from the table in your narrative. Instead, interpret the important points from the table, pointing out the major findings, trends, contradictions, and the like.

Use well-designed line, bar, pie, and other charts to aid in reader comprehension, emphasize certain data, create interest, and save time and space. Avoid using too many, too large, too garish, or too complicated charts. Also avoid misrepresenting your information—through distorting charts or statistics or omitting relevant information. The competent reporter of business information is an ethical reporter of business information.

KEY TERMS

Bar chart A graph with horizontal or vertical bars representing values.

Cross-tabulation The process by which two or more pieces of data are analyzed together.

Data editing The process of reviewing the data for accuracy and completeness before data analysis.

Line chart A graph based on a grid, with the vertical axis representing values and the horizontal axis representing time.

Map chart A visual representation of data based on geography.

Mean The arithmetic average of a group of numbers.

Median The middle value (or midpoint) in a group of numbers arranged from low to high (or vice versa).

Mode The value in a group of numbers that occurs most frequently.

Pictograph A graph with relevant symbols representing values.

Pie chart A circle graph whose area is divided into component wedges.

Range A measure of variability computed by subtracting the highest and lowest figures in a group and adding 1.

Statistics The branch of mathematics dealing with the collection, organization, and interpretation of numerical data.

Table An orderly arrangement of data into columns and rows.

Visual aids Tables, charts, photographs, and other graphic materials used in communications to aid comprehension and add interest.

For an exercise on matching terms, refer students to the *Study Guide*, pp. 162–163.

REVIEW AND DISCUSSION

The answers to the review and discussion questions appear in the *Instructor's Resource Manual*, beginning on p. 238.

1. **Communication at Oshkosh B'Gosh Revisited** ▪ Jim Solum of Oshkosh B'Gosh knows that charts, graphs, and other visual aids are very useful tools for portraying data in a report. At the same time, he stresses that graphics alone—especially those that show percentages rather than numbers—may not tell the whole story.
   a. What type of visual aid might Solum use to present Oshkosh B'Gosh's five-year profits? Why?
   b. What type of visual aid would be appropriate for comparing Oshkosh B'Gosh's domestic and foreign sales over a five-year period? Why?
   c. What symbol(s) can you suggest for an Oshkosh B'Gosh pictograph showing the growth in the number of major retailers carrying the company's baby overalls in 1985, 1990, and 1995?
2. Give an example of a specific incident in which editing the research data might be necessary.
3. What are the advantages of presenting numerical data in tables as opposed to presenting the data in narrative form?
4. Assume you have surveyed a sample of students at your institution to determine their career objectives and expectations. List three possible cross-tabulation analyses that might be appropriate for this study.
5. In what order should data be arranged in tables?
6. What types of visual aid would probably be most appropriate for each of the following situations? Explain your decisions.
   a. Data showing the percentage breakdown of employees by ethnic background.
   b. Data showing the state-by-state analysis of market share for the company's major product.
   c. A news release announcing the appointment of a new executive vice president.
   d. Data showing the number of employees by year from 1990 to 1995.
   e. An explanation of how to replace the cartridge in a laser printer.
   f. Data showing the average number of employees per department last year.
7. What types of material from a table should be discussed in the narrative of the report? What types of material need not be discussed?
8. What is meant by "overvisualizing" data? Why should this be avoided?
9. How do the mean, median, and mode differ?
10. What are the major types of misrepresentation that can occur in analysis of business data?
11. List one right and one obligation of the researcher and of the organization sponsoring the research.

EXERCISES

Exercise 1 is linked with Exercise 1 of Chapter 13. Sample solution for Exercise 1 appears in the *Instructor's Resource Manual*, p. 240.

1. **Microwriting: Analyzing Data** ▪

   PROBLEM

   As training manager for Gothic Manufacturing Company, you have been asked to determine the need for developing a communication-skills training program for the entry-level managers at your firm. As part of your research, you conducted a survey in which you asked 100 of your entry-level managers how important they thought the following five communication skills were when communicating with their superiors, coworkers, and subordinates:

Exchanging routine information
Giving oral reports
Listening
Participating in small groups
Persuading

The 100 managers responded on a scale from 1 to 5, with 5 representing the highest importance and 1 representing the lowest importance. The mean responses were as follows (responses are given in order of the five skills listed above): communicating with superiors—4.1, 3.2, 4.7, 1.7, 4.7; communicating with subordinates—4.0, 3.6, 4.2, 1.2, 3.6; communicating with coworkers—4.3, 3.0, 4.2, 3.9, 4.2.

Your job is to analyze the data for management.

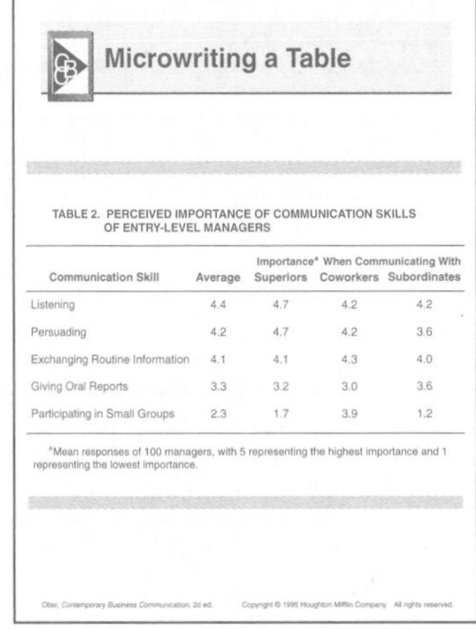

Microwriting a Table

TABLE 2. PERCEIVED IMPORTANCE OF COMMUNICATION SKILLS OF ENTRY-LEVEL MANAGERS

Communication Skill	Average	Importance[a] When Communicating With Superiors	Coworkers	Subordinates
Listening	4.4	4.7	4.2	4.2
Persuading	4.2	4.7	4.2	3.6
Exchanging Routine Information	4.1	4.1	4.3	4.0
Giving Oral Reports	3.3	3.2	3.0	3.6
Participating in Small Groups	2.3	1.7	3.9	1.2

[a]Mean responses of 100 managers, with 5 representing the highest importance and 1 representing the lowest importance.

Ober, *Contemporary Business Communication*, 2d ed.

See Master 12.1, Exercise 1, Microwriting, in the *Instructor's Resource Manual.*

PROCESS

a. Prepare a draft table; that is, list the three levels of communication (superiors, coworkers, and subordinates) across the top and the five communication skills down the left side. Then fill in the responses for each cell.
b. Assuming that the three levels of communication are equally important, add a new column before the *Superiors* column, labeled "Average," and compute the average score for each skill (total the three scores, divide by 3, round off to the nearest tenth). Now you can tell the overall importance attributed to each communication skill.
c. Rearrange the five skills in some logical order.
d. Compose an appropriate title for this table (assume that it is Table 2 of your report).
e. Overall, how important do the respondents consider communication skills to be?
f. Based on this data, if you could offer a communication workshop on only one topic, what would that topic be?

PRODUCT

Submit both your revised table and your responses to the process activities to your instructor.

Collaborative Research: Exercises 2–8 below are based on the survey results shown in Figure 12.18. Next year Broadway Productions will move its headquarters from Manhattan to Stamford, Connecticut, in the building where Tri-City Bank occupies the first floor. The bank hopes to secure many Broadway Productions employees as customers and has conducted a survey to determine their banking habits. The handwritten figures on the questionnaire show the number of respondents who checked each alternative.

Exercises 2–8 are linked with Exercise 11 of Chapter 13. Sample solutions for Exercises 2–11 appear in the *Instructor's Resource Manual*, pp. 240–245.

2. Constructing Tables ■

a. Is a table needed to present the information in Question 1?
b. Would any cross-tabulation analyses help readers understand the data in this questionnaire? Explain.
c. Construct a table that presents the important information from Question 4 of the questionnaire in a logical, helpful, and efficient manner. Give the table an appropriate title and arrange it in final report format.

FIGURE 12.18 Survey Results

BROADWAY PRODUCTIONS SURVEY

1. Do you currently have an account at Tri-City Bank?
   58 yes
   170 no

2. At which of the following institutions do you currently have an account? (Please check all that apply.)
   201 commercial bank
   52 employee credit union
   75 savings and loan association
   6 other (please specify ______)
   18 none

3. In terms of location, which one of the following bank locations do you consider most important in selecting your main bank?
   70 near home
   102 near office
   12 near shopping
   31 on way to and from work
   13 other (please specify ______)

4. How important do you consider each of the following banking services?

	Very Important	Somewhat Important	Not Important
Bank credit card	88	132	8
Check-guarantee card	74	32	122
Convenient ATM machines	143	56	29
Drive-in service	148	47	33
Free checking	219	9	0
Overdraft privileges	20	187	21
Personal banker	40	32	156
Telephone transfer	6	20	202
Trust department	13	45	170

5. If you have changed banks within the past three years, what was the major reason for the change?
   33 relocation of residence
   4 relocation of bank
   18 dissatisfaction with bank service
   7 other (please specify ______)

Thank you so much for your cooperation. Please return this questionnaire in the enclosed envelope to Customer Service Department, Tri-City Bank, P.O. Box 1086, Stamford, CT 06902.

3. **Checking Raw Data** ▪
   a. How would you expect the responses to Question 2 to differ from those of Questions 1, 3, and 4?
   b. How would you expect the responses to Question 5 to differ from those of Question 1? Question 2?
   c. How can you verify that you have tabulated all the answers to Questions 3 and 4?
4. **Interpreting Data** ▪
   a. Give a one- or two-sentence interpretation of the data for each of the five questions.
   b. Assume you need to present the important information from this questionnaire in one paragraph of no more than 50 or 60 words. Compose this summary paragraph.
5. **Constructing Charts** ▪ You decide to use a chart rather than a table to convey the data in Question 4 of the questionnaire.
   a. Can you use a line chart to present the data? Why or why not? If a line chart is appropriate, construct it and label the vertical and horizontal axes.
   b. Can you use a bar chart to present the data? Why or why not? If a bar chart is appropriate, construct it, arranging the bars in a logical order and clearly labeling each bar as well as the vertical axis.
   c. Can you use a pie chart to present the data? Why or why not? If a pie chart is appropriate, construct it, label each wedge, and clearly differentiate the wedges.
   d. Can you use a pictograph to present the data? Why or why not? If a pictograph is appropriate, construct it; explain your choice of symbols.
6. **Constructing Charts** ▪ You want to construct a visual aid to emphasize the proportion of respondents who have changed banks within the past three years. Calculate this percentage using the survey results. Decide which type of chart would most effectively convey this information. Then construct the chart, using appropriate values and helpful labels.
7. **Interpreting Data** ▪ Looking at the results of Question 5, Tri-City Bank managers decide to find out more about the problems with bank service that have caused 18 Broadway Productions employees to change financial institutions. The results of a second study show that 7 people were dissatisfied with the monthly service charges; 5 people felt the fees for returned checks were too high; 3 were annoyed about chronically long lines at the teller windows; and 3 found their branch's banking hours inconvenient. How would you arrange these responses into two meaningful categories? Referring to the two categories, write a brief paragraph summarizing the survey results.
8. **Constructing Charts** ▪
   a. Construct a chart that would most effectively present the important information in Question 2.
   b. For Question 3, construct both a bar chart and a pie chart. Which do you think is more effective? Why?

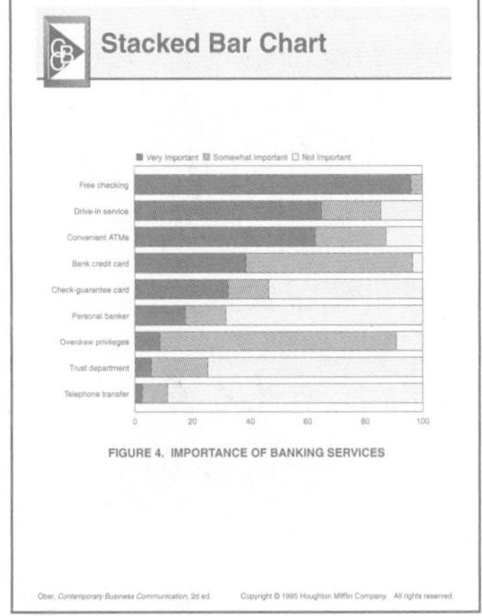

See Master 12.2, Exercise 5, Constructing Charts, in the *Instructor's Resource Manual.*

9. **Misrepresenting Data—Interpreting Charts** ▪ Examine the following interpretations of the data shown in Figure 12.9, Charts A, B, and C, page 375. Indicate whether each statement accurately represents the data in those charts.

   a. The industrial sector has provided most of Apex's sales and profits since 1990.
   b. The average age of Apex customers has increased since 1970.
   c. The average age of Apex customers reached a peak of 45 in 1985.
   d. Nearly half of Apex's sales in 1995 were to the industrial sector.
   e. More than half of Apex's sales in 1990 were to the industrial sector.
   f. Nearly half of Apex's sales in 1970 were to the consumer sector.
   g. The decline in Apex's consumer sales is due to the increase in the average age of the firm's consumer customers.
   h. Sales to the industrial sector have risen steadily since 1970.
   i. Sales to the consumer sector have fallen steadily since 1970.

10. **Misrepresenting Data—Interpreting a Table** ▪ The following sentences interpret the table in Figure 12.5 on page 369: Analyze each sentence to determine whether it represents the data in the table accurately.

   a. Males and females alike believe Apex is an asset to the community.
   b. More than one-fifth of the females (22.4%) did not respond.
   c. Age and the generation gap bring about different beliefs.
   d. Married males over age 50 had the most positive opinions.
   e. Females disagree more than males–probably because most of the workers at Apex are male.
   f. Female respondents tend to disagree with the statement.
   g. Apex should be proud of the fact that four-fifths of the residents believe the company is an asset to the community.
   h. Thirteen percent of the younger residents have doubts about whether Apex is an asset to the community.
   i. More single than married residents didn't care or had no opinion about the topic.
   j. Overall, the residents believe that 8% of the company is not an asset to the community.

11. **Misrepresenting Data—Use of Statistics** ▪ Politicians, business people, and others love to quote statistics to support their viewpoints. Locate three news stories in which someone quotes statistics to support a particular case. Then find an unbiased source that either confirms or refutes those statistics. Write a memo to your instructor discussing your findings. Include a photocopy of both the original news articles and your supporting statistics.

CONTINUING CASE 12

Light at the End of the Carpal Tunnel

Review the Continuing Case at the end of Chapter 11, in which Jean Tate asked Pat Robbins to write a report on "repeated-motion" illnesses, especially carpal tunnel syndrome (CTS). As part of her data gathering, Pat interviewed Terry Vaughn, executive director of the National Right-to-Safety Task Force, a government-supported task force. The NRSTF has been active in seeking a safer work environment for office workers. The following typed transcript shows part of this interview. (Note: "ER" stands for "Interviewer" and "EE" stands for "Interviewee.")

ER: What is the extent of the problem? How many people are afflicted with CTS each year?

EE: CTS is the largest of several injuries that are classified as cumulative trauma disorders. NIOSH estimates that 156,000 employees suffered from one of these disorders in 1990, up from 45,000 in 1986. The Bureau of Labor Standards estimates that for the years 1985 through 1990, these repeated trauma disorders accounted for 29, 33, 38, 39, and 41% of all occupational injuries, respectively. So it's a major problem, that's for sure.

ER: What is NIOSH?

EE: The National Institute for Occupational Safety and Health—or maybe it's "of" instead of "for." Anyway, it's a government agency located in Cincinnati, Ohio. NIOSH is also heavily involved in studying the effect of smoking in the workplace. One recent study showed that 25% of all U.S. firms have now imposed an across-the-board ban on workplace smoking and fully 60% have set up some form of smoking policy.

ER: Do VDT operators represent most of the CTS cases?

EE: No, but they do represent a growing percentage. Victims are still most likely to be physical laborers, such as meat packers and jackhammer operators. Interestingly, musicians also suffer inordinately from this disorder. I personally believe that women are most often the victim of this disease.

ER: Do you have any data to back that up?

EE: I don't need data; I just know it. When you have 160,000 people who suffered from this painful disorder in 1990, you just know it's a major problem for everyone. I know if I ever experienced that problem, I'd quit on the spot and sue the company.

ER: What can be done to alleviate the problem?

EE: In the office, you need wrist rests for each keyboard and rest breaks each hour, and also the furniture needs to be designed to eliminate awkward posture and the use of needless force.

A possible solution to the Continuing Case is described in the *Instructor's Resource Manual*, pp. 245–246.

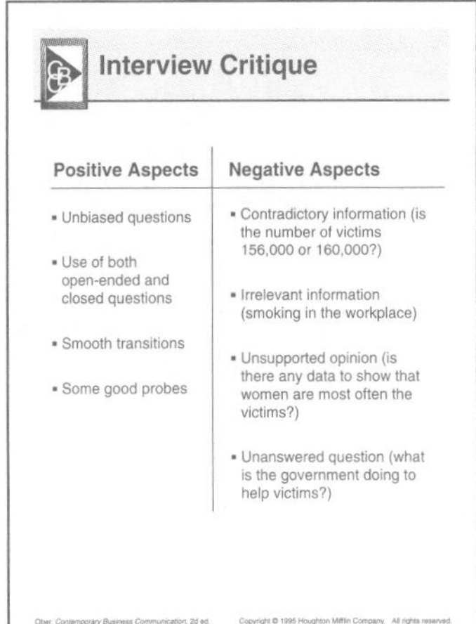

See Master 12.3, Continuing Case 12, Item 1, in the *Instructor's Resource Manual.*

ER: What is the government doing to help victims of this disorder?

EE: Not enough. The American Academy of Orthopedic Surgeons estimates that lost earnings and expenses for medical costs and treatment for this disorder now cost more than $42 billion annually.

Critical Thinking

1. How skillful was Pat in conducting this interview? Give some examples of both positive and negative aspects of the interview, especially in terms of probing.
2. What specific part(s) of the interview should you *not* use? Why?

Writing Projects

3. Write one or two paragraphs analyzing part of this interview; include both a paraphrase and a direct quotation in your narrative.
4. Assume that you have verified the Bureau of Labor Standards figures given in the interview. Construct both a table and a chart to communicate this information. Which one would you probably use in your report to Jean? Why?

WORDWISE *Numbers*

- You have to count all the way to one thousand before you get to a number that contains the letter *a*.
- *Forty* is the only number in English that, when spelled out, has all its letters in alphabetical order.
- The year *1961* reads the same upside down. The next year in which this will happen is *6009*.

CHAPTER

13

Writing the Report

Before members of the U.S. Congress vote on legislation related to nutrition research, food labeling, or food safety, they learn about the issues by reading informational reports written by Donna V. Porter and her colleagues in the Science Policy Research Division of the Congressional Research Service (CRS), which is part of the Library of Congress. Dr. Porter is a specialist in life sciences, and her job is to research and prepare reports that will give senators and representatives the background they need to make informed decisions about legislation dealing with these subjects.

Although the primary audience for these reports is members of Congress and their staff, Dr. Porter also takes into consideration her secondary audience. "Frequently, constituents from across the United States will contact their legislators to request information on a particular topic," she explained. "Federal agencies and Congressional offices often respond to these requests by sending a copy of a report provided by CRS."

These reports, which are not allowed to include recommendations, provide an unbiased, nonpartisan review of the issue. "The Congressional Research Service has high credibility because it provides balanced reports," said Dr. Porter. "Our reports always give both sides of an issue. No matter which side of the debate a member of Congress may be on, it's important to understand all the arguments on the other side as well."

Dr. Porter aims to educate her audiences about the science behind the issue as well as the impact on consumers and industry. For example, her recent report on food labeling explained how the science of nutrition had ad-

Communication Objectives

After you have finished this chapter, you should be able to

1. Determine an appropriate report structure based on the needs of the reader and the nature of the report problem.
2. Organize the report in a logical manner.
3. Develop an effective report outline.
4. Write each part of the report body and all supplementary pages.
5. Use an effective writing style.
6. Provide appropriate documentation when quoting, paraphrasing, or summarizing someone else's work.
7. Revise a report for content, style, and correctness.
8. Format a report for readability and consistency.
9. Proofread a report to ensure that it reflects pride of authorship.

Donna Porter
Specialist in life sciences, Congressional Research Service, Washington, D.C.

A chapter overview appears in the *Instructor's Resource Manual*, pp. 247–252.

vanced since the 1970s. She also examined the position of the manufacturers, the role of the various regulatory agencies, and the needs of the general public. "I try to show the larger context of an issue and describe the implications that an issue might have for all the affected parties," she added.

Many of her reports are long and detailed. "I think one comprehensive report that covers everything about an issue—and provides readers with 99% of what they will need—is much more valuable than a series of short reports," Dr. Porter observed. Because of their length, all her reports contain a one-page summary of the background and findings. In addition, an abstract of each report is entered into a computerized system that members of Congress can scan to decide which reports they need to read in full.

A formal outline is essential when writing these lengthy reports. "I start every report with a generic outline that covers the background of the issue, the science behind the issue, the activities of regulatory agencies and Congress, and other important items that must be covered. I also keep a running list of important points that I want to incorporate, which helps me remember important ideas that should be included.

Once she completes a report, she searches for typographical and spelling errors and then asks a colleague to read the report as a final check for clarity before CRS review. Dr. Porter stressed that "what may have seemed a clear thought when I wrote it may not be understood by the uninitiated. That's why it's important to ask someone who is detached from the issue to read and critique a report. I always bear in mind that my readers are not specialists in nutrition."

PLANNING

As we have seen throughout our study of business communication, the writing process consists of planning, drafting, revising, formatting, and proofreading. You follow this same process when writing a report.

For an exercise in writing an informal memorandum report, see Video Case Study 3, Lotus Notes.

Although much of the planning in the report process is, of necessity, done even before collecting the data, the written presentation of the results requires its own stage of planning. You need to make decisions about the structure of the report, the organization of the content, and the heading structure before and as you write.

Determining the Report Structure

The physical structure of the report and such general traits as complexity, degree of formality, and length depend on the audience for the report and the nature of the problem that the report addresses. The three most common formats for a report are manuscript, memorandum, and letter format.

Most reports are formatted as manuscripts, memos, or letters.

Manuscript reports, the most formal of the three, are formatted in narrative (paragraph) style, with headings and subheadings separating the different sections. If the problem that the report addresses is complex and has serious consequences, the report will likely follow a manuscript format and a formal writing style. A formal writing style typically avoids the use of first- and second-person pronouns, such as *I* and *you*. In addition, the more formal the report, the more supplementary parts are included (such as table of contents, executive summary, and appendixes) and, therefore, the longer the report.

Memorandum and letter reports contain the standard correspondence parts (for example, lines identifying the names of the sender and receiver). They use a more informal writing style and may or may not contain headings and subheadings. Compare the informal, simple, and short report in memo format shown in Figure 13.1 with the formal, complex, and long report (only the first page is shown) in manuscript format shown in Figure 13.2.

So that your written presentation will have an overall sense of proportion and unity, decide beforehand on the complexity, formality, length, and format of the report. The "right" decision depends on the needs and desires of the reader.

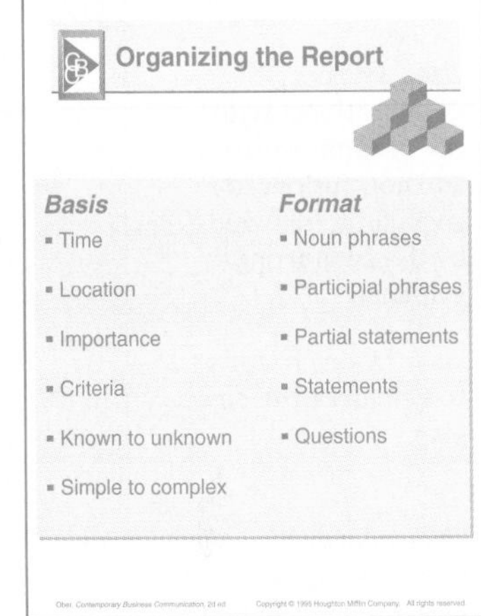

See Transparency 13.1, Organizing the Report.

Organizing the Report

A sculptor creating a statue of someone doesn't necessarily start at the head and work down to the feet in lock-step fashion. Instead, he or she may first create part of the torso, then part of the head, then another part of the torso, and so on. Likewise, a movie director may film segments of the movie out of narrative order. But in the end, both creations are put together in such a way as to show unity, order, logic, and beauty.

In a report using the direct organizational plan, students might use questions or verbal phrases for headings. Janice Redish of the American Institute for Research observes that "nouns name things, they do not explain . . . the nouns may be be too vague, too general, or too abstract" to show readers how the text is organized. (Janice Redish, "Writing in Organizations," *Writing in the Business Professions*, ed. Myra Kogen, NCTE, Urbana, IL, 1989 pp. 105–107.)

Similarly, you may have organized the collection and analysis of data in a way that suited the investigation of various subtopics of the problem. But now that it is time to put the results of your work together into a written presentation, you may need a *new* organization, one that integrates the whole and takes into account what you have learned throughout your research.

Planning your written presentation to show unity, order, logic, and, yes, even beauty involves selecting an organizational basis for the findings (the data you've collected and analyzed) and developing an outline. You must decide in what order to present each piece of the puzzle and when to "spill the beans"—when to present your overall **conclusions** (the answers to the research questions raised in the introduction) and any recommendations you may wish to make.

Organizational Basis As shown in Figure 13.3, the four most common bases for organizing your findings are *time*, *location*, *importance*, and *criteria*. There are, of course, other patterns for organizing data; for example, you can move from the known to the unknown or from the simple to the com-

FIGURE 13.1 Informal Memorandum Report

The memo format indicates the reader is someone from within the firm.

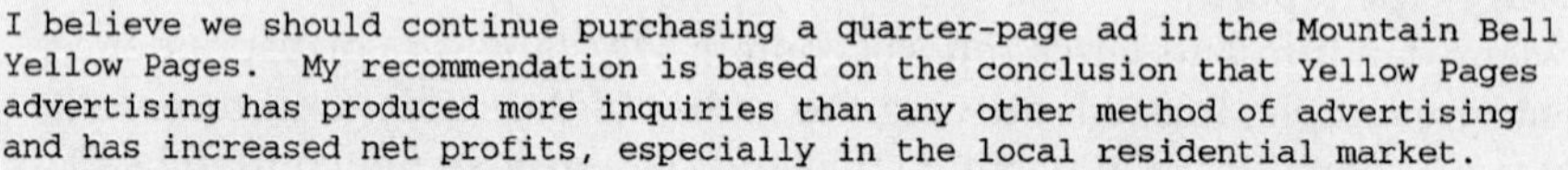

All Systems Go Moving Company

MEMO TO: Hiram Cooper, Director of Marketing

FROM: Barbara Novak, Sales Assistant *BN.*

DATE: August 9, 19--

SUBJECT: Yellow Pages Advertising

Uses a direct organizational style: the recommendation and conclusions are given first, followed by the supporting evidence.

I believe we should continue purchasing a quarter-page ad in the Mountain Bell Yellow Pages. My recommendation is based on the conclusion that Yellow Pages advertising has produced more inquiries than any other method of advertising and has increased net profits, especially in the local residential market.

Uses talking headings to reinforce the direct plan.

A PILOT TEST WAS SET UP

Uses informal language; makes extensive use of first- and second-person pronouns such as *I*, *we*, *you*, and *me*.

On March 1 you asked me to conduct a three-month test of the effectiveness of Yellow Pages advertising. I subsequently purchased a quarter-page ad for the edition of the Yellow Pages that was distributed the week of June 2-6. For six weeks thereafter, we queried all telephone and walk-in customers to determine how they had learned about our company. I also compared the percentage of signed contracts resulting from each source. Precise before-and-after sales data could not be generated because of other factors that affected sales for each period (for example, time of year and other promotional campaigns).

RESULTS WERE POSITIVE

My analysis of the data shows that 38% of the callers after June 2-6 first learned about our company from the Yellow Pages. The next highest source was referrals and repeat business, which accounted for 26% of the calls. In addition, 21% of the Yellow Pages inquiries resulted in signed contracts, as compared with our 19% overall average.

The new business that resulted from this advertising substantially affects the local residential market (11%-12% increase), has some effect on the commercial market (5%-6% increase), and has little or no effect on the long-haul or large-job market (0%-2% increase). Our last quarterly sales report indicated that the residential market accounts for 78% of our total sales.

WE SHOULD CONTINUE ADVERTISING

Does not include the detailed statistical information but makes it available if needed.

Based on the $358 monthly cost of our quarter-page ad, each dollar of ad cost is producing $3.77 in sales revenue and $0.983 toward product margin. These results clearly support the continuation of our Yellow Pages advertising. I would be happy to discuss the results of this research with you in more detail and to provide the supporting statistical data if you wish.

jeo

2443 South Canton
Mesa, AZ 85202
602-555-0143

Grammar and Mechanics Note

See the Reference Manual at the end of the text for guidance on how to format memorandums.

FIGURE 13.2 Formal Manuscript Report

The first page of a formal manuscript report is shown.

THE EFFECTIVENESS OF YELLOW PAGES ADVERTISING

FOR ALL SYSTEMS GO COMPANY

Barbara Novak, Sales Assistant

According to Mountain Bell, display advertising typically accounts for 55% of total sales for a firm in the moving business (Dye, 1994, p. 17). Thus, Hiram Cooper, director of marketing, requested a three-month test be conducted of the effectiveness of Yellow Pages advertising for All Systems Go.

This report describes the procedures used to gather the data and the results obtained. Based on the data, a recommendation is made regarding the continuation of Yellow Pages advertising.

Uses an indirect organizational style: the conclusions and recommendations will be given after the supporting data is presented.

Procedures

A quarter-page ad was purchased in the edition of the Mountain Bell Yellow Pages that was distributed the week of June 2-6. For the six-week period encompassing June 9-July 17, all telephone and walk-in customers were queried to determine how they had learned about the company. Comparisons were made of the percentage of signed contracts resulting from each source.

One delimitation of this study was that precise before-and-after sales data could not be generated because of other factors that affected sales for each period (for example, time of year and other promotional campaigns).

Uses generic report headings to reinforce the indirect plan.

Uses formal language; avoids first- and second-person pronouns.

Findings

The findings of this study are reported in terms of the sources of information for learning about All Systems Go, the amount of new business generated, and a cost-benefits comparison for Yellow Pages advertising.

Sources of Information

As shown in Table 1, 38% of the callers during the test period first learned about All Systems Go from the Yellow Pages display. This figure is

Uses visual aids (such as tables and charts) and multilevel headings, which are typical of formal reports.

Grammar and Mechanics Notes

See the Reference Manual at the end of the text for guidance on how to format manuscript reports.

FIGURE 13.3 How Should You Organize the Data?

Basis: Time
 	
Format:
Noun Phrases
	`A. EASTERN ELECTRONICS: A CASE STUDY`
	`1. Start-up of firm: 1987`
	`2. Rapid expansion: 1987-90`
	`3. Industry-wide slowdown: 1991`
	`4. Retrenchment: 1992-93`
	`5. Return to profitability: 1994`

Basis: Location
 	
Format:
Participial Phrases
	`B. RENOVATION NEEDS`
	`1. Expanding the mailroom`
	`2. Modernizing the reception area`
	`3. Installing a humidity system in Warehouse C`
	`4. Repaving the north parking lot`

Basis: Importance
 	
Format:
Partial Statements
	`C. PROGRESS REPORT ON AUTOMATION PROJECT`
	`1. Conversion on budget`
	`2. Time schedule slipped one month`
	`3. Branch offices added to project`
	`4. Software programs upgraded`

Basis: Criteria
 	
Format:
Statements
	`D. EVALUATION OF APPLICANTS FOR COMMUNICATIONS DIRECTOR`
	`1. Sefcik has higher professional training`
	`2. Jenson has more relevant work experience`
	`3. Jenson's written work samples are more effective`

Format:
Questions
	`E. ESTABLISHING A POLICY ON AIDS IN THE WORKPLACE`
	`1. What are the firm's legal and social responsibilities?`
	`2. What policies have other firms established?`
	`3. What policies are needed to deal with the needs of AIDS-infected employees?`
	`4. What policies are needed to deal with the concerns of noninfected employees?`
	`5. How should these policies be implemented?`

Most reports are organized by time, location, importance, or criteria.

plex. The purpose of the report (information, analysis, or recommendation), the nature of the problem, and your knowledge of the reader will help you select the organizational framework that will be most useful.

Time The use of chronology, or time sequence, is appropriate for agendas, minutes of meetings, programs, many status reports, and similar projects. Discussing events in the order in which they occurred or in the order in which they will or should occur is an efficient way to organize many informational reports—those whose purpose is simply to inform.

Despite its usefulness and simplicity, time sequence should not be overused. Because events *occur* one after another, chronology is often the most efficient way to *record* data, but it may not be the most efficient way to *present* that data to your readers. Assume, for example, that you are writing a progress report on a recruiting trip you made to four college campuses. Each day you interviewed candidates for the three positions you have open. The first passage, given in time sequence, requires too much work of the reader. The second version saves reader time.

> *Not:* On Monday morning, I interviewed one candidate for the budget-analyst position and two candidates for the junior-accountant position. Then, in the afternoon, I interviewed two candidates for the asset-manager position and another for the budget-analyst position. Finally, on Tuesday, I interviewed another candidate for budget analyst and two for junior accountant.
>
> *But:* On Monday and Tuesday, I interviewed three candidates for the budget-analyst position, four for the junior-accountant position, and two for the asset-manager position.

Obviously, a blow-by-blow description is not necessarily the most efficient means of communicating information to the reader—sometimes it forces the reader to do too much work. Organize your information in time sequence only when it is important for the reader to know the sequence in which events occurred.

Location Like the use of time sequence, the use of location as the basis for organizing a report is often appropriate for simple informational reports. Discussing topics according to their geographical or physical location (for example, describing an office layout) may be the most efficient way to present the data. Again, however, be sure that such an organizational plan helps the reader process the information most efficiently and that it is not merely the easiest way for you to report the data. Decisions should be based on reader needs rather than on writer convenience.

Importance For the busy reader, the most efficient organizational plan may be to have the most important topic discussed first, followed in order by topics of decreasing importance. The reader then gets the major idea up front and can skim the less important information as desired or needed. This organizational plan is routinely used by newspapers, where the most important points are discussed in the lead paragraph.

For some types of reports, especially recommendation reports, the opposite plan might be used effectively. If you've analyzed four alternatives and will recommend the implementation of Alternative 4, you might first present each of the other alternatives in turn and show why they're *not* feasible. Then, you save your "trump card" until last, thus making the alternative you're recommending the freshest in the reader's mind because it is the last one read. If you use this option, make sure that you effectively "slay all the dragons" except your own and that the reader will agree that your recommendation is the most logical one.

The most logical organization for most analytical and recommendation reports is by criteria.

Criteria For most analytical and recommendation reports, where the purpose is to analyze the data and possibly recommend a solution, the most logical arrangement is to organize the data by criteria. One of the important steps in the reporting process is to develop hypotheses regarding causes or solutions for the problem you're exploring. This process requires factoring, or breaking down, your problem into its component subproblems. These factors, or criteria, then, become the bases for organizing the report.

In Example D in Figure 13.3, for instance, the three factors presented—professional training, work experience, and written work samples—are the bases on which you will evaluate each candidate. Thus, they should also form the bases for presenting the data. By focusing attention on the criteria, you help lead the reader to the same conclusion you reached. Thus, organizing data by criteria is an especially effective organizational plan when the reader might be initially resistant to your recommendations.

If you're evaluating three sites for a new facility, for example, avoid the temptation to use the *locations* of these sites as the report headings. Such an organizational plan focuses attention on the sites themselves instead of the criteria by which you evaluated them and on which you based your recommendations. Instead, use the criteria as the headings. Similarly, avoid using "Advantages" and "Disadvantages" as headings. Keep your reader in step with you by helping the reader focus on the same topics—the criteria—that you focused on during the research and analysis phases of your project.

In actual practice, you might use a combination of these organizational plans. For instance, you might organize your first-level headings by criteria but your second-level headings in simple-to-complex order. Or you might organize your first-level headings by criteria but present these criteria in their order of importance. Competent communicators select an organizational plan with a view toward helping the reader comprehend and appreciate the information and viewpoints being presented in the most efficient manner possible.

In general, prefer the direct plan (conclusions and recommendations first) for business reports.

Presenting Conclusions and Recommendations Once you've decided how to organize the findings of your study, you must decide where to present the conclusions and/or recommendations that have resulted from these findings. The differences among findings, conclusions, and recommendations can be illustrated by the following examples:

Finding:	The computer monitor sometimes goes blank during operation.
Finding:	Nonsense data sometimes prints out on the screen for no reason.
Conclusion:	The computer is broken.
Recommendation:	We should repair the computer before May 3, when payroll processing begins
Finding:	Our Statesville branch has lost money four out of the past five years.
Conclusion:	Our Statesville branch is not profitable.
Recommendation:	We should close our Statesville branch.

The conclusions answer the research questions raised in the introduction.

Academic reports and many business reports have traditionally presented the conclusions and recommendations of a study at the end of the report, the rationale being that conclusions cannot logically be drawn until the data has been presented and analyzed; similarly, recommendations cannot be made until conclusions have been drawn.

Cristi Cawood, a CPA with a practice serving small businesses and individual investors in Portland, Oregon, often prepares reports for clients on complicated tax questions. While the reports present the regulations and data relevant to the case, the most important part is the conclusions Cawood draws. Clients rely on Cawood's ability to present complicated information clearly and concisely.

Figures 13.1 and 13.2, presented earlier, illustrate the two approaches. The informal memo report presents the conclusions and recommendations in the first paragraph; the formal manuscript report delays such presentation until after the findings have been presented and analyzed.

Although hard and fast rules cannot be given for when to use the direct and indirect organizational plans in reports, some guidance can be given. Generally, it is better to use the direct organizational plan (in which the conclusions and recommendations are presented at the beginning of the report) when

- The reader prefers the direct plan for reports.
- The reader will be receptive to your conclusions and recommendations.
- The reader can evaluate the information in the report more efficiently if the conclusions and recommendations are given up front.
- You have no specific reason to prefer the indirect pattern.

Similarly, the indirect plan (in which the evidence is presented first, followed by conclusions and recommendations) is more appropriate when

- The reader prefers the indirect plan for reports.
- The reader will be initially uninterested in or resistant to the conclusions and recommendations.
- The topic is so complex that detailed explanations and discussions are needed in order for the conclusions and recommendations to be understood and accepted.

The decision isn't necessarily an either/or situation. Instead of putting all the conclusions and recommendations either first or last, you may choose to split them up, discussing each in the appropriate subsection of your report. Similarly, even though you write a report using an indirect plan, you may add an executive summary or letter of transmittal that communicates the conclusions and recommendations to the reader before the report itself has been read.

Outlining the Report

Although we've not used the term *outlining* thus far, whenever we've talked about organizing, we've actually been talking about outlining as well. For example, early in the report process you factored your problem statement into its component subproblems. Thus, your problem statement and subproblems served as your first working outline.

The outline provides a concise visual picture of the structure of your report.

Many business writers find it useful at this point in the report process to construct a more formal outline. A formal outline provides an orderly visual representation of the report, showing clearly which points are to be covered, in what order they are to be covered, and what the relationship of each is to the rest of the report. The purpose of the outline is to guide you, the writer, in structuring your report logically and efficiently. Consider it a working draft, subject to being revised as you compose the report.

Use the working title of your report as the title of your outline. Then use upper roman numerals for the major headings, uppercase letters for first-level subheadings, arabic numerals for second-level subheadings, and lowercase letters for third-level subheadings. Only rarely will you need to use all four levels of headings. Figure 13.4 shows an outline for a formal report.

As part of the process of developing a formal outline, you should compose the actual wording for your headings and decide how many headings you will need. Headings play an important role in helping to focus the reader's attention and in helping your report achieve unity and coherence, so plan them carefully, and revise them as needed as you work toward a final version of your report.

Use descriptive and parallel headings for unity and coherence.

Talking Versus Generic Headings **Talking headings** identify not only the topic of the section but also the major conclusion. For instance, Example C in Figure 13.3 uses talking headings to indicate not only that the first section of the report is about the budget for the conversion but also that the conversion is proceeding on budget.

Talking headings, which are typically used in newspapers and magazines, are often also useful for business reports, where they can serve as a preview or executive summary of the entire report. They are especially useful when directness is desired—the reader can simply skim the headings in the report (or in the table of contents) and get an overview of the topics covered and the conclusions reached for each topic.

Generic headings, on the other hand, identify only the topic of the section, without giving the conclusion. Most formal reports and any report written in an indirect pattern would use generic headings, similar to the headings used for Examples A and B in Figure 13.3 and used throughout Figure 13.4.

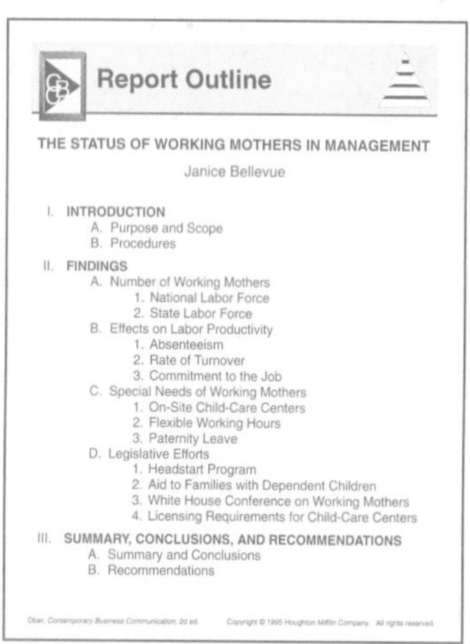
Report Outline

THE STATUS OF WORKING MOTHERS IN MANAGEMENT

Janice Bellevue

I. INTRODUCTION
  A. Purpose and Scope
  B. Procedures
II. FINDINGS
  A. Number of Working Mothers
    1. National Labor Force
    2. State Labor Force
  B. Effects on Labor Productivity
    1. Absenteeism
    2. Rate of Turnover
    3. Commitment to the Job
  C. Special Needs of Working Mothers
    1. On-Site Child-Care Centers
    2. Flexible Working Hours
    3. Paternity Leave
  D. Legislative Efforts
    1. Headstart Program
    2. Aid to Families with Dependent Children
    3. White House Conference on Working Mothers
    4. Licensing Requirements for Child-Care Centers
III. SUMMARY, CONCLUSIONS, AND RECOMMENDATIONS
  A. Summary and Conclusions
  B. Recommendations

Ober, Contemporary Business Communication, 2d ed.

See Transparency 13.2, Report Outline.

Parallelism As illustrated in Figure 13.3, you have wide leeway in selecting the formats of headings you wish to use in your report. Noun phrases are probably the most common form of heading, but you may also choose participial phrases, partial statements (in which a verb is missing—the kind often used in newspaper headlines), statements, or questions. Perhaps there are other forms you might choose as well.

FIGURE 13.4 Report Outline

STAFF EMPLOYEES' EVALUATION OF THE BENEFITS PROGRAM

AT ATLANTIC STATE UNIVERSITY

David Riggins

Uses the working title of the report as the outline title.

1 I. INTRODUCTION

A. Purpose and Scope
B. Procedures

II. FINDINGS

2 A. Knowledge of Benefits
1. Familiarity with Benefits
2. Present Methods of Communication
a. Formal Channels
b. Informal Channels
3. Preferred Methods of Communication
B. Opinions of Present Benefits
1. Importance of Benefits
2. Satisfaction with Benefits
C. Desirability of Additional Benefits

Organizes the findings by criteria.

Each level of subdivision contains at least two items.

III. SUMMARY, CONCLUSIONS, AND RECOMMENDATIONS

A. Summary of the Problem and Procedures
B. Summary of the Findings
C. Conclusions and Recommendations

Uses parallel structure (noun phrases are used for each heading and subheading).

APPENDIX

A. Cover Letter
3 B. Questionnaire

Grammar and Mechanics Notes

1 Align the roman numerals vertically on the periods. 2 Type each entry in upper- and lowercase letters. 3 Identify each appendix item by letter.

Regardless of the form of heading you select, be consistent within each level of heading. If the first major heading (a first-level heading) is a noun phrase, all first-level headings should be noun phrases. If the first major heading is a talking heading, the others should be too. As you move from level to level, you may switch to another form of heading if it would be more appropriate. Again, however, the headings within the same level must be parallel.

Length and Number of Headings Four to eight words is about the right length for most headings. Headings that are too long lose some of their effectiveness; the shorter the heading, the more emphasis it receives. Yet headings that are too short are ineffective because they do not convey enough meaning.

Use headings to break up a long report and refocus the reader's attention.

Similarly, choose an appropriate number of headings. Having too many headings weakens the unit of a report—they chop the report up too much, making it look more like an outline than a discussion. Having too few headings, however, confronts the reader with page after page of solid copy, without the chance to stop periodically and refocus attention on the topic.

In general, consider having at least one heading or visual aid to break up each single-spaced page or each two consecutive, double-spaced pages. Make your report inviting to read.

Balance Maintain a sense of balance within and among sections. It would be unusual to give one section of a report eight subsections (eight second-level headings) and give the following section none. Similarly, it would be unusual to have one section ten pages long and another section only half a page long. Finally, ensure that the most important ideas are in the highest levels of headings. If you're discussing four criteria for a topic, for example, all four of these should be in the same level of heading—presumably in first-level headings.

When you do divide a section into subsections, break it into at least two subsections. You cannot logically have just one second-level heading within a section, because when you divide something, it divides into more than one "piece."

DRAFTING

Although it is the last step of a long and sometimes complex process, the written presentation of your research is the only evidence your reader has of the effort you have invested in the project. The success or failure of all your work depends directly on this physical evidence. Prepare the written report carefully to bring out the full significance of your data and to help the reader reach a decision and solve a problem.

Everything that you learned in Chapter 5 about the writing process applies directly to report writing—choosing a productive work environment; scheduling a reasonable block of time to devote to the drafting phase; letting ideas flow quickly during the drafting stage, without worrying about style, correctness, or format; and revising for content, style, correctness, and readability. However, report writing requires several additional considerations as well.

Drafting the Body

The report body consists of the introduction, the findings, and the summary, conclusions, and recommendations. As stated earlier, the conclusions may go first or last in the report. Each part may be a separate chapter in long reports or a major section in shorter reports.

The introduction presents the information the reader needs to make use of the findings.

Introduction The introduction sets the stage for understanding the findings that follow. In this section, present such information as the following:

- Background of the problem
- Need for the study
- Authorization for the report
- Hypotheses or problem statement and subproblems
- Definition of terms (if needed)
- Procedures used to gather and analyze the data

The actual topics and amount of detail presented in the introductory section will depend on the complexity of the report and the needs of the reader. For example, if the procedures are extensive, you may want to place them in a separate section, with their own first-level heading. Here is an example of an introductory section for a formal report.

> Employee benefits are a rapidly growing and an increasingly important form of employee compensation for both profit and nonprofit organizations. According to a recent U.S. Chamber of Commerce survey, benefits now constitute 37% of all payroll costs, averaging $8,732 yearly for each employee (Berelson, 1992, p. 183). Thus, on the basis of cost alone, an organization's benefits program must be carefully monitored and evaluated.
>
> To ensure that the benefits program for Atlantic State University's 2,500 staff personnel is operating as effectively as possible, David Riggins, director of personnel, authorized this report on October 15, 1994.
>
> **Purpose and Scope**
>
> Specifically, the following problem statement was addressed in this study: what are the opinions of staff employees at Atlantic State University regarding their employee benefits? To answer this question, the following subproblems were addressed:
>
> 1. How knowledgeable are the employees about the benefits program?
> 2. What are the employees' opinions of the value of the benefits presently available?
> 3. What benefits, if any, would the employees like to have added to the program?
>
> This study attempted to determine employee preferences only. The question of whether employee preferences are economically feasible is not within the scope of this study.

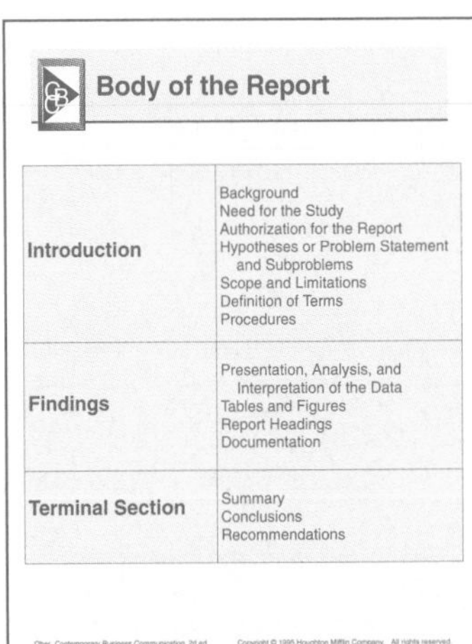
Body of the Report

Introduction	Background Need for the Study Authorization for the Report Hypotheses or Problem Statement and Subproblems Scope and Limitations Definition of Terms Procedures
Findings	Presentation, Analysis, and Interpretation of the Data Tables and Figures Report Headings Documentation
Terminal Section	Summary Conclusions Recommendations

See Transparency 13.3, Body of the Report.

Procedures

A list of the 2,489 staff employees who are eligible for benefits was generated from the October 15 payroll run. By means of a 10% systematic sample, 250 employees were selected for the survey. On November 3, each of the selected employees was sent the cover letter and questionnaire shown in Appendixes A and B via campus mail. A total of 206 employees completed usable questionnaires, for a response rate of 82%.

In addition to the questionnaire data, personal interviews were held with Lois White, compensation specialist at ASU; Roger Ray, chair of the Staff Personnel Committee at ASU; and Lewis Rigby, director of the State Personnel Board. The primary data provided by the survey and personal interviews was then analyzed and compared with findings from secondary sources to determine the staff employees' opinions of the benefits program at ASU.

Don't just present your findings; analyze and interpret them for the reader.

Findings The findings of the study represent the major contribution of the report and make up the largest section of the report. Discuss and interpret any relevant primary and secondary data you gathered. Organize this section using one of the plans discussed earlier (for example, by time, location, importance, or criteria). Using objective language, present the information clearly, concisely, and accurately.

Many reports will display numerical information in tables and figures (such as bar, line, or pie charts). The information in such displays should be self-explanatory; that is, readers should understand it without having to refer to the text. Nevertheless, all tables and figures must be mentioned and explained in the text so that the text, too, is self-explanatory. All text references should be by number (for example, "as shown in Table 4")—never by a phrase such as "as shown below," because the table or figure might actually appear at the top of the following page.

Summarize the important information from the display (see Figure 13.5). Give enough interpretation to help the reader comprehend the table or figure, but don't repeat all the information it contains. Discussing display information in the narrative *emphasizes* that information, so discuss only what merits such emphasis.

The table or figure should be placed immediately below the first paragraph of text in which the reference to the display occurs. (Of course, if the display contains supplementary information, you may place it in an appendix rather than in the body of the report itself.) Avoid splitting a table or figure between two pages. If not enough space is available on the page for the display, continue with the text to the bottom of the page and then place the display at the very top of the following page.

For all primary and secondary data, point out important items, implications, trends, contradictions, unexpected findings, similarities and differences, and the like. Use emphasis, subordination, preview, summary, and transition to make the report read clearly and smoothly. Keep the reader's needs and desires uppermost in mind as you organize, present, and discuss the information.

Summary, Conclusions, and Recommendations A one- or two-page report may need only a one-sentence or one-paragraph summary. Longer or

FIGURE 13.5 Presenting and Analyzing Tables in Reports

Recent studies (Egan, 1992; Ignatio, 1993) have shown that employees' satisfaction with benefits is directly correlated with their knowledge of such benefits. Thus, the ASU staff employees were asked to rate their level of familiarity with each benefit. As shown in Table 2, most staff employees believe that most benefits have been adequately communicated to them.

TABLE 2. EMPLOYEE LEVEL OF FAMILIARITY WITH ASU'S BENEFIT PROGRAM

Benefit	Level of Familiarity				
	Familiar	Unfamiliar	Undecided	No Resp.	Total
Sick leave	94%	4%	1%	1%	100%
Vacation	94%	4%	1%	1%	100%
Paid holidays	92%	4%	3%	1%	100%
Hospital/Medical ins.	90%	7%	2%	1%	100%
Life insurance	84%	10%	5%	1%	100%
Retirement	84%	11%	4%	1%	100%
Long-term disability ins.	55%	33%	12%	0%	100%
Auto insurance	36%	57%	6%	1%	100%

At least four-fifths of the employees are familiar with all major benefits except for long-term disability insurance, which is familiar to only a slight majority. The low level of knowledge about auto insurance (36% familiarity) may be explained by the fact that this benefit started just six weeks before the survey was taken.

more complex reports, however, should include a more extensive summary. Briefly review the problem and procedures used to solve the problem, and provide an overview of the major findings. Repeating the main points or arguments immediately before presenting the conclusions and recommendations reinforces the reasonableness of those conclusions and recommendations. To avoid monotony when summarizing, use wording that is different from the original presentation.

Findings lead to conclusions; conclusions lead to recommendations.

If your report only analyzes the information presented and does not make recommendations, you might label the final section of the report "Summary" or "Summary and Conclusions," as appropriate. If your report includes both conclusions and recommendations, ensure that the conclusions stem directly from your findings and that the recommendations stem directly from the conclusions. Provide ample evidence to support all your conclusions and recommendations. An example of a closing section of a report is shown below.

> **Conclusions and Recommendations**
>
> These findings show that staff employees at Atlantic State University are extremely knowledgeable about all benefits except long-term disability and automobile insurance; however, a majority would prefer to have an individualized benefits statement instead of the brochures now used to explain the benefits program. They consider paid time off as the most important benefit and automobile insurance as the least important. A majority are satisfied with all benefits, although retirement benefits generated substantial dissatisfaction. The only additional benefit desired by a majority of the employees is compensation for unused sick leave.
>
> The following recommendations are based on these conclusions:
>
> 1. Determine the feasibility of generating an annual individualized benefits statement for each staff employee.
> 2. Reevaluate the attractiveness of the automobile insurance benefit in one year to determine staff employees' knowledge about, use of, and desire for this benefit. Consider the feasibility of substituting compensation for unused sick leave for the automobile insurance benefit.
> 3. Conduct a follow-up study of the retirement benefits at ASU to determine how competitive they are with those offered by comparable public and private institutions.

End your report with an overall concluding statement that provides a definite sense of project completion. Don't leave your reader wondering if additional pages will follow.

> These recommendations, as well as the findings of this study, should help the university administration ensure that its benefits program is accomplishing its stated objectives of attracting and retaining high-quality employees and meeting their needs once employed.

Drafting the Supplementary Sections

The length, formality, and complexity of the report, as well as the needs of the reader, affect the number of report parts that precede and follow the body of the report. Use any of the following components that will help you achieve your report objectives. Each of these parts is illustrated in the Reference Manual at the end of the text.

Title Page A title page is typically used for reports typed in manuscript (as opposed to letter or memorandum) format. It shows such information as the title of the report, the names (and perhaps titles and departments) of the reader and writer, and the date the report was transmitted to the reader. Other information may be included at the writer's discretion. The information on the title page should be arranged attractively on the page.

Transmittal Document Formal reports and all reports that are not hand-delivered to the reader should be accompanied by a transmittal document.

Supplementary Report Sections

Title Page	Report Title Names of Reader and Writer Transmittal Date Other Relevant Information
Transmittal Document	Letter or Memorandum Conveying the Completed Report
Executive Summary	Synopsis or Abstract
Table of Contents	Identification of Report Headings Page Numbers on Which the Report Headings Are Found
Appendix	Supplemental Information
References	Complete Citations of All Sources Referred to in the Report

See Transparency 13.4, Supplementary Report Sections.

As its name implies, a **transmittal document** conveys the report to the reader. If the reader is outside the organization, you would use a transmittal letter; if the reader is within the organization, you would typically use a transmittal memo. Whether the report is written in formal or informal style, use a conversational, personal style of writing for the transmittal document.

Write the transmittal memo or letter in a direct pattern.

Because the completion of the report assignment is good news (whether the information it contains is good or bad news), use the direct organizational plan. Begin by actually transmitting the report. Briefly discuss any needed background information, and perhaps give an overview of the conclusions and recommendations of the report (unless you want the reader to read the evidence supporting these conclusions and recommendations first). Include any other information that will help the reader understand, appreciate, and make use of the information presented in the report. End with such goodwill features as an expression of appreciation for being given the report assignment, an offer of willingness to discuss the report further, or perhaps an offer of assistance in the future.

> Here is the report on our staff benefits program you requested on October 15.
>
> The report shows that the staff is familiar with and values most of the benefits we offer. At the end of the report, I've made several recommendations regarding issuing individualized benefits statements annually and determining the usefulness of the automobile insurance benefit, the feasibility of offering compensation for unused sick leave, and the competitiveness of our retirement program.
>
> I enjoyed working on this assignment, Dave, and learned quite a bit from my analysis that will help me during the upcoming labor negotiations. Please let me know if you have any questions about the report.

The letter or memo may simply be transmitted along with the report, or it may be a part of the report. In the latter case, it is placed immediately after the title page but before the executive summary or table of contents.

Executive Summary An **executive summary**, also called an *abstract* or *synopsis*, is a condensed version of the body of the report (including introduction, findings, and any conclusions or recommendations). Although some readers may simply scan the report itself, most will read the executive summary carefully. Like the transmittal document, the executive summary is an optional part of the report. It is especially appropriate when the conclusions and recommendations will be welcomed by the reader, when the report is long, or when you know your reader appreciates having such information up front.

The report summary may be read more carefully than the report itself.

Because the purpose of the executive summary is to save the reader time, the summary should be short—generally no more than 10% of the length of the report. The summary should contain the same emphasis as the report itself and should be independent of the report; that is, you should not refer to the report itself in the summary. Assume that the person reading the summary will not have a chance to read the whole report, so include as much useful information as possible.

Use the same writing style for the summary as you used in the report. Position the summary immediately before the table of contents.

Table of Contents Long reports with many headings and subheadings usually benefit from a table of contents. The wording used in the headings in the table of contents must be identical to the wording used in the headings in the body of the report. Typically, only two or three levels of headings are included in the table of contents—even if more levels are used in the body of the report. The page numbers identify the page on which the section heading appears, even though the section itself may comprise many pages. Obviously, the table of contents cannot be written until after the report itself has been typed.

An appendix might include supplementary reference material not important enough to go in the body of the report.

Appendix The appendix is an optional report part that contains supplementary information or documents. For example, in an appendix you might include a copy of the questionnaire and cover letter used to collect data, supplementary tables, forms, or computer printouts that might be helpful to the reader but that are not important enough to include in the body of the report. Label each appendix separately, by letter—for example, "Appendix A: Questionnaire" and "Appendix B: Cover Letter." In the body of the report, refer by letter to any items placed in an appendix.

References The reference list contains the complete record of any secondary sources cited in the report. Different disciplines use different formats for citing these references; whichever you choose, be consistent and include enough information that the reader can easily locate any source if he or she wants to.

A good indication of a researcher's scholarship is the accuracy of the reference list—in terms of both content and format—so proofread this part of your report carefully. The reference list is the very last section of the report.

Developing an Effective Writing Style

You can enhance the effectiveness of your written reports by paying attention to appropriate tone, pronouns, verb tenses, and emphasis and subordination.

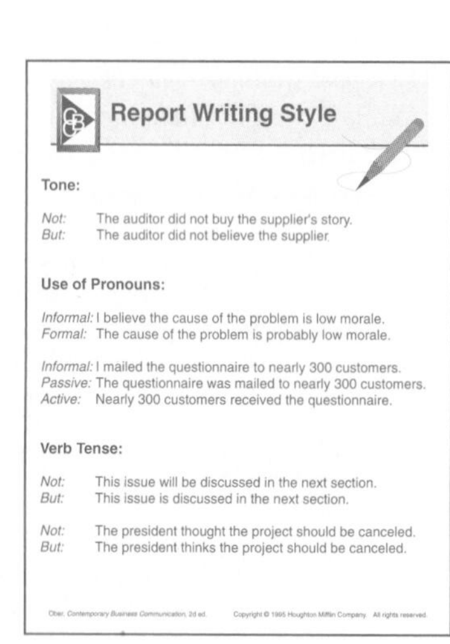

Report Writing Style
Tone:
Not: The auditor did not buy the supplier's story.
But: The auditor did not believe the supplier.
Use of Pronouns:
Informal: I believe the cause of the problem is low morale.
Formal: The cause of the problem is probably low morale.
Informal: I mailed the questionnaire to nearly 300 customers.
Passive: The questionnaire was mailed to nearly 300 customers.
Active: Nearly 300 customers received the questionnaire.
Verb Tense:
Not: This issue will be discussed in the next section.
But: This issue is discussed in the next section.
Not: The president thought the project should be canceled.
But: The president thinks the project should be canceled.

See Transparency 13.5, Report Writing Style.

Tone Regardless of the structure of your report, the writing style used is typically more objective and less conversational than, for example, the style of an informal memorandum. Avoid colloquial expressions, attempts at humor, subjectivity, bias, and exaggeration.

Not: The company hit the jackpot with its new MRP program.
But: The new MRP program saved the company $125,000 the first year.

Not: He claimed that half of his projects involved name-brand advertising.
But: He stated that half of his projects involved name-brand advertising.

Pronouns For most business reports, the use of first- and second-person pronouns is not only acceptable but also quite helpful for achieving an effective writing style. Formal language, however, focuses attention on the information being conveyed instead of on the writer; therefore, reports written in the formal style should use third-person pronouns and avoid using *I, we,* and *you.*

First- and second-person pronouns can be used appropriately in most business reports.

You can avoid the awkward substitute "the writer" by recasting the sentence. Most often, it is evident that the writer is the person doing the action communicated.

Informal:	I recommend that the project be canceled.
Awkward:	The writer recommends that the project be canceled.
Formal:	The project should be canceled.

Using the passive voice is a common device for avoiding the use of *I* in formal reports, but doing so weakens the impact. Instead, recast the sentence to avoid undue use of the passive voice.

Informal:	I interviewed Jan Smith.
Passive:	Jan Smith was interviewed.
Formal:	In a personal interview, Jan Smith stated . . .

You may also want to avoid using *he* as a generic pronoun when referring to an unidentified person. Chapter 4 discusses many ways to avoid such discriminatory language.

Verb Tense Use the verb tense (past, present, or future) that is appropriate at the time the reader *reads* the report—not necessarily at the time that you *wrote* the report. Use past tense to describe procedures and to describe the findings of other studies already completed, but use present tense for conclusions from those studies.

Verb tenses should reflect the reader's *(not the* writer's*) time frame.*

When possible, use the stronger present tense to present the data from your study. The rationale for doing so is that we assume our findings continue to be true; thus, the use of the present tense is justified. (If we cannot assume the continuing truth of any findings, we should probably not use them in the study.)

Not:	These findings *will be discussed* later in this report.
But:	These findings *are discussed* later in the report. (*But:* These findings *were discussed* earlier in this report.)
Not:	Three-fourths of the managers *responded* that they *believed* quality circles *were* effective at the plant.
But:	Three-fourths of the managers *believe* that quality circles *are* effective at the plant.
Procedure:	Nearly 500 people *responded* to this survey.
Finding:	Only 11% of the managers *received* any specific training on the new procedure.
Conclusion:	Most managers *do not receive* any specific training on the new procedure.

As discussed in Chapter 3, encourage students to choose the simple word over the more formal one. Here are some words that commonly appear in business writing and the simpler words that can replace them:

ameliorate/improve
commence/begin
finalize/finish
remunerate/pay
prioritize/rank or set priorities

Emphasis and Subordination Only rarely does all the data consistently point to one conclusion. More likely, you will have a mixed bag of data from which you will have to evaluate the relative merits of each point. For your report to achieve its objective, the reader must evaluate the importance of each point the same way you do. At the very least, your reader must be *aware* of the importance you attached to each point. Therefore, you

Use emphasis and subordination ethically—not to pressure the reader.

should employ the emphasis and subordination techniques learned in Chapter 4 when discussing your findings.

By making sure that the amount of space devoted to a topic reflects the importance of that topic, by carefully positioning your major ideas, and by using language that directly tells what is more and less important, you can help ensure that you and your reader are on the same wavelength when your reader analyzes the data.

Use emphasis and subordination to let the reader know what you consider most and least important—but *not* to unduly sway the reader. If the data honestly leads to a strong, definite conclusion, then by all means make your conclusion strong and definite. But if the data permits only a tentative conclusion, then say so.

Use previews, summaries, and transitions to achieve coherence and unity.

Coherence One of the difficulties of writing any long document—especially when the document is drafted in sections and then put together—is making the finished product read smoothly and coherently, like a unified presentation rather than a cut-and-paste job.

One effective way to achieve coherence in a report is to use previews, summaries, and transitions regularly. At the beginning of each major section, preview what is discussed in that section. At the conclusion of each section, summarize what was presented and provide a smooth transition to the next topic. For long sections, the preview, summary, and transition might each be a separate paragraph; for short sections, a sentence might suffice.

Advise students to review their reports for these commonly misused words and to make sure they are using the correct one:

accept/except
affect/effect
beside/besides
may be/maybe
principal/principle

Note how preview, summary, and transition are used in the following example of a report section opening and closing.

Training of System Users

The training program can be evaluated in terms of the opinions of the users and in terms of the cost of training in proportion to the cost of the system itself. . . . *(After this topic preview, several paragraphs follow that discuss the opinions of the users and the cost of the training program.)*

Even though a slight majority of users now feel competent in using the system, the training provided falls far short of the 20% of total system cost recommended by experts. This low level of training may have affected the precision of the data generated by the MRP system. *(The first sentence contains the summary of this section; the second, the transition to the next.)*

Don't depend on your heading structure for coherence. Your report should read smoothly and coherently without the headings. Avoid repeating the exact words of the heading in the following narrative, and avoid using the heading as part of the narrative.

Not: **THE TWO DEPARTMENTS SHOULD BE MERGED.** The reason is that there is a duplication of services.

Not: **THE TWO DEPARTMENTS SHOULD BE MERGED.** The two departments should be merged. The reason is that there is a duplication of services.

But: **THE TWO DEPARTMENTS SHOULD BE MERGED.** Merging the two departments would eliminate the duplication of services.

Always introduce a topic before dividing it into subtopics. Thus, you should never have one heading following another without some intervening text. Preview for the reader how the topic will be divided before you actually make the division.

Documenting Your Sources

Documentation is the identification of one's sources by giving credit to another person, either in the text or in the reference list, for using his or her words or ideas. You may, of course, use the words and ideas of others, provided such use is properly documented; in fact, for many business reports such secondary information may be the *only* data you use. You must, however, provide appropriate documentation whenever you quote, paraphrase, or summarize someone else's work (see the Spotlight on Law and Ethics).

Plagiarism is the use of another person's words or ideas without giving proper credit. One's writings are considered one's legal property; someone else who wrongfully uses such property is guilty of theft. Plagiarism, therefore, carries stiff penalties. In the classroom, the penalty ranges from failure in a course to expulsion from school. On the job, the penalty for plagiarism ranges from loss of credibility to loss of employment.

What Needs to Be Documented Except as noted below, all material in your report that comes from secondary sources must be documented; that is, enough information about the original source must be given to enable the reader to locate the source if he or she so desires. If the secondary source is published (for example, a journal article), the documentation should appear as a reference citation. If the source is unpublished, sufficient documentation can generally be given in the narrative, making a formal citation unnecessary, illustrated below:

Provide a reference citation for material that came from others, unless that material is common knowledge or can be verified easily.

> According to Board Policy 91-18b, all position vacancies above the level of C-3 must be posted internally at least two weeks prior to being advertised.

> The contractor's letter of May 23, 1994, stated, "We agree to modify Blueprint 3884 by widening the southeast entrance from 10 feet to 12 feet 6 inches for a total additional charge of $273.50."

Occasionally, enough information can be given in the narrative so that a formal citation is unnecessary even for published sources. This format is most appropriate when only one or two sources are used in a report.

> Widmark made this very argument in a guest editorial entitled "Here We Go Again" in the May 4, 1989, *Wall Street Journal* (p. A12).

Once a study has been cited once, it may be mentioned again in continuous discussion on the same page or even on the next pages without further citation if no ambiguity results. If several pages intervene or if ambiguity might result, the citation should be given again.

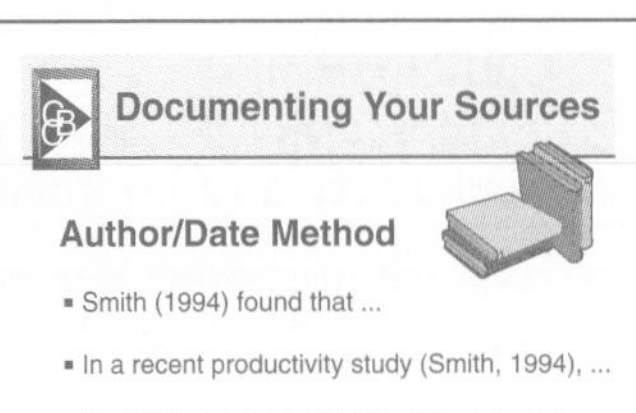

Documenting Your Sources
Author/Date Method
▪ Smith (1994) found that ...
▪ In a recent productivity study (Smith, 1994), ...
▪ As Smith and Jones (1993) demonstrated, ...
▪ As has been shown (Smith & Jones, 1993), ...
▪ Several studies (Abel, 1990, 1993a, 1993b; Brooks, 1980; Curtin, 1994) ...
▪ Johnson's answer was, "Not in your lifetime" (Dye, 1989, p. 230).
▪ Medco sold its Akron plant for $2.4 million ("Medco Lights Up," 1991, p. 14B).
Ober, Contemporary Business Communication, 2d ed.
Copyright © 1995 Houghton Mifflin Company. All rights reserved.

See Transparency 13.6, Documenting Your Sources.

What Does *Not* Need to Be Documented The use of two types of material by others does not need to be documented: (1) facts that are common

SPOTLIGHT ON LAW AND ETHICS

Who Said So?

Plagiarism is a potential problem for anyone who writes. For example, the head of Harvard University's psychiatric hospital resigned when it was found he had committed plagiarism in four papers he published. A nationally known minister was accused of plagiarizing numerous sections from someone else's book to include in his own popular book. A director of the Cooley Law School resigned immediately after admitting he used "substantial unattributed quotations" in a law-review article. Problems of dishonesty in research have, in fact, become so serious that the federal government has issued specific rules designed to police scientific fraud by researchers.

CHECK YOUR SOURCES

Business writers have also been guilty of shoddy scholarship. In *Pacific Rim Trade,* a book published by the American Management Association, the writers stated that Lakewood Industries, a small Minnesota firm, sells the most chopsticks in Japan. *Forbes* magazine investigated and found that the company doesn't sell the most chopsticks in Japan, never did, and never will. In fact, the three-year-old firm went bankrupt trying to perfect a technique for manufacturing the chopsticks.

You can, of course, go too far in the other direction and provide excessive documentation. Such a practice not only is distracting but also leaves the impression that the writer is not an original thinker. As an example of excessive documentation, a study of criminal procedure published in the *Georgetown Law Journal* was accompanied by 3,917 footnotes!

In addition to citing your sources, you should also verify any information you include in a report, regardless of who said it. For example, according to the book *They Never Said It,* despite widespread belief, Voltaire never said, "I disapprove of what you say, but I will defend to the death your right to say it"; Leo Durocher never said, "Nice guys finish last"; and W. C. Fields never said, "Anybody who hates children and dogs can't be all bad."

Similarly, James Cagney never used the line "You dirty rat," nor did Humphrey Bogart say, "Play it again, Sam," in any of his films. And Sherlock Holmes never uttered "Elementary, my dear Watson" in any of A. Conan Doyle's novels.

GIVE CREDIT WHERE CREDIT IS DUE

As a competent communicator, you must give appropriate credit to your sources and ensure the accuracy of your data. Make certain that you have answered completely and fairly the question "Who said so?" Your organization's reputation and welfare—not to mention your own—demand no less.

Sources: Kenneth H. Bacon, "U.S. Issues Rules Aimed at Policing Fraud in Research," *Wall Street Journal,* August 9, 1989, p. B3; Paul M. Barrett, "To Read This Story in Full, Don't Forget to See the Footnotes," *Wall Street Journal,* May 10, 1988, p. 1; Paul Boller and John George, *They Never Said It,* Oxford University Press, Oxford, England, 1989; Christopher Cook, "Judge Reportedly Plagiarized in Article," *Detroit Free Press,* March 19, 1989, p. 3A; John Harris, "Chop-Stuck," *Forbes,* August 21, 1989, p. 14; Ralph Keyes, "The Greatest Quotes Never Said," *Readers Digest,* June 1993, pp. 97–100; Rob Stein, "Plagiarism Charges End in Departure at Harvard," *Detroit Free Press,* November 29, 1988, p. 8A.

knowledge to the readers of your report and (2) facts that can be verified easily.

> Apple Computer is a large manufacturer of microcomputers.
> The stock market closed at 2,506 on November 8.

But such statements as "Sales of the original Macintosh were disappointing" and "Only 4,000 Macintosh computers were sold in 1984" would need to be documented. If in doubt about whether you need to document, provide the citation.

Forms of Documentation The three major forms for documenting the ideas, information, and quotations of other people in a report are endnotes, footnotes, and author-date references (see the Reference Manual at the back of this text for examples and formatting conventions). Let the nature of the report and the needs of the reader dictate the documentation method used. Regardless of the method you select, ensure that the citations are accurate, complete, and consistently formatted and that your bibliography format is compatible with your documentation format.

Standard citation formats are footnotes, endnotes, and author-year citations.

1. *Endnotes:* The endnote format uses superscript (raised) numbers to identify secondary sources in the text and then provides the actual citations in a numbered list entitled "Notes" at the end of the report. The endnotes are numbered consecutively throughout the report. Some readers prefer the endnote format because it avoids the clutter of footnotes and because it's easy to use.

Word processing has simplified the generation of endnotes and footnotes.

In the past, using endnotes for a long or complex report was somewhat risky because of the possibility of introducing errors when revising text. Every time text with a reference was inserted, deleted, or moved, all following endnote references in the text and in the list at the back of the report had to be renumbered. Today, however, most word processors have an endnote feature that automatically numbers and keeps track of endnote references. Still, some readers prefer one of the other formats because endnotes provide no clues in the text regarding the source.

The author-date format discussed in this chapter is also known as the APA method, and is fully documented in the *Publication Manual of the American Psychological Association.* Students who are not sure of the format for a citation should consult this manual.

2. *Footnotes:* For years, footnotes were the traditional method of citing sources, especially in academic reports. A bibliographic footnote provides the complete reference at the bottom of the page on which the citation occurs in the text. Thus, a reader interested in exploring the source does not have to turn to the back of the report. Today's word processors can format footnotes almost painlessly—automatically numbering and positioning each note correctly. Some readers, however, find the presence of footnotes on the text page distracting.

3. *Author-Date Format:* Many business report readers prefer the author-date format of documentation, regarding the method as a reasonable compromise between endnotes (which provide *no* reference information on the text page) and footnotes (which provide *all* the reference information on the text page). In the author-date format, the writer inserts at an appropriate point in the text the last name of the author and the year of publication in parentheses. Complete bibliographic information is included in the Notes section at the end of the report.

The author-date format is preferred by many users of business reports.

REVISING

Once you have produced a first draft of your report, put it away for a few days. Doing so will enable you to view the draft with a fresh perspective and perhaps find a more effective means of communicating your ideas to the reader. Don't try to correct all problems in one review. Instead, look at this process as having three steps—revising first for content, then for style, and finally for correctness.

Revise first for content. Make sure you've included sufficient information to support each point, that you've included no extraneous information

In addition to revising for content, style, and correctness, remind students to review their drafts for unintentional plagiarism. They should be sure they have cited their sources not only for direct quotations but also for summaries and paraphrases.

Though he presents his reports on air instead of on paper, revising is just as important for Al Sigala of Portland, Oregon's KATU as it is for those preparing written reports. Because the amount of time he has on air is often determined at the last minute, Sigala must be able to cut or expand quickly while keeping his main points clearly focused for his audience.

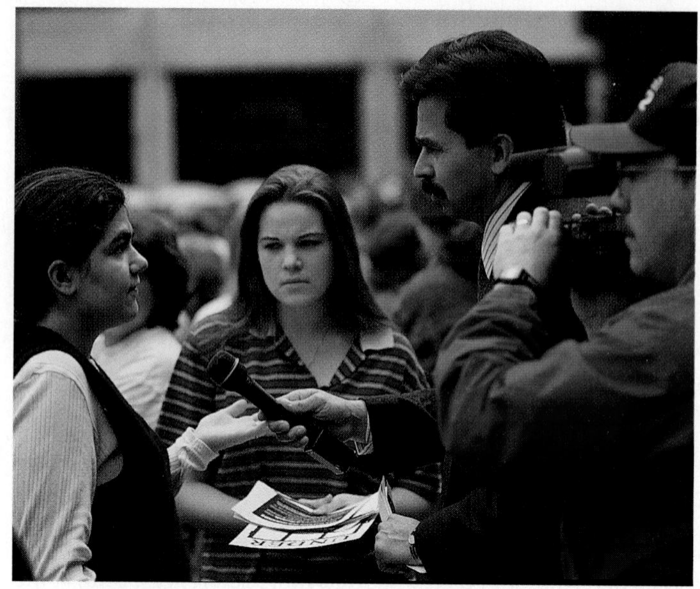

(regardless of how interesting it might be), that all the information is accurate, and that the information is presented in an efficient and logical sequence. Keep the purpose of the report and the reader's needs and desires in mind as you review for content.

For an exercise on revising an internal technical report, refer students to the *Study Guide*, pp. 174–176.

Once you're satisfied with the content of the report, revise for style (refer to Checklist 1: Writing with Style on page 100). Ensure that your writing is clear and that you have used short, simple, vigorous, and concise words. Check to see that you have used a variety of sentence types and have used active and passive voice appropriately. Do your paragraphs have unity and coherence, and are they of reasonable length? Have you maintained an overall tone of confidence, courtesy, sincerity, and objectivity? Finally, review your draft to ensure that you have used nondiscriminatory language and appropriate emphasis and subordination.

Edit for grammar, spelling, punctuation, and word usage.

After you're confident about the content and style of your draft, revise once more for correctness. This revision step, known as *editing*, identifies and resolves any problems with grammar, spelling, punctuation, and word usage—the topics covered in the LABs in the Reference Manual at the back of this text. Do not risk losing credibility with the reader by careless English usage. If possible, have a colleague review your draft to catch any errors you may have overlooked.

FORMATTING

The physical format of your report (margins, spacing, and the like) depends to a certain extent on the length and complexity of the report and the format preferred by either the organization or the reader.

General Formatting Guidelines

Consistency and readability are the hallmarks of an effective format. For example, be sure that all your first-level headings are formatted consistently; if they are not, the reader may not be able to tell which headings are superior or subordinate to other headings. Regardless of the format used, make sure the reader can instantly tell which are major headings and which are minor headings. You can differentiate among headings by using different fonts, font sizes, styles (such as bold or italic), and horizontal placement.

Adopt a consistent, logical format, keeping the needs of the reader in mind.

If the organization or reader has a preferred format style, use it. Otherwise, follow the report formatting guidelines provided in the Reference Manual at the back of this text.

Enhancing Reports Through Document Design

Contemporary word processing software makes it easy for writers to take the report process one step further—that is, to *design* their business reports for maximum impact and effectiveness. Although the product is always more important than the packaging, there is no denying the fact that an attractively formatted document, with legible type and plenty of white space, will help you achieve your report objectives.

With that in mind, consider the following ten design guidelines, which are illustrated in the Spotlight on Technology. Both versions of the Spotlight report contain the same information. Compare the typed version with the designed version for impact and readability.

1. Keep It Simple. The most important guideline is to use a simple, clean, and consistent design. It would be distracting, for example, to use many different type styles and sizes in the same document. Instead, select one serif typeface (*serifs* are the small strokes at the tops and bottoms of characters, such as the "feet" at the bottom of a *T;* sans serif typefaces have no such ornamental strokes) for the body of your report and one sans serif typeface for headings and subheadings. One popular combination is Times Roman for body type and Helvetica for special treatments such as headings, subheadings, and captions for figures.

Use a simple, consistent design.

> This is an example of Times Roman in 11-point type. Because the serifs aid in readability, Times Roman is a good choice for the body of your report.
>
> This is an example of Helvetica in 11-point type. Because it contrasts nicely with Times Roman, Helvetica is a good choice for headings.

Similarly, it would be distracting if a reader is accustomed to seeing lists arranged in a certain format to encounter a list formatted differently.

Designing Business Reports

Staff Employees' Evaluation of the Benefits Program at Atlantic State University

EMPLOYEE BENEFITS ARE a rapidly growing and an increasingly important form of employee compensation for both profit and nonprofit organizations. According to a recent U.S. Chamber of Commerce survey, benefits now constitute 37% of all payroll costs, averaging $8,732 yearly for each employee (Berelson, 1992, p. 183). Thus, on the basis of cost alone, an organization's benefits program must be carefully monitored and evaluated.

To ensure that the benefits program for Atlantic State University's 2,500 staff personnel is operating as effectively as possible, David Riggins, director of personnel, authorized this report on October 15, 1994.

Purpose and Scope

Specifically, the following problem statement was addressed in this study: What are the opinions of staff employees at Atlantic State University regarding their benefits? To answer this question, the following subproblems were addressed:

- How knowledgeable are the employees about the benefits program?
- What are the employees' opinions of the value of the benefits now available?
- What benefits, if any, would the employees like to have added to the program?

This study attempted to determine employee preferences only. Whether the preferences are economically feasible is not within the scope of the study.

Procedures

A list of the 2,489 staff employees who are eligible for benefits was generated from the October 15 payroll run. By means of a 10% systematic sample, 250 employees were selected for the survey. On November 3, each of the selected employees was sent the cover letter and questionnaire shown in Appendixes A and B via campus mail. A total of 206 employees completed questionnaires, for a response rate of 82%.

In addition to the questionnaire data, personal interviews were held with Lois White, compensation specialist at ASU; Roger Ray, chair of the Staff Personnel Committee at ASU; and Lewis Rigby, director of the State Personnel Board. The primary data provided by the survey and personal interviews was then analyzed and compared with findings from secondary sources to determine the staff employees' opinions of the benefits program at ASU.

1

Document-Designed Version

STAFF EMPLOYEES' EVALUATION OF THE BENEFITS PROGRAM

AT ATLANTIC STATE UNIVERSITY

Employee benefits are a rapidly growing and an increasingly important form of employee compensation for both profit and nonprofit organizations. According to a recent U.S. Chamber of Commerce survey, benefits now constitute 37% of all payroll costs, averaging $8,732 yearly for each employee (Berelson, 1992, p. 183). Thus, on the basis of cost alone, an organization's benefits program must be carefully monitored and evaluated.

To ensure that the benefits program for Atlantic State University's 2,500 staff personnel is operating as effectively as possible, David Riggins, director of personnel, authorized this report on October 15, 1994.

Purpose and Scope

Specifically, the following problem statement was addressed in this study: What are the opinions of staff employees at Atlantic State University regarding their employee benefits? To answer this question, the following subproblems were addressed:

1. How knowledgeable are the employees about the benefits program?
2. What are the employees' opinions of the value of the benefits presently available?
3. What benefits, if any, would the employees like to have added to the program?

This study attempted to determine employee preferences only. The question of whether employee preferences are economically feasible is not within the scope of this study.

Procedures

A list of the 2,489 staff employees who are eligible for benefits was generated from the October 15 payroll run. By means of a 10% systematic sample, 250 employees were selected for the survey. On November 3, each of the selected employees was sent the cover letter and questionnaire shown in Appendixes A and B via campus mail. A total of 206 employees completed usable questionnaires, for a response rate of 82%.

In addition to the questionnaire data, personal interviews were held with Lois White, compensation specialist at ASU; Roger Ray, chair of the Staff Personnel Committee at ASU; and Lewis Rigby, director of the State Personnel Board. The primary data provided by the survey and personal interviews was then analyzed and compared with findings from secondary sources to determine the staff employees' opinions of the benefits program at ASU.

Typewritten Version

The reader would have to pause to figure out what is different, and why. Make sure that whatever decisions you initially make about margins, spacing, headings, and the like are followed consistently throughout your report.

2. Use White Space to Advantage. Use generous top, bottom, and side margins to make your report inviting to read. Consider white space (the blank sections of the report) as part of your overall design. In general, the more white space, the better. Break up long paragraphs into shorter ones, and leave generous space before and after headings. Also separate lengthy areas of text with subheadings. Subheadings not only break up solid blocks of type but also enhance readability by periodically providing signals for the reader.

The empty space on a page also communicates.

3. Select a Suitable Line Length and Type Size. Line length can have a major impact on the readability of a document. Lines that are too short weaken coherence because they needlessly disrupt the normal horizontal pattern of reading. Lines that are too long cause readers to lose their place when they return to the beginning of the next line.

> Using too many columns on a page will result in line lengths that are so short they are difficult to read. The line length is partially a function of the size and style of typeface you select. Larger typefaces should be formatted on longer lines than smaller typefaces.

> Lines that are too long for the size of type used cause the reader to lose his or her place too easily. Using long line lengths simply to get more information on the page is counterproductive if it results in a less readable document. Format the report for the convenience of the reader—not the writer.

The first line of the first column above contains only 14 characters and spaces; it is too short. The first line of the second paragraph contains 91 characters and spaces; it is too long for easy readability. In general, use a line no shorter than 25 characters and no longer than 65 to 75 characters for business documents. Although one column is standard for business reports, any business document can also be typed in two or three columns on a standard-sized page.

For the body of most business reports, you should select a type size between 10 points (elite size) and 12 points (pica size); 1 point equals $\frac{1}{72}$ of an inch. Proportionately larger type should be used for headings and subheadings.

4. Determine an Appropriate Justification Format. All text lines in the body of your report should be left-justified; that is, they should all begin at the left margin. However, the end of each line may be either right-justified (sometimes called *full justification*) or ragged right. In general, a justified line presents a clean, formal look, whereas a ragged-right line gives an informal, casual appearance. In addition, you should limit your use of full justification to documents printed on laser printers.

Use full justification for a formal appearance and an uneven right margin for an informal appearance.

This is an example of a justified column, which produces even left and right margins. You should always have the hyphenation feature of your word processor turned on when justifying your lines.

This is an example of a column with a ragged right margin, that is, one where the lines end unevenly. Ragged-right lines do not typically require as many distracting hyphenations as justified lines of type.

5. Use a Contemporary Punctuation Style. In monospaced type (where each character is the same size, as in most typewriter type), you are accustomed to leaving two spaces after a period at the end of a sentence and after a colon. Designed documents use proportional type, where the width of each letter varies according to the shape of the letter (in proportional type, for example, an *m* is much wider than an *i*). In designed documents, it is customary to leave only one space after each punctuation mark instead of two.

```
This is typewriter type.  Leave two spaces after a
period at the end of a sentence.
```

This is proportional type. Leave one space after a period at the end of a sentence.

Also, in typewriter type, you are accustomed to using generic quotation marks; that is, you use the same character for both the opening and closing quotation mark. Designed documents use different marks for each.

```
Use "generic" quotation marks on a typewriter.
```

Use “differentiated” quotation marks in desktop publishing.

Finally, in typewriter type, you make a dash by typing two hyphens with no space before, between, or after. Designed documents use a special character for the dash.

```
Type a dash--two hyphens--like this on a typewriter.
```

Type a dash—a special character—like this in desktop publishing.

6. Format Paragraphs Correctly. Business reports prepared on a typewriter may be single- or double-spaced. Designed documents use only single spacing. New paragraphs are indicated either by leaving a blank line before the paragraph or by indenting the first line. Do not, however, both indent *and* leave a blank line; that would be too much. Even when paragraphs are indented, designed documents typically do not indent the first line of a paragraph that immediately follows a heading or subheading; it is obvious that what follows a heading is a new paragraph.

Writers sometimes use various techniques at the start of a document to engage the reader immediately: beginning the first word of the document with an extra-large, decorative letter; typing the first three or four words in solid capitals; or setting the first paragraph in larger type than the rest of the document. The purpose of such techniques is to make the copy attractive and inviting to read.

Use special emphasis techniques sparingly.

7. Emphasize Words and Ideas Appropriately. On a typewriter, underlining and solid capitals are about the only way to emphasize an idea. Thus, report headings and subheadings have traditionally been formatted in one of these two styles.

Designed documents, however, have a variety of techniques readily available—larger type size, boldface lettering, and italic type, for example. Any of these techniques is preferable to underlining and solid capitals. Solid capitals are appropriate only for very short headings. Unlike lowercase letters, capital letters are all the same size, and are therefore more difficult to read. Also avoid using nonstandard type styles, such as outline or shadow type, in business reports; they provide visual clutter and are distracting.

Use boldface for strong emphasis and italic for medium emphasis in the body of a report. Both boldface and italic type, along with a larger type size, may be used for headings and subheadings; just be sure your main headings stand out more than your subheadings. When headings are displayed prominently, they may be typed in upper- and lowercase letters or with only the first word and proper names in uppercase. Any of the following three styles would be appropriate for a report heading:

Opinions of Present Benefits

Opinions of Present Benefits

Opinions of present benefits

8. Format Lists for Readability. Because lists or enumerations are surrounded by white space, with each item by itself on a separate line, they tend to stand out more than when the same material is presented in narrative form. You have the choice of using either numbered lists or bulleted lists. Number your lists when *sequence* is important ("Here are the five steps for requesting temporary help") or when the list is long and numbering will help when referring to a specific point. When sequence is not important and the list is short, use bullets (small squares or circles) to call attention to each item. Keep the bullets small and close to the items they relate to. For both numbered and bulleted lists, either a hanging style or a first-line-indented style may be used. Both of the following lists are formatted appropriately:

Use numbered lists when order is important; otherwise, use bulleted lists.

To insert a chart into your report file, follow these steps:

1. Create the chart using a graphics or spreadsheet program, such as *Harvard Graphics* or *Lotus 1-2-3.*
2. Open your report file.
3. Use your word processor's command to insert the graphic.
4. Resize the graphic so that it is in proper scale and position it below the paragraph where it is introduced.

Each typeface can vary in a number of important ways:

- Posture: Roman (vertical) and italic (oblique)
- Weight: Hairline, thin, light, book, regular, medium, demibold, bold, heavy, black, and ultra
- Width: Condensed, regular, and expanded
- Size: Text (all type sizes up to 12 points) and display (type sizes larger than 12 points)

9. Use Graphics—In Moderation. When used in moderation, graphics can add interest and aid comprehension. This is especially the case when using charts and tables. In addition, writers today can make use of files of computerized drawings, called *clip art,* that can be electronically inserted into their documents.

Use graphics only when they help you achieve your report objectives.

To be effective, such clip art must be used sparingly and be well drawn, relevant, and in proper scale. Unless you are certain that a particular piece of clip art will help you tell your story more effectively, save clip art for more informal communications such as company newsletters and advertising documents. Most business reports should have a dignified, businesslike appearance.

Horizontal and vertical lines (called *rules*), another graphic device, can also be used in moderation to separate different elements of the document. Horizontal rules can be narrow or wide; vertical rules (sometimes used to separate columns) should be very narrow. If horizontal rules are used at the top and bottom of a page, the top rule is generally wider than the bottom.

10. Have Fun! Just as the arrival of the personal computer gave the average manager easy access to strategic information, so also has the arrival of desktop publishing and document design given the average business person more control over the documents he or she produces. You don't have to be an artist to *design* your documents. The features you'll need are available on any contemporary word processing or desktop publishing pro-

CHECKLIST 14

Reviewing Your Report Draft

INTRODUCTION

1. Is the report title accurate, descriptive, and honest?
2. Is the research problem or the purpose of the study stated clearly and accurately?
3. Is the scope of the study identified?
4. Are all technical terms, or any terms used in a special way, defined?
5. Are the procedures discussed in sufficient detail?
6. Are any questionable decisions justified?

FINDINGS

7. Is the data analyzed completely, accurately, and appropriately?
8. Is the analysis free of bias and misrepresentation?
9. Is the data interpreted (its importance and implications discussed) rather than just presented?
10. Are all calculations correct?
11. Is all relevant data included and all irrelevant data excluded?
12. Are visual aids correct, needed, clear, appropriately positioned, and correctly labeled?

SUMMARY, CONCLUSIONS, AND RECOMMENDATIONS

13. Is the wording used in the summary different from that used earlier to present the data initially?
14. Are the conclusions drawn supported by ample, credible evidence?
15. Do the conclusions answer the questions or issues raised in the introduction?
16. Are the recommendations reasonable in light of the conclusions?
17. Does the report end with a sense of completion?

gram. Buy a book or two on basic design, and perhaps subscribe to one of the many desktop or personal publishing magazines. Begin to pay attention to the layout and design of professionally prepared documents, and learn from them. Be creative and don't be afraid to experiment. And, most important, have fun! Document design is empowering—to you and your ideas.

PROOFREADING

Do not risk destroying your credibility by failing to proofread carefully.

First impressions are important. Even before reading the first line of your report, the reader will have formed an initial impression of the report—and of *you*. Make this impression a positive one by ensuring that the report carries with it a professional appearance.

After making all your revisions and formatting the various pages, give each page one final proofreading. Check closely for typographical errors.

SUPPLEMENTARY PAGES

18. Is the executive summary short, descriptive, and in proportion to the report itself?
19. Is the table of contents accurate, with correct page numbers and wording that is identical to that used in the report headings?
20. Is any appended material properly labeled and referred to in the body of the report?
21. Is the reference list accurate, complete, and in an appropriate format?

WRITING STYLE AND FORMAT

22. Does the overall report take into account the needs and desires of the reader?
23. Is the material properly organized?
24. Are the headings descriptive, parallel, and appropriate in number?
25. Are emphasis and subordination used effectively?
26. Does each major section contain a preview, summary, and transition?
27. Has proper verb tense been used throughout?
28. Has an appropriate level of formality been used?
29. Are all references to secondary sources properly documented?
30. Is each needed report part included and in an appropriate format?
31. Is the length of the report appropriate?
32. Are the paragraphs of an appropriate length?
33. If the report is formatted on a computer, have the principles of document design been followed to enhance the report's effectiveness?
34. Is the report free from spelling, grammar, and punctuation errors?
35. Does the overall appearance of the report provide a positive first impression?
36. Does the entire project reflect care, neatness, and scholarship?

Check for appearance. Have you arranged the pages in correct order and stapled them neatly? If you're submitting a photocopy, are all the copies legible and of even darkness? Is each page free of wrinkles and smudges?

If you formatted the report on a computer, ensure that in moving passages about, you did not inadvertently delete a line or two or repeat a passage. Run the spelling checker a final time after making all changes. (Remember, however, that a spelling checker will not locate an incorrect word that is spelled correctly.) If you have a grammar software program, evaluate your writing electronically. The grammar checker will check for use of passive voice, sentence length, misuse of words, unmatched punctuation (for example, an opening parenthesis not followed by a closing parenthesis), and readability. Use every aid at your disposal to ensure that your report reflects the highest standards of scholarship, critical thinking, and care.

In short, let your pride of authorship show through in every facet of your report. Appearances count. Review your entire document to ensure that you can answer "yes" to every question contained in Checklist 14: Reviewing Your Report Draft.

MICROWRITING

A Section of a Report

PROBLEM

Review the Microwriting project in Chapter 12, Analyzing Data, page 390. You have constructed your report table (see Figure 12.16) and analyzed the data (see Question 2, Table Interpretation); you are now ready to write this section of your report.

PROCESS

1. Develop an effective talking heading and an effective generic heading for this section of the report. Which one will you use?

   Talking Heading: **MAIL ORDERS CATCHING UP WITH RETAIL SALES**

   Generic Heading: **SOURCES OF SOFTWARE PURCHASES**

   Because I do not personally know the readers of the report and their preferences, I'll make the conservative choice and use a generic heading.

2. Compose an effective topic (preview) sentence for this section.

   Respondents were asked to indicate the source of the last software program they purchased.

3. Where will you position the table for this section?

   At the end of the first paragraph that refers to the table.

4. What verb tense will you use in this section?

   Past tense for the procedures; present tense for the findings.

5. Assume that the next report section discusses the cost of software. Compose an effective summary/transition sentence for this section of the report.

   Perhaps the increasing reliance on mail-order purchases is one reason why the cost of communication software has decreased since 1990.

6. Skip to the recommendations section of your report. What recommendations, if any, will you make regarding these findings?

   Because of the increased importance of mail-order purchases, XYZ Company should explore the feasibility of increasing its marketing efforts to mail-order firms in such areas as volume discounts, better technical support, and more in-depth training efforts.

4

SOURCES OF SOFTWARE PURCHASES

Respondents were asked to indicate the source of the last software program they purchased. As shown in Table 8, retail outlets and mail-order companies are now equally important sources for obtaining software, together accounting for more than four-fifths of all sources. HAL and Pear users obtain their software in different ways: the majority of HAL users obtain theirs from retail outlets whereas the majority of Pear users obtain theirs from mail-order firms.

TABLE 8. SOURCE OF LAST SOFTWARE PROGRAM

(In percentages)

Source	1995			1990		
	Total (*N* = 146)	HAL (*N* = 81)	Pear (*N* = 65)	Total (*N* = 132)	HAL (*N* = 92)	Pear (*N* = 40)
Retail outlet	43.2	54.3	29.2	53.0	50.0	60.0
Mail-order company	41.1	30.9	53.9	21.2	26.1	10.0
Software publisher	6.8	4.9	9.2	6.8	4.3	12.5
Unauthorized copy	4.1	3.7	4.6	15.9	16.3	15.0
Other	4.8	6.2	3.1	3.1	3.3	2.5
Total	100.0	100.0	100.0	100.0	100.0	100.0

The market share for retail outlets decreased by almost 20% from 1990 to 1995 while the market share for mail-order companies almost doubled, increasing by 95%. Also, the use of unauthorized copies appears to be decreasing (although the actual figure is probably somewhat higher than these self-reported figures).

Perhaps the increasing reliance on mail-order purchases is one reason that the cost of communication software has declined since 1990.

COST OF SOFTWARE

...

SUMMARY

The most common report formats are manuscript (for formal reports) and letter or memorandum (for informal reports). The most common plans for organizing the findings of a study are by time, location, importance, and criteria. Conclusions should be presented at the beginning of the report unless the reader prefers the indirect plan, the reader will not be receptive toward the conclusions, or the topic is complex. Report headings should be composed carefully—in terms of their type, parallelism, length, and number.

The body of the report consists of the introduction, findings (the major part of the report), and, as needed, the summary, conclusions, and recommendations. Long, formal reports might also require such supplementary components as a title page, transmittal document, executive summary, table of contents, appendix, and reference list.

Use an objective writing style, appropriate pronouns, and verb tenses that reflect the reader's time frame (rather than the writer's). Use emphasis and subordination techniques to help alert the reader to what you consider important, and use preview, summary, and transitional devices to help maintain coherence. Provide appropriate documentation whenever you quote, paraphrase, or summarize someone else's work by using endnotes, footnotes, or the author-date method of citation.

Delay revising the report until a few days after completing the first draft. Revise in three distinct steps: first for content, then for style, and finally for correctness.

The report's format should enhance the report's appearance and readability and should be based on the organization's and reader's preferences. Unless directed otherwise, follow generally accepted formatting guidelines for margins, report headings, and pagination. Use a simple, consistent design and make generous use of white space. Select an appropriate line length, type size, justification format, and punctuation style; format paragraphs and lists correctly; use graphics in moderation, if needed; and emphasize words and ideas appropriately.

After all revisions and formatting have been completed, give each page one final proofreading. Make sure the final report reflects the highest standards of scholarship, critical thinking, and care.

KEY TERMS

For an exercise on matching terms, refer students to the *Study Guide*, pp. 170–171.

Conclusions The answers to the research questions raised in the introduction.

Documentation Giving credit to another person for his or her words or ideas that you have used.

Executive summary A condensed version of the report body; also called an *abstract* or *synopsis*.

Plagiarism Using another person's words or ideas without giving proper credit.

Talking heading A report heading that identifies not only the topic of the report section but also the major conclusion.

Transmittal document A letter or memorandum that conveys the finished report to the reader.

REVIEW AND DISCUSSION

The answers to the review and discussion questions appear in the *Instructor's Resource Manual*, beginning on p. 252.

1. **Communication at Congressional Research Service Revisited ▪** When elected officials consider how to vote on a particular nutrition-related issue, they can learn more about the background by reading reports prepared by Dr. Donna Porter and her colleagues in the Congressional Research Service of the Library of Congress.
   a. Would Dr. Porter use formal or informal language in a report to members of Congress? Why?
   b. Dr. Porter's reports are informational only; should they be organized according to the direct or the indirect plan? Explain.
   c. Why is documentation important in a report submitted to the U.S. Congress?
2. What factors influence the format and general traits of a report?
3. Give an example of a report topic for which it would be most logical to organize the findings by (a) time, (b) location, (c) importance, and (d) criteria.
4. Under what circumstances should a direct versus an indirect organizational pattern be used for presenting conclusions and recommendations?
5. Assume that your report evaluating three business texts discusses the following topics (the author of the book that rated highest in each category is shown in parentheses):
   a. Content and organization (Bates)
   b. What types of supplementary aids (such as transparencies and student guide) are available (Bates)
   c. How much the book costs (Arnold)
   d. What kind of national reputation the author has (Bates)
   e. Whether the book is up to date in its content coverage (Carroll)

   Compose two sets of headings for these five sections, first generic headings, then talking headings. Make sure each set of headings is parallel.
6. What is the difference between merely *presenting* data and *analyzing* data? Give an example.
7. What verb tense (past, present, or future) should be used for presenting the following information from a study on the effectiveness of a new accounting software program?
   a. A preview of the topics covered in the following section
   b. The procedures of this study
   c. The conclusion regarding the effectiveness of the program
   d. Recommendations for conducting a follow-up study
   e. A discussion of the product reviews contained in computer magazines
8. Assume you surveyed your firm's 50 sales representatives in April. Your survey results showed that they felt left out of the product-planning phase. As a result, you're recommending that the sales manager (the reader of your report) include a two-hour session on this topic at the next sales conference. Write a paragraph presenting this information, first using an informal writing style and then using a formal writing style.
9. Describe some techniques that can be used to emphasize and subordinate findings in a report. What is the appropriate use of such techniques?
10. Give an example of a fact that does and one that does not need to be documented by a citation.
11. What are the advantages and disadvantages of each of the three documentation methods discussed in this chapter?

12. Why should a report not be revised immediately after it is written?
13. Why is white space important in a document?
14. What special proofreading steps should you take if you formatted your report on a computer?

EXERCISES

Exercise 1 is linked with Exercise 1 of Chapter 12. Sample solutions for Exercises 1–18 appear in the *Instructor's Resource Manual*, pp. 254–259.

1. **Microwriting a Report Section ▪**

PROBLEM

Review Exercise 1 of Chapter 12 (page 394). You have constructed your report table and analyzed the data. Now you are ready to write this section of the report.

PROCESS

a. Compose an effective talking heading and an effective generic heading for this section of the report. Which one will you use?
b. Compose an effective topic sentence for this section.
c. Compose the sentence that contains your recommendation.
d. Assume that the next section of the report discusses similar training programs used at other companies. Compose an effective summary/transition sentence for this section of the report.

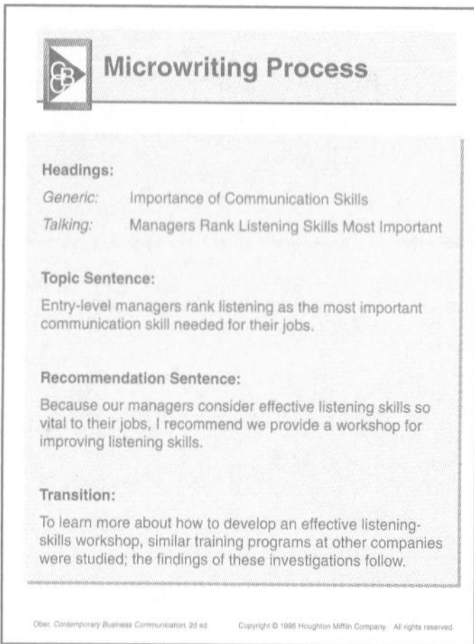
Microwriting Process

Headings:
Generic: Importance of Communication Skills
Talking: Managers Rank Listening Skills Most Important

Topic Sentence:
Entry-level managers rank listening as the most important communication skill needed for their jobs.

Recommendation Sentence:
Because our managers consider effective listening skills so vital to their jobs, I recommend we provide a workshop for improving listening skills.

Transition:
To learn more about how to develop an effective listening-skills workshop, similar training programs at other companies were studied; the findings of these investigations follow.

See Master 13.1, Exercise 1, Microwriting a Report Section, in the *Instructor's Resource Manual*.

PRODUCT

Prepare this section of your report (one to three paragraphs). Include the table in the appropriate position. Submit both your report section and your responses to the process activities to your instructor.

2. **Organizing the Report—Government Report ▪** From the library or a government source, obtain a copy of a recent federal, state, or local government report about an important issue such as crime, education, or immigration. Analyze the organizational structure of the report, and write a memo to your instructor answering the following questions:
   a. What is the purpose of the report?
   b. Who is the audience?
   c. Were the findings organized according to time, location, importance, or criteria? How does the choice of organizational basis relate to the purpose of the report?
   d. Does the report use the indirect or direct organizational plan?
   e. List the main conclusion(s) and indicate where in the report this information was presented.
   f. List the recommendation(s) and indicate where in the report this information was presented.
   g. Prepare an outline of the report. Are all headings in the report parallel? If not, suggest appropriate changes.

Exercise 3 may be linked with Exercise 6 of Chapter 14.

3. **Report Section—Secondary Statistical Data Furnished ▪** You are the vice president of marketing for Excelsior, a small manufacturer located in Asheboro, North Carolina. Although your firm manufactures consumer products such as toothpaste, plastic food wrap, and floor wax, you have the capability of manufacturing numerous different types of small, inexpensive products. The CEO of your firm has asked you to prepare an extensive report on the feasibility of Excelsior's entering the international market.

One strategy that you're considering is the possibility of becoming a supplier for a large multinational company. As part of your research, you have located data on the world's 100 largest public companies (see Figure 13.7). You are interested, first, in the nonbanking firms in this group that have the largest sales, and second, in the percentage change in sales from the previous year. (You are not interested in market value and profit data because they are too much affected by extraneous market conditions that are irrelevant to your purposes, and you are not interested in banks, mortgage companies, and holding companies because they would not be potential purchasers of your products.)

Compose the section of your report that presents and discusses this data. Include a table of the 25 largest firms (in terms of 1992 sales) that meet your criteria. Discuss the data in terms of the largest companies, their countries of origin, changes in sales from the previous year, and similar factors. Format the section in appropriate report format (beginning with page 5 of your report), provide an effective heading for this section, a topic sentence, summary, and transition to the next section, which discusses the largest companies in terms of the major products they sell.

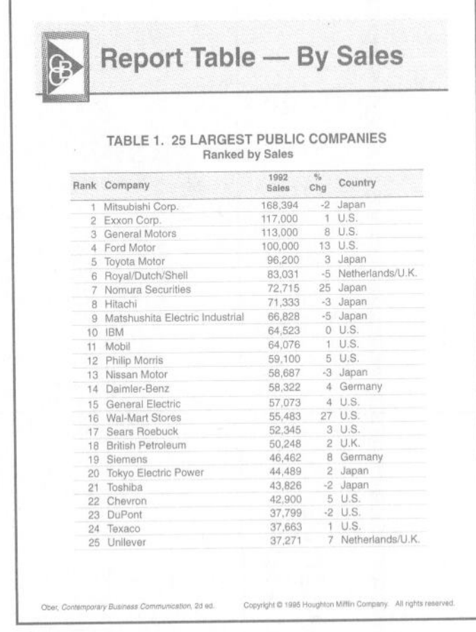

Report Table — By Sales

TABLE 1. 25 LARGEST PUBLIC COMPANIES
Ranked by Sales

Rank	Company	1992 Sales	% Chg	Country
1	Mitsubishi Corp.	168,394	-2	Japan
2	Exxon Corp.	117,000	1	U.S.
3	General Motors	113,000	8	U.S.
4	Ford Motor	100,000	13	U.S.
5	Toyota Motor	96,200	3	Japan
6	Royal/Dutch/Shell	83,031	-5	Netherlands/U.K.
7	Nomura Securities	72,715	25	Japan
8	Hitachi	71,333	-3	Japan
9	Matshushita Electric Industrial	66,828	-5	Japan
10	IBM	64,523	0	U.S.
11	Mobil	64,076	1	U.S.
12	Philip Morris	59,100	5	U.S.
13	Nissan Motor	58,687	-3	Japan
14	Daimler-Benz	58,322	4	Germany
15	General Electric	57,073	4	U.S.
16	Wal-Mart Stores	55,483	27	U.S.
17	Sears Roebuck	52,345	3	U.S.
18	British Petroleum	50,248	2	U.K.
19	Siemens	46,462	8	Germany
20	Tokyo Electric Power	44,489	2	Japan
21	Toshiba	43,826	-2	Japan
22	Chevron	42,900	5	U.S.
23	DuPont	37,799	-2	U.S.
24	Texaco	37,663	1	U.S.
25	Unilever	37,271	7	Netherlands/U.K.

Ober, *Contemporary Business Communication*, 2d ed.

See Master 13.2, Exercise 3, Report Section, in the *Instructor's Resource Manual.*

4. **Supplementary Sections—Going International** ▪ Resume the role of vice president of marketing for Excelsior (see Exercise 3 above). Your report to Victor Trillingham, Excelsior's CEO, needs several supplementary sections.
   a. Assuming that the report will be submitted tomorrow, prepare a title page.
   b. Using the data you analyzed in Exercise 3, draw conclusions and make recommendations. Then write a transmittal memo to accompany this report. Include brief statements of your conclusions and recommendations.
   c. Decide whether you need an appendix; if so, note what it should contain.
5. **Short Memorandum Report—New Analysis** ▪ Excelsior's CEO has read your report (see Exercise 4 above). He would like the data on the 25 companies you identified as potential purchasers analyzed from a different perspective: he wants you to group the companies according to the country in which they are based. Put the data into a table and, based on your findings, draw conclusions about the geographic concentration of prospects. Write a brief memorandum report to the CEO; include your table and your conclusion.

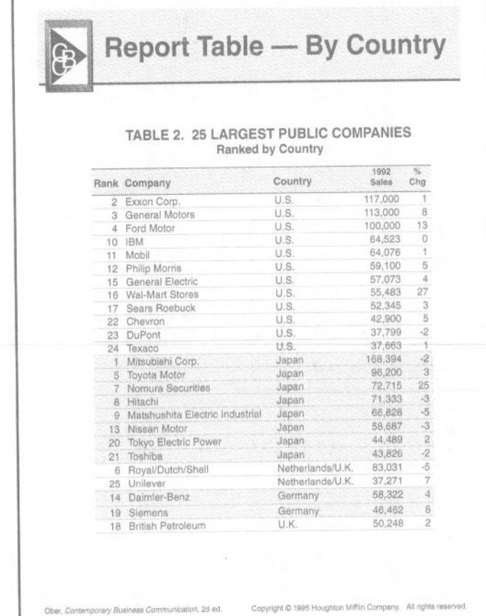

Report Table — By Country

TABLE 2. 25 LARGEST PUBLIC COMPANIES
Ranked by Country

Rank	Company	Country	1992 Sales	% Chg
2	Exxon Corp.	U.S.	117,000	1
3	General Motors	U.S.	113,000	8
4	Ford Motor	U.S.	100,000	13
10	IBM	U.S.	64,523	0
11	Mobil	U.S.	64,076	1
12	Philip Morris	U.S.	59,100	5
15	General Electric	U.S.	57,073	4
16	Wal-Mart Stores	U.S.	55,483	27
17	Sears Roebuck	U.S.	52,345	3
22	Chevron	U.S.	42,900	5
23	DuPont	U.S.	37,799	-2
24	Texaco	U.S.	37,663	1
1	Mitsubishi Corp.	Japan	168,394	-2
5	Toyota Motor	Japan	96,200	3
7	Nomura Securities	Japan	72,715	25
8	Hitachi	Japan	71,333	-3
9	Matshushita Electric Industrial	Japan	66,828	-5
13	Nissan Motor	Japan	58,687	-3
20	Tokyo Electric Power	Japan	44,489	2
21	Toshiba	Japan	43,826	-2
6	Royal/Dutch/Shell	Netherlands/U.K.	83,031	-5
25	Unilever	Netherlands/U.K.	37,271	7
14	Daimler-Benz	Germany	58,322	4
19	Siemens	Germany	46,462	8
18	British Petroleum	U.K.	50,248	2

Ober, *Contemporary Business Communication*, 2d ed.

See Master 13.3, Exercise 5, Report Section, in the *Instructor's Resource Manual.*

6. **Secondary Data—International Competition** ▪ Excelsior CEO Victor Trillingham (see Exercises 3, 4, and 5) is concerned about the international activities of Nestlé, which competes with Excelsior in the United States and would be a formidable rival in international markets. Conduct secondary research to uncover the answers to Trillingham's questions.
   a. In how many countries does Nestlé sell its products? List the countries.
   b. What percentage of Nestlé's overall sales are made outside the United States?
   c. What companies (if any) has Nestlé acquired during the past 12 months?
   d. What major new consumer products has Nestlé introduced in the United States during the past 12 months?

   Using talking headings, outline an informational report in manuscript format to present your findings. Prepare visual aids to convey the answers to Questions a and b. Include a reference list of secondary sources used in

FIGURE 13.7 The World's 100 Largest Public Companies

Ranked by market value as of June 30, 1993, as determined by Morgan Stanley Capital International Perspective (In millions of U.S. dollars; financial data at Dec. 31, 1992, exchange rates ; percentage change based on home currency).

RANK 1993	RANK 1992	COMPANY (COUNTRY)	MARKET VALUE	FISCAL 1992 SALES*	PERCENT CHANGE FROM 1991	FISCAL 1992 PROFIT	PERCENT CHANGE FROM 1991
1	3	**NT&T** (Japan)	$127,287	$61,565	2%	$1,590	-12%
2	7	**AT&T** (U.S.)	84,409	64,900	45	3,850	640
3	2	**Exxon Corp.** (U.S.)	82,127	117,000	1	4,800	-14
4	5	**General Electric** (U.S.)	81,907	57,073	4	4,305	8
5	1	**Royal Dutch/Shell** (Netherlands/U.K.)	81,606	83,031	-5	4,623	27
6	17	**Mitsubishi Bank** (Japan)	73,237	469,734	-4	530	-25
7	16	**Sumitomo Bank** (Japan)	67,195	583,937	-2	199	-82
8	25	**Industrial Bank of Japan** (Japan)	65,662	419,376	9	388	-30
9	24	**Dai-Ichi Kangyo Bank** (Japan)	64,688	561,957	-1	445	-44
10	22	**Fuji Bank** (Japan)	64,134	572,919	8	549	-37
11	29	**Sanwa Bank** (Japan)	61,225	559,922	-4	899	-11
12	6	**Wal-Mart Stores** (U.S.)	60,331	55,483	27	1,995	24
13	10	**Coca-Cola Co.** (U.S.)	56,191	13,074	13	1,905	18
14	11	**Toyota Motor** (Japan)	53,546	96,200	3	2,253	-45
15	32	**Sakura Bank** (Japan)	51,130	508,495	-10	546	-29
16	28	**Tokyo Electric Power** (Japan)	44,630	44,489[1]	2	698[1]	-2
17	4	**Philip Morris** (U.S.)	43,299	59,100	5	4,940	26
18	8	**Merck & Co.** (U.S.)	40,637	9,663	12	2,447	15
19	12	**British Telecom** (U.K.)	39,990	19,982	-1	1,930	-37
20	52	**Nomura Securities** (Japan)	36,218	72,715	25	38	-86
21	19	**Procter & Gamble** (U.S.)	35,329	29,362	9	1,872	6
22	26	**GTE** (U.S.)	33,921	19,984	2	1,787	5
23	40	**Roche Holding** (Switzerland)	31,896	8,658	13	1,282	30
24	15	**DuPont** (U.S.)	31,632	37,799	-2	1,438	-46
25	20	**General Motors** (U.S.)	31,462	113,000	8	-2,620	-47
26	14	**Bristol-Myers Squibb** (U.S.)	29,914	11,155	6	2,208	7
27	33	**Mobil** (U.S.)	29,812	64,076	1	1,308	-32
28	18	**Unilever** (Netherlands/U.K.)	29,654	37,271	7	1,942	12
29	27	**PepsiCo** (U.S.)	29,563	21,970	14	1,302	21
30	30	**Nestle** (Switzerland)	29,368	36,435	8	1,805	9
31	79	**Bank of Tokyo** (Japan)	28,951	275,527	-8	358	-6
32	37	**Chevron** (U.S.)	28,534	42,900	5	2,210	71
33	97	**Tokai Bank** (Japan)	28,419	317,999	-4	239	-51
34	9	**IBM** (U.S.)	28,215	64,523	0	-6,865	1,048[2]
35	35	**BellSouth** (U.S.)	27,406	15,200	6	1,660	10
36	56	**American Int'l Group** (U.S.)	27,300	9,139	0	1,625	5
37	36	**Amoco** (U.S.)	27,235	28,200	0	850	-44
38	21	**Johnson & Johnson** (U.S.)	27,199	13,753	10	1,625	11
39	—	**Asahi Bank** (Japan)	27,014	285,948	0	342	-5
40	66	**Kansai Electric Power** (Japan)	26,781	22,434[1]	1	738[1]	7
41	13	**Glaxo Holdings** (U.K.)	25,716	6,181	21	1,559	13
42	42	**Ford Motor** (U.S.)	25,576	100,000	13	-80	-96
43	53	**Bell Atlantic** (U.S.)	25,472	12,600	1	1,380	12
44	47	**British Petroleum** (U.K.)	25,214	50,248	2	-691	-211
45	43	**Matsushita Electric Industrial** (Japan)	24,986	66,828	-5	360	-71
46	23	**Allianz Holding** (Germany)	24,823	32,372	12	N.A.	0
47	51	**Hitachi** (Japan)	24,810	71,333	-3	729	-40
48	55	**Microsoft** (U.S.)	24,770	3,753	36	953	35
49	—	**HSBC Holdings** (U.K.)	24,166	257,276	-5	1,842	108
50	88	**Nippon Steel** (Japan)	23,870	27,924	-9	19	-97
51	45	**Minnesota Mining & Mfg.** (U.S.)	$23,656	$13,883	4%	$1,236	7%
52	93	**Long-Term Credit Bank** (Japan)	23,330	321,672	13	221	-63
53	60	**Southwestern Bell** (U.S.)	23,240	10,015	7	1,302	13
54	—	**Motorola** (U.S)	23,102	13,303	17	576	27
55	—	**Intel** (U.S.)	23,022	5,844	30	1,067	30
56	89	**Federal Nat'l Mortgage** (U.S.)	22,625	181,000	23	1,649	13[3]
57	31	**Abbott Laboratories** (U.S.)	21,920	7,852	14	1,239	14
58	69	**Ameritech** (U.S.)	21,715	11,150	3	1,346	15
59	—	**Walt Disney** (U.S.)	21,369	7,504	23	817	28
60	34	**Pfizer** (U.S.)	21,335	7,230	4	1,094	52
61	71	**Seven-Eleven** (Japan)	20,761	11,094[1]	10	118[1]	-69
62	92	**Mitsubishi Heavy Industries** (Japan)	20,734	26,740	1	768	-23
63	39	**Siemens** (Germany)	20,529	46,462	8	1,062	-3
64	64	**Hewlett-Packard** (U.S.)	20,375	16,410	13	881	17
65	72	**Toshiba** (Japan)	20,373	43,826	-2	195	-48
66	41	**American Home Products** (U.S.)	20,155	7,874	11	1,151	-16
67	75	**Pacific Telesis** (U.S.)	19,698	9,935	0	1,142	13
68	100	**Chubu Electric Power** (Japan)	19,630	18,553[1]	2	521[1]	-11
69	50	**British Gas** (U.K.)	19,442	15,473	-2[4]	1,028	-41[4]
70	90	**Home Depot** (U.S.)	19,407	7,148	39	363	46
71	65	**BTR** (U.K.)	19,171	13,341[5]	31	1,022	22
72	96	**Sears Roebuck** (U.S.)	19,035	52,345	3	-2,567	-380
73	87	**U S West** (U.S.)	19,013	10,281	-3	1,179	3
74	48	**Deutsche Bank** (Germany)	18,892	293,430	11	1,062	30
75	76	**Nynex** (U.S.)	18,657	13,155	-1	1,311	14
76	46	**B.A.T. Industries** (U.K.)	18,634	16,206	10	1,311	138
77	67	**Atlantic Richfield** (U.S.)	18,475	18,668	3	1,193	68
78	—	**Tokio Marine & Fire** (Japan)	18,292	10,176	7[1]	194	-45
79	59	**Elf Aquitaine** (France)	18,199	35,198	0	1,084	-37
80	62	**Assicurazioni Generali** (Italy)	17,771	N.A.	0	375	2
81	73	**McDonald's** (U.S.)	17,621	7,133	7	959	12
82	—	**UBS** (Switzerland)	17,504	178,366	7	896	10
83	38	**Daimler-Benz** (Germany)	16,988	58,322	4	839	-24
84	94	**Ito-Yokado** (Japan)	16,979	28,728	4	613	-12
85	44	**SmithKline Beecham Group** (U.K.)	16,842	7,875	11	1,073	11
86	58	**Hanson** (U.K.)	16,474	13,276	14	1,643	5
87	—	**Chrysler** (U.S.)	16,438	36,900	26	723	-191
88	77	**Texaco** (U.S.)	16,350	37,663	1	1,012	-22
89	—	**Nissan Motor** (Japan)	16,288	58,687	-3	530	40
90	—	**Eastman Kodak** (U.S.)	16,247	20,577	5	994	5,747
91	84	**Alcatel Alsthom** (France)	16,062	28,368	1	1,238	14
92	—	**WMX Technologies** (U.S.)	15,981	8,661	15	921	52
93	—	**Daiwa Securities** (Japan)	15,891	54,588	-11	-123[1]	-70
94	—	**Mitsubishi Corp.** (Japan)	15,847	168,394	-2	271	-46
95	—	**All Nippon Airways** (Japan)	15,705	8,415	2	11	-84
96	—	**Mitsubishi Trust & Banking** (Japan)	15,655	177,472	2	262	-21
97	—	**American Express** (U.S.)	15,479	175,800	20	436	-45
98	83	**Dow Chemical** (U.S.)	15,435	18,971	1	276	-71[2]
99	80	**Sandoz** (Switzerland)	15,416	9,640	8	999	34
100	85	**BankAmerica** (U.S.)	15,408	115,500[6]	4	1,492	33

NOTE: Rank calculated for Royal Dutch/Shell Group by combining market value of Netherland's Royal Dutch Petroleum and Britain's Shell Transport & Trading. Rank calculated for Unilever by combining market value of Netherland's Unilever NV and Britain's Unilever PLC. Sales and profits are for combined companies.

*Assets are used instead of sales for financial companies and are calculated without contingent liabilities and Treasury stock items

[1]Based on nonconsolidated results

[2]1991 earnings include extraordinary pretax charges

[3]1991 earnings include extraordinary pretax gains

[4]Changed fiscal year in 1991

[5]In January 1992 acquired Hawker Siddeley

[6]In April 1992 acquired Security Pacific

your research. Then draft a transmittal memorandum to Trillingham (assume that the report will be submitted next Monday).

7. **Report Section—Document Design** ▪ Reformat the report section shown on page 435 to incorporate the elements of document design discussed in this chapter. You may edit the report as needed, as long as you do not change the basic information.

8. **Short Formal Report—Primary and Secondary Statistical Data Furnished** ▪ North Star is a producer of consumer products with annual sales of $47.2 million. It has 4.5% of the consumer market for its six consumer products (soap, deodorant, ammonia, chili, canned ham, and frozen vegetables).

   On July 8 of this year, Paul Gettisfield, sales manager, asked you, a product manager, to study the feasibility of North Star's entering the generic-products market. Generic products are products that do not have brand names but instead carry a plain generic label, such as "Paper Towels." Generic products are typically not advertised; they involve less packaging, less processing, and cheaper ingredients than brand names; and they compete both with private brands (those distributed solely by individual store chains such as A&P and Kroger) and with national brands (those available for sale at all grocery stores and advertised nationally). At the present time, North Star produces only national brands.

   Paul specifically asked you *not* to explore whether North Star had the necessary plant capacity. He wanted you only to provide up-to-date information on the generic market in general and to explore likely consumer acceptance of generic brands for the products North Star produces. He is quite interested in learning the results of your research.

   In August you conducted a mail survey of 1,500 consumers in the three states (California, Texas, and Arizona) that constitute your largest market. Responses were received from 832 consumers to the following questions; responses are provided for all 832 consumers and for the 237 largest consumers (those who indicated that they did 51%–100% of their household shopping):

   ```
   Have you purchased a food generic product (such as canned
   fruit or vegetables) in the last month?
     All consumers: 36% yes, 64% no
     Largest consumers: 29% yes, 71% no

   Was this the first time you had purchased a food generic
   product?
     All consumers: 18% yes, 82% no
     Largest consumers: 20% yes, 80% no

   Have you purchased a nonfood generic product (such as
   paper towels or soap) in the last month?
     All consumers: 60% yes, 40% no
     Largest consumers: 59% yes, 41% no

   Was this the first time you had purchased a nonfood ge-
   neric product?
     All consumers: 5% yes, 95% no
     Largest consumers: 7% yes, 93% no
   ```

```
If you could save at least 30% by purchasing a generic
brand rather than a national brand, would you purchase a
generic brand of any of the following products?
  Bar of soap:  43% yes, 57% no, 0% don't use this product
  Deodorant:  31% yes, 67% no, 2% don't use this product
  Ammonia:  80% yes, 10% no, 10% don't use this product
  Chili:  34% yes, 52% no, 14% don't use this product
  Canned ham:  19% yes, 44% no, 37% don't use this product
  Frozen vegetables:  54% yes, 30% no, 16% don't use this
                      product
```

You also asked the local North Star sales representatives to audit 20 randomly selected chain supermarkets in each of these three states in August. Personal observation showed that 39 of the stores stocked generic brands, 37 of these 39 stocked 100 or more generic items, and 15 had separate generic-product sections. All but 3 of the 60 stores stocked all six products that North Star produces.

In gathering your data, you also made the following notes from three secondary sources:

1. *Hammond's Market Reports*, Gary, IN, 1995, pp. 1027-1030: This annual index lists various information for more than 2,000 consumer products. The percentages of market share for the six products North Star produces are as follows:

	1985	*1990*	*1995*
Generic brands	1.5%	2.6%	7.3%
Private labels	31.6%	30.7%	27.8%
National brands	66.9%	66.7%	64.9%

2. H. R. Nolan, "No-Name Brands: An Update," *Supermarket Management*, April 1994, pp. 31-37.
   a. Generic brands are typically priced 30% to 50% below national brands. (p. 31)
   b. Consumers require a 36% saving on a bar of soap and 40% savings on deodorant to motivate them to switch to a generic. (p. 32)
   c. Consumer awareness of generics has tripled since 1978. (p. 33)
   d. "The easiest way to become a no-name store is to ignore no-name brands." (direct quotation from p. 33)
   e. Many leading brand manufacturers feel compelled to produce the lower-profit generic brands because either the market has grown too big to ignore or the inroads generic brands have made on their own brands have left them with idle capacity. (p. 35)

3. Edward J. Rauch and Pamela G. McCleary, "National Brands to Play a Bit Part in the Future," *Grocery Business*, Fall 1993, pp. 118-120.
   a. Eight out of ten food-chain officers believe their costs will rise more than their prices this year. (p. 118)

b. Generics are now available in 84% of the stores nationwide and account for about 4% of the store space. (p. 118)
c. "Supermarket executives foresee a drop in shelf space allocated to brand products and an increase in the space allocated to generics and private labels. Many experts predict that supermarkets will ultimately carry no more than the top two brands in a category plus a private label and a generic label." (direct quotation from p. 119)
d. Today, 37% of the grocery stores have switched from paper bags to the less expensive plastic bags for packaging customer purchases, even though the plastic bags are nonbiodegradable. (p. 119)
e. Starting from nearly zero in 1977, generics have acquired 7% of the $275 billion grocery market. Many observers predict they will go up to 25% by the turn of the century. (p. 120)

Analyze the data, prepare whatever visual aids would be helpful, and then write a formal report for Gettisfield. Include any supplementary report pages you think would be helpful.

9. **Memorandum Report—Primary Statistical Data Furnished** ▪ You are a systems analyst, reporting to Hilda Brandt, vice president of information services at General Resources, Inc. The executive vice president of GRI has asked Brandt to develop a style and procedures manual for all internally produced office documents.

In preparation for this task, Brandt has asked you to analyze the documents prepared at GRI offices to determine the kinds of documents typed, the input source for these documents, the amount of time required to type each document, and the number of copies made of each. She then asked you to prepare an informal memorandum report, summarizing your findings.

For a period of one week, you asked a random sample of 100 office workers to make an extra copy of the first item they typed either at their typewriters or at their computers after 9 a.m., 11 a.m., and 2 p.m. each day and to complete a short form answering several questions about the document. A total of 531 documents were submitted for analysis—173 letters, 77 memos, 21 reports, 222 forms, and 18 miscellaneous other items.

Analyze the data contained in Figure 13.8, prepare whatever visual aids would be helpful (keep them simple for this memo report), and then write the requested analytical report.

10. **Short Memorandum Report—Nonstatistical Data Furnished** ▪ You are the research assistant for Congresswoman Anna Murray. A constituent has written her asking that she introduce legislation to ban telephone call identification. Congresswoman Murray sent you the letter with this handwritten message attached: "I really don't know much about this telephone service. Please research it and prepare a short informal report (no tables, charts, or footnotes, please) so that I can make an informed decision about this matter. Should I or should I not introduce legislation to ban this type of telephone service?"

FIGURE 13.8 Analysis of GRI Documents

Origin of Typing Tasks, Classified by Kind of Item								
		Kind of Item						
Origin		**Forms**	**Letters**	**Memos**	**Reports**	**Tables**	**Other**	**Totals**
Handwritten—	No.	66	44	17	8	12	9	156
not on same form	%	29.7%	25.4%	22.1%	38.1%	60.0%	50.0%	29.4%
Handwritten on same form	No.	56	2	4		3		65
	%	25.2%	1.2%	5.2%		15.0%		12.2%
Typed and handwritten	No.	16	15	7	3	2	3	46
	%	7.2%	8.7%	9.1%	14.3%	10.0%	16.7%	8.7%
All typed	No.	21	35	15	6		4	81
	%	9.5%	20.2%	19.5%	28.6%		22.2%	15.3%
Shorthand dictation	No.	4	36	16	1			57
	%	1.8%	20.8%	20.8%	4.8%			10.7%
Machine dictation	No.	3	8	12	3			26
	%	1.4%	4.6%	15.6%	14.3%			4.9%
Self-composed	No.	29	33	6			2	70
	%	13.1%	19.1%	7.8%			11.1%	13.2%
Other	No.	27				3		30
	%	12.2%				15.0%		5.6%
Totals	No.	222	173	77	21	20	18	531
	%	41.8%	32.6%	14.5%	4.0%	3.8%	3.4%	100.0%

Amount of Time Required by Office Workers to Type Items, Classified by Kind of Item								
		Kind of Item						
Minutes required		**Forms**	**Letters**	**Memos**	**Reports**	**Tables**	**Other**	**Totals**
Less than 5	No.	144	72	40	2		4	262
	%	64.9%	41.6%	51.9%	9.5%		22.2%	49.3%
5–9	No.	37	77	17	4	9	5	149
	%	16.7%	44.5%	22.1%	19.0%	45.0%	27.8%	28.1%
10 or more	No.	41	24	20	15	11	9	120
	%	18.5%	13.9%	26.0%	71.4%	55.0%	50.0%	22.6%
Totals	No.	222	173	77	21	20	18	531
	%	41.8%	32.6%	14.5%	4.0%	3.8%	3.4%	100.0%

Number of Copies of Typed Items Required (Including Original), Classified by Kind of Item								
		Kind of Item						
Number of copies (including original)		**Forms**	**Letters**	**Memos**	**Reports**	**Tables**	**Other**	**Totals**
1 (original only)	No.	27	9	5	1	2	4	48
	%	12.2%	5.2%	6.5%	4.8%	10.0%	22.2%	9.0%
2	No.	35	88	15	5	6		149
	%	15.8%	50.9%	19.5%	23.8%	30.0%		28.1%
3–4	No.	82	56	22	4	1	6	171
	%	36.9%	32.4%	28.6%	19.0%	5.0%	33.3%	32.2%
5 or more	No.	78	20	35	11	11	8	163
	%	35.1%	11.6%	45.5%	52.4%	55.0%	44.4%	30.7%
Totals	No.	222	173	77	21	20	18	531
	%	41.8%	32.6%	14.5%	4.0%	3.8%	3.4%	100.0%

You've talked to numerous people at the telephone company and have read brochures, magazine articles, and editorials about this topic. You've jotted down the following notes—in no particular order:

a. Automatic number identification (ANI): A telephone service that displays the phone number of the person calling you.
b. You can use ANI to decide which calls you want to answer and simply ignore the others.
c. It can threaten the privacy and personal safety of users.
d. Every caller's number would be displayed—even those with unpublished numbers who have paid extra for their privacy.
e. Delivery businesses (taxis and pizzerias, for example) can use ANI to ensure that telephone orders are legitimate.
f. The device that displays the callers' numbers costs up to $80.
g. Emergency services can use the number to dispatch help quickly for people who may be too panicky to give an address.
h. Customer service agents at your local utility or your stockbroker can immediately call up your file when you call to serve you more efficiently. A computer can even be programmed to do this automatically as soon as your call goes through.
i. ANI allows businesses to record the number of every caller—and perhaps even to sell your number to telemarketers.
j. New Jersey Bell Telephone Co. began the service after learning that a whopping 1.2 million of their customers had received threatening or obscene calls.
k. If you receive a threatening, obscene, or harassing call, you can record the number to notify the police or phone company without their having to tap your phone. (You can even call the person back yourself, although that might not be wise.)
l. People who make calls from their home may have legitimate reasons for not wanting their private numbers revealed—law enforcement officers, doctors, psychiatrists, or social workers, for example.
m. New Jersey Bell reported that phone-trace requests in Hudson County dropped 49% after ANI was established—even though only 2.3% of its customers used it.
n. It's now available in a growing number of states.
o. You can even program ANI to prevent your phone from receiving calls from a specified number, thus preventing harassers from repeatedly calling your number from the same phone.
p. Runaway children might be scared to call home for fear of being traced.
q. Only a few states require a feature that lets callers prevent their numbers from being displayed (which defeats the whole purpose of the service).

r. New Jersey Bell says complaints about obscene or harassing phone calls have dropped nearly 50% since it began offering ANI.
s. You can refuse to answer telephone sales pitches that come in the middle of dinner.
t. It threatens the privacy of individuals who call suicide-prevention, drug-treatment, AIDS, and abortion-counseling hotlines.
u. It took 23 years to catch and convict Bobby Gene Stice, who used the telephone for two decades to terrorize thousands of California women. ANI could have stopped him in a day.
v. The service charge for the ANI feature is as much as $8.50 monthly.

Organize and analyze the data, and then write the requested recommendation report. Use whatever report headings would be helpful.

Exercise 11 is linked with Exercises 2–8 in Chapter 12.

11. Letter Report—Primary Statistical Data Supplied ■ Review the Broadway Productions Survey exercises (Exercises 2–8) at the end of Chapter 12, including the completed questionnaire (Figure 12.18). Assume that you are a management consultant for Banking Services, Inc., and were hired by Carol J. Green, vice president of Tri-City Bank (65 Washington Avenue, Stamford, CT 06902), to conduct this survey.

Write a letter report presenting the information you gathered and analyzed. Include any appropriate visual aids and helpful headings in your report. You may assume any reasonable data needed.

12. Collaborative Writing—Long Formal Report Requiring Library Research ■ Assume that your group of four has been asked by Jim Miller, executive vice president of Jefferson Industries, to write an exploratory report on the feasibility of Jefferson's opening a frozen yogurt store in Akron, Ohio. If the preliminary data your group gathers warrants further exploration of this project, a professional venture-consultant group will be hired to conduct an in-depth, "dollars-and-cents" study. Your job, then, is to recommend whether such an expensive follow-up study is warranted. Assume that Jefferson has the financial resources to support such a venture if it looks promising.

You can immediately think of several areas you'll want to explore: the general market outlook for frozen yogurt stores, the demographic makeup of Akron (home of the University of Akron), the local economic climate, franchise opportunities in the industry, and the like. Undoubtedly, other topics (or criteria) will surface as you brainstorm the problem.

Working as a group, carry through the entire research process for this project—planning the study, collecting the data, organizing and analyzing the data, and writing the report. (*Note:* If you gathered any data by completing the exercises at the end of Chapter 11, integrate that data into your study as needed.)

Write the body of the report using formal language, organize the study by criteria, and place the conclusions and recommendations at the end. Include a title page, transmittal memo (addressed to James H. Miller), executive summary, table of contents, and reference list (use the author-date method of citation).

Regardless of how your group decides to divide up the work, everyone should review and comment on the draft of the final report. If different members wrote different parts, edit as needed to ensure that the report reads smoothly and coherently.

Note: For Exercises 13–17, follow the desires of your instructor (the audience) in terms of length, format, degree of formality, number of report parts, and the like.

13. **Secondary Data—Electronic Communications** ▪ You are a technical specialist for a large pharmaceutical firm located in Bayamon, Puerto Rico. As one way of connecting the employees in your worldwide organization, your superior, Chris Rice, director of information systems, is exploring the feasibility of having your organization join the Internet, a high-speed data communications network that links hundreds of thousands of university, corporate, and government computers. She has asked you to prepare a background report, describing what Internet is, how it is used, to what extent business uses it, advantages and disadvantages of using Internet, costs associated with its use, and the like. Since this is a report of background information, you will not make any recommendations regarding whether your organization should join.
14. **Secondary Data—The Female Manager** ▪ Using the appropriate business indexes (print or computer), identify three women who are presidents or CEOs of companies listed on the New York Stock Exchange. Provide information on their backgrounds. Did they make it to the top by rising through the ranks, by starting the firm, by taking over from another family member, or in some other manner?

    Analyze the effectiveness of these three individuals. How profitable are the firms they head in relation to others in the industry? Are their firms more or less profitable now than when they assumed the top job? Finally, try to uncover data regarding their management styles—how they see their role, how they relate to their employees, problems they've experienced, and the like.

    From your study of these three individuals, are there any valid conclusions you can draw? Write a report objectively presenting and analyzing the information you've gathered.
15. **Secondary Data—Keyboarding Skills** ▪ You are the director of training for an aerospace firm located in Seattle, Washington. Your superior, Charles R. Underwood, personnel manager, is concerned that so many of the firm's 2,000 white-collar employees use their computers for hours a day but still do not know how to touch-keyboard. He believes the hunt-and-peck method is inefficient and increases the possibility of making errors when inputting data, thus lowering its reliability.

    He has asked you to recommend a software program that teaches the user how to type. He is specifically interested in a program that is IBM-compatible, is geared to adults, is educationally sound, and can be learned on an individual basis without an instructor present.

    Identify and evaluate three to five keyboarding software programs that meet these criteria, and write a report recommending the best one to Underwood. Justify your choice.
16. **Primary Data—Career Choices** ▪ Explore a career in which you are interested. Determine the job outlook, present level of employment, salary trends, typical duties, working conditions, educational or experience requirements, and the like. If possible, interview someone holding this position to gain firsthand impressions. Then write up your findings in a report to your instructor. Include at least five secondary sources and at least one table or visual aid in your report.
17. **Primary Data—Intercultural Dimensions** ▪ To what extent does network and cable television accurately portray members of cultural, ethnic, and racial minorities? To what extent are they portrayed at all during

prime time (8 p.m. to 11 p.m.)? In what types of roles are they shown, and what is their relationship with nonminority characters? As assistant to the director of public relations of the National Minority Alliance, you are interested in such questions.

Locate and review at least three journal articles on this topic. Then develop a definition of the term *minority*. Randomly select and view at least ten prime-time television shows, and develop a form for recording the needed data on minority representation in these shows. As part of your research, compare the proportion of minority members in this country with their representation on prime-time television. Integrate your primary and secondary data into a report. Use objective language, being careful to present ample data to support any conclusions or recommendations you may make.

18. **Primary Data—Student Living Arrangements** ■ Darlene Anderson, a real estate developer and president of Anderson and Associates, is exploring the feasibility of building a large student-apartment complex on a lot her firm owns two blocks from campus. Even though the city planning commission believes there is already enough student housing, Anderson thinks she can succeed if she addresses specific problems of present housing. She has asked you, her executive assistant, to survey students to determine their views of off-campus living. Specifically, she wants you to develop a ranked listing of the most important attributes of student housing. How important to students are such criteria as price, location (nearness to campus, shopping, public transportation, and the like), space and layout, furnishings (furnished versus unfurnished), social activities, parking, pets policy, and the like?

    In addition, the architect has drawn a plan that features the following options: private hotel-like rooms (sleeping and sitting area and private bath but no kitchen); private, one-room efficiency apartments; one-bedroom, two-person apartments; and four-bedroom, four-person apartments. Which of these arrangements would students most likely rent, given their present economic situation? Would another alternative be more appealing to them?

    Develop a questionnaire and administer it to a sample of students. Then analyze the data and write a report to Anderson.

URBAN SYSTEMS

A possible solution to the Continuing Case is described in the *Instructor's Resource Manual*, p. 259.

CONTINUING CASE 13

Reporting—A Pain in the Wrist

Review the Continuing Case accounts at the ends of Chapters 11 and 12, in which Jean Tate asked Pat Robbins to write a report on carpal tunnel syndrome, a neuromuscular wrist ailment caused by repeated hand motions as in typing.

Now, administer the questionnaire you developed in Chapter 11 to a sample of at least 50 clerical workers at your institution, where you work, or at some other office. For the purposes of this assignment, assume that the responses you receive were actually those from Urban Systems clerical workers. Then analyze the questionnaire data carefully. Construct whatever tables and charts would be helpful to the reader.

Critical Thinking

1. Considering the findings from your questionnaire, the interview with Terry Vaughn, and the secondary sources you checked, what does all this information mean in terms of your problem statement?
2. For each subproblem you specified (see Chapter 11), what conclusion can you draw? In view of each of these individual conclusions, what overall conclusion is merited? In view of your individual and overall conclusions, what recommendations are appropriate?

Writing Project

3. Prepare a recommendation report in manuscript format for Tate. Use formal language for the body of the report, organize the study by criteria, and place the conclusions and recommendations at the end. Include a title page, transmittal memo, executive summary, table of contents, abstract, appendix (copy of the questionnaire), and reference list (use the author-date method of citation).

WORDWISE *Spelling*

- According to columnist Dave Barry, it's no wonder kids today can't spell: they're surrounded by signs like "Suzi's All-Nite E-Z Drive-Thru Donut Shoppe."
- Americans are the worst spellers in the English-speaking world. The best spellers are in Australia, followed by Canada, the United Kingdom, and then the United States.
- From a letter written in the 1700s by the fourth earl of Chesterfield to his son: "One false spelling may fix a stigma upon a man for life."

PART V

Oral Communication

CHAPTER 14

Business Presentations

CHAPTER 15

Other Types of Nonwritten Communication

CHAPTER

14

Business Presentations

Communication Objectives

After you have finished this chapter, you should be able to

1. Describe the important role that business presentations play in the organization.
2. Plan a presentation by determining its purpose, analyzing the audience, and determining the timing and method of delivery.
3. Write a presentation by collecting the data and organizing it in a logical format.
4. Develop effective visual aids for a presentation.
5. Practice a presentation to develop an effective speaking style.
6. Deliver a presentation in a clear, confident, and efficient manner.
7. Plan and deliver other types of presentations, such as impromptu remarks, introductions, special recognitions, collaborative presentations, and video presentations.

Jim Garrity knows that computer jargon can be confusing and intimidating to people outside the field. As director of marketing communications for Compaq Computer Corporation, he is responsible for all marketing-oriented external communications, including advertising, product brochures, promotions, and direct marketing. At least once a month, Garrity makes a presentation to an audience of reporters, industry analysts, or other people whose opinions influence computer purchasers at all levels, from corporate executives to individual consumers.

When planning a presentation, the Compaq executive carefully considers the audience's level of sophistication, areas of interest, and familiarity with technical terms. "I try to use terminology that most of the audience will understand," Garrity said. "Half the audience may know the meaning of a certain term, but I take care to define it for everybody in the room."

Because people start to form their opinions of a speaker within the first minute or two, Garrity pays particular attention to the way he opens his presentations. On occasion, he will create an unexpected, dramatic, or humorous title for his presentation, then begin by explaining the title as a way to set up the premise of his talk. At other times, he will use humor to build a relationship with the audience. "Humor gets you and the audience off to a good start," he noted. "What works best is situational humor, humor that is relevant to this audience at this point in time. This type of humor shows the audience that you're aware of what's on their minds."

Properly used, humor can make the audience more comfortable with the speaker, but Garrity observes that it can also help the speaker become

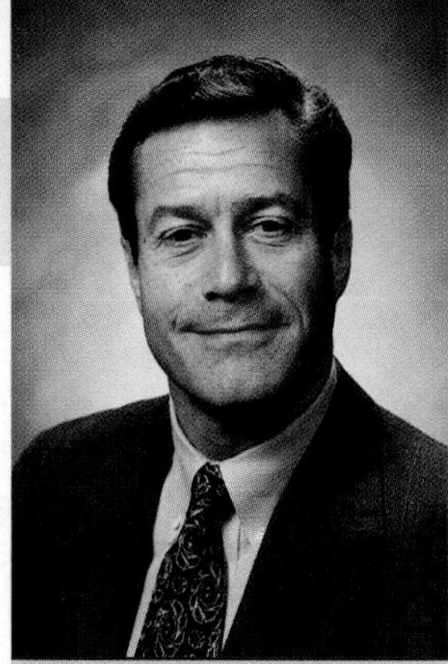

Jim Garrity
Director of marketing communications, Compaq Computer Corporation, Houston, Texas

more comfortable with the audience. "Audience feedback is important. Hearing the audience react builds the speaker's confidence and shows that the audience is listening and responding to what you have to say."

If Garrity expects to be quoted by the media, he may read from a prepared script. However, this delivery method leaves little room for spontaneity. "A speaker needs to be able to react to a comment from the audience or to an unforeseen development, like a slide being upside down," he said. To maintain flexibility, Garrity usually speaks from prepared notes. "I work out a detailed outline in advance, then keep it in front of me on a single sheet of paper to make sure I stay in sequence and make the points I want to make."

Visual aids are an integral part of Garrity's presentations, and he often uses electronic projection of computer images. "I can take a portable computer on the airplane and be revising visuals until the time the wheels hit the ground," he explained. "With the right equipment, I can connect the portable computer to a projector and run the visual aids directly from the podium. The computer monitor shows what my audience is seeing; I don't have to turn around to look at the screen behind me." If that sounds convenient, consider that in the future, visual aids will be even more affordable, easier to use, and more portable. "By the year 2000," according to Garrity, "anything that can be seen on a screen today—video, animation, graphics, and text—will be stored on a platter the size of a compact disk."

A chapter overview appears in the *Instructor's Resource Manual*, pp. 262–267.

ROLE OF BUSINESS PRESENTATIONS

Anyone who plans a career in sales, training, or education expects to make many oral presentations to customers, employees, or students each week. What you may not realize, though, is that just about *everyone* in business will probably give at least one major presentation and many smaller ones each year, to customers, superiors, subordinates, or colleagues—not to mention presentations at PTA meetings, homeowners' association meetings, civic clubs, and the like. Here are some typical business presentations and examples:

Almost everyone in business is required to give a presentation occasionally.

- *Sales pitches:* Why you should purchase our products
- *Status reports:* How we're progressing on our network conversion
- *Briefing sessions:* What I learned at the OSHA workshop last week
- *Proposals:* Why you should adopt my idea
- *Training:* How to operate the new electronic mail software program
- *Explanation of policies and procedures:* How our new insurance plan will affect you and your family

It is estimated that 20 million face-to-face meetings take place *every day* in the United States,[1] and many of these meetings include oral presentations. Thus, it is not surprising that the ability to speak effectively is considered a strategic managerial skill. Unfortunately, many managers haven't acquired this skill. In one survey of vice presidents in the nation's largest corporations, 44% described most presentations they hear as "boring," and 40% admitted to having dozed off while listening to a presentation.[2] It is clear, then, that many executives who are otherwise highly competent in their fields have much to learn about how to make interesting and effective oral presentations of their knowledge.

The costs of ineffective presentations are immense. With many top executives earning $100,000 or more a year, a presentation that discusses ideas incompletely and inefficiently wastes time and money. Sales are lost, vital information is not communicated, training programs fail, policies are not implemented, and profits fall.

No wonder, then, that large companies spend millions of dollars each year trying to teach their executives how to polish their speaking skills. For instance, Arthur Anderson & Co., the large accounting and consulting firm, annually runs hundreds of partners and managers through a two-day training course in how to make effective presentations. The course has long been one of the most popular offerings at the company's training center, and executives routinely report that they learned more in this course than in any other they had taken.[3]

For those who seriously want to improve communication skills, crash courses in communicating are available. Bert Decker, of San Francisco–based Decker Communications, offers a one-day course for $2,500. "I've trained 32,000 people, and there isn't anyone who comes here who really wants to be here," says Decker. (Dick Janssen, "Putting More Oomph in Your Oratory," *Business Week*, June 4, 1990, p. 165.)

Written Versus Oral Presentations

Written reports and oral presentations both play important roles in helping an organization achieve its objectives. An oral presentation may be made either in conjunction with or in place of a written report. Effective communicators must recognize the advantages and disadvantages of presenting business information orally.[4]

Oral presentations provide immediate feedback, allow speaker control, and require little work of the audience.

Advantages of Oral Presentations Probably the most important advantage of oral presentations is the *immediate feedback* that is possible from the audience. Questions can be answered and decisions can be made on the spot. In addition, the speaker can pick up cues from the audience regarding how well they understand and agree with his or her points and then can adjust content and delivery accordingly.

A second advantage concerns *speaker control.* A written report may never even be read, let alone studied carefully. But speakers have a captive audience. They can control the pace of the presentation, question the audience to ensure attention and understanding, and use nonverbal cues such as pauses, gestures, and changes in voice speed and volume to add emphasis. In addition, visual aids used in an oral presentation are often more effective than those used in a written report.

A third advantage of the oral presentation has to do with the listener: presentations are simply *less work for the audience.* Listening is less strenuous and often more enjoyable than reading. The written report presents mostly verbal clues, whereas the oral presentation is filled with a variety of verbal and nonverbal clues to make comprehension easier and more interesting.

Oral presentations do not provide a permanent record and are often very expensive.

Disadvantages of Oral Presentations Considering the advantages of immediate feedback, speaker control, and reduced audience effort, why isn't *all* business information communicated orally? The major reason is that oral presentations are *impermanent.* They "disappear," and within hours of delivery much of the information presented has been forgotten. Also, listeners have only one opportunity to understand what they're hearing. In contrast, the written report provides a permanent record that can be reread and referred to in the future.

Oral presentations may also be very *expensive.* It is much more cost-effective to have 1,000 managers scattered around the country read a written report than to have them hear the same information in a mass meeting. In addition to the expense, the sheer logistics of assembling such a large group can be overpowering. Furthermore, the visual aids used in oral presentations are often more expensive than those used in written reports (which is perhaps one reason that they're also typically more effective). For example, a color slide of a graph or chart costs many times more to produce than a black-and-white paper copy that has been printed directly from the computer.

It's not surprising, then, that many presentations include both an oral and a written component. As a business communicator, you'll need to weigh a number of factors when you decide whether to communicate orally or in writing: the complexity of the material, the size of the audience, your need for immediate feedback, and the cost of the presentation, among others.

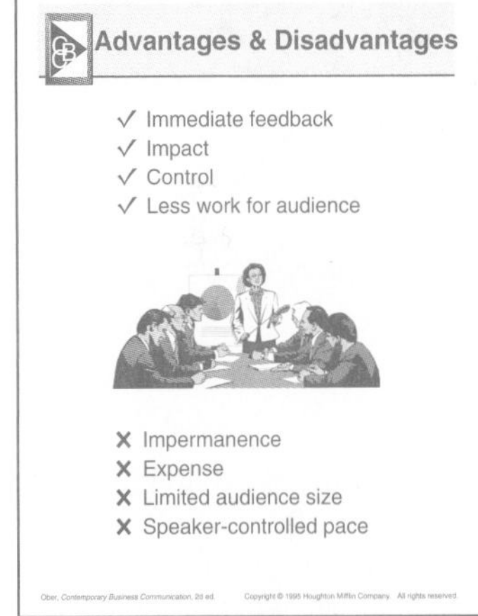

See Transparency 14.1, Advantages and Disadvantages of Oral Presentations.

The Process of Making a Business Presentation

The presentation process requires planning, organizing, developing visual aids, practicing, and delivering the presentation.

As you will remember, we followed a specific process when learning to communicate business information in written form; the process consisted of planning, drafting, revising, formatting, and finally proofreading the written document. We follow a similar logical process for making an oral presentation.

1. *Planning:* Determining the purpose of the presentation, analyzing the audience, and determining the timing and method of delivery.

2. *Organizing:* Collecting the data and outlining it in a logical order.

3. *Developing visual aids:* Selecting the appropriate type, number, and content of visual aids.

4. *Practicing:* Rehearsing by simulating the actual presentation conditions as closely as possible.

5. *Delivering:* Dressing appropriately, maintaining friendly eye contact, speaking in an effective manner, and answering questions confidently.

PLANNING THE PRESENTATION

When assigned the task of making a business presentation, your first impulse might be to sit down at your desk or computer and begin writing. Resist the temptation. As in written communications, several important steps precede the actual writing. These steps involve determining the purpose of the presentation, analyzing the audience, planning the timing of the presentation, and selecting a delivery method.

In addition to helping you decide what to include in your presentation, these planning tasks will give you important information about the degree of formality appropriate for the situation. The more formal the presentation, the more time you'll devote to the project. In general, complex topics or proposals with "high stakes" demand more formal presentations, with well-planned visuals, a carefully thought-out organizational plan, and extensive research. Likewise, the larger the audience (and especially if there is a need to repeat the presentation) and the greater the audience's opposition to your ideas, the more formal the presentation should be. Finally, if the audience is made up of nationals from other countries, you will need to take their needs and expectations into consideration and will probably prepare a more formal presentation (see Spotlight Across Cultures).

Purpose

Most presentations seek either to report, explain, persuade, or motivate.

Keeping your purpose uppermost in mind helps you decide what information to include and what to omit, in what order to present this information, and which points to emphasize and subordinate. Most business presentations have one of these four purposes:

- *Reporting:* Updating the audience on some project or event.
- *Explaining:* Detailing how to carry out a procedure or how to operate a new piece of equipment.
- *Persuading:* Convincing the listener to purchase something or to accept an idea you're presenting.
- *Motivating:* Inspiring the listeners to take some action.

Assume, for example, that you have been asked to make a short oral presentation on the topic of absenteeism at the Limerick Generating Station. If you're speaking to the management committee, your purpose would be to *report* the results of your research. Using a logical organization, you would discuss the effects of the problem on productivity, its causes, and possible solutions.

If you're speaking to the union personnel, however, your purpose might be to *motivate* the employees to reduce their absenteeism. You might then briefly discuss the extent of the problem, devote your major efforts to showing how the employees ultimately benefit from lower absenteeism, and finally introduce a monthly recognition program.

After your presentation is over, your purpose provides a criterion—the *only* important criterion—by which to judge the success of your presenta-

SPOTLIGHT ACROSS CULTURES

Presenting Abroad

Increasingly, managers are being required to make presentations abroad to nationals from other countries. Many of the principles discussed in this chapter hold true; however, those discussed in Chapter 2 regarding international communications also apply. Because each culture is different, we cannot make broad generalizations. The following discussion, then, simply points out some factors you will want to be aware of as you try to make your presentation appropriate for the specific country.

PLANNING THE PRESENTATION

Planning the presentation should really begin with deciding *who* should make the presentation. In the Japanese culture, age is highly respected and the credibility of a younger presenter, regardless of his or her expertise or communication skills, may be questioned by an older audience. Similarly, female presenters may experience difficulty in some Middle Eastern countries.

The culture also affects the content and organization of your presentation, and you should adopt a strategy that will help you accomplish your goal. In their book, *Managing Cultural Differences,* Harris and Moran recommend the following dual strategy—one that reflects both your culture and the host country's:

1. Describe the problem as understood by both cultures.
2. Analyze the problem from two cultural perspectives.
3. Identify the cause(s) of the problem from both viewpoints.
4. Solve the problem through cooperative strategies.
5. Determine if the solution is working multiculturally.

Well-planned visual aids and printed handouts are especially desirable in helping an audience for whom English is a second language to follow your presentation. The use of examples and frequent preview and summary is also helpful. Know the customs and attitudes of your audience. For example, beginning a presentation with a joke, discussing incidents from one's private life, or holding a question-and-answer period might or might not be considered appropriate.

GIVING THE PRESENTATION

In many cultures, a formal presentation will be expected, with the presenter speaking from a full script and using elaborate visual aids. Some audiences may misinterpret an extemporaneous speech given from notes as implying the speaker didn't respect the audience enough to prepare his or her remarks fully.

Writing out your remarks in full beforehand will also help you plan your choice of words carefully. Restrict your vocabulary to the most common English words and your word meanings to the most common ones. Avoid using figures of speech such as jargon, slang, and clichés.

Speak slowly and clearly, using short, simple sentences, and keep gestures to a minimum. Do not be surprised if some members of the audience do not look at you directly as you speak. Eye contact is not as important in some cultures as it is to many Americans. If possible, try to include some phrase from the local language in your remarks. When using overhead and slide projectors, the American custom is normally to stand next to the projector, whereas the European custom is to present while seated, with the projector alongside on a low table.

An overall attitude of sensitivity, empathy, respect, and flexibility will help you achieve success in giving presentations—both here and abroad.

Sources: Philip R. Harris and Robert T. Moran, *Managing Cultural Differences,* 2d ed., Gulf Publishing, Houston, 1987; Dona Z. Meilach, "Visually Speaking," *Presentation Products Magazine,* undated supplement, pp. A–L; Robert T. Moran, "Tips on Making Speeches to International Audiences," *International Management,* April 1989, p. 59.

tion. In other words, did the management committee understand the results of your research? Were the union members motivated to reduce their absenteeism? No matter how well or how poorly you spoke and no matter how impressive or ineffective your visual aids, the important question is whether or not you accomplished your purpose.

Audience Analysis

Analyze the audience in terms of demographics, level of knowledge, and psychological needs.

In addition to identifying such demographic factors as the size, age, and organizational status of your audience, you will also need to determine their level of knowledge about your topic and their psychological needs (values, attitudes, and beliefs). These factors provide clues to everything from the overall content, tone, and types of examples you should use to the types of questions to expect and even the way you should dress.

The principles by which you analyze your audience are the same as those we discussed in the chapters on writing letters, memos, and reports. Consider the effect of your message on your audience and your credibility with them. The key is to put yourself in your audience's place so that you can anticipate their questions and reactions. The "you" attitude applies to oral as well as to written communication.

Large audiences require a more formal presentation.

The larger your audience, the more formal your presentation will be. When you speak to a large group, you should speak louder and slower and use more emphatic gestures and larger visuals. Usually, you should allow questions only at the end of your talk. If you're speaking to a small group, you can be more flexible about questions, and your tone and gestures will be more like those used in normal conversation. Furthermore, when presenting to small groups, your options in terms of visual aids increase.

If your audience is unfamiliar with your topic, you will need to use clear, easy-to-understand language, with extensive visual aids and many examples. If the audience is more knowledgeable, you can proceed at a faster pace. Suppose, however, that you have an audience composed of both novices and experts. One option, of course, would be to separate the two groups and to give two presentations—each geared to the level of that particular audience.

If the gulf in understanding is not quite that wide, you should determine who the key decision maker is in the group—frequently, but not always, the highest-ranking member present—and then provide a level of detail necessary to secure that person's understanding. Take time especially to understand this decision maker's needs, objectives, and interests as they relate to your objective.

The audience's psychological needs will also affect your presentation. If, for example, you think your listeners will be hostile—either to you personally or to your message—then you'll have to oversell yourself or your idea. Instead of giving one or two examples, you'll need to give several. In addition to establishing your own credibility, you may need to quote other experts to bolster your case.

In the presentation on absenteeism discussed earlier, the first audience was the management committee. They have very high organizational status and probably expect a somewhat formal presentation. Although they may not be very familiar with the specific problem, they are very familiar with the organization overall and are probably quite interested in the bottom-line implications of the problem.

Regarding the second presentation, however, the union members are probably a more heterogeneous group than the management committee. Thus, you must make sure the language and examples used are appropriate for a broad range of knowledge, interests, and attitudes. In addition,

FIGURE 14.1 The Audience and Purpose Determine the Content

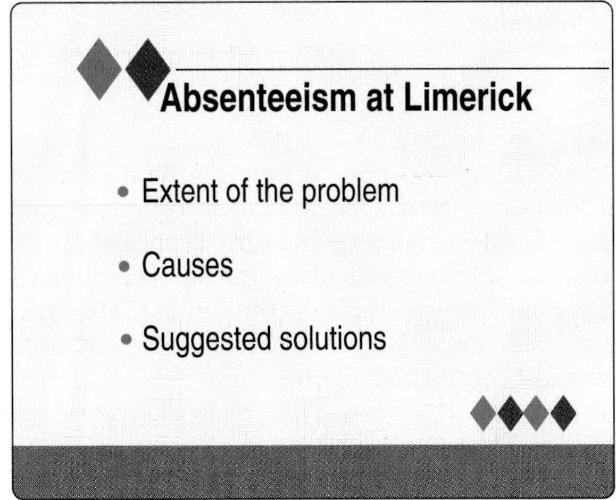

OR

you'll probably want to use a more informal, conversational style for the presentation.

Sample overhead transparencies that might be used for each of these two presentations are shown in Figure 14.1.

Once you've identified your audience, it is often helpful to meet with key people before your presentation, especially with the key decision makers. These meetings can help you predispose the audience in your favor or, at the very least, help you discover sources of opposition. Knowing ahead of time about their concerns will let you build relevant information into your presentation to address those concerns.

Timing of the Presentation

Time the presentation to allow adequate preparation and to avoid rushed periods.

Often the timing of a presentation is beyond your control. If you've been asked to update the management committee about the absenteeism problem and the committee typically meets at 2 p.m. the first Tuesday of each month, that is the precise time you must be available. Sometimes, however, you will have some flexibility. For example, if you want to present a proposal for a pet project to several managers whose cooperation is crucial for your success, you would be in charge of scheduling the meeting.

Consider two factors when scheduling presentations. First, allow yourself enough time to prepare—including gathering data, writing and revising, producing visual aids, and practicing the presentation. Second, consider the needs of your audience. Avoid times when they will be away or be so occupied with other matters that they will not be able to concentrate on your presentation. In general, early or midmorning presentations are preferable to late afternoon sessions. Try to avoid giving a presentation immediately before lunch, when the audience may be hungry or eager to make lunch appointments, or, worse, immediately after lunch, when the audience may be late or not very alert.

Delivery Method

At some point during your planning, you must decide on the method of delivery—that is, will you memorize your speech, read it, or speak from notes? (Impromptu speaking—speaking without any formal preparation—is covered later.) Your choice will be determined by the answers to such questions as, How long is your talk? How complex is the content? How formal is the presentation? And, very important, what method (or combination of methods) are you the most comfortable with?

Of the three common methods of presentation (memorizing, reading, and speaking from notes), the last is the most common for business presentations.

Memorizing Unless a presentation is short and significant, memorizing an entire speech is risky, not to mention very time-consuming. You always run the risk (a very real one if you're nervous) of forgetting your lines and thus ruining your entire presentation if you have no notes to fall back on. In addition, memorized presentations often sound mechanical and do not let you adapt the material to the needs of the audience. However, memorizing the first or last section of your presentation, a telling quotation, or a humorous story may be extremely effective for presenting a key part of your talk.

Reading Reading speeches is quite common in academic settings, where a professor or researcher might be asked to read a paper at a professional conference. Writing out a speech and reading from the prepared text is helpful if you're dealing with a highly complex or technical topic, if the subject is controversial (making a statement to the press, for example), or if you have a lot of information to present in a short time. Such delivery is *not* recommended for most business settings because the presenter's eyes are typically too much on the paper and not enough on the audience, because spontaneity and flexibility are lost, and because, after all, if the speech is going to be read word for word, why not just duplicate and distribute it to the audience for them to read at their leisure?

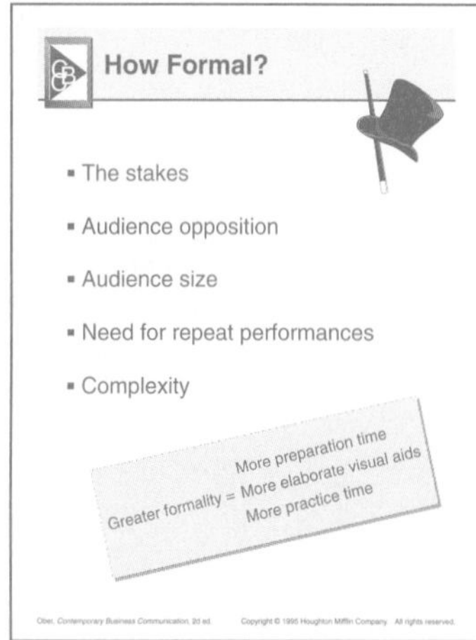
How Formal?
The stakes
Audience opposition
Audience size
Need for repeat performances
Complexity
Greater formality = More preparation time
More elaborate visual aids
More practice time
Ober, Contemporary Business Communication, 2d ed.
Copyright © 1995 Houghton Mifflin Company. All rights reserved.

See Transparency 14.2, Level of Formality.

Speaking from Notes By far the most common (and generally the most effective) method for business presentations is speaking from prepared notes, such as an outline. The notes contain key phrases rather than complete sentences, and you compose the exact wording as you speak. Although you may occasionally stumble in choosing a word, the spontaneous, conversational quality and the close audience rapport that result are generally superior to those of other presentation methods. The notes help ensure that you will cover all the material and in a logical order, yet this method provides enough flexibility that you can adapt your remarks in reaction to verbal and nonverbal cues from the audience.

The specific content and format of the notes is not important; choose whatever works best for you. Some people use a formal outline on full

If you are using overhead transparencies, you may find that they can serve as your notes. If you are comfortable enough to do so, moving away from the podium (or in this case, the projector) and using gestures can add a bit of variety and help your audience stay focused.

sheets of paper; others prefer notes jotted on index cards. Some use complete sentences, others, short phrases. If desirable, include notes to yourself, such as when to pause, what phrases to emphasize, and when to change a slide or transparency.

Whether you use full sheets or index cards, be sure to number each page (in case the pages are dropped). For ease in moving from sheet to sheet or card to card, write on just one side and do not staple. Typed copy is better than handwritten copy and large type is better than small type. Type your notes in standard upper- and lowercase letters rather than in all capitals, which are more difficult to read because all the letters are the same size.

Use larger type and upper- and lowercase letters for outline notes.

Examples of an excerpt from a written report, an oral presentation using a complete script, and an oral presentation using just outline notes are shown in Figure 14.2. Note several things about the content and format of the excerpts from the oral presentation:

- Both the complete script and the outline notes are typed in larger type for ease of reading, and both contain prompts showing when to display each visual aid (transparency).
- The complete script is written in a more informal, conversational style than the written report and uses a shorter line length and extra spacing between paragraphs (to help the speaker find his or her place easily).
- The outline notes contain mostly phrases, with each subtopic indented to show its relationship to the main idea.

Of course, you can tailor any combination of these methods to suit your needs. Some people, especially those who give speeches only occasionally, do best by writing out the entire speech and then practicing it until they can recite whole paragraphs or thoughts with ease. Doing so enables them to maintain eye contact with the audience. Some insert delivery

FIGURE 14.2 Complete Script Versus Outline Notes

Original Written Report Page
Note the formal language.

The staff employees were asked to rate their level of familiarity with each benefit. As shown in Table 1, most staff employees believe that most benefits have been adequately communicated to them.

At least three-fourths of the employees are familiar with all major benefits except for long-term disability insurance, which is familiar to only a slight majority. The low level of knowledge about automobile insurance can be explained by the fact that this benefit had been in effect for only six weeks at the time of the survey.

In general, benefit familiarity is not related to length of employment at ASU. Most employees are familiar with most benefits, regardless of their length of employment. However, as shown in Figure 1, the one benefit for which this is not true is life insurance. The longer a person has been employed at ASU, the more likely he or she is to know about this benefit.

Complete Script of an Oral Presentation
Note the conversational language, larger type size, and shorter line length.

We asked our employees how familiar they are with our benefits (TRANSPARENCY 1). As you can see, most employees know about most of our benefits.

At least three-fourths of them are familiar with all but two of our benefits, and those two are long-term disability and automobile insurance. Only a slight majority know about our long-term disability insurance, and slightly more than a third know about our automobile insurance. As you may remember, we began offering automobile insurance just six weeks before conducting this survey.

In general, there's no correlation between how long employees have worked here and how familiar they are with our benefits. Most employees are familiar with our benefits, no matter how long they've worked here. The one exception is life insurance (TRANSPARENCY 2). The longer a person has worked for us, the more likely that person is to know about our life insurance program.

Outline Notes for an Oral Presentation
Note the incomplete sentences and abbreviations.

FAMILIARITY WITH BENEFITS—TRANSP 1

- Most know about most benefits
- +3/4 know about all but 2 benefits:
  —Long-term disability = slight majority
  —Auto insur = +1/3 (begun 6 wks before survey)

- No correlation between employment length & familiarity
  —Not true for life insur—TRANSP 2
  —Life insur: Longer employment = more familiarity

cues, indicating when to pause, smile, make a gesture, display a visual aid, slow down, and the like.

Some professionals start off by writing out the entire speech and then practice extensively from the prepared script. Only after they are thoroughly familiar with their verbatim script do they condense it into an outline and then speak from the outline. Whatever method you use, the key to a successful delivery is practice, practice, practice.

What Are You Trying to Accomplish?

- **Reporting** *Telling what happened at the OSHA meeting last week*
- **Explaining** *Showing how to complete the new expense report forms*
- **Persuading** *Convincing the executive committee to adopt a tuition-reimbursement plan*
- **Motivating** *Inspiring the employees to volunteer to become a Big Brother or Big Sister*

See Transparency 14.3, Purpose of the Presentation.

ORGANIZING THE PRESENTATION

For most presentations, the best way to begin is simply to brainstorm: write down every point you can think of that might be included in your presentation. Don't worry about the order or format—just get it all down. During the next several days, carry a pen and paper with you so that you can jot down random thoughts as they occur—during a meeting, at lunch, going to and from work, or in the evening at home.

Later, separate your notes into three categories: opening, body, and ending. As you begin to analyze and organize your material, you may find that you need additional information. You may need to retrieve records from files, consult with a colleague, or perhaps visit your corporate or local library to fill in the gaps.

The Opening

Your opening should introduce the topic, identify the purpose, and preview the presentation.

The purpose of the opening is to capture the interest of your audience, and the first 90 seconds of your presentation are crucial. The audience will be observing every detail about you—your dress, posture, facial features, and voice qualities, as well as what you're actually saying—for clues about you and your topic, and they will be making preliminary judgments accordingly.

Begin immediately to establish rapport and build a relationship with your audience—not just for the duration of your presentation but for the long term. If you're making a proposal, you need not only the audience's attention during your presentation but also their cooperation later to implement your proposal. Because the opening is so crucial, many professionals write out the entire opening and practice it word for word until they almost know it by heart.

The kind of opening that will be effective depends on your topic, how well you know the audience, and how well they know you. If, for example, you're giving a status report on a project about which you've reported before, you can immediately announce your main points (for example, that the project is on schedule and proceeding as planned) and go immediately to the body of your remarks. If, however, you're presenting a new proposal to your superiors, you'll first have to introduce the topic and provide background information.

If most of the listeners don't know you, you'll first have to gain their attention with a creative opening. The following types of attention-getting openings have proven successful for business presentations; the examples given are for the presentation to union employees on the topic of absenteeism:

Effective openings include a quotation, question, hypothetical situation, story, or startling fact or visual aid.

- *Quote a well-known person:* "Comedian Woody Allen once noted that just showing up is 90% of the job."
- *Ask a question:* "If we were able to cut our absenteeism rate by half during the coming six months, exactly how much do you think that would mean for each of us in our end-of-year bonus checks?"
- *Present a hypothetical situation:* "Assume that as you were leaving home this morning to put in a full day at work, your son came up to you and said he was too tired to go to school because he had stayed up so late last night watching 'Wrestle Mania.' What would be your reaction?"
- *Relate an appropriate anecdote, story, joke, or personal experience:* "George, a friend of mine who had recently changed jobs, happened to meet his former boss on the street and asked her whom she had hired to fill his vacancy. 'George,' his former boss said, 'when you left, you didn't *leave* any vacancy!' Perhaps the reason George didn't leave any vacancy was that. . . .
- *Give a startling fact:* "During the next 24 hours, American industry will lose $136 million because of absenteeism."
- *Use a dramatic prop or visual aid:* (holding up a paper clip) "What do you think is the *true* cost of this paper clip to our company?"

Don't apologize or make excuses (for example, "I wish I had had more time to prepare my remarks today" or "I'm not really much of a speaker"). The audience may agree with you! At any rate, you'll turn them off immediately and weaken your credibility.

Your opening should lead into the body of your presentation by previewing your remarks: "Today, I'll cover four main points. First, . . ." Let the audience know the scope of your remarks. For example, if you're discussing the pros and cons of a plant closing from a strictly dollars-and-cents standpoint, alert the audience immediately that your analysis does not include political or human relations considerations. If you don't first define the scope of your remarks, you may invite needless questions and second-guessing during your presentation.

For most business presentations, let the audience know up front what you expect of them. Are you simply presenting information for them to absorb, or will the audience be expected to react to your remarks? Are you asking for their endorsement, their resources, their help, or what? Let the audience know what their role will be so that they can then place your remarks in perspective.

The Body

The body of your presentation conveys the real content. Here you'll develop the points you introduced in the opening, giving background information, specific evidence, examples, implications, consequences, and other needed information.

Choose a Logical Sequence Just as when writing a letter or report, you should choose an organizational plan that suits your purpose and your audience's needs. The most commonly used organizational plans are these:

Organize the body logically, according to your topic and audience needs.

- *Direct sequence:* Give the major conclusions first, followed by the supporting details (typically used for presenting routine information).
- *Indirect sequence:* Present the reasons first, followed by the major conclusion (typically used for persuasive presentations).
- *Chronology:* Present the points in the order in which they occurred (typically used in status reports or when reporting on some event).
- *Cause/effect/solution:* Present the sources and consequences of some problem and then pose a solution.
- *Order of importance:* Arrange the points in order of importance and then pose each point as a question and answer it (an effective way of ensuring that the audience can follow your arguments).
- *Elimination of alternatives:* List all alternatives and then gradually eliminate each one until only one option remains—the one you're recommending.

Whatever organizational plan you choose, make sure your audience knows at the outset where you're going and is able to follow your organization. In a written document, signposts such as headings tell the reader how the parts fit together. In an oral presentation, you must compensate for the lack of such aids by using frequent and clear transitions that tell your listeners where you are. Pace your presentation of data so that you do not lose your audience.

Establish Your Credibility Convince the listener that you've done a thorough job of collecting and analyzing the data and that your points are reasonable. Support your arguments with credible evidence—statistics, actual experiences, examples, and support from experts. Use objective language; let the data—not exaggeration or emotion—persuade the audience. Be guided by the same principles you used when writing a persuasive letter or report.

Avoid saturating your presentation with so many facts and figures that your audience won't be able to absorb them. Regardless of their relevance, statistics will not strengthen your presentation if the audience is unable to digest all the data. A more effective tactic is to prepare handouts of detailed statistical data to distribute for review at a later time.

Deal with Negative Information It would be unusual if *all* the data you've collected and analyzed supports your proposal. (If that were the case, persuasion would not be needed.) What should you do, then, about negative information, which, if presented, might weaken your argument? You cannot simply ignore negative information. To do so would surely open up a host of questions and subsequent doubts that would seriously weaken your position.

Do not ignore negative information.

Think about your own analysis of the data. Despite the negative information, you still concluded that your solution has merit. Your tactic, then, is to present all the important information—pro and con—and to show through your analysis and discussion that your recommendations are still valid, in spite of the disadvantages and drawbacks. Use the techniques you learned in Chapter 4 about emphasis and subordination to let your listeners know which points you considered major and which you considered minor.

Although you should discuss the important negative points, you may safely omit discussing minor ones. You must, however, be prepared to discuss these minor negative points if any questions about them arise at the conclusion of your presentation.

The Ending

Finish on a strong, upbeat note, leaving your audience with a clear and simple message.

The ending of your presentation is your last opportunity to achieve your objective. Don't waste it. A presentation without a strong ending is like a joke without a punchline.

Your closing should summarize the main points of your presentation, especially if it has been a long one. Even if the members of your audience have had an easy time following the structure of your talk, they won't necessarily remember all your important points. Let the audience know the significance of what you've said. Draw conclusions, make recommendations, or outline the next steps to take. Leave the audience with a clear and simple message.

To add punch to your ending, you may want to use one of the same techniques discussed for opening a presentation. You might tell a story, make a personal appeal, or issue a challenge. However, resist the temptation to end with a quotation. It won't sound dramatic enough. Besides, you want your listeners to remember *your* words and thoughts—not someone else's. Also avoid fading out with a weak "That's about all I have to say" or "I see that our time is running out."

After you've developed some experience in giving presentations, you will be able to judge fairly accurately how long to spend on each point in order to finish on time. Until then, practice your presentation with a stopwatch. If necessary, insert reminders at critical points in your notes indicating where you should be at what point in time. Avoid having to drop important sections or rush through the conclusion of your presentation because you misjudged your timing.

Because your audience will remember best what they hear last, think of your ending as one of the most important parts of your presentation. Finish on a strong, upbeat note. If you've used a slide projector during your presentation, turn it off and turn the room lights on so that *you* are the center of attention. Also remember that no one ever lost any friends by finishing a minute or two ahead of schedule. As Toastmasters International puts it, "Get up, speak up, shut up, and sit down."

For an exercise on revising a business presentation, refer students to the *Study Guide*, pp. 185–186.

The Use of Humor in Business Presentations

Memory research indicates that when ideas are presented with humor, the audience is not only able to recall more details of the presentation but is also able to retain the information longer.[5]

Most of us are not capable of being a Jerry Seinfeld or Roseanne Arnold, even if we wanted to be. If you know you do not tell humorous stories well, the moment you're in front of an audience is not the time to try to rectify that situation. Both you and your audience will suffer. If, however, you feel that you can use humor effectively, doing so might add just the appropriate touch to your presentation.

Use humor if it is appropriate and you are adept at telling humorous stories.

Jokes, puns, satire, and, especially, funny real-life incidents are just a few examples of humor, all of which serve to form a bond between the speaker and audience. Humor can be used anywhere in a presentation—in the opening to get attention, in the body to add interest, or in the closing to drive home a point. Humor should, of course, be avoided if the topic is very serious or has negative consequences for the audience.

If you tell a funny story, it must always be appropriate to the situation and in good taste. Never tell an off-color or sexist joke; never use offensive language; never single out an ethnic, racial, or religious group; and never use a dialect or foreign accent in telling a story. Such tactics are always in bad taste. The best stories are directed at yourself; they show that you are human and can laugh at yourself.

Before telling a humorous story, make sure you understand it and think it's funny. Then personalize it for your own style of speaking and for the particular situation. Avoid beginning jokes by saying, "I heard a funny story the other day about. . ." A major element of humor is surprise, so don't warn the audience a joke is coming. If you do, they're mentally preparing for a funny punch line, and you may disappoint them. If, on the other hand, you're already halfway into the story before the audience even realizes it's a joke, your chances of success are greater.

Resist the temptation to laugh at your own stories. A slight smile is more effective. Wait for the (hoped-for) laughter to subside; then continue your presentation by relating the punch line to the topic at hand.

Regardless of your expertise as a joke teller, do not use humor too frequently. Humor is a means to an end—not an end in itself. When all is said and done, you don't want your audience to remember that you were funny. You want them to remember that what you had to say was important and made sense.

Making a presentation while seated is more difficult than while standing, and delivery must often be modified, communications consultants advise. To appear impressive and in control while seated, speakers should remember to work hard to appear energetic, keep the voice strong, try not to move around in the seat, keep hands on or above the table, and maintain eye contact. ("Don't Be a Sitting Duck," *Sales & Marketing Management*, April 1991, p. 29.)

DEVELOPING APPROPRIATE VISUAL AIDS

Today's audiences are accustomed to multimedia events that bombard the senses. They often assume that any formal presentation must be accompanied by some visual element, whether it is a flipchart, overhead transparency, slide, film, videotape, or actual model. This expectation helps explain why worldwide sales of overhead transparencies are expected to top 4 billion sheets annually by 1996; two-thirds of these are sold in the United States.[6]

Visual aids are relatively simple to create (see the Spotlight on Technology) and help the audience understand the presentation, especially if it includes complex or statistical material. A University of Pennsylvania study found that presenters who used visual aids were successful in persuading 67% of their audience, whereas those who did not use them persuaded

SPOTLIGHT ON TECHNOLOGY

Desktop Presentations

Desktop presentation software is a special type of software that combines the functions of outline, word processing, and graphics programs into one easy-to-use program that enables you to design professional-looking overhead transparencies and 35-mm slides easily, as well as produce miniature print copies to use as audience handouts.

Presentation programs come with slide and transparency templates—that is, built-in designs that specify such features as background and font colors, borders, and the size, face, and position of type. Templates are available for title slides, bulleted lists, all types of charts, and illustrations. These templates, which can be changed, ensure a professional and consistent appearance.

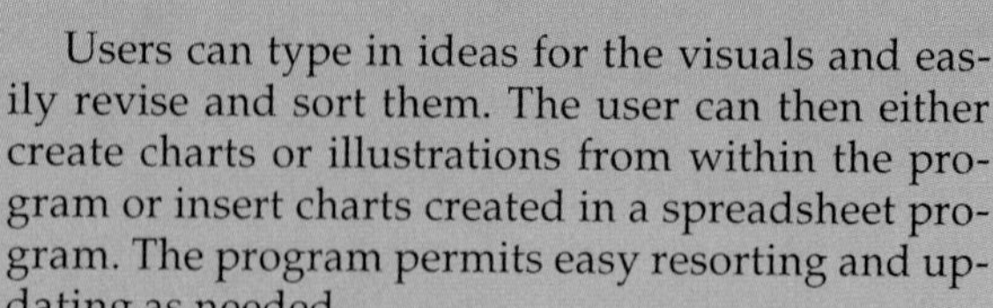

Users can type in ideas for the visuals and easily revise and sort them. The user can then either create charts or illustrations from within the program or insert charts created in a spreadsheet program. The program permits easy resorting and updating as needed.

When everything is perfect, the user either prints them out on a color printer (for color transparencies) or uses a modem and communication software program to send the data file electronically to a film processing company. The finished sides and transparencies are shipped back to the user within 24 hours, at a cost of a few dollars per visual. (Black-and-white transparencies can, of course, be produced directly from a laser printer.)

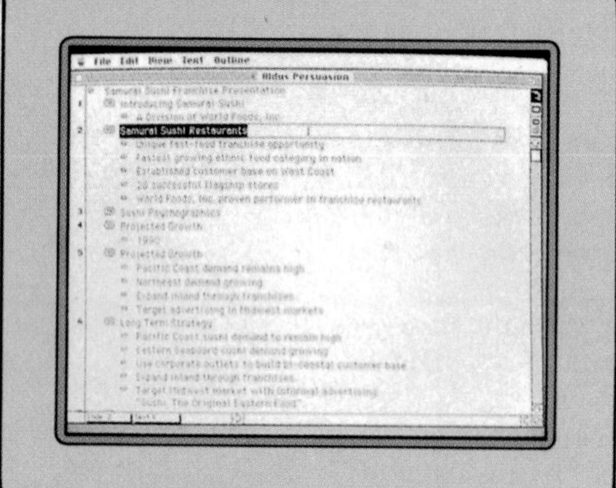

Outline your ideas.

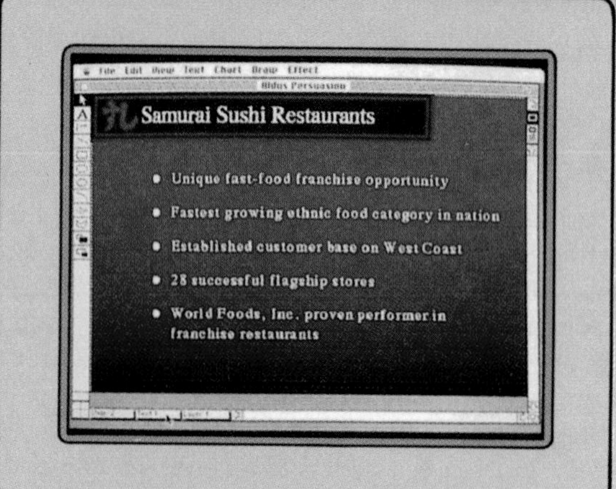

View the finished slides.

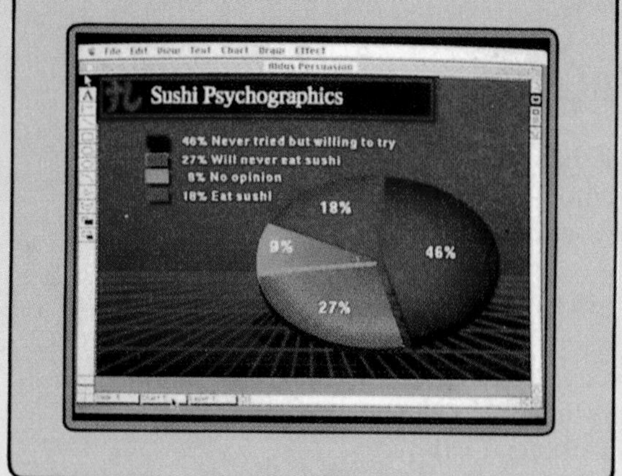

Chart numerical data.

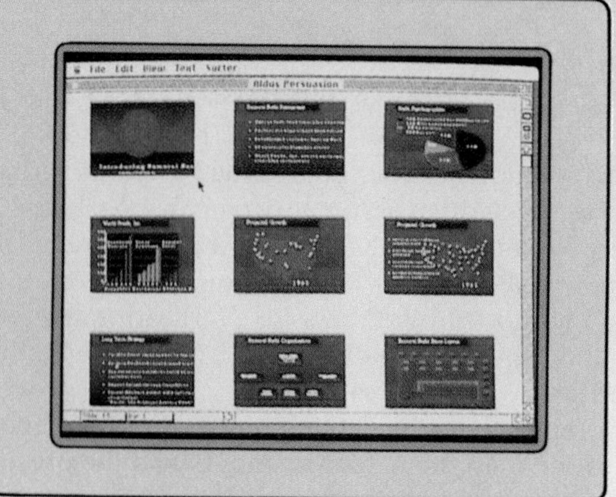

Produce speaker notes and handouts.

only 50% of their audience. In addition, meetings in which visual aids were used were 28% shorter than those with no such aids. Similarly, a University of Minnesota study found that the use of graphics increased a presenter's persuasiveness by 43%. Presenters who used visual aids were also perceived as being more professional, better prepared, and more interesting than the group who didn't use visual aids.[7]

Types of Visual Aids

Transparencies, slides, and handouts are the most common visual aids.

Transparencies for overhead projection are probably the most commonly used visual aid in business presentations. Inexpensive, easy to produce, and simple to update, they can be used without darkening the room and while you face the audience. Thus, your audience can see to take notes, and you can maintain eye contact with them. Thanks to presentation software, overhead transparencies can now make use of color, designed fonts, charts, and artwork, instead of being limited to hard-to-read and overcrowded typewriter type.

Although 35-mm slides are best projected in a somewhat darkened room, their high quality adds a distinctly professional touch to a presentation, and they can be used with very large audiences. However, slides lack the flexibility of transparencies; it is difficult to review an earlier slide or skip forward several slides during a presentation. Slides are moderately expensive to produce and require somewhat more preparation time than transparencies. However, the use of computer-generated slides is decreasing both the cost and production time.

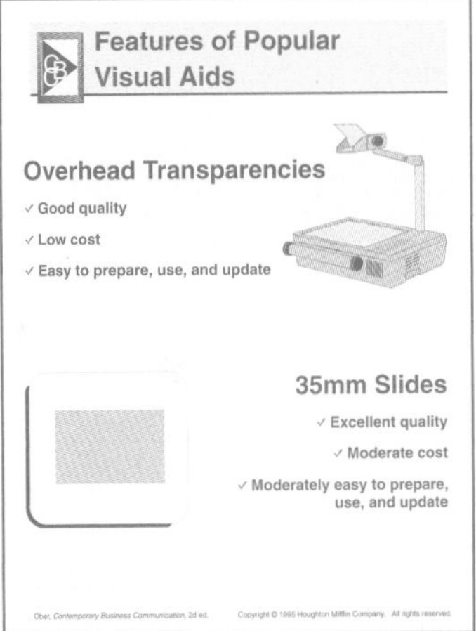

See Transparency 14.4, Features of Popular Visual Aids.

Electronic slide presentations are the newest medium for visual aids. They consist of slides shown directly from a computer and projected onto a screen by use of a display panel sitting on top of an overhead projector. Because the slide images come directly from the computer file, actual transparencies and slides do not have to be made. Electronic slide presentations provide more flexibility than traditional slide presentations, but they do require high-powered overhead projectors for best results.

Handouts—printed copies of notes, tables, or illustrations—are often important in helping the audience follow a presentation. In addition, they provide a permanent record of the major points of the presentation and reduce or eliminate the need for note taking. Handouts are especially helpful for presenting complex information such as detailed statistical tables, which would be ineffective if projected as a slide or transparency.

The appropriate use of these and other types of visual aids is shown in Figure 14.3.

Preparing Visual Aids

Visual aids should be used only when needed, and be simple, readable, and of high quality.

The key to effective visual aids is to use them only when needed, keep them simple and readable, and ensure they're of the highest quality.

Avoid using too many visual aids. Novice presenters sometimes use them as a crutch. Such overuse keeps the emphasis on the visual aid rather than on the presenter. Use visual aids only when they will help the audience grasp an important point, and remove them when they're no longer

FIGURE 14.3 Criteria for Selecting Visual Aids

Criteria	Transpar-encies	35-mm slides	Electronic presenta-tions	Films	Videotape	Flipcharts	Handouts
Quality	Good	Excellent	Good	Excellent	Excellent	Poor	Good
Cost	Low	Moderate	Moderate	High	High	Low	Low
Ease of use	Easy	Moderate	Difficult	Moderate	Easy	Easy	Easy
Ease of preparation	Easy	Moderate	Moderate	Difficult	Difficult	Easy	Easy
Ease of updating	Easy	Moderate	Moderate	Difficult	Difficult	N/A	Easy
Degrees of formality	Either	Formal	Formal	Either	Either	Informal	Either
Adaptability to audience size	Excellent	Excellent	Moderate	Excellent	Moderate	Poor	Moderate
Dependence on equipment	Moderate	Moderate	High	Moderate	Moderate	Low	None

needed. One or two relevant, helpful visual aids are better than an entire armload of irrelevant ones—no matter how attractive they are.

One of the most common mistakes presenters make in developing visual aids is to simply photocopy tables or illustrations from reports, printouts, or journals and project them on a screen. Print graphics usually contain far too much information to serve effectively as presentation graphics. Using print graphics in a presentation will often do more to hinder your presentation than to help it.

As a general rule, each slide or transparency should contain no more than 40 characters per line, no more than six or seven lines per visual, and no more than three columns of data. Use upper- and lowercase letters (rather than all capitals) in a large, simple typeface and plenty of white (empty) space. Use bulleted lists to show a group of related items that have no specific order and numbered lists to show related items with a specific order.

Establish a color scheme and stay with it for all your visual aids; that is, use the same background color for each slide or transparency. For handouts and overheads, use dark type on a light background; for slides, use light type on a dark background. Figure 14.4 illustrates these principles for developing effective visual aids.

If you do not keep your visual aids clear and simple, your audience can easily become overwhelmed, with their attention drawn to the technology rather than to the content. As always, seek to *express*—not to *impress*. With visual aids, less is more.

The only real way to ensure that your visual aids are readable is to test them beforehand from the back seat of the room in which you will be presenting. If that is not possible, follow these guidelines: the smallest image projected on the screen should be 1 inch tall for each 30 feet of viewing distance, and no one should be seated farther from the screen than ten times the height of the projected image. Thus, if you're projecting onto a screen 6 feet high, the back seat should be no farther than 60 feet from the screen, and the projector should be positioned so that the projected letters are at least 2 inches tall.

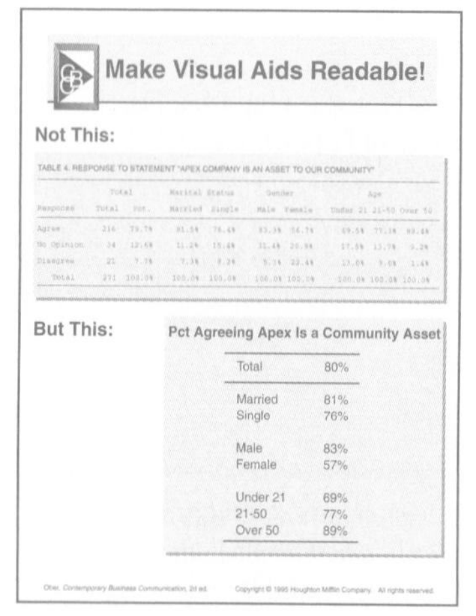

See Transparency 14.5, Making Visual Aids Readable.

FIGURE 14.4 Making Your Visual Aids Effective

Be obvious. You can get a lot of impact from a large headline and straightforward text.

Be direct. Using a concise title and limiting yourself to one idea per slide helps to make the point stick.

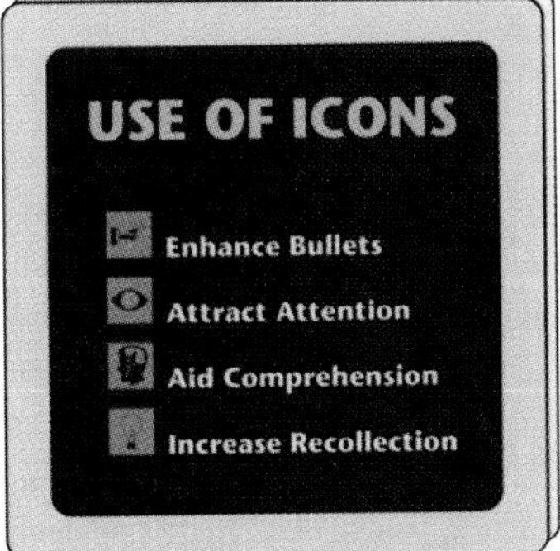

Icons, often more appealing than text, can be used to tie together parts of a presentation.

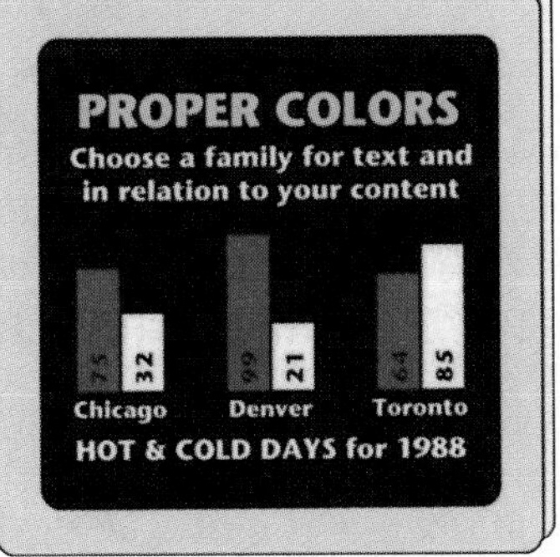

Be sparing in your use of color, and try to use colors that relate directly to your subject matter.

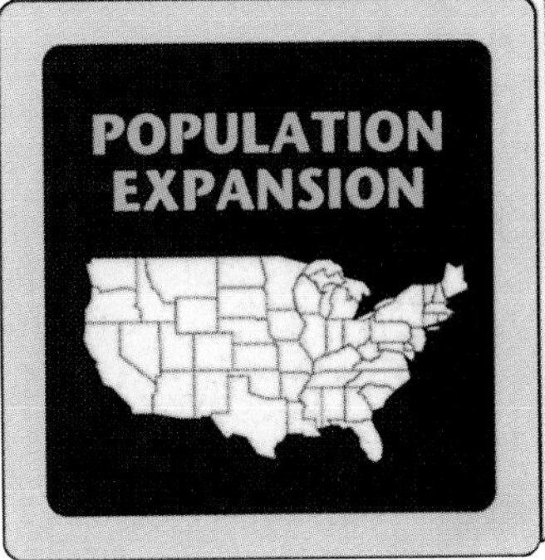

Good overheads don't need to be entirely self-explanatory. They can reinforce ideas being put forth by the speaker.

The quality of your visual aids sends a nonverbal message about your competence and your respect for your audience. Just as you don't want your audience's attention distracted by the razzle-dazzle of your slides, neither do you want their attention distracted by their poor quality. If the visual aid isn't readable or attractive, don't use it.

Using Visual Aids

In the fall of 1993, President Clinton addressed a joint session of Congress and a national television audience to outline his national health-care plan. He smiled at the audience and looked into the teleprompter, preparing to begin his speech. Unfortunately, the words he saw scrolling by were those of his State-of-the-Union speech, given months earlier—not his health-care

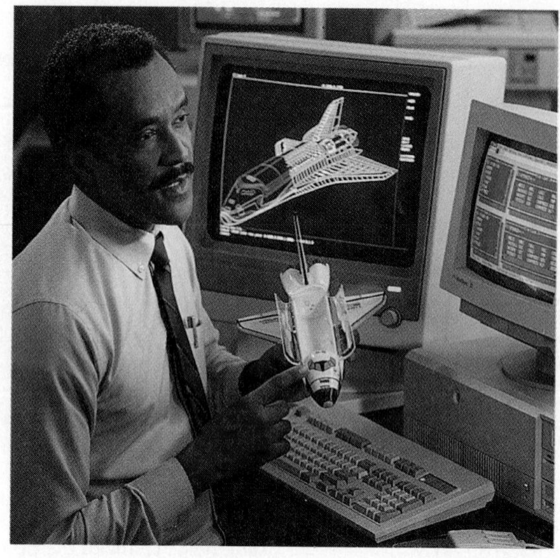

Visual aids can include not only overhead transparencies, slides, and computer presentations but also actual models, as in this design presentation at the National Aeronautics and Space Administration presentation. If you are using more than one type of aid, plan ahead of time which you will use at each point of your presentation.

Practice using your visual aids smoothly and effectively.

speech. Fortunately, the President had prepared a contingency plan and began delivering his speech from a written copy he had brought with him, while aides scrambled to load the correct cassette into the teleprompter.

As this real-life incident attests, even the best visual aid will not be effective if it is not used properly during the presentation or if the equipment doesn't work. Using equipment smoothly does not come naturally; it takes practice and a keen awareness of audience needs, especially when using a slide or overhead projector. If you have the option of positioning the projection equipment (slide or overhead projector) and screen, ensure that the image is readable from every seat and that neither you nor the projector blocks anyone's view (see Figure 14.5).

Confirm that your equipment is in top working order and that you know how to operate it and how to secure quickly a spare bulb or spare machine if one becomes necessary. Adjust the projector and focus the image so that it is clearly readable from the farthest seat. However, do not make the image larger than necessary; the presenter should be the center of attention. The image should be a square or rectangle. Avoid the common keystoning effect (where the top of the image is wider than the bottom) by tilting the top of the screen forward slightly toward the projector.

When using slide projectors, have a blank opaque slide or a generic title slide as the last slide so that the audience is not suddenly hit with a bright flash of light when you finish your presentation. And with both types of projectors, avoid walking in front of the projected image.

Try to avoid problems. Lock your slides in place in the tray; number your slides and transparencies so that they can be resorted quickly if dropped; have your film already threaded into the projector; clean the overhead projector glass before using it; tape the device used to advance the slides to the lectern to avoid having it tumble off; and have an extra bulb handy (and know how to insert it). Finally, be prepared to give your presentation without visual aids if that should become necessary.

Be prepared to give your presentation without visual aids if necessary.

With practice, you can learn to stand to the side of the screen, facing the audience with your feet pointed toward them. Then, when you need to re-

FIGURE 14.5 Positioning the Projector Correctly

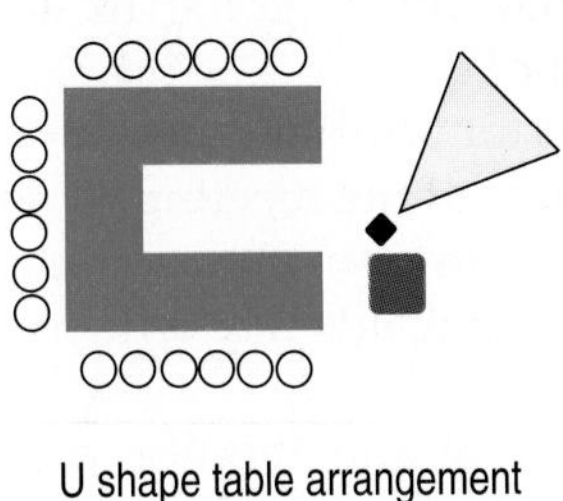

U shape table arrangement

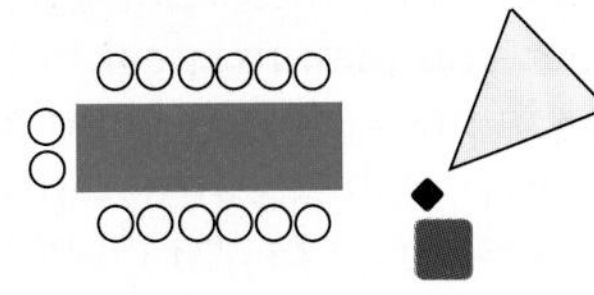

Center table arrangement

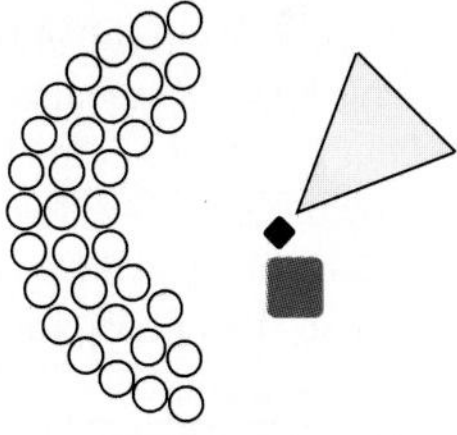

Amphitheater

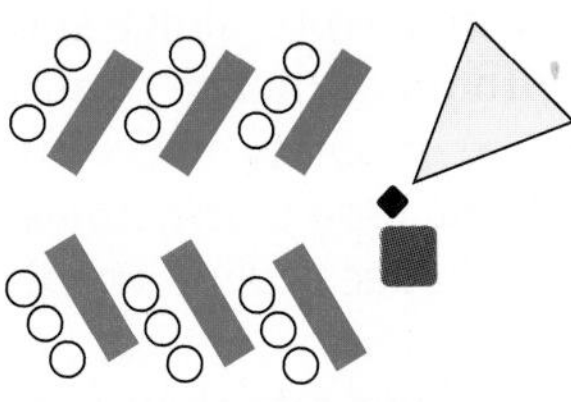

Chevron arrangement

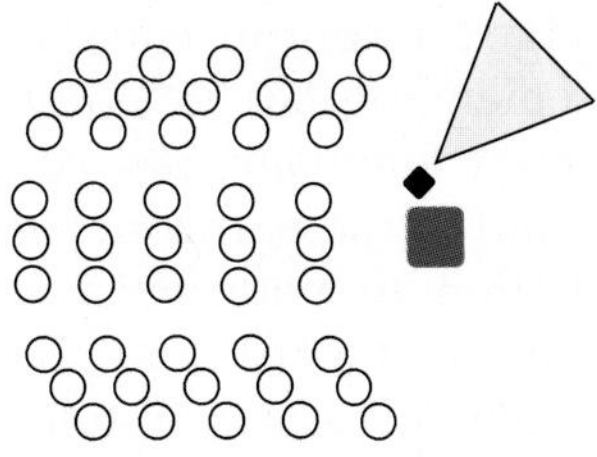

Auditorium or theater arrangement

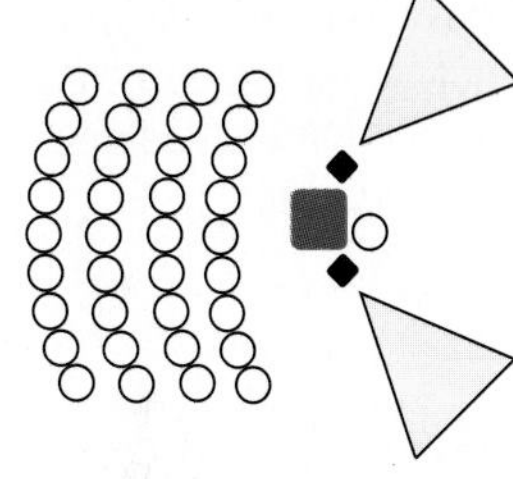

Dual projector meetings

fer to an item on the screen, point with either a finger, pointer, or pen. Turn your body from the waist, keeping your feet pointed toward the audience. Doing so enables you to maintain better eye contact with the audience as well as better control of the presentation.

Distribute handouts before your presentation if they contain information the audience will need during your presentation. Otherwise, distribute them at the end of your presentation (to avoid distracting the audience from your remarks). Do, however, alert the audience at the start that you will be distributing a printed summary of your remarks so that people won't take unneeded notes.

PRACTICING THE PRESENTATION

Use appropriate language, voice qualities, gestures, and posture.

The language of oral presentations must be simple. Because the listener has only one chance to comprehend the information presented, shorter sentences and simpler vocabulary should be used for oral presentations than for written presentations. Presenters have trouble articulating long, involved sentences with complex vocabulary, and listeners have trouble understanding them. A long sentence that reads easily on paper may leave the speaker breathless when he or she says it aloud. Avoid such traps. Use short, simple sentences and a conversational style. Use contractions freely, and avoid using words that you may have trouble pronouncing. (Compare, for example, the different styles used in the excerpt from the written report and the oral presentation shown earlier in Figure 14.2.)

What should you do if, on your way to the podium, you trip over an electric cord and go sprawling? Executive Elaine Moncur kept her composure and her sense of humor. "It was awful," she cheerfully recalls. But she picked herself up, got to the microphone, and told the audience, "This reminds me of starting my own business—a fast slide down and a slow climb up." She received a standing ovation. (Judy Linscott, "Getting on and Off the Podium," *Savvy*, October 1985, p. 44.)

Use frequent preview, summary, transition, and repetition to help your audience follow your presentation. The old advice to preachers is just as pertinent for business presenters: "Tell them what you're going to tell them, tell them, and then tell them what you told them."

Whether you plan to speak from a complete script or from notes or an outline, begin practicing by simulating the conditions of the meeting room as closely as possible. Always practice standing, with your notes at the same level and angle as at a podium, and use any visual aids that will be a part of your presentation.

Videotaping your rehearsal can help you review and modify your voice qualities, gestures, and speech content. If videotaping is not possible, two good substitutes are a large mirror and a tape recorder. The mirror can help you judge the appropriateness of your posture, facial expressions, and gestures. Remember that 55% of your credibility with an audience comes from your body language, 38% comes from your voice qualities, and only 7% comes from the actual words you use.[8] Play back the tape many times, paying attention to your voice qualities (especially speed and pitch), pauses, grouping of words and phrases, and pronunciation.

Use an Outline — Not a Script

Absenteeism Rate — Transp 1

- 4.7% first 6 mo.
  - 5% higher than last yr.
  - 14% increase in 3 yrs.
- Industry average = 3.6% (steady)

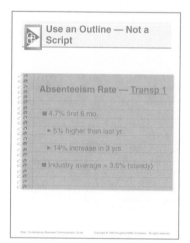

See Transparency 14.6, Example of Presentation Script.

Speak in a conversational tone, but at a slightly slower rate than normally used in conversation. For interest and to fit the situation, vary both the volume and the rate of speaking, slowing down when presenting important or complex information and speeding up when summarizing. Use periodic pauses to emphasize important points. Use correct diction, avoid slurring or dropping off the endings of words, and practice pronouncing difficult names.

Occasional hand and arm gestures are important for adding interest and emphasis, but only if they are appropriate and appear natural. If you never "talk with your hands" in normal conversation, it is unlikely you will do so naturally while presenting. Avoid annoying and distracting mannerisms and gestures, such as jingling coins or keys in your pocket; coughing or clearing your throat excessively; wildly waving your hands; gripping the lectern tightly; nervously swaying or pacing; playing with jewelry, pens, or paper clips; or peppering your remarks with "and uh" or "you know."

Practice smiling occasionally, standing tall and naturally, with the body balanced on both feet. Rest your hands on the podium, by your side, or in any natural, quiet position. Your voice and demeanor should reflect professionalism, enthusiasm, and self-confidence.

DELIVERING THE PRESENTATION

Dress comfortably—just slightly dressier than your audience.

Your clothing is a part of the message you communicate to your audience, so dress appropriately—in comfortable and businesslike attire. Try to dress just slightly better than the average member of your audience; the audience will be complimented by your efforts.

If you're speaking after a meal, eat lightly, avoiding heavy sauces, desserts, and alcoholic beverages. As you're being introduced, take several deep breaths to clear your mind, walk confidently to the front of the room, take enough time to arrange yourself and your notes, look slowly around you, establish eye contact with several members of the audience, and then, in a loud, clear voice, begin your presentation.

In most environments, a microphone is not needed if you're speaking to a group smaller than 150 people—10 to 12 rows of people. Your voice should carry that far. Not using a microphone gives you more freedom to move about and avoids problems with audio feedback and volume adjustments. If you will need to use a microphone, test it beforehand to see how it operates and to determine the appropriate setting and height; the microphone normally should be 4 to 6 inches from your mouth.

You should know your presentation well enough that you can maintain eye contact easily with your audience, taking care to include members in all corners of the room. If you lose your place in your notes or script, relax and take as much time as you need to regroup.

If your mind actually does go blank, try to keep talking—even if you repeat what you've just said. The audience will probably think you intentionally repeated the information for emphasis, and the extra time may jog your memory. If this doesn't work, simply skip ahead to another part of your presentation that you do remember; then come back later to the part you omitted.

If someone in the audience exposes an error or weakness in a presentation, the speaker should not get defensive. "Speakers who admit to imperfections, thank people for pointing them out, and assure the audience that steps will be taken to correct the inaccuracies do better than speakers who take the opposite position." (Michael E. Cavanagh, "Make Effective Speeches," *Personnel Journal*, March 1988, pp. 51–55.)

Stage Fright

For some people, making a presentation is accompanied by such symptoms as these:

- Gasping for air
- Feeling faint or nauseated ("butterflies in the stomach")
- Having shaking hands or legs and sweaty palms
- Feeling the heart beat rapidly and loudly
- Speaking too rapidly and in a high-pitched voice

If you've ever experienced any of these symptoms, take comfort in the fact that you're not alone. Fear of giving a speech is the Number 1 fear of most Americans. In a national poll of 3,000 people, 42% said the one thing they're most afraid of in life—even more than having cancer or a heart attack—is giving a speech.[9] Fortunately, behavior-modification experts have found that, of the full range of anxiety disorders, people can most predictably overcome their fear of public speaking.[10]

Recognize that you have been asked to make a presentation because someone obviously thinks you have something important to say. You should feel complimented. Unless you are an exceptionally good or exceptionally bad speaker, the audience will more likely remember *what* you say rather than how you say it. Most of us fall somewhere between these two extremes as presenters.

To avoid anxiety, practice, develop a positive attitude, and concentrate on friendly faces.

The best way to minimize any lingering anxiety is to overprepare. For the anxious presenter, there is no such thing as overpractice. The more familiar you are with the content of your speech and the more trial runs you've made, the better you'll be able to concentrate on your delivery once you're actually in front of the group. You may want to memorize the first several sentences of your presentation just so you can approach those critical first moments (when anxiety is highest) with more confidence.

Before your presentation, take a short walk to relax your body. While waiting for your presentation to begin, let your arms drop loosely by your sides and shake your wrists gently, all the while breathing deeply several times. As you begin to speak, look for friendly faces in the crowd, and concentrate on them initially.

Some nervousness, of course, is good. It gets the adrenalin flowing and gives your speech an edge. If you do find that you're exceedingly nervous as you begin your speech, don't say something like, "I'm so nervous this morning, my hands are shaking." Probably your audience hadn't noticed; but as soon as you bring it to their attention, their eyes will immediately move to your shaking hands, thus creating a needless distraction and weakening your credibility.

Finally, the professional who is anxious about speaking in public should consider taking a public speaking course or joining Toastmasters International, the world's oldest and largest nonprofit educational organization. The purpose of Toastmasters is to improve the speaking skills of their members. They meet weekly or monthly and deliver prepared speeches, evaluate one another's oral presentations, give impromptu talks, develop their listening skills, conduct meetings, and learn parliamentary procedure.

Answering Questions

Plan your answers to possible questions ahead of time.

One advantage of oral presentations over written reports is the opportunity to engage in two-way communication. The question-and-answer session is a vital part of your presentation; plan for it accordingly.

Normally, you should announce at the beginning of your presentation that you will be happy to answer any questions when you're through. Holding questions until the end prevents you from being interrupted and losing your train of thought or possibly running out of time and not being able to complete your prepared remarks. Also, there is always the possibility that the listener's question will be answered in the course of your presentation.

The exception to a questions-at-the-end policy is when your topic is so complex that a listener's question must be answered immediately, so he or she can follow the rest of the presentation. Another exception is informal (and generally small) meetings, where questions and comments naturally occur throughout the presentation.

As you prepare your presentation, anticipate what questions you might expect from the audience. Make a list of them and think through possible answers. If necessary, make notes to refer to while answering. If your list of questions is very long, you should probably consider revising your presentation to incorporate some of the answers into your prepared remarks.

Always listen carefully to the question; repeat it, if necessary, for the benefit of the entire audience; and look at the entire audience as you answer—not just at the questioner. Treat each questioner with unfailing courtesy. If the question is antagonistic, be firm but fair and polite.

If you don't know the answer to a question, freely say so and promise to have the answer within a specific period. Then write down the question to remind yourself to find the answer later. Do not risk embarrassing another member of the audience by referring the question to him or her.

If your call for questions results in absolute silence, you may conclude either that you did a superb job of explaining your topic or that no one wishes to be the first to ask a question. If you suspect the latter, to break the ice, you might start the questions yourself, by saying something like, "One question I'm frequently asked that might interest you is . . ." Or you may ask the program chair ahead of time to be prepared to ask the first question if no one in the audience begins.

After the presentation is over and you're back in your office, evaluate your performance using the guidelines presented in Checklist 15 so that you can benefit from the experience. What seemed to work well and what not so well? Analyze each aspect of your performance—from initial research through delivery. Regardless of how well the presentation went, vow to improve your performance next time.

A chart used in a visual presentation must be at least twice as simple and four times as bold as one used in a report. It's the same as the distinction between a billboard that must be read and understood in the time you drive past it and a magazine advertisement that you can study in detail. (Gene Zelazny, *Say It with Charts: The Executive's Guide to Successful Presentations in the 1990s*, Second Edition, Business One Irwin, Homewood, IL, 1991, p. 5.)

OTHER BUSINESS PRESENTATIONS

In the standard type of business presentation discussed so far, you, the presenter, are the star of the show. Occasionally, you may be asked to participate in other types of presentations—ones in which you are a supporting player. Such situations include giving impromptu remarks, making introductions, and giving special recognitions. In addition, you may sometimes be asked to participate in collaborative or video presentations.

Impromptu Remarks

During the course of a meeting or in conjunction with another person's presentation, you may unexpectedly be asked to come to the podium to "say a few words about" or "bring us up to date on" some topic. In truth, most such situations are not completely unexpected; you can often predict when you may be called on and should prepare accordingly. (Remember the words of Mark Twain: "It takes three weeks to prepare a good impromptu speech.")

Anticipate and plan for situations when you may be asked to make impromptu remarks.

Do not be put off by the fact that you may sometimes prepare remarks that will never be given because you were not called on to speak. As a management strategy and as preparation for future speaking opportunities, it is helpful to review a situation and define your ideas about it.

If, in fact, you truly have no warning, stay calm. You would not have been called on unless you had something positive to contribute. Remember also that the audience knows you are giving impromptu remarks, so they won't expect the same polish as for a prepared presentation. There is no need to apologize. Keep to the topic, limiting your remarks to those areas

CHECKLIST 15

The Oral Presentation Process

PLANNING

1. Determine if an oral presentation will be more effective than a written report.
2. Determine your purpose: what response do you want from your audience?
3. Analyze your audience in terms of demographic factors, level of knowledge, and psychological needs.
4. If possible, schedule the presentation to permit adequate preparation and to avoid rushed periods for the audience.
5. Select an appropriate delivery method.

ORGANIZING

1. Brainstorm. Write down every point you think you might cover in the presentation.
2. Separate your notes into the opening, body, and ending. Gather additional data if needed.
3. Write an effective opening that introduces the topic, discusses the points you'll cover, and tells the audience what you hope will happen as a result of your presentation.
4. In the body, develop the points fully, giving background data, evidence, and examples.
   a. Organize the points logically.
   b. To maintain credibility, discuss any major negative points and be prepared to discuss any minor negative points.
   c. Pace the presentation of data to avoid presenting facts and figures too quickly.

in which you do have some expertise or insight, and speak for no more than a few minutes.

Introductions

Be gracious when introducing a speaker and keep the focus on the speaker.

When introducing a speaker, remember that the speaker is the main event—not you. All your remarks should be directed at welcoming the speaker and establishing his or her qualifications to speak on the topic. Avoid inserting your own opinions about the topic or speaking for too long, thereby cutting into the speaker's time.

Before the event, ask the speaker for a data sheet. Select from it those accomplishments that are particularly relevant to the current topic, add any personal asides such as hobbies or family information to show the speaker as human, and conclude with a statement such as, "We're delighted to have with us Ms. Jane Doe, who will now speak on the topic of . . . . Ms. Doe." Lead the applause as the speaker arises and also when he or she finishes speaking. Also open the question-and-answer session if there is one, and be prepared to ask the first question if no one else does. At the conclusion, extend sincere appreciation to the speaker.

If you are responsible for seating and introducing a head table, you and the speaker should be seated on either side of the podium, with the speaker at the immediate left as you face the audience and you, as master of ceremonies, at the immediate right side of the podium. When making the intro-

5. Finish on a strong, upbeat note by summarizing your main points, adding a personal appeal, drawing conclusions and making recommendations, discussing what needs to be done next, or using some other logical closing.
6. Use humor only when appropriate and only if you are effective at telling humorous stories.
7. Ensure that your visual aids are needed, simple, easily readable, and of the highest quality.

PRACTICING

1. Rehearse your presentation extensively, simulating the actual speaking conditions as much as possible and using your visual aids.
2. Use simple language and short sentences, with frequent preview, summary, transition, and repetition.
3. Stand tall and naturally, and speak in a loud, clear, enthusiastic, and friendly voice. Vary the rate and volume of your voice.
4. Use correct diction and appropriate gestures.

DELIVERING

1. Dress appropriately—in comfortable, businesslike, conservative clothing.
2. Use a microphone effectively.
3. Maintain eye contact with the audience, including all corners of the room in your gaze.
4. To avoid anxiety, practice extensively, develop a positive attitude, and concentrate on the friendly faces in the audience.
5. Plan your answers to possible questions ahead of time. Listen to each question carefully and address your answer to the entire audience.

ductions, indicate whether each person should stand when introduced or remain seated, and ask the audience to hold their applause until everyone has been introduced. Then introduce each person, saying a few appropriate remarks about each. Proceed from your extreme right to the podium and then from your extreme left to the podium.

The speaker should be at the immediate left of the podium as you face the audience, and the master of ceremonies at the immediate right.

Give similar types and amounts of information about each person and be sure that you pronounce everyone's name correctly. Be consistent in identifying each person—all first names or all personal titles and last names. When you get to the speaker (who will be your last introduction), introduce him or her in a similar manner, indicating that a more complete introduction will follow. Lead the applause when all have been introduced.

Special Recognitions

When presenting an award or recognizing someone for special achievement, first provide some background about the award—its history and the criteria for recipient selection. Then discuss the awardee's accomplishments, emphasizing those most relevant to the award. Under such happy circumstances, extensive praise is appropriate. Lead the applause as the awardee rises.

When accepting such an honor yourself, show genuine appreciation and graciously thank those responsible for the award. You may briefly

Business presentations sometimes involve demonstrations. Here Coffee Connection's Raymond Trevino instructs a group in the niceties of making steamed milk for specialty coffee drinks.The key to success in demonstrations is to know your equipment and to practice with it enough to be sure it will work as you expect.

thank those who helped in your accomplishments, but do not bore the audience by thanking a long list of people the audience may never have heard of.

Collaborative Presentations

Collaborative presentations are quite common for communicating about complex projects. For example, when presenting the organization's marketing plan to management or when updating the five-year plan, it is unlikely that any one person has the expertise or time to prepare the entire presentation. Instead, a cooperative effort would be most effective.

Collaborative presentations, whether written or oral, require extensive planning, close coordination, and a measure of maturity and goodwill. If you are responsible for coordinating such efforts, allow enough time and assign responsibilities based on individual talents and time constraints.

Make individual assignments for collaborative presentations based on individual strengths and preferences.

Your major criterion for making assignments is what division of duties will result in the most effective presentation. Some members may be better at collecting and analyzing the information to be presented, others may be better at developing the visual aids, and others may be better at delivering the presentation. Everyone need not share equally in each aspect of the project. As coordinator, you should ensure that all efforts are recognized publicly and equally during the actual presentation, regardless of how much "podium time" each person is assigned.

Just as people have different writing styles, they also have different speaking styles, and you must ensure that your overall presentation has coherence and unity—that it sounds as if it were prepared and given by one individual. Thus, the group members should decide beforehand the most appropriate tone, format, organization, style for visual aids, manner of dress, format for handling questions, and similar factors that will help the presentation flow smoothly from topic to topic and from speaker to speaker.

A full-scale rehearsal—in the room where the presentation will be made and using all visual aids—is crucial. If possible, it should be videotaped for later analysis by the entire group. Critiquing the performance of a colleague requires tact, empathy, and goodwill; and accepting such feedback requires grace and maturity. For the entire presentation to succeed, each individual element must also succeed. And if it does, each contributor shares in the success and any rewards that may result.

Video Presentations

Practice your video presentation using a camcorder and VCR.

Increasingly, organizations are videotaping not just rehearsals but the presentations themselves, which can then be shown on a television monitor using a videocassette recorder (VCR). For example, as part of an orientation program for new employees, the president of the organization may videotape a welcome speech and a personnel specialist may tape a presentation of employee benefits. Or a marketing manager may announce a new product via videotape to be sent to important customers and the news media around the country. In fact, any presentation that must be given many times is a candidate for videotaping.

Most of the same principles presented earlier apply equally to video presentations. In addition, peculiar effects may result from facing the camera because gazing into the eye of the camera for a long time is such an artificial situation. The only solution is to practice. Fortunately, handheld video camcorders and VCRs are now so common that you can practice easily in the comfort of your own home or office.

The best colors to wear are shades of blue; a light blue shirt or blouse with a blue jacket or blazer is ideal. Avoid contrasting colors and stripes. Makeup is recommended for both men and women to reduce sweat and even out skin tone. When recording, sit or stand straight and look into the camera as long as possible while talking. Always focus your eyes on one of two places—either directly at the camera or at your notes; never gaze off to the side or over the camera. Because television exaggerates movements, stand or sit as still as possible and keep gestures to a minimum.

MICROWRITING

A Business Presentation

THE PROBLEM

You are Matt Kromer, an information specialist at Lewis & Smith, a large import/export firm in San Francisco. Your company publishes three major external documents—a quarterly customer newsletter, a semiannual catalog, and an annual report. All three are currently prepared by an outside printing company. However, the decision was recently made to switch to some form of in-house publishing for these publications.

Your superior asked you to research the question of whether your firm should use word processing or desktop publishing software for these documents. You were asked to make a formal 20-minute presentation of your findings and recommendations to the firm's administrative committee.

THE PROCESS

1. What is the purpose of your presentation?

   To present the findings from my research, to recommend a type of software program, and to persuade the audience that my recommendation is sound.

2. Describe your audience.

   The administrative committee consists of the five managers (including my superior) who report to the vice president for administration. I have met them all, but with the exception of my own superior, I do not know any of them well.

   Their role will be to make the final decision regarding which type of software program to use. Once that decision has been made, the actual users will decide which brand to purchase. Four of the five managers are casual users of word processing software. They've all likely heard of desktop publishing but have never used it.

3. What type of presentation will be most appropriate?

   This will be a normal business presentation to a small audience, so I'll speak from notes and use transparencies. Because I have only 20 minutes to present, I'll hold off answering questions until the end–to make sure I have enough time to cover the needed information.

4. What kind of data have you collected for your presentation?

   I studied each publication's formatting requirements, analyzed the features of the most popular word processing (Final Word) and desktop publishing (Personal Editor®) programs, and spoke with a colleague from a firm that recently began publishing its documents in-house.

   Based on the criteria of cost, ease of use, and features, I'll recommend the use of word processing software to publish our three documents.

5. How will you organize the data?

   First I'll present the background information. Then I could organize my research data by presenting the advantages and disadvantages of each type of program. However, I think it would be more effective to organize my findings by criteria instead; that is, I will show how each program rates in terms of cost, ease of use, and features.

6. Outline an effective opening section for your presentation.

   a. <u>Introduction</u>: "Freedom of the Press" (Computer software now gives us the freedom to publish our own documents at lower cost and with greater flexibility.)
   b. <u>Purpose</u>: to recommend whether to use WP or DTP software
   c. <u>Organization</u>: by criteria (cost, ease of use, and features)
   d. <u>Audience role</u>: to make the final decision

7. How will you handle negative information?

   Although I'm recommending word processing software, the desktop publishing program has more features. However, I'll show that (a) we don't need those features and (b) those features make the program more difficult to learn.

8. What types of visual aids will you use?

   <u>Transparencies</u>

   - Two at the beginning—to preview the topic and to illustrate our three publications
   - Two in the middle—to compare the costs and features of the two programs
   - Two at the end—to give my recommendations and to show what needs to be done next

   <u>Handout</u>

   A one-page handout showing miniature copies of the six transparencies—as a summary of my important points and for future reference.

9. How will you practice your presentation?

   I'll do a dry run in the conference room where I'll be speaking, standing where I'll actually be giving the presentation and using my transparencies. I'll also set up a cassette recorder at the far end of the conference table to tape my practice presentation to ensure that I can be heard, to check for clarity and voice qualities, and to ensure that I'm within my time limits. I'll also practice answering any questions I think the managers might ask.

PRODUCT

Provides identifying information in the opening—in case of loss or for future reference.

Uses an attention-getting opening that is written verbatim for a stress-free start.

Uses the opening to give the purpose, preview the topics, and identify the audience's role.

Alerts the audience to prevent interrupting questions and unnecessary note taking.

Marks the transparency references for easy identification.

SELECTING DESKTOP PUBLISHING SOFTWARE

Presentation to the Administrative Committee
Matt Kromer, 10/3/--

I. **OPENING**

A. I'd like to talk to you today about freedom of the press—specifically about our recent decision to switch to in-house publishing. And though our publications won't be completely "free," in-house publishing will provide us with more flexibility—at a greatly reduced cost.

B. Purpose of presentation: to recommend whether to use word processing or desktop publishing software to publish our company newsletter, catalog, and annual report.

TRANSP 1 — FREEDOM OF THE PRESS

C. Organization:

1. Background information

2. Criteria for decision:
   a. Cost
   b. Ease of use
   c. Features

3. Recommendation

D. Your job: to make final decision regarding which type of software to support. You will not decide which brand of software; that decision will be left up to the users.

E. Will be happy to answer any questions at the conclusion of my remarks. Also have handout of my transparencies to distribute later.

II. **BODY**

TRANSP 2 — PUBLICATIONS

A. Background:

1. We publish 3 major external documents, all of which have strategic marketing value:

   a. Newsletter: *The Forum*, sent quarterly to 2,000 customers; 8 pp; 1-color (black) on ivory stock, with brown masthead; photos and line art.

   b. Catalog: semiannual; 36-42 pp; 1-color (black) interior with 4-color cover; 4,000 copies.

Grammar and Mechanics Notes Type the outline in large upper- and lowercase letters, either on individual note cards or on full sheets of paper. Leave plenty of white space (perhaps more than is shown here) between sections so that you won't lose your place.

2

c. Annual report: annual; 24-28 pp; 1-color (blue) interior on grey stock with 4-color cover; 1,500 copies.

2. All 3 presently prepared by Medallion Printing Co.

3. Research:

a. Analyzed each publication tô determine formatting requirements.

b. Analyzed features of Final Word, the WP program we presently support, and Personal Editor, the most popular DTP software program (other DTP programs have similar features).

c. Spoke with Paula Henning from Crown Busch; her co. began producing their documents in-house using DTP last year.

B. Criteria:

TRANSP 3 — COST COMPARISON

1. Cost:

a. Either program will require
   (1) Font cartridge for each laser printer: cost—$195 ea.
   (2) One flatbed scanner and software to be shared by all: cost—$1,450.

b. Final Word: $595 list; $475 mail order. But we already own.

c. Personal Editor: $795 list; $595 mail order; cost for 3 copies—$1,785.

d. Conclusion: Personal Editor costs $1,800 more than Final Word.

2. Ease of use:

a. Final Word:
   (1) Operators already know how to use because they use it every day for routine typing.
   (2) 1/2 day seminar must be developed to teach advanced features needed for DTP (taught by local community college faculty member); cost—$500.

b. Personal Editor:
   (1) Difficult to learn to use because of its many features. However, once learned, many features are easier to implement than on Final Word.
   (2) Danger of forgetting and having to relearn because Personal Editor will be used infrequently.
   (3) Would need to send 3 primary users to 1-week seminar sponsored by Personal Editor at their Denver headquarters; cost—$450 tuition each plus travel, room, and board; estimated total cost—$3,750.

c. Considering all costs, Personal Editor costs 3 times more than Final Word—$5,000 difference.

Discusses research procedures to help establish credibility.

Organizes the main part of the speech body by the criteria used for making the decision.

Presents both positive and negative information and discusses the importance and implications of each feature.

Grammar and Mechanics Notes You do not have to write your presentation notes in parallel format; no one will see them but you. You may need complete sentences to jog your memory for some parts but only partial sentences, individual words, or abbreviations for other parts. Underline important points for easy referral.

3

TRANSP 4 — FEATURE COMPARISON

3. Features:

   a. Font flexibility: both have.

   b. Column feature: both have.

   c. Import/manipulate graphics: both have; Personal Editor has more options.

   d. Horizontal and vertical rules: both have; Personal Editor has more options.

   e. Color separations: Personal Editor has; Final Word does not (don't need now; maybe in the future).

   f. Predesigned templates: both have; Personal Editor permits more elaborate designs (not needed).

   g. Ease of revisions (important criterion): both allow, but easier in Final Word (which has full WP features).

III. CLOSING

Puts the final recommendation and the rationale on transparency—for emphasis.

TRANSP 5 — RECOMMENDATION

A. Recommendation: Final Word

   1. Cheaper
   2. Easier to use/less training needed
   3. Has all the features we presently need

TRANSP 6 — SCHEDULE

B. Schedule:

Today:	Make decision regarding software
November:	Purchase and install hardware and software
December:	Conduct user training
January:	Begin producing 3 documents in-house

Closes by giving the recommendation and telling what happens next. Ends on a confident, forward-looking note.

C. Conclusion:

Our entry into desktop publishing is an exciting project because it gives us greater control over our publications at less cost. In addition, DTP will open up opportunities for even more publishing projects in the future to help us better fulfill our corporate mission.

HANDOUT — SELECTING DESKTOP PUBLISHING SOFTWARE

Follows presentation by a question-and-answer session.

IV. QUESTIONS

Grammar and Mechanics Notes You would no doubt have to insert some last-minute handwritten changes in your final outline prior to actually giving the presentation.

Selecting Desktop Publishing Software

Presention to the Administrative Committee
Matt Kromer, October 3, 19--

Freedom of the Press

1. Background
2. Criteria
   - Cost
   - Ease of Use
   - Features
3. Recommendation

Transparency 1

Publications

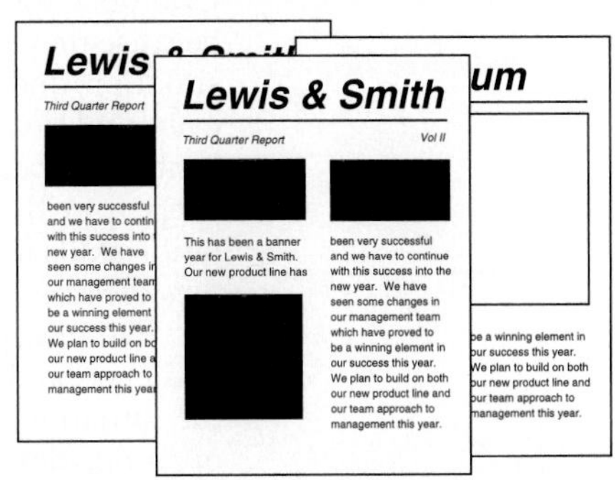

Transparency 2

Cost Comparison

	Word Proc.	Desktop Pub.
Font Cartridge	585	585
Scanner	1,450	1,450
Software	—	1,785
	2,035	3,620
Training	500	3,750
TOTAL	2,535	7,570

Transparency 3

Feature Comparison

	Word Proc.	Desktop Pub.
Fonts	Good	Good
Columns	Yes	Yes
Graphics	Good	Excellent
Rules	Good	Excellent
Color	No	Yes
Templates	Good	Excellent
Revisions	Excellent	Fair

Transparency 4

Recommendation: Word Processing

- Costs $5,000 less
- Is easier to use
- Requires less training
- Includes all needed features

Transparency 5

Schedule

Today	*Make decision*
November	*Purchase and install*
December	*Conduct user training*
January	*Begin publishing*

Transparency 6

SUMMARY

Oral business presentations are a vital part of the contemporary organization because they provide immediate feedback, give the presenter full control of the situation, and require less audience effort than do written presentations. However, oral presentations are also impermanent and expensive, and the speaker-controlled pace means that some people in the audience may not be able to keep up with the flow of information. Managers need to develop their presentation skills in order to take advantage of these strengths and to minimize these weaknesses.

Planning the presentation requires determining the purpose, analyzing the audience, and planning the timing and method of presentation appropriate for the situation. Organizing the presentation requires developing an effective opening, developing each point logically in the middle, and closing on a strong, confident note. Visual aids should be relevant, simple, easily readable, and of high quality. Practice your presentation as much as necessary. When actually delivering the presentation, dress appropriately, speak in a clear and confident manner, and maintain eye contact with the audience. Evaluate your performance afterward to ensure that your presentation skills improve with each opportunity to speak.

Other common types of oral presentations in business include impromptu remarks, introductions, and special recognitions. In addition to giving individual presentations before a live audience, managers frequently give collaborative presentations and occasionally may be called on to make a video presentation.

REVIEW AND DISCUSSION

The answers to the review and discussion questions appear in the *Instructor's Resource Manual*, beginning on p. 267.

For an exercise on matching terms, refer students to the *Study Guide*, p. 181.

1. **Communication at Compaq Revisited** ■ Before Jim Garrity of Compaq makes a business presentation to people outside his own organization, he thinks about the audience's level of sophistication, areas of interest, and familiarity with computer jargon. He also thinks about the visual aids he will use; often his choice is electronic projection of computer images during a speech.
   a. What are the advantages and disadvantages of revising computerized visual aids right up to the start of the presentation?
   b. Why would Garrity choose to read his speech if he expects to be quoted by the media?
   c. How might an unusual presentation title affect Garrity's audience before and during the presentation?
2. What are the advantages and disadvantages of oral presentations as opposed to written reports?
3. Identify and give an example of each of the four principal purposes of oral presentations.
4. Give an example of a business situation in which it would be appropriate to deliver a presentation (a) by reading the speech and (b) by speaking from notes.
5. What types of information should be presented in the opening section of a presentation?
6. List six possible plans for organizing the body of a presentation.
7. What types of humor are appropriate in a business presentation, and under what circumstances should humor be used?

8. What criteria should be used for deciding to use visual aids in a business presentation?
9. What are the specific advantages of using transparencies, 35-mm slides, and handouts for a business presentation?
10. What type of language is most appropriate for business presentations?
11. What voice qualities are important when presenting business information orally?
12. What are some effective strategies for dealing with stage fright?
13. Why is it best to delay audience questions until the end of a presentation? Under what circumstances is this strategy not recommended?
14. Explain the meaning of Mark Twain's observation that "It takes three weeks to prepare a good impromptu speech."
15. What special considerations must be addressed when preparing a collaborative presentation?

EXERCISES

1. Microwriting a Proposal Presentation ▪

PROBLEM

Review Exercise 1 of Chapter 10 (page 319), in which the Hospitality Services Association at your university proposes to start University Hosts, a business that would provide hospitality services for campus visitors. Assume that you have been given 10 minutes to present your proposal orally to the President's Council at your institution.

PROCESS

a. What is the purpose of your presentation?
b. Describe your audience.
c. What type of delivery would be most appropriate—reading, memorizing, or speaking from notes?
d. Because of the importance of both the topic and the audience, you decide to write in full your opening remarks. Write a 1- to 1½-minute opening section for your presentation. Include an attention-getter.
e. Outline the topics you will discuss and the order in which you will discuss them. Be sure to include reader benefits.
f. Write a 1- to 1½-minute closing section for your presentation.
g. Prepare rough drafts of the transparencies you will use for your presentation.

PRODUCT

Prepare (a) a complete presentation outline, including where the transparencies will be used and (b) final paper copies of the transparencies for the presentation.

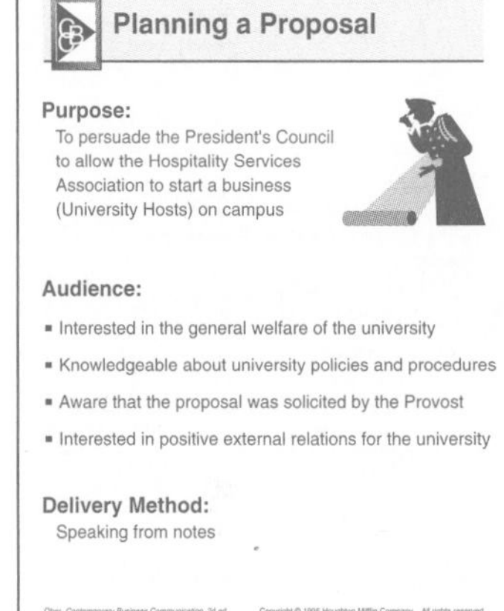

Planning a Proposal
Purpose:
To persuade the President's Council to allow the Hospitality Services Association to start a business (University Hosts) on campus
Audience:
▪ Interested in the general welfare of the university
▪ Knowledgeable about university policies and procedures
▪ Aware that the proposal was solicited by the Provost
▪ Interested in positive external relations for the university
Delivery Method:
Speaking from notes
Ober, *Contemporary Business Communication*, 2d ed.
Copyright © 1995 Houghton Mifflin Company. All rights reserved.

See Master 14.1, Exercise 1, Microwriting, in the *Instructor's Resource Manual.*

Exercise 1 is linked with Exercise 1 in Chapter 10. Sample solutions for Exercises 1–11 appear in the *Instructor's Resource Manual*, pp. 269–272.

2. Understanding the Role of Business Presentations ▪

Interview two business people in your community who hold positions in your area of interest to learn more about their experiences in making oral presentations. Write a memorandum to your instructor summarizing what you've learned. You may want to ask such questions as the following:

a. How important has the ability to make effective oral presentations been to your career?
b. What kinds of oral presentations do you make in and out of the office and how often?

c. How do you typically prepare for them?
d. What kinds of audiovisual aids do you use?

3. **Evaluating a Presentation** ■ Attend a presentation given by a business person, perhaps a speaker at an event sponsored by a campus business organization or one of the business or professional organizations in your community. Critique the speaker's presentation in light of what you've learned in this chapter, and submit a memorandum report to your instructor.
4. **Planning a Presentation** ■ You decided at the last minute to apply to the graduate school at your institution to work toward an MBA degree. Even though you have a 3.4 GPA (on a 4.0 scale), you were denied admission because you had not taken the GMAT, which is a prerequisite for admission. You have, however, been given 10 minutes to appear before the Graduate Council to try to convince them to grant you a temporary waiver of this requirement and permit you to enroll in MBA classes next term, during which time you will take the GMAT. The Graduate Council consists of the director of the MBA program and two senior faculty members, one of whom is your business communication professor.
   a. What is the purpose of your presentation?
   b. What do you know or what can you surmise about your audience that might help you prepare a more effective presentation?
   c. What considerations affect the timing of your presentation?
   d. What method of delivery should you use?

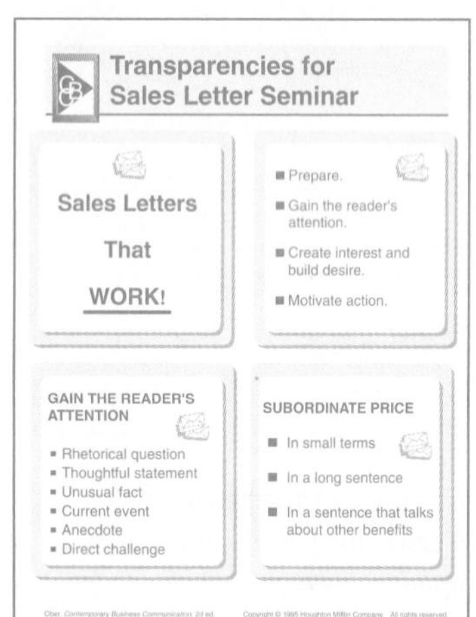

See Master 14.2, Exercise 5, Planning the Visual Element, in the *Instructor's Resource Manual.*

5. **Planning the Visual Element** ■ You are the trainer for an in-house survey course in effective advertising techniques that is being offered to franchise owners of your Mexican fast-food chain. As part of the course, you are scheduled to present a 30-minute session on writing effective sales letters; and you decide to use the sales-letter section of Chapter 7 in this text (beginning on page 194) as the basis for your presentation.

   Prepare four to six transparency masters that you might use for your presentation to the 25 participants. Submit full-sized photocopies of the transparencies (rather than the transparencies themselves) to your instructor.
6. **Presenting Research Data** ■ Review the analytical or recommendation report you prepared in Chapter 13. Assume that you have been given 15 minutes to present the important information from your written report to a committee of your superiors who will not have an opportunity to read the written report.
   a. Write your presentation notes, using either full sheets of paper or note cards.
   b. Develop four to six overhead transparencies to use during your presentation.
   c. Practice your presentation several times—at least once in the classroom where you will actually give it.
   d. Give your presentation to the class.

   Your instructor may ask the audience to evaluate each presentation in terms of the effectiveness of its content, use of visual aids, and delivery.
7. **Presenting Narrative Information** ■ Locate two journal articles on some aspect of business communication (the topics in the table of contents of this text will provide clues for searching). The two articles should be about the same topic. Integrate the important information from both articles, and present your findings to the class in a 5-minute presentation. Include at least one visual aid in your presentation. Prepare a one-page

abstract that synthesizes the important information from both articles, and distribute it as a handout to the class after your presentation. Submit to your instructor (a) a photocopy of each article, (b) a copy of your presentation notes, (c) a copy of your visual aids, and (d) a copy of your handout.

8. **Presenting Negative Information** ■ Your library should have copies of the latest annual reports from many Fortune 500 companies. Select an annual report from a company that lost money last year. Assuming the role of that company's CEO, prepare and give a 10-minute presentation designed for a breakfast meeting of the New York Investment Council, a group made up of institutional investors and large private investors. Your purpose is to persuade the audience that your organization is still a good investment. Assume that the audience will have already seen a copy of your annual report. Select two visual aids contained in the annual report and simplify them as necessary for use in your oral presentation.
9. **Collaborative Presentation** ■ Divide into groups of four or five students per team. Your instructor will assign you to either the pro or con side for one of the following topics:

   - Drug testing should/should not be mandatory for all employees.
   - All forms of smoking should/should not be banned completely from the workplace.
   - Employers should/should not provide flextime (flexible working hours) for all office employees.
   - Employers should/should not provide on-site child-care facilities for the preschool children of their employees.
   - Employees who deal extensively with the public should/should not be required to wear a company uniform.
   - Employers should/should not have the right to hire the most qualified employees without regard to affirmative action guidelines.

   Assume that your employee group has been asked to present its views to a management committee that will make the final decision regarding your topic. The presentations will be given as follows:

   a. Each side (beginning with the pro side) will have 8 minutes to present its views.
   b. Each side will then have 3 minutes to confer.
   c. Each side (beginning with the con side) will have a 2-minute rebuttal—to refute the arguments and answer the issues raised by the other side.
   d. Each side (beginning with the pro side) will have a 1-minute summary.
   e. The management committee (the rest of the class) will then vote by secret ballot regarding which side (pro or con) presented its case most effectively.

   Gather whatever data you feel will be helpful to your case, organize it, prepare suitable visual aids, and divide up the speaking roles as you deem best. (*Hint:* It might be helpful to gather information on both the pro and con sides of the issue in preparation for the rebuttal session, which will be given impromptu.)
10. **Presenting to an International Audience** ■ The west coast manager of Honda has approached your school of business about the possibility of sending 30 of its Japanese managers to your institution to pursue a three-month intensive course in written and oral business communication. The

purpose of the course is to make the Japanese managers better able to interact with their American counterparts.

You, the assistant provost at your institution, have been asked to give a 6- to 8-minute presentation to the four Japanese executives who will decide whether to fund this program at your institution. The purpose of your presentation is to convince them to select your school.

Because of the care with which you will want to select your wording for this international audience and because of the high stakes involved, you decide to prepare a full script of your presentation (approximately 1,000 words), along with several overhead transparencies. Submit your script and transparency masters to your instructor.

11. **Evaluating Your Oral Communication Skills** ▪ Arrange to have videotaped one of the oral presentations that you prepared and delivered for this chapter. (Either use your institution's audiovisual services or have a colleague videotape your presentation using a personal camcorder.) Review the tape and evaluate your performance, using each of the criteria given in Checklist 15 (pages 478–479).

    Prepare a memorandum to your instructor in which you objectively discuss the strengths and weaknesses of your presentation. Your grade for this assignment will be based on your *evaluation* of your presentation—not on the presentation itself. Submit both the videotape and the memorandum to your instructor.

A possible solution to the Continuing Case is described in the *Instructor's Resource Manual*, p. 272.

CONTINUING CASE 14

The Typists Who Lost Their Touch

Review the Continuing Case presented at the ends of Chapters 11, 12, and 13. As you recall, in response to increasing sick-leave among data-entry personnel, Jean Tate asked Pat Robbins to write a report on carpal tunnel syndrome, a neuromuscular wrist injury caused by repeated hand motions such as in typing. Assume the role of Pat Robbins. You have now been asked to present the results of your research in a 20-minute session to the executive committee, composed of Dave Kaplan and the three vice presidents. This is your first opportunity to speak to this high-ranking group, and the speech is on a topic about which you've developed strong feelings over the past few months as you've researched the topic in depth.

Critical Thinking

1. Analyze your audience. Specifically, what do you know (or what can you learn) about each of the executive committee members that will affect your presentation?
2. How will your strong feelings about this topic affect your presentation—either positively or negatively?

Speaking/Writing Projects

Prepare as many of the following projects as assigned by your instructor. (*Note:* If you did not conduct any primary research for this project, base your presentation on secondary data.)

3. Write your presentation notes, using either full sheets of paper or note cards.
4. Develop five to eight overhead transparencies to use during your presentation.
5. Arrange to have a full-scale practice session of your presentation videotaped. Evaluate your taped practice session in light of the guidelines presented in this chapter. Prepare a memo to your instructor critiquing your performance. Submit both your memo and the videotape.
6. Divide into groups of five students, with each student in turn giving his or her presentation to the other four. Each presenter should conduct a question-and-answer session immediately after each presentation. Be prepared to ask a question of the presenter and to answer any questions directed to you when you present. Prepare a memo to your instructor critiquing the performance of each presenter.

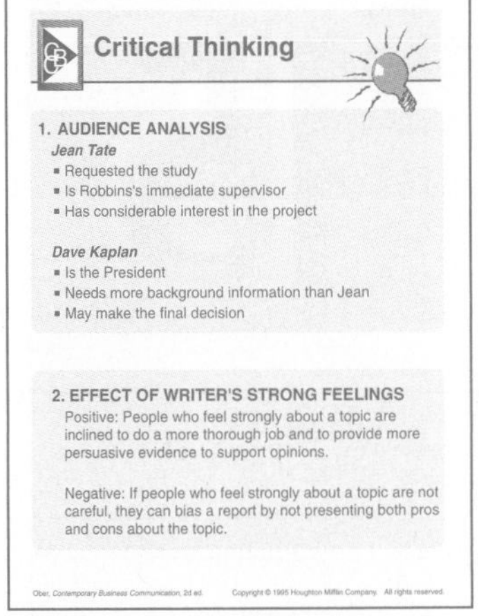

See Master 14.3, Continuing Case 14, in the *Instructor's Resource Manual.*

WORDWISE *Word Puzzles*

1. Rearrange the following letters to make one long word: *D O O R N O L N W E G*
2. Can you use the same seven consecutive letters in the same sequence three times in a sentence and not repeat yourself?
3. What do you get when you break the language barrier?

Answers: 1. *one long word;* 2. *The NOTABLE surgeon was NOT ABLE to operate because she had NO TABLE;* 3. a phonic boom.

CHAPTER

15

Other Types of Nonwritten Communication

Communication Objectives

After you have finished this chapter, you should be able to

1. Communicate effectively in small groups.
2. Plan and conduct a business meeting.
3. Listen effectively in business situations.
4. Use effective techniques for conducting business via the telephone.
5. Dictate business messages.
6. Use etiquette to maintain effective working relationships.

Need a decision? Call a meeting. That's the advice of Amy Hilliard-Jones, senior vice president and director of integrated marketing services for Burrell Communications Group in Chicago. Burrell is a marketing communications firm that helps clients such as Procter & Gamble, Kmart, McDonald's, Coca-Cola, and L'Eggs develop advertising, promotion, and public relations programs to reach out to the African-American consumer.

Although organizations hold meetings for a variety of reasons, one of the most important reasons is to come to a decision. "Face-to-face meetings expedite decisions," Hilliard-Jones noted. "Many times, if you have the right people at the meeting, you can get a decision right away."

When a meeting is called, the leader should let people know why they are sitting down together. "Every meeting should have a purpose, a strategy, and some sort of desired outcome. Otherwise a meeting will be a waste of time," she said. "It helps people focus their thoughts if you tell them in a sentence or two why they are there. If you send an agenda in advance showing who is responsible for each topic to be covered, this is a signal that participants should come to the meeting prepared to provide the needed information."

An agenda can also be a useful tool for directing a meeting. "I go over the objective at the beginning of the meeting, then I use the agenda to keep people on track," Hilliard-Jones explained. "Meetings tend to evolve, but the leader can bring people back to the desired focus as long as an agenda was established up front."

The Burrell executive often uses brainstorming as a way to stimulate creativity in a problem-solving meeting. "If you start by saying, 'There is no right answer,' people will be encouraged to contribute their ideas. By doing so, you get many more options to choose from. You can't be too specific in a brainstorming session because then you might not get the kind of 'out-of-the-box' thinking that often is the clue to the solution."

Amy Hilliard-Jones

Director of integrated marketing services, Burrell Communications Group, Chicago

Once a meeting is over, the leader is responsible for communicating the results. At Burrell, key meetings are summarized in a synopsis that outlines the decisions made. When the meeting includes only Burrell personnel, the synopsis is sent to the participants and to managers who need to be informed about actions taken on specific issues. When the meeting includes clients, the summary is sent to a designated person on the client side, who in turn distributes copies as needed to others in the client organization.

Hilliard-Jones attends at least two—and as many as six—meetings on any given day. As a leader and a participant, she understands the value of listening. "Sometimes it's difficult to listen without having your response percolating in your mind, but you need to clear your mind and concentrate on what the other person is saying," she said. "Not interrupting is one of the best listening techniques because speakers know they will have the opportunity to finish their thoughts. And before answering with an opinion that's different, you should acknowledge what the other person has said. If you don't acknowledge other people's viewpoints, then they're not going to listen to you."

In Chapter 14 we discussed oral presentations. As important as such presentations are, most managers spend more of their time communicating in other ways, such as communicating in small groups, participating in business meetings, listening, using the telephone, and dictating messages. To be effective at such tasks and to maintain effective working relationships, managers must communicate in a polite and appropriate manner. These important topics—communicating in small groups, conducting a business meeting, listening, using the telephone, dictating, and behaving appropriately and politely in the business environment—are introduced in this chapter.

A chapter overview appears in the *Instructor's Resource Manual*, pp. 273–277.

SMALL-GROUP COMMUNICATION

Regardless of the size of the organization, members must periodically divide into small groups to accomplish some objective. Small groups range from one-time, on-the-spot meetings to permanent committees. Some of the more common types of small-group sessions are as follows:

Even in large organizations or large departments, workers tend to come together in small groups to accomplish their goals.

- *Operating groups:* Operating groups are the more or less permanent committees within the organization that meet periodically to give and receive information, consult, and reach decisions. Members typically see such groups as

For more on small-group communication, see Video Case Study 1, Chiat/Day.

very important to success in their present jobs and future promotions. Whether members typically seek to enhance organizational goals or their own personal goals is, to a large extent, determined by the type of communication climate that exists in the organization.

- *Negotiating groups:* Negotiating groups are formed when two groups in conflict meet to work out an agreement. An obvious example is the labor-management team that meets to develop a new contract. The communication climate in such groups may be quite staged, with each side sometimes trying to mislead, confuse, or bluff the other. Also, members may use such nonverbal tactics as a "poker face" or simulated anger to gain advantage.
- *Creative groups:* Brainstorming sessions are sometimes called to dream up creative ideas and novel solutions. Here, the communication environment encourages freewheeling ideas, with no criticism of ideas being allowed. The quantity of ideas generated, rather than their quality, is emphasized.
- *Training groups:* In-house training sessions are held to help members become more proficient at their jobs. The training leader should encourage an atmosphere of openness, encouraging questions and soliciting frequent feedback to ensure that the members are following the instruction. A supportive communication environment is necessary to motivate participation and encourage learning.
- *Ad hoc groups:* The Latin term *ad hoc* means "for this special purpose." An ad hoc group is formed to carry out a temporary, special purpose. It may meet once or several times, but it is not a permanent group. Because the group is temporary, there is no team spirit or established way of doing things, and members are usually willing to accept imposed leadership and direction for the short duration of the group.

Guidelines for Communicating in Small Groups

The following guidelines will help you achieve your communication goals when communicating collaboratively.

If the group is too large, group members begin to form cliques, or subgroups.

Select an Appropriate Group Size Two to seven members seems to be the maximum size range for effective work groups. Small-group research indicates that five is an ideal size.[1] Smaller groups often do not have enough diversity of skills and interests to function effectively as a group, whereas larger groups may lack healthy group interaction because just a few people dominate the discussions.

Develop a Team Spirit It is difficult to work effectively as a group if the group members do not know each other well and are not aware of each other's strengths and weaknesses, styles of working, experiences, attitudes, and the like. Thus, the first task of most new groups is to get to know one another.

For small groups to function effectively, not only the task dimension but also the social dimension must be considered. Some amount of "small talk" about family, friends, current happenings, and the like before and

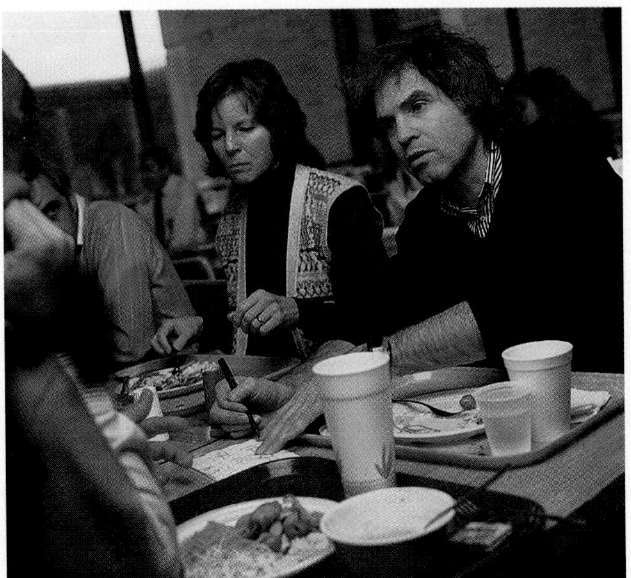

Small group communication happens throughout an organization—both formally and informally. At Bell Labs, Horst Stormer believes that lunchtime exchanges can spark creative ideas.

after the meetings is natural and helps to establish a supportive and open environment.

Some companies find less formal meetings valuable. For example, Du Pont executives have regular, informal talks with managers to set personal growth goals and to focus on a path to attain them. Suggestions might include management training or volunteer work.

Avoid "Groupthink" Although group cohesiveness is a necessary condition for successful small-group communication, too much cohesiveness can result in what has been termed **groupthink,** the barrier to communication that results from an overemphasis on unity, which stifles opposing ideas and the free flow of information.[2] When groupthink emerges, the pressure to conform is so great that negative information and contrary viewpoints are never even aired and discussed. Thus, the group loses the advantage of hearing and considering varying perspectives. In effective small-group communications, conflicts, different opinions, and questions are considered an inevitable and essential part of the collaborative process.

Deal with Conflict Constructively It is pointless and counterproductive to try to avoid conflict in small-group communication. Indeed, one purpose of collaborating on a project is to ensure that various viewpoints are heard so that a consensus as to the most appropriate course of action can emerge. Thus, conflict is a necessary part of the collaborative experience. If the group has worked to develop cohesiveness, to build a team spirit or "groupness," it will be able to deal with disagreements as they arise.

Competent communicators welcome all contributions from group members, regardless of whether the members agree or disagree with their own views. They evaluate each contribution objectively and respond in a nonthreatening manner, with comments that are factual, constructive, and goal-oriented. If the atmosphere becomes tense, they make a light comment, laugh, compliment, recall previous incidents, or take other helpful actions to defuse the situation and move the group forward. If conflict appears to be developing into a more or less permanent part of the group discussions, the group should put the topic of conflict on its agenda and

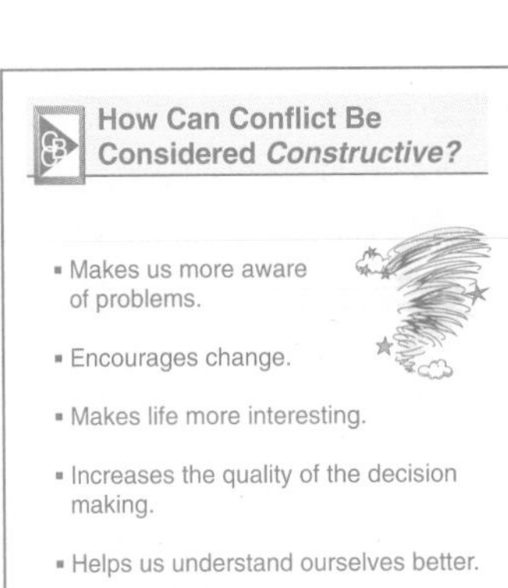

How Can Conflict Be Considered *Constructive?*
• Makes us more aware of problems.
• Encourages change.
• Makes life more interesting.
• Increases the quality of the decision making.
• Helps us understand ourselves better.
• Increases our self-confidence.

See Transparency 15.1, How Can Conflict Be Considered *Constructive?*

then devote sufficient meeting time to discussing and working through the conflict.

Groups should avoid the temptation to resolve conflicts by making a scapegoat out of one member—for example, "We'd be finished with this report now if Sam had done his part; you never can depend on him." Rarely is one person solely responsible for the success or failure of a group effort. Because every member's role is a function of both his or her own personality and the group's personality, the group should consider how to help the person contribute more to the collaborative efforts. Figure 15.1 provides guidelines for dealing with nonproductive group members.

The Ethical Dimension of Small-Group Communication

Concentrate on group goals rather than individual goals.

Accepting membership in a group implies acceptance of certain standards of ethical behavior. One of the most basic of these is to put the good of the group ahead of personal gain. Just as the successful ball player adopts the tenet "I don't care if I score so long as my team wins," so also should the successful team player in the organization adopt the attitude "I don't care who gets the credit so long as we achieve our goal." Group members should set aside hidden agendas in their group actions and avoid advocating positions that might benefit them personally but that would not be best for the group.

Group members also have an ethical responsibility to respect the integrity and emotional needs of one another. Everyone's ideas should be treated with respect, and no action should be taken that results in a loss of self-esteem for a member.

Finally, each member has an ethical responsibility to promote the group's welfare—by contributing his or her best efforts to the group's mission and by refraining from destructive gossip, domination of meetings, and other counterproductive actions.

BUSINESS MEETINGS

Effective managers know how to run and participate in business meetings.

For more on business meetings, see Video Case Study 4, Chemical Bank.

Meetings serve a wide variety of purposes in the organization. They keep members informed of events related to carrying out their duties; they provide a forum for soliciting input, solving problems, and making decisions; and they promote unity and cohesiveness among the members through social interaction.

Considering these important purposes, it is not surprising that as many as 20 million meetings take place each day in America. The average executive spends 25% to 70% of his or her day in meetings—and considers about a third of them to be unproductive. No wonder, then, many managers complain that "meetingitis" has become a national plague in American business. The typical American business meeting is a staff meeting held in a company conference room for just under two hours and has no written agenda distributed in advance.[3]

FIGURE 15.1 Solving Problems in Small Groups

If a Group Member Creates a Problem

Symptoms	Reasons	What to do
Member won't participate.	Excessive primary tension. Feels lack of acceptance and status.	Involve him in conversation. Find out about his personal interests. Listen with interest to what he says. Devote some time to him outside the discussion. When he does take part, make a special note of it. "That is a good point, Joe. We haven't been hearing enough from you. We appreciate hearing your position." Use questions to draw him out. Ask a direct, open-ended question so that only he can answer. Do not use a question that can be answered "yes" or "no," and, of course, do not ask a question that he might be unable to answer for lack of information.
Member is joker, life of the party.	Feels tension, wants to relieve it. Enjoys spotlight and likes to get laughs.	Encourage him when tensions need release. Laugh; compliment his wit. Ignore him when it is time to go to work and tensions are eased. He will soon learn that his role is the productive releaser of tensions and that he must not waste time laughing it up when the group should be discussing.
Member monopolizes discussion.	(a) Is involved in a role struggle. Is trying to impress group to achieve high status or leadership.	(a) Encourage her if she is contending for a role that will benefit the group the most. If not, interrupt her and move to another discussant. In general, encourage the group to take care of her. OR
	(b) Is full of the subject and is sincerely eager to get to work.	(b) Don't embarrass him or be sarcastic. You will need him in this role later. Do not let him monopolize or give long speeches. Interrupt politely and throw the ball to another discussant with a question.
Member is argumentative, obstinate.	(a) Involved in role struggle.	(a) Keep your own temper. Understand she is not inherently obstinate but is so in the context of this discussion. Don't let the group get too tense and excited. Antagonism breeds further antagonism and secondary tension. Remember, the group is partly responsible for her behavior. What can the group do to change it? OR
	(b) Has strong personal convictions on topic.	(b) Examine his position carefully. Find merit in it if possible. Do not close your mind to the ideas just because they are expressed in an opinionated way. The group must examine all sides. In an emergency, tell him time is short and you will be glad to talk to him later. Talk to him privately before the next meeting. Explain that his view is important, the group will consider it, but he must not destroy group effectiveness.

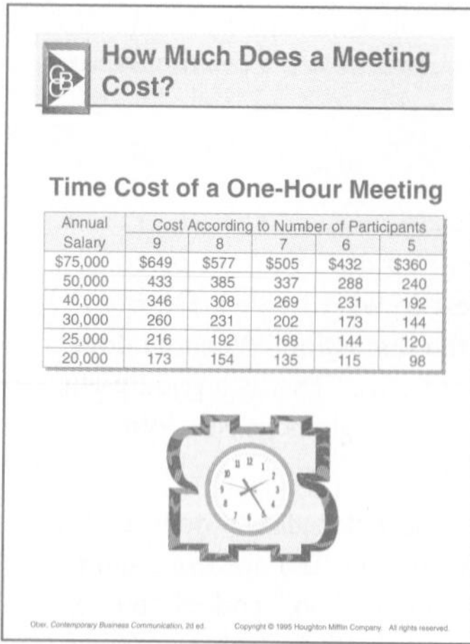

How Much Does a Meeting Cost?

Time Cost of a One-Hour Meeting

Annual Salary	Cost According to Number of Participants				
	9	8	7	6	5
$75,000	$649	$577	$505	$432	$360
50,000	433	385	337	288	240
40,000	346	308	269	231	192
30,000	260	231	202	173	144
25,000	216	192	168	144	120
20,000	173	154	135	115	98

Ober, *Contemporary Business Communication*, 2d ed.

See Transparency 15.2, Time Cost of a One-Hour Meeting.

The ability to conduct and participate in meetings is a crucial managerial skill. One survey of more than 2,000 business leaders showed that executives who run a meeting well are perceived to be better managers by both their superiors and their peers.[4]

To use meetings as an effective managerial tool, you need to know not only how to run them but also when to call them and how to follow up afterward. Like so many decisions you will have to make about communication, your choices will be guided by what you hope to accomplish.

Planning the Meeting

When you add up the hourly salaries and fringe benefits of those planning and attending a meeting, the cost can be considerable. Managers must make sure they're getting their money's worth from a meeting, and that guarantee requires careful planning: identifying the purpose and determining whether a meeting is in fact necessary, preparing an agenda, deciding who should attend, and planning the logistics.

Identifying Your Purpose The first step is always to determine your purpose. The more specific you can be, the better results you will get. A purpose such as "to discuss how to make our marketing representatives more effective" is vague and therefore not as helpful as "to decide whether to purchase cellular phones for our marketing representatives." The more focused your purpose, the easier it will be to select a means of accomplishing that purpose.

First, determine if a meeting is the best way to accomplish your goal.

Determining Whether a Meeting Is Necessary Sometimes meetings are not the most efficient means of communication. For example, a short memo or E-mail message is more efficient than a face-to-face meeting to communicate routine information. Similarly, it doesn't make sense to use the weekly staff meeting of ten people to hold a long discussion involving only one or two of the members. A phone call or smaller meeting would accomplish that task quicker and at less cost.

However, alternative means of conveying or securing information often present their own problems. Some people don't read written messages carefully or they interpret them differently. Time is lost in transmitting and responding to written messages. And information may be garbled as it moves from person to person and from level to level.

An agenda helps focus the attention of both the leader and the participants.

Preparing an Agenda Once you've established your specific purpose, you need to consider in more detail what topics the meeting will cover and in what order. This list of topics, or **agenda,** will accomplish two things: (1) it will help you prepare for the meeting by showing what background information you'll need, and (2) it will help you run the meeting by keeping you focused on your topic.

Knowing what topics will be discussed will also help those attending the meeting to plan for the meeting effectively—reviewing needed documents, bringing pertinent records, deciding what questions need to be raised, and the like. The survey of 2,000 business leaders mentioned earlier revealed that three-fourths of the managers consider agendas to be essential for efficient meetings; yet nearly half the meetings they attended are *not* accompanied by written agendas.[5]

Formal, recurring business meetings might follow an agenda like this one; of course, not every meeting will contain all these elements:

1. Call to order
2. Roll call (if necessary)
3. Reading and approval of minutes of previous meeting (if necessary)
4. Reports of officers and standing committees
5. Reports of special committees
6. Unfinished business
7. New business
8. Announcements
9. Program
10. Adjournment

Each item to be covered under these headings should be identified, including the speaker (if other than the chair), for example:

7. NEW BUSINESS
   a. Review of December 3 press conference
   b. Recommendation for annual charitable contribution
   c. Status of remodeling—Jan Fischer

Everyone at the meetings should have a direct reason for being there.

Deciding Who Should Attend A great number of ad hoc meetings take place each business day for the purpose of solving a specific problem. If you must decide who will attend a particular meeting, your first concern is how the participants relate to your purpose. Who will make the decision? Who will implement the decision? Who can provide needed background information? On the one hand, you want to include all who can contribute to solving the problem; on the other, you want to keep the meeting to a manageable number of people.

Consider also how the potential group members differ in status within the organization, in knowledge about the issue, in communication skills, and in personal relationships. The greater the differences, the more difficult it will be to involve everyone in a genuine discussion aimed at solving the problem.

Don't underestimate the impact of hidden agendas on the part of potential group members. If any member's personal goals for the meeting differ from the group goals, conflicts can arise and the quality of the resulting decisions can be impaired. Meeting separately with some of the important participants ahead of time might help to identify sources of potential problems and provide clues for dealing with them.

Membership in recurring meetings (such as a weekly staff or committee meeting) is relatively fixed. Even for these meetings, however, the planner must decide whether outsiders will be invited to observe, participate, or simply be available as resource people.

Determining Logistics It would be unwise to schedule a meeting that requires extensive discussion and creative problem solving at the end of the workday, when members may be exhausted emotionally and physically. Likewise, it would be counterproductive to schedule a three-hour meeting in a room equipped with uncushioned fold-up chairs, poor lighting, and extreme temperatures.

Instead, facilitate group problem solving by making intelligent choices about the timing and location of the meeting, room and seating arrangements, types of audiovisual equipment, and the like. Doing so will increase the likelihood of achieving the goals of the meeting.

Increasingly, another logistical consideration is whether to hold a face-to-face meeting or a **teleconference**, a meeting in which members in different locations are linked by simultaneous electronic communications, using camera, projection screens, microphones, and computer equipment (see the Spotlight on Technology).

Conducting a Meeting

Planning for a meeting goes a long way toward ensuring its success, but the manager's job is by no means over when the meeting begins. A manager must be a leader during the meeting, keeping the group focused on the point and encouraging participation.

An efficient leader begins and ends each meeting on time.

Punctuality Unless a high-level member or one whose input is vital to the business at hand is tardy, make it a habit to begin every meeting on time. Doing so will send a powerful nonverbal message to chronic late arrivers that business will be conducted and decisions made whether they're present or not.

If you wait for latecomers, you send the message to those who *were* punctual that they wasted their time by being prompt. As a result, they will probably arrive late for subsequent meetings. And the habitual late arrivers will then begin arriving even later! Avoid this vicious cycle by beginning (and ending) at the appointed times.

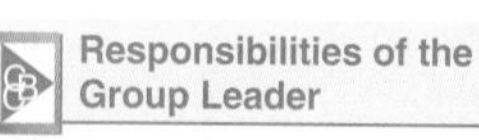

Responsibilities of the Group Leader

1. Determine the purpose of the meeting and who will attend.
2. Prepare and distribute an agenda.
3. Start the meeting on time.
4. Keep the group aware of the goals; discourage digressions.
5. Encourage quiet members and politely control those who try to monopolize the meeting.
6. Provide frequent internal summaries as well as a final summary.
7. End the meeting on time.

Ober, *Contemporary Business Communication*, 2d ed.

See Transparency 15.3, Responsibilities of the Group Leader.

Following the Agenda One of the keys to a focused meeting is to follow the agenda. At formal meetings you will be expected to discuss all items on the published agenda and no items not on the agenda. The less formal the meeting, the more flexibility you have in allowing new topics to be introduced. It's always possible that new information that has a bearing on your problem may arise. To prevent discussion simply because you didn't include the item on your agenda would make it more difficult for you to achieve your purpose. But as leader of the meeting, you must make certain that new topics are directly relevant.

Leading the Meeting Begin the meeting with a statement of your purpose and an overview of the agenda. As the meeting progresses, keep track of time. Don't let the discussion get bogged down in details.

Preventing people from talking too much or digressing from the topic requires tact. Comments like "I see your point, and that relates to what we were just discussing" can keep you on track without offending the speaker. You'll also need to encourage the participation of the quieter members of the group with comments like "John, how does this look from the perspective of your department?"

SPOTLIGHT ON TECHNOLOGY

The Electronic Meeting

Video conferencing and other forms of electronic meetings have been enjoying extraordinary growth throughout the industrialized world. The possibility of holding electronic meetings became a reality when American Telephone and Telegraph introduced its Picturephone at the 1964 World's Fair in New York. Since that time, advances in computer and communication technology have made video conferencing more affordable and more effective.

VIDEO CONFERENCES

In a video conference, meetings are held in two or more specially equipped meeting rooms in different parts of the country. These conference rooms, in the company's own buildings or at hotels, contain cameras, projection screens, and microphones that enable participants at one location to see and hear what transpires at the other(s).

The major advantage of video conferencing is, of course, the savings in time and cost for executive travel; the days of executives traveling two days to attend a one-hour meeting may be over. Also, because no travel is involved, more executives can participate in video conferences, and as many visual aids can be used as needed. A final advantage is that most people are more comfortable on their own turf and are more likely to be able to contribute more effectively than if interacting in an unfamiliar environment.

Despite these advantages, video conferences have not replaced face-to-face meetings partly because of the cost of the initial investment and partly because of the communication environment. Some managers are uncomfortable in front of a camera and worry about how they look, act, and sound. Also, some managers miss being able to assess nonverbal cues easily and prefer the personal chemistry that develops more easily in face-to-face meetings. These self-conscious feelings are likely to diminish as managers become more familiar with the medium and develop more experience in conducting business this way.

COMPUTERIZED MEETINGS

In addition in installing video conference rooms to facilitate *distance* communication, some organizations are installing computerized meeting rooms to facilitate *local* communication. Such facilities are especially helpful for brainstorming.

Typically, a computerized meeting will start with each manager typing out ideas on a subject for perhaps a half hour using a computer at his or her seat. As fast as they are written, the ideas appear on a large screen at the front of the room. Because the ideas are anonymous, there is little showing off or intimidation.

Then, using special software, the meeting participants are able to categorize and rank the ideas to bring some order out of the chaos. Boeing Company found that using such facilities cut meeting times 71%; IBM reported average time reductions of 56%.

Whether managers meet across the table or across the country, technology is helping them communicate more effectively in meetings.

Sources: William M. Bulkeley, "Computerizing Dull Meetings Is Touted as an Antidote to the Mouth That Bored," *Wall Street Journal,* January 28, 1992, p. B1; "Computers the Key to More Productive Meetings," *Presentation Products Magazine,* August 1989, p. 48; Janet Guyon, "Video Conference May Soon Come Alive," *Wall Street Journal,* January 16, 1989, p. B1; Pamela Sebastian, "Business Bulletin: Video Conferencing Locks on a Market," *Wall Street Journal,* February 7, 1991, p. 1; Julie Sturgeon, "Meeting the Future," *Indianapolis C.E.O.,* February 1993, pp. 53–59.

Determine which problem-solving strategy is appropriate.

If your purpose is to solve a problem, you should consider ahead of time how you will structure the discussion. The particular strategy you use (such as brainstorming or role-playing) will, of course, depend on the nature and importance of the problem and the skills of the group members. For many topics and groups, a simple discussion is all that is needed.

As leader, you'll sometimes have to resolve conflicts among members. Your first step is to make sure all members understand the facts involved

When a meeting leader wants to pay more attention to what is said at the meeting than to keeping order, he or she might have a facilitator lead the meeting. Facilitators express no opinion but keep the group focused and move the meeting along. Ford, Du Pont, and Apple Computer have all used facilitators to lead meetings. (Walter Kiechel III, "How to Lead a Meeting," *Fortune*, August 29, 1988, pp. 97–98.)

and that you and everyone else understand each person's position. You then need to examine what each person's goals are and search for alternatives that will satisfy the largest number of goals.

At the end of the meeting, summarize for everyone what the meeting has accomplished. What was decided? What are the next steps? Review any assignments and make sure everyone understands his or her responsibilities.

During the meeting, someone—either an assistant, the leader, or someone the leader designates—should record what happens. That person must report objectively and not impose his or her own biases.

In parliamentary procedure, the minority is heard and the majority prevails.

Parliamentary Procedure Every group needs to adopt rules that permit the orderly transactions of business in meetings. The larger the group and the more important their mission, the more important it is to establish written rules of order (called **parliamentary procedure**). Imagine, for example, the chaos that could result if a meeting did not follow the basic rule that only one person can have the floor and speak at a time!

The basis for parliamentary procedure is that the minority shall be heard, but that the majority shall prevail. The basic reference for parliamentary procedure—the authority used by governments, associations, and business organizations the world over—is *Robert's Rules of Order.*[6] The rationale for using parliamentary procedure is given in the preface of that classic:

> The application of parliamentary law is the best method yet devised to enable assemblies of any size, with due regard for every member's opinion, to arrive at the general will on a maximum number of questions of varying complexity in a minimum time and under all kinds of internal climate ranging from total harmony to hardened or impassioned division of opinion.[7] [*Note:* Incidentally, this 61-word sentence is probably as good an example as you're likely to find of a long sentence that communicates its message clearly and concisely.]

Robert's Rules of Order was written in 1896 by Gen. Henry M. Robert, a U.S. Army officer who was active in many civic and educational organizations; it has been revised periodically since then. The current edition contains more than 650 pages of rules and procedures; those that are most helpful for running the typical business meeting are summarized in Figure 15.2.

Knowledge of basic parliamentary procedures is a strategic communication skill for managers. Anyone who runs a business meeting, whether at work or in connection with a professional, civic, or social organization, would do well to become familiar with the basic requirements of conducting business in a parliamentary manner.

Following Up the Meeting

Formal meetings require formal minutes of what took place.

Routine meetings may require only a short memorandum as a follow-up to what was decided. Formal meetings or meetings where controversial ideas were discussed may require a more formal summary.

Minutes are an official record of the proceedings; they summarize what was discussed and what decisions were made. Generally, they should

Current management theory suggests that cross-functional teams can work creatively and quickly. At Hallmark Cards, new-product teams like this one combine artists, designers, printers, and finance people. Collaborative decision making increases the importance of running group meetings productively.

emphasize what was *done* at the meeting, not what was *said* by the members. Minutes may, however, present an intelligent summary of the points of view expressed on a particular issue, without names attached, followed by the decision made. Avoid presenting minutes that are either so short they lack the "flavor" of what transpired or so long they tend to be ignored.

For an exercise on revising a follow-up letter, refer students to the *Study Guide*, pp. 198–200.

The first paragraph of minutes should identify the type of meeting (regular or special); the meeting date, time, and place; the presiding officer; the names of those present (or absent) if customary; and the fact that the minutes of the previous meeting were read and approved.

The minutes should be accurate, objective, and complete.

The body of the minutes should contain a separate paragraph for each topic. According to parliamentary procedure, the name of the maker of a motion, but not the seconder, should be entered in the minutes. It is often helpful to use the same subheadings as in the agenda. A sample portion of the minutes of a business meeting is shown below:

Review of December 3 Press Conference

A videotape of the December 3 press conference conducted by Donita Doyle was viewed and discussed. Roger Eggland's motion that "Donita Doyle be commended for the professional and ethical manner in which she presented the company's view at the December 3 press conference" was adopted unanimously without debate.

Recommendation for Annual Charitable Contribution

Tinrah Porisupatani moved "that American Chemical donate $15,000 to a worthwhile charity operating in Essex County." Linda Peters moved to amend the motion by inserting the words "an amount not exceeding" after the word "donate." On a motion by Todd Chandler, the motion to make a donation, with the pending amendment, was referred for further study to the Social Responsibility Committee with instructions to recommend a specific amount and charity and report at the next meeting.

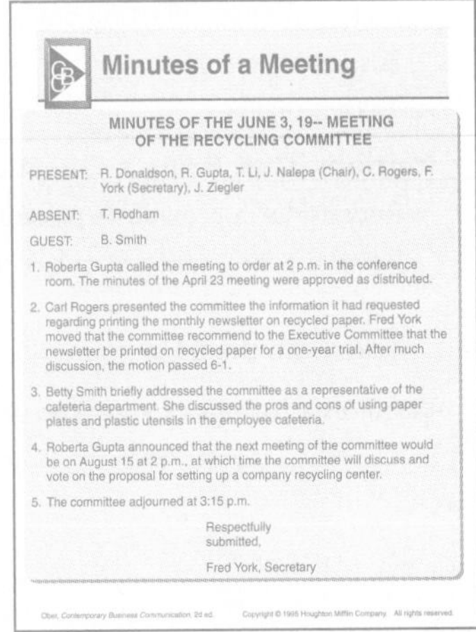

Minutes of a Meeting

MINUTES OF THE JUNE 3, 19-- MEETING
OF THE RECYCLING COMMITTEE

PRESENT: R. Donaldson, R. Gupta, T. Li, J. Nalepa (Chair), C. Rogers, F. York (Secretary), J. Ziegler

ABSENT: T. Rodham

GUEST: B. Smith

1. Roberta Gupta called the meeting to order at 2 p.m. in the conference room. The minutes of the April 23 meeting were approved as distributed.
2. Carl Rogers presented the committee the information it had requested regarding printing the monthly newsletter on recycled paper. Fred York moved that the committee recommend to the Executive Committee that the newsletter be printed on recycled paper for a one-year trial. After much discussion, the motion passed 6-1.
3. Betty Smith briefly addressed the committee as a representative of the cafeteria department. She discussed the pros and cons of using paper plates and plastic utensils in the employee cafeteria.
4. Roberta Gupta announced that the next meeting of the committee would be on August 15 at 2 p.m., at which time the committee will discuss and vote on the proposal for setting up a company recycling center.
5. The committee adjourned at 3:15 p.m.

Respectfully submitted,

Fred York, Secretary

Ober, *Contemporary Business Communication*, 2d ed.

See Transparency 15.4, Minutes of a Meeting.

FIGURE 15.2 Parliamentary Procedure for Business Meetings

To Do This:	You Say This:	Interrupt the speaker?	Need a second?	Debatable?	Amendable?	Vote needed?
Main Motion						
Make a main motion	*I move that . . .*	yes	yes	yes	yes	maj
Secondary Motions						
Adjourn	*I move that we adjourn.*	no	yes	no	no	maj
Amend a motion	*I move to amend by . . .*	no	yes	yes	yes	maj
Appeal a chair's ruling	*I appeal the decision of the chair.*	yes	yes	yes	no	maj
Ask a question	*I rise to a point of information.*	yes	no	no	no	none
Call for a secret ballot	*I move the vote be taken by ballot.*	no	yes	no	yes	maj
Call for standing or show-of-hands vote	*I call for a division.*	yes	no	no	no	none
Close debate	*I move the previous question.*	no	yes	no	no	2/3
Close nominations	*I move to close nominations.*	no	yes	no	yes	2/3
Consider parts of a motion separately	*I move to divide the question.*	no	yes	no	yes	maj
Lay the pending motion aside temporarily	*I move to lay the question on the table.*	no	yes	no	no	maj
Point out a rule violation	*I rise to a point of order.*	yes	no	no	no	none
Postpone to a certain time	*I move to postpone the question until . . .*	no	yes	yes	yes	maj
Postpone indefinitely	*I move to postpone the question indefinitely.*	no	yes	yes	no	maj
Raise a point of parliamentary procedure	*I rise to a parliamentary inquiry.*	yes	no	no	no	none
Refer a motion to a committee	*I move to refer the question to . . .*	no	yes	yes	yes	maj
Require that the agenda be followed	*I call for orders of the day.*	yes	no	no	no	none
State a request affecting one's rights	*I rise to a question of privilege.*	yes	no	no	no	none
Suspend the rules	*I move to suspend the rule . . .*	no	yes	no	no	2/3
Take a recess	*I move that we take a . . . recess.*	no	yes	no	yes	maj
Motions That Bring a Question Again Before the Assembly						
Reconsider a previously passed motion	*I move to reconsider the vote on . . .*	no	yes	yes	no	maj
Revoke action taken at previous meeting	*I move to rescind the motion relating to . . . adopted at the May meeting.*	no	yes	yes	yes	2/3[a]
Take from the table	*I move to take the question from the table.*	no	yes	no	no	maj

[a]Requires a two-thirds vote if no prior notice has been given, majority vote if prior notice has been given.

FIGURE 15.2 (*Continued*)

Miscellaneous Notes

1. Types of motions:
   a. A main motion brings an action before the group. It may be made only when no other motion is pending and must be made and seconded before it can be discussed.
   b. A secondary motion may be made and considered while a main motion is pending and must be acted on before the main motion can be considered further.
   c. A motion that brings a question again before the assembly enables the group to reconsider an action disposed of earlier.
2. Special rules adopted by the group take precedence over *Robert's Rules of Order.*
3. Unless otherwise specified, a majority of the membership constitutes a quorum (the minimum number of members who must be present to transact business).
4. A vote is not required to approve the minutes of the previous meeting. They are simply accepted as read and/or distributed, or they are accepted as corrected.
5. A vote is not required to accept a committee report. However, committee recommendations that require action must be voted on. Motions made on behalf of the committee do not require a second.
6. The purpose of tabling a motion is to enable the group to consider a more urgent matter that has arisen. If the tabled motion is not taken from the table by the next regularly scheduled meeting, the question dies.
7. The purpose of postponing a motion definitely is to defer action until a later date (e.g., when more information has been gathered). The purpose of postponing a motion indefinitely is to avoid taking action on the motion, thereby killing it.
8. The motion to reconsider a previously passed motion must be made at the same meeting as the original vote and must be made by someone from the prevailing (majority) side of the original vote.
9. After a motion has been made and seconded, the chair repeats the motion before calling for discussion and again before calling for the vote.

The last paragraph of the minutes should state the time of adjournment and, if appropriate, the time set for the next meeting. The minutes should be signed by the person preparing them. If someone other than the chair prepares the minutes, they should be read and approved by the chair before being distributed.

Guidelines for conducting business meetings are summarized in Checklist 16.

LISTENING

Effective communication requires both sending and receiving messages—both transmission and reception. Whether you are making a formal presentation to 500 people or conversing with one person over lunch, your efforts will be in vain if your audience does not listen.

Listening involves much more than just hearing. Hearing is simply perceiving sound; sound waves strike the eardrum, sending impulses to

CHECKLIST 16

Business Meetings

PLANNING THE MEETING

1. Identify the purpose of the meeting.
2. Determine whether a meeting is the most appropriate method for achieving your purpose.
3. Prepare an agenda for distribution to the participants.
4. Decide who should attend the meeting.
5. Determine the logistics of the meeting—timing, location, room and seating arrangements, and types of audiovisual equipment needed.
6. Assign someone (even if it is yourself) the task of making notes during the meeting. These notes should be objective, accurate, and complete.

CONDUCTING THE MEETING

7. Encourage punctuality by beginning and ending the meeting on time.
8. Begin each meeting by stating the purpose of the meeting and reviewing the agenda.
9. Establish ground rules that permit the orderly transaction of business. Many organizations follow parliamentary procedure.
10. Control the discussion to ensure that it is relevant, that a few members do not monopolize the discussion, and that all members have an opportunity to be heard.
11. At the end of the meeting, summarize what was decided, what the next steps are, and what each member's responsibilities are.

FOLLOWING UP THE MEETING

12. If the meeting was routine and informal, follow it up with a memorandum summarizing the major points of the meeting. For more formal meetings, prepare and distribute minutes.

There is a difference between hearing and listening.

the brain. Hearing is a passive process, whereas listening is an active process. When you *perceive* a sound, you're merely aware of it; you don't necessarily comprehend it. When you *listen,* you interpret and assign meaning to the sounds.

Consider the automobile you drive. When the car is operating normally, even though you *hear* the sound of the engine as you're driving, you're barely aware of it; you tend to tune it out. But the minute the engine begins to make a strange sound—not necessarily louder or harsher, but just *different*—you immediately tune back in, listening intently to try to discern the nature of the problem. You *heard* the normal hum of the engine but *listened* to the strange noise.

The Problem of Poor Listening Skills

Listening is the communication skill we use the most. White-collar workers typically devote at least 40% of their workday listening. Yet, immediately after hearing a ten-minute oral presentation, the average person retains only 50% of the information. Forty-eight hours later, only 25% of what was heard can be recalled.[8] Thus, listening is probably the least developed of the four verbal communication skills (writing, reading, speaking, and listening).

One of the major causes of poor listening is that most people have simply not been taught how to listen well. Think back to your early years in school. How much class time was devoted to teaching you to read and write? How many opportunities were you given to read aloud, participate in plays, or speak before a group? Chances are that reading, writing, and perhaps speaking were heavily stressed in your education. But how much formal training have you had in listening? If you're typical, the answer is, "not much."

Although listening is the communication skill we use the most, most people have not been taught how to listen effectively.

Another factor that contributes to poor listening skill is the disparity between the speed at which we normally speak versus the speed at which our brains can process data. We can think faster than we can speak—about four times faster, as a matter of fact. Thus, when listening to others, our minds begin to wander, and we lose our ability to concentrate on what is being said.

The results of ineffective listening include such problems as instructions not being followed, equipment broken from misuse, sales lost, feelings hurt, morale lowered, productivity decreased, rumors started, and health risks increased. Still, poor listening skills are not as readily apparent as poor speaking or writing skills. It's easy to spot a poor speaker or writer but much more difficult to spot a poor listener because a poor listener can fake attention. In fact, the poor listener may not even be aware of this weakness. He or she may mistake hearing for listening.

Keys to Better Listening

To learn to listen more effectively, whether you're involved in a one-on-one dialogue or are part of a mass audience, give the speaker your undivided attention, stay open-minded, avoid interrupting, and involve yourself in the communication.

Give the Speaker Your Undivided Attention During a business presentation, a member of the audience may hear certain familiar themes, think, "Oh no, not again," and proceed to tune the speaker out. Or during a conference with a subordinate, an executive may make or take phone calls, doodle, play around with a pen or pencil, or do other distracting things that give the speaker the impression that what he or she has to say is unimportant or uninteresting.

Physical distractions are the easiest to eliminate. Simply shutting the door or asking your assistant to hold all calls will eliminate many interruptions during personal conferences. If you're in a meeting where the environment is noisy, the temperature too cold or hot, or the chairs uncomfortable, try to tune out the distractions rather than the speaker. Learn to ignore those annoyances over which you have no control and concentrate instead on the speaker and what he or she is saying.

Mental distractions are more difficult to eliminate. But with practice and effort, you can discipline yourself, for example, to temporarily forget

- Work at listening (Concentrate).
- Resist distractions.
- Maintain eye contact with the speaker.
- Focus on the message content and on key ideas.
- Mentally summarize.
- Keep emotions in check; recognize personal biases.
- Listen and watch for nonverbal messages.
- Don't interrupt.
- Develop empathy.

See Transparency 15.5, Keys to Better Listening.

about your fatigue or to put competing thoughts out of your mind so that you can give the speaker your attention.

Just as it is important for the speaker to maintain eye contact with the whole audience, it is also important for the *listener* to maintain eye contact with the speaker. Doing so sends the message that you're interested in what the speaker has to say, and the speaker will be more likely to open up to you and provide the information you need.

Pay more attention to what the speaker says than to how he or she says it.

We talk about giving the speaker your undivided attention. Actually, it would be more accurate to say that you give the speaker's *comments* your undivided attention; that is, you focus on the content of the talk and are not overly concerned about how the talk is delivered. It is true, of course, that nonverbal clues do provide important information. However, do not be put off by the fact that the speaker may have dressed inappropriately, spoken too fast or in an unfamiliar accent, or appeared nervous. Almost always, *what* is said is more important than how it is said.

Likewise, avoid dismissing a topic simply because it is uninteresting or is presented in an uninteresting manner. "Boring" does not mean unimportant. Some information that may be boring or difficult to follow may in fact prove to be quite useful to you and thus well worth your effort to give it your full attention.

Stay Open-Minded Regardless of whom you're listening to or what the topic is, keep your emotions in check. Listen objectively and empathetically. Be willing to accept new information and new points of view, regardless of whether they mesh with your existing beliefs. Concentrate on the content of the message rather than on its source.

Don't look at the situation as a win/lose proposition; that is, don't consider that the speaker wins and you lose if you concede the merits of his or her position. Instead, think of it as a win/win situation: the speaker wins by convincing you of the merits of his or her position, and you win by gaining new information and insights that will help you perform your duties more effectively.

Maintain neutrality as long as possible, and don't jump to conclusions too quickly. Instead, try to understand *why* the speaker is arguing a particular point of view and what facts or experience convinced the speaker to adopt this position. When you assume this empathetic frame of reference, you will likely find that you neither completely agree nor completely disagree with every point the speaker makes. This ability to evaluate the message objectively will help you gain the most from the exchange.

Interrupting a speaker creates a barrier to effective communication.

Don't Interrupt Perhaps because of time pressures, we sometimes get impatient. As soon as we've figured out what a person is going to say, we tend to interrupt to finish the sentence for the speaker; this practice is especially a problem when listening to a slow speaker. Or, as soon as we can think of a counterargument, we tend to rush right in—whether or not the speaker has finished or even paused for a breath.

Such interruptions have many negative consequences. First of all, they are considered rude. Also, instead of speeding up the exchange, such interruptions tend to drag it out because they often interfere with the speaker's train of thought, causing backtracking. The most serious negative consequence, however, is the nonverbal message such an interruption sends: I have the right to interrupt you because what I have to say is more important than what you have to say! Is it any wonder, then, that such a message hinders effective communication?

There is a difference between listening and simply waiting to speak. Even if you're too polite to interrupt, don't simply lie in wait for the first available opportunity to barge in with your version of the truth. If you're constantly planning what you'll say next, you can hardly listen attentively to what the other person is saying.

Americans tend to have low tolerance for silence. Yet, waiting a moment to two after someone has finished before you respond has several positive effects—especially in an emotional exchange. It gives the person speaking a chance to elaborate on his or her remarks, thereby drawing out further insights. It also helps create a quieter, calmer, more respectful atmosphere, one that is more conducive to solving the problem at hand.

Involve yourself mentally in what the speaker is saying.

Involve Yourself As we have said, hearing is passive whereas listening is active. You should be *doing* something while the other person is speaking (and we don't mean doodling, staring out the window, or planning your afternoon activities).

Much of what you should be doing is mental. Summarize to yourself what the speaker is saying; create what the experts call an *internal paraphrase* of the speaker's comments. We can process information much faster than the speaker can present it, so use that extra time for active listening—ensuring that you really are hearing not only what the person is saying but the motives and implications as well.

Some listeners find it helpful to jot down points, translating their mental notes into written notes. If you do this, keep your notes brief; don't become so busy writing down the facts that you miss the message. Concentrate on the main ideas; if you get these, you'll be much more likely to remember the supporting details later. Recognize also that even if a detail or two of the speaker's message might be inaccurate or irrelevant, the major points may still be valid. Evaluate the validity of the overall argument; don't get bogged down in trivia.

Be selfish in your listening. Constantly ask yourself, How does this affect me? How can I use this information to further my goals or to help me perform my job more effectively? Personalizing the information will help you to concentrate more easily and to weigh the evidence more objectively—even if the topic is difficult to follow or uninteresting and even if the speaker has some annoying mannerisms or an unpleasant personality.

Encourage the speaker by letting him or her know that you're actively involved in the exchange. Maintain eye contact, nod in agreement, lean forward, utter encouraging phrases such as "uh huh" or "I see." In a conversation, ensure that your mental paraphrases are on target by summarizing aloud for the speaker what you think you're hearing. You can give such feedback as "So you believe. . . , is that true?" or "Do you mean that . . . ?" which in turn enables the speaker to clarify remarks, add new information, or to clear up any misconceptions. Further, it tells the speaker that you're paying attention to the exchange.

COMMUNICATING BY TELEPHONE

There are more than 285 million telephones in the world, 115 million of them in the United States. That is the equivalent of about one telephone for every two people in this country. American Telephone and Telegraph (AT&T) processes 75 million calls on these phones every single day.[9] No wonder, then, that communicating effectively by telephone is a crucial managerial skill, one that becomes increasingly important as the need for instantaneous information increases. Your telephone demeanor may be taken by the caller as the attitude of the entire organization. Every time the phone rings, your organization's future is on the line.

Calling Versus Writing

Sometimes even the most motivated salespeople can't reach sales goals. Some of the reasons? Fear of appearing too pushy and reluctance in using a telephone for prospecting purposes.

Before you pick up the phone to make a call, consider whether you'll accomplish your purpose better by calling or by writing. If your message is long and complicated, it may be easier for your audience to understand in writing, plus the person can refer back to the document when necessary. If you are conveying bad news, a phone call may soften the blow, whereas a letter may strengthen the force of your message. You'll need to have a clear purpose and understand the effect the form of your message will have on your audience.

Written messages, of course, provide a record of communication. Even if you decide to telephone, remember that you should often follow a call with a written note, both to make sure there has been no misunderstanding and to document your communication.

Your Telephone Voice

Your voice is a primary means of accomplishing your objective on the phone.

Much of what you have learned about body language is useless when you're talking on the phone. You cannot maintain eye contact or observe facial expression and body posture through telephone lines (yet!). That is one reason why ear-to-ear communication is often not as effective as person-to-person communication in solving difficult problems. You are, however, able to make use of such voice qualities as rate of speech and pitch to provide nonverbal clues about the other person (and, of course, the other person is able to make use of the same information about you).

Because the person to whom you're speaking has no visual clues to augment the auditory clues, a voice that is raspy, hoarse, shrill, loud, or weak can make you sound angry, excited, depressed, or bored—even if you aren't. Therefore, try to control your voice and project a friendly, competent, enthusiastic image to the other party.

To make your voice as clear as possible, sit or stand tall and avoid chewing gum or eating while talking. If your head is tilted sideways to cradle the phone between your head and shoulder, your throat is strained and your words may sound unclear.

Greet the telephone caller with a smile—just as you would greet someone in person. Your voice sounds more pleasant when you're smiling. An experiment was once conducted in which telephone salespeople were instructed to smile when they talked to their customers on one day and to scowl on the next. The salespeople sold almost twice as much on the days they were smiling.[10]

When the phone rings, pause, shift gears mentally, smile, and then answer the phone. Some firms even attach a sticker to the phone to remind employees to smile. "Smile," the sticker says, "it might be the boss calling."

In an article in *Working Woman* magazine, Gil Schwartz advises against informing people that you're calling them from your car phone. They're liable to think you're not giving them your undivided attention—and they're right. (Gil Schwartz, " 'Hi! I'm Calling from the Car Phone!'...and Other Breaches of High-Tech Etiquette," *Working Woman*, December 1990, pp. 66–67.)

Your Telephone Technique

Although every office worker will answer phones, the people who answer the firm's main number are vital to the firm's public image. These people must be trained and highly qualified—not the newest or least informed workers, as is often the case. These people's contacts with customers can have more impact on the organization's public image than the best advertising and promotional campaign.

Always answer the phone by the second or third ring. Regardless of how busy you are, you do not want to give the impression that your company doesn't care about its callers. Answer clearly and slowly, giving the company's name. Remember that even if you give the same greeting 50 times a day, your callers probably hear it only once. Make sure they can understand it.

Answer promptly and courteously, providing as much helpful information as possible.

Be a good listener. Just as you would never continue writing or reading while someone speaks to you in person, do not engage in such distracting activities during phone calls. Pay attention especially to getting names correct and use the person's name during the conversation to personalize the message.

As with most other communication forms, emphasize positive language. Instead of saying, "I don't know," say, "Let me check and call you right back." Instead of "you'll have to . . . ," say, "We'll be happy to handle that if you'll just . . ."

Encourage employees to answer the phones of coworkers who are temporarily away from their desks. If you're answering calls for someone else, take the message graciously, using language such as "Ms. Hall will be attending a meeting most of the day but would be happy to return your call tomorrow morning. May I give her your message?" Always give the impression that callers are important (they are!) and that you will do anything you reasonably can to assist them.

If you must put a caller on hold, always ask, "May I put you on hold?" and then give the caller an opportunity to respond. Long-distance callers may prefer to call back rather than to be put on hold. When you get back on the line, do not appear rushed or exasperated. Give the patient caller your complete attention.

Voice Mail

Whether you love it or hate it, voice mail (for example, "Press 1 to leave a message or press 2 to speak to an operator") is here to stay. Although some callers find voice mail impersonal and irritating, most are grateful for the opportunity to leave a message when they're unable to reach their party.

Answer your phone in person when possible.

A notebook computer, a pager, a cellular phone—with this six pounds of equipment, Harriet Donnelly, an AT&T managing director of consumer products, can work anywhere. Electronic mail and voice mail have become major media for much business communication today.

Before you even make a call, recognize that you might have to leave a message (using voice mail or an answering machine), so plan your message beforehand. Be polite and get to the point quickly. Clearly define the purpose of the call and the desired action and always give your phone number—even if the caller has it on file. The calls that get returned the fastest are those that are easiest to make.

If you have voice mail on your own phone, follow these guidelines:

- Never use voice mail as a substitute for answering your phone when you are available. Your customers, suppliers, and fellow workers deserve more consideration than that.
- Record your outgoing message in your own voice and keep it short (today, almost everyone knows how to use voice mail or an answering machine). Here is an example: "Hello, this is John Smith. Please leave me a message and I'll get back to you as quickly as I can. Thank you." Change your message when you will be away from the office for an extended period of time.
- Check your messages at least daily and return calls promptly. Callers assume that you've received their messages and may interpret a lack of response as rudeness.

Telephone Tag

The telephone would be a much more efficient instrument if we could be assured of reaching our party each time we call. Instead, we're often forced to play an unproductive game of **telephone tag**, in which Party A calls Party B, is unable to reach her, and leaves a message. Party B then returns A's call, is unable to reach him, and leaves a message. And the process continues until the connection is finally made or until one party gives up in frustration.

Only 17% of business callers reach their intended party on the first try, 26% by the second try, and 47% by the third try.[11] Thus, it takes the majority of business callers at least three tries to reach their intended party. These false starts add up to an estimated four work weeks each year wasted on unproductive or unnecessary telephone calls.[12]

Here are some suggestions for avoiding telephone tag:

Develop specific strategies to minimize telephone tag.

- *Plan the timing of your calls.* Try to schedule them at times when you're most likely to reach the person. (Likewise, make yourself available in the office at established hours so that your contacts will know when they can likely reach you.)
- *Announce when you're returning a call.* If you're returning someone's call and get a secretary on the line, begin by saying you're returning the boss's call. This will clue the secretary that the boss wanted to speak to you.
- *Explore alternatives.* Find out what time would be best to call back or whether someone else in the organization can help.
- *Make use of technology.* Know how and be willing to use answering machines, voice mail, electronic mailboxes, call processing, and other automated devices that will help you achieve your purposes. If your organization has a computer network, you'll find that electronic mail often eliminates telephone tag; employees can send and receive mail at their convenience, and there's no need for both parties to be available at the same time.

Finally, know when to call it quits. If you haven't reached your intended party after numerous attempts, it is unlikely that further attempts will be successful. When all else fails, stop calling and write a letter.

DICTATING

There are, of course, many input methods for written communication. You can jot a note on a personal memo form and send it through interoffice mail in handwritten form, you can keyboard and format your own message, or you can dictate your message for transcription by someone else.

Machine dictation is more efficient than writing in longhand or dictating to a secretary taking shorthand.

Dictation is the process of transmitting information orally for subsequent transcription. (**Transcription** is the process of preparing a typed copy of a document from longhand notes, shorthand notes, or machine dictation.) Dictation is usually accomplished either by dictating to a secretary who records your message in shorthand or, more typically, by dictating to a machine that records your message on magnetic media.

In the future, it is likely that voice input into a computer will become a third major form of dictation. A **voice-input system** translates human speech into electronic signals that are readable by computer software. Such systems let the operator speak rather than type the information into the computer.

Preparing to Dictate

Become familiar with the operation of the equipment you'll be using. Dictation systems range from large centralized systems that are accessed via the telephone to battery-operated handheld units that can be carried and used anywhere. The operator's manual that comes with the machine will tell you how to use the machine's features for maximum efficiency.

To prepare for a particular dictation session, first gather the resource materials you'll need—copies of past correspondence, notes, files, and the like. Then arrange your dictation jobs in order from highest to lowest priority. That way, if you are interrupted before you finish, you will have the most important jobs dictated and on their way to being transcribed.

If you're answering a piece of correspondence, mark it up: underline or highlight the important points and jot notes to yourself in the margins. Then make a rough outline of what you intend to say, keeping in mind the purpose of the message and the needs of the audience.

Dictating the Message

Unless the same person transcribes all your correspondence and is familiar with your voice, begin by giving your name, title, department, and phone number. Then identify the document you're dictating, indicating, for example, whether it is a letter, memorandum, or report. If your organization has not adopted a standard style for each type of document, give formatting instructions (e.g., modified block style) and any special stationery requirements (e.g., monarch stationery). Finally, indicate whether the document is to be a draft or final copy, the number of copies needed, and the turnaround time needed for the typed document. All this information is needed *before* the transcriber can begin typing the document.

Dictate any needed instructions for transcribing your message.

Special instructions should always precede the passage to which they apply. If you want a passage indented from each margin or set in all capitals or underlined, tell the transcriber *before* he or she types the passage. Otherwise, the passage will have to be reformatted. Complicated sections, such as tables and diagrams, are often best prepared as handwritten rough drafts that are then submitted for typing along with the dictation.

When dictating, speak distinctly and at a speed somewhat slower than in normal conversation. Pause between each sentence and at punctuation points. By tone of voice, indicate when you're giving dictation to be transcribed and when you're giving special instructions to the transcriber that are not to be transcribed. Avoid eating, chewing gum, pacing back and forth, or making other distractions while dictating. It is to your advantage to be heard clearly and distinctly.

Spell out proper names, and indicate punctuation if needed.

Spell out any proper nouns that might possibly be misspelled. Is it *Louis* or *Lewis* (or even *Lois*)? For example, you might say, "This letter is to Robert Batz; that's *B* as in *Bertha, A* as in *Alice, T* as in *Thomas,* and *Z* as in *Zebra.*"

Unusual punctuation should be indicated. Indicate which words or phrases should be underlined, typed in all capitals, or be enclosed in quotation marks. It is generally unnecessary to indicate the ends of sentences; your voice inflection will provide sufficient guidance for the transcriber. You should, however, indicate each new paragraph (generally, by saying "Paragraph" at the end of a paragraph and in a different tone of voice).

Whether or not to indicate such internal punctuation as commas, semicolons, colons, and apostrophes depends on your language skills and those of the transcriber. If you're confident about your own skills but unsure of those of the transcriber's, your best bet is to insert all punctuation. If you choose not to, you're indicating your willingness to accept the transcriber's judgment.

If your dictation unit is not voice-activated, use the pause or stop button to turn the machine off temporarily when you're thinking or searching for information. It would be inefficient to make the transcriber listen to long periods of silence.

When you make an error or decide to rephrase a passage, do so immediately. Simply reverse the tape to the point where the correction begins and tape over the original version. Or, using a different tone of voice, say something like "Transcriber (or, the transcriber's name, if known), let's rephrase that last sentence." If you need to revise an earlier passage or if you omitted needed instructions, use the *cuing* feature of the machine—the function that places a tone on the recording to give special instructions to the transcriber or to indicate where corrections are to be made.

If the same person always transcribes your dictation, it will probably not be necessary to dictate all the closing lines; typically "Sincerely yours," will be enough for the transcriber to know to then insert your name and title as you prefer them. Otherwise, dictate all the closing lines. In either case, don't forget to indicate any enclosures and copy notations, and if necessary, tell where the enclosures may be found. End each session by thanking the transcriber. A simple dictation session might begin as follows:

> This is Betty Johnson, assistant manager, purchasing department, extension 4056. Please prepare a letter in standard format to Mr. Edward LaPaz; that's capital *L* as in *Lewis, A* as in *Alice,* capital *P* as in *Peter* (no space before the *P*), *A* as in *Apple,* and *Z* as in *Zebra.* His address is American General Corporation, ten twenty-six Woodland (one word) Street, Milwaukee, Wisconsin 53172.
>
> Dear Ed: The following items we received from your company on Invoice (capital I) 3076 arrived in damaged condition. Operator, please arrange the following items in two columns. The heading for the first column is *Item No.* (abbreviated *N-o-period*) and for the second column *Description.* Please underline each column heading . . .

The transcribed pages will be returned to you for your approval, signature, and distribution. Proofread each transcribed document carefully before signing it or approving it for distribution. Remember that documents are sent out under *your* name—not under the transcriber's name. You are responsible for their accuracy and appearance. Whether the mistake was your own or the transcriber's, now is the time to correct it. Use appropriate proofreader's marks to indicate corrections (see the Reference Manual at the end of the text).

You are ultimately responsible for the accuracy and appearance of documents going out under your name.

BUSINESS ETIQUETTE

Business etiquette is the practice of polite and appropriate behavior in the business setting. It dictates what behaviors are proper and under what circumstances; thus, business etiquette is really concerned with interaction between people—not meaningless ritual.

Learn what is considered appropriate behavior in your organization.

Each organization has its own rules about what is and is not considered fitting in terms of dress, ways of addressing superiors, importance of punctuality, and the like. In addition, every country and every culture has its own rules. Generally, these rules are not written down but must be learned informally or through observation. Executives who follow correct business etiquette are more confident and appear more in charge; and the higher you advance in your career, the more important such behavior will become.

Business etiquette differs in many ways from social etiquette. The manager who enumerates all his or her accomplishments to the superior during a performance appraisal is simply being savvy, but if the manager does so during a social engagement, he or she is being a boor. You must be sensitive to what is appropriate under any given circumstances.

Good manners are good business; they communicate a strong positive message about you as a person. As Mark Twain once observed about etiquette, "Always do right: you will please some people and astonish the rest."

Making Introductions

The important point to remember about making introductions is simply to *make them*. The format you use is less important than the fact that you avoid the awkwardness of requiring two people to introduce themselves.

Traditionally, a man is introduced to a woman (saying the woman's name first), the lower ranking person is introduced to the higher ranking person (saying the higher ranking person's name first), and other people are introduced to the guest (saying the guest's name first). However, when introducing a newcomer to a group of people, simply mention the newcomer's name first and then go around the group introducing each person in turn.

The format for an introduction might be like this: "Helen, I'd like you to meet Carl Byrum. Carl just began working here as an account manager. Carl, this is Helen Smith, our vice president." Or, in a social situation, you might just say, "Rosa, this is Gene Stauffer. Gene, Rosa Bennett." The appropriate response to an introduction is "How do you do, Gene?" Regardless of the gender of the two people being introduced, either may initiate the handshake—a gesture of welcome.

Use a person's name in the conversation to help you remember it.

To help you remember the name of someone you've met, make a point of using his or her name when shaking hands. And using the person's name again at least once during the conversation will help fix that name in your mind. If you cannot remember someone's name, when the person approaches you, simply extend your hand and say your name. The other person will typically respond by shaking your hand and also giving his or her name.

Whenever you greet an acquaintance whom you've met only once some time ago, introduce yourself and immediately follow it with some information to help the other person remember, unless he or she immediately recognizes you—for example, "Hello, Mr. Wise, I'm Eileen Wagoner. We met at the Grahams' party last month."

Dining

The restaurant you select for a business meal reflects on you and your organization. Choose one where the food is of top quality and the service dependable. In general, the more important your guest, the more exclusive the restaurant. If a maitre d' (headwaiter) seats you and your guest, your guest should precede you to the table. If you're seating yourselves, take the lead in locating an appropriate table. Give your guest the preferred seat, facing the window with an attractive view or facing the dining room if you're seated next to the wall.

Although customs vary, it is typical for a man to hold the woman's chair as she is being seated and for the nearest man to rise when a woman excuses herself for a moment and when she returns. Female managers and professionals do not mistake genuine gestures of courtesy as chauvinism. Let common sense and your knowledge of the person's preferences guide your actions.

Unfold your napkin and place it in your lap immediately upon being seated. To avoid grabbing the wrong glass of water, remember "solids on the left, liquids on the right." When making a food recommendation or announcing, when asked, what you intend to order, recognize your guest will take your choice as a guideline to suitable price ranges. Each guest should order for himself or herself at a business meal. If the server mistakenly begins by asking you, the host, for your order, simply say, "My guests will order first," thereby letting him or her also know that you should get the check.

Always pass food or condiments to the right, offering it to someone else before you serve yourself. Avoid salting your food before tasting it. At the conclusion of the meal, return your folded napkin to the table just before rising and leaving the table. In most parts of the country, the usual tip for standard service is 15% of the food and bar bill and 10% of the cost of the wine.

Giving Gifts

Avoid giving gifts that are extravagant or personal, or that might be perceived as a bribe.

Giving gifts to suppliers, customers, or workers within one's own organization is typical at many firms, especially in December during the holiday period. Although such gifts are often deeply appreciated, you must be sensitive in terms of whom you give a gift to and the type of gift you select. Most people would consider a gift appropriate if it meets these four criteria:

- *It is an impersonal gift.* Gifts that can be used in the office or in connection with one's work are always appropriate.
- *It is for past favors.* Gifts should be used to thank someone for past favors, business, or performance—*not* to create obligations for the future. A gift to a prospective customer who has never ordered from you before might be interpreted as a bribe.
- *It is given to everyone in similar circumstances.* Singling out one person for a gift and ignoring others in similar positions would not only embarrass the one selected but create bad feelings among those who were ignored.

- *It is not extravagant.* A very expensive gift might make the recipient uneasy, create a sense of obligation, and call into question the motives of the giver.

Although it is often the custom for a superior to give a subordinate a gift, especially one's secretary, it is less usual for the subordinate to give a personal gift to a superior. More likely, coworkers will contribute to a joint gift for the boss, again selecting one that is neither too expensive nor too personal. As always, follow local customs when giving gifts to international colleagues (see the Spotlight Across Cultures).

Around the Office

Many situations occur every day in the typical office that call for common courtesy. The basis for appropriate behavior is always the golden rule: "Treat others as you yourself would like to be treated."

Follow the golden rule in your dealings with others at work.

Drinking Coffee If there is a container provided to pay for the coffee, do so every time you take a cup; don't force others to treat you to a cup of coffee. Also, take your turn making the coffee and cleaning the pot if that is a task performed by the group. Although in most offices it is acceptable to drink coffee or some other beverage while working, some offices have an unwritten rule against snacking at one's desk. Regardless, never eat while talking to someone in person or on the telephone.

Smoking Most offices today have designated smoking areas, and many prohibit smoking anywhere on the premises. If you smoke, follow the rules strictly. Smoking in public anywhere is increasingly considered bad manners, not to mention a health hazard.

Using Electronic Mail Because E-mail is often written "on the fly"—composed and sent as one keyboards the message—there is sometimes a tendency to forget the niceties and to let emotions take over. Such behavior is called "flaming" and should be avoided. Always assume the message you send will never be destroyed but will be saved permanently on somebody's computer file.

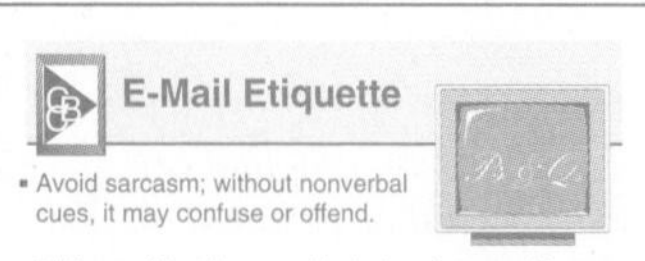

E-Mail Etiquette
▪ Avoid sarcasm; without nonverbal cues, it may confuse or offend.
▪ Fill in a subject line—and include only one subject per message.
▪ Avoid using all-capital letters.
▪ Avoid marking every message urgent; it's like crying wolf.
▪ Don't clutter the airwaves with a lot of copied messages.
▪ Don't use blind carbon copies (BCCs) too often—they hint of schemes and secrets.
▪ Check your mail often and respond to messages promptly.
▪ Assume that any message you send will be made public.

See Transparency 15.6, E-Mail Etiquette.

Using Cellular Phones and Paging Devices Nothing is more disconcerting than to have your business presentation interrupted by the ringing of someone's handheld cellular phone or the beeping of someone's pager. In public locations where conversation is expected (such as in airline terminals), using a cellular phone or answering a page is appropriate. However, at formal meetings, restaurants, movies, and social occasions, you should either turn off your machine or switch it to the "silent-alert" mode (typically either a light or vibrating device).

When calling someone on a cellular phone, get down to business quickly; both you and the recipient are paying by-the-minute charges for using the phone. And when driving, remember that safety comes first. Do not make (or even answer) a call while maneuvering in difficult traffic.

SPOTLIGHT ACROSS CULTURES

Gift Giving—Japanese-Style

When conducting business in Japan, there are very few occasions when giving a gift is not considered appropriate. There are two occasions, however, when gift giving is mandatory—for the Japanese as well as for those doing business with the Japanese. These two occasions are *O-chugen,* which falls in midsummer, and *O-seibo,* at year's end. *O-seibo,* which can only be compared with our Christmas, is an especially important gift-giving occasion, with more than $10 billion spent on gifts during this one season.

WHAT TO GIVE

As incongruous as it might sound, your best bet in selecting a gift for your Japanese colleague is to "Buy American." Your best choices for gifts are items that are either not easily available in Japan or are quite expensive there. Anything with a prominent American label might be appropriate. Brand names such as Gucci, Ralph Lauren, and L. L. Bean are understood and valued in Japan.

Regional gifts are always popular—such as Vermont maple syrup, mugs with your city name, university sweatshirts, baseball caps from famous teams, and even subscriptions to popular American magazines. Food selections are also appropriate—including such items as fruit and preserves, cheese, beef, and wine and spirits (especially bourbon, which is a uniquely American product).

Make sure that whatever items you choose are of the highest quality, but never ostentatious. Tact is the key to successful gift giving: nothing too large and extravagant nor too small and cheap. Take your cue from your Japanese colleagues. And remember that hierarchical relationships are important. Never give the same gift (or an equally priced gift) to people at different levels in the same organization.

HOW TO GIVE

The presentation of the gift may be as important as the gift itself. The gift should be wrapped attractively in top-quality gift wrap, and it is customary to transport the gift in a neat paper bag (so as not to call attention to the fact that you're bringing a gift).

When presenting the gift, extend it to the recipient with both hands (a sign of respect and humility), while making a self-deprecating comment such as "This is really nothing at all." It is customary for the recipient to then put the gift aside, unopened in the presence of the giver.

When you give a gift to a Japanese colleague, you can expect to receive one of similar value in the near future. Similarly, if you receive a gift, you will be expected to reciprocate. The Japanese (and many other Asian societies) value relationships highly, and giving gifts is one way of maintaining relationships.

Sources: Dean Foster, "Business Across Borders: International Etiquette for the Effective Global Secretary," *The Secretary,* October 1992, pp. 20–24; "Gift Giving Japanese-Style," *Business Tokyo,* November 1990, pp. 9–12; Yumiko Ono, "There's an Old Saying: Never Look for a Gift, of Course, in the Mouth," *Wall Street Journal,* December 13, 1989, p. B1.

Dealing with the Handicapped When talking with a blind person, deal in words rather than gestures or glances. As you approach a blind person, make your presence known; and if in a group, address the person by name so that he or she will know when you're talking directly to him or her. Identify yourself and use a normal voice and speed.

When interacting with a physically handicapped person, always ask before providing special assistance, and follow the person's wishes. When possible, place yourself at eye level and in front of the person to facilitate communication.

Most important, relax. Insofar as possible, forget about the handicap, and treat the person as you would anyone else. That person was hired because of the contribution he or she could make to the organization—not because of the handicap.

A Plan for a Business Meeting

PROBLEM

You are Dieter Ullsperger, director of employee relations for the city of Portland, Oregon. The city manager has asked your department to develop a policy statement regarding the solicitation of funds from employees during work hours for employee weddings, retirements, and anniversaries.

Despite the good intentions of their efforts, the city manager questions whether such efforts put undue pressure on some employees and take unreasonable time from their official duties. You have already gathered secondary data regarding this matter and have spoken with your counterparts in Jacksonville, Florida; Milwaukee, Wisconsin; and Memphis, Tennessee. You are now ready to prepare a first draft of the policy statement.

PROCESS

1. What is the purpose of your task?

   To prepare a policy statement on soliciting funds from employees during business hours.

2. Is a meeting necessary?

   Because this policy will affect every employee in the city government, it should be developed based on input from representatives of the work force. Therefore, a planning meeting is desirable.

3. What will be the agenda?

   My first reaction is that the meeting agenda is to write the new policy. However, I recognize that it is not reasonable for a policy statement to be written in a meeting. Thus, the real agenda is to develop the broad outlines for the policy. The policy will be planned collaboratively, drafted individually, reviewed collaboratively, and finally revised individually.

4. Who should attend the meeting?

   Because I want to ensure broad consensus on this policy, I'll ask the union steward of our two unions to attend (I'll represent management). I'll also ask the city attorney to attend to ensure that our policy is legal. Finally, I'll ask Lyn Peterson in transportation to attend; she is a veteran city employee who is well respected among her peers and has served as the unofficial social chairperson for numerous fund-raising events over the past several years. I'll telephone each of them to ask for their voluntary participation in this project.

5. What about logistics?

   We'll hold the meeting in the small conference room downstairs, which has an oval table. The only audiovisual equipment I'll need is a chalkboard to display any ideas we might have. I'll ask my secretary to take notes. Since I was not given a specific deadline, I'll delay the meeting for three weeks, because two retirement parties are already scheduled in the meantime.

PRODUCT

M · E · M · O

To: Betty Haggblade, Union Steward, OPEIU Local 146
Harold Inacker, City Attorney
David Ma, Employee Representative, AFGE Local 38
Lyn Peterson, Chief Dispatcher

From: Dieter Ullsperger, Director of Employee Relations D.U.

Re: Planning Meeting for New Policy Statement

Date: December 14, 19--

Thanks so much for agreeing to serve on a committee to help draft a policy statement on soliciting funds from employees during office hours. As I indicated to each of you, the city manager has requested such a statement.

Let's plan to meet on Friday, January 9, from 1:30 until 3:30 p.m. in the downstairs conference room (HG 204). Our agenda will be as follows:

1. Review the city manager's charge
2. Describe policies in effect in other cities
3. Identify and evaluate possible alternatives
4. Reach consensus on the major outlines of the new policy
5. Schedule assignments and future meetings

Before our meeting, I would appreciate your discussing this matter with your colleagues so that we might have the benefit of their thoughts as we develop this policy that will affect each city employee.

tgh

SUMMARY

Within the organization, members periodically form small groups such as operating, negotiating, creative, training, and ad hoc groups. For small groups to function effectively, the group should be of an appropriate size, develop a team spirit, avoid groupthink, and deal with conflict constructively. In addition, each group member should follow high standards of ethical conduct in order to help achieve the group's goals.

Planning a business meeting requires determining your purpose and deciding whether a meeting is the most efficient way of accomplishing that purpose. You must then determine your agenda, decide who should attend, and plan such logistics as timing, location, and room arrangements.

When conducting a meeting, begin with a statement of your purpose and agenda. Then follow the agenda, keeping things moving along. Control those who talk too much, and encourage those who talk too little. Use whatever strategies seem appropriate for solving problems and managing conflicts. At the end of the meeting, send a follow-up memo if needed or distribute minutes of the meeting.

Listening is the most used but least developed of the four verbal communication skills. Whether listening to a formal presentation or conversing with one or two people, you can learn to listen more effectively by giving the speaker your undivided attention, staying open-minded about the speaker and the topic, avoiding interrupting the speaker, and involving yourself actively in the communication.

When communicating by telephone, give the person to whom you're speaking your undivided attention, speak clearly, listen carefully, and treat the other party with courtesy. Take positive steps to avoid the inconvenience of not being able to reach your party (telephone tag) and use voice mail appropriately.

To dictate a message, first gather your resources and outline what you intend to say. While dictating, avoid interruptions and distractions, speak slowly and distinctly, and indicate unusual directions or punctuation. Because the transcribed message carries your name, edit and proofread it carefully.

Business etiquette is a guide to help people behave appropriately in business situations. To be effective in business, learn how to make introductions, conduct business lunches, give suitable gifts, and maintain good working relationships around the office. Good manners are good business.

KEY TERMS

For an exercise on matching terms, refer students to the *Study Guide*, pp. 194–195.

Agenda An ordered list of topics to be considered at a meeting, along with the name of the person responsible for each topic.

Business etiquette The practice of polite and appropriate behavior in a business setting.

Dictation The process of transmitting information orally for subsequent transcription.

Groupthink A barrier to communication that results from an overemphasis on group cohesiveness, which stifles opposing ideas and the free flow of information.

Minutes The official record of the proceedings of a meeting that summarizes what was discussed and what decisions were made.

Parliamentary procedure Written rules of order that permit the efficient transaction of business in meetings.

Teleconference A meeting in which members in different locations are linked by simultaneous electronic communications, using cameras, projection screens, microphones, and computer equipment.

Telephone tag The communication barrier caused by the repeated inability to reach someone by phone.

Transcription The process of preparing a typed copy of a document from longhand notes, shorthand notes, or machine dictation.

Voice-input systems A combination of recording, computer, and software technology that translates human speech into electronic signals that are readable by computer software, thereby avoiding the need for keyboarding.

REVIEW AND DISCUSSION

The answers to the review and discussion questions appear in the *Instructor's Resource Manual*, beginning on p. 278.

1. **Communication at Burrell Revisited** ■ Amy Hilliard-Jones of Burrell Communications Group calls a meeting when she needs a decision. She starts every meeting by restating the objective, and she uses an agenda to keep participants on track.
   a. Should Hilliard-Jones schedule a lengthy, creative, problem-solving meeting during the late morning? the late afternoon? When? Why?
   b. Should the leader hold a brainstorming meeting to a strict schedule? Explain your answer.
   c. Should the minutes of a problem-solving meeting name the participants who propose particular solutions? Why or why not?
2. What types of small groups typically operate in the organization?
3. Describe four techniques for enhancing small-group communication.
4. Under what circumstances is a meeting the most efficient way of accomplishing business objectives?
5. What are some ways of encouraging punctuality at meetings?
6. What is the difference between a main motion and a secondary motion?
7. What is the difference between tabling a motion and postponing a motion?
8. What types of information should be included in minutes of a meeting and what types should be excluded?
9. What is the difference between listening and hearing?
10. What are the major causes and effects of poor listening skills?
11. What is meant by the tip, "Be selfish in your listening"?
12. Is a boring presentation necessarily an unimportant one? Explain.
13. Why is it important to greet the telephone caller with a smile?
14. What are some suggestions for avoiding telephone tag?
15. What steps are necessary before beginning to actually dictate a message?
16. How should you introduce your professor and the person who sits beside you in class?
17. What guidelines should you follow for giving business gifts?

EXERCISES

Sample solutions for Exercises 1–10 appear in the *Instructor's Resource Manual*, pp. 279–281.

1. **Microwriting a Plan for a Business Meeting ▪**

   PROBLEM

   Assume you are a dean at your institution, which does not now celebrate Martin Luther King Jr.'s birthday with a paid holiday. You are seeking the support of the college's other four deans for making the third Monday in January a holiday for all college employees and students.

   PROCESS

   a. What is the purpose of your task?
   b. Will a meeting best serve your purpose? Why or why not?
   c. Assuming you've decided to call a meeting with the deans, who should attend (use your own institution for your decisions)?
   d. Determine the logistics of the meeting—timing, location, room and seating arrangements, and types of audiovisual equipment needed (again, use your own institution).
   e. Prepare an itemized agenda for your meeting.

   PRODUCT

   Prepare a memorandum, including the agenda, to the other deans. Submit both your memo and your responses to the questions to your instructor.
2. **Collaborative Communication—Conducting a Meeting ▪** Divide into groups of five, with each person assuming the role of a dean at your institution (see Exercise 1). Draw straws to determine who will be the dean calling the meeting and use this person's agenda. Conduct a 15- to 20-minute meeting. Following the meeting, evaluate its effectiveness. Did you achieve your objective? Explain your answer.
3. **Collaborative Writing—Conducting a Meeting ▪** Divide into groups of five, with each member playing the role of a president of one of the five business student organizations on campus. The dean of the School of Business has proposed requiring all students to purchase a certain brand of portable computer (student price of $1,450) before being allowed to take upper-division business courses. Your group is meeting to either support or oppose this proposal. Draw straws to determine who will be group leader. Each person other than the group leader must either make or amend a motion during the meeting.

   Conduct a 15- to 20-minute meeting on this topic, following parliamentary procedure. Do not adjourn until you have approved a motion one way or the other. After adjournment, evaluate the meeting. Discuss how efficiently it was conducted, how well each person's role was performed, and whether correct parliamentary procedure was followed. Write up your evaluation in a joint memo to your instructor.
4. **Preparing Minutes of a Meeting ▪** Attend a business meeting on campus this week—either a meeting of a student organization or a faculty or staff meeting (most of them are open to visitors). Take minutes of the meeting, edit them, and turn them in.
5. **Listening ▪** Your instructor will assign you a television show to watch this week—either a news program, talk show, or documentary. Using the listening techniques you learned in this chapter, take notes on the important points covered in the meeting. Listen for the major themes, not the details.

Write a one-page memo to your instructor summarizing the important information you heard. Should every student's paper contain basically the same information? Explain your answer.

6. **Communicating by Telephone** ▪ Role-play the situation described below. Record the conversations for later evaluation. While two students are role-playing, the others in the class should be making notes of what went well and what might have been improved. To help simulate a telephone environment, have the two student actors sit back to back so that they cannot see each other or the other class members.

   Situation: You are Chris Renshaw, administrative assistant for Ronald Krugel, the marketing manager at Kraft Enterprises. Terry Plachta, an important customer whom you've never met, calls your boss with a complaint that an item ordered two weeks ago does not work as advertised. Your boss won't be back in the office until tomorrow afternoon.
7. **Evaluating Telephone Communications** ▪ Telephone two organizations in your area. Your purpose is to speak to the director of human relations to learn how much time he or she spends in meetings each week and to get an evaluation of the effectiveness of these meetings. Call at least three times if you're not successful the first time. Leave a message if necessary. Keep a log of each person with whom you speak at each organization, and evaluate the effectiveness of that person's telephone communication skills. Finally, write a summary of what you learned about meetings in that organization. Submit both your log and your summary to your instructor.
8. **Leaving Effective Telephone Messages** ▪ Assume that on your third try (see Exercise 7) you were still unsuccessful in reaching the director of human relations by telephone. Instead you got a recording, asking you to leave a message of no more than 30 seconds. Compose the message you would leave.
9. **Dictating** ▪ For this assignment, you will need to work with a partner and have a cassette recorder and blank tape. Set up the tape recorder so that it is ready to record. Your instructor will give each of you in turn a simple letter or memo to write—perhaps a routine message from Chapter 6. You will have 10 minutes to study the assignment, make whatever notations you wish (but not a verbatim script), and then dictate your message using the cassette recorder. Your partner will then do the same thing using his or her assigned problem. After you have both recorded your dictation, exchange cassettes and transcribe the dictation in final format. You may insert any punctuation you feel is needed, but you may not change the dictator's wording. Submit both your transcribed document and the cassette to your instructor.
10. **Using Business Etiquette** ▪ Assume that you're the dean of your college. Think of three people to whom it would be appropriate to give a gift during December holidays and three people to whom it would not be appropriate to give a gift. Identify the individuals and their positions, and give reasons for your decisions. For the three people to whom you *would* give, suggest an appropriate gift, and a recommended price range.

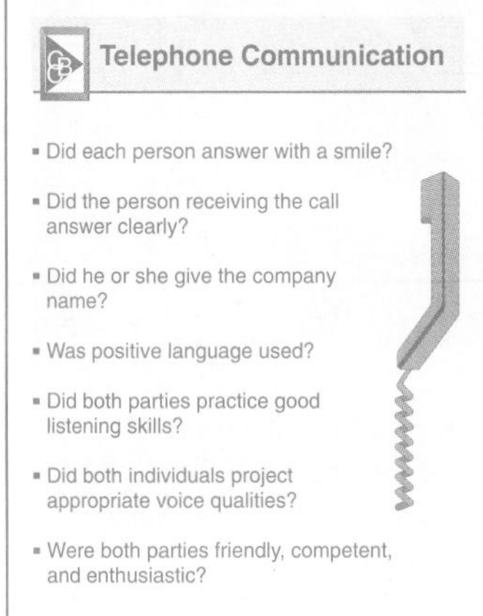

Telephone Communication
▪ Did each person answer with a smile?
▪ Did the person receiving the call answer clearly?
▪ Did he or she give the company name?
▪ Was positive language used?
▪ Did both parties practice good listening skills?
▪ Did both individuals project appropriate voice qualities?
▪ Were both parties friendly, competent, and enthusiastic?

See Master 15.1, Exercise 6, Communicating by Telephone, in the *Instructor's Resource Manual.*

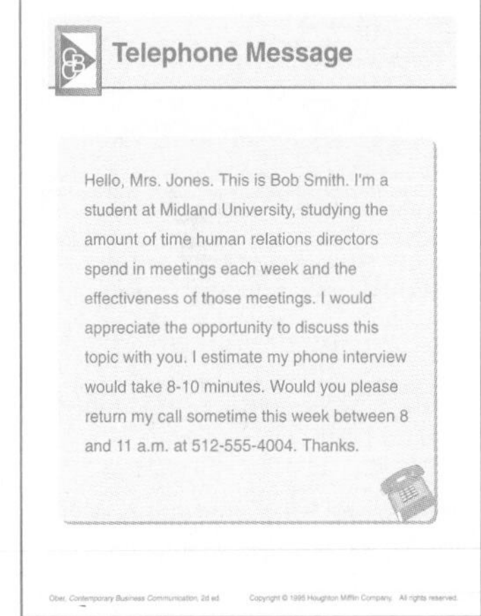

Telephone Message
Hello, Mrs. Jones. This is Bob Smith. I'm a student at Midland University, studying the amount of time human relations directors spend in meetings each week and the effectiveness of those meetings. I would appreciate the opportunity to discuss this topic with you. I estimate my phone interview would take 8-10 minutes. Would you please return my call sometime this week between 8 and 11 a.m. at 512-555-4004. Thanks.

See Master 15.2, Exercise 8, Leaving Effective Telephone Messages, in the *Instructor's Resource Manual.*

URBAN SYSTEMS

A possible solution to the Continuing Case is described in the *Instructor's Resource Manual*, p. 281.

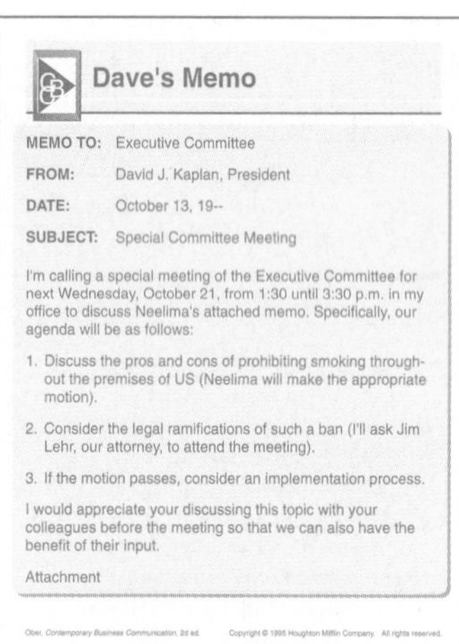

Dave's Memo

MEMO TO: Executive Committee
FROM: David J. Kaplan, President
DATE: October 13, 19--
SUBJECT: Special Committee Meeting

I'm calling a special meeting of the Executive Committee for next Wednesday, October 21, from 1:30 until 3:30 p.m. in my office to discuss Neelima's attached memo. Specifically, our agenda will be as follows:

1. Discuss the pros and cons of prohibiting smoking throughout the premises of US (Neelima will make the appropriate motion).
2. Consider the legal ramifications of such a ban (I'll ask Jim Lehr, our attorney, to attend the meeting).
3. If the motion passes, consider an implementation process.

I would appreciate your discussing this topic with your colleagues before the meeting so that we can also have the benefit of their input.

Attachment

Ober, *Contemporary Business Communication*, 2d ed.

See Master 15.3, Continuing Case 15, in the *Instructor's Resource Manual*.

CONTINUING CASE 15

Don't Let the Smoke Get in Your Eyes

Marc Kaplan ground his cigarette into the ashtray and thought, "Here go those save-the-earth people again." He had just read a copy of a memo that Neelima had sent to Dave Kaplan asking that smoking be prohibited throughout the premises of Urban Systems—both in Ann Arbor and in Charlotte. Neelima cited health dangers, lessened productivity, rights of nonsmokers, and damage to company property. Marc knew he could cite some arguments also: the rights of smokers, the unfairness of imposing new restrictions that were not in place when workers were hired, the lessened productivity due to stress from not smoking or to time spent on outside smoking breaks, and the fact that other health productivity hazards (such as gross obesity) were not banned. He felt he could enlist the support of O. J. Drew and Wendy Janish—the other two smokers in the management offices. Arnie McNally, an ex-smoker, was an unknown.

At any rate, Dave Kaplan had decided to hold a special meeting of the executive committee, made up of himself and the three vice presidents, next week to discuss and resolve the issue. Parliamentary procedure is followed at these meetings.

Oral and Written Communication Projects

1. Assume the role of Dave Kaplan. Compose a memo to the executive committee announcing the meeting and giving the agenda.
2. Have four members play the roles of Dave and the three vice presidents; Dave conducts the meeting. The other class members should listen actively, take notes, and be prepared to discuss the events afterward. Each observer should also serve as the secretary and submit a set of minutes for the meeting.

Critical Thinking

3. After role-playing, discuss the situation. How did each actor feel? Was anyone arguing a position he or she didn't really agree with? Was correct parliamentary procedure followed? Was the meeting successful? Did anyone win? lose?

WORDWISE *Language Origins*

Laser is an acronym for Light Amplification by Stimulated Emission of Radiation.

Epcot (amusement park) at Disney World is an acronym for Experimental Prototype Community of Tomorrow.

Alexander Graham Bell invented the telephone, but Thomas Edison coined the telephone salutation "Hello"; Bell favored "Ahoy."

PART VI

Employment Communication

CHAPTER 16

Your Résumé and Job-Application Letter

CHAPTER 17

The Job Interview and Follow-Up

CHAPTER

16

Your Résumé and Job-Application Letter

Communication Objectives

After you have finished this chapter, you should be able to

1. Analyze your interests, strengths, weaknesses, and preferred lifestyles as the first step in choosing a career.
2. Research possible professions, demographic trends, industries, and prospective employers.
3. Use different types of techniques to locate job leads and secure a job interview.
4. Determine the appropriate length and format for your résumé.
5. Determine the appropriate content for your résumé.
6. Compose solicited and unsolicited job-application letters.

Paul Orvos reads a lot of résumés and job-application letters. Orvos is corporate manager of employment for Computer Sciences Corporation (CSC), a leading information systems technology company, and he is also responsible for the company's college relations program. Every year, CSC's offices in Falls Church, Virginia, receive 4,000 letters and résumés—many from college graduates starting their careers—and a good number of these wind up on Orvos's desk.

Competition for entry-level positions, which is fierce now, is likely to become even more intense in the future; but don't despair. According to Orvos, a well-crafted letter and résumé can boost a candidate's chances for consideration. "The cover letter is your first opportunity to communicate with an employer," he explained. "Letters can show who you are and what you want to accomplish with your education, training, and life experience. Always send a cover letter, because a résumé alone won't distinguish you from many others who have a similar educational background. Your letter should gain the reader's attention quickly and be a quick read, so express your thoughts concisely."

Orvos suggests that as applicants develop their letters and résumés, they take the employer's perspective and ask themselves these four questions: What can I bring to this company? How can I help the company achieve its goals? How will I adapt to changes in the company's business? What long-term role might I play in this company? "Employers look far into the future and they are in effect hiring their future managers and executives from the pool of entry-level college graduates," he noted, "If you have had leadership responsibilities in school, in work, in a club, or in another organization, don't neglect to mention it."

A common mistake is to assume that a résumé should include only job history and functional responsibilities. "While that information is important, it's only half of what an employer needs to see. What's missing is the applicant's assessment of what has been learned on each job or project. Every experience is a learning experience. If the applicant's background has little relation to an employer's business, the résumé should stress communication skills, mediation skills, organizational skills, time-management skills, or other skills that translate across business and industry lines."

The statement of objective on a résumé is so important that Orvos believes it can make or break a candidacy. "A generic or meandering statement of objective can leave a weak impression," he said. "Take the time to research the company and then compose a statement of objective that shows you understand where and how you might fit into an employer's organization. Ideally, the statement of objective should be customized for every employer."

One way to sell yourself to an employer is to emphasize your ability to adapt to change and to continue the learning process on the job. "Business is dynamic and ever-changing," observed the CSC executive. "We're looking for people who can change with the business environment, and that involves the willingness and the ability to learn."

Finally, pay attention to physical presentation. "Choose a type style that's easy on the reader's eyes, and use a lot of white space to punctuate sections of the résumé," Orvos advised. "Double- and triple-check your grammar, spelling, and punctuation, because employers view résumés and letters as samples of the quality of work they can expect from you."

Paul Orvos

Corporate manager of employment, Computer Sciences Corporation, Falls Church, Virginia

PLANNING YOUR CAREER

Although we've stressed throughout this text the importance of communication skill for success on the job, one of your first professional applications of what you've learned will be in actually securing a job. Think for a moment about some of the important communication skills you've developed thus far—for example, how to analyze your audience, write effective letters, research and analyze data, speak persuasively, and use nonverbal communication to achieve your objectives.

Communication skills play an important role in the job campaign.

A chapter overview appears in the *Instructor's Resource Manual,* pp. 284–286.

All these communication skills will serve you well when you begin your job-getting campaign—from researching career, industry, and company information to writing effective résumés and application letters to conducting yourself effectively during the job interview. To refine these skills further, in this chapter you will learn how to plan your career, develop a résumé, and write application letters. The following chapter covers interviewing and writing post-interview letters.

A "Job Seeker's Handbook," with the following chapters, appears in the *Study Guide:*
Chapter 1: "Planning Your Job Search," pp. 1–3
Chapter 2: "Conducting a Self-Assessment," pp. 4–7
Chapter 3: "Targeting Potential Employers," pp. 8–11
Chapter 4: "Preparing Your Résumé," pp. 12–30
Chapter 5: "Writing Letters of Application," pp. 31–35
Chapter 6: "Completing Application Forms," pp. 36–41
Chapter 7: "Attending Interviews," pp. 42–54
Chapter 8: "Evaluating Job Offers," pp. 55–58

As you begin to think about your career, consider these facts about the American work force:[1]

- Three to four million new jobs are created each year, but job seekers have to beat odds of at least six to one to secure a job because there are typically six candidates *equally qualified* in terms of education and experience for each vacancy.
- Less than half (41%) of the work force deliberately *chose* their jobs or careers; instead, most got their jobs through chance, by having no other choice, or as the result of pressure from family or friends.
- About half (51%) of American workers say they would choose a different line of work if they had it to do over again.
- One in four entry-level employees fails to make it through the first year, and nearly one-third of the entire work force expects to change jobs within the next three years.

As these statistics make clear, you must put considerable time, effort, and thought into getting a job if you want to have a rewarding and fulfilling work life. The process is the same whether you're beginning your first job, changing careers, or returning to the workplace after an extended absence; and it begins with a self-analysis.

Self-Analysis

Your job campaign begins with a self-analysis.

If you are typical of many students, you have changed your major at least once during your college career. Thus, you've already made many important decisions about your life and career. When it is time to decide how to use your college education, you must do some soul-searching to decide exactly how you wish to spend the working hours of your life. Recognize that during the typical week you will probably spend as many of your waking hours at the workplace as at home.

Think about your life, your interests, things you're good at (and those you're not), and the experiences that have given you the most satisfaction. Such introspection will help you make sound career decisions. Take a few moments now to answer these questions:

1. Which courses have you enjoyed most and least in school?
2. Recalling projects on which you've worked in class, in organizations, or at work, which kinds have you been most successful at and enjoyed the most? Which have you disliked?
3. Do you enjoy working most with records (reports, correspondence, and forms), people, ideas, or things? Do you enjoy working more with your mind or with your body?
4. Do you prefer working independently on a project or with a group?
5. How important to you is being your own boss?
6. In what type of work setting do you function best: a quiet office, an environment with lots of activity and people, or an outside location? Would you most enjoy working in the organization's home office, a branch, while traveling, or at home?

7. What type of work schedule would you prefer: fixed or flexible? days, nights, or weekends? How willing or eager are you to work overtime?
8. What is important about the geographical location of your job in terms of climate, size of metropolitan area, and location (downtown, suburban, or rural)? Do you prefer a particular city, state, region of the country, or international setting (see the Spotlight Across Cultures)? How willing or eager are you to relocate?
9. For what kind of organization would you like to work: large or small? established or new? commercial, government, or nonprofit?
10. What is important about the personalities of the people with whom you will work? Describe your ideal boss, subordinates, and colleagues.
11. How would you like to dress for work?
12. What types of material rewards are important for you in terms of salary, commissions, fringe benefits, job security, and the like?
13. How willing or eager are you to participate in an extensive on-the-job training program?
14. What are your career goals five years from now?

Your answers to these questions will help you identify the type of career that would offer you the most satisfaction and success. Remember that for any particular college major, many jobs are available. One of them will likely meet your needs and desires.

Research

Armed with your self-assessment, you are now ready to secure additional information—about possible occupations, demographic trends, and industries and companies in which you're interested. Many job seekers begin their search for occupational information by interviewing one or more people currently employed in the career or industry that interests them. Such sources can provide the current and detailed information you seek, and they're likely to be more objective than a recruiter. Locate such sources by reading the business section of the local newspaper, asking family and friends, or consulting with your college placement office or your professors.

Research possible professions, demographic trends, industries, and prospective employers.

For more on job research, see the supplemental lecture/discussion notes in the *Instructor's Resource Manual*, p. 286–287.

Although the major purpose of such interviews is data gathering, these sessions also advertise your availability for and interest in a position. The interviewee may volunteer information about possible job leads. Avoid, however, turning the informational interview into an employment interview.

Occupational Information One of the most comprehensive sources of up-to-date information about jobs is the *Occupational Outlook Handbook*, published by the U.S. Department of Labor.

This handbook describes in detail the 225 occupations that account for 80% of all jobs in the U.S. economy. For each occupation, the volume gives detailed and accurate information regarding (1) the nature of the work; (2) working conditions; (3) employment levels; (4) training, qualifications, and advancement; (5) job outlook (that is, projected employment levels and

Learn as much as you can about the occupations in which you're interested.

SPOTLIGHT ACROSS CULTURES

Working in the International Arena

Many recent graduates elect to work temporarily overseas before "settling down" to a career stateside. Fortunately, many countries allow students or recent graduates to receive a temporary work permit with little hassle. For example, the United Kingdom issues $100 permits, enabling Americans to work in England, Scotland, Wales, or Northern Ireland for up to six months. Many of these temporary employees work as waiters, bartenders, hotel staff, secretaries, or retail clerks and then return to the United States to attend graduate school or begin their careers with an international experience added to their résumés.

WORKING FOR A JAPANESE FIRM

Suppose, however, you wish to secure a more or less permanent position at an American subsidiary of a Japanese firm. You may wonder how to conduct yourself during the intensive interviewing that precedes a job offer. The best advice is just to be yourself. When you meet your interviewers, for example, you do not need to bow; neither, however, should you appear to be too effervescent—wildly shaking hands and talking in a loud voice, with exaggerated body language.

If you're the type of person who needs an immediate decision and who dislikes meetings, you will quickly decide that you should look for a job elsewhere. The Japanese style of consensus management means that you will attend lots of meetings in which every nuance of every decision is discussed. The advantage of such a strategy is that all issues are raised and debated, everyone has his or her say, and everyone thus feels a part of the final decision. Therefore, although decision making may take longer than in an American firm, implementation is likely to be faster and easier.

Job interviews are often very involved and time-consuming. The Japanese view the organization as an extended family and are quite interested in how the applicants as well as their families would fit into the organizational family. Look for an opportunity to show that you are a team member, are eager to work with others, and get along well with your colleagues.

You will likely rise faster and higher in a Japanese-owned firm if you're in the sales or human resources area, which is often headed by an American. Finance, however, which requires close coordination with the headquarters in Japan, is typically headed by a Japanese. And the chief executive officer is invariable Japanese.

SPEAKING THE LANGUAGE

Although it is not absolutely necessary in all cases, competence in the native language is a very strong qualification—and one that will set you apart from most of your competitors. Only through learning the native language is a person truly able to appreciate a culture, understand how its members think, and become accepted by them. Even if the native business people speak English, as many of them surely will, the fact that you've taken the trouble to learn their language, albeit haltingly and with a pronounced accent, will demonstrate vividly your interest in and respect for them.

TAPPING INTO A TREND

The opportunities for important and satisfying careers in the international arena are enormous and growing rapidly each year. In addition to large international firms, small and medium-sized companies are finding a ready market for their products and services on both sides of both oceans—as well as in Mexico and Canada. Also don't overlook U.S. government positions, including positions in the foreign service and in such organizations as the U.S. Agency for International Development.

If you are adventuresome, self-confident, independent, flexible, curious, and open-minded, perhaps the *world,* rather than any particular country or city, will become your new home.

Sources: Philip R. Harris and Robert T. Moran, *Managing Cultural Differences,* 2d ed., Gulf Publishing, Houston, TX, 1987; Bill Powell, "How to Win Over a Japanese Boss," *Newsweek,* February 2, 1987, p. 46; Chip Rowe, "Working in Europe After Graduation," *National Business Employment Weekly,* Spring 1991, pp. 18–20.

factors influencing the future of the occupation); (6) earnings; (7) related occupations; and (8) sources of additional information.

Other sources of job information are your college placement office, professional associations (see the *Encyclopedia of Associations*, published by Gale Research Company of Detroit, Michigan, for a list of professional associations in your area of interest), and business periodicals, such as the *Wall Street Journal*, *Business Week*, and *Forbes*. The latter two publications are especially helpful because each issue contains an index of those companies mentioned in that issue.

Study the environment in which you will be working.

Demographic Information Smart career choices are dictated not only by personal interest but also by demographic characteristics, with which you should become familiar. For example, no matter how much you enjoy handwriting and no matter how clear and lovely your lettering is, it is unlikely that you would be able to make a good living today as a scribe (a copier of manuscripts) because technology has preempted that occupation. Some of the demographic trends that the U.S. Department of Labor believes will affect employment through the year 2000 are as follow:[2]

- *Population:* There will be a smaller proportion of children and youth in the future and a considerably greater proportion of middle-aged and older people. Blacks, Hispanics, and Asians will make up a larger share of the population. The West and the South will grow in population, the Midwest will remain the same, and the Northeast will decline.
- *Labor force:* Blacks, Hispanics, and Asians will account for 58% of the growth in the labor force between 1986 and 2000; women will account for 47% of the labor force in 2000. The fastest-growing jobs will be in executive, managerial, professional, and technical fields—those requiring the highest levels of education and skill.
- *Industrial profile:* Nearly four out of every five jobs in the year 2000 will be in industries that provide services—such as banking, health care, hospitality, and consulting. In the goods-producing industries, only the construction industry is expected to grow; manufacturing, mining, and agriculture will decline.

Suggest that your students look for jobs in small companies rather than large ones. Since 1980, the 500 largest U.S. companies have lost 3.9 million jobs, but since 1970, two of every three new jobs have been created by firms with 100 or fewer employees. (Richard Bolles, *What Color Is Your Parachute?*, Ten Speed Press, Berkeley, CA, 1993, p. 76.)

Industry and Company Information Now that you have analyzed yourself in relation to a career, investigated possible professions, and studied demographic trends, you probably have a good idea of the career you want to pursue. You're now ready to research industry and company information. No organization exists in a vacuum. Each is affected by the economic, political, and social environment in which it operates.

Start with the Standard Industry Classification (SIC) code for the industry in which you're interested. Also helpful are the *U.S. Industrial Outlook*, published by the U.S. Department of Commerce, and *Standard and Poor's Industry Surveys*.

After learning about the industry, pick out a few companies to explore further. Be guided by your interests—large versus small firms, geographical constraints, and so forth. This research will give you a better framework for evaluating the specific companies with whom you will be interviewing.

One handy reference is the *CPC Annual*, a three-volume directory of employment opportunities for college graduates (both two- and four-year)

Sources for Locating Jobs

Personal Contacts
- Friends and relatives
- Professors
- Business acquaintances
- Counselors

Placement and Employment Services
- University placement office
- Career counseling center
- State employment agency
- Private employment agencies

Literature
- Government publications
- Professional journals
- Private company publications
- Magazines and newspapers
- Directories, indexes, and databases

See Transparency 16.1, Sources for Locating Jobs.

published by the College Placement Council (Bethlehem, Pennsylvania). This directory, which is available in most college placement offices and libraries, contains narrative information about more than 600 large employers and the types of positions they have available. It is indexed by employer, occupation, and geographical region.

Analyzing the specific organization enables you to tailor your credentials in terms of the organization's needs.

Audience Analysis As noted throughout this text, the task of audience analysis is pivotal to every type of communication skill. Learn as much as you can about the specific employment environment so that you can customize your employment communications to the needs of the employer.

For example, an effective résumé is tailored to the needs of the prospective employer. Analyzing the audience—your potential employer—will show you how to emphasize what you have gained from your education or work experience that will benefit the company. Employers do not hire you as a reward for what you've accomplished in the past but rather for the promise of what you can do for them in the future. So treat your résumé as an advertisement of good things to come rather than as an obituary of what has already happened.

Currently an organization spends $7,500 just to hire an executive,[3] so the cost of making a wrong decision is great. And if you multiply your likely salary times three or four years in a job, you'll see that the organization is making a very expensive purchase when it hires you. If you were making that large an investment, wouldn't you go to great lengths to make the right choice?

To convince the employer that you're worth the investment, learn as much about the organization as possible so that you can then present your credentials in terms of specific reader benefits.

Job-Getting Techniques

Do not depend on any single technique for landing the ideal job. Instead, use every technique at your disposal that might benefit you—including the computer (see the Spotlight on Technology). Some of the more popular techniques are networking, using professional employment services, answering advertisements, and advertising yourself.

Seek the help of professional and personal acquaintances in your job campaign.

Networking In the job-getting process, "networking" refers to developing a group of acquaintances who might provide job leads and career guidance. The term has been used so much recently that it has perhaps become a buzzword, but it is still an important job-getting tool. Everyone searching for a job—from the most recent college graduate to the president of a Fortune 500 firm—has a network on which to draw.

Your initial network might include friends, family, professors, former employers, social acquaintances, college alumni, your dentist, family doctor, insurance agent, local business people, your minister or rabbi—in short, anyone you know who might be able to help. Ideally, your network will combine both personal and professional connections. That's one benefit of belonging to professional associations, and college isn't too early to start. Most professional organizations either have student chapters of their associations or provide reduced-rate student memberships in the parent organization.

SPOTLIGHT ON TECHNOLOGY

Getting A Job—Electronically

Both employers and job seekers are making increasing use of technology to make the job-selection process more effective and more efficient. Let's follow the case of Robin Gryder, a records management major, as he begins his job search.

USING RÉSUMÉ SOFTWARE

To begin, Robin purchases PFS:Resume & Job Search Pro for Windows®, a $79 software program from Spinnaker Software (Cambridge, Massachusetts), to help him prepare his résumé. PFS: Resume takes Robin through a sequential process that helps him organize his skills, experience, and education into a clear and concise format of his choice. After he selects from the many sample formats included, the spacing, fonts, boldfacing, tabs, and underlining are done automatically. The result is a customized résumé in minutes. The data base feature then helps Robin organize his job campaign by keeping track of meeting dates, phone calls, and appointments.

REGISTERING ON-LINE

Next, using his computer and modem, Robin logs onto Internet, a worldwide computer network comprising 11,000 public and private computer systems used by more than 10 million people (most universities offer students free access to Internet). On Internet, he signs up with the nonprofit service Online Career Center (also available on such online systems as America On-Line and CompuServe). Robin now transmits his résumé to the Career Center via computer.

Company recruiters from around the country (or even around the world) access the data base to enter job openings and sort through the posted résumés by region, profession, and other criteria. More than 3,000 companies use the Internet for employment; and at any time, approximately 8,000 jobs are listed, none more than a few weeks old.

MAKING A VIDEO RÉSUMÉ

Recognizing that a printed résumé does little to communicate how he talks, acts, and looks, Robin takes his job search one step further by contacting Res-A-Vue, a video marketing company in Connecticut. For a fee ranging from a few hundred to several thousand dollars, Res-A-Vue will prepare a professionally produced video résumé for a job candidate.

Such résumés typically last about five minutes and give the candidate an opportunity to tell about his or her abilities and ambitions before a studio camera. Res-A-Vue then edits the tape to delete any weak or distracting footage and adds on-screen titles and background music. Robin can then send copies of the videotape to prospective employers to give them an opportunity to "meet" him before the job interview takes place.

SCHEDULING INTERVIEWS

At his computer again, Robin bids for an open interview slot with one of the on-campus recruiters. He can do this from the comfort of his dormitory room, 24 hours a day, seven days a week—not just when the placement office is open. He also uploads his résumé to the placement office computer for the recruiter to review electronically.

As soon as Robin has scheduled an on-campus interview, he logs onto Dialog Information Services and accesses the Disclosure data base to learn more about the company with whom he will be interviewing. Disclosure contains detailed information about all publicly held U.S. corporations. It costs approximately $20 to print out three years of information about the company, such as income statements and balance sheets; names, ages, and salaries of corporate officers and directors; the management discussion from the annual report; and a description of the products or services the company sells. Finally, Robin accesses the *Wall Street Journal Index* to print out copies of any recent news articles that mention the company.

Like all savvy job applicants, Robin uses every communication tool possible to help in this most important undertaking.

Sources: William Bulkeley, "Job-Hunters Turn to Software and Databases to Get an Edge," *Wall Street Journal,* June 16, 1992, p. B13; William B. Flanagan, "Interview . . . Take One!" *Forbes,* November 18, 1992, pp. 244–245; Laurianne McLaughlin, "Software to the Rescue for Creating Your Résumé," *PC World,* October 1993, p. 113; Franklynn Peterson and Judi K. Turkel, "Computer Programs Can Teach and Help Land a Job," *Indianapolis Star,* June 2, 1992, p. C12; John Strauss, "Computer Listing Links Job Seekers, Employers," *Indianapolis Star,* October 7, 1993, p. C1.

Certainly, you don't develop a network of acquaintances purely for personal gain; the friendships gained through such contacts can last a lifetime. But don't forget to seek the advice and help of everyone who can be of assistance in this important endeavor.

Professional Employment Services Professional employment services include your college career center, the state employment service, private employment agencies, and private career consulting services. The college career center is generally the first, the most effective, and often the only source of help used by most graduating students. Such offices typically provide career information, critique student résumés, and arrange interviews with campus recruiters.

Your state employment service can provide information on job vacancies, job requirements, available training programs, and local economic conditions. For a fee, private employment agencies seek to match vacancies at a firm with qualified applicants. Their primary allegiance is to whoever pays their fee; the fee is sometimes paid by the applicant and sometimes by the employer. Career consultants charge a fee for helping people identify and promote their own strengths; their services range from résumé preparation, to administering interest and aptitude tests, to career counseling.

Answering Advertisements Any large daily newspaper contains hundreds of classified ads of job openings, and you would be wise to scan them. Often you can pick up important words and phrases that will help you describe yourself appropriately in your résumé and application letter.

Be aware, however, that most jobs are *not* filled though want ads; in fact only 14% are. The methods by which all jobs are typically filled are shown here as percentages of the whole:[4]

Most jobs are filled through personal contacts.

Networking or personal contacts	70%
Help-wanted ads	14%
Executive search firms	11%
Mass mailing of résumés	5%
	100%

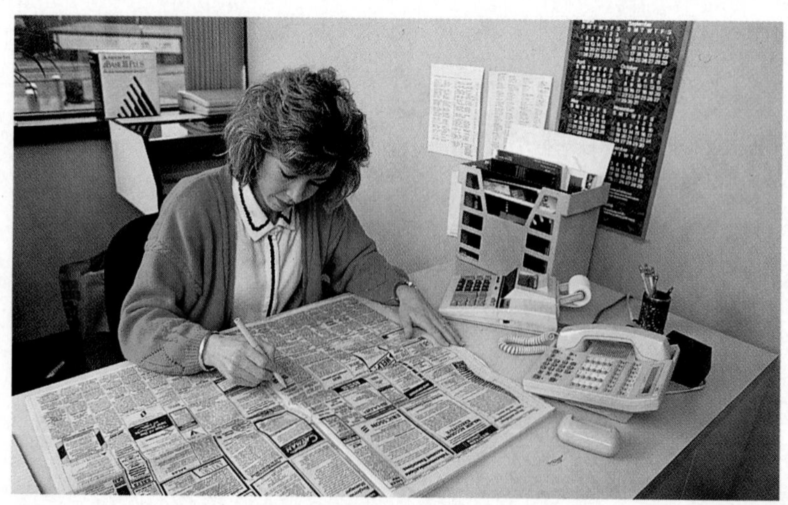

Reading the want ads may not be glamorous, but doing so can provide information, whether or not you ultimately find a job that way. Newspaper ads will give you a sense of what types of businesses are thriving in an area and what kinds of skills are in demand.

For hiring new college graduates, on-campus interviewing is the major source of jobs, accounting for 42% of all selections, with responses from help-wanted ads accounting for 8%.[5]

If you do use want ads, don't rely on them exclusively; follow other leads as well. In addition, to increase your chances, respond as soon as you see a suitable position advertised.

Many newspaper ads are "blind" ads; that is, instead of listing a company name and address, they simply provide a box number for responding to the ad. Although most such ads are legitimate, a word of caution is in order. There have been instances of people submitting their résumés in response to these blind ads who have been victimized by harassing phone calls, burglary, or even bodily harm. After all, your résumé often contains your home address, home phone number, and perhaps even the hours when you're most likely to be at home. Anyone expecting to make heavy use of newspapers ads would be well advised to rent a post-office box for this purpose.

Use common sense when responding to blind ads.

Advertising Yourself Suppose you've followed every lead you can find and still have not been able to locate a suitable vacancy. If, for example, you go to college in the Midwest and plan to seek employment in Southern California, you won't be able to make as effective use of your institution's career center because many of the midwestern recruiters will be interviewing for regional vacancies.

In such circumstances, an aggressive job seeker goes "prospecting"; that is, you begin contacting companies you identified during earlier research and ask if they have openings for which you might qualify. Enclose your résumé with your prospecting (or unsolicited application) letters—letters of inquiry written to organizations that have not advertised vacancies.

Suppose you have learned, for example, that XYZ Corporation is building an assembly plant in Nogales, Mexico. Wouldn't it be reasonable to expect that they might need a personnel specialist (you) who is fluent in Spanish? Write a prospecting letter to find out. Although "blind" prospecting—simply mailing out hundreds of résumés along with a duplicated application letter—will seldom lead to an interview, using the knowledge from your research to customize your appeal to each company *can* prove effective.

PREPARING YOUR RÉSUMÉ

A **résumé** is a brief record of one's personal history and qualifications that is typically prepared by an applicant for a job. Although recruiters sometimes refer to the résumé as a *wilawid* ("What I've learned and what I've done"), the emphasis in the résumé should be on the future rather than on the past: you must show how your education and work experience have prepared you for future jobs—specifically, the job for which you are applying.

For more on résumés, see the supplemental lecture/discussion notes in the *Instructor's Resource Manual*, p. 287.

Right from the start, be realistic about the purpose of your résumé. Few people are actually hired on the basis of their résumés alone. (However,

Job fairs are another way to gather information about an industry. You'll be able to pick up literature describing the companies represented at the fair and to talk to employees about what jobs are available, what the career paths are at the company, and what the salary ranges are, among other things.

many people are *not hired* because of their poorly written or poorly presented résumés.) Instead, applicants are generally hired on the basis of their performance during a job interview.

The purpose of a résumé is to get you a job interview—not to get you a job.

Thus, the purpose of the résumé is to get you an interview, and the purpose of the interview is to get you a job. Remember, however, that the résumé and accompanying application letter (cover letter) are crucial in advancing you beyond the mass of initial applicants and into the much smaller group of potential candidates invited to an interview.

Résumé Length

Most recruiters prefer a one-page résumé for entry-level positions.

Decisions about résumé length become much easier when you consider what happens on the receiving end: recruiters typically spend no more than 35 seconds looking at each résumé during their initial screening to pare down the perhaps hundreds of applications for a position into a manageable number to study in more detail.[6] How much information can the recruiter be expected to read in less than a minute? It won't matter how well qualified you are if no one ever reviews those qualifications.

As one recruiter for a larger corporation has noted, the perfect résumé is "like a Henny Youngman two-liner. No fat. Get to the point and then say goodbye. . . . Remember: You're trying to get us to hire you, not to marry you."[7]

How much is too much? Surveys of employment and human resource executives consistently show that most managers prefer a one-page résumé for the entry-level positions typically sought by recent college graduates, with a two-page résumé being reserved for unusual circumstances or for higher-level positions.[8] True or not, take note of the old placement office adage, "The thicker the résumé, the thicker the applicant."

According to one survey of 200 executives from major U.S. firms, the most serious mistake job candidates make is including too much information in their résumés. Their ranking (in percentages of the whole) of the most serious résumé errors is as follows:[9]

Too long	32%
Typographical or grammatical errors	25%
No descriptions of job functions	18%
Unprofessional appearance	15%
Achievements omitted	10%
	100%

A one-page résumé is *not* the same as a two-page résumé crammed onto one page by means of small type and narrow margins. Your résumé must be attractive and easy to read. Shorten your résumé by making judicious decisions about what to include and then by using concise language to communicate what is important.

Do not, on the other hand, make your résumé *too* short. A résumé that does not fill one page may tell the prospective employer that you have little to offer. It has been estimated that one page is ideal for 85% of all résumés, and that is the length you should target.[10]

Here are a few more books on preparing résumés that Richard Bolles recommends in *What Color Is Your Parachute?: Who's Hiring Who?* by Richard Lathrop, *The Résumé Solution* by David Swanson, *The Perfect Résumé* by Tom Jackson, *The Damn Good Résumé Guide* by Yana Parker, and *The Overnight Résumé* by Donald Asher.

Résumé Format

Although the content of your résumé is obviously more important than the format, remember that first impressions are lasting. As pointed out earlier, those first impressions are formed during the half-minute that is typically devoted to the initial screening of each résumé. Therefore, even before you begin writing your résumé, think about the format, because some format decisions will affect the amount of space available to discuss your qualifications and background.

One of your first decisions will be whether to prepare your résumé yourself or to hire someone to do it for you. In years past, it was often advantageous to have your résumé prepared and typeset at a print shop. Although typeset résumés do look professional, the danger is that most résumé-preparation services tend to use similar formats and type styles for many résumés, so your résumé tends to look like many others. Experienced résumé readers can also spot a professionally prepared résumé and may wonder why the applicant did not feel qualified to prepare his or her own. Recruiters want to learn about you, not about someone else's interpretation of you.

Design and prepare your own résumé.

Another problem is that once you've gone to the trouble and expense of having your résumé professionally prepared, you'll probably be reluctant to change it. But as any experienced job seeker can attest, you'll learn things during each interview that will help you sharpen your résumé, and you'll want to revise, add, delete, and reorganize the information.

Thus, a far better option is to design and prepare your résumé yourself. Your college placement office will likely have on file many résumés that you can review for format and content ideas. And consult some of the many employment guides available, such as *How to Write a Winning Résumé,* by Deborah Bloch (VGM Career Horizons); *Your First Résumé,* by

Ronald Fry (Career Press); and *What Color Is Your Parachute?* by Richard Bolles (Ten Speed Press).

If you prepare your résumé and application letter on a computer, you can easily customize them for each employment opportunity. In addition, you'll be sending the employer a nonverbal message that you know how to use a computer and word processing software.

If you print your résumé on a laser printer, it will be nearly indistinguishable from a typeset one. With laser printers, you have the option of using different typefaces (such as Times Roman or Helvetica) and different sizes and styles (such as boldface and italics) to make different parts stand out. Consider, for example, the two versions of the same résumé shown in the Spotlight on Technology. Both contain identical information; which one makes the better first impression?

Use a clear, simple design, with plenty of white space.

Choose a simple, easy-to-read typeface, and avoid the temptation to use a lot of "special effects" just because they're available on your computer. One or two typefaces in one or two different sizes should be enough. Use a simple format, with lots of white space, short paragraphs, and a logical organization. Through the use of type size and style, indentation, bullets, and the like, make clear which parts are subordinate to main features.

Format your résumé on standard-sized paper (8½ by 11 inches) so that it can be filed easily. Also, avoid brightly colored papers: they'll get attention but perhaps the wrong kind. Dark colors do not photocopy well, and you want photocopies of your résumé (whether prepared by you or by the potential employer) to look professional. Choose white or an off-white (cream or ivory) paper of good quality—at least 20-pound bond.

Unless you're applying for a creative position (such as a copywriter of advertising material) and know your intended audience well, avoid being too artistic and original in formatting your résumé. If you are applying for the typical business position, the overall appearance of your résumé should present a professional, conservative appearance—one that adds to your credibility. Don't scare off your readers before they have a chance to meet you.

Finally, your résumé and application letter must be 100% free from error—in content, spelling, grammar, and format. Ninety-nine percent accuracy is simply not good enough when seeking a job. One recent survey of large company executives showed that fully 80% of them had decided against interviewing a job seeker simply because of poor grammar, spelling, or punctuation in his or her résumé.[11] Don't write, as one job applicant did, "Education: Advanced Curses in Accounting," or as another did, "I have an obsession for detail; I make sure that I cross my i's and dot my t's." Show right from the start that you're the type of person who takes pride in his or her work.

Résumé Content

Fortunately, perhaps, there is no such thing as a standard résumé; each is as individual as the person it represents. There are, however, standard parts of the résumé—those parts recruiters expect and need to see to make valid judgments. For example, one survey of 152 Fortune 500 company per-

First Impressions Count!

PATRICIA L. BAILEY

(Address until May 10, 1995)
112 Campus Drive, Apt. B
Bloomington, IN 47401
Phone: 812-555-9331

(Address after May 10, 1995)
915 North Jay Street
Indianapolis, IN 46204
Phone: 317-555-0328

JOB OBJECTIVE

Professional position in hotel management in the Chicago metropolitan area

EDUCATION

Bachelor of Science in Business Administration
Indiana University: May 1995
Major: Hospitality Services Administration
Minor: Marketing
Achieved overall grade-point average of 3.4 (on a 4.0 scale).
Received Board of Regents' tuition scholarship.
Financed 75% of college expenses through savings and part-time work.

WORK EXPERI

Assistant Manager, McDonald's Restaurant
Bloomington, Indiana: 1991-Present (f
during school year)
Advanced to this position after
and cook; developed work schedu
designed and administered sever
projects; gained considerable p
employees and handling human-re

Student Intern, Valley Hideaway
South Bend, Indiana: September-Decem
sponsored by Indiana University)
Worked as the assistant to the
gained experience in operating
was responsible for producing d
wrote two articles for the empl

PERSONAL

Active member of Sigma Iota Epsilon (busine
Treasurer of Hospitality Services Associati
Special Olympics volunteer--Summer 1994

REFERENCES AVAILABLE

This version of the résumé was typed on an electronic typewriter and arranged in an attractive, easy-to-read format. However, the absence of different type styles and sizes limits design flexibility.

Patricia L. Bailey

(Address until May 10, 1995)
112 Campus Drive, Apt. B
Bloomington, IN 47401
Phone: 812-555-9331

(Address after May 10, 1995)
915 North Jay Street
Indianapolis, IN 46204
Phone: 317-555-0328

Job Objective

Professional position in hotel management in the Chicago metropolitan area

Education

Bachelor of Science in Business Administration — Indiana University, May 1995
Major: Hospitality Services Administration
Minor: Marketing
- Achieved overall grade-point average of 3.4 (on a 4.0 scale).
- Received Board of Regents' tuition scholarship.
- Financed 75% of college expenses through savings and part-time work.

Work Experience

Assistant Manager, McDonald's Restaurant — Bloomington, Indiana
1991-Present (full-time during summers; part-time during school year)
- Advanced to this position after only six months as a counter clerk and cook.
- Developed work schedules for 23 part-time employees.
- Designed and administered several successful employee incentive projects.
- Gained considerable practical experience in supervising employees and handling human-relations problems.

Student Intern, Valley Hideaway — South Bend, Indiana
September-December 1994 (full-time internship sponsored by Indiana University)
- Worked as the assistant to the night manager of a 200-room resort.
- Gained experience in operating the GuestServ management system.
- Was responsible for producing daily and weekly occupancy reports.
- Wrote two articles for the employee newsletter.

Personal

Active member of Sigma Iota Epsilon (business honor society)
Treasurer of Hospitality Services Association
Special Olympics volunteer—Summer 1994

References Available upon Request

This version was typed on a microcomputer using word processing software and printed on a laser printer. It contains the same information as the typewritten version, but it is much more attractive and readable.

A growing number of companies are now filing résumés in electronic databases or turning to commercial résumé databases. By searching its database for key qualifications, Nike turned up Peg Donovan's résumé and promptly hired her. But characteristics like italic type and colored paper that might make a résumé attractive to a human reader make it difficult to scan into a database.

sonnel indicated that 90% or more wanted the following information on a résumé:[12]

Include the information employers want; exclude the information they do not want.

- Name, address, and telephone number
- Job objective
- College major, degree, name of college, and date of graduation
- Jobs held, employing company or companies (but not complete mailing address or the names of your supervisors), dates of employment, and job duties
- Special aptitudes and skills

Similarly, items *not* wanted on the résumé (items rated unimportant by over 90% of those surveyed) related primarily to bases for discrimination: religion, ethnicity, age, gender, photograph, and marital status. Additionally, most of the employers questioned thought high school activities should not be included on the résumés of college graduates.

The standard and optional parts of the résumé are discussed here in the order in which they typically appear on the résumé of a recent (or soon-to-be) college graduate.

Display your name, address, and phone number in a prominent position.

Identifying Information It doesn't do any good to impress a recruiter if he or she cannot locate you easily to schedule an interview; therefore, your name and complete address (including phone number) are crucial.

Your name should be the very first item on the résumé, arranged attractively at the top. Use whatever form you typically use for signing your name (for example, with or without initials). Give your compete name, avoiding nicknames, and do not use a personal title such as *Mr.* or *Ms.*

It is not necessary to include the heading "Résumé" at the top (any more than it is necessary to use the heading "Letter" at the top of a business letter). The purpose of the document will be evident to the recruiter. Besides, you want your name to be the main heading—where it will stand out in the recruiter's mind.

If you will soon be changing your address (as from a college address to a home address), include both, along with the relevant dates for each. If you are away from your telephone most of the day and no one is at home to answer it and take a message, you would be wise to invest in an answering machine or get permission to use the telephone number where you work as an alternate phone listing. The important point is to be available for contact.

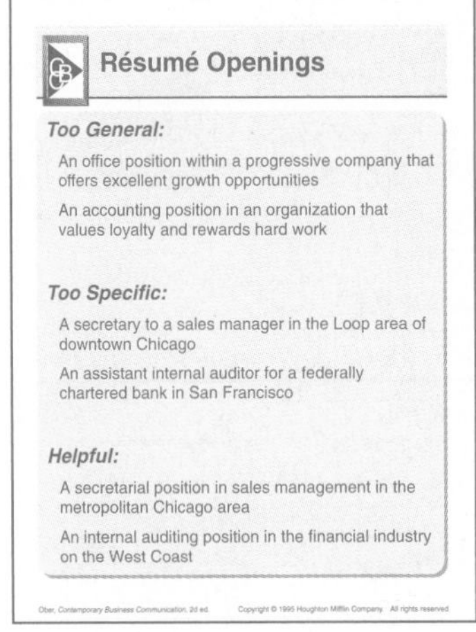

Résumé Openings
Too General:
An office position within a progressive company that offers excellent growth opportunities
An accounting position in an organization that values loyalty and rewards hard work
Too Specific:
A secretary to a sales manager in the Loop area of downtown Chicago
An assistant internal auditor for a federally chartered bank in San Francisco
Helpful:
A secretarial position in sales management in the metropolitan Chicago area
An internal auditing position in the financial industry on the West Coast

See Transparency 16.2, Résumé Openings.

Job Objective The job objective is a one-sentence summary of your area of expertise and career interest. As indicated, most recruiters want the objective stated so that they will know where you might fit into their organization. Don't force the employer to guess about your career goals.

Furthermore, don't waste the objective's prominent spot at the top of your résumé by giving a weak, over-general goal like these:

Not: "A position that offers both a challenge and an opportunity for growth."

Not: "Challenging position in a progressive organization."

Not: "A responsible position that lets me use my education and experience and that provides opportunities for increased responsibilities."

The problem with such goals is not that they're unworthy objectives; they are *very* worthwhile. That is why everyone—including the recruiter presumably—wants such positions. The problem is that such vague, high-flown goals don't help the recruiter find a suitable position for *you*. They waste valuable space on your résumé.

Include a job objective if you have specific requirements.

For your objective to help you, it must be personalized—both for you and for the position you're seeking. Also, it must be specific enough to be useful to the prospective employer but not so specific as to exclude you from many types of similar positions. The following job objectives meet these criteria:

- "Position in personal sales in a medium-sized manufacturing firm."
- "Opportunity to apply my accounting education and Spanish-language skills in a corporation overseas."
- "A public relations position requiring well-developed communication, administrative, and computer skills."

Note that after reading these three objectives, you feel you know a little about each candidate, a feeling you did not get from reading the earlier general objectives. If your goals are so broad that you have difficulty specifying a job objective, consider either eliminating this section of your résumé or developing several résumés, each with a different job objective and emphasis.

You should be aware that an increasing number of large corporations have begun scanning the résumés they receive into their computer systems and then searching this computerized data base by key word. Be certain, therefore, that the title of the actual position you desire and other relevant terms are included somewhere in your résumé.

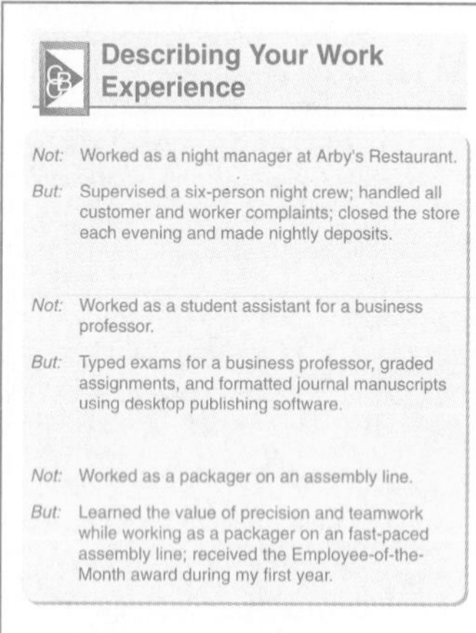

See Transparency 16.3, Describing Work Experience on a Resumé.

Regardless of which type of organizational pattern you use, provide complete information about your work history.

Education Unless your work experience has been extensive, fairly high level, and directly related to your job objective, your education is probably a stronger job qualification than your work experience and should therefore come first on the résumé.

List the title of your degree, the name of your college and its location if needed, your major and (if applicable) minor, and your expected date of graduation (month and year).

List your grade-point average if it will set you apart from the competition (generally, at least a 3.0 on a 4.0 scale). If you've made the dean's list or have financed any substantial portion of your college expenses through part-time work, savings, or scholarships, mention that. Unless your course of study provided distinctive experiences that uniquely qualify you for the job, avoid including a lengthy list of college courses.

Work Experience Today, almost half of all full-time college students are employed, most of them working between 15 and 29 hours a week.[13] And most other students have had at least some work experience in the past—for example, summer jobs. Thus, most students will have some work experience to bring to their future jobs.

Work experience—*any* work experience—is a definite plus. It shows the employer that you've had experience in satisfying a superior, following directions, accomplishing objectives through group effort, and being rewarded for your labors. If your work experience has been directly related to your job objectives, consider putting it ahead of the education section, where it will receive more emphasis.

In relating your work experience, use either a chronological or a functional organizational pattern.

- *Chronological:* In a chronological arrangement, you organize your experience by date, describing your most recent job first and working backward. This format is most appropriate when you have had a strong continuing work history and much of your work has been related to your job objective (see Figure 16.1, page 548). About 95% of all résumés are chronological, beginning with the most recent information and working backward.[14]
- *Functional:* In a functional arrangement, you organize your experience by type of function performed (such as *supervision* or *budgeting*) or by type of skill developed (such as *human relations* or *communication skills*). Then, under each, give specific examples (evidence) as illustrated in Figure 16.2, page 549. Functional résumés are most appropriate when you're changing industries, moving into an entirely different line of work, or are reentering the work force after a long period of unemployment, because they emphasize your skills rather than your employment history and let you show how these skills have broad applicability to other jobs.

In actual practice, the two patterns are not mutually exclusive; you can use a combination. And regardless of which arrangement you ultimately decide on, remember that more than 90% of the employers in the survey cited earlier indicated they want to see on a résumé the jobs held, employing company or companies, dates of employment, and job duties.

Remember that the purpose of describing your work history is to show the prospective employer what you've learned *that will benefit the organization.* No matter what your previous work, you've developed certain traits or had certain experiences that can be transferred to the new position. Based on your research into the duties of the job you are seeking, highlight those transferable skills.

If you can honestly do so, show in your résumé that you have developed as many of the following characteristics as possible:

Show how your work experience qualifies you for the type of job for which you are applying.

- Ability to work well with others
- Communication skills
- Competence and good judgment
- Innovation
- Reliability and trustworthiness
- Enthusiasm
- Honest and moral character
- Increasing responsibility

Complete sentences are not necessary. Instead, start your descriptions with action verbs, using present tense for current duties and past tense for previous job duties or accomplishments. Concrete words such as the following make your work experience come alive:

Use concrete, achievement-oriented words to describe your experience.

accomplished	designed	operated
achieved	determined	ordered
administered	developed	organized
analyzed	diagnosed	oversaw
approved	directed	planned
arranged	edited	prepared
applied	established	presented
assisted	evaluated	presided
authorized	forecast	produced
balanced	generated	purchased
budgeted	guided	recommended
built	handled	reported
changed	hired	researched
collected	implemented	revised
communicated	increased	scheduled
completed	instituted	screened
conceived	interviewed	secured
concluded	introduced	simplified
conducted	investigated	sold
consolidated	led	studied
contracted	maintained	supervised
controlled	managed	taught
constructed	marketed	trained
coordinated	modified	transformed
created	motivated	updated
delegated	negotiated	wrote

FIGURE 16.1 Résumé in Chronological Format

Provides specific enough objective to be useful.

Places work experience before education because applicant considers it to be her stronger qualification.

Uses action words like *assisted* and *developed;* uses incomplete sentences to emphasize the action words and to conserve space.

Provides degree, institution, major, and graduation date.

Provides additional data to enhance her credentials.

Does not include actual names and addresses of references.

Aurelia Gomez 1

225 West 70 Street, New York, NY 10023
Phone: Days—212-555-3079; Evenings—212-555-3821

--- 2

Career Objective

Entry-level staff accounting position with a public accounting firm

Experience 3

Summer 1994 — ***Accounting Intern:*** Coopers & Lybrand, New York City
Assisted in preparing corporate tax returns; attended meetings with clients; conducted research in corporate tax library and wrote research reports; was invited to work again the following summer.

Nov. 1990- Aug. 1993 — ***Payroll Specialist:*** City of New York
Full-time civil service position in Department of Administration. Used payroll software on both DEC 1034 minicomputer and IBM microcomputers; audited all overtime billing; developed two new forms for requesting independent-contractor status that are now used throughout all branches of city government; represented 28-person work unit on the department's management-labor committee; left job to pursue college degree full-time.

Education

Jan. 1988- Present — Pursuing a bachelor of business administration degree from New York University 4
Major: Accounting
Expected graduation date: June 1995
Attended part-time from 1988 until 1993 while holding down a full-time job; have financed 100% of all college expenses through savings, part-time work, and student loans; plan to sit for the CPA exam in November 1995.

Personal Data

- Helped start the Minority Business Student Association at New York University and served as program director for two years; secured the publisher of *Black Enterprise* magazine as a banquet speaker
- Have traveled extensively throughout the Caribbean
- Member of the Accounting Society
- Willing to relocate

References — Available on Request

Grammar and Mechanics Notes

1 The name is formatted in larger type for emphasis. 2 A horizontal rule separates the heading information from the body of the résumé. 3 The major section headings are parallel in format and in wording. 4 The side headings for the dates are formatted in a vertical column for ease of reading. Note that abbreviations may be used.

FIGURE 16.2 Résumé in Functional Format

Raymond J. Arnold

15 Turner Hall
Northern Arizona University
Flagstaff, AZ 86001-8134
Phone: 602-555-9833

Address after June 15, 1995:
801 Benjamin Avenue, Apt. 16-G
Norfolk, NE 68701
Phone: 308-555-3714

Provides both temporary and permanent addresses.

1 **OBJECTIVE**
Labor relations position in a large multinational firm that requires well-developed labor relations, management, and communication skills

LABOR RELATIONS SKILLS
- Majored in labor relations; minored in psychology
- Belong to Local 463 of International Office Workers Union (member since 1992)
- 2 Was crew chief for the second-shift work team at Valley National Bank
- Served as the student member of the faculty senate at Northern Arizona University

Introduces three skill areas and expands on each with bulleted examples.

MANAGEMENT SKILLS
- Learned time-management skills by working 30 hours per week while attending school full-time
- Was promoted twice in three years at Valley National Bank
- Sharpened interpersonal and human relations skills while dealing extensively with the public as a teller and salesperson
- Practiced discretion while dealing with the financial affairs of others; treated all transactions confidentially

Relates each listed item directly to the desired job.

Provides specific evidence to support each skill.

COMMUNICATION SKILLS
- Was the newsletter editor for Alpha Kappa Psi, professional business fraternity
- Ran for senior class vice president, making frequent campaign speeches and impromptu remarks
- 3 Took elective classes in report writing and business research
- Know how to use word processing and desktop publishing software

Weaves work experiences, education, and extracurricular activities into the skill statements.

EDUCATION
Bachelor of Science degree from Northern Arizona University
Degree to be awarded June 1995
Major: Labor Relations; Minor: Psychology

4

EXPERIENCE
- Bank teller, Valley National Bank, Flagstaff, Arizona: 1992-Present
- Salesperson, Penney's, Norfolk, Nebraska: Summer 1990

Avoids repeating the duties given earlier.

REFERENCES
Available from the Placement and Career Information Center, Northern Arizona University, Flagstaff, AZ 86001-8134; phone: 602-555-2000

Grammar and Mechanics Notes

1 Putting the headings along the side and indenting the copy opens up the résumé, providing more white space. 2 Bullets are used to highlight the individual skills; asterisks would have worked just as well. 3 All items are in parallel format. 4 More space is left *between* the different sections than *within* sections (to clearly separate each section).

A few more gender-specific words you can remind your students to avoid are cameraman, congressman, pressman, spokesman, stock boy, tradesman, and workman's compensation. Instead, use camera operator, representative or senator, press operator, spokesperson, stock clerk, shopkeeper, and worker's compensation. (Helen Gorenstein, *Put It in a Memo*, Houghton Mifflin, Boston, MA, 1991, p. 51.)

Avoid weak verbs such as *attempted, endeavored, hoped,* and *tried,* and avoid sexist language such as *manpower* or *chairman*. When possible, ensure credibility by listing specific accomplishments, giving numbers or dollar amounts. Highlight especially those accomplishments that have direct relevance to the desired job. Here are some examples:

Weak: I was responsible for a large sales territory.

Better: Managed a six-county sales territory; increased sales 13% during first full year.

Weak: I worked as a clerk in the cashier's office.

Better: Balanced the cash register every day; was the only part-time employee entrusted to make nightly cash deposits.

Weak: Worked as a bouncer at a local bar.

Better: Maintained order at Nick's Side-Door Saloon; learned firsthand the importance of compromise and negotiation in solving problems.

Weak: Worked as a volunteer for Art Reach.

Better: Personally sold more than $1,000 worth of tickets to annual benefit dance; introduced an "Each one, reach one" membership drive that increased membership every year during my three-year term as membership chairperson.

Work experience need not be restricted to paid positions.

As illustrated in the last example, if you have little or no actual work experience, show how your involvement with professional, social, or civic organizations has helped you develop skills that are transferable to the workplace. Volunteer work, for example, can help develop valuable skills in time management, working with groups, handling money, speaking, accepting responsibility, and the like. In addition, many schools offer internships in which a student receives course credit and close supervision while holding down a temporary job.

It has been said that the closest any of us comes to perfection is when we develop our résumé, which has also been called "a balance sheet without any liabilities." Employers recognize your right to put your best foot forward in your résumé—that is, to highlight your strengths and minimize your weaknesses. However, you must never lie about anything and must never take credit for anything you did not do. A simple telephone call can verify any statement on your résumé.

Be ethical in all aspects of your résumé.

The *Wall Street Journal* calls the background checking of job applicants a growth industry.[15] Screening firms can electronically tap into public records and purchase the computerized files of credit-reporting firms, often producing résumé verifications within 24 hours at a cost of a few dollars per search. Don't risk destroying your credibility before being hired, and don't risk the possibility of being dismissed later for misrepresenting your qualifications.

Other Relevant Information If you have special skills that might give you an edge over the competition (such as knowledge of a foreign language), list them. Although competence in common software programs such as spreadsheets, word processing, and data bases was considered a special skill in the past, today employers assume that most business graduates will have such skills; therefore, listing them will not be of special benefit to you. However, nonbusiness majors should list these and any other specific business skills on their résumés.

Include any honors or recognitions that have relevance to the job you're seeking. Memberships in business-related organizations demonstrate your commitment to your profession, and you should list them if space permits. Likewise, involvement in volunteer, civic, and other extracurricular activities gives evidence of a well-rounded individual and reflects your values and commitment.

Avoid including any data that can become grounds for a discrimination suit—such as information about age, gender, race, religion, handicaps, marital status, and the like. Do not include a photograph with your application papers. Some employers like to have the applicant's Social Security number included as an aid in verifying college or military information. If you have military experience, include it. If your name stereotypes you as a possible noncitizen and citizenship is important for the job you want, you may want to explicitly state your citizenship.

Other optional information includes hobbies and special interests, travel experiences, willingness to travel, and health status. (However, because it is unlikely that anyone has ever written "Health—Poor" on a résumé, a health statement may be meaningless.) Such information may be included if it has direct relevance to your desired job and if you have room for it, but it may be safely omitted if you need space for more important information.

As space permits, include other information that uniquely qualifies you for the type of position for which you're applying.

References A **reference** is a person who has agreed to provide information to a prospective employer regarding a job applicant's fitness for a job. As a general rule, the names and addresses of references should not be included on the résumé itself. Instead, give a general statement that references are available. This policy ensures that you will be contacted before your references are called. The exception to this practice is if your references are likely to be known by the person reading the résumé; in this case, list their names.

The names of references are generally not included on the résumé.

Your references should be professional references rather than character references. The best ones are employers, especially your present employer. University professors with whom you have had a close and successful relationship are also valuable references. When asking for references, be prepared to sign a waiver stating that you forgo your right to see the recommendation or that you won't claim that a reference prevented you from getting a job. Many firms are becoming reluctant to authorize their managers to provide reference letters because of the possibility of being sued.

Study the résumé presented earlier in the Spotlight on Technology (page 543) and the two résumés shown in Figures 16.1 and 16.2. Note the different formats that can be used to present the data. As stated earlier, there is no standard résumé format. Use these résumés or others to which you have access (available from your college career center office or from job-hunting books) to glean ideas for formatting your own.

Note also the different organizational patterns used to convey work experience. The résumé in Figure 16.1 is arranged in a chronological pattern (with the most recent work experience listed first), whereas the one in

CHECKLIST 17

Résumés

LENGTH AND FORMAT

1. Use a one-page résumé (neither longer nor shorter) when applying for most entry-level positions.
2. For maximum impact and flexibility, format your résumé on a computer with word processing software and print it on a laser printer.
3. Use a simple format, with lots of white space and short blocks of text. By means of type size, indenting, bullets, boldface, and the like, show which parts are subordinate to other parts.
4. Print your résumé on standard-sized (8 ½ x 11 inches), good-quality, white or off-white (cream or ivory) paper.
5. Make sure the finished document looks professional, attractive, and conservative and that it is 100% error-free.

CONTENT

6. Type your complete name without a personal title at the top of the document (omit the word *résumé*), followed by an address (both temporary and permanent if needed) and a daytime phone number.

Figure 16.2 is arranged in a functional pattern that stresses the skills learned rather than the jobs held. Note how job descriptions and skills are all geared to support the applicant's qualifications for the desired job. Note also the concise, concrete language used and the overall tone of quiet confidence.

Because your résumé is about you, it is perhaps the most personal business document you'll ever write. Use everything you know about successful communication techniques to ensure that you tell your story in the most effective manner possible. After you're satisfied with the content and arrangement of your résumé, proofread your document carefully and have several others proofread it also. Then have it photocopied on high-quality white or off-white 8½- by-11-inch paper, and turn your attention to your cover letters.

The guidelines for developing a résumé are summarized in Checklist 17.

For more on application letters, see the supplemental lecture/discussion notes in the *Instructor's Resource Manual*, p. 287.

WRITING JOB-APPLICATION LETTERS

A résumé itself is all that is generally needed to secure an interview with an on-campus recruiter. However, you will likely not want to limit your job search to those employers that interview on campus. Campus recruiters typically represent large organizations or regional employers. Thus, if you want to work in a smaller organization or in a distant location, you will need to contact those organizations by writing application letters.

For more on writing job-application letters, see Video Case Study 4, Chemical Bank.

An **application letter** communicates to the prospective employer your interest in and qualifications for a position within the organization. The letter is also called a *cover letter*, because it introduces (or "covers") the major

7. Include a one-sentence job objective that is specific enough to be useful to the employer but not so specific as to preclude consideration for similar jobs.
8. Decide whether your education or work experience is your stronger qualification, and list it first. For education, list the title of your degree, the name of your college and its location, your major and minor, and your expected date of graduation (month and year). List your grade-point average if it is impressive and any academic honors. Avoid listing college courses that are part of the normal preparation for your desired position.
9. For work experience, determine whether to use a chronological (most recent job first) or a functional (list of competencies and skills developed) organizational pattern. For either, stress those duties or skills that are transferable to the new position. Use short phrases and action verbs, and provide specific evidence of the results you achieved.
10. Include any additional information (such as special skills, professional affiliations, and willingness to travel or relocate) that will help to distinguish you from the competition. Avoid including such personal information as age, gender, ethnicity, religion, disabilities, or marital status.
11. Provide a statement that references are available on request.
12. Throughout, highlight your strengths and minimize any weaknesses, but always tell the truth.

points in your résumé, which you should include with the application letter. A **solicited application letter** is written in response to an advertised vacancy, whereas an **unsolicited application letter** (also called a *prospecting letter*) is written to an organization that has not advertised a vacancy.

Use the application letter, which is often your first contact with the potential employer, to personalize your qualifications for one specific job.

Most job applicants use the same résumé when applying for numerous positions and then use their application letter to personalize their qualification for the specific job for which they are applying. Even so, much of the information in cover letters remains constant; therefore, using word processing software will result in less input time and higher-quality output.

Because the application letter is the first thing the employer will read about you, it is of crucial importance. Make sure the letter is formatted appropriately, looks attractive, and is free from typographical, spelling, and grammatical errors. Don't forget to sign the letter and don't forget to enclose a copy of your résumé.

More than half of 500 executives surveyed thought unsolicited résumés indicated that the sender was unemployed and had sent the résumé to many corporations. "When you're trying to get your foot in the door to set up your first meeting, the best tactic is to concentrate your efforts on a letter of introduction." (Quote from outplacement firm Swain and Swain founders Madeleine and Robert Swain in "How to Write Letters that Win Jobs," *Working Woman*, April 1989, p. 120.)

Some personnel specialists say they learn more about the applicant from reading a cover letter than from reading a résumé. According to one recruiter, "A résumé tells what they [job applicants] have done. A cover letter tells who they are. I can learn a person's style, poise, confidence, humbleness, skills, control of the language, and potential from a cover letter."[16]

Your cover letter is a sales letter—you're selling your qualifications to the prospective employer. You should use the same persuasive techniques you learned earlier; for example, provide specific evidence, stress reader benefits, avoid exaggeration, and show confidence in the quality of your product.

An application letter should be no longer than one page. Let's examine each part of a typical letter. Figure 16.3 shows a solicited application letter, written to accompany the résumé presented in Figure 16.1. (An unsolicited application letter appears in Microwriting on page 558.)

FIGURE 16.3 Solicited Job-Application Letter

This is an example of a solicited application letter; it accompanies the résumé in Figure 16.1.

March 13, 1995

Mr. David Norman, Partner
Ross, Russell & Weston
452 Fifth Avenue
New York, NY 10018

Dear Mr. Norman: 1

Begins by identifying the job position and the source of advertising.

My varied work experience in accounting and payroll services, coupled with my accounting degree, has prepared me for the position of EDP specialist that you advertised in the March 9 <u>New York Times</u>. 2

Emphasizes a qualification that might distinguish her from other applicants.

In addition to taking required courses in accounting and business information systems as part of my accounting major at New York University, I also took an elective course in EDP auditing and control. The training I received in this course in applications, software, systems, and service-center records would immediately enable me to become a productive member of your EDP consulting staff. 3

Relates her work experience to the specific needs of the employer.

My college training has been supplemented by an internship in a large public accounting firm. In addition, my two and a half years of experience as a payroll specialist for the city of New York have given me firsthand knowledge of the operation and needs of nonprofit agencies. This experience should help me to contribute to your large consulting practice with governmental agencies.

Provides a telephone number (may be done either in the body of the letter or in the last line of the address block).

After you have had an opportunity to review my enclosed résumé, I would appreciate having the opportunity to discuss with you in person why I believe I have the right qualifications and personality to serve you and your clients. I can be reached by phone at 212-555-3821 after 3 p.m. daily. 4

Sincerely,

Aurelia Gomez

Aurelia Gomez 5
225 West 70 Street
New York, NY 10023

Enclosure

Grammar and Mechanics Notes

1 This letter is formatted in modified-block style with standard punctuation (colon after the salutation and comma after the complimentary closing). 2 <u>*New York Times*</u>: Underline (or italicize) the names of newspapers. 3 *accounting and business information systems:* Do not capitalize the names of college courses unless they include a proper noun. 4 *résumé:* This word may also properly be written without the accent marks: *resume.* 5 Putting the writer's name and address together at the bottom of the letter makes it convenient for the reader to respond.

Address and Salutation

Your letter should be addressed to an individual rather than to an organization or department. Remember, the more hands your letter must go through before it reaches the right person, the more chance for something to go wrong. Ideally, your letter should be addressed to the person who will actually interview you and who will likely be your supervisor if you get the job.

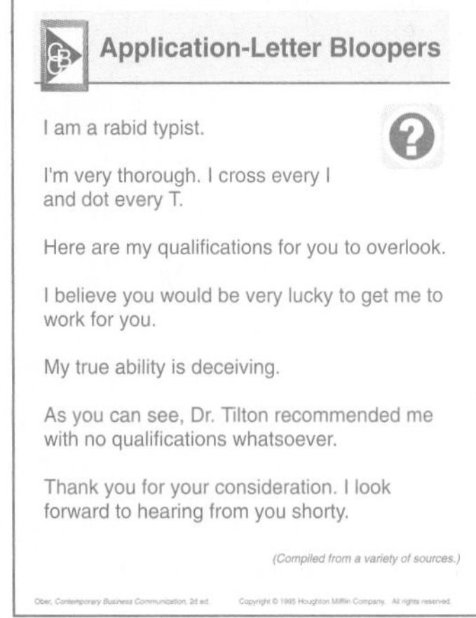

See Transparency 16.4, Application-Letter Bloopers.

If you do not know enough about the prospective employer to know the name of the appropriate person (the decision maker), you have probably not gathered enough data. If necessary, call the organization to make sure you have the right name—including the correct spelling—and position title. In your salutation, use a courtesy title (such as *Mr.* or *Ms.*) along with the person's last name.

Some job-vacancy ads are blind ads; they do not identify the hiring company by name and provide only a box number address, often in care of the newspaper or magazine that contains the ad. In such a situation, you (and all others responding to that ad) have no choice but to address your letter to the newspaper and to use a generic salutation, such as "Dear Personnel Manager."

Opening

Use the direct organizational plan for writing a solicited application letter.

The opening paragraph of a solicited application letter is fairly straightforward. Because the organization has advertised an opening, it is eager to receive quality applications, so use a direct organization: state (or imply) the reason for your letter, identify the particular position for which you're applying, and indicate how you learned about the opening.

Gear your opening to the job and to the specific organization. For positions that are widely perceived to be somewhat conservative (such as finance, accounting, and banking), use a restrained opening. For more creative work (like sales, advertising, and public relations), you might start out on a more imaginative note. Here are two examples:

Conservative: Mr. Adam Storkel, manager of your Fleet Street branch, has suggested that I submit my qualifications for the position of assistant loan officer that was advertised in last week's *Indianapolis Business.*

Creative: If quality is Job 1 at Ford, then Job 2 must surely be communicating that message effectively to the public. My degree in journalism and work experience at the Kintzell agency will enable me to help you achieve that objective. The enclosed résumé further describes my qualifications for the position of advertising copywriter posted in the June issue of *Automotive Age.*

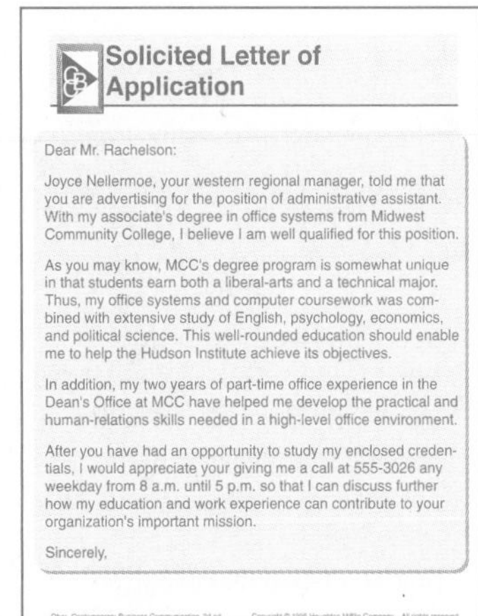
Solicited Letter of Application

Dear Mr. Rachelson:

Joyce Nellermoe, your western regional manager, told me that you are advertising for the position of administrative assistant. With my associate's degree in office systems from Midwest Community College, I believe I am well qualified for this position.

As you may know, MCC's degree program is somewhat unique in that students earn both a liberal-arts and a technical major. Thus, my office systems and computer coursework was combined with extensive study of English, psychology, economics, and political science. This well-rounded education should enable me to help the Hudson Institute achieve its objectives.

In addition, my two years of part-time office experience in the Dean's Office at MCC have helped me develop the practical and human-relations skills needed in a high-level office environment.

After you have had an opportunity to study my enclosed credentials, I would appreciate your giving me a call at 555-3026 any weekday from 8 a.m. until 5 p.m. so that I can discuss further how my education and work experience can contribute to your organization's important mission.

Sincerely,

See Transparency 16.5, Solicited Letter of Application.

For unsolicited application letters, you must first get the reader's attention. You can gain that attention most easily by talking about the company rather than about yourself. One effective strategy is to show that you know something about the organization—its recent projects, awards, changes in personnel, and the like—and then to show how you can contribute to the corporate effort.

> Now that EDS has expanded operations to Central America, can you use a marketing graduate who speaks fluent Spanish and who knows the culture of the region?

Your opening should be short, interesting, and reader-oriented. Avoid tired openings such as "This is to apply for . . ." or "Please consider this letter my application for . . ." Also maintain an air of formality. Don't address the reader by first name and don't try to be cute. Avoid such attention-grabbing stunts as sending a worn, once-white running shoe with the note "Now that I have one foot in the door, I hope you'll let me get the other one in" or writing the application letter beginning at the bottom of the page and working upward (to indicate a willingness to start at the bottom and work one's way up). Such gimmicks send a nonverbal message to the reader that the applicant may be trying to deflect attention from a weak résumé.

Body

Don't repeat all the information from the résumé.

In a paragraph or two, highlight your strongest qualifications and show how they can benefit the employer. Show—don't tell; that is, provide specific, credible evidence to support your statements, using wording different from that used in the résumé. Tell an anecdote about yourself ("For example, recently I . . ."). Your discussion should reflect modest confidence rather than a hard-sell approach. Avoid starting too many sentences with *I*.

Not: I am an effective supervisor.
But: Supervising a staff of five counter clerks taught me . . .

Not: I am an accurate person.
But: In my two years of experience as a student secretary, none of the letters, memorandums, and reports I typed were ever returned with a typographical error marked.

Not: I took a course in business communications.
But: The communication strategies I learned in my business communication course will enable me to solve customer problems as a customer-service representative at Allegheny Industries.

The outside of the envelope can affect the reader's response to the cover letter and résumé inside. A survey suggests that managers don't open envelopes with dot matrix-printed labels (looks too much like junk mail) and envelopes addressed by title, not by name. Envelopes most likely to be opened are those that are neatly handwritten. (Martin Yate, *Cover Letters That Knock 'Em Dead*, Bob Adams Publishers, Holbrook, MA, p. 44.)

Refer the reader to the enclosed résumé. Subordinate the reference to the résumé, and emphasize instead what it contains.

Not: I am enclosing a copy of my résumé for your review.
But: As detailed in the enclosed résumé, my extensive work experience in records management has prepared me to help you "take charge of this paperwork jungle," as headlined in your classified ad.

Closing

You are not likely to get what you do not ask for, so close by asking for a personal interview. Indicate flexibility regarding scheduling and location.

CHECKLIST 18

Job-Application Letters

1. Use your job-application letter to show how the qualifications listed in your résumé have prepared you for the specific job for which you're applying.
2. If possible, address your letter to the individual in the organization who will interview you if you're successful.
3. When applying for an advertised opening, begin by stating (or implying) the reason for the letter, identify the position for which you're applying, and tell how you learned about the opening.
4. When writing an unsolicited application letter, first gain the reader's attention by showing that you are familiar with the company and can make a unique contribution to its efforts.
5. In one or two paragraphs, highlight your strongest qualifications and relate them directly to the needs of the specific position for which you're applying. Refer the reader to the enclosed résumé.
6. Treat your letter as a persuasive sales letter: provide specific evidence, stress reader benefits, avoid exaggeration, and show confidence in the quality of your product.
7. Close by tactfully asking for an interview.
8. Maintain an air of formality throughout the letter. Avoid cuteness.
9. Make sure the finished document presents a professional, attractive, and conservative appearance and that it is 100% error-free.

Provide your phone number, either in the last paragraph or (preferably) immediately below your name and address in the closing lines.

Politely ask for an interview.

> After you have reviewed my qualifications, I would appreciate your calling or writing to let me know when we can meet to discuss further my employment with Connecticut Power and Light. I will be in the Hartford area from December 16 through January 4 and could come to your office at any time that is convenient for you.

Or:

> I will call your office next week to see if we can arrange a meeting at your convenience to discuss my qualifications for working as a financial analyst with your organization.

Use a standard complimentary closing (such as "Sincerely"), leave enough space to sign the letter, and then type your name, address, and phone number. Even though you may be sending out many application letters at the same time, take care with each individual letter. You never know which one will be the one that actually gets you an interview. Sign your name neatly in blue or black ink, fold each letter and accompanying résumé neatly, and mail.

For an exercise on revising an application letter, refer students to the *Study Guide*, pp. 208–209.

The guidelines for writing an application letter are summarized in Checklist 18.

MICROWRITING

An Application Letter

PROBLEM

You are Ray Arnold, a senior labor relations major at Northern Arizona University. You have analyzed your interests, strengths and weaknesses, and preferred lifestyle and have decided you would like to work in some area of labor relations for a large multinational firm in Southern California. Because you attend a medium-sized school in a small Arizona town some distance from Southern California, you decide not to limit your job search to on-campus interviewing.

In your research you learned that Precision Systems, Inc. (PSI), has recently been awarded a $23 million contract by the U.S. Department of State to develop a high-level computerized message system to provide fast and secure communications among U.S. government installations throughout Europe. PSI, which is headquartered in Los Angeles, will build a new automated factory in Cuidad Juárez, Mexico, to assemble the electronic components for the new system.

You decide to write to PSI to see whether they might have an opening for someone with your qualifications. You will, of course, include a copy of your résumé with your letter. (See Figure 16.2 for the résumé.) Send your letter to Ms. Phyllis Morrison, Assistant Director of Personnel, Precision Systems, Inc., PO Box 18374, Los Angeles, CA 90018.

PROCESS

1. Will this be a solicited or unsolicited (prospecting) letter?

   `Unsolicited—I don't know whether or not PSI has an opening.`

2. Write an opening paragraph for your letter that gets attention and that relates your skills to PSI's needs. Make sure the purpose of your letter is made clear in your opening paragraph.

   `PSI's recently accepted proposal to the State Department estimated that you would be adding up to 3,000 new staff for the Cuidad Juárez project. With this dramatic increase in personnel, do you have an opening in your human resources department for a college graduate with a major in labor relations and a minor in psychology?`

3. Compare your education with PSI's likely requirements. What will help you stand out from the competition?

   - `It's somewhat unusual for a labor relations major to have a psychology minor.`
   - `My course work in my major and minor were pretty standard, so there's no need to list individual courses.`

An Application Letter, continued

4. Compare your work experiences with PSI's likely requirements. What qualifications from your résumé should you highlight in your letter?

   - The interpersonal and human relations skills developed as a teller will be an important asset in labor management.
   - Written and oral communications skills developed through work and extracurricular activities will enable me to communicate effectively with a widely dispersed work force.

5. What other qualifications should you mention?

   My degree in labor relations, combined with my union membership, will help me look at each issue from the perspective of both management and labor.

6. Write the sentence in which you request the interview.

   I would welcome the opportunity to come to Los Angeles to discuss with you the role I might play in helping PSI manage its human resources in an efficient and humane manner.

PRODUCT

This prospecting letter accompanies the résumé in Figure 16.2.

15 Turner Hall 1
Northern Arizona University
Flagstaff, AZ 86001-8134
February 7, 1995

Ms. Phyllis Morrison
Assistant Director of Personnel
Precision Systems, Inc.
PO Box 18734
Los Angeles, CA 90018

Begins with an attention-getting opening that relates the writer's skills to the needs of the company.

Dear Ms. Morrison 2

PSI's recently accepted proposal to the State Department estimated that your organization would be adding up to 3,000 new positions for the Ciudad Juárez project. With this dramatic increase in personnel, will you have an opening in your human resources department for a recent college graduate with a major in labor relations and a minor in psychology? 3

Shows how the writer's unique qualifications will benefit the company.

My combination of course work in business and liberal arts will enable me to approach each issue from both a management and a behavioral point of view. Further, my degree in labor relations along with my experience as a union member will help me consider each issue from the perspective of both management and labor.

Provides specific evidence to support his claims: *shows* rather than *tells.*

During my term as editor of a student newsletter, the Scholastic Press Association recognized our publication for its "original, balanced, and refreshingly candid writing style." On the job, dealing successfully with customers' 4
overdrawn accounts, bank computer errors, and delayed-deposit recording has taught me the value of active listening and has provided me experience in explaining and justifying the company's position. As detailed on the enclosed résumé, these communication and human relations skills will help me to interact and communicate effectively with PSI employees at all levels and at widely dispersed locations.

Gives the reader the option of phoning the applicant or having him phone her.

I would welcome the opportunity to come to Los Angeles at your convenience to discuss with you the role I might play in helping PSI manage its human resources in an efficient and humane manner. I will call your office on February 15, or you may call me at any time after 2 p.m. daily at 602-555-9833.

Sincerely

Raymond J. Arnold

Raymond J. Arnold

Enclosure

Grammar and Mechanics Notes 1 In a personal business letter, the writer's return address may be typed above the date (as shown here) or below the sender's name in the closing. 2 This letter is formatted in block style, with all lines beginning at the left margin, and in open punctuation style, with no punctuation after the salutation and complimentary closing. 3 *major in labor relations:* Do not capitalize the names of college majors and minors. 4 *writing style.":* A period goes inside the closing quotation mark.

SUMMARY

One of the most important communication tasks you will ever face is securing a rewarding and worthwhile job. The job-seeking campaign thus requires considerable time, effort, and thought.

The planning phase begins with a self-analysis of your interests, strengths, weaknesses, and needs. Then you should gather data about possible jobs, demographic trends, and industries and companies that interest you. Use all available sources of information and strategies, including networking, professional employment services, job announcements and advertising, and self-promotion.

The purpose of your résumé is to get you a job interview. Strive for a one-page document, preferably typed in a simple, readable format on a computer and output on a laser printer. Include your name, address, phone number, job objective, information about your education and work experience, and special aptitudes and skills. Include other information only if it will help distinguish you favorably from the other applicants. Use either a chronological or functional organization for your work experience, and stress those skills and experiences that can be transferred to the job you want.

You will typically use the same résumé when applying for numerous positions and then construct an application letter that discusses how your education and work experience qualify you specifically for the job at hand. If possible, address your letter to the person who will interview you for the job. When writing a solicited application letter, begin by stating the reason for your letter, identify the position for which you're applying, and tell how you learned about the position. When writing an unsolicited letter, first gain the reader's attention. Then use the body of your letter to highlight one or two of your strongest qualifications, relating them to the needs of the position for which you're applying. Close by politely asking for an interview.

If your application efforts are successful, you will be invited to come for an interview. Successful interviewing strategies are covered in the next chapter.

KEY TERMS

Application letter A letter from a job applicant to a prospective employer explaining the applicant's interest in and qualifications for a position within the organization; also called a "cover" letter.

Reference A person who has agreed to provide information to a prospective employer regarding a job applicant's fitness for a job.

Résumé A brief record of one's personal history and qualifications that is typically prepared by a job applicant.

Solicited application letter An application letter written in response to an advertised job vacancy.

Unsolicited application letter An application letter written to an organization that has not advertised a vacancy; also called a "prospecting" letter.

For an exercise on matching terms, refer students to the *Study Guide*, p. 205.

REVIEW AND DISCUSSION

The answers to the review and discussion questions appear in the *Instructor's Resource Manual*, beginning on p. 288.

1. **Communication at Computer Sciences Corporation Revisited ▪** Paul Orvos of Computer Sciences Corporation appreciates application letters and résumés that do more than merely list job titles and responsibilities. He believes applicants should research the company before they start to develop their résumés or application letters.
   a. You want to apply for a job as a UNIX computer programmer with CSC; where will you look for information on the company?
   b. What job objective might you state on your résumé when you apply for the job?
   c. If no job opening for computer programmer had been advertised, write the first sentence of your unsolicited application letter.
2. Think of two different occupations. How might the answers to the 14 self-assessment questions on page 532–533 differ for someone interested in each of these occupations?
3. What types of career information are contained in the *Occupational Outlook Handbook?*
4. What services does the placement office or career-information center at your institution provide?
5. What is the purpose of a résumé?
6. How long should a résumé be?
7. What are the advantages of preparing your own résumé rather than having a professional résumé service prepare it?
8. Under what conditions should the education section of a résumé precede the work experience section?
9. What kinds of information should *always* go in a résumé?
10. What kinds of information should *never* go in a résumé?
11. What is the difference between a chronological and a functional organizational pattern?
12. How should references be treated in a résumé?
13. What is the difference between a solicited and an unsolicited application letter?
14. When might it be necessary *not* to address the application letter to the specific person who will be interviewing you?
15. Should the focus of an application letter be on the past or the future? Explain.

EXERCISES

Suggestions and sample solutions for exercises appear in the *Instructor's Resource Manual*, beginning on p. 289.

1. **Microwriting a Résumé—Getting To Know You ▪**

   PROBLEM

   Assume that you are beginning your last term of college before graduating. Using factual data from your own education, work experience, and so on (include any data that you expect to be true at the time of your graduation), prepare a résumé in an effective format. (*Note:* You will probably want to complete Exercises 2–6 on pages 563–564 before composing your résumé.)

PROCESS

a. How will you word your name at the top of your résumé—for example, with or without any initials? (Remember *not* to include a personal title before your name.)
b. What is your mailing address? If you will be changing addresses during the job search, include both addresses, along with the effective dates of each.
c. What is your daytime phone number? When can you typically be reached at this number?
d. For what type of position are you searching? Prepare an effective one-sentence job objective—one that is neither too general nor too specific.
e. What is the title of your degree? name of your college? location of the college? major and minor? expected date of graduation (month and year)?
f. What is your grade-point average overall and in your major? Is either one high enough to be considered a personal selling point?
g. Have you received any academic honors throughout your collegiate years, such as scholarships or being named to the dean's list? If so, list them.
h. Did you take any elective courses (courses that most applicants for this position probably did *not* take) that might be especially helpful in this position? If so, list them.
i. List in reverse chronological order (most recent job first) the following information for each job you've held during your college years: job title, organizational name, location (city and state), inclusive dates of employment, and full- or part-time status. Describe your specific duties at each position, stressing those duties that helped prepare you for your job objective. Use short phrases, beginning each duty or responsibility with one of the action verbs on page 547 and showing, where possible, specific evidence of the results you achieved.
j. Will your education or your work experience be more likely to impress the recruiter?
k. What additional information might you include, such as special skills, professional affiliations, offices held, or willingness to relocate or travel?
l. Are your reference letters on file at your school's placement office? If so, provide the office name, address, and phone number. (If not, you should include a statement such as "References available on request" at the bottom of your résumé.)

PRODUCT:

Using the above information, draft, revise, format, and then proofread your résumé. Submit both your résumé and your responses to the process questions to your instructor.

2. **Self-Assessment** ■ As a first step in your job campaign, answer the 14 questions given on page 532–533. Type each question and then your answer. Although the content of the answer is certainly more important than mechanics and format, use this exercise as a measure of your basic writing skills as well, taking care to use complete sentences, correct grammar, and competent writing style.

3. **Tell Me About Yourself** ■ One of the most common strategies an interviewer uses to start an interview is to ask you to tell something about yourself. Of course, you need to think about this question much earlier than the interview; the start of your job campaign is the time for this self-disclosure.

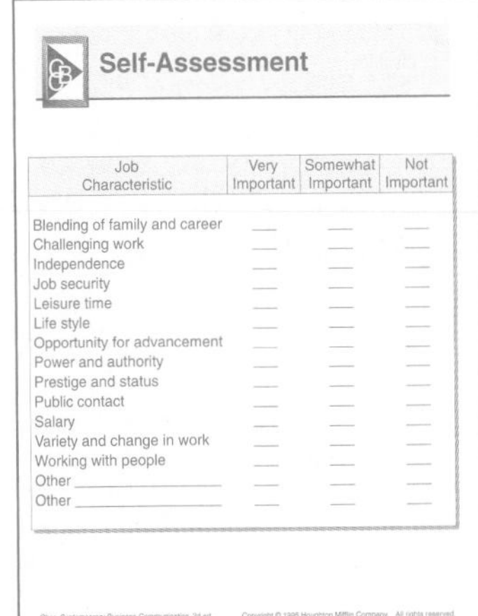

Self-Assessment

Job Characteristic	Very Important	Somewhat Important	Not Important
Blending of family and career	___	___	___
Challenging work	___	___	___
Independence	___	___	___
Job security	___	___	___
Leisure time	___	___	___
Life style	___	___	___
Opportunity for advancement	___	___	___
Power and authority	___	___	___
Prestige and status	___	___	___
Public contact	___	___	___
Salary	___	___	___
Variety and change in work	___	___	___
Working with people	___	___	___
Other ________	___	___	___
Other ________	___	___	___

Ober, *Contemporary Business Communication*, 2d ed.

See Master 16.1, Exercise 2, Self-Assessment, in the *Instructor's Resource Manual.*

In approximately 250 words (about a one-page double-spaced report), respond to the interviewer's request to "tell me about yourself." Keep in mind your job objective.

4. **Audience Analysis—International** ▪ Assume that you wish to work in another country upon graduation from college. Select a company headquartered abroad and research that organization. Learn about its products, economic outlook, employment needs, politics, organizational climate, and the like. Considering what you know about the company, what points about your own background might you stress in your application letter and résumé that would be of particular interest to this employer? Write a two-page memo report to your instructor detailing what you've learned about the organization (and about yourself).

5. **Career Planning** ▪ Select a career in which you might be interested. Using at least four references (one of which should be the latest edition of the *Occupational Outlook Handbook*), write a two- or three-page memo report to your instructor with the following sections:

   a. *Job description:* Include in this section a description of the job, including perhaps a definition of the job, typical duties, working conditions, and the kinds of knowledge, skills, and education needed.

   b. *Employment levels:* Nationally, how many people are employed in this type of job? Are employment levels increasing or decreasing? Why? What industries or what parts of the country are experiencing the greatest and the least demand for this job. What are the projected employment levels in the future?

   c. *Salary:* Discuss the latest salary statistics for this job—actual salaries, changes, trends, and projections.

   d. *Expected changes:* What changes are expected in this career within the next ten years or so? Discuss both the expected changes and the factors causing such changes. For example, will technology have any impact on this job? international business competition? federal or state regulations?

   Provide a concluding paragraph for your memo report that summarizes the career information you've discussed, and then indicate whether your initial opinion about the job has changed as a result of your research.

6. **Collaborative Project—Job-Getting Techniques** ▪ Working in a group of four to five students, complete the following tasks:

   a. Select an occupation (perhaps to be fair to everyone, you might select one that none of you plans to pursue as a career).

   b. Compose a list of five people any of you know who might provide information about this career or possible job leads. Tell why each person in your network of contacts was chosen.

   c. Interview (either in person or by telephone) a counselor at a nearby private employment service to determine what help the service could provide in securing a job in this occupation.

   d. Review the help-wanted ads in your local newspaper to determine what types of jobs are available in this occupation.

   Write a memo report to your instructor presenting the results of your research.

7. **Résumé Feedback** ▪ Make five photocopies of the résumé you created in Exercise 1 on appropriate paper—the kind you would use for your job campaign. Meet with three professionals who have expertise in your career area—the type of people who might be interviewing you for a job. Ask them to critique your résumé for you, commenting both on positive aspects and on any areas that should be strengthened. Revise your résumé based on this

feedback. Submit a copy of both your original résumé and your revised version to your instructor, along with a memo explaining what you revised and why.

8. **Résumé Project—Format** ▪ Review the final résumé you developed in Exercise 7. Using the same information, prepare another résumé in a different format; that is, include the same content but arrange it on the page differently. Which format do you think works better? Why? Submit both résumés, along with a short memo to your instructor evaluating the format of each document.

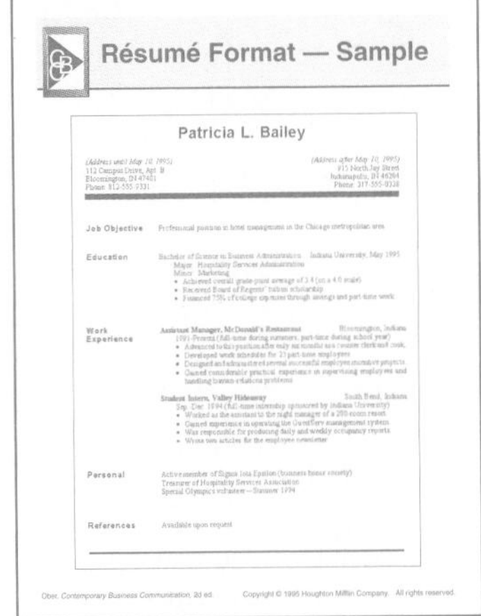

Résumé Format — Sample

Patricia L. Bailey

Job Objective

Education

Work Experience

Personal

References — Available upon request

Ober, *Contemporary Business Communication*, 2d ed. Copyright © 1995 Houghton Mifflin Company. All rights reserved.

See Master 16.2, Exercise 8, Résumé Project Format, in the *Instructor's Resource Manual*.

9. **Application Letter Project** ▪ This project consists of writing both a solicited and an unsolicited application letter. Prepare each letter in an appropriate format and on appropriate paper. Include a copy of your résumé with each letter. Submit each letter to your instructor folded and inserted into a correctly addressed envelope (don't forget to sign your letter).
    a. Identify a large prospective employer—one that has not advertised for an opening in your field. Using one of the résumés you developed earlier, write an unsolicited application letter.
    b. For various reasons, you might not secure a position directly related to your college major. In such a situation, it is especially important to be able to show how your qualifications (no matter what they are) match the needs of the employer. Using your own background, apply for the following position, which was advertised in last Sunday's *New York Times:*

> MANAGER-TRAINEE POSITION. Philip Morris is looking for recent college graduates to enter its management-trainee program in preparation for an exciting career in one of the diversified companies that make up Philip Morris. Excellent beginning salary and benefits, good working conditions, and a company that cares about you. (Reply to Box 385-G in care of this newspaper.)

CONTINUING CASE 16

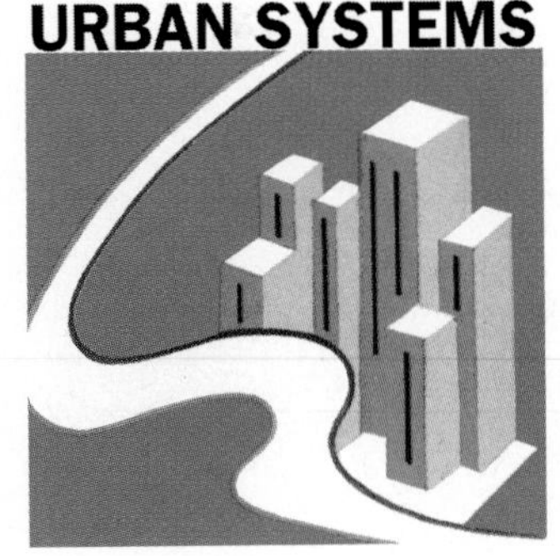

"Help Wanted"

When Neelima Shrikhande accepted the position of vice president of administration at Urban Systems, she knew she would have to work closely with Marc Kaplan, vice president of marketing. However, she resented Marc's condescending attitude toward her and his chauvinistic remarks toward female employees in general.

Despite her best efforts, their relationship has now deteriorated to the point that Neelima believes it is adversely affecting her ability to perform her job effectively. Knowing that Marc (one of the two founders of the company) has no plans to leave, Neelima has decided to explore other career opportunities.

Neelima is savvy enough to recognize that she is highly marketable and that many organizations would be eager to create a position for her even if they had no advertised openings. She is interested in finding a position in information management at a large organization located in a metropolitan area. She is free to relocate anywhere in the country. Hoping to

A possible solution to the Continuing Case is described in the *Instructor's Resource Manual*, pp. 290–291.

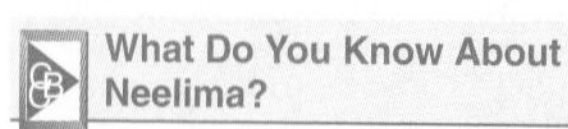

What Do You Know About Neelima?

- She is single, willing to relocate, likes a large-city atmosphere, and prefers to work in a large organization.
- She has highly marketable skills and a master's degree in MIS from Stanford University.
- She has been successful in her current position, is very self-confident, and is interested in the welfare of her subordinates and the organization.
- She is a feminist and is politically active.

See Master 16.3, Continuing Case 16, in the *Instructor's Resource Manual.*

avoid the kind of situation she presently faces, she would like to become associated with a progressive organization, preferably one whose top-level officers are active in social and political causes. An organization with other females in prominent executive positions who could serve as her mentors would be especially attractive.

Note: Although you already know quite a bit about Neelima, you may assume any additional, reasonable information you need to complete this project.

Critical Thinking

1. Is Neelima making the right decision in leaving? Why or why not?
2. Review what you know about Neelima—both from the background information contained in the Appendix to Chapter 1 and from the case studies in previous chapters. Develop a list of short phrases that describe her. What implication might each of these characteristics have for choosing a suitable, new work environment?

Writing Project

3. Locate three organizations that would be top prospects for Neelima to explore for a career move. Identify the organizations for Neelima in terms of the criteria just discussed. Present a balanced view of the organizations, incorporating both positive and negative information. Finally, provide the name, address, and phone number of an appropriate person for Neelima to contact. Organize your information in a logical manner, and present it as a letter report to Neelima.

WORDWISE *Company Slogans*

- *Let us remove your shorts.* (Art's Electric Co., Pullman, WA)
- *Your pane is our pleasure.* (Hogan's Window Cleaning Co., Lake Havasu City, AZ)
- *We run a shady business.* (Tarpman Tent and Awning Co., Quartzsite, AZ)
- *Drop your pants here.* (Air Lee Cleaners, Roanoke, VA)
- *Get your buns in here.* (Schumann's Bakery, Pine City, MN)
- *We dry harder.* (Concrete Products Co., Salt Lake City, UT)
- *More experienced than our name would suggest.* (Virgin Airlines)

The Job Interview and Follow-Up

CHAPTER

17

Communication Objectives

After you have finished this chapter, you should be able to

1. Prepare for an employment interview.
2. Conduct yourself appropriately during an employment interview.
3. Complete the communication tasks needed after the employment interview.

Ben & Jerry's is a self-proclaimed "left-of-center" ice cream company located in rural Vermont. Many of the company's 350 employees have been interviewed by Liz Lonergan, the human resources manager, who has been with the company in different capacities since 1983. Ben & Jerry's often attracts job candidates who, in Lonergan's words, "think this is a different company." But even a company that has business practices outside of the "norm" must do some things traditionally in order to be successful. "And recruiting," Lonergan said, "happens to be one of them."

The company—which sponsors an annual folk music festival, donates 7.5% of its pretax profits to charity, and does not have a dress code for its managers—interviews many people who could not imagine working in a "normal" corporate environment. In fact, some candidates believe Ben & Jerry's is the only company they could work for. But while enthusiasm is important, the "only-place-for-me" attitude shows immaturity on a candidate's part. "It's a great company, but it's not perfect. It makes me nervous when people tell me this is the *only* place they want to work," Lonergan said. "There are lots of good companies out there."

Lonergan noted that quite a few company employees are former city dwellers who decided that Ben & Jerry's location would help provide them with a change in lifestyle. Although the company's country setting gives Ben & Jerry's an almost romantic appeal, it seems to stop some candidates from doing a little basic research on the company's hiring and paying practices. Following an interview, some managerial candidates have left Vermont shaking their heads after Lonergan told them that, up until 1994, the com-

Liz Lonergan
Human resources manager, Ben & Jerry's Homemade, Inc., Waterbury, Vermont

pany had a seven-to-one management-to-staff salary ratio with a salary cap of $163,000 a year.

A pompous attitude is another handicap for a job seeker at Ben & Jerry's. "I don't mean a healthy 'I'm the one for the job.' There is a difference," Lonergan said. A candidate bound to be rejected is someone "who doesn't give me the impression that he or she can relate to employees at all levels. I don't like prima donnas. I enjoy the fact that when I walk into the plant there are people at every level whom I know. I feel it's really important, especially when you're hiring managers, that people be able to relate from the boardroom to the boiler room, so to speak."

A few candidates under consideration have ruined their chances by calling Lonergan a day or two after being interviewed and treating her assistant shabbily—an indication of arrogance that wasn't evident during an interview. Her assistant, she said, works too hard to be treated as if she doesn't matter. "Basically, if they won't tell her who they are or insist that they have to speak to only me, they don't get anywhere," she said.

The success of Ben & Jerry's, like that of any company, rests largely on the employees' maturity, enthusiasm, and ability to work with others. Just because a company is "different" doesn't mean that it will hire candidates who lack those fundamental qualities.

A chapter overview appears in the *Instructor's Resource Manual*, pp. 292–293.

PREPARING FOR A JOB INTERVIEW

Ninety-five percent of all employers require one or more employment interviews before extending a job offer, resulting in up to 150 million employment interviews being conducted annually.[1] The employer's purpose in these interviews is to verify information on the résumé, explore any issues raised by the résumé, and get some indication of the probable chemistry between the applicant and the organization. (It is estimated that 90% of all job failures result from personality clashes or conflicts—not incompetence.[2]) The job applicant will use the interview to glean important information about the organization and to decide whether the culture of the organization meshes with his or her personality (see the Spotlight on Law and Ethics for some ethical dimensions of the job campaign).

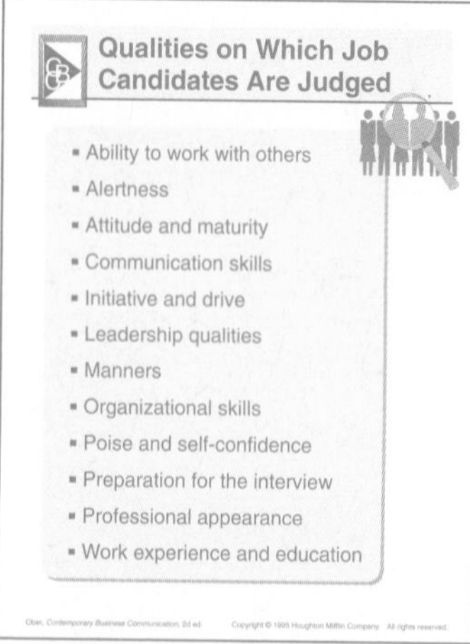

Qualities on Which Job Candidates Are Judged
• Ability to work with others
• Alertness
• Attitude and maturity
• Communication skills
• Initiative and drive
• Leadership qualities
• Manners
• Organizational skills
• Poise and self-confidence
• Preparation for the interview
• Professional appearance
• Work experience and education

See Transparency 17.1, Qualities on Which Job Candidates Are Judged.

Consider the employment interview as a sales presentation. Just as any good sales representative would never attempt to walk into a potential customer's office without having a thorough knowledge of the product, neither should you. You are both the product and the product promoter, so do your homework—both on yourself and on the potential customer.

Researching the Organization

As a result of having developed your résumé and written your application letters, you have probably done enough general homework on yourself.

SPOTLIGHT ON LAW AND ETHICS

The Ethical Dimensions of the Job Campaign

Most recruiters have heard the story about the job applicant who, when told that he was overqualified for a position, pleaded in vain, "But I lied about my credentials." When constructing your résumé and application letter, when completing an application form, and when answering questions during an interview, you will constantly have to make judgments about what to divulge and what to omit. Everyone would agree that outright lying is unethical (and clearly illegal as well). But when is hedging or omitting negative information about yourself simply being smart, and when is it unethical?

THE ETHICS OF CONSTRUCTING A RÉSUMÉ

Recruiters believe that the problem they call "résumé inflation" has increased in recent years, and plenty of research backs them up. One survey of executives found that 26% of them reported hiring employees during the previous year who had misrepresented their qualifications, education, or salary history. By far, the most frequent transgression is misrepresenting one's qualifications.

Acting ethically does not, of course, require that you emphasize every little problem that has occurred in your past. Indeed, one study showed that the majority of Fortune 500 human resource directors agree with the statement "Interviewees should stress their strengths and not mention their weaknesses unless the interviewer asks for information in an area of weakness."

Recognize, however, that many employers have a standard policy of terminating all employees who are found to have falsely represented their qualifications on their résumés. Generally, the employer must show evidence that the employee intentionally misrepresented his or her qualifications so as to fraudulently secure a job. Claiming to have a college degree when, in fact, one does not, would likely be grounds for termination, whereas an unintentional mistake in the dates of previous employment would probably not be.

THE ETHICS OF ACCEPTING A POSITION

For some applicants, another ethical dilemma occurs when they receive a second, perhaps more attractive, job offer after having already accepted a prior offer. Most professionals believe that such a situation should not present a dilemma. A job acceptance is a promise that the applicant is expected to keep. The hiring organization has made many decisions based on the applicant's acceptance, not the least of which was to notify all other candidates that the job had been filled. Reneging on the commitment to the employer not only puts the applicant in a bad light (and don't underestimate the power of the network in spreading such information) but also puts the applicant's school in a bad light.

If you're unsure about whether to accept a job offer, ask for a time extension. Once you've made your decision, however, stick to it and have no regrets. If you decide to accept the job, immediately notify all other employers that you are withdrawing from further consideration. If you decide to decline the job, move on to your next interviews without looking back. Learn to live with your decisions.

Sources: "Creative Résumés," *Dun's Business Month,* June 1985, p. 20; Nelda Spinks and Barron Wells, "Employment Interviews: Trends in the Fortune 500 Companies—1980–1988," *ABC Bulletin,* December 1988, p. 17; "Will Ethical Conflicts Undo Your Career?" *Mt. Pleasant (MI) Morning Sun,* May 12, 1988, p. 9.

Learn as much as you can about the organization—your possible future employer.

You are likely to have a reasonably accurate picture of who you are and what you want out of your career. Now is the time to zero in on the organization.

It is no exaggeration to say that you should learn everything you possibly can about the organization. Research the specific organization in depth, using the research techniques you developed in Chapter 11. Search the current business periodical indexes to learn what has been happening recently

Job-seeking skills will be useful throughout your career, especially in an economic climate where fewer and fewer people spend their entire careers in a single industry, let alone at a single company. Edward Andrews made the leap from banking to health care. He landed a job as financial services director at New York University Medical Center, in part by interviewing people in health care about how they handled medical billing.

with the company. Many libraries maintain copies of the annual reports from large companies, either in hard copy or on microfiche. Study these or other sources for current product information, profitability, plans for the future, and the like. Learn about the company's products and services, its history, the names of its officers, what the business press has to say about the organization, its recent stock activity, financial health, corporate structure, and the like.

For an exercise on preparing for a job interview, see Video Case Study 4, Chemical Bank.

Relate what you discover about the individual company to what you've learned about competing companies and about the industry in general. By trying to fit what you've learned into the broader perspective of the industry, you will be able to discuss matters more intelligently during your interview instead of just having a bunch of jumbled facts at your disposal.

If you're interviewing at a governmental agency, determine its role, recent funding levels, recent activities, spending legislation affecting the agency, and the extent to which being on the "right" side (that is, the official side) of a political question matters. If you're interviewing for a teaching position at an educational institution, determine the range of course offerings, types of students, conditions of the facilities and equipment, professionalism of the staff, and funding levels. In short, every tidbit of information you can learn about your prospective employer will help you make the most appropriate career decision.

Avoid "showing off" your knowledge of the organization.

You will use this information as a resource to help you understand and discuss topics with some familiarity during the interview. No one is impressed by the interviewee who, out of the blue, spouts, "I see your stock went up 5½ points last week." However, in response to the interviewer's comment about the company's recent announcement of a new product line, it would be quite appropriate to respond, "That must have been the reason your stock jumped 5½ points last week."

In short, bring up such information only if it flows naturally into the conversation. Even if you're never able to discuss some of the information you've gathered, the knowledge itself will still provide perspective in helping you to make a reasonable decision if a job offer is extended.

Practicing Interview Questions

Practice your responses to typical interview questions.

Following is a sample of typical questions that are often asked during an employment interview. Questions such as these provide the interviewer important clues to the applicant's qualifications, personality, poise, and communication skills. The interviewer is interested not only in the content of your responses but also in your reaction to the questions themselves and how you communicate your thoughts and ideas.

Before going for your interview, practice dictating a response to each of these questions into a cassette recorder. Then assume the role of the interviewer and play back your responses. How acceptable and appropriate was each response?

- Tell me about yourself.
- How would you describe yourself?
- Tell me something about yourself that I won't find on your résumé.
- What do you take real pride in?
- Why would you like to work for our organization?
- Why should we hire you?
- What are your long-range career objectives?
- What types of work do you enjoy doing most? least?
- What accomplishment has given you the greatest satisfaction?
- What would you change in your past?
- What courses did you like best and least in college?
- How does your education or experience relate to this job?

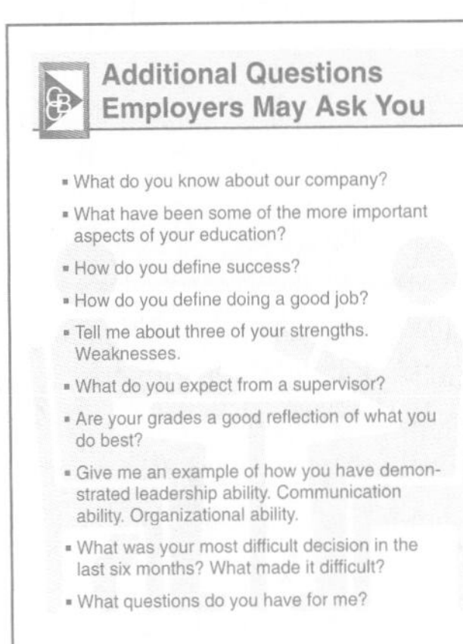

Additional Questions Employers May Ask You
▪ What do you know about our company?
▪ What have been some of the more important aspects of your education?
▪ How do you define success?
▪ How do you define doing a good job?
▪ Tell me about three of your strengths. Weaknesses.
▪ What do you expect from a supervisor?
▪ Are your grades a good reflection of what you do best?
▪ Give me an example of how you have demonstrated leadership ability. Communication ability. Organizational ability.
▪ What was your most difficult decision in the last six months? What made it difficult?
▪ What questions do you have for me?
Ober: Contemporary Business Communication, 2d ed.
Copyright © 1995 Houghton Mifflin Company. All rights reserved.

See Transparency 17.2, Additional Questions Employers May Ask.

These questions are fairly straightforward and not especially difficult to answer if you have practiced them. Not infrequently, however, interviewers may pose more difficult questions—ones that seemingly have no "right" answer. Sometimes they even try to create a stressful situation by asking pointed questions, interrupting, or feigning disbelief in an attempt to gauge your behavior under stress.

Answer each question honestly, but in a way that highlights your qualifications.

The strategy to use in such a circumstance is to keep the desired job firmly in mind and to formulate each answer—no matter what the question—so as to highlight your ability to perform the desired job competently. You don't have to accept each question as asked. You can ask the interviewer to be more specific or to rephrase the question. Doing so not only will provide guidance for answering the question but will give you a few additional moments to prepare your response.

Here are examples of some challenging questions you might be asked, along with possible strategies for answering these and similar questions. Again, you should recognize that the interviewers may be more interested in your reaction and poise under stress than in your actual words, so be aware of the nonverbal signals you are communicating.

- *Tell me about your strengths and weaknesses.* When asked about a strength, mention one of your qualifications that is directly related to the specific job. If asked about a weakness, you might identify a relatively harmless matter or even a strength that you sometimes carry to excess, such as "I tend to work too hard"; "I'm very tenacious; once I've started a project, I won't relax until I've finished it"; or "I tend to ask a lot of questions." Answer the weakness part of the question first, ending with a discussion of some job-related strength. Relate an anecdote or give some examples when possible.

- *Suppose you had to pick between two equally qualified subordinates for promotion. One was a black male and the other a handicapped female. Whom would you select?* Whenever you're asked a question that has no right answer, avoid answering the question directly. Instead, talk about related issues—in this case, your respect for affirmative action and equal opportunity efforts, your interest in working for an organization that had such a wonderful "problem," or some other issue that relates to the question but does not force an unreasonable choice. If you're asked for the "most important" something, you're generally safer instead to list several items as being very important, without assigning any one of them the top position.

How *you respond to difficult questions may be as important as* what *you say.*

- *What position do you expect to hold in five years?* Avoid telling the interviewer, "your job." He or she won't appreciate it, even if that is an accurate answer. Instead, talk about what you hope to have accomplished by then, the types of increasing responsibility you hope to be given, or the opportunities to make a greater contribution to the organization's efforts.

- *Tell me about your personal interests.* Your investigation of the organization should have revealed its attitudes and "personality." Rightly or wrongly, most organizations reflect upper-middle-class attitudes and mores. If you wish to fit in at such organizations, you should provide honest, middle-of-the-road responses. This would not be the time then to discuss your preoccupation with the occult. Also avoid appearing *too* interested in any outside pursuit. Organizations are looking for well-rounded individuals who enjoy outside interests but who do not have such a consuming interest that it might interfere with their jobs.

Employers tend to hire applicants who spend about half the interview speaking and half listening, revealed a Massachusetts Institute of Technology study. Another study suggested that applicants who make the best impression speak no longer than two minutes at a time during the interview. (Richard Bolles, *What Color is Your Parachute?*, Ten Speed Press, Berkeley, CA 1993, p. 317.)

- *What do you like most or least about your present job?* For the most-liked part of this question, select an aspect of your present job that you both enjoy and that is directly related to the new position. For the least-liked part of the question, select an aspect of your present job that you dislike and that the new position does not involve.

- *Can you work effectively in an environment that emphasizes diversity?* The ability to fit in and function productively around people of widely varying backgrounds is becoming increasingly important. Emphasize whatever experiences you have had in working with people of different cultures, ages, economic backgrounds, religions, and the like. Provide evidence that you value diversity.

Preparing Your Own Questions

During the course of the interview, many of the questions you may have about the organization or the job will probably be answered. However, an interview is a two-way conversation, so it is legitimate for you to pose relevant questions at appropriate moments, and you should prepare those questions beforehand.

Ensure that any relevant questions you may have are answered during the interview.

Questions such as the following will provide useful information on which to base a decision if a job is offered:

- How would you describe a typical day on the job?
- How is an employee evaluated and promoted?
- What types of training are available?
- What are your expectations of new employees?
- What are the organization's plans for the future?
- To whom would I report? Would anyone report to me?
- What are the advancement opportunities for this position?

Here are a few hints on asking effective questions that might help your students during an interview: start slowly, with easy questions; preface questions with facts; be direct and to the point—ask short questions; and demonstrate that you listened by repeating key words, paraphrasing, or summarizing. (Milt Grassell, "The Power of Questions," *Nation's Business*, November 1986, p. 58.)

Each of these questions not only provides needed information to help you make a decision but also sends a positive nonverbal message to the interviewer that you are interested in this position as a long-term commitment. Do not, however, ask so many questions that the roles of the interviewer and the interviewee become blurred, and avoid putting the interviewer on the spot.

Finally, avoid asking about salary and fringe benefits during the initial interview. There will be plenty of time for such questions later, after you've convinced the organization that you're the person they want. In terms of planning, however, you should know ahead of time the market value of the position for which you're applying. Check the classified ads, reports collected by your college career service, and library sources to learn what a reasonable salary figure for your position would be.

Avoid appearing to be overly concerned about salary.

Dressing for Success

The importance of making a good first impression during the interview can hardly be overstated. One study has shown that 75% of the interviewees who made a good impression during the first five minutes of the interview received a job offer, whereas only 10% of the interviewees who made a bad impression during the first five minutes received a job offer.[3]

Prefer well-tailored, clean, conservative outfits for the interview.

The most effective strategy for making a good impression is to pay careful attention to your dress, grooming, and posture. Dress in a manner that flatters your appearance while conforming to the office norm. The employment interview is not the place for a fashion statement. You want the interviewer to remember what you had to say and not what you wore. Although different positions, different companies, different industries, and different parts of the country and world have different norms, in general prefer well-tailored, clean, conservative clothing for the interview.

For most business interviews, men should dress in a blue or gray suit and a white or pale blue shirt with a subtle tie, dark socks, and black shoes. Women should dress in a blue or gray tailored suit with a light-colored blouse and medium-height heels. Avoid excessive or distracting jewelry, heavy perfumes or after-shave lotions, and elaborate hairstyles. Impeccable grooming is a must, including clothing clean and free of wrinkles, shoes shined, teeth brushed, and hair neatly styled and combed. Blend in; you will have plenty of opportunity to express your individual style once you've been hired.

Controlling Nervousness

Overpreparation is the best way to control nervousness.

Control nervousness during the interview the same way you control it when making an oral presentation; that is, practice until you're confident you can face whatever the interviewer throws your way. The placement offices at many colleges conduct mock interviews to prepare prospective interviewees. If yours does not, ask a professor or even another student to interview you. Practice answering lists of common questions.

Become so thoroughly familiar with your résumé, application letter, and (if used) application blank that you won't have to search for some particular item or try to remember exactly how you responded to a particular question.

Interviewers know that you may be nervous and will probably begin the interview with some fairly innocuous, easy-to-answer questions to break the ice. It is to their advantage to put you at ease so that the real you can shine through, and they will try to do so. Recognize also that some nervousness is helpful; a bit of nervous energy will keep you alert and give sharper focus to the verbal exchange.

One way to avoid excessive nervousness is to arrive properly equipped—with a pen and notebook, a list of questions you want to ask, two copies of your résumé, any past correspondence with the organization, a list of references (including addresses and phone numbers), and, if applicable, work samples.

Map out the route you will take to the interview site, and avoid the stress of having to rush to arrive on time. Plan to arrive 10 to 15 minutes early, but no more than that. Arriving too early makes you appear too eager and may disrupt the interviewer's prior plans. If you're a bit nervous, plan to arrive a half-hour early, find your way to the correct office, and then go for a walk. It will release some of the pent-up energy you may have stored on the drive over.

CONDUCTING YOURSELF DURING THE INTERVIEW

Observe the organizational environment very carefully and treat everyone you meet, including the receptionist and the interviewer's secretary, with scrupulous courtesy. Maintain an air of formality. When shown into the in-

Making eye contact and maintaining a pleasant demeanor are important to a successful interview.

terview room, greet the interviewer by name, with a firm handshake, direct eye contact, and a smile.

At the beginning, address the interviewer as "Mr." or "Ms.," switching to a first-name basis only if specifically requested to do so. If you're not asked to be seated immediately, wait until the interviewer is seated and then take your seat. Sit with your feet planted firmly on the floor, lean forward a bit in your seat, and maintain comfortable eye contact with the interviewer. Avoid taking notes, except perhaps for a specific name, date, or telephone number.

Assume a confident, courteous, and conservative attitude during the interview.

Recognize that certain parts of the office are off-limits—especially the interviewer's desk and any area behind the desk. Do not rest your hands, purse, or notes on the desk and never wander around the office. Show interest in everything the interviewer is saying; don't concentrate so hard on formulating your response that you miss the last part of any question. Answer each question in a positive, confident, forthright manner. Recognize that more than yes-or-no answers are expected.

Throughout the interview, your attitude should be one of confidence and courtesy. Assume a role that is appropriate for you. Don't go in with the attitude that "You're lucky to have me here." The interviewer might not agree. Likewise, you needn't fawn or grovel. You're *applying*—not begging—for a job. If the match works, both you and the employer will benefit. Finally, don't try to take charge of the interview. Follow the interviewer's lead, letting him or her determine which questions to ask, when to move to a new area of discussion, and when to end the interview.

Answer each question put to you as honestly as you can (see the Spotlight on Law and Ethics). Keep your mind on the desired job and how you

SPOTLIGHT ON LAW AND ETHICS

The Legal Dimensions of the Job Campaign

I applied for a job and was told I will be hired if I take a lie-detector test. Must I take this test?

In most states, yes, if you want the job. A few states, however (including Oregon, Washington, Alaska, Delaware, and Minnesota), prohibit employers from requiring a lie-detector test as a condition of employment.

The computer firm where I want to work requires all job applicants to take a psychological test as part of the application process. Is this legal?

Yes. Aptitude, personality, and psychological tests are legal as long as the results are accurate, are related to success on the job, and do not tend to eliminate anyone on the basis of gender, age, race, religion, or national origin.

I work full-time and have been offered a dream job by another employer—if I can start the new job immediately. Do I have to give my current employer a certain number of days' notice?

No. You are not legally required to do so unless the contract you signed specifies how far in advance you must notify the company.

I'm an older student who will be applying for positions along with much younger ones. Can the interviewer ask my age?

No, not unless the employer can show that most people beyond a certain age cannot perform the job competently or safely. If you're worried about the possible impact of your age, you might wish to volunteer certain information to allay the interviewer's concerns—for example, mentioning some vigorous physical activity you regularly engage in.

What types of information may not be asked for on an application form or during a job interview?

- Race or national origin (including origin of a surname or place of birth; however, you may be asked to prove that you have legal authorization to work in the United States)
- Family information (including marital status, plans for marriage or children, number of children or their ages, child-care arrangements, spouse's occupation, roommate arrangements, and home ownership)
- Disabilities (unless they relate directly to the job)
- Arrests (you may, however, be asked about convictions for serious offenses)

How should I respond to an illegal question during a job interview?

The best response, assuming you want to continue to be considered for the position, may be to deflect the question by focusing on how you can contribute to the job. For example, if you were asked about your plans to have children in the immediate future, you might respond, "I assure you that I'm fully committed to my career and to making a real contribution to the organization for which I work." Or you may respond by saying you don't believe such questions are relevant to your ability to do the job, or by asking the interviewer to explain the relevance of the question. You could also, of course, file a complaint with the Equal Employment Opportunity Commission.

Sources: Ronald A. Anderson, Ivan Fox, and David P. Twomey, *Business Law and the Legal Environment*, 14th ed., South-Western, Cincinnati, OH, 1990; Gordon W. Brown, Edward E. Byers, and Mary Ann Lawlor, *Business Law: With UCC Applications*, 7th ed., McGraw-Hill, New York, 1989; Gordon W. Brown and R. Robert Rosenberg, *Understanding Business and Personal Law*, 7th ed., McGraw-Hill, New York, 1984; Neil Story and Lynn Ward, *American Business Law and the Regulatory Environment*, South-Western, Cincinnati, OH, 1989.

can show that you are qualified for that job. Don't try to oversell yourself, or you may end up in a job for which you're unprepared. However, if the interviewer doesn't address an area in which you believe you have strong qualifications, be on the alert to volunteer such information at the appropriate time, working it into your answer to one of the interviewer's questions.

If asked about your salary expectations, try to avoid giving a salary figure, indicating that you would expect to be paid in line with other employees at your level of expertise and experience. If pressed, however, be prepared to reveal your salary expectations, preferably using a broad range.

When discussing salary, talk in terms of what you think the position and responsibilities are worth rather than what you think *you* are worth. If salary is not discussed, be patient. Few people have ever been offered a job in industry without first being told what they would be paid.

It is possible that you may perceive an immediate rapport problem with the interviewer—either that the interviewer dislikes you or that you dislike the interviewer. In the former situation, take stock immediately of yourself and the verbal and nonverbal signals you're sending out, and try to adjust them to send a more appropriate message.

If your first impression of the interviewer is unfavorable, recognize that first impressions are not always valid. Also, remember that the interviewer may not be your superior or may not be your superior for long. Evaluate the long-term situation before making any immediate decision. At any rate, conduct yourself as professionally and as effectively as possible throughout the interview. You can make a final decision later, after you've had more time to evaluate the situation more clearly.

You might participate in a group interview, in which several people interview you at once. If possible, find out about this ahead of time so that you can learn the name, position, and rank of each interviewer. Address your responses to everyone, not just to the person who asked the question or to the most senior person present.

It is also likely that you will be interviewed more than once—having either multiple interviews the same day or, if you survive the initial interview, a more intense set of interviews to be scheduled for some later date. Be on the alert for clues you can pick up from your early interviews that might be of use to you in later interviews and be sure to provide consistent responses to the same questions asked by different interviewers. Assume that the different interviewers will get together to discuss their reactions to you and your responses.

When the interview ends, if you've not been told, you have a right to ask the interviewer when you might expect to hear from him or her. You will likely be evaluated on these four criteria:

- *Education and experience:* Your accomplishments as they relate to the job requirements, evidence of growth, breadth and depth of your experiences, leadership qualities, and evidence of willingness to assume responsibility.
- *Mental qualities:* Intelligence, alertness, judgment, logic, perception, creativity, organization, and depth.
- *Manner and personal traits:* Social poise, sense of humor, mannerisms, warmth, confidence, courtesy, aggressiveness, listening ability, manner of oral expression, emotional balance, enthusiasm, initiative, energy, ambition, maturity, stability, and interests.
- *Appearance:* Grooming, dress, posture, cleanliness, and apparent health.

An activity test may be administered as part of an interview. Dave Wiegand, president of Advance Network Design, tests his sales candidates during an interview by setting up a simulated sales call. The candidate must go into a separate room, call Wiegand's office, and try to make an appointment. Wiegand makes the candidate ask for an appointment three times. Activity tests help employers identify weak candidates. (Ellyn Spragins, "Test-driving Job Applicants," *Inc.*, May 1992, p. 148.)

You will likely be evaluated on education and experience, mental qualities, manner and personal traits, and appearance.

COMMUNICATING AFTER THE INTERVIEW

Although you may be exhausted (mentally and physically) from your interview sessions, there are several tasks that remain to be done. Some must be completed immediately after the interview; others must wait until you receive notice of the hiring decision.

Following Up the Interview

After the interview, critique your performance, your résumé, and your application letter.

Immediately after the interview, conduct a self-appraisal of your performance. Try to recall each question that was asked and evaluate your response. If you're not satisfied with one of your responses, take the time to formulate a more effective answer. Chances are that you will be asked a similar question in the future.

Also reevaluate your résumé. Were any questions asked during the interview that indicated some confusion about your qualifications? Does some section need to be revised or some information added or deleted? If you have composed your résumé on a computer, making the needed changes will be easy.

Determine too whether you can improve your application letter based on your interview experience. Were the qualifications you discussed in your letter the ones that seemed to impress the interviewers the most? Were these qualifications discussed in terms of how they would benefit the organization? Did you provide specific evidence to support your claims?

You should also take the time to send the interviewer (or interviewers) a short thank-you note as a gesture of courtesy and to reaffirm your interest in the job. The interviewer, who probably devoted quite a bit of time to

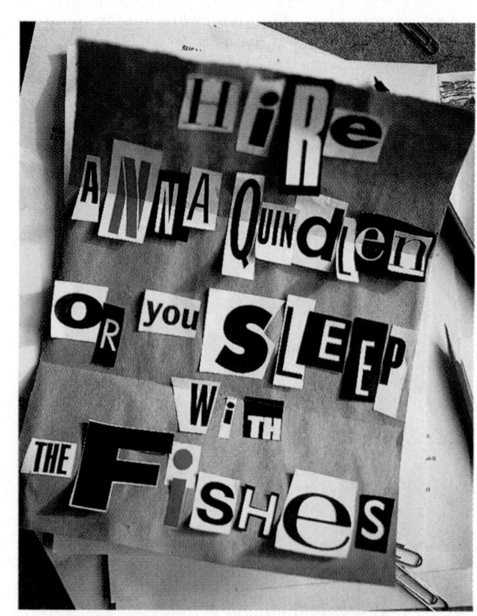

Here's a technique definitely not *appropriate for all situations: When author and* New York Times *columnist Anna Quindlen applied for a job at the* New York Post, *she sent this mock kidnapping note as a follow-up to her interview. Quindlen had judged her audience correctly; she got the job. You should use unusual techniques only when you know enough about the person you're dealing with to know that they'll appreciate the gesture.*

you before, during, and after the interview session, deserves to have his or her efforts on your behalf acknowledged.

Recognize, however, that your thank-you note may or may not have any effect on the hiring decision. Most decisions to offer the candidate a job or to invite him or her back for another round of interviewing are made the day of the interview, often during the interview itself. Thus, your thank-you note may arrive after the decision, good or bad, has been made.

Send a short thank-you note immediately after the interview.

The real purpose of a thank-you note is to express genuine appreciation for some courtesy extended to you; you do not write to earn points. Also, avoid trying to resell yourself. You've already made your case through your résumé, cover letter, and interview.

Your thank-you note should be short and may be either typed or handwritten. Consider it a routine message that should be written in a direct organizational pattern. Begin by expressing appreciation for the interview; then achieve credibility by mentioning some specific incident or insight gained from the interview. Close on a hopeful, forward-looking note. The thank-you note in Figure 17.1 corresponds to the résumé and application letter presented in Chapter 16 (Figures 16.1 and 16.3).

If you have not heard from the interviewer by the deadline date he or she gave you for making a decision, telephone the interviewer for a status report. If no decision has been made, your inquiry will keep your name and your interest in the position in the interviewer's mind. If someone else has been selected, you need to know so that you can continue your job search.

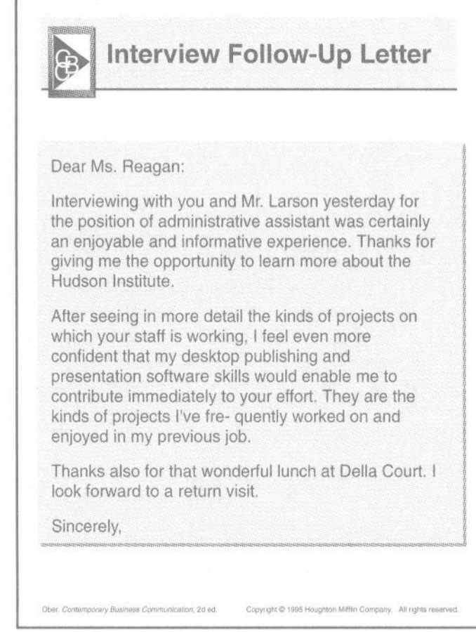
Interview Follow-Up Letter

Dear Ms. Reagan:

Interviewing with you and Mr. Larson yesterday for the position of administrative assistant was certainly an enjoyable and informative experience. Thanks for giving me the opportunity to learn more about the Hudson Institute.

After seeing in more detail the kinds of projects on which your staff is working, I feel even more confident that my desktop publishing and presentation software skills would enable me to contribute immediately to your effort. They are the kinds of projects I've fre- quently worked on and enjoyed in my previous job.

Thanks also for that wonderful lunch at Della Court. I look forward to a return visit.

Sincerely,

Ober, *Contemporary Business Communication*, 2d ed.

See Transparency 17.3, Interview Follow-Up Letter.

Handling Rejection

Some job applicants become discouraged at the long wait between mailing out their initial résumés and being invited for an interview. You should recognize, however, that the first responses you will get are the rejections because it takes less time to eliminate those who are obviously unsuited for a specific position than to evaluate those who might qualify. Each of us is unsuitable for *some* position, but that doesn't mean we're unsuitable for *all* positions.

Similarly, don't spend your time after a job interview sitting by the phone waiting for word on the hiring decision. You may have to go on several employment interviews at different organizations before being offered a job, so don't waste valuable time. Immediately schedule additional interviews; you can always cancel them if necessary, but they will give you something to fall back on if you're passed over for one position. In addition, the perspective that comes from having interviewed at numerous organizations will help you make an informed decision when a job offer is made.

Job-hunting support groups can help job hunters deal with rejection. Your students can find these groups at federal and state employment offices, the Chamber of Commerce, colleges, or community or adult education centers. The *National Business Employment Weekly*, available on newsstands, lists these types of groups in its Calendar of Career Events. (Richard Bolles, *What Color Is Your Parachute?*, Ten Speed Press, Berkeley, CA, 1993, p. 88.)

The job applicant who presents a well-groomed and confident appearance, who is well qualified, and who is well prepared for the interview has an excellent chance of being offered a position. You should know, however, that despite the employer's best efforts, job selection is as much an art as a science. Personal likes and dislikes and the right personal chemistry also play a role.

Although feelings of hurt and disappointment are natural in such circumstances, there is no reason to feel anger at the organization that rejects

FIGURE 17.1 Interview Follow-Up Letter

The interview follow-up letter should be written within a day or two of the job interview.

April 5, 1995

Mr. David Norman, Partner
Ross, Russell & Weston 1
452 Fifth Avenue
New York, NY 10018

Addresses the person in the salutation as he or she was addressed during the interview.

Dear Mr. Norman: 2

Begins directly, with a sincere expression of appreciation.

Thank you for the opportunity to interview for the position of EDP specialist yesterday. I very much enjoyed meeting you and Arlene Worthington and learning more about the position and about Ross, Russell & Weston.

Mentions a specific incident that occurred and relates it to the writer's background.

I especially appreciated the opportunity to observe the long-range planning meeting yesterday afternoon and to learn of your firm's plans for increasing your consulting practice with nonprofit agencies. My experience working in city government leads me to believe that nonprofit agencies can benefit 3
greatly from your expertise.

Closes on a confident, forward-looking note.

Again, thank you for taking the time to visit with me yesterday. I look 4
forward to hearing from you.

Sincerely,

Aurelia Gomez

Aurelia Gomez
225 West 70 Street
New York, NY 10023

Grammar and Mechanics Notes

1 Use the ampersand (&) in a firm name only if it is used by the firm itself. 2 Use a colon (not a comma) even if the salutation uses the reader's first name. 3 *nonprofit:* Write most words beginning with "non" solid—without a hyphen. 4 *Again:* Use a comma after an introductory expression.

your application. If there are 200 applicants for the position, 199 of them are going to receive the same letter you did. Instead of getting mad, write a gracious note to the interviewer, such as the following:

The smart applicant sends a gracious note following a rejection.

> Although I'm naturally disappointed that I was not selected for the position, I do appreciate the professionalism and courtesy you showed me and hope you will keep me in mind if a position for which I might qualify opens in the future.

Such a note speaks volumes about the maturity of the applicant and might open the door for future employment. Besides, it is not unusual for any successful job applicant to receive several offers, all but one of which must be declined. Your gracious note might just put you at the top of the list for a second interview if the chosen applicant declines the job.

Remember that the job campaign is a job itself—perhaps one of the most important jobs you'll ever undertake and maybe even one of the most difficult. Depersonalize any early rejections. Look at them objectively, determine what went wrong (if anything), and learn from the experience. As with most endeavors, perseverance, preparation, and a positive attitude will pay off in ultimate success.

Accepting, Delaying, and Refusing a Job Offer

Use the direct organizational style when writing an acceptance letter.

Remember that a job offer is never "official" until it is in writing, so avoid making permanent plans until the confirming letter arrives. Accepting a job offer is easy. An acceptance letter is, of course, a good-news letter and should be written in the direct organizational pattern. Give the good news first, follow it with any necessary details, including salary, starting date, and other contractual details. Close with a positive look to the future. Always accept in writing, so that you and the organization have a permanent record of your decision (see Figure 17.2 for an acceptance letter that corresponds to the résumé in Figure 16.2 and application letter in Chapter 16 Microwriting.

Suppose you receive a job offer from one organization while you still have other job interviews pending. In such a case, you may be unsure whether to accept and need more time to make a decision. Recruiters are certainly aware that you are interviewing at more than one organization; on the other hand, they may be facing deadlines or putting other qualified candidates on hold until you respond, so your request for a time extension must be diplomatic. Your best strategy is to express appreciation for the job offer, tactfully ask for an extension, and close by reaffirming your interest in the job.

Job-Acceptance Letter

Dear Mr. Haversham:

Thanks so much for your telephone call this morning offering me the position of office manager at Holland Graphic Services at an annual salary of $21,300. Of course I accept and look forward to beginning work on September 15.

I'm also happy to accept your invitation to the company picnic on September 13 at Raleigh State Park. Unfortunately, my husband will be away on business and will be unable to accompany me.

Thanks, Mr. Haversham, for giving me this opportunity to put my computer and office systems skills to work at HGS. I look forward to contributing to your efforts.

Sincerely,

Ober, *Contemporary Business Communication*, 2d ed.

See Transparency 17.4, Accepting a Job Offer.

> Thank you for your letter of May 30 offering me the position of manager-trainee at a salary of $24,500. This position represents a wonderful professional opportunity for me, and I'm giving it careful consideration.
>
> I had previously scheduled another job interview on June 14, the day before you asked me for my acceptance decision. I feel obligated

FIGURE 17.2 Job-Acceptance Letter

15 Turner Hall
Northern Arizona University
Flagstaff, AZ 86001-8134 1
March 17, 1995

Ms. Phyllis Morrison
Assistant Director of Personnel
Precision Systems, Inc.
PO Box 18734
Los Angeles, CA 90018

Dear Ms. Morrison:

Gives the good news (that you accept the job offer) first, where it will receive the most attention.

I am delighted to accept your offer of a position as EEOC coordinator for PSI at an annual salary of $25,600. I look forward to beginning my new position on July 5. 2

Provides the needed additional details.

Enclosed are the completed medical examination and the insurance forms. I plan to be in the Los Angeles area on May 13 through 15 to secure an apartment and would be happy to meet with you then if any further matters related to my employment need to be resolved. 3

Closes on a friendly, forward-looking note.

Thanks, Ms. Morrison, for giving me this opportunity to make a contribution to the Human Resources Division and to Precision Systems, Inc. 4

Cordially,

Raymond J. Arnold

Raymond J. Arnold

Enclosures

Grammar and Mechanics Notes

1 Using a nine-digit Zip Code is optional. 2 You may indent paragraphs (as shown here) or block paragraphs in a letter. 3 *an apartment_and:* Do not use a comma here because the second part of the sentence lacks a subject. 4 *Thanks, Ms. Morrison,:* Use commas to set off nouns of address.

> to keep this appointment and would appreciate being able to give you my decision June 21—one week after this final interview.
>
> The position you have offered is an exciting one, especially since you indicated the strong possibility of an overseas assignment after my one-year training program. But because my decision is so important to both of us, I'd be grateful to have one additional week to consider it.

Consider your acceptance of a job as a binding commitment.

Once you've accepted one job offer, you should immediately inform all other organizations at which you're being seriously considered for a position to withdraw your name from further consideration. Similarly, if you receive any subsequent job offers, you should immediately decline them. When withdrawing your name from further consideration for a job or declining a job, you may communicate either by letter or by telephone. Phone calls are faster, but you run the risk of being asked for more details than you care to divulge about either your reasons for declining or the job you've accepted. You have more control of what you communicate in a letter; in addition, letters provide a permanent record—both for you and for the employer.

Your refusal letter should be brief and written in the indirect organizational plan.

Refusal letters are best written in the indirect organizational pattern, beginning on a neutral but relevant note, stating the refusal in neutral or positive terms, and closing on a pleasant, supportive note. Such letters may be brief and need not go into great detail. The important point is to convey in a professional manner the news that the organization needs to continue its search process. Figure 17.3 shows a refusal letter.

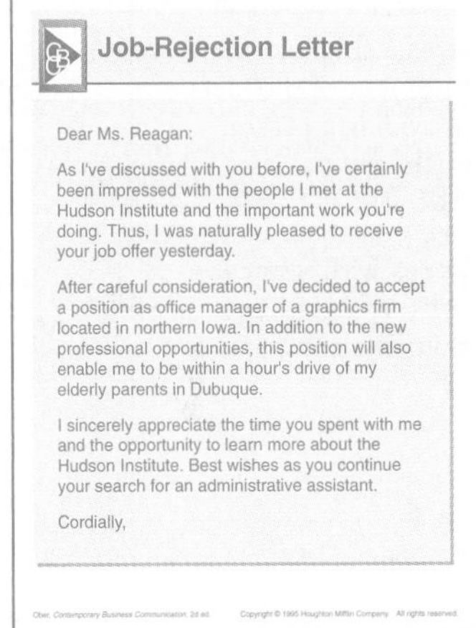

Job-Rejection Letter

Dear Ms. Reagan:

As I've discussed with you before, I've certainly been impressed with the people I met at the Hudson Institute and the important work you're doing. Thus, I was naturally pleased to receive your job offer yesterday.

After careful consideration, I've decided to accept a position as office manager of a graphics firm located in northern Iowa. In addition to the new professional opportunities, this position will also enable me to be within a hour's drive of my elderly parents in Dubuque.

I sincerely appreciate the time you spent with me and the opportunity to learn more about the Hudson Institute. Best wishes as you continue your search for an administrative assistant.

Cordially,

Ober, *Contemporary Business Communication*, 2d ed.

See Transparency 17.5, Rejecting a Job Offer.

If you accept a job while employed elsewhere, you must resign immediately from your present job. Your resignation may or may not come as a surprise to your employer; either way, it should be in writing. Because you're writing to someone within the organization, an interoffice memorandum is the appropriate type of communication.

Because you're writing to your superior, you may decide to use a direct organizational pattern. Surely, however, your resignation will be bad news to the reader and so should be buffered somewhat. Regardless of your reason for leaving, now is not the time to bring up past injustices or to tell your superior how he or she should manage the organization's affairs. Dwell on the positive—what you've learned on the job and the satisfaction that came from making a contribution to the organization's welfare. Provide any additional details needed and close on a positive note (see Figure 17.4).

FIGURE 17.3 Job-Rejection Letter

15 Turner Hall 1
Northern Arizona University
Flagstaff, AZ 86001-8134
March 17, 1995

Mr. Stanley Scukanec, Director
Personnel Department
Occidental Life, Inc.
1901 Avenue of the Stars
Los Angeles, CA 90067

Dear Mr. Scukanec:

Begins with a supportive, relevant, and neutral opening.

I certainly enjoyed meeting with you and your colleagues on March 3 and was pleased to receive an invitation to join your firm as wage and salary 2
administrator.

Gives a simple statement of the facts (providing a reason for the refusal is optional).

After careful consideration of the offers I've received, I've decided to accept a position as EEOC coordinator at an electronics firm. This position will require substantially less travel time than would have been necessary with the Occidental position.

Closes with a sincere, gracious statement about the company.

I want to thank you and your colleagues for the time you spent with me.
As I stated in my letter of March 5, I've always been impressed with the 3
professionalism of your insurance agents and look forward to continuing my relationship with Occidental as a satisfied customer.

Cordially,

Raymond J. Arnold

Raymond J. Arnold

Grammar and Mechanics Notes

1 You may type the writer's return address above the date (as shown here) or as part of the closing lines, immediately below the writer's name. 2 Do not capitalize job titles in the body of a letter unless they are used in place of a personal title (for example *Vice President Smith.*) 3 *March 5:* Use cardinal (rather than ordinal) numbers for dates unless the day precedes the month (for example, *the 5th of March*).

FIGURE 17.4 Job-Resignation Memo

Valley National Bank

Fulton Street Branch
Phone: 602-555-3889

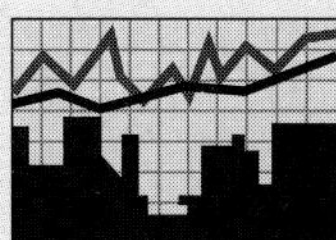

1 **MEMO TO:** Austin Gibson

FROM: Ray Arnold RA

DATE: May 1, 1995

My position as a teller at the Fulton Street branch of Valley National Bank
2 has certainly been a rewarding experience—both in terms of providing funds for my college education and, just as important, in terms of the experience I gained in dealing with the public, learning time-management skills, and handling the confidential affairs of our customers.

These skills will surely be of help to me in my chosen field of labor relations. Although you indicated to me earlier that a management position would be available for me at VNB when I graduate in June, I think you know of my
3 desire to live on the West Coast. Therefore, I've accepted a position as EEOC coordinator for Precision Systems, Inc., in Los Angeles.

My first day of work at PSI will be July 5, and I would like to terminate my present position on Friday, June 7. The intervening five weeks should allow sufficient time for you to hire a replacement and for me to provide whatever on-the-job training you might desire.

I will always be grateful for the opportunities you provided me, Mr. Gibson,
4 and will remember my two and one-half years here with great fondness.

5 c: Personnel Department

Begins directly by acknowledging what has been learned from the present job.

Explains in a positive manner the reason for the resignation before actually communicating the bad news.

Provides needed details and offers to help.

Closes on a positive note.

Grammar and Mechanics Notes

1 Use the memo format when writing to another employee within the same organization. Memos do not contain a salutation or closing lines. 2 *experience—both:* If your keyboard does not contain a dash, type two hyphens with no space before, between, or after. 3 *West Coast:* Capitalize a direction only when it is part of a proper name representing a part of the country. 4 *one-half:* Hyphenate fractions. 5 Use a copy notation to let the recipient know that a copy of the document is being sent to another party.

A Job-Rejection Letter

PROBLEM

You are Aurelia Gomez, whose résumé is shown in Figure 16.1, page 548. As a result of your application letter to David Norman, partner at Ross, Russell & Weston (see Figure 16.3, page 554), you participated in two job interviews at the accounting firm and just received the following letter:

> Dear Aurelia:
>
> I am pleased to offer you the position of EDP specialist with our firm, effective July 1, at an annual salary of $31,400. Your duties are outlined in the enclosed job description.
>
> This offer is conditional upon your passing a comprehensive medical examination (see enclosed). In addition, your probationary period, during which time you may be released with two weeks' notice, will extend until you receive a passing score on all parts of the New York State CPA examination.
>
> I look forward to having you join our firm, Aurelia, and would appreciate receiving a written acceptance of this offer by May 30.
>
> Sincerely,

Your excitement at receiving this letter is tempered by the fact that last week you orally accepted an offer of $27,000 from Modlin and Associates, another accounting firm, and their confirming letter arrived yesterday. Although you've not yet answered Modlin's letter, you planned to do so this weekend. You had also planned to write Ross, Russell & Weston this weekend, asking them to withdraw your name from further consideration.

PROCESS

1. Which job offer is more appealing to you?

   In addition to their offering a larger salary, another factor I like about Ross, Russell is that they are more active in city politics than Modlin. If their offer had arrived first, I would definitely have taken it.

2. Because you haven't responded in writing to the Modlin offer, are you still free to accept the Ross, Russell offer?

   No, I definitely did accept the Modlin offer over the phone. In addition to the ethical dimension, public accounting firms are a very "clubby" group. Partners in different firms tend to have frequent contacts with one another, and it is likely that my action would become known to both firms.

3. Should your rejection letter be written in the direct or indirect organizational pattern?

   Indirect. Presumably, they will consider my rejection of their job offer as bad news because they will have to reopen their search process.

4. Can you leave open the possibility of future employment with Ross, Russell?

   Considering the fact that one in four entry-level employees fails to make it through the first year, there is always that possibility. However, any direct reference to future employment would be inappropriate.

5. Should you express regret that you cannot accept their offer?

   No. It might invite additional job negotiations from Ross, Russell, which would not be in my best interests. I accepted the Modlin offer because I thought it would be a good career move. Despite the new offer, I still feel I will be happy and productive at Modlin.

PRODUCT

April 20, 19--

Mr. David Norman, Partner
Ross, Russell & Weston
452 Fifth Avenue
New York, NY 10018

Dear Mr. Norman:

The opportunity to join a progressive accounting firm in New York City, especially one that is active in the political life of our city, is certainly attractive.

I am sure, therefore, that you can appreciate the mixed feelings with which I inform you that I accepted another job offer last week. Your letter arrived before I had a chance to inform you of my decision.

I thank you sincerely for the opportunity I had to learn about your firm, its employees, and its management philosophy. I found the entire process very educational and rewarding, and I look forward to continuing to get to know you and your firm better as my career in public accounting progresses.

Sincerely,

Aurelia Gomez

Aurelia Gomez
225 West 70 Street
New York, NY 10023

CHECKLIST 19

Employment Interviews

PREPARING FOR AN EMPLOYMENT INTERVIEW

1. Before going on an employment interview, learn everything you can about the organization.
2. Practice answering common interview questions and prepare questions of your own to ask.
3. Select appropriate clothing to wear.
4. Control your nervousness by being well prepared, well equipped, and on time.

CONDUCTING YOURSELF DURING THE INTERVIEW

5. Throughout the interview, be aware of the nonverbal signals you are communicating through your body language.
6. Answer each question completely and accurately, always trying to relate your qualifications to the specific needs of the desired job.
7. Whether you are interviewed by one person or a group of people, you will be evaluated based on your education and experience, mental qualities, manner and personal traits, and general appearance.

COMMUNICATING AFTER THE INTERVIEW

8. Immediately following the interview, critique your performance and also send a thank-you note to the interviewer.
9. Recognize that several interviews at different organizations may be needed before you are offered a worthwhile job, so continue scheduling interviews.
10. When you receive a job offer you want to accept, write the organization an acceptance letter and telephone or write all other employers withdrawing your name from further consideration.
11. If you need additional time to consider a job offer, write a tactful letter expressing appreciation for the offer, justifying your request, and assuring the organization of your continuing interest in the position.
12. If you receive additional offers, reject them immediately. Similarly, if you are presently employed, write a letter of resignation.

SUMMARY

To succeed at the interview phase of the job campaign, prepare for the interview, conduct yourself appropriately during the interview, and complete the communication tasks needed after the interview. The specific steps are summarized in Checklist 19.

REVIEW AND DISCUSSION

1. **Communication at Ben & Jerry's Revisited ▪**
   When Liz Lonergan interviews applicants for management positions at Ben & Jerry's Homemade, she looks for people who can relate to colleagues at every level, "from the boardroom to the boiler room." However, some appli-

The answers to the review and discussion questions appear in the *Instructor's Resource Manual*, beginning on p. 295.

cants are so eager to work in a country setting that they neglect to do even basic research on the company's hiring and paying practices.

a. You are going to interview with Ben & Jerry's for the position of advertising manager, and you know that the firm's managers do not have to adhere to a dress code. What will you wear to the interview?
b. Knowing that Lonergan doesn't want to hire a prima donna, what might you say or do during your interview to show that you can comfortably relate to employees at all levels?
c. What specific company information would you want to research in advance of your interview?

2. What types of information should you research about the organization with which you will be interviewing?
3. What overall strategy should you use when answering questions during the interview?
4. Describe item by item what articles of clothing and accessories from your own wardrobe you might wear to a job interview.
5. What should you do if an interviewer does not ask about an area in which you feel you are uniquely qualified for the position?
6. What criteria does an organization generally use to assess the interviewee?
7. Should you ask about salary during the interview? Why or why not?
8. Why should a thank-you note follow the interview?
9. What are the disadvantages of declining a job offer by phone?
10. If you accept one job offer and then receive a better offer a few days later from another firm, what are the ethical implications of accepting the second job offer?
11. What organizational pattern should be used for writing job-rejection letters?

EXERCISES

Suggestions and sample solutions for exercises appear in the *Instructor's Resource Manual,* beginning on p. 296.

1. Microwriting a Letter Asking to Delay a Job-Offer Decision ▪

PROBLEM

Assume that you were offered the position of manager-trainee at Philip Morris (see Exercise 9b in Chapter 16) at a salary of $24,500, starting June 15. However, you've interviewed at two other firms and expect to learn their decisions by May 5 (10 days after Ms. Trimmer from Philip Morris asked you to respond to her job offer). Write to Ms. Trimmer, tactfully asking for a delay.

PROCESS

a. Describe your audience.
b. Should your letter be written in the direct or indirect organizational pattern? Why?
c. Compose the first paragraph of your letter, in which you express appreciation for the job offer.
d. Compose the middle paragraph of your letter, in which you tactfully ask for a time extension, explaining the reason for the request.
e. Compose the last paragraph of your letter, in which you reaffirm your interest in the job.

PRODUCT

Revise, format, and proofread your letter (addressed to Ms. Janice Trimmer, Personnel Manager, Kraft Food Division, Philip Morris Companies, 120 Park Avenue, New York, NY 10017). Be careful to maintain a tone of sincerity throughout. Submit both your letter and your responses to the process questions to your instructor.

2. **Preparing for the Interview** ■ Page 571 contains a list of commonly asked interview questions. Prepare a written answer for each of these questions based on your own qualifications and experience. Then select two of the stress questions on page 572 and answer them in terms of your own situation. Type each question and then your answer.
3. **Researching the Employer** ■ Refer to Exercise 9b in Chapter 16. Assume that Philip Morris has invited you to interview for the manager-trainee position. Research this company prior to your interview. Prepare a two-page, double-spaced report on your findings. You will, of course, concentrate on that information most likely to help you during the interview. As you're conducting your research, some questions are likely to occur to you that you'll want to get answered during the interview. Prepare a list of these questions and attach it as an appendix to your report.
4. **Collaborative Project—Mock Interviews** ■ This project uses information collected as part of Exercise 3. Divide into groups of six students. Draw straws to determine which three members will be interviewers and which three will be job applicants. Both groups now have homework to do. The interviewers must get together to plan their interview strategy (10 to 12 minutes for each candidate); and the applicants, working individually, must prepare for this interview.

   The interviews will be conducted in front of the entire class, with each participant dressed appropriately. On the designated day, the three interviewers as a group will interview each of the three job applicants in turn (while the other two are out of the room). Given the short length of each interview, the applicant should refrain from asking any questions of his or her own, except to clarify the meaning of an interviewer's question.

   After each round of interviews, the class as a whole will vote for the most effective interviewer and interviewee.
5. **Accepting a Job Offer** ■ Neither of the other two jobs panned out (see the Microwriting Exercise 1 above). Write your acceptance letter to Ms. Trimmer.
6. **Rejecting a Job Offer** ■ Assume that you were offered the job in Exercise 1 above. Even though the position is with the Kraft Food Division of Philip Morris, you've had second thoughts about working for an organization so closely associated with tobacco products. You prefer to take your chances on getting another job offer, one with which you will be more comfortable. Write your letter of rejection to Ms. Trimmer.

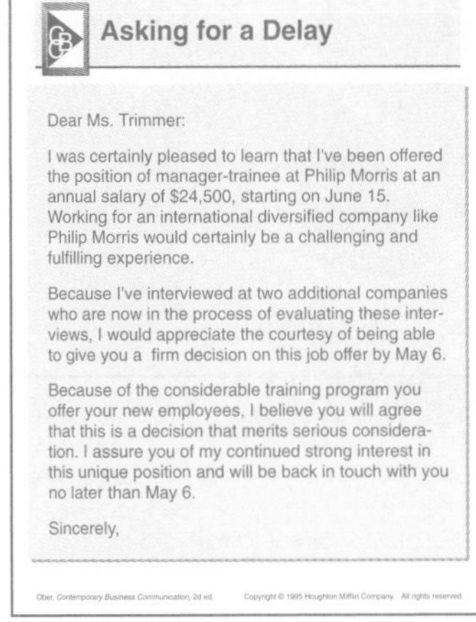

Asking for a Delay

Dear Ms. Trimmer:

I was certainly pleased to learn that I've been offered the position of manager-trainee at Philip Morris at an annual salary of $24,500, starting on June 15. Working for an international diversified company like Philip Morris would certainly be a challenging and fulfilling experience.

Because I've interviewed at two additional companies who are now in the process of evaluating these interviews, I would appreciate the courtesy of being able to give you a firm decision on this job offer by May 6.

Because of the considerable training program you offer your new employees, I believe you will agree that this is a decision that merits serious consideration. I assure you of my continued strong interest in this unique position and will be back in touch with you no later than May 6.

Sincerely,

See Master 17.1, Exercise 1, Microwriting a Letter Asking to Delay Job-Offer Decision, in the *Instructor's Resource Manual*.

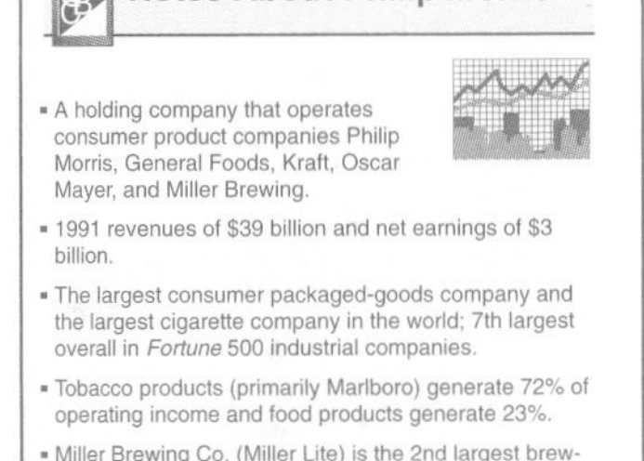

Notes About Philip Morris

- A holding company that operates consumer product companies Philip Morris, General Foods, Kraft, Oscar Mayer, and Miller Brewing.
- 1991 revenues of $39 billion and net earnings of $3 billion.
- The largest consumer packaged-goods company and the largest cigarette company in the world; 7th largest overall in *Fortune* 500 industrial companies.
- Tobacco products (primarily Marlboro) generate 72% of operating income and food products generate 23%.
- Miller Brewing Co. (Miller Lite) is the 2nd largest brewing company in the world (Anheuser-Busch is first).
- Company started in 1847 when Philip Morris opened his London tobacco store.
- Headquarters in New York city; Chairman and CEO is Hamish Maxwell, who earned $1.9 million last year.

See Master 17.2, Exercise 3, Researching the Employer, in the *Instructor's Resource Manual*.

CONTINUING CASE 17

Neelima Takes a Walk

Neelima Shrikhande has been on two job interviews and is scheduled to go on a third next week. Yesterday in the mail she received a job offer from Applied Biosystems (James R. Douglas, Vice President, 850 Lincoln Centre Drive, Foster City, CA 94404) to begin work on September 1 as director of management information systems at an annual salary of $78,500. Today, she received a phone call from Anne McKenzie, president of Stride Rite (5 Cambridge Center, Cambridge, MA 02142), offering her the newly created position of director of corporate communications at an annual salary of $69,000, effective at her convenience but not later than 60 days from acceptance of the job offer.

Despite the lower salary, Neelima immediately decides to accept the position at Stride Rite. She will report directly to Anne McKenzie, and she feels she will enjoy living in the Boston metropolitan area. She will cancel her interview next week with Victor DeJorgè at Southeast Banking in Miami.

A possible solution to the Continuing Case is described in the *Instructor's Resource Manual*, p. 298.

Critical Thinking

1. How should Neelima inform Victor DeJorgè of her decision?
2. One week later, Neelima received an overnight express letter from Jim Douglas proposing a counteroffer: Neelima's salary will be increased to $82,000, and she will be named to head a corporate-wide task force to coordinate Applied Biosystems' efforts to increase the role of women in technical and engineering positions within the organization. What should Neelima do?

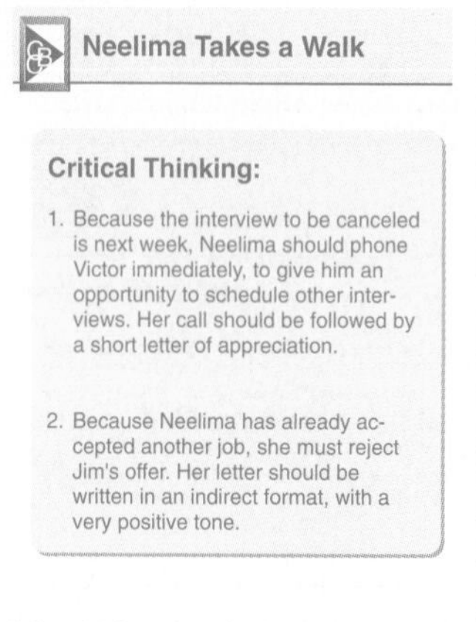
Neelima Takes a Walk

Critical Thinking:

1. Because the interview to be canceled is next week, Neelima should phone Victor immediately, to give him an opportunity to schedule other interviews. Her call should be followed by a short letter of appreciation.
2. Because Neelima has already accepted another job, she must reject Jim's offer. Her letter should be written in an indirect format, with a very positive tone.

See Master 17.3, Continuing Case 17, in the *Instructor's Resource Manual.*

Writing Projects

3. Assume the role of Neelima Shrikhande. Write letters to Anne McKenzie and James R. Douglas giving your decision.

WORDWISE *Proper Names*

- To be eligible to compete in the Kentucky Derby, a horse must bear a name of no more than 18 letters and three words.
- More than 70 million people in China have the surname *Wang*. In fact, a fourth of the Chinese population has one of four family names: *Wang*, *Li*, *Zhang*, and *Liu*.
- The word *Main* is only the 11th most common street name in America (*Park* is the most common).

REFERENCE MANUAL

SECTION A
Language Arts Basics

LAB 1: Punctuation—Commas

Punctuation serves as a roadmap to help guide the reader through the twists and turns of your message—pointing out what is important (underscores), subordinate (commas), copied from another source (quotation marks), explained further (colon), considered as a unit (hyphens), and the like. Sometimes correct punctuation is absolutely essential for comprehension. Consider, for example, the different meanings of the following sentences, depending upon the punctuation:

What's the latest, Dope?
What's the latest dope?

The social secretary called the guests names as they arrived.
The social secretary called the guests' names as they arrived.

Our new model comes in red, green and brown, and white.
Our new model comes in red, green, and brown and white.

The play ended, happily.
The play ended happily.

A clever dog knows it's master.
A clever dog knows its master.

We must still play Michigan, which tied Ohio State, and Minnesota.
We must still play Michigan, which tied Ohio State and Minnesota.

"Medics Help Dog Bite Victim"
"Medics Help Dog-Bite Victim"

The comma rules presented below and the other punctuation rules presented in LAB 2 do not cover every possible situation; comprehensive style manuals, for example, routinely present more than 100 rules just for using the comma rather than just the 12 rules presented below. These rules cover the most frequent uses of punctuation in business writing. Learn them—because you will be using them frequently.

Commas are used to connect ideas and to set off elements within a sentence. When typing, leave one space after a comma. Many writers use commas inappropriately. No matter how long the sentence, make sure you have a legitimate reason before inserting a comma.

1.1 Adjectives Use a comma to separate two or more adjectives that modify the same noun if the adjectives are *not* joined by a coordinate conjunction.

He was an aggressive, unpleasant manager.
But: He was an aggressive_and unpleasant manager.

Note: The major coordinate conjunctions are *and, but, or,* and *nor;* they join elements of equal rank. Do not use a comma if the first adjective modifies the combined idea of the second adjective plus the noun: *Please order a new*

bulletin board *for the conference room.* Do not use a comma between the last adjective and the noun: *Wednesday was a long, hot, humid_day.*

1.2 Complimentary Closing Use a comma after the complimentary closing of a business letter formatted in the standard punctuation style.

> Yours truly,
> Sincerely yours,

Note: No punctuation follows the complimentary closing if the open punctuation style is used.

1.3 Date Use commas to set off the year in a complete date.

> The note is due on May 31, 1998, at 5 p.m.

Note: Do not forget the comma *after* the year. A comma should not be used after a partial date: *The note is due on August 31_at 5 p.m.*

1.4 Direct Address Use commas to set off a name used in direct address.

> Thank you, Ms. Cross, for bringing the matter to our attention.
> Ladies and gentlemen, we appreciate your attending our session today.

1.5 Independent Clauses Use a comma to connect independent clauses joined by a coordinate conjunction (unless both clauses are short and closely related).

> Mr. Karas discussed last month's performance, and Ms. Daniels presented the sales projections.
> The meeting was running late, but Mr. Mears was in no hurry to adjourn.
> The firm hadn't paid_and John was angry.

Note: Do not confuse two independent clauses joined by a coordinate conjunction and a comma with a compound predicate, whose verbs are not to be separated by a comma:

> Mrs. Ames had read the merger report, but she had not discussed it with her colleagues.
> Mrs. Ames had read the merger report_but had not discussed it with her colleagues.

1.6 Interrupting Expression Use commas to set off an interrupting expression.

> I believe it was John, not Nancy, who raised the question.
> It is still not too late to make the change, is it?

1.7 Introductory Expression Use a comma to set off an introductory expression (unless it is a short prepositional phrase).

> No, the status report is not ready.
> When the status report is ready, I shall call you.

But: I shall call you_when the status report is ready.

To finish the task on time, Frank hired temporary help.
But: In 1990_we expanded into South America.

Note: An introductory expression is a word, phrase, or clause that comes before the subject and verb of the independent clause. Do not use a comma between the subject and verb: *To finish that boring and time-consuming task in time_for the monthly sales meeting_was a major challenge.*

1.8 Nonrestrictive Expression Use commas to set off a nonrestrictive expression.

Nonrestrictive:	Ann Cosgrave, who has had some experience, should apply for the position.
Restrictive:	Anyone_who has had some experience_should apply for the position.
Nonrestrictive:	Those papers, which we had left on the conference table, are missing.
Restrictive:	Only those papers_that we had left on the conference table are missing.
Nonrestrictive:	Wagner's latest book, *Merger Mania*, was the topic of the session.
Restrictive:	The book_*Merger Mania*_was the topic of the session.

Note: A nonrestrictive expression is a word, phrase, or clause that may be omitted without changing the basic meaning of the sentence. A restrictive expression, on the other hand, limits (restricts) the meaning of the noun or pronoun that it follows; because it is essential to the meaning of the sentence, it is *not* set off by commas. Always examine the noun or pronoun that comes before the expression to determine whether the noun or pronoun needs that expression to complete its meaning; it if does, do *not* use a comma.

In the last pair of sentences, note that an appositive (a noun that renames the preceding noun) is set off by commas only if it is nonrestrictive.

1.9 Place Use commas to set off a state or country that follows a city.

The sales conference will be held in Phoenix, Arizona, on May 13–15.

Our business agent is located in Brussels, Belgium, in the P.O.M. Building.

Note: Do not forget to insert the comma *after* the state or country.

1.10 Quotation Use commas to set off a direct quotation in narrative material.

The president said, "You have nothing to fear," and I believed him.

"I assure you," the vice president said, "that no positions will be terminated."

Note: If a quotation at the beginning of a sentence is a question, use a question mark instead of a comma: *"How many have applied?" she asked.*

1.11 Series

Use commas to separate three or more items in a series.

> The committee may meet on Wednesday, Thursday, or Friday.
> Carl wrote the questionnaire, Anna distributed it, and Tim tabulated the results.

Note: Some style manuals indicate that the last comma (before the conjunction) is optional. However, to avoid ambiguity in business writing, you should insert this comma. Do not use a comma after the last item in a series: *Planning the agenda, preparing the handouts, and recording the minutes_are the three jobs left to complete.*

1.12 Transitional Expression

Use commas to set off a transitional expression or independent comment.

> You may, of course, cancel your subscription at any time.
> One suggestion, for example, was to undertake a leveraged buyout.

Note: Examples of transitional expressions and independent comments are *in addition, as a result, therefore, in summary, on the other hand, however, unfortunately,* and *as a matter of fact.*

APPLICATION

Directions Insert any needed commas in the following sentences. In the blank at the left, write the abbreviation for the comma rule (or rules) being applied. If a sentence is correctly punctuated as shown, write a C in the blank.

Examples: __*tran*__ We cannot, therefore, accept your offer.
__C__ I hoped to receive permission but was disappointed.

______ 1. The contracts to be signed were left on the supervisor's desk.

______ 2. Portland Oregon is a lovely city.

______ 3. Leonard has prepared numerous reports news releases and sales presentations.

______ 4. At the sales manager's specific direction we are extending store hours until 7 p.m.

______ 5. I will attend the conference in August and let you know what happens.

______ 6. You may make the slides yourself or you may request assistance from audiovisual services.

______ 7. I assumed as a matter of fact that the project was finished.

______ 8. We signed the original lease on January 1 1990.

______ 9. I hope you will purchase Lotus 1-2-3 and will make use of it in budgeting.

______ 10. They must have your answer by June 15 before the board meeting.

1. C
2. Portland, Oregon, (, place)
3. reports, news releases, (, ser)
4. direction, (, intro)
5. C
6. yourself, (, ind)
7. assumed, as a matter of fact, (, tran)
8. January 1, (, date)
9. C
10. June 15, (, nonr)

11. C	________	11. The group of co-op students from Los Angeles visited our offices today.
12. C	________	12. Ross hopes to get the figures to you soon but cannot promise delivery by a certain date.
13. C	________	13. The consultant was pressed for time to complete the analysis before closing time.
14. department, for example, (, tran)	________	14. Their software-support department for example handles more than a thousand calls daily.
15. C	________	15. To end the quarter with a small surplus is the major goal for the division.
16. concise, (, adj)	________	16. Richardson gave a concise reasoned explanation of the process.
17. note, Bonnie, (, dir ad)	________	17. You will note Bonnie that your signature appears on the document.
18. early, I suspect, (, interr)	________	18. It is not too early I suspect to begin planning our tenth-anniversary sale.
19. states, (, quot)	________	19. Their catalog states "All merchandise is guaranteed for 90 days."
20. surplus, (, intro)	________	20. To end the quarter with a small surplus we must reduce costs by at least 8%.
21. Everyone, (, dir ad)	________	21. Everyone please be seated so that President Mary Webler can tell us about her short but interesting conversation.
22. C	________	22. His attempt to conceal his role in the cover-up of the savings-and-loan scandal was not successful.
23. prospects, qualifying them, (, ser) June 13, 1996, (, date)	________	23. Identifying prospects qualifying them and determining their preferences will consume most of the afternoon of June 13 1996 for Anne's group.
24. C	________	24. I agree with you but do not feel that such drastic action is necessary.
25. well, (, intro)	________	25. To do your job well you will require some assistance from another department.
26. C	________	26. To do your job well will require a major time commitment.
27. comma, (, ind)	________	27. A noun that comes before a nonrestrictive expression is followed by a comma but one that comes before a restrictive expression is not.
28. hard, (, intro) Phoenix, (, interr)	________	28. By working hard we gained approval to hold our conference in Phoenix not in Springfield.
29. C	________	29. John drove and I navigated.
30. C	________	30. The fact that Pete Johnson and I both came from San Francisco and had been with the company for a total of 32 years did not persuade the human resources director to approve our request that the retirement plan be modified to permit early retirements.

LAB 2: Punctuation—Other Marks

APOSTROPHES

Apostrophes are used to show that letters have been omitted (as in contractions) and to show possession. When typing, do not space before or after an apostrophe (unless a space after is needed to end the word).

2.1 Gerund Use the possessive form for a noun (or pronoun) that comes before a gerund.

> Garth questioned Karen**'s** leaving so soon.
> **Stockholders'** raising so many questions delayed the adjournment.
> Mr. Matsumoto knew Karl and objected to **his** going to the meeting.

Note: A gerund is the *-ing* form of a verb used as a noun.

2.2 Pronoun Use an apostrophe plus the letter *s* to form the possessive of indefinite pronouns; do not use an apostrophe to form the possessive of personal pronouns.

It is someone's responsibility.	The responsibility is theirs.
I will review everybody's figures.	The company used its credit.

Note: Examples of indefinite possessive pronouns are *anybody's, everyone's, no one's, nobody's, one's,* and *somebody's.* Examples of personal possessive pronouns are *hers, his, its, ours, theirs,* and *yours.* Do not confuse the possessive pronouns *its, theirs,* and *whose* with the contractions *it's, there's,* and *who's: **It's** time to put litter in **its** place. **There's** no reason to take **theirs**. **Who's** determining **whose** jobs will be eliminated?*

2.3 Singular Nouns Use an apostrophe plus *s* to form the possessive of a singular noun.

Al Brown's office	Gil Hodges's record
brother-in-law's problem	a year's time
Mr. and Mrs. Smith's home	the CPA's opinion
Michigan National Bank's assets	the boss's contract
the buyer's and the seller's signatures	Clinton and Gore's administration

Note: To indicate joint ownership, make only the last noun possessive: *John and Mary's report.* To indicate separate ownership, make both nouns possessive: *John's and Mary's reports.* Add the apostrophe plus *s* to the last word in a compound possessive (*attorney general's opinion*).

2.4 Plural Nouns Use only an apostrophe, without an *s*, to form the possessive of plural nouns that end in *s*.

the two companies' agreement	*But:* the children's books
both girls' statements	the men's dressing room
the Smiths' home	
all the doctors' offices	
two years' worth	

Note: Make sure that what comes before the apostrophe is a complete word: *juries' verdicts* and not *jurie's verdicts*. To avoid problems with plural possessives, first make the noun plural; then form the possessive of the plural noun: *child, children, children's shoes; city, cities, the two cities' boundaries.* Do not confuse plural nouns with possessive nouns (singular or plural). Whenever a noun ending in *s* is followed by another noun, the first noun is probably a possessive, requiring an apostrophe; for example, write *company's policies* or *companies' policies*, but not *companies_ policies.*

COLONS

Colons are used (1) after an independent clause that introduces explanatory material and (2) after the salutation of a business letter. When typing, leave two spaces after a colon; do not begin the following word with a capital letter unless it begins a quoted sentence.

2.5 Explanation Use a colon to introduce explanatory material that is preceded by an independent clause.

> Just remember this: you may need a reference from her in the future.
>
> The fall trade show offers the following advantages: inexpensive show space, abundant traffic, and free press publicity.

Note: An independent clause is a subject-verb combination that can stand alone as a complete sentence. Expressions commonly used to introduce explanatory material are *the following, as follows,* and *these.* The explanatory material may be a listing, a restatement, an example, or a quotation.

Make sure the clause preceding the explanatory material can stand alone as a complete sentence. Otherwise, no punctuation is needed: *The fall trade show offers_inexpensive show space, abundant traffic, and free press publicity.*

2.6 Salutation Use a colon after the salutation of a business letter that uses the standard punctuation style.

> Dear Mr. Jones:
> Dear Alice:

Note: Never use a comma after the salutation in a business letter. (A comma would be used only in a personal letter.) With standard punctuation, a colon follows the salutation and a comma follows the complimentary closing. With open punctuation, no punctuation follows the salutation or complimentary closing.

ELLIPSIS

An ellipsis is an omission. Three periods, with one space before and after each, are used to show that something has been left out of a quotation. Four periods (the sentence period plus the three ellipsis periods) indicate the omission of the last part of a quoted sentence, the first part of the next sentence, or a whole sentence or paragraph. Here is an example:

> *Complete Quotation:*
>
> The average age of homebuyers has risen to 31.5 years from 29.6 years in 1989. This increase is partly due to the rising cost of new home mortgages. Adjustable-rate mortgages now account for 60% of all new mortgages.
>
> *Shortened Quotation:*
>
> The average age of homebuyers has risen to 31.5 years. . . . Adjustable-rate mortgages now account for 60% of all new mortgages. (The typing sequence is *years.*(space).(space).(space).(2 spaces)*Adjustable.*)

2.7 Omission Use ellipsis periods to indicate that one or more words have been omitted from quoted material.

> According to *Business Week,* "A continuing protest could shut down . . . Pemex, which brought in 34% of Mexico's dollar income last year."

HYPHENS

Hyphens are used to form some compound adjectives, to link some prefixes to root words (such as *quasi-public*), and to divide words at the ends of lines. When typing, do not leave a space before or after a regular hyphen. Likewise, do not use a hyphen with a space before and after to substitute for a dash. (If your keyboard does not have a dash character, make a dash by typing two hyphens with no space before, between, or after.)

2.8 Compound Adjective Hyphenate a compound adjective that comes *before* a noun (unless the adjective is a proper noun or unless the first word is an adverb ending in *-ly*). Leave one space after a "suspended" hyphen unless it is followed by a punctuation mark.

> We hired a first-class management team.
> *But:* Our new management team is first_class.
>
> The long-term outlook for our investments is excellent.
> *But:* We intend to hold our investments for the long_term.
>
> The General_Motors warranty received high ratings.
>
> Alice presented a poorly_conceived proposal.
>
> Only first- and second-class mail will arrive on time.

Note: Don't confuse compound adjectives (which are generally temporary combinations) with compound nouns (which are generally well-established concepts). Compound nouns (such as *social security, life insurance, word processing,* and *high school*) are not hyphenated when they come before a noun; thus, use *income_tax form, real_estate agent, public_relations firm,* and *data_processing center.* In the last sentence, note that when two hyphenated adjectives have a common base you should use a "suspended" hyphen rather than repeating the base word (*class* is the base word in this example).

2.9 Numbers Hyphenate fractions and compound numbers 21 through 99 when they are spelled out.

Nearly three-fourths of our new applicants were unqualified.
Seventy-two orders were processed incorrectly.

PERIODS

Periods are used at the ends of declarative sentences and polite requests and in abbreviations. When typing, leave two spaces after a period (or any other punctuation mark) that ends a sentence.

2.10 Request Use a period to end a sentence that is a polite request.

Would you please sign the form on page 2.
May I please have the report by Friday.

Note: Consider the statement a polite request if you expect the reader to respond by *acting* rather than by giving a yes-or-no answer. *Would you be willing to take this assignment?* is a real question, requiring a question mark, whereas *Would you let me know your answer by Friday.* is a polite request, requiring a period.

QUOTATION MARKS

Quotation marks are used around direct quotations, titles of some publications and conferences, and special terms. When typing, do not space after the opening quotation mark or before the closing quotation mark. Type the closing quotation mark after a period or comma but before a colon or semicolon. Type the closing quotation mark after a question mark or exclamation point if the quoted material itself is a question or an exclamation; otherwise, type it before the question mark or exclamation point. Capitalize the first word of a quotation that begins a sentence.

2.11 Quotation Use quotation marks around a direct quotation.

"When we return on Thursday," Luis said, "we would like to meet with you."
Did Helen say, "He will represent us"?

Note: Do not confuse a direct quotation with an indirect quotation, which is not enclosed in quotation marks: *Warren said that he wanted to meet with me on Thursday.*

2.12 Term Use quotation marks around a term to clarify its meaning or to show that it is being used in a special way.

Net income after taxes is known as "the bottom line."
The job title was changed from "chairman" to "chief executive officer."
The president misused the word "effect" in last night's press conference.

2.13 Title Use quotation marks around the title of a newspaper or magazine article, chapter in a book, report, conference, and similar items.

Read the article entitled "Wall Street Recovery."

Chapter 4, "Market Segmentation," of Industrial Marketing is of special interest.

The theme of this year's sales conference is "Quality Sells."

The report "Common Carriers" shows the extent of the transportation problems.

Note: The titles of *complete* published works are underscored or shown in italics. The titles of *parts* of published works and most other titles are enclosed in quotation marks.

SEMICOLONS

Semicolons are used to show where elements in a sentence are separated. The separation is stronger than a comma but not as strong as a period. When typing, leave one space after a semicolon and begin the following word with a lowercase letter.

2.14 Comma If a misreading might otherwise occur, use a semicolon (instead of a comma) to separate independent clauses that contain internal commas.

Confusing: I ordered juice, toast, and bacon, and eggs, toast, and sausage were sent instead.

Clear: I ordered juice, toast, and bacon; and eggs, toast, and sausage were sent instead.

But: Although high-quality paper was used, the photocopy machine still jammed, and neither of us knew how to repair it. (*no misreading likely to occur*)

Note: Make sure the semicolon is inserted *between* the independent clauses—not within one of the clauses.

2.15 Independent Clauses Use a semicolon to separate closely related independent clauses that are not connected by a coordinate conjunction.

The president was eager to proceed with the plans; the board still had some reservations.

I slept through my alarm; consequently, I was late for the meeting.

Note: If a coordinate conjunction (such as *and, but, or,* or *nor*) connects the two clauses, use a comma: *The president was eager to proceed with the plans, but the board still had some reservations.* Do not use a comma to separate two independent clauses that are not joined by a coordinate conjunction (such an error is called a *comma splice*).

2.16 Series Use semicolons to separate items in a series if any of the items already contain commas.

The personnel department will be interviewing in Dallas, Texas; Stillwater, Oklahoma; and Little Rock, Arkansas, for the new position.

Among the guests were Henry Halston, our attorney; his wife, Edith; and Lisa Hart-Wilder, our new controller.

Note: Make sure the semicolon is inserted between (not within) each item in the series. Even if only one of the items contains an internal comma, separate all of them with semicolons.

UNDERSCORES

An underscore (or underline) is a line typed under an expression to show emphasis or to substitute for italic type. When typing a title, underscore the spaces between the words, but do not underscore any punctuation after the title. When underscoring individual words, do not underscore the spaces between the words: *Does the author of* The Last Almighty Dollar *spell her name* *Joanne*, *Joann*, *or* *Jo* *Ann*?

2.17 Title Underscore the title of a book, magazine, newspaper, and other complete published works.

> Roger's newest book, All That Glitters, was reviewed in The New York Times.
>
> The Alaco oil spill was the cover story in last week's Time.

Note: Instead of underscoring, you may type the words in italics.

APPLICATION

Directions Insert any needed punctuation (including commas) in the following sentences. In the blank at the left, write abbreviations for the punctuation rules being applied; some sentences will apply more than one rule. If a sentence is correctly punctuated as shown, write a C in the blank. Each numbered item is one sentence.

Examples: __*sing*__ We received our money's worth.
__C__ Your presentation to the president was first class.

______ 1. I plan to attend Judys session Gretchen does not.

______ 2. Doris finished the newsletter on time but in the meantime her other duties were left undone.

______ 3. Please consult with Mr. McGlynn training director Ms. Little forms analyst and me before taking any action.

______ 4. You must read the article in Business Week entitled Japanese Carmakers Flash Their Cash.

______ 5. Chris Overmans updating of the lobbies furnishings was widely appreciated.

______ 6. Will your remarks be off the record?

______ 7. If Agnes intends to go she should notify Mark he will make all the arrangements.

______ 8. They will first paint my office then after five minutes rest they will paint yours.

1. Judy's (' sing)
   session; (; noconj)
2. time, (, ind)
   meantime, (, intro)
3. McGlynn, training director;
   Ms. Little, forms analyst;
   (, ser ; ser)
4. Business Week (_ title)
   "Japanese . . . Cash."
   (" title)
5. Overman's (' ger)
   lobbies' (' plur)
6. C
7. go, (, intro)
   Mark; (; noconj)
8. office; (; noconj)
   minutes' (' plur)
   rest, (, intro)

_______ 9. These are the new requirements three years experience and union membership.

_______ 10. Those peoples computers are privately owned.

_______ 11. They were careful workers nevertheless two errors slipped by them.

_______ 12. Its about time your division was given its due share of resources.

_______ 13. Dayle is certainly a highly valued employee of ours.

_______ 14. Betty wanted to attend the APICS meeting but she was out of town.

_______ 15. Mens wallets and womens handbags are featured in this weeks sale.

_______ 16. The award ceremony was a never to be forgotten experience for that workers family.

_______ 17. You may test up to three fourths of the workers said Mr. Palmer if you notify them ten days prior to the testing.

_______ 18. The two dates to remember are March 15 1994 and April 15 1995.

_______ 19. It took Mavis only two hours to do the five hour job.

_______ 20. The Browns automobile is two years newer than the Wilsons.

_______ 21. Bills leaving delayed our new product introduction by two weeks.

_______ 22. My superiors wife used the term nonboring to describe their new family life.

_______ 23. Twenty one of the reports were prepared on the secretaries computers.

_______ 24. The inns guests complained about the geeses honking.

_______ 25. Here is the latest development Business Week will feature the company in its next issue.

_______ 26. The mayors voted to coordinate their efforts in attracting the new firm we should be receiving their joint plan soon.

_______ 27. Would you please photocopy the article entitled Green Is the Color of Money that appeared in last weeks Money magazine.

_______ 28. The commerce official said We will trim imports by two thirds by the end of the quarter.

_______ 29. You will be meeting our agent in Milan next week but do not forget to visit Rudolpho Angeletti our distributor in Rome on your way home.

_______ 30. Casey nominated Maria Tony and Ken and Barbie Andy and Jo seconded the nomination.

9. requirements: (: exp)
   years' (' plur)

10. people's (' plur)

11. workers; (; noconj)
    nevertheless, (, tran)

12. It's (' contract)

13. C

14. meeting, (, ind)

15. Men's (' plur)
    women's (' plur)
    week's (' sing)

16. never-to-be-forgotten (- adj)
    worker's (' sing)

17. "You . . . workers," (" quot , quot)
    three-fourths (- num)
    Palmer, "if . . . testing." (, quot " quot)

18. March 15, 1994, and April 15, 1995 (, date)

19. five-hour (- adj)

20. Browns' (' plur)
    Wilsons' (' plur)

21. Bill's (' ger)

22. superior's (' sing)
    "nonboring" (" term)

23. Twenty-one (- num)
    secretaries' (' plur)

24. inn's (' sing)
    geese's (' plur)

25. development: (: exp)
    <u>Business Week</u> (_ title)

26. firm; (; noconj)

27. "Green . . . Money" (" title)
    week's (' sing)
    <u>Money</u> (_ title)

28. said, (, quot)
    "We . . . quarter." (" quot)
    two-thirds (- num)

29. week, (, ind)
    Angeletti, our distributor in Rome, (, nonr)

30. Maria, Tony, (, ser)
    Ken; (; comma)
    Barbie, Andy, (, ser)

LAB 3: Grammar

Suppose the vice president of your organization asked you, a systems analyst, to try to locate a troublesome problem in a computer spreadsheet. After some sharp detective work, you finally resolved the problem and wrote a memo to the vice president saying, "John and myself discovered that one of the formulas were incorrect, so I asked he to revise it."

Instantly, you've turned what should have been a "good-news" opportunity for you into, at best, a "mixed-news" situation. The vice president will be pleased that you've uncovered the bug in the program but will probably focus entirely too much attention on your poor grammar skills.

Grammar refers to the rules for combining words into sentences. The most frequent grammar problems faced by business writers are discussed below. Learn these common rules well so that your use of grammar will not present a communication barrier to the message you're trying to convey.

MODIFIERS (ADJECTIVES AND ADVERBS)

An adjective modifies a noun or pronoun; an adverb modifies a verb, an adjective, or another adverb.

3.1 Modifiers Use a comparative adjective or adverb (*-er, more,* or *less*) to refer to two persons, places, or things and a superlative adjective or adverb (*-est, most,* or *least*) to refer to more than two.

> The Datascan is the fast**er** of the two machines.
> The XR-75 is the slow**est** of all the machines.
>
> Rose Marie is the **less** qualified of the two applicants.
> Rose Marie is the **least** qualified of the three applicants.

Note: Do not use double comparisons, such as "more faster."

AGREEMENT (SUBJECT/VERB/PRONOUN)

Agreement is correspondence in number between related subjects, verbs, and pronouns. All of them are singular if they refer to one, plural if they refer to more than one.

3.2 Agreement Use a singular verb or pronoun with a singular subject and a plural verb or pronoun with a plural subject.

> The four **workers have** a photocopy of **their** assignments.
> Roger's **wife was** quite late for **her** appointment.
> **Mr. Tibbetts and Mrs. Downs plan** to forgo **their** bonuses.
> Included in this envelope **are a contract and an affidavit.**

Note: This is the general rule; variations are discussed below. In the first sentence, the plural subject (*workers*) requires a plural verb (*have*) and a plural pronoun (*their*). In the second sentence, the singular subject (*wife*) requires a singular verb (*was*) and a singular pronoun (*her*). In the third sentence, the plural subject (*Mr. Tibbetts and Ms. Downs*) requires a plural verb (*plan*) and a plural pronoun (*their*). In the last sentence, the subject is *a contract and an affidavit*—not *envelope*.

3.3 Company Names Company names may be singular or plural so long as consistency is maintained.

> Bickley and Bates **has** paid for **its** last order. **It** is now ready to reorder.
>
> Bickley and Bates **have** paid for **their** last order. **They** are now ready to reorder.
>
> *Not:* Bickley and Bates **has** paid for **its** last order. **They** are ready to reorder.

3.4 Expletives In sentences that begin with an expletive, the true subject follows the verb. Use *is* or *are,* as appropriate.

> There **is** no **reason** for his behavior.
>
> There **are** many **reasons** for his behavior.

Note: An expletive is an expression such as *there is, there are, here is,* and *here are* that comes at the beginning of a clause or sentence. Because the topic of a sentence that begins with an expletive is not immediately apparent, such sentences should be used sparingly in business writing.

3.5 Intervening Words Disregard any words that come between the subject and verb when establishing agreement.

> Only **one** of the mechanics **guarantees his** work. (not *their work*)
>
> The **appearance** of the workers, not their competence, **was** being questioned.
>
> The **secretary**, as well as the clerks, **was** late filing **her** form. (not *their forms*)

Note: First determine the subject; then make the verb agree. Other intervening words that do not affect the number of the verb are *together with, rather than, accompanied by, in addition to,* and *except.*

3.6 Pronouns Some pronouns (*anybody, each, either, everybody, everyone, much, neither, no one, nobody,* and *one*) are always singular. Other pronouns (*all, any, more, most, none,* and *some*) may be singular or plural, depending on the noun to which they refer.

> **Each** of the laborers **has** a different view of **his or her** job.
>
> **Neither** of the models **is** doing **her** job well.
>
> **Everybody** is required to take **his or her** turn at the booth. (not *their turn*)
>
> **All** the **dessert has** been eaten. **None** of the **work is** finished.
>
> **All** the **reports have** been filed. **None** of the **workers are** finished.

3.7 Subject Nearer to Verb If two subjects are joined by correlative conjunctions (*or, either/or, nor, neither/nor,* or *not only/but also*), the verb and any pronoun should agree with the subject that is nearer to the verb.

> Either Robert or **Harold is** at **his** desk.
>
> Neither the receptionist nor the **operators were** able to finish **their** tasks.
>
> Not only the actress but also the **dancer has** to practice **her** routine.
>
> The tellers or the **clerks have** to balance **their** cash drawers before leaving.

Note: The first noun in this type of construction may be disregarded when determining whether the verb should be singular or plural. Pay special attention to using the correct pronoun; do not use the plural pronoun *their* unless the subject and verb are plural. Note that subjects joined by *and* or *both/and* are always plural: *Both* ***the actress and the dancer have*** *to practice* ***their*** *routines.*

3.8 Subjunctive Mood Verbs in the subjunctive mood require the plural form, even when the subject is singular.

I wish the situation **were** reversed.

If I **were** you, I would not mention the matter.

Note: Verbs in the subjunctive mood refer to conditions that are impossible or improbable.

CASE

Case refers to the form of a pronoun and indicates its use in a sentence. There are three cases: nominative, objective, and possessive. (Possessive pronouns are covered under "Apostrophes" in the section on punctuation in LAB 2.) Reflexive pronouns, which end in *-self* or *-selves*, refer to nouns or other pronouns.

3.9 Nominative Case Use nominative pronouns (*I, he, she, we, they, who, whoever*) as subjects of a sentence or clause and with the verb *to be.*

The customer representative and **he** are furnishing the figures. (***he*** *is furnishing*)

Mrs. Quigley asked if Oscar and **I** were ready to begin. (***I*** *was ready to begin*)

We old-timers can provide some background. (***we*** *can provide*)

It was **she** who agreed to the proposal. (***she*** *agreed*)

Who is chairing the meeting? (***he*** *is chairing*)

Mr. Lentzner wanted to know **who** was responsible. (***she*** *was responsible*)

Anna is the type of person **who** can be depended upon. (***she*** *can be depended upon*)

Note: If you have trouble determining which pronoun to use, ignore the plural subject or substitute another pronoun. See the reworded clauses in parentheses above.

3.10 Objective Case Use objective pronouns (*me, him, her, us, them, whom, whomever*) as objects in a sentence, clause, or phrase.

Thomas sent a fax to Mr. Baird and **me**. (*sent a fax to* ***me***)

This policy applies to Eric and **her**. (*applies to* ***her***)

Joe asked **us** old-timers to provide some background. (*Joe asked* ***us*** *to provide*)

The work was assigned to **her** and **me**. (*she assigned the work to* ***me***)

To **whom** shall we mail the specifications? (*mail them to* ***him***)

Anna is the type of person **whom** we can depend upon. (*we can depend upon* ***her***)

Note: For *who/whom* constructions, if *he/she* can be substituted, *who* is the correct choice; if *him/her* can be substituted, *whom* is the correct choice. Remember: *who-he, whom-him.* The difference is apparent in the final examples shown here and under "Nominative Case" above: ***who*** *can be depended upon* versus ***whom*** *we can depend upon.*

3.11 Reflexive Pronouns Use reflexive pronouns (*itself, myself, yourself, himself, herself, ourselves, yourselves,* or *themselves*) to refer to or emphasize a noun or pronoun that has already been named. Do not use reflexive pronouns to *substitute for* nominative or objective pronouns.

I **myself** have some doubts about the proposal.
You should see the exhibit **yourself**.

Not: Virginia and **myself** will take care of the details.
But: Virginia and **I** will take care of the details.

Not: Mary Louise administered the test to Thomas and **myself**.
But: Mary Louise administered the test to Thomas and **me**.

APPLICATION

Directions Select the correct word or words in parentheses.

1. Sherrie Marshall, in addition to James M. Smith, (are/is) in line for an appointment to the Federal Trade Commission. (Who/Whom) do you know on the FTC staff? None of the people I contacted (has/have) heard of them. Smith, I believe, is the (younger/youngest) of the two.

   1. is, Whom, have, younger

2. Tower and Associates is moving (its/their) headquarters. (It/They) (are/is) selling (its/their) old furniture and equipment at auction. Not only a conference table but also a high-speed collator (are/is) for sale. The facilities manager asked that all inquiries be directed to (her/she).

   2. its, It, is, its, is, her

3. If he (was/were) honest about his intentions, Carl Ichan would talk directly to Ivan and (me/myself). After all, he knows that it was (I/me) (who/whom) made the offer originally. Between the two of us, Ivan is the (more/most) supportive of Ichan's position.

   3. were, me, I, who, more

4. Here (are/is) the reports on Hugo's bankruptcy. It seems that (us/we) investors were a little overconfident, but it is generally the early investors (who/whom) make the most money.

   4. are, we, who

5. Neither our savings account nor our long-term securities (are/is) earning adequate interest. Everybody in finance (are/is) trying to improve the performance of (his or her/their) portfolio. Each of the analysts (are/is) trying to maintain quarterly investment goals.

   5. are, is, his or her, is

6. There (was/were) several people in the audience (who/whom) questioned whether each of our divisions (was/were) operating efficiently. The CEO asked (us/we) division managers to respond to their questions.

   6. were who, was, us

7. Neither Lan Yang nor the two programmers (was/were) able to resolve the problem. In fact, neither of the two programmers (was/were) successful in

   7. were, was, is, her

locating the source of the problem. However, Lan Yang, as well as the programmers, (are/is) continuing (her/their) efforts.

8. slower, has, him

8. John is the (more slower/most slower/slower/slowest) of the two welders. Only one of his jobs (has/have) been finished, so I asked (he/him) to work overtime this weekend.

9. Whom, me, most accurate, who

9. (Who/Whom) will you ask to assist (I/me/myself)? Alex is the (more accurate/most accurate) typist on our entire staff; however, Jill is the type of worker (who/whom) can coordinate the entire project.

10. were, me, their, is, I, who

10. I wish it (was/were) possible for Ella and (I/me) to ask both Roger and David about (his/their) experience in using temporary help. Getting their answers to our questions (are/is) going to require some real detective work, and it is (I/me) (who/whom) will have to do it.

LAB 4: Mechanics

Writing mechanics include those elements in communication that are evident only in written form: abbreviations, capitalization, number expression, spelling, and word division. (Punctuation, also a form of writing mechanics, was covered in LABS 2 and 3.) While creating a first draft, you need not be too concerned about the mechanics of your writing. However, you should be especially alert during the editing and proofreading stages to follow the common rules that follow.

ABBREVIATIONS

Use abbreviations sparingly in narrative writing; many abbreviations are appropriate only in technical writing, statistical material, and tables. Consult a dictionary for the correct form for abbreviations, and follow the rule "When in doubt, write it out." When typing, do not space within abbreviations except to separate each initial of a person's name. Leave one space after an abbreviation unless another mark of punctuation follows immediately.

4.1 Not Abbreviated In narrative writing, do not abbreviate common nouns (such as *acct.*, *assoc.*, *bldg.*, *co.*, *dept.*, *misc.*, and *pkg.*) or the names of cities, states (except in addresses), months, and days of the week.

4.2 With Periods Use periods to indicate many abbreviations.

No.	8 a.m.	4 ft.
Dr. M. L. Peterson	P.O. Box 45	e.g.

4.3 Without Periods Write some abbreviations in all capitals, with no periods—including all two-letter state abbreviations used in addresses with Zip Codes.

CPA	IRS	CT
TWA	UNESCO	OK

Use two-letter state abbreviations in bibliographic citations.

CAPITALIZATION

The function of capitalization is to emphasize words or to show their importance. For example, the first word of a sentence is capitalized to emphasize that a new sentence has begun.

4.4 Compass Point Capitalize a compass point that designates a definite region or that is part of an official name. (Do not capitalize compass points used as directions.)

Margot lives in the **S**outh.
Our display window faces **w**est.
Is **E**ast Orange in **W**est Virginia?

4.5 Letter Part Capitalize the first word and any proper nouns in the salutation and complimentary closing of a business letter.

Dear Mr. Smith:	Sincerely yours,
Dear Mr. and Mrs. Ames:	Yours truly,

4.6 Noun Plus Number Capitalize a noun followed by a number or letter (except for page and size numbers).

Table 3	page 79
Flight 1062	size 8D

4.7 Position Title Capitalize an official position title that comes before a personal name, unless the personal name is an appositive set off by commas. Do not capitalize a position title used alone.

Vice President Alfredo Tenegco	Shirley Wilhite, dean,
our president, Joanne Rathburn,	The chief executive officer retired.

4.8 Proper Noun Capitalize proper nouns and adjectives derived from proper nouns. Do not capitalize articles, conjunctions, and prepositions of four or fewer letters (for example, *a, an, the, and, of*). The names of the seasons and the names of generic school courses are not proper nouns and are not capitalized.

Xerox copier	Amherst College (the college)
New York City (the city)	the Mexican border
the Fourth of July	Friday, March 3,
Chrysler Building	Bank of America
First-Class Storage Company	Margaret Adams-White
business communication	the winter holidays

4.9 Quotation Capitalize the first word of a quoted sentence. (Do not capitalize the first word of an indirect quotation.)

According to Hall, "The goal of quality control is specified uniform quality."

Hall thinks we should work toward "specified uniform quality."

Hall said that uniform quality is the goal.

4.10 Title In a published title, capitalize the first and last words, the first word after a colon or dash, and all other words except articles, conjunctions, and prepositions of four or fewer letters.

"A Word to the Wise"

Pricing Strategies: The Link with Reality

NUMBERS

Authorities do not agree on a single style for expressing numbers—whether to spell out the number in words or write it in figures. The following guidelines apply to typical business writing. (The alternative is to use a *formal* style, in which all numbers that can be expressed in one or two words are spelled out.) When typing numbers in figures, separate thousands, millions, and billions with commas; and leave a space between a whole-number figure and its fraction unless the fraction is a character on the keyboard.

4.11 General Spell out numbers for zero through ten and use figures for 11 and over.

the first three pages	ten complaints
18 photocopies	5,376 stockholders

Note: Follow this rule only when none of the following special rules apply.

4.12 Figures Use figures for

- dates. (Use the endings *-st, -d, -rd,* or *-th* only when the day precedes the month.)
- all numbers if two or more *related* numbers both above and below ten are used in the same sentence.
- measurements—such as time, money, distance, weight, and percentage. Be consistent in using either the word *percent* or (more typically) the symbol %.
- mixed numbers.

May 9 (or the 9th of May)	10 miles
4 men and 18 women	*But:* The **18** women had **four** cars.
$6	5 p.m. (or 5 o'clock)
5% (or 5 percent)	6 ½
	But: 6 3/18

4.13 Words Spell out

- numbers used as the first word of a sentence.
- the smaller number when two numbers come together.
- fractions.
- the words *million* and *billion* in even numbers.

Thirty-two people attended.	nearly two-thirds of them
three 29-cent stamps	150 two-page brochures
37 million	$4.8 billion

Note: When fractions and the numbers 21 through 99 are spelled out, they should be hyphenated.

SPELLING

Correct spelling is essential to effective communication. A misspelled word can distract the reader, cause misunderstanding, and send a negative message about the writer's competence. Because of the many variations in the spelling of English words, no spelling guidelines are foolproof; there are exceptions to every spelling rule. The five rules that follow, however, may be safely applied in most business writing situations. Learning them will save you the time of looking up many words in a dictionary. (Although it is no substitute for a dictionary, Section B of this Reference Manual contains a list of 1,000 words that are frequently misspelled in business writing.)

4.14 Doubling a Final Consonant If the last syllable of a root word is stressed, double the final consonant when adding a suffix.

Last Syllable Stressed		*Last Syllable Not Stressed*	
prefer	preferring	prefer	preference
control	controlling	total	totaling
occur	occurrence	differ	differed

4.15 One-Syllable Words If a one-syllable word ends in a consonant preceded by a single vowel, double the final consonant before a suffix starting with a vowel.

Suffix Starting with Vowel		*Suffix Starting with Consonant*	
ship	shipper	ship	shipment
drop	dropped	glad	gladness
bag	baggage	bad	badly

4.16 Final *E* If a final *e* is preceded by a consonant, drop the *e* before a suffix starting with a vowel.

Suffix Starting with Vowel		*Suffix Starting with Consonant*	
come	coming	hope	hopeful
use	usable	manage	management
nerve	nervous	sincere	sincerely

Note: Words ending in *ce* or *ge* usually retain the *e* before a suffix starting with a vowel: *noticeable, advantageous.*

4.17 Final *Y* If a final *y* is preceded by a consonant, change *y* to *i* before any suffix except one starting with *i.*

Most Suffixes		*Suffix Starting with I*	
company	companies	try	trying
ordinary	ordinarily	forty	fortyish
hurry	hurried		

4.18 *EI* and *IE* Words Remember the rhyme:

Use *i* before *e*	believe	yield
Except after *c*	receive	deceit
Or when sounded like *a*	freight	their
As in *neighbor* and *weigh.*		

WORD DIVISION

When possible, avoid dividing words at the end of a line, because word divisions tend to slow down or even confuse a reader (for example, *rear-*

range for *rearrange* or *read- just* for *readjust*). However, when necessary to avoid grossly uneven right margins, use the following rules. Although other optional word-division guidelines are sometimes given, these rules are absolute—they must always be followed. Most word processing software programs have a hyphenation feature that automatically divides words to make a more even right margin. When you are typing, do not space before a hyphen.

4.19 Compound Word Divide a compound word either after the hyphen or where the two words join to make a solid compound.

self- service free- way battle- field

4.20 Division Point Leave at least two letters on the upper line and carry at least three letters to the next line.

ex- treme typ- ing

4.21 Not Divided Do not divide a one-syllable word, contraction, or abbreviation.

straight shouldn't
UNESCO approx.

4.22 Syllables Divide words only between syllables.

per- sonnel knowl- edge

Note: When in doubt about where a syllable ends, consult a dictionary.

APPLICATION

Directions Rewrite the following paragraphs to make sure that all words and numbers are expressed correctly. Do not change the wording in any sentences.

1. 5,000 of our employees will receive their bonus checks at 4 o'clock tomorrow. According to dorothy k. needles, human resources director, employees in every dept. will receive a bonus of at least 4% of their annual salary.

   1. Five thousand, Dorothy K. Needles, department

2. As of june 30th, nearly ¾ of our inventory consisted of overpriced computer chips. The vice president for finance, o. jay christensen, presented this and other information in figure 14 of our quarterly status report.

   2. June 30, three-fourths, O. Jay Christensen, Figure 14

3. The public relations director of our firm gave 14 1-hour briefings during the 3-day swing. Then he drove west to columbus, oh, for a talk-show interview.

   3. 14 one-hour, three-day, Columbus, Ohio

4. In response to the $4 drop in price that was reported on page 45 of yesterday's newspaper, president ronald bradley said that next quarter's earnings are expected to be 1⅔ times higher than this quarter's earnings.

   4. President Ronald Bradley

5. Today's los angeles herald-examiner quoted jason fowler as saying, "we're proud of the fact that 4 of our regional managers and 13 of our representatives donated a total of 173 hours to the hospice project."

   5. Los Angeles Herald-Examiner, Jason Fowler, "We're

Section A

Directions Correct the one misspelling in each line.

1.	phenomenon	hypocricy	assistance
2.	liaison	precedant	miniature
3.	surprise	harrass	nickel
4.	similiar	occasionally	embarrassing
5.	concensus	innovate	irresistible
6.	benefited	exhaustible	parallell
7.	seperately	inadvertent	exhilarated
8.	efficiency	insistance	disapproval
9.	accidentally	camouflage	alloted
10.	criticize	innocence	indispensible
11.	accommodate	perserverance	plausible
12.	apparent	deterrant	license
13.	category	occurrence	wierd
14.	recommend	changeable	hairbrained
15.	argument	boundry	deceive

1. hypocrisy
2. precedent
3. harass
4. similar
5. consensus
6. parallel
7. separately
8. insistence
9. allotted
10. indispensable
11. perseverance
12. deterrent
13. weird
14. harebrained
15. boundary

Directions Write the following words, inserting a hyphen at the first correct division point. If a word cannot be divided, write it without a hyphen.

Examples: mis-spelled
thought

1.	desktop	released	safety
2.	abundant	rhythm	masterpiece
3.	ILGWU	loudly	planned
4.	importance	couldn't	senator-elect
5.	ahead	extremely	going

1. desk-top, re-leased, safety
2. abun-dant, rhythm, master-piece
3. ILGWU, loudly, planned
4. im-portance, couldn't, senator-elect
5. ahead, ex-tremely, go-ing

LAB 5: Word Usage

The following words and phrases are often used incorrectly in everyday speech and in business writing. Learn to use them correctly to help you achieve your communication goals.

In some cases in the following list, one word is often confused with another similar word; in other cases, the structure of our language requires that certain words be used only in certain ways. Because of space, only brief and incomplete definitions are given here. Consult a dictionary for more complete or additional meanings.

5.1 Accept/Except *Accept* means "to agree to"; *except* means "to leave out" or "to exclude."

I will **accept** all the recommendations **except** the last one.

5.2 Advice/Advise *Advice* is a noun meaning "counsel"; *advise* is a verb meaning "to recommend."

If I ask for her **advice**, she may **advise** me to quit.

5.3 Affect/Effect *Affect* is most often used as a verb meaning "to influence" or "to change"; *effect* is most often used as a noun meaning "result" or "impression."

The legislation may **affect** sales but should have no **effect** on gross margin.

5.4 All Right/Alright Use *all right*. (*Alright* is considered substandard.)

The arrangement is **all right** (not *alright*) with me.

5.5 A Lot/Alot Use *a lot*. (*Alot* is considered substandard.)

We used **a lot** (not *alot*) of overtime on the project.

5.6 Among/Between Use *among* when referring to three or more; use *between* when referring to two.

Among the three candidates was one manager who divided his time **between** London and New York.

5.7 Amount/Number Use *amount* to refer to money or to things that cannot be counted; use *number* to refer to things that can be counted.

The **amount** of interest was measured by the **number** of cards returned.

5.8 Anxious/Eager Use *anxious* only if great concern or worry is involved.

Jon was **eager** to get the new car although he was **anxious** about making such high payments.

5.9 Any One/Anyone Spell as two words when followed by *of;* spell as one word when the accent is on *any*.

Anyone is allowed to attend **any one** of the sessions.

Between See *Among/Between.*

5.10 Can/May *Can* indicates ability; *may* indicates permission.

I **can** finish the project on time if I **may** hire an additional secretary.

5.11 Cite/Sight/Site *Cite* means "to quote" or "to mention"; *sight* is either a verb meaning "to look at" or a noun meaning "something seen"; *site* is most often a noun meaning "location."

The **sight** of the high-rise building on the **site** of the old battlefield reminded Monica to **cite** several other examples to the commission members.

5.12 Complement/Compliment *Complement* means "to complete" or "something that completes"; *compliment* means "to praise" or "words of praise."

I must **compliment** you on the model, which will **complement** our line.

5.13 Could Of/Could've Use *could've* (or *could have*). (*Could of* is incorrect.)

We **could've** (not *could of*) prevented that loss had we been more alert.

5.14 Different From/Different Than Use *different from.* (*Different than* is considered substandard.)

Your computer is **different from** (not *different than*) mine.

5.15 Each Other/One Another Use *each other* when referring to two; use *one another* when referring to three or more.

The two workers helped **each other**, but the three visitors would not even look at **one another**.

Eager See *Anxious/Eager.*

Effect See *Affect/Effect.*

5.16 e.g./i.e. The abbreviation *e.g.* means "for example"; *i.e.* means "that is." Use *i.e.* to introduce a restatement or explanation of the preceding expression. Both abbreviations, like the expressions for which they stand, are followed by commas. (Many writers prefer the full English wordings to the abbreviations because they are clearer.)

The proposal has merit; **e.g.**, it is economical, forward-looking, and timely. Unfortunately, it is also a hot potato; **i.e.**, it will generate unfavorable publicity.

5.17 Eminent/Imminent *Eminent* means "well-known"; *imminent* means "about to happen."

The arrival of the **eminent** scientist from Russia is **imminent**.

5.18 Enthused/Enthusiastic Use *enthusiastic.* (*Enthused* is considered substandard.)

I have become quite **enthusiastic** (not *enthused*) about the possibilities.

Except See *Accept/Except.*

5.19 Farther/Further *Farther* refers to distance; *further* refers to extent or degree.

We drove 10 miles **farther** while we discussed the matter **further**.

5.20 Fewer/Less Use *fewer* to refer to things that can be counted; use *less* to refer to money or to things that cannot be counted.

Alvin worked **fewer** hours at the exhibit and therefore generated **less** interest.

Further See *Farther/Further.*

5.21 Good/Well *Good* is an adjective; *well* is an adverb or (with reference to health) an adjective.

Joe does a **good** job and performs **well** on tests, even when he does not feel **well**.

i.e. See *e.g./i.e.*

Imminent See *Eminent/Imminent.*

5.22 Imply/Infer *Imply* means "to hint" or "to suggest"; *infer* means "to draw a conclusion." Speakers and writers *imply;* readers and listeners *infer.*

The president **implied** that changes will be forthcoming; I **inferred** from his tone of voice that these changes will not be pleasant.

5.23 Irregardless/Regardless Use *regardless.* (*Irregardless* is considered substandard.)

He wants to proceed, **regardless** (not *irregardless*) of the costs.

5.24 Its/It's *Its* is a possessive pronoun; *it's* is a contraction for "it is."

It's time to let the department increase **its** budget.

5.25 Lay/Lie *Lay* (principal forms: *lay, laid, laid, laying*) means "to put" and requires an object to complete its meaning; *lie* (principal forms: *lie, lay, lain, lying*) means "to rest."

Please **lay** the supplies on the shelf.	I **lie** on the couch after lunch each day.
I **laid** the folders in the drawer.	The report **lay** on his desk yesterday.
She had **laid** the notes on her desk.	The job has **lain** untouched for a week.

Less See *Fewer/Less.*

Lie See *Lay/Lie.*

5.26 Loose/Lose *Loose* means "not fastened"; *lose* means "to be unable to find."

Do not **lose** the **loose** change in your pocket.

May See *Can/May.*

Number See *Amount/Number.*

One Another See *Each Other/One Another.*

5.27 Percent/Percentage With figures, use *percent;* without figures, use *percentage.*

We took a commission of 6 **percent** (or 6%), which was a lower **percentage** than last year.

5.28 Personal/Personnel *Personal* means "private" or "belonging to one individual"; *personnel* means "employees."

I used my **personal** time to draft a memo to all **personnel.**

5.29 Principal/Principle *Principal* means "primary" (adjective) or "sum of money" (noun); *principle* means "rule" or "law."

The guiding **principle** is fair play, and the **principal** means of achieving it is a code of ethics.

5.30 Real/Really *Real* is an adjective; *really* is an adverb. Do not use *real* to modify another adjective.

She was **really** (not *real*) proud that her necklace contained **real** pearls.

5.31 Reason Is Because/Reason Is That Use *reason is that.* (*Reason is because* is considered substandard.)

The **reason** for such low attendance **is that** (not *is because*) the weather was stormy.

Regardless See *Irregardless/Regardless.*

5.32 Same Do not use *same* to refer to a previously mentioned item. Use *it* or some other wording instead.

We have received your order and will ship **it** (not *same*) in three days.

5.33 Set/Sit *Set* (principal forms: *set, set, set, setting*) means "to place"; *sit* (principal forms: *sit, sat, sat, sitting*) means "to be seated."

Please **set** your papers on the table. Please **sit** in the chair.

She **set** the computer on the desk. I **sat** in the first-class section.
I have **set** the computer there before. I had not **sat** there before.

5.34 Should Of/Should've Use *should've* (or *should have*). (*Should of* is incorrect.)

We **should've** (not *should of*) been more careful.

Sight See *Cite/Sight/Site.*

Sit See *Set/Sit.*

Site See *Cite/Sight/Site.*

5.35 Stationary/Stationery *Stationary* means "remaining in one place"; *stationery* is writing paper.

I used my personal **stationery** to write them to ask whether the minicomputer should remain **stationary.**

5.36 Sure/Surely *Sure* is an adjective; *surely* is an adverb. Do not use *sure* to modify another adjective.

I'm **surely** (not *sure*) glad that she is running and feel **sure** that she will be nominated.

5.37 Sure And/Sure To Use *sure to.* (*Sure and* is considered substandard.)

Be **sure to** (not *sure and*) attend the meeting.

5.38 Their/There/They're *Their* means "belonging to them"; *there* means "in that place"; and *they're* is a contraction for "they are."

They're too busy with **their** reports to be **there** for the hearing.

5.39 Theirs/There's *Theirs* is a possessive pronoun; *there's* is a contraction for "there is."

We finished our meal but **there's** no time for them to finish **theirs.**

They're See *their/there/they're.*

5.40 Try And/Try To Use *try to.* (*Try and* is considered substandard.)

Please **try to** (not *try and*) attend the meeting.

Well See *Good/Well.*

5.41 Whose/Who's *Whose* is a possessive pronoun; *who's* is a contraction for "who is."

Who's going to let us know **whose** turn it is to make coffee?

5.42 Your/You're *Your* means "belonging to you"; *you're* is a contraction for "you are."

> **You're** going to present **your** report first.

APPLICATION

Directions Select the correct words in parentheses.

1. advise, eminent, real

1. Please (advice/advise) the (eminent/imminent) educator of the (real/really) interest we have in his lecture.

2. stationary, may, one another

2. The three workers on the (stationary/stationery) platform (can/may) help (each other/one another) if they are running late.

3. implied, their, between

3. The writer (implied/inferred) that she and her colleagues divided (their/there/they're) time about evenly (among/between) the two projects.

4. Who's, fewer, can

4. (Whose/Who's) convinced that (fewer/less) of our employees (can/may) elect this option?

5. lose, your, affected

5. If you (loose/lose) seniority, (your/you're) work schedule might be (affected/effected).

6. cited, really, well

6. Mary Ellen (cited/sighted/sited) several examples showing that our lab employees are (real/really) (good/well) protected from danger.

7. between, percent, theirs

7. In comparing performance (among/between) the two companies, Brenda noted that our company earned 7 (percent/percentage) more than (theirs/there's).

8. to, compliment, its

8. Try (and/to) (complement/compliment) the advertising group for (its/it's) stunning new brochure.

9. laid, number, i.e.

9. When Susan (laid/lay) the models on the table, I was surprised at the (amount/number) of moving parts; (e.g./i.e.), I had expected simpler designs.

10. personnel, could've, that

10. The reason the (personal/personnel) department (could of/could've) been mistaken is (that/because) we failed to keep them informed.

11. accept, stationery, less

11. Sherry refused to (accept/except) the continuous-form (stationary/stationery) because it had (fewer/less) absorbency than expected.

12. You're, number, sight

12. (Your/You're) being paid by the (amount/number) of defective finished products you (cite/sight/site) while observing on the assembly line.

13. principal, anxious, a lot

13. The (principal/principle) reason we're (anxious/eager) to solve this problem is that (a lot/alot) of workers have complained of dizziness.

14. enthusiastic, except, it

14. All our customers are (enthused/enthusiastic) about the new pricing (accept/except) for Highland's, which asked for a quantity discount and expected (it/same) to be granted.

15. sure to, percentage, from

15. Be (sure and/sure to) point out to her that the (percent/percentage) of commission we pay new agents is no different (from/than) that which we pay experienced agents.

16. eager, it's, whose

16. I am (anxious/eager) to see if (its/it's) going to be Arlene (whose/who's) design will be selected.

17. I (implied/inferred) from Martin's remarks that Austin is a (sure/surely) bet as the (cite/sight/site) for our new plant.

17. inferred, sure, site

18. The (principal/principle) (advice/advise) that Michelle gave was to (set/sit) long-term goals and stick to them.

18. principal, advice, set

19. Although (their/there/they're) located (farther/further) from our office than I would like, I believe their expertise will (complement/compliment) our own.

19. they're, farther, complement

20. (Any one/Anyone) who can (farther/further) refine the (loose/lose) ends of our proposal should come back this afternoon.

20. Anyone, further, loose

21. In the previous shot, Joyce and Kathy (should of/should've) been (laying/lying) next to (each other/one another) on the beach, discussing their plans for the evening.

21. should've, lying, each other

22. Please (set/sit) awhile and tell them about your experiences in the Foreign Service, (e.g./i.e.), the time you were arrested in Buenos Aires for doing a (good/well) deed for a local shopkeeper.

22. sit, e.g., good

23. (Theirs/There's) no reason to pry into an applicant's (personal/personnel) life; however, it is (all right/alright) to ask about the applicant's general state of health.

23. There's, personal, all right

24. (Any one/Anyone) of the stockbrokers, (irregardless/regardless) of his or her philosophy, would (sure/surely) question such a strategy.

24. Any one, regardless, surely

25. (Their/There/They're) will be little (affect/effect) on operations from the (eminent/imminent) change in ownership of the firm.

25. There, effect, imminent

SECTION B

Basic Spelling List for Business Writing

This list contains 1,000 words that are frequently misspelled in business writing. The list is long enough to serve as a useful first reference for checking the spelling of a suspect word, yet short enough for efficient use.*

A

abandon
abbreviation
abscess
absence
accede
accelerated
acceptable
acceptance
access
accessible
accessory
accidentally
acclaim
accommodate
accommodation
accompanying
accomplice
accordance
accountant
accumulate
accuracy
accrual
accrued
achievement
acknowledgment
acquaintance
acquiesce
acquire
acquisition
across
actuary
adapt
address
adequate
adherent
adhesive
adjacent
adjustment
administrative
admirable
advantageous
advertisement
advisable
advisory
aeronautics
affidavit
affirmative
affluent
agenda
aggravate
aggressive
aging
agreeable
agreement
aisle
alien
alignment
alkali
all right
alleged
allegiance
allocate
allotment
allotted
allowable
allowance
almost
alphanumeric
already
altogether
aluminum
amateur
amendment
amortize
analysis
analyze
announcement
annoyance
annual
annuity
anonymous
answer
antagonistic
anticipate
anxiety
anxious
apathy
apologize
appall
apparatus
apparel
apparent
appearance
appliance
applicable
applicant
appointment
appraisal
appreciable
appropriate
approximate
approximately
arbitrary
arbitration
architect
archive
arguing
argument
arrangement
article
articulate
artificial
ascertain
asinine
assassinate
assessment
assignment
assistance
associate
assured
athletic
atrocious
attendance
attention
attorneys
auctioneer
auspices
authorize
automation
autumn
auxiliary
available
awkward

B

bachelor
baggage
bankruptcy
bargain
barometer
basically
basis
beginning
believe
belligerent
beneficial
beneficiary
benefited
biased
binary
boisterous
bookkeeping
booster
boundary
breakfast
brilliant
brochure
budget
bulletin
bullion
bureau
bureaucracy
buses
business
busy
buyout
byte

C

cabinet
calculator
calendar
calorie
camouflage
campaign
cancel

*Scot Ober, *The Spelling Problems of First-Year Typewriting Students,* Delta Pi Epsilon Research Foundation, Little Rock, AR, 1984.

canceled
cancellation
candor
cannot
capital
capitol
carburetor
career
carriage
cashier
casualty
catalog
category
cause
cellular
cemetery
census
ceremony
certificate
chairperson
changeable
chaplain
chargeable
chattel
chief
chronological
circumstances
circumstantial
clerical
client
clientele
coding
coincidence
collateral
collator
collectible
colonel
colossal
column
columnar
coming
commentator
commercial
commission
commitment
committee
comparable
comparatively
comparison
compatible
compelled
competent
competitive
competitor
complete
composite
compromise
computer
concealment
concede
conceivable
conceive
concern
concession
concurred
condemn
condenser
conference
confident
confidential
congratulate
congregation
connoisseur
conquer
conscience
conscientious
conscious
consensus
consequence
consign
consignment
consistent
contagious
container
contingent
continuous
contract
controlling
controversy
convenience
convenient
conversion
converter
cooperative
coordinate
cordially
corduroy
corporation
correspondence
courteous
courtesy
coverage
creditor
criticism
criticize
current
cursor
customer
cycle

D

debtor
deceive
decide
decimal
decision
deductible
defamation
defendant
defense
deferred
deficiency
deficit
definite
definitely
dehydrate
delegate
democracy
demonstration
denominator
dependent
depositor
depreciation
descendant
describe
description
desirable
destination
deteriorate
deterrent
detrimental
development
device
devise
dexterity
diagraming
dictionary
difference
differential
digital
dignitary
dilemma
director
disappear
disappointed
disaster
disastrous
disbursement
discernible
discipline
discrepancy
disguise
diskette
dissatisfied
distortion
distribution
docket
document
double
duplicating
duress

E

eagerly
easement
economical
economics
economy
education
efficiency
eighth
either
electronic
elementary
eligible
eliminate
embarrass
embezzlement
emergency
eminent
emphasis
emphasize
employee
employer
emptied
empty
enclosure
encumbrance
encyclopedia
endeavor
endorsement
ensemble
enterprise
enthusiasm
enthusiastic
entree
entrepreneur
entries
enumerate
envelope
environment
equality
equipment
equipped
equity
ergonomics
escalate
escrow
especially
essential
establish
etiquette
exaggerate
exceed
excellence
excellent
excessive
exclamation
excusable
exercise
exhaustible
exhibit
exhilarated
existence
exonerate
exorbitant

expedite
expenditure
expense
expensive
experience
explanation
extemporaneous
extension
external
extraordinary
extremely
eyeing

F

facilities
facsimile
fallacy
familiarize
fascinate
favorable
favorite
feasible
February
fiery
finally
financial
financier
flexible
fluorescent
forbade
forcible
foreclosure
foreign
foresee
forfeit
forfeiture
fortieth
forty
fourteen
fourth
fraud
freight
friend
frustrate
fulfillment
fundamental
furniture
furthermore

G

gauge
genuine
gigantic
glamorous
glamour
government
governor
grammar
grateful
gratuitous
gray
grievance
grievous
grudge
gruesome
guarantee
guardian

H

handled
harassment
hardware
hazardous
hectic
height
heir
hesitant
heterogeneous
hindrance
hoping
hors d'oeuvre
humanitarian
hygiene
hypocrisy

I

identical
illegality
illegible
illiterate
illuminate
immediate
immediately
impasse
imperative
impossible
inasmuch as
incidentally
incontestable
inconvenience
incurred
indebtedness
indelible
indemnity
independence
independent
indispensable
individual
inducement
industry
inevitable
infinite
inflammable
influential
initial
innocence
innocuous
innovation
innuendo
inquiry
insistence
installation
installment
integrated
intelligence
intention
intercede
interest
interfere
interfered
interfering
interim
intern
interpret
interrupted
intestate
inventory
investor
irrelevant
irreparable
irresistible
irreverent
issuing
itemized
itinerary

J

jeopardize
jeopardy
journal
jubilee
judgment
judicious
justifiable

K

kilocycle
kilowatt
knowledge
knowledgeable

L

label
labeled
labeling
laboratory
language
lawyer
ledger
legible
legitimate
leisure
length
letterhead
leverage
liable
liaison
libel
librarian
library
license
lien
lieutenant
lightning
likable
limousine
linear
linoleum
litigation
livelihood
luxury

M

magazine
magnetic
magnificent
maintenance
malignment
manageable
management
maneuver
manifestation
manipulate
manufacturer
manuscript
marriage
material
mathematics
matrix
maximum
mediocre
memento
memorandum
menu
menus
mercantile
merchandise
meticulous
microcomputer
mileage
millionaire
miniature
minimum
minuscule
minutiae
miscellaneous
mischievous
misdemeanor
misspell
modem
modernize

mortgage
motion
motor
movable
murmur

N

necessary
negative
negligible
negotiate
negotiation
neighborhood
neither
nevertheless
nickel
nineteenth
ninety
ninth
nonessential
notice
noticeable
novice
nuclear
nucleus
numerator

O

oblige
oblivious
obsolete
obstinate
obvious
occasion
occasionally
occupant
occupation
occurred
occurrence
occurring
offense
offered
offering
official
offset
omission
omitted
operator
opinion
opportunity
optical
optimism
option
ordinary
organization
organize
original
originator
orphan
output
overconfident
overdue

P

pageant
paid
pamphlet
panic
panicked
paragraph
parallel
paralyze
parenthesis
parochial
partial
partially
participant
participate
particularly
partnership
patience
pastime
patronage
penalize
percent
peripheral
permanent
permissible
permitted
perseverance
persistent
personal
personnel
persuade
persuasion
pharmacist
phase
phenomenal
phenomenon
phony
photocopy
physician
plagiarism
plaintiff
planning
plausible
pleasant
pleasure
pneumatic
positive
possession
practical
practically
practice
precarious
precede
precedent
precision
preferable
preference
preferred
prejudice
preliminary
premium
prerequisite
prerogative
pressurized
prestige
presumptuous
pretense
previous
printout
privilege
probably
procedure
proceed
processing
professor
programmed
prominent
promissory
prompt
pronounce
pronunciation
propeller
proprietor
propulsion
prosecute
psychiatric
psychology
publicly
punctuation
pursue

Q

quantitative
quantity
questionnaire
quorum

R

ratification
reaffirm
realize
reasonable
rebellious
rebuttal
receipt
receive
recently
receptacle
receptionist
recipe
recipient
reciprocate
recognition
recognize
recommendation
reconcile
reconciliation
reconnaissance
recruit
recurrence
reference
referendum
referred
referring
regrettable
reimbursement
reinforce
relevant
remember
reminiscent
remittance
remunerate
rendezvous
renewal
renowned
repetition
repetitively
replica
representative
repudiate
requirement
requisition
reservoir
rescind
resistance
response
responsibility
responsible
restaurant
résumé
retrieval
retroactive
reveal
rhetorical
rhyme
rhythm
ridiculous
rotary
route
rudiment

S

salable
salary
satellite
satisfactorily
scarcity
schedule
scissors
secretary
securities

seize
seniority
separate
sergeant
serviceable
settlement
shipment
shipping
siege
significant
similar
simplified
simultaneous
sincerely
sincerity
sizable
skeptic
skiing
skillful
socialism
solar
sources
souvenir
sovereign
specialize
specialty
specifications
specimen
sponsor
stabilize
statement
statistics
stenographer
stockholder
straight
strategy
strength
strictly
submitted
subpoena
subscriber
subscription
subsidiary
substantial
subtle
subtlety
succeed
successful
successor
sufficient
suing
summary
superintendent
supersede
supervisor
surgeon
surprise
surveillance
susceptible
survey
sympathize
synonymous
synthetic
system

T

tangible
tariff
taxiing
technique
technology
telecommunication
temperament
temperature
temporary
tempt
tenacious
tenancy
tenant
territory
theater
theory
thorough
threshold
throughout
totaled
tragedy
tranquil
transcribe
transferred
transistor
transit
traveler
trivial
truly
turbine
turnaround
twelfth
twentieth
typewritten
typing

U

ultimately
unanimous
undoubtedly
unforgettable
unfortunately
unique
unmanageable
unnecessary
until
unwieldy
upheaval
urgent
usable
usage
usually
usury
utterance

V

vacancies
vacillate
vacuum
valuable
vandalism
variable
various
vegetable
vehicle
vendor
veracity
verbatim
vetoes
vicinity
vicious
victim
visible
vitalize
vocational
void
volume
voluntary
volunteer

W

waiver
warehouse
warranty
wealthiest
weather
Wednesday
weird
whether
whiskey
wholesale
wholly
wield
withhold
witness
workstation
worthwhile
wraparound
writing
wrought

Y

yield

SECTION C

Formatting Business Documents

FORMATTING LETTERS AND MEMOS

The most common features of business letters and memos are discussed below and illustrated in Figures C.1 and C.2.

Letter and Punctuation Styles

The *block style* is the simplest letter style to type because all lines begin at the left margin. In the *modified block style,* the date and closing lines begin at the center point. Offsetting these parts from the left margin enables the reader to locate them quickly. In the *simplified style,* which is actually seldom used, all lines begin at the left margin, the salutation and complimentary closing are omitted, and the subject line and writer's identification are typed in all-capital letters.

The *standard punctuation style*—the most common format—contains a colon (never a comma) after the salutation and a comma after the complimentary closing. The *open punctuation style,* on the other hand, uses no punctuation after these two lines. Figure C.3 shows how these styles differ.

Stationery and Margins

Most letters are typed on standard-sized stationery, 8½ by 11 inches. The first page of a business letter is typed on letterhead stationery, which shows company information printed at the top. Subsequent pages of a business letter and all pages of a personal business letter (a letter written to transact one's personal business) are typed on good-quality, plain paper.

Side and bottom margins should be 1 to 1½ inches (most word processing programs have default margins of 1 inch, which works just fine). Leave a 2-inch top margin on the first page and a 1-inch top margin for subsequent pages. Set a tab at the center point (4¼ inches) if you're formatting a modified block style letter.

Required Letter Parts

The required letter parts are as follows:

Date Line Type the current month (spelled out), day, and year 2 inches from the top of the page. Begin either at the center point for modified block style or at the left margin for all other styles.

Inside Address The inside address gives the name and location of the person to whom you're writing. Include a personal title (such as *Mr., Mrs., Miss,* or *Ms.*). If you use the addressee's job title, type it on the same line as the name (separated from the name by a comma) or on the following line by itself. In the address, use the two-letter U.S. Postal Service abbreviation,

FIGURE C.1 Standard Business Letter

This letter is shown in block style with standard punctuation.

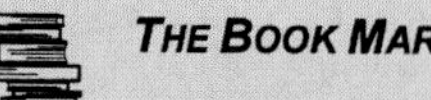

THE BOOK MARK

18615 SILVER CENTER
BOZEMAN, MT 59715

Ph: 406-555-3856
Fax: 406-555-3893
E-Mail: jdye@bookmark.com

↓ 2 inches

Date Line: Date the letter is typed.

November 18, 19-- ↓ 1 inch

Inside Address: Name and address of the person to whom you're writing.

Ms. Ella Shore, Professor
Department of Journalism
Mountainside College
Paseo Canyon Drive
Great Falls, MT 59404 ↓ 2

Salutation: Greeting.

Dear Ms. Shore: ↓ 2

Subject Line

Subject: Yearbook Advertising ↓ 2

Body: Text of the letter.

Thank you for thinking of The Book Mark when you were planning the advertising for next year's yearbook at Mountainside College. We appreciate the wide acceptance your students and faculty give our merchandise, and we are proud to be represented in the *Mountain Lark*. Although budget restrictions prevent us from taking a full-page ad, we are happy to purchase a quarter-page ad, as follows:

1. The ad should include our standard trademark and the words "Welcome to The Book Mark." Please note that the word "The" is part of our name and should begin with a capital letter.

2. We would prefer that our ad appear in the top right corner of a right-facing page, if possible.

Our trademark is enclosed for you to duplicate. I am also enclosing a check for $275 to cover the cost of the ad. Best wishes as you prepare the fifty-fifth edition of your yearbook. ↓ 2

Complimentary Closing: Parting farewell.

Sincerely, ↓ 4

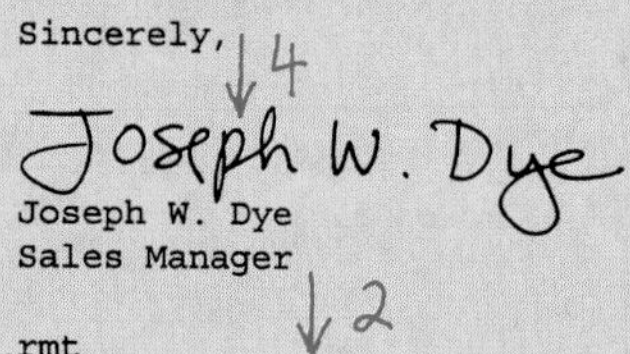

Writer's Identification: Name and/or title of the writer.

Joseph W. Dye
Sales Manager
↓ 2

Reference Initials: Initials of the person who typed the letter.

rmt

Notations: Indications of items being enclosed with the letter, copies of the letter being sent to another person, special delivery instructions, and the like.

Enclosures
c: Advertising Supervisor

Grammar and Mechanics Notes

The arrows indicate how many lines or inches to space down before typing the next part. For example, ↓*2 inches* before the date means to begin typing the date 2 inches from the top of the page, and ↓*4* after the complimentary closing means to press Enter four times before typing the writer's name.

FIGURE C.2 Standard Memorandum

A memorandum is sent to someone within the same organization.

2 inches

TAB

Heading

MEMO TO: Max Dillon, Sales Manager

FROM: Richard J. Hayes RH.

DATE: February 25, 19--

SUBJECT: New-Venture Proposal

Body

The purpose of this memorandum is to propose the purchase or lease of a van to be used as a mobile bookstore. We could then use this van to generate sales in the outlying towns and villages throughout the state.

We have been aware for quite some time that many small towns around the state do not have adequate bookstore facilities, but the economics of the situation are such that we would not be able to open a comprehensive branch and operate it profitably. However, we could afford to stock a van with books and operate it for a few days at a time in various small towns throughout the state. As you are probably aware, the laws of this state would permit us to acquire a statewide business license fairly easily and inexpensively.

With the proper advance advertising, we should be able to generate much interest in this endeavor. It seems to me that this idea has much merit because of the flexibility it offers us. For example, we could tailor the length of our stay to the size of the town and the amount of business generated. Also, we could customize our inventory to the needs and interests of the particular locales.

The driver of the van would act as the salesperson, and we would, of course, have copies of our complete catalog so that mail orders could be taken as well. Please let me have your reactions to this proposal. If you wish, I can explore the matter further and generate cost and sales estimates.

Reference Initials

jmc

Grammar and Mechanics Notes

Key the standard heading entries (*MEMO TO:, FROM:, DATE:,* and *SUBJECT:*) in bold and all-capital letters. Then turn off bold and press Tab (tabs are preset at ½-inch intervals) to get to the position for typing the variable information. Memos may be typed on plain paper or on letterhead stationery.

FIGURE C.3 Letter and Punctuation Styles

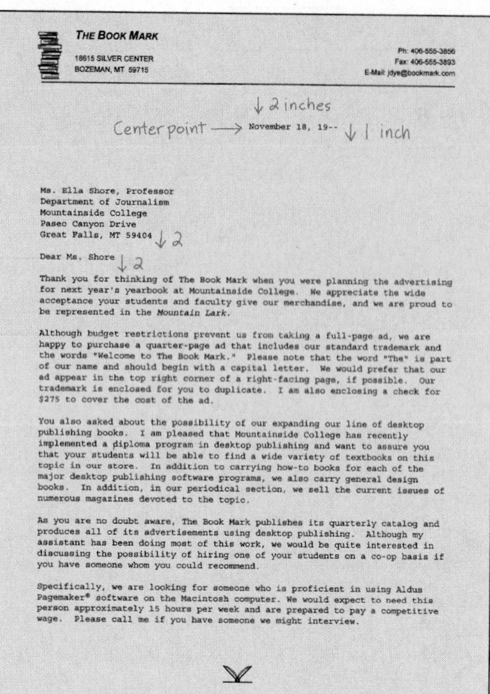

THE BOOK MARK
18615 SILVER CENTER
BOZEMAN, MT 59715

Ph: 406-555-3856
Fax: 406-555-3893
E-Mail: jdye@bookmark.com

↓ 2 inches
Centerpoint ⟶ November 18, 19-- ↓ 1 inch

Ms. Ella Shore, Professor
Department of Journalism
Mountainside College
Paseo Canyon Drive
Great Falls, MT 59404 ↓ 2

Dear Ms. Shore ↓ 2

Thank you for thinking of The Book Mark when you were planning the advertising for next year's yearbook at Mountainside College. We appreciate the wide acceptance your students and faculty give our merchandise, and we are proud to be represented in the *Mountain Lark*.

Although budget restrictions prevent us from taking a full-page ad, we are happy to purchase a quarter-page ad that includes our standard trademark and the words "Welcome to The Book Mark." Please note that the word "The" is part of our name and should begin with a capital letter. We would prefer that our ad appear in the top right corner of a right-facing page, if possible. Our trademark is enclosed for you to duplicate. I am also enclosing a check for $275 to cover the cost of the ad.

You also asked about the possibility of our expanding our line of desktop publishing books. I am pleased that Mountainside College has recently implemented a diploma program in desktop publishing and want to assure you that your students will be able to find a wide variety of textbooks on this topic in our store. In addition to carrying how-to books for each of the major desktop publishing software programs, we also carry general design books. In addition, in our periodical section, we sell the current issues of numerous magazines devoted to the topic.

As you are no doubt aware, The Book Mark publishes its quarterly catalog and produces all of its advertisements using desktop publishing. Although my assistant has been doing most of this work, we would be quite interested in discussing the possibility of hiring one of your students on a co-op basis if you have someone whom you could recommend.

Specifically, we are looking for someone who is proficient in using Aldus Pagemaker® software on the Macintosh computer. We would expect to need this person approximately 15 hours per week and are prepared to pay a competitive wage. Please call me if you have someone we might interview.

Modified block style letter with open punctuation

↓ 1 inch
Ms. Ella Shore
Page 2
November 18, 19-- ↓ 2

In the meantime, best wishes to you and your staff as you prepare the fifty-fifth edition of your yearbook—and the first edition to be desktop published. I look forward to receiving a copy. ↓ 2

Centerpoint ⟶ Sincerely ↓ 4
Joseph W. Dye

Joseph W. Dye
Sales Manager ↓ 2

rmt
Enclosures
By Federal Express
c: Advertising Supervisor ↓ 2

PS: Because The Book Mark is such an important part of the lives of many Mountainside College students, we would be happy to have your *Mountain Lark* photographer take candid photographs of students in our store. Just have him or her call to arrange an appointment.

Page 2 of modified block style letter with open punctuation

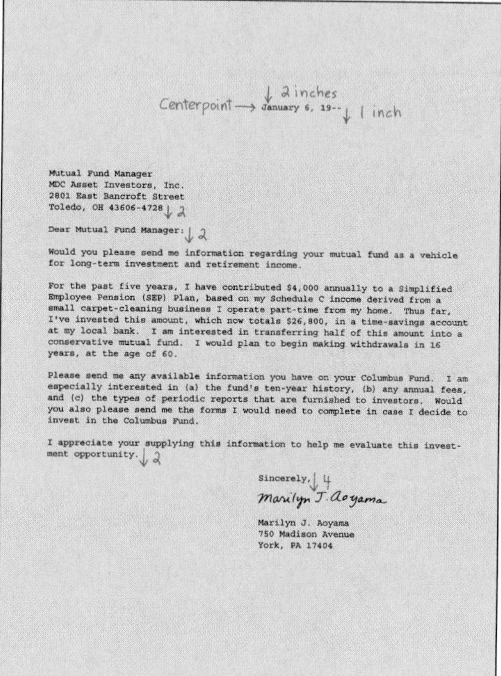

↓ 2 inches
Centerpoint ⟶ January 6, 19-- ↓ 1 inch

Mutual Fund Manager
MDC Asset Investors, Inc.
2801 East Bancroft Street
Toledo, OH 43606-4728 ↓ 2

Dear Mutual Fund Manager: ↓ 2

Would you please send me information regarding your mutual fund as a vehicle for long-term investment and retirement income.

For the past five years, I have contributed $4,000 annually to a Simplified Employee Pension (SEP) Plan, based on my Schedule C income derived from a small carpet-cleaning business I operate part-time from my home. Thus far, I've invested this amount, which now totals $26,800, in a time-savings account at my local bank. I am interested in transferring half of this amount into a conservative mutual fund. I would plan to begin making withdrawals in 16 years, at the age of 60.

Please send me any available information you have on your Columbus Fund. I am especially interested in (a) the fund's ten-year history, (b) any annual fees, and (c) the types of periodic reports that are furnished to investors. Would you also please send me the forms I would need to complete in case I decide to invest in the Columbus Fund.

I appreciate your supplying this information to help me evaluate this investment opportunity. ↓ 2

Sincerely, ↓ 4
Marilyn J. Aoyama

Marilyn J. Aoyama
750 Madison Avenue
York, PA 17404

Personal business letter in modified block style

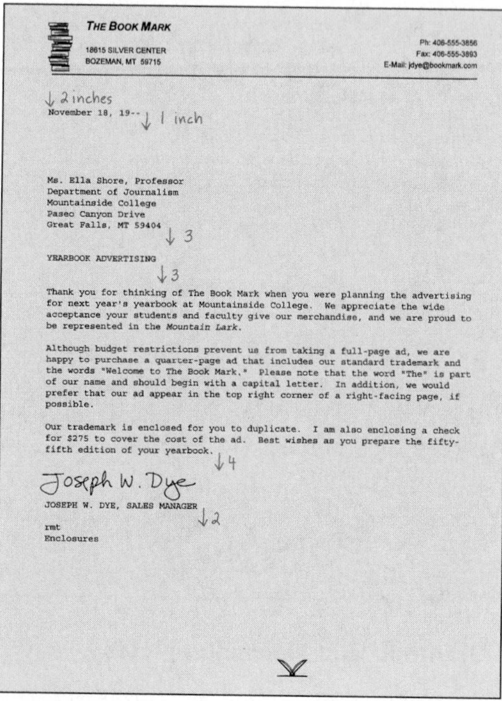

THE BOOK MARK
18615 SILVER CENTER
BOZEMAN, MT 59715

Ph: 406-555-3856
Fax: 406-555-3893
E-Mail: jdye@bookmark.com

↓ 2 inches
November 18, 19-- ↓ 1 inch

Ms. Ella Shore, Professor
Department of Journalism
Mountainside College
Paseo Canyon Drive
Great Falls, MT 59404 ↓ 3

YEARBOOK ADVERTISING ↓ 3

Thank you for thinking of The Book Mark when you were planning the advertising for next year's yearbook at Mountainside College. We appreciate the wide acceptance your students and faculty give our merchandise, and we are proud to be represented in the *Mountain Lark*.

Although budget restrictions prevent us from taking a full-page ad, we are happy to purchase a quarter-page ad that includes our standard trademark and the words "Welcome to The Book Mark." Please note that the word "The" is part of our name and should begin with a capital letter. In addition, we would prefer that our ad appear in the top right corner of a right-facing page, if possible.

Our trademark is enclosed for you to duplicate. I am also enclosing a check for $275 to cover the cost of the ad. Best wishes as you prepare the fifty-fifth edition of your yearbook. ↓ 4

Joseph W. Dye
JOSEPH W. DYE, SALES MANAGER ↓ 2

rmt
Enclosures

Simplified style letter

typed in all capitals with no period (see Figure C.4), and leave one to two spaces between the state and the Zip Code. Type the inside address at the left margin 1 inch below the date—for most word processing programs, just press Enter six times. For international letters, type the name of the country in all-capital letters on the last line by itself.

Salutation Use the same name in both the inside address and the salutation. If the letter is addressed to a job position rather than to a person, use a generic but nonsexist greeting, such as "Dear Personnel Manager." If you typically address the reader in person by first name, use the first name in the salutation (for example, "Dear Lois:"); otherwise, use a personal title and the surname only (for example, "Dear Ms. Lane:"). Leave one blank line before and after the salutation.

Body Single-space the lines of each paragraph and leave one blank line between paragraphs. Follow correct word-division rules (see LAB 4 on page 614) when hyphenating a word at the end of a line.

Page 2 Heading Type the addressee's name, the page number, and the date beginning 1 inch from the top of the page, blocked at the left margin. Leave one blank line (that is, press Enter two times) before continuing with the text. You should carry forward to a second page at least two lines of the body of the message.

Complimentary Closing Begin the complimentary closing at the same horizontal point as the date line, capitalize the first word only, and leave one blank line before and three blank lines after, to allow room for the signature. If a colon follows the salutation, use a comma after the complimentary closing; otherwise, no punctuation follows.

Signature Some women insert the personal title they prefer (*Ms., Miss,* or *Mrs.*) in parentheses before their signature. Men never include a personal title.

Writer's Identification The writer's identification (name or job title or both) begins on the fourth line immediately below the complimentary closing. Do not use a personal title. The job title may go either on the same line as the typed name, separated from the name by a comma, or on the following line by itself.

Reference Initials When used, reference initials (the initials of the typist) are typed at the left margin in lowercase letters without periods, with one blank line before. Do not include reference initials if you type your own letter.

Envelopes Business envelopes have a printed return address. You may type your name above this address, if you wish. Use plain envelopes for personal business letters; you should type the return address (your home address) at the upper left corner. Envelopes may be typed either in standard upper- and lowercase style or in all-capital letters without any

FIGURE C.4 Correspondence Formats

LARGE (No. 10) ENVELOPES

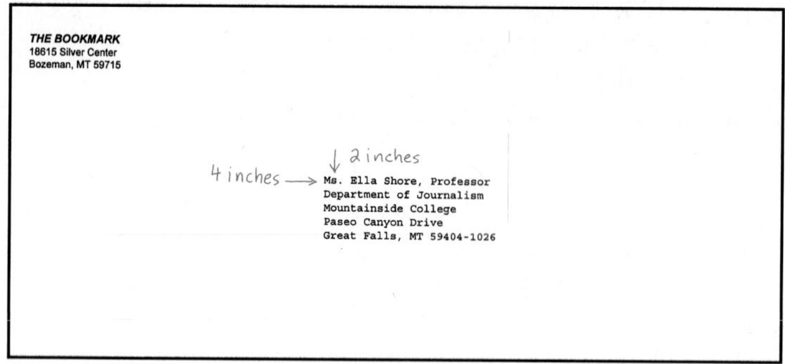

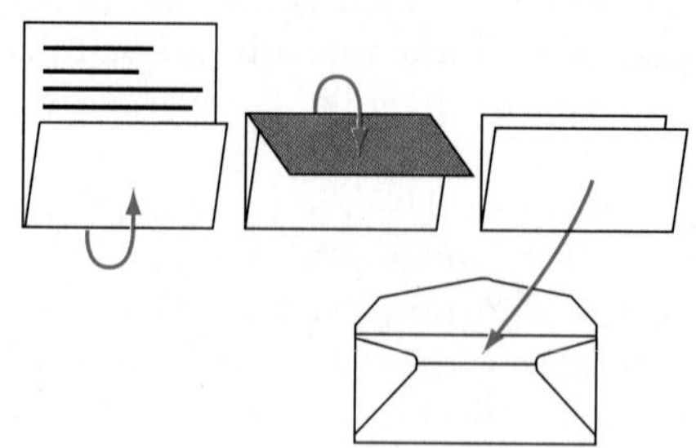

SMALL (No. 6 3/4) ENVELOPES

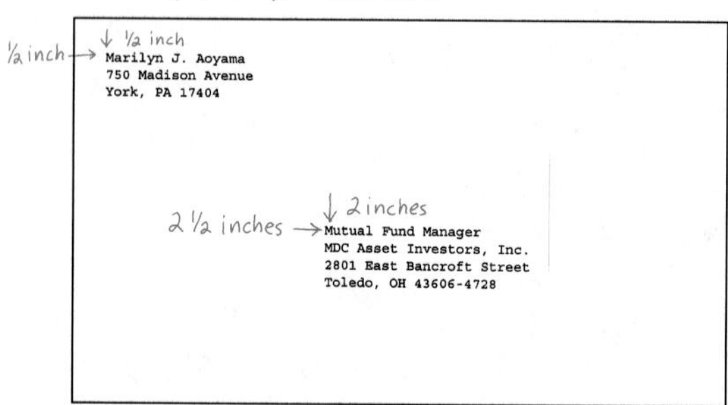

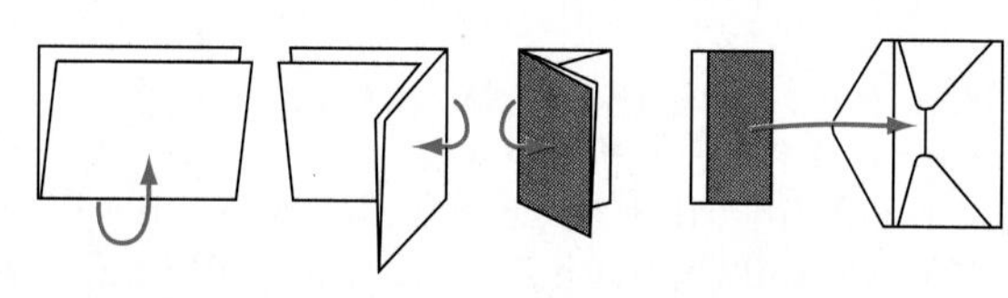

POSTAL SERVICE ABBREVIATIONS

U.S. POSTAL SERVICE ABBREVIATIONS FOR STATES, TERRITORIES, AND CANADIAN PROVINCES

States and Territories

Alabama	AL
Alaska	AK
Arizona	AZ
Arkansas	AR
California	CA
Colorado	CO
Connecticut	CT
Delaware	DE
District of Columbia	DC
Florida	FL
Georgia	GA
Guam	GU
Hawaii	HI
Idaho	ID
Illinois	IL
Indiana	IN
Iowa	IA
Kansas	KS
Kentucky	KY
Louisiana	LA
Maine	ME
Maryland	MD
Massachusetts	MA
Michigan	MI
Minnesota	MN
Mississippi	MS
Missouri	MO
Montana	MT
Nebraska	NE
Nevada	NV
New Hampshire	NH
New Jersey	NJ
New Mexico	NM
New York	NY
North Carolina	NC
North Dakota	ND
Ohio	OH
Oklahoma	OK
Oregon	OR
Pennsylvania	PA
Puerto Rico	PR
Rhode Island	RI
South Carolina	SC
South Dakota	SD
Tennessee	TN
Texas	TX
Utah	UT
Vermont	VT
Virgin Islands	VI
Virginia	VA
Washington	WA
West Virginia	WV
Wisconsin	WI
Wyoming	WY

Canadian Provinces

Alberta	AB
British Columbia	BC
Labrador	LB
Manitoba	MB
New Brunswick	NB
Newfoundland	NF
Northwest Territories	NT
Nova Scotia	NS
Ontario	ON
Prince Edward Island	PE
Quebec	PQ
Saskatchewan	SK
Yukon Territory	YT

Section C

punctuation. On large (No. 10) envelopes, begin typing the mailing address 2 inches from the top edge and 4 inches from the left edge. On small (no. 6¾) envelopes, begin typing the mailing address 2 inches from the top edge and 2½ inches from the left edge. Fold letters as shown in Figure C.4.

Optional Letter Parts

Optional letter parts are as follows:

Subject Line You may include a subject line (identified by the words *Subject, Re,* or *In Re* followed by a colon) to identify the topic of the letter. Type it below the salutation, with one blank line before and one after.

Enumerations in the Body Begin an enumeration (a numbered list) at the left margin and leave two spaces between the period after the number and the following text. Indent runover lines four spaces (typically 0.4 inch). If every item takes up only a single line, single-space between items; otherwise, single-space the lines within each item and double-space between items. Either way, leave one blank line before and after the list.

Enclosure Notation Use an enclosure notation if any additional items are to be included in the envelope. Type "Enclosure" on the line immediately below the reference initials, and as an option, add the description of what is enclosed. (Note: For memos, the correct term is "Attachment" instead of "Enclosure" if the items are to be physically attached to the memo instead of being enclosed in an envelope.)

Copy Notation If someone other than the addressee is to receive a copy of the letter, type a copy notation ("c:") immediately below the enclosure notation or reference initials, whichever comes last. Then follow the copy notation with the names of the people who will receive copies.

Postscript If you add a postscript to a letter, type it as the last item, preceded by one blank line. The heading "PS:" is optional. Postscripts are used most often in sales letters.

International Formatting Styles In most respects, letters sent to and received from a foreign country are formatted similarly. One analysis of business letters received from abroad by U.S. firms found that the majority were formatted in modified block style, used the American format for the date (month-day-year), used either a title and surname or first name only in the salutation, and used "Sincerely" or "Sincerely yours" as the complimentary closing. (Retha H. Kilpatrick, "International Business Communication Practices," *Journal of Business Communication,* Vol. 21, Fall 1984, pp. 40–42.)

Formatting Reports and Documenting Sources

If the reader or organization has a preferred format style, use it. Otherwise, follow these generally accepted guidelines for formatting business reports. Be sure to make use of any automatic or formatting features of your computer to enhance the appearance and readability of your report and to increase the efficiency of the process.

Margins

Memo and letter reports use regular correspondence margins as discussed earlier in this manual. For reports typed in manuscript (formal report) format, use a 2-inch top margin for the first page of each special part (for example, the table of contents, the executive summary, the first page of the body of the report, and the first page of the reference list). Leave a 1-inch top margin for all other pages and at least a 1-inch bottom margin on all pages. If the report is to be bound at the left, set a 1½-inch left margin and a 1-inch right margin. If the report is to be unbound, set 1-inch side margins on both the left and right.

Spacing

Memo and letter reports are typed single-spaced. Manuscript reports may be either single- or double-spaced. Double spacing is preferred if the reader will likely make many comments on the pages. Note that double spacing leaves one blank line between each line of type; do not confuse double spacing with 1½ spacing, which leaves only *half* a blank line between lines of type.

Regardless of the spacing used for the body of the report, single spacing is typically used for the table of contents, the executive summary, long quotations, tables, and the reference list. Use a 5-space paragraph indention for double-spaced paragraphs. Do not indent single-spaced paragraphs; instead, double-space between them.

Report Headings

The number of levels of headings used will vary from report to report. Memo reports may have only first-level subheadings, with no part titles or other headings. Long reports may have as many as four levels of headings. One standard format for the various levels is given here. Recognize, however, that the format presented here is only one of several that might be used. Again, consistency and readability should be your major goals. Regardless of the format used, make sure that the reader can instantly tell which are major headings and which are subordinate headings.

Part Title Center a part title (for example, "Contents" or "References") in all capitals and in bold on a new page, leaving a 2-inch top margin. Leave two blank lines after a part title—that is, triple-space below it. Double-space titles of two or more lines, using an inverted pyramid style (the first line longer).

First-Level Subheading Center and bold the first-level subheading in all-capital letters. Triple-space before and double-space after the heading.

Second-Level Subheading Begin the second-level subheading at the left margin. Use bold type and all-capital letters as in first-level headings. Triple-space before and double-space after the heading.

Third-Level Subheading Double-space before the third-level subheading, indent, and bold. Capitalize the first letter of the first and last words and all other words except articles, prepositions with fewer than five letters, and conjunctions. Leave a period and two spaces after the subheading, and begin typing the text on the same line.

Pagination

Number the preliminary pages, such as the table of contents, with lowercase roman numerals centered on the bottom margin. The title page is counted as page i, but no page number is shown. Page numbers appear on all other preliminary pages centered at the bottom margin. For example, the executive summary might be page ii and the table of contents page iii.

Number all pages beginning with the first page of the body of the report with arabic numerals. The first page of the body is counted as page 1, but no page number is typed (in word processing terminology, the page number is *suppressed*). Beginning with page 2 of the body and continuing through the reference pages, number all pages consecutively at the top right of the page.

FIGURE C.5 Sample Report

Center each line; type the title in all capitals and in bold, perhaps in a larger font than normal. Double-space and use inverted pyramid style for multiline titles.

Use upper- and lowercase letters for all other lines.

Leave the same amount of blank space between each of the sections.

Leave equal top and bottom margins.

STAFF EMPLOYEES' EVALUATION OF THE BENEFIT PROGRAM

AT ATLANTIC STATE UNIVERSITY

Prepared for

David Riggins
Director of Personnel
Atlantic State University

Prepared by

Loretta J. Santorini
Assistant Director of Personnel
Atlantic State University

December 8, 19--

Title Page

A title page is typically used for manuscript reports but not for memo or letter reports. The report title, reader's name, writer's name, and submission date are required; other information is optional. An academic report might also contain a section immediately after the title with this wording (diagonals indicate line breaks): "A Research Report / Submitted in Partial Fulfillment / of the Requirements for the Course / *Course Number and Title.*"

MEMO TO: David Riggins, Director of Personnel

FROM: Loretta J. Santorini, Assistant Director of Personnel

DATE: December 8, 19--

SUBJECT: Staff Employees' Evaluation of the Benefit Program at Atlantic State University

Here is the report evaluating our staff benefits program that you requested on October 15.

The report shows that, overall, the staff is familiar with and values most of the benefits we offer. At the end of the report, I've made several recommendations regarding issuing individualized benefits statements annually and determining the usefulness of the automobile insurance benefit, the feasibility of offering compensation for unused sick leave, and the competitiveness of our retirement program.

I enjoyed working on this assignment, Dave, and learned quite a bit from my analysis of the problem that will help me during the upcoming labor negotiations. Please let me know if you have any questions about the report.

emc
Attachment

ii

Use a memo format for an internal reader and a letter format for an external reader. Ensure that the memo date agrees with the date on the title page.

Triple-space after the subject line.

Use standard correspondence margins and format.

Type the page number in lowercase roman letters at the bottom margin (the title page is considered page i).

Transmittal Document

The transmittal document—either a letter or a memo—is an optional part of a report. Use a direct organizational pattern and conversational language, even if the report itself uses formal language. Give a brief overview of the major conclusions and recommendations unless you expect the reader to react negatively to such information. Close with goodwill comments.

FIGURE C.5 Sample Report (*Continued*)

Use an inverse pyramid style for multiline titles.

Triple-space after the date.

Single-space the body of the summary, with double spacing between paragraphs.

Margins:
- 2-inch top
- 1-inch left and right (1½-inch left for bound reports)
- 1-inch bottom

Type the page number in lowercase roman letters at the bottom margin.

EXECUTIVE SUMMARY

STAFF EMPLOYEES' EVALUATION OF THE BENEFIT PROGRAM

AT ATLANTIC STATE UNIVERSITY

Loretta J. Santorini
December 8, 19--

Employee benefits now account for over a third of all payroll costs. Thus, on the basis of cost alone, an organization's benefits program must be carefully monitored and evaluated.

The problem in this study was to determine the opinions of the nearly 2,500 staff employees at Atlantic State University regarding the employee benefits program. Specifically, the investigation included determining the employees' present level of knowledge about the program, their opinions of the benefits presently offered, and their preferences for additional benefits. A survey of 206 staff employees and interviews with three managers familiar with the ASU employee benefits program provided the primary data for this study.

Overall, nearly 70% of the employees feel the benefits program has been explained adequately to them. However, a majority of the employees would prefer to have an individualized benefits statement instead of the brochures now used to explain the program.

Employees are most familiar with the benefits having to do with paid time off; more than 90% are familiar with ASU policies concerning vacation, holidays, and sick leave. Similarly, more than 95% of the employees rank these three benefits as most important to them; they rank auto insurance and bookstore discounts as least important. Employees are most satisfied with the ASU vacation policy (90% satisfied) and least satisfied with the retirement policy (20% dissatisfied). The only benefit that a majority of the staff employees would like to see added is compensation for unused sick leave.

The university should study further the offering of individualized benefits statements, automobile insurance, compensation for unused sick leave, and retirement benefits. This assessment of ASU's benefits program should help the administration ensure that the program operates as effectively as possible.

iii

Executive Summary

The executive summary, also called an *abstract* or *synopsis,* is an optional part of a report. If used, it goes immediately before the table of contents. If a transmittal document is not included, the summary page would be numbered ii.

CONTENTS

iv

Triple-space after the *CONTENTS* heading.

Triple-space before each part title and double-space after.

Align numbers at the right.

Indent each lower-level heading three spaces.

Use either leaders or spaced leaders (period, space, period) between the headings and page numbers.

Margins:
2-inch top
1-inch left and right (1½-inch left for bound reports)
1-inch bottom

Table of Contents

Use a table of contents for long reports with numerous headings. The wording in the headings on the contents page must be identical with that used in the report itself. Identify only the page on which each heading is located, even though the section may comprise several pages. Generic headings (noun phrases) are used in this sample.

Triple-space after the title; double-space after the first-level subheading (*INTRODUCTION*). Format all headings in bold.

STAFF EMPLOYEES' EVALUATION OF THE BENEFITS PROGRAM

AT ATLANTIC STATE UNIVERSITY

INTRODUCTION

Begin the introduction by providing background information and establishing a need for the study.

Employee benefits are a rapidly growing and an increasingly important form of employee compensation for both profit and nonprofit organizations. According to a recent U.S. Chamber of Commerce survey, benefits now constitute 37% of all payroll costs, costing an average of $7,832 a year for each employee (Berelson, Lazarsfield, and Connell, 1993, p. 183). Thus, on the basis of cost alone, an organization's benefits program must be carefully monitored and evaluated.

Cite references appropriately; the author-date method is used here.

Atlantic State University employs nearly 2,500 staff personnel, and they have not received a cost-of-living increase in two years. As a result, staff salaries may not have kept pace with private industry, and the university's employee benefits program may become more important in attracting and retaining good workers. In addition, the contracts of three of the four staff unions expire next year, and the benefits program is typically a major area of bargaining.

PURPOSE AND SCOPE OF THE STUDY

Count the first page of the body of the report as page 1, even though the page number is not typed on the page.

As has been noted by one management consultant, "The success of employee benefits programs depends directly on whether employees need, understand, and appreciate the value of the benefits provided" (Egan, 1993, p. 220). Thus, to help ensure that the benefits program is

Body of the Report

This recommendation report is written in manuscript format and in formal style (note the absence of first- and second-person pronouns). An indirect organizational pattern is used.

operating as effectively as possible, David Riggins, director of personnel, authorized this report on October 15, 19--.

Specifically, the following problem was addressed in this study: What are the opinions of staff employees at Atlantic State University regarding their employee benefits? To answer this question, the following subproblems were addressed:

1. How knowledgeable are the employees about the benefits program?
2. What are the employees' opinions of the value of the benefits presently available?
3. What benefits, if any, would the employees like to have added to the program?

This study explored the attitudes of the staff employees at Atlantic State University. Although staff employees at all three state universities receive the same benefits, no attempt has been made to generalize the findings beyond Atlantic State University because the communication of the benefits may be different, and because geographical differences may make some benefits of more use at one institution than at another.

In addition, this study attempted to determine employee preferences only. The question of whether employee preferences are economically feasible is not within the scope of this study.

PROCEDURES

A list of the 2,489 staff employees who are eligible for benefits (that is, those who are employed at least 20 hours a week) was generated from the October 15 payroll run. By means of a 10% systematic sample, 250 employees were selected for the survey. On November 3, each of the selected employees was sent the cover letter

Use your word processing program's pagination feature to number pages at the top right.

Begin enumerations at the paragraph point: indented for indented paragraphs, as shown here, or beginning at the left margin for blocked paragraphs. Either way, indent runover lines 0.4 inch.

Early in the report, discuss the parameters of your study (the scope) to avoid questions by the reader.

Use a double-spaced format (as shown here) for reports if you expect the reader to insert numerous comments or if your reader prefers. In a single-space format, leave a blank line between paragraphs but do not indent.

Provide an appropriate closing statement for the Introduction section.

First-level subheadings: Center, bold, and type in all capitals; leave two blank lines before and one blank line after.

Second-level subheadings: Begin at the left margin, bold, and type in all capitals; leave two blank lines before and one blank line after.

3

and questionnaire shown in Appendixes A and B via campus mail. A total of 206 employees completed usable questionnaires, for a response rate of 82%.

In addition to the questionnaire data, personal interviews were held with Lois White, compensation specialist at ASU; Roger Ray, chair of the Staff Personnel Committee at ASU; and Lewis Rigby, director of the State Personnel Board. The primary data provided by the survey and personal interviews was then analyzed and compared with findings from secondary sources to determine the staff employees' opinions of the benefits program at ASU.

FINDINGS

For a benefits program to achieve its goals, employees must be aware of the benefits provided. Thus, the first section that follows discusses the effectiveness of the university's present method of communicating benefits as well as those methods that employees would prefer. An effective benefits package must also include benefits that are relevant to employee needs. Thus, the employees' opinions of the importance of and their satisfaction with each benefit offered are discussed next. The section concludes with a discussion of those benefits employees would like to see added to the benefits program at ASU.

KNOWLEDGE OF BENEFITS

Several studies (Egan, 1993; Ignatio, 1994; Meany, 1990) have shown that employees' satisfaction with benefits is directly correlated with their knowledge of such benefits. Thus, an indication of

The Findings (also called *Results*) begins by providing an overview of the organization of this section. Each of the subsections that follow discusses one of the subproblems; thus, the organizational basis used in this report is the criteria identified earlier for solving this problem.

the staff employees' level of familiarity with their benefits and suggestions for improving communication were solicited.

Familiarity with Benefits. The staff employees were asked to rate their level of familiarity with each benefit. As shown in Table 1, most staff employees believe that most benefits have been adequately communicated to them.

TABLE 1. LEVEL OF FAMILIARITY WITH THE BENEFIT PROGRAM

Benefit	Level of Familiarity				
	Familiar	Unfamil.	Undecid.	No Resp.	Total
Sick leave	94%	4%	1%	1%	100%
Vacation	93%	4%	2%	1%	100%
Paid holidays	92%	3%	4%	1%	100%
Hospital/medical ins.	90%	7%	3%	0%	100%
Life insurance	84%	10%	5%	1%	100%
Retirement	76%	14%	8%	2%	100%
Long-term disability ins.	53%	33%	14%	0%	100%
Auto ins.*	34%	58%	7%	1%	100%

* This benefit started six weeks before the survey was taken.

At least three-fourths of the employees are familiar with all major benefits except for long-term disability insurance, which is familiar to only a slight majority, and auto insurance, which is familiar to only a third of the respondents. The low level of knowledge about auto insurance is probably attributable to the fact that this benefit started only six weeks before the survey was taken.

In general, benefit familiarity is not related to length of employment at ASU. Most employees are familiar with most benefits,

If you must divide a paragraph between pages, leave at least two lines of the paragraph at the bottom of the previous page and bring at least two lines forward to the next page.

Third-level subheading: Indent, use initial capitals, bold, and end with a period; leave one blank line before and begin the first word of the paragraph two spaces following the period.

Leave two or three blank lines before and after each table or figure.

Introduce each table before showing it. Always refer to tables by table number instead of by their location (that is, avoid phrases like "as shown below"). Discuss only the most important data from the table in the narrative. Tables may be presented in any standard table format, but be consistent throughout the report.

regardless of their length of employment. However, as shown in Figure 1, the only benefit for which this is not true is life insurance. The longer a person has been employed at ASU, the more likely he or she is to know about this benefit.

FIGURE 1. KNOWLEDGE OF LIFE INSURANCE BENEFIT

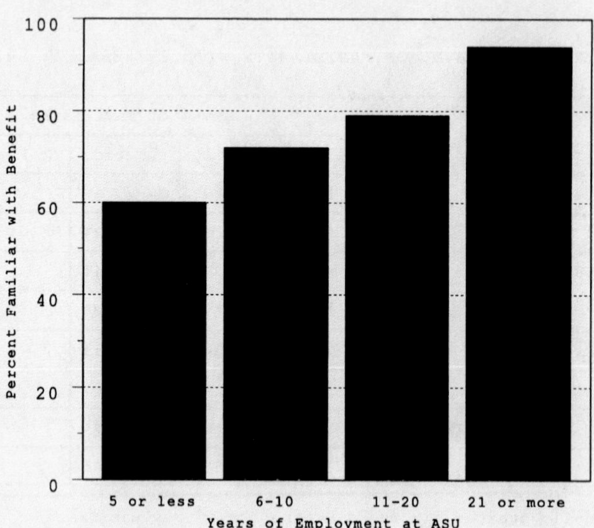

Present Methods of Communication. A variety of methods is presently being used to communicate the fringe benefits to employees. According to Lewis Rigby, director of the State Personnel Board, every new state employee views a 30-minute video entitled "In Addition To Your Salary" as part of the new-employee orientation. Also, the major benefits are explained during one-on-one counseling during the first that showed that such compensation has been cost-effective over the long run for companies in the manufacturing and service industries.

Keep charts simple and of an appropriate size. All visual aids should be in typed, rather than handwritten, format. If necessary, create the chart in another program, leave space for the chart on your report page, tape the chart onto the page, and then submit a good-quality photocopy of the entire report (never photocopy just one page).

that showed that such compensation has been cost-effective over the long run for companies in the manufacturing and service industries.

CONCLUSIONS AND RECOMMENDATIONS

If your Conclusions and Recommendations section is short, omit second-level subheadings.

These findings show that staff employees at Atlantic State University are extremely knowledgeable about all benefits except long-term disability and automobile insurance. However, a majority would prefer to have an individualized benefits statement instead of the brochures now used to explain the benefits program. They consider paid time off as the most important benefit and automobile insurance as the least important. A majority are satisfied with all benefits, although retirement benefits generated substantial dissatisfaction. The only additional benefit desired by a majority of the employees is compensation for unused sick leave.

The following recommendations are based on these conclusions:

1. Determine the feasibility of generating for each staff employee an annual individualized benefits statement.

2. Reevaluate the attractiveness of the automobile insurance benefit in one year to determine staff employees' knowledge about, use of, and desire for this benefit. Consider the feasibility of substituting compensation for unused sick leave for the automobile insurance benefit.

3. Conduct a follow-up study of the retirement benefits at ASU to determine how competitive they are with comparable public and private institutions.

Single-space the lines within an enumeration; double-space between enumerations.

These recommendations, as well as the findings of this study, should help the university ensure that its benefits program is accomplishing its stated objectives of attracting and retaining high-quality employees and meeting their needs once employed.

Provide an appropriate concluding paragraph that gives a sense of completion to the report.

This is the last page of the report. Ensure that the conclusions and recommendations stem directly from the findings and that you have presented ample supporting evidence. Avoid extreme or exaggerated language.

FIGURE C.5 Sample Report (*Continued*)

18

REFERENCES

Book—one author

Adams, J. B. (1994). *Compensation systems*. Boston: Benson, Inc.

Book—two authors

Adams, J. M. & Stearns, G. R. (1991). *Personnel administration*. Cambridge, MA: All-State Press.

Book—three or more authors

Berelson, B. R., Lazarsfield, P. F., & Connell, W., Jr. (1993). *Managing your benefit program* (2nd ed.). Chicago: Novak-Siebold.

Book—organization as author

Directory of business and financial services. (1995). New York: Corporate Libraries Association.

Book—edited volume

Egan, J. D. (Ed.). (1993). *Human resources*. London: Varsity Press.

Book—component part

Gowens, J. A. (1995). Cafeteria-style benefits. In R. Anshen (Ed.), *Personnel management* (pp. 661-672). New York: Gump Bros.

Journal article

Ignatio, E. (1994). Flexible benefits are the key to compensation. *Personnel Quarterly*, *61*, 113-125.

Second work by same author—in chronological order

Ignatio, E. (1995). Employee benefits in transition: Managers look to the past to move employee benefits into the future. *Supervisory Management in the 21st Century*, *28*, 36-39.

Magazine article

Kean, T. J., III. (1993, November). Employee benefits: Then and now. *Business Monthly*, pp. 39-41.

Newspaper article (unsigned)

Letting employees determine their own benefits. (1995, January 12). *New York City Times*, p. E21.

Dissertation or thesis

Meany, G. (1990). Employee benefits at American universities. (Doctoral dissertation, Atlantic State University, 1989). *Dissertation Abstracts International*, *60*, 4509C.

Paper presented at a meeting

Potts, R. (1993, August). Tuition reimbursement. Paper presented at the meeting of the National Mayors' Conference, Trenton, NJ.

Computerized data base

Trademark search data base. (1995). [Tristar On-Line File 305, Item 0119 473]. Denver, CO: Tristar Information Systems.

Nonprint media

Varney, J. L. (Producer). (1990, August 5). *Weekly business report* [Television show]. Los Angeles: Valhalla Broadcasting Company.

Government document

U.S. Department of Commerce. Bureau of the Census. (1992). *United States census of the population: 1990, Vol. 1: Characteristics of the population*. Washington, DC: U.S. Government Printing Office.

This reference list is shown in APA format. For all formats, arrange all entries in one alphabetical listing according to the author's last name. Include only those sources actually cited in the report, not every source read. Begin each entry at the left margin and indent runover lines five spaces. Single-space each entry and double-space between entries. Type magazine, journal, and newspaper titles in upper- and lowercase letters. Type book and article titles sentence style: capitalize the first word, proper nouns, and the first word after a colon. Do not enclose article titles in quotation marks. Underlined titles may be typed in italics instead.

FIGURE C.6 Three Documentation Formats

Endnotes

One out of ten adults nationwide inquires about moving or storage every year, and a slight majority of these people turn to the Yellow Pages for guidance.[1] Consumers in general do not have a specific company in mind when they begin searching the Yellow Pages for a particular product or service.[2]

Size appears to be the single most important factor in a Yellow Pages
display ad because "the eye focuses first on a large ad and later on
1 the smaller ads."[3] Color, design, and illustrations seem to be much
less important than size.

Number the endnotes consecutively throughout the report, using superior numbers (or your word processing program's endnote feature). The actual citations are given on a separate Notes page at the back of the report.

Footnotes

One out of ten adults nationwide inquires about moving or storage every year, and a slight majority of these people turn to the Yellow Pages for guidance.[1] Consumers in general do not have a specific company in mind when they begin searching the Yellow Pages for a particular product or service.[2]

Size appears to be the single most important factor in a Yellow Pages display ad because "the eye focuses first on a large ad and later on the smaller ads."[3] Color, design, and illustrations seem to be much less important than size.

2 ____________________

[1]Max Voight, Marketing Techniques for the Moving and Storage
3 Industry, Midwest Publishing Co., Chicago, 1991, p. 54.

[2]Lisa Poston, "Eye-Perception Research: A Marketing Tool," Journal of Telecommunications, Vol. 15, No. 4, May 1993, pp. 75-76.

[3]Larry R. Chilton and Harry M. Raines, "Who Really Reads the Yellow Pages?" Business Monthly, October 1994, p. 13.

Number the footnotes consecutively, starting with 1 on each page, using superior numbers (or your word processing program's footnote feature). Position the actual citations at the bottom of the same page as the text references.

Author-Date Method

One out of ten adults nationwide inquires about moving or storage
every year, and a slight majority of these people turn to the Yellow
4 Pages for guidance (Voight, 1991, p. 54). Consumers in general do not
have a specific company in mind when they begin searching the Yellow
Pages for a particular product or service (Poston, 1993).

Size appears to be the single most important factor in a Yellow Pages display ad because "the eye focuses first on a large ad and later on the smaller ads" (Chilton and Raines, 1994, p. 13). Color, design, and illustrations seem to be much less important than size.

The author-date method refers readers to the References section of the report. Put the author's name and the publication date in parentheses. If the author's name is given in the narrative, put only the year in parentheses. Include page numbers for direct quotations and for cited statistics.

Mechanics Notes

1 Insert the superior numbers immediately after punctuation and after closing quotation marks. 2 Single-space before and double-space after a 2-inch divider line. 3 Single-space the lines within a citation; double-space between citations. 4 Type the parenthetical reference before any punctuation but after the closing quotation mark.

FIGURE C.7 Three Bibliographic Formats

Use the same basic format for the notes as for the footnote citations, except that numbers should be followed by periods instead of formatted as superior numbers. Arrange the entries in the order in which they appear in the body of the report.

Arrange the entries in alphabetical order according to the first author's last name. List the first author's name in reverse order (last name first), but type the other author names in normal order. Use capital and lowercase letters for publication titles.

Arrange the entries in alphabetical order according to the first author's last name. List all authors' names in reverse order, and use initials only for the given names. Capitalize only the first word, proper nouns, and the first word following a colon or dash in the titles of journal and magazine articles and of books. Do not use quotation marks around article titles. (The format shown here follows APA style.)

For Endnotes 1

1. Max Voight, Marketing Techniques for the Moving and Storage Industry, Midwest Publishing Co., Chicago, 1991, p. 54. 2

2. Lisa Poston, "Eye-Perception Research: A Marketing Tool," Journal of Telecommunications, Vol. 15, No. 4, May 1993, pp. 75-76.

3. Larry R. Chilton and Harry M. Raines, "Who Really Reads the Yellow Pages?" Business Monthly, October 1994, p. 13.

For Footnotes

Chilton, Larry R., and Harry M. Raines, "Who Really Reads the Yellow Pages?" Business Monthly, October 1994, pp. 12-17. 3

Poston, Lisa, "Eye-Perception Research: A Marketing Tool," Journal of Telecommunications, Vol. 15, No. 4, May 1993, pp. 75-79.

Voight, Max, Marketing Techniques for the Moving and Storage Industry, Midwest Publishing Co., Chicago, 1991.

For Author-Date Method

Chilton, L. R., & Raines, H. M. (1994, October). Who really reads the Yellow Pages? Business Monthly, pp. 12-17.

Poston, L. (1993, May). Eye-perception research: A marketing tool. Journal of Telecommunications, 15(4), 75-79.

Voight, M. (1991). Marketing techniques for the moving and storage industry, Chicago: Midwest Publishing Co.

Mechanics Notes

1 No matter which format you use, begin the list on a separate page, leaving a 2-inch top margin. 2 Indent the first line of each endnote citation five spaces. Single-space the lines of each citation, but double-space between citations. 3 Begin the first line at the left margin, and indent runover lines five spaces.

FIGURE C.8 Report Page in MLA Style

Santorini 1

Loretta J. Santorini

Professor Riggins

Management 348

8 December 19--

Staff Employees' Evaluation of the Benefits Program

at Atlantic State University

Employee benefits are a rapidly growing and an increasingly important form of employee compensation for both profit and nonprofit organizations. According to a recent U.S. Chamber of Commerce survey, benefits now constitute 37% of all payroll costs, costing an average of $7,832 a year for each employee (Berelson, Lazarsfield, and Connell 183). Thus, on the basis of cost alone, an organization's benefits program must be carefully monitored and evaluated.

Atlantic State University employs nearly 2,500 staff personnel, and they have not received a cost-of-living increase in two years. As a result, staff salaries may not have kept pace with private industry, and the university's employee benefits program may become more important in attracting and retaining good workers. In addition, the contracts of three of the four staff unions expire next year, and the benefits program is typically a major area of bargaining.

As has been noted by one management consultant, "The success of employee benefits programs depends directly on whether employees need, understand, and appreciate the value of the benefits provided" (Egan 220). Thus, to help ensure that the benefits program is operating as effectively as possible, David Riggins, director of personnel, authorized this report on 15 October 19--. Specifically, the following problem was addressed in this study:

Type the author's name and the page number at the right margin ½ inch from the top.

Type the heading information as shown on the first page of the report.

Leave 1-inch margins on all four sides (other than for the page number).

Double-space every single line of the report—including enumerated lists, tables, and the reference list (entitled "Works Cited").

Include the author's last name and page number (if citing a part of a source)—but not the date—in the parenthetical reference.

For further information, see Joseph Gibaldi and Walter S. Achtert, *MLA Handbook for Writers of Research Papers,* 3rd ed. New York: Modern Language Association, 1988.

FIGURE C.9 Works-Cited Page

Santorini 18

Works Cited

Book—one author

Adams, John B. Compensation Systems. Boston: Benson, 1994.

Book—two authors

Adams, J. Marlene, and George R. Stearns. Personnel Administration. Cambridge: All-State, 1991.

Book—three or more authors

Berelson, Bret R., Paul Lazarsfield, and Will Connell, Jr. Managing Your Benefit Program. 2nd ed. Chicago: Novak-Siebold, 1993.

Book—organization as author

Corporate Libraries Association. Directory of Business and Financial Services. New York: Corporate Libraries Association, 1995.

Book—editor as author

Egan, Jean, ed. Human Resources. London: Varsity, 1993.

Book—component part

Gowens, Joanne. "Cafeteria-Style Benefits." Personnel Management. Ed. Rose Anshen. New York: Gump, 1995. 661-672.

Journal article

Ignatio, Earl. "Flexible Benefits Are the Key to Compensation." Personnel Quarterly 61 (1994): 113-125.

Second work by same author—in chronological order

---. "Employee Benefits in Transition: Managers Look to the Past to Move Employee Benefits into the Future." Supervisory Management in the 21st Century 28 (1995): 36-39.

Magazine article

Kean, T. J., III. "Employee Benefits: Then and Now." Business Monthly Nov. 1993: 39-41.

Newspaper article (unsigned)

"Letting Employees Determine Their Own Benefits." New York City Times 12 Jan. 1995: E21.

Dissertation or thesis

Meany, Grant. Employee Benefits at American Universities. Diss. Atlantic State U, 1989. Ann Arbor: UMI, 1990. 4509C.

Government document

United States Dept. of Commerce. Bureau of the Census. United States Census of the Population: 1990, Vol. 1: Characteristics of the Population. Washington: GPO, 1992.

Center the heading "Works Cited" 1 inch from the top in upper- and lowercase letters. Double-space the lines within and between each citation. Compare the format of this listing with the References list shown in APA format on Reference Manual page 648.

SECTION D
Grading Symbols

Style and Mechanics Grading Checklist

SYMBOL	MEANING	REVIEW PAGES	COMMENTS
Abb	Do not abbreviate this word.	611	
Act	Use active voice.	73–74, 92	
Agr	Make sure subjects, verbs, and pronouns agree; use plural verbs and pronouns with plural subjects and singular verbs and pronouns with singular subjects.	606–608	
Apol	Do not apologize in this instance.	158	
Apostrophes: 'ger	Use the possessive form for a noun or pronoun that comes before a gerund.	599	
'plur	Use only an apostrophe to form the possessive of a plural noun ending in *s*.	599–600	
'pro	Use *'s* to form the possessive of an *indefinite* pronoun (such as *someone's*); do not use an apostrophe with a *personal* pronoun (such as *hers*).	599	
'sing	Use *'s* to form the possessive of a singular noun.	599	
App	Make sure that the appearance of your document does not detract from its effectiveness.		
Aud	Make sure the content and tone of your message are appropriate for your specific audience.	112–115, 180–182 458–459	
Cit	Use the correct format for reference citations in a report.	418, 423, 648, 651	
Colons: : exp	Use a colon: To introduce explanatory material that follows an *independent* clause.	600	
: salut	After a salutation in a business letter formatted with standard punctuation.	600	
Commas: , adj	Use a comma: Between two adjacent adjectives not joined by a conjunction.	594	
, clos	After a complimentary closing in a business letter formatted with standard punctuation.	595	
, date	Before and after the year in a complete date.	595	
, ind	Between independent clauses joined by a conjunction.	595	
, intro	After a long introductory expression.	595–596	

SYMBOL	MEANING	REVIEW PAGES	COMMENTS
, nonr	Before and after a nonrestrictive expression.	596	
, place	Before and after a state or country that follows a city (but not before a Zip Code).	596	
, ser	Between each item in a series of three or more.	597	
, tran	Before and after a transitional expression (such as *therefore* or *nevertheless*).	597	
Conc	Be more concise; use fewer words to express this idea.	67–70	
Conf	Use a more confident style of writing; avoid doubtful expressions.	88–89	
Cons	Be consistent; do not contradict yourself.		
Dang	Avoid dangling expressions; place modifiers close to the words they modify.	61–62	
Disc	Avoid discriminatory language.	93–96	
Div	Divide words only between syllables.	614–615	
Emp	Emphasize this point.	90–93, 419–420	
End	Make the ending of your message more effective—more interesting, more positive, or more original.	148, 160, 188, 223–224	
Evid	Give more evidence to support this point.	187–188, 197–200	
Expl	Use expletive beginnings (such as *there are* or *it is*) sparingly.	70, 607	
For	Use correct format.	629–635 (corresp); 636–652 (reports)	
Head	Use report headings effectively—descriptive, concise, parallel, and not too many or too few.	410–412	
Hyphens: - adj	Hyphenate: A compound adjective that comes *before* a noun.	601	
Info	Use all the relevant information in the problem; make only *reasonable* assumptions.		
Int	Interpret this point. Don't simply present the facts or repeat the data from tables and figures; give more information so that the reader understands the importance and implications.	384	
Mean	Reword to make your meaning clearer or to be more precise.	60–63	
Mod	Use modifiers (adjectives and adverbs) correctly.	606	
Num	Express numbers correctly (either in words or in figures).	612–613	
Obv	Avoid obvious statements.		
Org—Dir	Use a direct organizational pattern here—main idea before the supporting data.	143–144, 185, 217–218	

SYMBOL	MEANING	REVIEW PAGES	COMMENTS
Org—Ind	Use an indirect organizational pattern here—supporting data before the main idea.	185–187, 219–221	
Orig	Use more original wording; avoid clichés and avoid copying the wording from the text.	64–67	
Par	Use parallel structure; express similar ideas in similar grammatical form.	77–78, 410–411	
Para	Do not make paragraphs so long that they appear uninviting to read.	78–79	
Periods: . req	Use a period to end a sentence that is a polite request.	602	
Plur	Do not confuse plurals and possessives.	599–600	
Pos	Use positive language to express this idea.	70–71	
Pro	Use pronouns and antecedents correctly.	599, 606–608	
Quot	Use direct quotations sparingly; paraphrasing is usually more effective.	334–335, 388	
Read	Put the reader in the action; state this idea in terms of reader response or reader benefits; use the "you" attitude.	96–98	
Rep	Avoid needless repetition and redundancy.	67–68	
Sale	Include sales promotion or resale here.	159–160	
Semicolons: ; noconj	Use a semicolon: To join two closely related independent clauses that are *not* connected by a conjunction.	603	
; ser	To separate items in a series if any of the items already contain commas.	603	
Spec	Be more specific.	64–65	
Sp	Use correct spelling.	613–614, or 624 (spelling list)	
Sub	Subordinate this point.	90–93, 419–420	
Ten	Use proper verb tense—past, present, or future.	419	
Title	Express titles correctly—underline (or italicize) titles of complete works; enclose titles of parts of works in quotation marks.	602–603, 604	
Tone	Avoid a tone of insincerity, anger, flattery, condescension, preachiness, bragging, accusation, or exaggeration.	89–90	
Tran	Use transition and coherence to make sentences flow smoothly and to move smoothly from one topic to the next.	72–73, 76–77, 420–421	
Word	Choose your words carefully; do not confuse similar-sounding words.	617 (word list)	

PROOFREADERS' MARKS

Proofreaders Mark	Draft	Final Copy
≡ Capitalize	Elmwood street	Elmwood Street
Delete	a true fact	a fact
∘∘∘ Don't delete	a true story	a true story
ds Double-space	ds first line second line	first line second line
∧ Insert	to Mr. Aaron Atlas	to Mr. Aaron Atlas
# Insert space	paperclip the receipt	paper clip the receipt
⊙ Make a period	for today John may	for today. John may
[Move left	Thank you	Thank you
] Move right	The second reason	The second reason
Omit space	at the book store	at the bookstore
¶ Paragraph	¶ To be sure	To be sure
ss Single-space	ss first line second line	first line second line
sp Spell correctly	Sincrly yours,	Sincerely yours,
Spell out	only 4 times	only four times
Transpose	to clearly see	to see clearly
___ Underline (or italicize)	in today's Tribune	in today's Tribune
/ Use lowercase letter	the President of	the president of

Section D

REFERENCES

CHAPTER 1

1. Leland V. Gustafson, Jack E. Johnson, and David H. Hovey, "Preparing Business Students—Can We Market Them Successfully?" *Business Education Forum,* Vol. 47, April 1993, pp. 23–26; "It's All Just Bossiness," *Indianapolis Star,* April 4, 1992, p. C3; "Mediocre Memos," *Detroit Free Press,* May 26, 1990, p. 9A; "Speak the Language," *Indianapolis Star,* January 30, 1991, p. A9; "Workplace Literacy," *USA Today,* September 21, 1992, p. B1.
2. Robert L. Montgomery, *Listening Made Easy: How to Improve Listening on the Job, at Home, and in the Community,* American Management Association, New York, 1981, p. 6.
3. Peter F. Drucker, quoted by Bill Moyers in *A World of Ideas,* Doubleday, Garden City, NY, 1990.
4. Albert Mehrabian, "Communicating Without Words," *Psychology Today,* September 1968, pp. 53–55.
5. Judee K. Burgoon and Thomas Saine, *The Unspoken Dialogue: An Introduction to Nonverbal Communication,* Houghton Mifflin, Boston, 1978, p. 123.
6. See, for example, Mark L. Knapp, *Essentials of Nonverbal Communication,* Holt, Rinehart & Winston, New York, 1980, pp. 21–26; "Study: Good Looks Bring Bigger Bucks in Business World," *USA Today,* August 8, 1989, p. 2B.
7. Edward T. Hall, *The Hidden Dimension,* Doubleday, Garden City, NY, 1966, pp. 107–122.
8. Donald B. Simmons, "The Nature of the Organizational Grapevine," *Supervisory Management,* Vol. 30, November 1985, p. 40; Alan Zaremba, "Working with the Organizational Grapevine," *Personnel Journal,* Vol. 67, July 1988, p. 40; Carol Hymowitz, "Spread the Word: Gossip Is Good," *The Wall Street Journal,* October 4, 1988, p. B1.

CHAPTER 2

1. *The Universal Almanac: 1992,* Andrews and McMeel, Kansas City, MO, p. 316.
2. *World Almanac and Book of Facts: 1992,* Pharos Books, New York, p. 573.
3. Margaret L. Usdansky, "Minority Majorities in One in Six Cities," *USA Today,* June 9, 1993, p. 10A.
4. Stephen Karel, "Learning Culture the Hard Way," *Consumer Markets Abroad,* Vol. 7, May 1988, pp. 1, 15.
5. George L. Beiswinger, "See What They're Doing with Voice Processing!" *The Office,* December 1991, p. 62.
6. "Fax Users Paper Offices," *USA Today,* May 18, 1993, p. 2B.
7. Bob Laird, "Business Facts on Fax," *USA Today,* June 11, 1992, p. B1.
8. Rick Friedman, "Cellular Telephones: Coming into Their Own," *The Office,* March 1992, p. 12.
9. Donald Harris, "A Matter of Privacy: Managing Personal Data in Company Computers," *Personnel,* Vol. 65, June 1988, p. 52.

CHAPTER 3

1. Scot Ober, "The Basic Vocabulary of Written Business Communications," Research Project 81-902-111-03, Arizona Department of Education, Phoenix, 1981.
2. Richard Lederer, "Strength of a Single Syllable," *Reader's Digest,* June 1991, p. 157.
3. Richard A. Lanham, *Revising Business Prose,* Scribner's, New York, 1981, p. 2.

4. Eve Nagler, "A Macaroni Company with Homespun Appeal," *The New York Times,* December 12, 1993, section 13, p. 22.

CHAPTER 4

1. Robert Gunning, *The Technique of Clear Writing,* McGraw-Hill, New York, 1968, pp. 38–39.
2. George R. Klare, "A Second Look at the Validity of Readability Formulas," *Journal of Reading Behavior,* Vol. 8, 1976, p. 147.
3. Gunning, p. 28.
4. "Will They Understand?" *Communication Briefings,* July 1990, p. 2.
5. Gunning, p. xiii.

CHAPTER 5

1. Marshall Cook, "Seven Steps to Better Manuscripts," *Writer's Digest,* September 1987, p. 30.
2. Marty Baumann, "More Executives Use PCs," *USA Today,* May 19, 1993, p. B1.
3. Julie Schmit, "Continental's $4 Million Typo," *USA Today,* May 25, 1993, p. B1.

CHAPTER 6

1. Marj Jackson Levin, "Don't Get Mad: Get Busy," *Detroit Free Press,* March 10, 1989, p. B1.

CHAPTER 7

1. Abraham Maslow, *Motivation and Personality,* 2d ed., Harper & Row, New York, 1970, pp. 35–58.
2. Herschell Gordon Lewis, *Direct Mail Copy That Sells!* Prentice-Hall, Englewood Cliffs, NJ, 1984, p. iii.
3. Ed Cerny, "Listening for Effect," *American Salesman,* May 1986, p. 28.
4. Linda Lynton, "The Fine Art of Writing a Sales Letter," *Sales & Marketing Management,* August 1988, p. 55.

CHAPTER 8

1. For a discussion of the empirical rationale for using an indirect versus a direct approach, see Marsha Bayless, "Business and Education: Perceptions of Written Communication," *NABTE Review,* 1991, pp. 32–35; D. Brent, "Indirect Structure and Reader Response," *Journal of Business Communication,* Spring 1985, pp. 5–7; Mohan Limaye, "Buffers in Bad News Messages and Recipient Perceptions," *Management Communication Quarterly,* August 1988, pp. 90–101; Kitty O. Locker, "The Rhetoric of Negative Messages," *English for Specific Purposes,* July 1984, pp. 1–2; and Douglas Salerno, "An Interpersonal Approach to Writing Negative Messages," *Journal of Advanced Composition,* 1985–86, pp. 139–149.

CHAPTER 9

1. Mark Memmott, "More Firms Stop Giving References," *USA Today,* December 5, 1989, p. B1.

CHAPTER 10

1. Scot Ober, "The Physical Format of Memorandums and Business Reports," *Business Education World,* November–December 1981, pp. 9–10, 24.
2. John Naisbitt, *Megatrends: Ten New Directions Shaping Our Lives,* Warner Books, New York, 1984, p. 17.

CHAPTER 11

1. *DIALOG Database Catalog,* DIALOG Information Services, Palo Alto, CA, 1992, p. 1.
2. Robert Rosenthal and Ralph L. Rosnow, *The Volunteer Subject,* John Wiley, New York, 1975, pp. 195–196.

CHAPTER 12

1. See, for example, "Tabling the Move to Computer Graphics," *Wall Street Journal*, January 30, 1991, p. B1; Jerimiah J. Sullivan, "Financial Presentation Format and Managerial Decision Making: Tables Versus Graphs," *Management Communication Quarterly*, Vol. 2, November 1988, pp. 194–216.
2. Edward Tufte, *The Visual Display of Quantitative Information*, Graphics Press, Cheshire, CT, 1983.
3. Mary Eleanor Spear, *Practical Charting Techniques*, McGraw-Hill, New York, 1969, pp. 56–59.

CHAPTER 14

1. E. J. McGarry, "Presentations Can Be Economical and Effective," *Office Dealer 92*, March/April 1992, p. 18.
2. "Wake Me When It's Over," *Presentation Products*, August 1989, p. 8.
3. Gilbert Fuchsberg, "Putting One Course to the Test," *Wall Street Journal*, September 10, 1993, p. R4.
4. Adapted from Leonard F. Meuse, Jr., *Mastering the Business and Technical Presentation*, CBI Publishing, Boston, 1980, pp. 2–7.
5. Kerry L. Johnson, "You Were Saying," *Managers Magazine*, February 1989, p. 19.
6. E. J. McGarry, "Presentations Can Be Economical and Effective," *Office Dealer 92*, March/April 1992, p. 18.
7. Wharton Applied Research Center, "A Study of the Effects of the Use of Overhead Transparencies on Business Meetings, Final Report," Philadelphia: University of Pennsylvania, September 14, 1981; "Why Presentations?" *MacWorld*, April 1988, p. 143.
8. Albert Mehrabian, "Communicating Without Words," *Psychology Today*, September 1968, pp. 53–55.
9. David Wallechinsky, Irving Wallace, and Amy Wallace, *The Book of Lists*, William Morrow, New York, 1977, pp. 469–470.
10. Jolie Solomon, "Executives Who Dread Public Speaking Learn to Keep Their Cool in the Spotlight," *Wall Street Journal*, May 4, 1990, p. B1.

CHAPTER 15

1. John R. Pierce, "Communication," *Scientific American*, Vol. 227, September 1972, p. 36.
2. Irving R. Janis, *Victims of Groupthink*, Houghton Mifflin, Boston, 1972.
3. Michael Doyle and David Straus, *How to Make Meetings Work*, Wyden Books, New York, 1976, p. 4; Marcy E. Mullins, "Are Meetings Worthwhile?" *USA Today*, August 28, 1989, p. B1; "Profile of the Typical Meeting," *Presentation Products Magazine*, February 1990, p. 8; E. F. Wells, "Rules for a Better Meeting," *Mainliner*, May 1978, p. 56; E. J. McGarry, "Presentations Can be Economical and Effective," *Office Dealer 92*, March/April 1992, p. 18.
4. "Managing Meetings: A Critical Role," *The Office*, November 1989, p. 20.
5. "Managing Meetings," p. 20.
6. Henry M. Robert, *The Scott, Foresman Robert's Rules of Order, Newly Revised*, Scott, Foresman, Glenview, IL, 1981.
7. Robert, p. xiii.
8. Ralph G. Nichols, "Listening Is a Ten-Part Skill," *Nation's Business*, September 1987, p. 40; "Listen Up!" *American Salesman*, July 1987, p. 29.
9. Alan Russell and Norris McWhirter (eds.), *1988 Guinness Book of World Records*, Bantam Books, New York, 1987, p. 418; Tom Heymann, *On an Average Day*, Fawcett Columbine, New York, 1989, p. 185.
10. John T. Molloy, "Dress for Success," *Detroit Free Press*, December 19, 1989, p. 3C.

11. "Only 17% Get Through on First Phone Call," *Office Systems '89,* March 1989, p. 13.
12. "Phone Calls Waste a Month Each Year," *Office Systems '89,* September 1989, p. 14.

CHAPTER 16

1. Karen Ball, "Poll: Chance a Big Factor in Job Choice," *Mt. Pleasant (MI) Morning Sun,* January 14, 1990, p. 1C; Selwyn Feinstein, "The Checkoff," *Wall Street Journal,* November 6, 1990, p. A1; Ronald W. Fry, *Your 1st Résumé,* 2d ed., Career Press, Hawthorn, NJ, 1989, p. 15; "Grass Always Greener for Most in Job Survey," *Office Systems '89,* March 1989, p. 16; "Job Search Data," *Administrative Management,* December 1985, p. 10; L. Patrick Scheetz, *Recruiting Trends 1989–90,* Michigan State University Career Development and Placement Services, East Lansing, MI, 1989.
2. U.S. Department of Labor, *Occupational Outlook Handbook,* 1988–89 ed., Government Printing Office, Washington, DC, pp. 8–13.
3. Selwyn Feinstein, "Labor Letter," *Wall Street Journal,* September 18, 1990, p. A1.
4. Keith Carter, "Networking Is the Key to Jobs," *USA Today,* August 7, 1989, p. B1.
5. John D. Singleton, "The Economics of the Job Market," in *CPC Annual,* Vol. 1, 32d ed., College Placement Council, Bethlehem, PA, 1988, p. 49.
6. Sandra L. Latimer, "First Impressions," *Mt. Pleasant (MI) Morning Sun,* May 8, 1989, p. 6.
7. Larry McCoy, "Tell Me About Yourself . . . That's Enough!" *Wall Street Journal,* April 5, 1989, p. A10.
8. See, for example, Jules Harcourt and A. C. "Buddy" Krizan, "A Comparison of Résumé Content Preferences of Fortune 500 Personnel Administrators and Business Communication Instructors," *Journal of Business Communication,* Spring 1989, pp. 177–190; Rod Little, "Keep Your Résumé Short," *USA Today,* July 28, 1989, p. B1; Darlene C. Pibal, "Criteria for Effective Résumés as Perceived by Personnel Directors," *Personnel Administrator,* May 1985, pp. 119–123.
9. "Most Serious Résumé Gaffes," *Communication Briefings,* March 1991, p. 6.
10. "To Be or Not To Be," *The Secretary,* April 1991, p. 6.
11. Albert P. Karr, "Labor Letter," *Wall Street Journal,* September 1, 1992, p. A1.
12. Harcourt and Krizan, pp. 177–190.
13. "Flashcard," *Education Life* (Supplement to the *New York Times*), November 5, 1989, p. 21.
14. Therese Droste, "Executive Résumés: The Ultimate Calling Card," *Hospitals,* March 5, 1989, p. 72.
15. Eugene Carlson, "Business of Background Checking Comes to the Fore," *Wall Street Journal,* August 31, 1993, p. B2.
16. Latimer, p. 6.

CHAPTER 17

1. Lynn Ulrich and Don Trumbo, "The Selection Interview Since 1949," *Psychological Bulletin,* Vol. 43, 1956, p. 100.
2. Shelley Liles, "Wrong Hire Might Prove Costly," *USA Today,* June 6, 1989, p. 6B.
3. Mary Bakeman et al., *Job-Seeking Skills Reference Manual,* 3d ed., Minnesota Rehabilitation Center, Minneapolis, MN, 1971, p. 57.

ACKNOWLEDGMENTS

Grateful acknowledgment is made to the following companies and individuals for allowing their interviews to be included in this book:

Chapter 1: The Home Depot/Deedy Taylor; *Chapter 2:* International Business Protocol/Dorothy Manning; *Chapter 3:* General Electric Company/George Bolln (published with permission General Electric Company, U.S.A.); *Chapter 4:* Frank Sanitate Associates/Frank Sanitate, President, Frank Sanitate Associates, 1152 Camino Manadero, Santa Barbara, CA 93111; *Chapter 5:* Keep America Beautiful, Inc./John Kazzi; *Chapter 6:* Kidder, Peabody and Company, Inc./Gwen Salley; *Chapter 7:* American Society for the Prevention of Cruelty to Animals/Joanne Lawson; *Chapter 8:* Digital Equipment Corporation/Alan Pike; *Chapter 9:* TRW Information Services/Janis Lamar; *Chapter 10: Worth* magazine/Richard Perkins; *Chapter 11:* Della Femina McNamee/Mary Hall; *Chapter 12:* Oshkosh B'Gosh/Jim Solum; *Chapter 13:* Congressional Research Service/Donna Porter; *Chapter 14:* Compaq Computer Corporation/Jim Garrity; *Chapter 15:* Burrell Communications Group/Amy Hilliard-Jones; *Chapter 16:* Computer Sciences Corporation/Paul Orvos; *Chapter 17:* Ben & Jerry's Homemade, Inc./Elizabeth Lonergan

TEXT CREDITS

Chapter 2

Spotlight on Law and Ethics, The Hanson Group, Los Altos, CA. Used with permission of the author.

Chapter 3

Excerpt on page 64: Richard Lederer, excerpted with permission from June 1991 *Reader's Digest*. Copyright © 1991 by Richard Lederer. Reprinted by permission of Pocket Books, a division of Simon & Schuster, Inc.

Spotlight Across Cultures, Ge-Lin Zhu, Chief Editor, *Practical Commercial English Handbook*, Commercial Publishing Company, Beijing, China, 1981, p. 49.

Chapter 5

Spotlight on Technology, "Writing Analysis Software" is reprinted by permission of RightSoft, Inc. Copyright © RightSoft, Inc.

Chapter 6

Microwriting a Routine Adjustment Letter, information from The Sharper Image advertising brochure.

Chapter 10

Figure 10.3, "Policy," is reprinted with the permission of Central Michigan University.

Figure 10.4, "Procedure for Hiring a Temporary Employee," is adapted by permission from Leslie H. Matthies, "Writing Your First Procedure—How to Go About It," *Journal of Systems Management,* November 1987, pp. 25–29.

Chapter 11

Wordwise, "Word Books," reprinted with permission of Children's Television Workshop; Used with permission of LUCASFILM, Ltd.

Figure 11.1, "A Fatty Stock," by Eric K. Schumuckler is reprinted by permission of *Forbes* magazine. Copyright © Forbes, Inc., 1989.

Chapter 14

Spotlight on Technology, © Aldus Corporation. Used with the express permission of Aldus Corporation. Aldus®, Pagemaker®, Persuasion®, and Aldus FreeHand® are registered trademarks of Aldus Corporation. All rights reserved.

Figure 14.4, Suzanne Waltzman, "Presentations with Power," *ITC Desktop:* No. 1. Reprint permission by International Typeface Corporation, New York, NY. Copyright ITC 1989.

Figure 14.5, used with permission by Robert W. Pike, President, Creative Training Techniques International, Inc., Eden Prairie, MN.

Chapter 15

Figure 15.1, "Solving Problems in Small Groups," is reprinted from Ernest G. Bormann and Nancy C. Bormann, *Effective Small Group Communication,* 4th Ed., Burgess Publishing, 1988, pp. 143–144.

PHOTO CREDITS

Chapter 1

Page 2: Courtesy Home Depot; 3: Steve Horwitz; 4: Francisco Rangel; 13: Wyatt McSpadden; 19: Steve Jennings; 27: Bill Varie/The Image Bank; 30: Jim Whitmer.

Chapter 2

Page 37: Mitsutaka Kuroshino; 40: Peter Sibbald; 46: Bill Nation/Sygma.

Chapter 3

Pages 56 & 57: Courtesy George Bolln, General Electric; 62: Theo Westenberger/Sygma; 69: James McGoon; 77: Brian Smale.

Chapter 4

Pages 87 & 88: Sean Brady; 92: John Storey; 97: Courtesy Nash-Finch; 98: Courtesy Dana Duke and Johnson & Johnson.

Chapter 5

Pages 108 & 109: Courtesy John Kazzi; 114: John Bohn/*Boston Globe*; 119: Sing Si Schwartz; 121: Smithsonian Institution photo by Michael Anderson.

Chapter 6

Pages 142 & 143: Courtesy Gwen Salley; 145: John Abbott; 157: Andy Freeburg; 159: John Abbott.

Chapter 7

Page 177: Dave McMichael/ASPCA; 178: Courtesy Joanne Lawson; 182: Michael O'Brien; 186: Courtesy Caesars Palace, Las Vegas; 196: Ted Morrison/Still Life Stock.

Chapter 8

Pages 215 & 216: Courtesy Alan Pike, Digital Equipment Corporation; 236: Gabe Kircheimer/Black Star.

Chapter 9

Pages 250 & 251: Courtesy Janis Lamar, TRW; 254: James Schnepf/Gamma Liaison; 263: Eli Reichman; 275: Michael Abramson.

Chapter 10

Pages 292 & 293: Courtesy Richard Perkins, *Worth* magazine; 297: Michael Abramson; 303: Jim Gund/Allsport.

Chapter 11

Page 324: Doug Vann/Photoreporters; 325: Della Femina McNamee/Mary Hall; 327: Courtesy Dean Foods Co.; 339: Andy Freeburg; 348: Barth Falkenberg.

Chapter 12

Page 362: Steve Winter/Black Star; 363: Oshkosh B'Gosh/Jim Solum; 370: Per Breiehagen; 373: Garth Vaughan; 388: By permission of *Texas Monthly*, photos by Kevin Van Diver/Texastock & Jim Myers.

Chapter 13

Page 401: Courtesy Michael M. Simpson; 402: Courtesy Donna Porter; 409 & 424: Francisco Rangel.

Chapter 14

Page 452: Courtesy Compaq Computer Corp.; 453: Courtesy Jim Garrity; 461: Ken Kaminsky/Picture Cube; 472: John Madere; 480: Lane Turner/*Boston Globe*.

Chapter 15

Page 494: Blair Jensen; 495: Courtesy Amy Hilliard-Jones, Burrell Communications Group; 497: Wyatt McSpadden; 505: James Schnepf; 514: Andy Freeburg.

Chapter 16

Page 530: Photo by Dennis Brack/Black Star, courtesy Computer Sciences Corporation; 531: Courtesy Paul Orvos, Computer Sciences Corporation; 538: Frank Siteman/Picture Cube; 540: Emily Strong/Picture Cube; 544: Jeffrey MacMillan/USNWR.

Chapter 17

Pages 567 & 568: Courtesy Liz Longerman, Ben & Jerry's; 570: Jeffrey MacMillan/USNWR; 575: Bob Daemmrich; 578: Lars Klove.

INDEX

A

B

D

E

F

J

K

L

M

Q

R

S

T